Honda CBR1100XX Super Blackbird
Service and Repair Manual

by Matthew Coombs

(3901-8AG1-304)

Models covered
CBR1100XX-V and XX-W (carburettor). 1137cc. 1997 to 1998
CBR1100XX-X to XX-7 (fuel injected). 1137cc. 1999 to 2007

© Haynes Publishing 2007

ABCDE
FGHIJ
KLMNO

A book in the **Haynes Service and Repair Manual Series**

All rights reserved. No part of this book may be reproduced or transmitted in any form or by any means, electronic or mechanical, including photo-copying, recording or by any information storage or retrieval system, without permission in writing from the copyright holder.

ISBN **978 1 84425 752 2**

British Library Cataloguing in Publication Data
A catalogue record for this book is available from the British Library

Library of Congress Control Number 2007934142

Printed in the USA

Haynes Publishing
Sparkford, Nr Yeovil, Somerset BA22 7JJ, England

Haynes North America, Inc
861 Lawrence Drive, Newbury Park, California 91320, USA

Haynes Publishing Nordiska AB
Box 1504, 751 45 UPPSALA, Sweden

Contents

LIVING WITH YOUR HONDA SUPER BLACKBIRD

Introduction

Daily (pre-ride checks)

MAINTENANCE

Routine maintenance and servicing

Contents

REPAIRS AND OVERHAUL

Engine, transmission and associated systems

Chassis and bodywork components

Electrical system

Wiring diagrams

REFERENCE

Index

The Birth of a Dream

by Julian Ryder

There is no better example of the Japanese post-war industrial miracle than Honda. Like other companies which have become household names, it started with one man's vision. In this case the man was the 40-year old Soichiro Honda who had sold his piston-ring manufacturing business to Toyota in 1945 and was happily spending the proceeds on prolonged parties for his friends.

However, the difficulties of getting around in the chaos of post-war Japan irked Honda, so when he came across a job lot of generator engines he realised that here was a way of getting people mobile again at low cost.

A 12 by 18-foot shack in Hamamatsu became his first bike factory, fitting the generator motors into pushbikes. Before long he'd used up all 500 generator motors and started manufacturing his own engine, known as the 'chimney', either because of the elongated cylinder head or the smoky exhaust or perhaps both. The chimney made all of half a horsepower from its 50 cc engine but it was a major success and became the Honda A-type.

Less than two years after he'd set up in Hamamatsu, Soichiro Honda founded the Honda Motor Company in September 1948. By then, the A-type had been developed into the 90 cc B-type engine, which Mr Honda decided deserved its own chassis not a bicycle frame. Honda was about to become Japan's first post-war manufacturer of complete motorcycles. In August 1949 the first prototype was ready. With an output of three horsepower, the 98 cc D-type was still a simple two-stroke but it had a two-speed transmission and most importantly a pressed steel frame with telescopic forks and hard tail rear end. The frame was almost triangular in profile with the top rail going in a straight line from the massively braced steering head to the rear axle. Legend has it that after the D-type's first tests the entire workforce went for a drink to celebrate and try and think of a name for the bike. One man broke one of those silences you get when people are thinking, exclaiming 'This is like a dream!' 'That's it!' shouted Honda, and so the Honda Dream was christened.

> 'This is like a dream!'
> 'That's it'
> shouted Honda

Mr Honda was a brilliant, intuitive engineer and designer but he did not bother himself with the marketing side of his business. With hindsight, it is possible to see that employing Takeo Fujisawa who would both sort out the home market and plan the eventual expansion into overseas markets was a masterstroke. He arrived in October 1949 and in 1950 was made Sales Director. Another vital new name was Kiyoshi Kawashima, who along with Honda himself, designed the company's first four-stroke after Kawashima had told them that the four-stroke opposition to Honda's two-strokes sounded nicer and therefore sold better. The result of that statement was the overhead-valve 148 cc E-type which first ran in July 1951 just two months after the first drawings were made. Kawashima was made a director of the Honda Company at 34 years old.

The E-type was a massive success, over 32,000 were made in 1953 alone, a feat of mass-production that was astounding by the

Honda C70 and C90 OHV-engined models

standards of the day given the relative complexity of the machine. But Honda's lifelong pursuit of technical innovation sometimes distracted him from commercial reality. Fujisawa pointed out that they were in danger of ignoring their core business, the motorised bicycles that still formed Japan's main means of transport. In May 1952 the F-type Cub appeared, another two-stroke despite the top men's reservations. You could buy a complete machine or just the motor to attach to your own bicycle. The result was certainly distinctive, a white fuel tank with a circular profile went just below and behind the saddle on the left of the bike, and the motor with its horizontal cylinder and bright red cover just below the rear axle on the same side of the bike. This was the machine that turned Honda into the biggest bike maker in Japan with 70% of the market for bolt-on bicycle motors, the F-type was also the first Honda to be exported. Next came the machine that would turn Honda into the biggest motorcycle manufacturer in the world.

The C100 Super Cub was a typically audacious piece of Honda engineering and marketing. For the first time, but not the last, Honda invented a completely new type of motorcycle, although the term 'scooterette' was coined to describe the new bike which had many of the characteristics of a scooter but the large wheels, and therefore stability, of a motorcycle. The first one was sold in August 1958, fifteen years later over nine-million of them were on the roads of the world. If ever a machine can be said to have brought mobility to the masses it is the Super Cub. If you add

The CB250N Super Dream became a favorite with UK learner riders of the late seventies and early eighties

in the electric starter that was added for the C102 model of 1961, the design of the Super Cub has remained substantially unchanged ever since, testament to how right Honda got it first time. The Super Cub made Honda the world's biggest manufacturer after just two years of production.

Honda's export drive started in earnest in 1957 when Britain and Holland got their first bikes, America got just two bikes the next year. By 1962 Honda had half the American market with 65,000 sales. But Soichiro Honda had already travelled abroad to Europe and the USA, making a special

The GL1000 introduced in 1975, was the first in Honda's line of GoldWings

Carl Fogarty in action at the Suzuka 8 Hour on the RC45

An early CB750 Four

point of going to the Isle of Man TT, then the most important race in the GP calendar. He realised that no matter how advanced his products were, only racing success would convince overseas markets for whom 'Made in Japan' still meant cheap and nasty. It took five years from Soichiro Honda's first visit to the Island before his bikes were ready for the TT. In 1959 the factory entered five riders in the 125 class. They did not have a massive impact on the event being benevolently regarded as a curiosity, but sixth, seventh and eighth were good enough for the team prize. The bikes were off the pace but they were well engineered and very reliable.

The TT was the only time the West saw the Hondas in '59, but they came back for more the following year with the first of a generation of bikes which shaped the future of motorcycling – the double-overhead-cam four-cylinder 250. It was fast and reliable – it revved to 14,000 rpm – but didn't handle anywhere near as well as the opposition. However, Honda had now signed up non-Japanese riders to lead their challenge. The first win didn't come until 1962 (Aussie Tom Phillis in the Spanish 125 GP) and was followed up with a world-shaking performance at the TT. Twenty-one year old Mike Hailwood won both 125 and 250 cc TTs and Hondas filled the top five positions in both races. Soichiro Honda's master plan was starting to come to fruition, Hailwood and Honda won the 1961 250 cc World Championship. Next year Honda won three titles. The other Japanese factories fought back and inspired Honda to produce some of the most fascinating racers ever seen: the awesome six-cylinder 250, the five-cylinder 125, and the 500 four with which the immortal Hailwood battled Agostini and the MV Agusta.

When Honda pulled out of racing in '67 they had won sixteen rider's titles, eighteen manufacturer's titles, and 137 GPs, including 18 TTs, and introduced the concept of the modern works team to motorcycle racing. Sales success followed racing victory as Soichiro Honda had predicted, but only because the products advanced as rapidly as the racing machinery. The Hondas that came to Britain in the early '60s were incredibly sophisticated. They had overhead cams where the British bikes had pushrods, they had electric starters when the Brits relied on the kickstart, they had 12V electrics when even the biggest British bike used a 6V system. There seemed no end to the technical wizardry. It wasn't that the technology itself was so amazing but just like that first E-type, it was the fact that Honda could mass-produce it more reliably than the lower-tech competition that was so astonishing.

When in 1968 the first four-cylinder CB750 road bike arrived the world of motorcycling changed for ever, they even had to invent a new word for it, 'Superbike'. Honda raced again with the CB750 at Daytona and won the

World Endurance title with a prototype DOHC version that became the CB900 roadster. There was the six-cylinder CBX, the CX500T – the world's first turbocharged production bike, they invented the full-dress tourer with the GoldWing, and came back to GPs with the revolutionary oval-pistoned NR500 four-stroke, a much-misunderstood bike that was more a rolling experimental laboratory than a racer. Just to show their versatility Honda also came up with the weird CX500 shaft-drive V-twin, a rugged workhorse that powered a new industry, the courier companies that oiled the wheels of commerce in London and other big cities.

It was true, though, that Mr Honda was not keen on two-strokes – early motocross engines had to be explained away to him as lawnmower motors! However, in 1982 Honda raced the NS500, an agile three-cylinder lightweight against the big four-cylinder opposition in 500 GPs. The bike won in its first year and in '83 took the world title for Freddie Spencer. In four-stroke racing the V4 layout took over from the straight four, dominating TT, F1 and Endurance championships with the RVF750, the nearest thing ever built to a Formula 1 car on wheels. And when Superbike arrived Honda were ready with the RC30. On the roads the VFR V4 became an instant classic while the CBR600 invented another new class of bike on its way to becoming a best-seller. The V4 road bikes had problems to start with but the VFR750 sold world-wide over its lifetime while the VFR400 became a massive commercial success and cult bike in Japan. The original RC30 won the first two World Superbike Championships is 1988 and '89, but Honda had to wait until 1997 to win it again with the RC45, the last of the V4 roadsters. In Grands Prix, the NSR500 V4 two-stroke superseded the NS triple and became the benchmark racing machine of the '90s. Mick Doohan secured his place in history by winning five World Championships in consecutive years on it.

In yet another example of Honda inventing a new class of motorcycle, they came up with the astounding CBR900RR FireBlade, a bike with the punch of a 1000 cc motor in a package the size and weight of a 750. It became a cult bike as well as a best seller, and with judicious redesigns continues to give much more recent designs a run for their money.

When it became apparent that the high-tech V4 motor of the RC45 was too expensive to produce, Honda looked to a V-twin engine to power its flagship for the first time. Typically, the VTR1000 FireStorm was a much more rideable machine than its opposition and once accepted by the market formed the basis of the next generation of Superbike racer, the VTR-SP-1.

One of Mr Honda's mottos was that technology would solve the customers' problems, and no company has embraced

The CX500 – Honda's first V-Twin and a favorite choice of dispatch riders

cutting-edge technology more firmly than Honda. In fact Honda often developed new technology, especially in the fields of materials science and metallurgy. The embodiment of that was the NR750, a bike that was misunderstood nearly as much as the original NR500 racer. This limited-edition technological tour-de-force embodied many of Soichiro Honda's ideals. It used the latest techniques and materials in every component, from the oval piston, 32-valve V4 motor to the titanium coating on the windscreen, it was – as Mr Honda would have wanted – the best it could possibly be. A fitting memorial to the

man who has shaped the motorcycle industry and motorcyles as we know them today.

The Stealth Tourer

When the Blackbird first emerged in late '96 for the 1997 model year, people had a problem pigeon-holing it (excuse the ornithological pun). Here was a bike with a modified FireBlade motor that was to set new outright speed records for production machinery but obviously wasn't intended for the racetrack. Much like the first VFR750, it was so visually very understated it came in a choice of three plain colours: black, gunmetal and a dark red.

The VFR400R was a cult bike in Japan and a popular grey import in the UK

The original carburettor-engined Super Blackbird

The 2001 fuel-injected CBR1100XX-1 model

The bike's name – and the black colour scheme most customers chose – derives from a US Air Force high-level reconnaissance plane, and somehow that image carries through to the on-road behaviour of the bike.

The fact it is astonishingly fast in a straight line is almost irrelevant, it's the way the bike covers ground so effortlessly that marks it out. On its launch it deposed the reigning king of the long-distance super-tourers, the Kawasaki ZZ-R1100. The Honda was faster (a largely irrelevant achievement), smoother and more efficient than it rival. Given that the ZZ-R1100 was a pretty fine way to transport two people and their luggage across a continent in comfort, this was some achievement. It was done with Honda's standard across-the-frame four-cylinder technology: chain-driven double-overhead cams and four-valve heads. The only deviation from standard practice were twin balancer shafts, one above and one under the crank. The cylinder bank was canted forward to make room for a bank of 42 mm carbs off the FireBlade. The high-frequency-vibration-cancelling balancer shafts meant the motor didn't have to have the 'Blade's rubber engine mountings so it could be used as a stressed member of the frame. If you bought a black 'Bird you also got a black finished frame. The frame is a conventional, but relatively lightweight, aluminium

twin spar wrapped in highly aerodynamically efficient bodywork. The wind tunnel dictated that the fairing nose should be pointy so that meant a specially developed headlamp with the main and dip beams riding piggyback one above the other.

The reason for the underwhelming response to the Blackbird's launch was that it was so understated. It took a few roadtests for the reality to sink in. Here was a bike that was totally effortless to ride fast for long distances, and being a Honda the detailing was well thought-out. It had a fuel gauge and reserve light, clock, bungee hooks, a stowage compartment for a shackle lock and – praise be! – a centrestand. If you put luggage on the bike it didn't look out of place and the touring capability was underlined by the fact that a pillion had been properly catered for.

The only point on which not everyone was agreed was the linked braking system, DCBS (dual combined braking system). Squeezing the front brake lever activated the outer two pistons of the three-piston front calipers, a torque arm on the left front caliper then operates a secondary master cylinder which progressively brings in the outer pistons in the rear caliper. The brake pedal operates the middle pistons on all three calipers.

Frankly, brakes aside, the Blackbird was very well sorted right from the start and set

new standards in its class by out-performing the ZZ-R1100 and it held its crown without a challenge until the Suzuki Hayabusa and ZX-12 arrived. Even then it was still a good fight for the crown. The only significant change to the Blackbird was the conversion to fuel injection for the CBR1100XX-X (1999 model year). The 'Bird got the same PGM-FI system as the VFR800 which filled in the hole in the power band just above 5000 rpm and smoothed out power delivery even more. Riders who'd experienced the carburetted V and W models were amazed at the improvement, mainly because they didn't think it was possible. Fuel injection plus a very small number of other modifications kept the Blackbird competitive in the marketplace when the Suzuki Hayabusa and ZX-12 came in.

The stealth metaphor works well for the Blackbird. Following the lack of understanding at its launch it gained a loyal following addicted to its seamless flow of effortless power. It wasn't a cutting-edge sportster although you certainly need one to out-pace it, it was a bike for mature riders with grown-up attitudes. Serious tourers who didn't want to go the full-house route of a GoldWing or even a Pan European embraced the Blackbird as the answer to their prayers.

Acknowledgements
Our thanks are due to Bransons Motorcycles of Yeovil who supplied the machines featured in the illustrations throughout this manual. We would also like to thank NGK Spark Plugs (UK) Ltd for supplying the colour spark plug condition photographs, the Avon Rubber Company for supplying information on tyre fitting and Draper Tools Ltd for some of the workshop tools shown.

Thanks are also due to Honda (UK) Ltd who supplied model photographs and to Julian Ryder who wrote the introduction 'The Birth of a Dream'.

About this Manual
The aim of this manual is to help you get the

best value from your motorcycle. It can do so in several ways. It can help you decide what work must be done, even if you choose to have it done by a dealer; it provides information and procedures for routine maintenance and servicing; and it offers diagnostic and repair procedures to follow when trouble occurs.

We hope you use the manual to tackle the work yourself. For many simpler jobs, doing it yourself may be quicker than arranging an appointment to get the motorcycle into a dealer and making the trips to leave it and pick it up. More importantly, a lot of money can be saved by avoiding the expense the shop must pass on to you to cover its labour

and overhead costs. An added benefit is the sense of satisfaction and accomplishment that you feel after doing the job yourself.

References to the left or right side of the motorcycle assume you are sitting on the seat, facing forward.

We take great pride in the accuracy of information given in this manual, but motorcycle manufacturers make alterations and design changes during the production run of a particular motorcycle of which they do not inform us. No liability can be accepted by the authors or publishers for loss, damage or injury caused by any errors in, or omissions from, the information given.

Frame and engine numbers

The frame serial number is stamped into the right-hand side of the steering head. The engine number is stamped into the top of the crankcase on the right-hand side of the engine. Both of these numbers should be recorded and kept in a safe place so they can be furnished to law enforcement officials in the event of a theft. There is also a colour code label on the top of the right-hand rail on the rear sub-frame, and a VIN plate on the right-hand frame beam. The carburettors or throttle bodies also have an ID number stamped into them.

The frame serial number, engine serial number, and colour code should also be kept in a handy place (such as with your driver's licence) so they are always available when purchasing or ordering parts for your machine.

Where necessary the procedures in this manual identify models by their code letter and production year, e.g. V (1997). The model code or production year is displayed on the machine's colour code label, but can also be established from the initial engine and frame numbers given below.

Buying spare parts

Once you have found all the identification numbers, record them for reference when buying parts. Since the manufacturers change specifications, parts and vendors (companies that manufacture various components on the machine), providing the ID numbers is the only way to be reasonably sure that you are buying the correct parts.

Whenever possible, take the worn part to the dealer so direct comparison with the new component can be made. Along the trail from the manufacturer to the parts shelf, there are numerous places that the part can end up with the wrong number or be listed incorrectly.

The two places to purchase new parts for your motorcycle – the accessory store and the franchised dealer – differ in the type of parts they carry. While dealers can obtain every part for your motorcycle, the accessory dealer is usually limited to normal high wear items such as shock absorbers, tune-up parts, various engine gaskets, cables, chains, brake parts, etc. Rarely will an accessory outlet have major suspension components, camshafts, transmission gears, or cases.

Used parts can be obtained for roughly half the price of new ones, but you can't always be sure of what you're getting. Once again, take your worn part to the breaker for direct comparison.

Whether buying new, used or rebuilt parts, the best course is to deal directly with someone who specialises in parts for your particular make.

The frame number is stamped into the right-hand side of the steering head

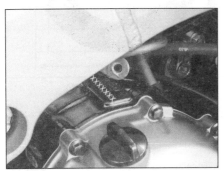

The engine number is stamped into the top of the crankcase on the right-hand side of the engine

The colour code label is on the top of the right-hand rail on the rear sub-frame

The VIN plate is on the right-hand frame beam

Model – UK/Europe	Year	Initial engine no.	Initial frame no.	Carb/Throttle body ID no.
CBR1100XX-V	1997	SC35E-2000001	JH2SC35A-VM000001	VPS0A-A
CBR1100XX-W	1998	SC35E-3000001	JH2SC35A-WM100001	VPS0D-A
CBR1100XX-X	1999	SC35E-3100001	JH2SC35A-XM200001	GQ40A-A
CBR1100XX-Y	2000	SC35E-3300001	JH2SC35A-YM300001	GQ40A-A
CBR1100XX-1	2001	SC35E-3400001	JH2SC35A-1M400001	GQ40E-A
CBR1100XX-2	2002	Not available		
CBR1100XX-3	2003	Not available		
CBR1100XX-4	2004	Not available		
CBR1100XX-5	2005	Not available		
CBR1100XX-6	2006/7	Not available		
Model – US	**Year**	**Initial engine no.**	**Initial frame no.**	**Carb/Throttle body ID no.**
CBR1100XX	1997	SC35E-2000001	JH2SC35A-VM000001	VPS2A-A (VPS1A-A*)
CBR1100XX	1998	SC35E-3000001	JH2SC35A-WM100001	VPS2D-A (VPS1D-A*)
CBR1100XX	1999	SC35E-3100001	JH2SC35A-XM200001	GQ40D-A (GQ40B-A*)
CBR1100XX	2000	SC35E-3300001	JH2SC35A-YM300001	GQ40D-A (GQ40B-A*)
CBR1100XX	2001	SC35E-3400001	JH2SC35A-1M400001	GQ40D-A (GQ40B-A*)
CBR1100XX	2002	Not available		
CBR1100XX	2003	Not available		
CBR1100XX	2004	Not available		

*Information relates to California market models

Bike spec

Weights and dimensions

Overall length . . . . .2160 mm (85.0 in)
Overall width . . . . .720 mm (28.3 in)
Overall height
   V, W, X and Y (1997 to 2000) models . . . . .1170 mm (46.1 in)
   1 (2001) models onward . . . . .1200 mm (47.2 in)
Wheelbase . . . . .1490 mm (58.7 in)
Seat height . . . . .810 mm (31.9 in)
Footrest height . . . . .372 mm (14.6 in)
Ground clearance . . . . .130 mm (5.1 in)
Weight (dry) . . . . .223 to 225 kg (492 to 496 lb)
Maximum weight capacity
   UK and European models . . . . .185 kg (408 lb)
   US 49 States and California models . . . . .174 kg (384 lb)
   Canada models . . . . .178 kg (392 lb)
Engine weight (dry) . . . . .83 kg (183 lb)

Engine

Type . . . . .Four-stroke in-line four
Capacity . . . . .1137 cc
Bore . . . . .79 mm
Stroke . . . . .58 mm
Compression ratio . . . . .11.0 to 1
Cooling system . . . . .Liquid cooled
Clutch . .Wet multi-plate
Transmission . . . . .Six-speed constant mesh
Final drive . . . . .Chain and sprockets
Camshafts . . . . .DOHC, chain-driven

Fuel system

V and W (1997 and 1998)
   models . . . . .4 x 42 mm flat-slide Keihin CV type
X (1999) models onward . . . . .PGM-FI fuel injection
Ignition system . . . . .Digital transistorised with electronic advance

Chassis

Frame type . . . . .Twin spar aluminium box section
Rake and trail . . . . .25°, 99 mm
Fuel tank capacity (including reserve)
   V and W (1997 and 1998) models . . .22 litres (4.8 Imp gal, 5.8 US gal)
   X (1999) models onward . . . . .24 litres (5.3 Imp gal, 6.3 US gal)
Front suspension
   Type . . . . .43 mm oil-damped telescopic forks
   Travel . . . . .120 mm (4.7 in)
Rear suspension
   Type . . . . .Single shock absorber, rising rate linkage,
      box-section aluminium swingarm
   Travel . . . . .120 mm (4.7 in)
   Adjustment . . . . .Rebound damping
Wheels . . . . .17 inch 3-spoke alloys
Tyres
   Front . . . . .120/70-ZR17 58W Radial
   Rear . . . . .180/55-ZR17 73W Radial
Front brake . . . .Twin 310 mm disc with Nissin 3-piston sliding calipers
Rear brake . . . .Single 256 mm disc with Nissin 3-piston sliding caliper
Braking system . . . . .Linked (Honda Dual Combined Braking System)

Model development

CBR1100XX-V (1997 model year)

The very first model was the CBR1100XX-V launched in late 1996 for the 1997 model year.

The Blackbird has an in-line four cylinder engine, with a twin balancer shaft to smooth out engine vibration. Drive to the double overhead camshafts which actuate the four valves per cylinder is by chain from the right-hand end of the crankshaft. The engine is liquid-cooled. The clutch is a conventional wet multi-plate unit and the gearbox is 6-speed. Drive to the rear wheel is by chain and sprockets.

The engine gets its fuel and air via four 42 mm CV carburettors, and this is ignited by an electronic ignition system. The exhaust system is a four-into-two design.

The engine sits in a twin-beam aluminium frame which uses the engine as a stressed member, with box-section tubing for the upper rails. Front suspension is by oil-damped 43 mm forks which have cartridge type dampers. Rear suspension is by a single shock absorber via a three-way rising rate linkage.

The brake system is the DCBS (dual combined braking system) that has been used on other models, notably the Pan European and the VFR800. It is a complicated system that is designed to provide equal and progressive braking by applying a proportion of rear brake when the front brake lever is applied, and a proportion of front brake when the rear brake pedal is applied.

Colours were Mute black metallic, Candy muthos magenta and Titanium metalic.

CBR1100XX-W (1998 model year)

Apart from a modification to the thermostat housing, there were no significant changes from the V (1997) model.

Colours were Mute black metallic, Candy glory red-U and Titanium metalic.

CBR1100XX-X (1999 model year)

Major changes were made to the X model, the most significant being the move to fuel injection instead of carburettors. Honda's PGM-FI engine managment system, as seen on other models in their range, was fitted to the Blackbird. German and Swiss market models gained a 3-way catalytic converter.

Other changes were made to the clutch, the oil cooler, the tail light, and the air filter housing and its air ducts. The suspension and brake systems remained unchaged. Fuel tank capacity was increased to 24 litres.

European models were fitted with Honda's HISS immobiliser system.

Colours were Pearl prism black, Candy phoenix blue and Candy glory red-U. A PGM-FI decal was added to the rear bodywork.

CBR1100XX-Y (2000 model year)

There were no significant changes from the X (1999) model.

CBR1100XX-1 (2001 model year)

The cooling fan motor was controlled by the ECM, via a relay and information received from the coolant temperature sender; previously the fan was triggered by a conventional fan switch. Iridium spark plugs were fitted. The 3-way catalytic converter fitted to certain earlier models was now available on the UK market model.

New digital instruments were fitted which featured electronic displays for all except the tachometer which remained analogue. LEDs were used for meter illumination and warning lights. The rear turn signals were restyled.

Colours were Accurate silver metalic, Darkness black metalic, Candy phoenix blue and Candy glory red-U.

CBR1100XX-2 (2002 model year)

There were no significant changes from the 1 (2001) model. Colours were Accurate silver metallic, Darkness black metallic, Candy Tahitian blue, Candy blazing red.

CBR1100XX-3 (2003 model year)

There were no significant changes from the 2 (2002) model apart from hard-wired lighting on Europe models. Colours were Accurate silver metallic, Darkness black metallic, Candy Tahitian blue and Candy blazing red.

CBR1100XX-4 (2004 model year)

There were no significant changes from the 3 (2003 model year). Colour changes were Accurate silver metallic, Darkness black metallic, Candy Tahitian blue and Mat gunpowder black metallic.

CBR1100XX-5 (2005 model year)

There were no significant changes from the 4 (2004 model year). Colours were Accurate silver metallic, Darkness black metallic and Candy Phoenix blue.

CBR1100XX-6 (2006/7 model year)

There were no significant changes from the 5 (2005 model year). Colours were Darkness black metallic and Iron silver metallic.

Professional mechanics are trained in safe working procedures. However enthusiastic you may be about getting on with the job at hand, take the time to ensure that your safety is not put at risk. A moment's lack of attention can result in an accident, as can failure to observe simple precautions.

There will always be new ways of having accidents, and the following is not a comprehensive list of all dangers; it is intended rather to make you aware of the risks and to encourage a safe approach to all work you carry out on your bike.

Asbestos

● Certain friction, insulating, sealing and other products - such as brake pads, clutch linings, gaskets, etc. - contain asbestos. Extreme care must be taken to avoid inhalation of dust from such products since it is hazardous to health. If in doubt, assume that they do contain asbestos.

Fire

● Remember at all times that petrol is highly flammable. Never smoke or have any kind of naked flame around, when working on the vehicle. But the risk does not end there - a spark caused by an electrical short-circuit, by two metal surfaces contacting each other, by careless use of tools, or even by static electricity built up in your body under certain conditions, can ignite petrol vapour, which in a confined space is highly explosive. Never use petrol as a cleaning solvent. Use an approved safety solvent.

● Always disconnect the battery earth terminal before working on any part of the fuel or electrical system, and never risk spilling fuel on to a hot engine or exhaust.

● It is recommended that a fire extinguisher of a type suitable for fuel and electrical fires is kept handy in the garage or workplace at all times. Never try to extinguish a fuel or electrical fire with water.

Fumes

● Certain fumes are highly toxic and can quickly cause unconsciousness and even death if inhaled to any extent. Petrol vapour comes into this category, as do the vapours from certain solvents such as trichloroethylene. Any draining or pouring of such volatile fluids should be done in a well ventilated area.

● When using cleaning fluids and solvents, read the instructions carefully. Never use materials from unmarked containers - they may give off poisonous vapours.

● Never run the engine of a motor vehicle in an enclosed space such as a garage. Exhaust fumes contain carbon monoxide which is extremely poisonous; if you need to run the engine, always do so in the open air or at least have the rear of the vehicle outside the workplace.

The battery

● Never cause a spark, or allow a naked light near the vehicle's battery. It will normally be giving off a certain amount of hydrogen gas, which is highly explosive.

● Always disconnect the battery ground (earth) terminal before working on the fuel or electrical systems (except where noted).

● If possible, loosen the filler plugs or cover when charging the battery from an external source. Do not charge at an excessive rate or the battery may burst.

● Take care when topping up, cleaning or carrying the battery. The acid electrolyte, evenwhen diluted, is very corrosive and should not be allowed to contact the eyes or skin. Always wear rubber gloves and goggles or a face shield. If you ever need to prepare electrolyte yourself, always add the acid slowly to the water; never add the water to the acid.

Electricity

● When using an electric power tool, inspection light etc., always ensure that the appliance is correctly connected to its plug and that, where necessary, it is properly grounded (earthed). Do not use such appliances in damp conditions and, again, beware of creating a spark or applying excessive heat in the vicinity of fuel or fuel vapour. Also ensure that the appliances meet national safety standards.

● A severe electric shock can result from touching certain parts of the electrical system, such as the spark plug wires (HT leads), when the engine is running or being cranked, particularly if components are damp or the insulation is defective. Where an electronic ignition system is used, the secondary (HT) voltage is much higher and could prove fatal.

Remember...

✗ **Don't** start the engine without first ascertaining that the transmission is in neutral.

✗ **Don't** suddenly remove the pressure cap from a hot cooling system - cover it with a cloth and release the pressure gradually first, or you may get scalded by escaping coolant.

✗ **Don't** attempt to drain oil until you are sure it has cooled sufficiently to avoid scalding you.

✗ **Don't** grasp any part of the engine or exhaust system without first ascertaining that it is cool enough not to burn you.

✗ **Don't** allow brake fluid or antifreeze to contact the machine's paintwork or plastic components.

✗ **Don't** siphon toxic liquids such as fuel, hydraulic fluid or antifreeze by mouth, or allow them to remain on your skin.

✗ **Don't** inhale dust - it may be injurious to health (see Asbestos heading).

✗ **Don't** allow any spilled oil or grease to remain on the floor - wipe it up right away, before someone slips on it.

✗ **Don't** use ill-fitting spanners or other tools which may slip and cause injury.

✗ **Don't** lift a heavy component which may be beyond your capability - get assistance.

✗ **Don't** rush to finish a job or take unverified short cuts.

✗ **Don't** allow children or animals in or around an unattended vehicle.

✗ **Don't** inflate a tyre above the recommended pressure. Apart from overstressing the carcass, in extreme cases the tyre may blow off forcibly.

✔ **Do** ensure that the machine is supported securely at all times. This is especially important when the machine is blocked up to aid wheel or fork removal.

✔ **Do** take care when attempting to loosen a stubborn nut or bolt. It is generally better to pull on a spanner, rather than push, so that if you slip, you fall away from the machine rather than onto it.

✔ **Do** wear eye protection when using power tools such as drill, sander, bench grinder etc.

✔ **Do** use a barrier cream on your hands prior to undertaking dirty jobs - it will protect your skin from infection as well as making the dirt easier to remove afterwards; but make sure your hands aren't left slippery. Note that long-term contact with used engine oil can be a health hazard.

✔ **Do** keep loose clothing (cuffs, ties etc. and long hair) well out of the way of moving mechanical parts.

✔ **Do** remove rings, wristwatch etc., before working on the vehicle - especially the electrical system.

✔ **Do** keep your work area tidy - it is only too easy to fall over articles left lying around.

✔ **Do** exercise caution when compressing springs for removal or installation. Ensure that the tension is applied and released in a controlled manner, using suitable tools which preclude the possibility of the spring escaping violently.

✔ **Do** ensure that any lifting tackle used has a safe working load rating adequate for the job.

✔ **Do** get someone to check periodically that all is well, when working alone on the vehicle.

✔ **Do** carry out work in a logical sequence and check that everything is correctly assembled and tightened afterwards.

✔ **Do** remember that your vehicle's safety affects that of yourself and others. If in doubt on any point, get professional advice.

● If in spite of following these precautions, you are unfortunate enough to injure yourself, seek medical attention as soon as possible.

Note: *The daily (pre-ride) checks outlined in the owner's manual covers those items which should be inspected on a daily basis.*

Engine/transmission oil level check

The correct oil
● Modern, high-revving engines place great demands on their oil. It is very important that the correct oil for your bike is used.
● Always top up with a good quality oil of the specified type and viscosity and do not overfill the engine.

Oil type	API grade SE, SF or SG
Oil viscosity	SAE 10W40

Before you start:
✔ Take the motorcycle on a short run to allow it to reach normal operating temperature. *Caution: Do not run the engine in an enclosed space such as a garage or workshop.*
✔ Stop the engine and support the motorcycle on its centre-stand. Allow it to stand undisturbed for a few minutes to allow the oil level to stabilise. Make sure the motorcycle is on level ground.

Bike care:
● If you have to add oil frequently, check whether you have any oil leaks from the engine joints, seals and gaskets. If not, the engine could be burning oil, in which case there will be white smoke coming out of the exhaust - (see *Fault Finding*).

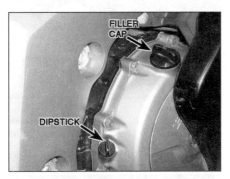

1 Unscrew the dipstick from the clutch cover.

2 Wipe off all the oil using a clean rag or paper towel.

3 Insert the dipstick back in the engine and allow it to rest on the cover - do not screw it in.

4 Remove the dipstick and observe the level of the oil, which should be somewhere in between the upper and lower level lines (arrowed).

5 If the level is below the minimum line, unscrew the oil filler cap from the top of the clutch cover.

6 Top the engine up with the recommended grade and type of oil to bring the level up to the upper line on the dipstick. Do not overfill. On completion, make sure the dipstick and filler cap are secure in the cover.

Suspension, steering and drive chain checks

Suspension and steering:
● Check that the front and rear suspension operates smoothly without binding.
● Check that the rear suspension is adjusted as required.
● Check that the steering moves smoothly from lock-to-lock.

Drive chain:
● Check that the chain isn't too loose or too tight, and adjust it if necessary (see Chapter 1).
● If the chain looks dry, lubricate it (see Chapter 1).

Brake fluid level checks

 Warning: Brake hydraulic fluid can harm your eyes and damage painted surfaces, so use extreme caution when handling and pouring it and cover surrounding surfaces with rag. Do not use fluid that has been standing open for some time, as it absorbs moisture from the air which can cause a dangerous loss of braking effectiveness.

Before you start:

✔ The front master cylinder reservoir is integral with the master cylinder on the right-hand handlebar. The rear master cylinder reservoir is located behind the seat cowl on the right-hand side of the machine.

✔ Make sure you have the correct hydraulic fluid. DOT 4 is recommended.

✔ Wrap a rag around the reservoir being worked on to ensure that any spillage does not come into contact with painted surfaces.

✔ Support the motorcycle on its centre-stand.

Bike care:

● The fluid in the front and rear brake master cylinder reservoirs will drop slightly as the brake pads wear down.

● If either fluid reservoir requires repeated topping-up there could be an hydraulic leak somewhere in the system, which must be investigated immediately.

● Check for signs of fluid leakage from the hydraulic hoses and components – if found, rectify immediately (see Chapter 7).

● Check the operation of both brakes before taking the machine on the road; if there is evidence of air in the system (spongy feel to lever or pedal), it must be bled (see Chapter 7).

1 The front brake fluid level, visible through the window in the reservoir body, must be above the LOWER line (arrowed).

2 If the level is below the LOWER level line, undo the two reservoir cover screws (note use of angled screwdriver).

3 Remove the cover, diaphragm plate and diaphragm.

4 Top up with new DOT 4 fluid until the level is up to the UPPER level line, marked on the inside of the reservoir. Do not overfill

5 Ensure that the diaphragm is correctly seated before installing the plate and cover.

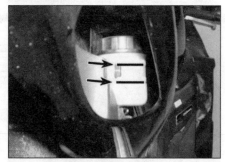

6 The rear brake fluid level is visible through the reservoir body via the aperture in the seat cowling.

7 If the level is below the LOWER level line, remove the seat cowling (see Chapter 8). Unscrew the reservoir cap and remove the diaphragm plate and diaphragm.

8 Top up with new DOT 4 fluid until the level is up to the UPPER level line. Do not overfill.

9 Ensure that the diaphragm is correctly seated before installing the plate and cap. Tighten the cap securely, then install the seat cowling.

Clutch fluid level check

> ⚠ **Warning: Brake and clutch hydraulic fluid can harm your eyes and damage painted surfaces, so use extreme caution when handling and pouring it and cover surrounding surfaces with rag. Do not use fluid that has been standing open for some time, as it absorbs moisture from the air which can cause a dangerous loss of braking and clutch effectiveness.**

Before you start:

✔ The clutch master cylinder reservoir is integral with the master cylinder on the left-hand handlebar.
✔ Make sure you have the correct hydraulic fluid. DOT 4 is recommended.
✔ Wrap a rag around the reservoir to ensure that any spillage does not come into contact with painted surfaces.

✔ Support the motorcycle on its centre-stand, and turn the handlebars to full right lock so that the top of the reservoir is level. Access to the cover screws is partially restricted by the windshield, so if a short or angled screwdriver is not available, slacken the screws before turning the handlebars, but do not remove the cover until the reservoir is level. Alternatively, remove the windshield (see Chapter 8).

Bike care:

● If the fluid reservoir requires repeated topping-up there could be an hydraulic leak somewhere in the system, which must be investigated immediately.
● Check for signs of fluid leakage from the hydraulic hose and components - if found, rectify immediately.
● Check the operation of the clutch before taking the machine on the road; if there is evidence of air in the system (spongy feel to the lever, difficulty in engaging gear, drag when in gear), bleed the clutch as described in Chapter 2.

1 The clutch fluid level is visible through the window in the reservoir body - it must be above the LOWER level line.

2 If the level is below the LOWER level line, undo the two reservoir cover screws (see *Before You Start* above).

3 Remove the cover, diaphragm plate and diaphragm.

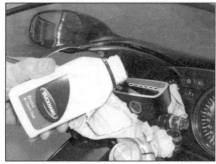

4 Top up with new clean DOT 4 fluid until the level is up to the UPPER line, marked on the inside of the reservoir. Do not overfill.

5 Ensure that the diaphragm is correctly seated before installing the plate and cover.

Legal and safety checks

Lighting and signalling:

● Take a minute to check that the headlight, taillight, brake light, instrument lights and turn signals all work correctly.
● Check that the horn sounds when the switch is operated.
● A working speedometer is a statutory requirement in the UK.

Safety:

● Check that the throttle grip rotates smoothly and snaps shut when released, in all steering positions. Also check for the correct amount of freeplay (see Chapter 1).

● Check that the engine shuts off when the kill switch is operated.
● Check that sidestand and centrestand return springs hold the stands up securely when retracted.

Fuel:

● This may seem obvious, but check that you have enough fuel to complete your journey. If you notice signs of fuel leakage – rectify the cause immediately.
● Ensure you use the correct grade fuel – see Chapter 4 Specifications.

Tyre checks

Tyre tread depth:

● At the time of writing UK law requires that tread depth must be at least 1 mm over 3/4 of the tread breadth all the way around the tyre, with no bald patches. Many riders, however, consider 2 mm tread depth minimum to be a safer limit. Honda recommend a minimum of 1.5 mm on the front and 2 mm on the rear.

● Many tyres now incorporate wear indicators in the tread. Identify the location marking on the tyre sidewall to locate the indicator bar and replace the tyre if the tread has worn down to the bar.

The correct pressures:

● The tyres must be checked when **cold**, not immediately after riding. Note that low tyre pressures may cause the tyre to slip on the rim or come off. High tyre pressures will cause abnormal tread wear and unsafe handling.

● Use an accurate pressure gauge. Many forecourt gauges are wildly inaccurate. If you buy your own, spend as much as you can justify on a quality gauge.

● Proper air pressure will increase tyre life and provide maximum stability and ride comfort.

Loading	Front	Rear
All loadings and speeds	42 psi (2.90 Bar)	42 psi (2.90 Bar)

Tyre care:

● Check the tyres carefully for cuts, tears, embedded nails or other sharp objects and excessive wear. Operation of the motorcycle with excessively worn tyres is extremely hazardous, as traction and handling are directly affected.

● Check the condition of the tyre valve and ensure the dust cap is in place.

● Pick out any stones or nails which may have become embedded in the tyre tread. If left, they will eventually penetrate through the casing and cause a puncture.

● If tyre damage is apparent, or unexplained loss of pressure is experienced, seek the advice of a tyre fitting specialist without delay.

1 Check the tyre pressures when the tyres are **cold** and keep them properly inflated.

2 Measure tread depth at the centre of the tyre using a depth gauge.

3 Tyre tread wear indicator bar and its location marking (usually either an arrow, a triangle or the letters TWI) on the sidewall.

Coolant level check

 Warning: DO NOT remove the radiator pressure cap to add coolant. Topping up is done via the coolant reservoir tank filler. DO NOT leave open containers of coolant about, as it is poisonous.

Before you start:

✔ Make sure you have a supply of coolant available (a mixture of 50% distilled water and 50% corrosion inhibited ethylene glycol anti-freeze is needed).

✔ Always check the coolant level when the engine is at normal working temperature. Take the motorcycle on a short run to allow it to reach normal temperature.

Caution: Do not run the engine in an enclosed space such as a garage or workshop.

✔ Stop the engine and support the motorcycle on its centre-stand. Make sure the motorcycle is on level ground.

Bike care:

● Use only the specified coolant mixture. It is important that anti-freeze is used in the system all year round, and not just in the winter. Do not top the system up using only water, as the system will become too diluted.

● Do not overfill the reservoir tank. If the coolant is significantly above the UPPER level line at any time, the surplus should be siphoned or drained off to prevent the possibility of it being expelled out of the overflow hose.

● If the coolant level falls steadily, check the system for leaks (see Chapter 1). If no leaks are found and the level continues to fall, it is recommended that the machine is taken to a Honda dealer for a pressure test.

1 The coolant reservoir is located on the right-hand side behind the engine, on the inside of the frame. The coolant UPPER and LOWER level lines (arrowed) are marked on the back of the reservoir.

2 If the coolant level is not in between the UPPER and LOWER markings, remove the seat (see Chapter 8), then remove the reservoir filler cap.

3 Top the coolant level up with the recommended coolant mixture. Fit the cap securely, then install the seat.

Chapter 1
Routine maintenance and servicing

Contents

Air filter – renewal 22
Battery – charging ....see Chapter 9
Battery – check 10
Battery – removal, installation, inspection
  and maintenance ....see Chapter 9
Brake caliper and master cylinder seal renewal 33
Brake fluid –change 24
Brake hoses – renewal 34
Brake pads – wear check 3
Brake system – check 14
Carburettors – synchronisation (V and W models) 12
Clutch – check 4
Clutch fluid – change 25
Clutch hose – renewal 36
Clutch master and slave cylinder seal renewal 37
Cooling system – check 13
Cooling system – draining, flushing and refilling 27
Cylinder compression – check 28
Drive chain and sprockets – check, adjustment, cleaning and
  lubrication 1
Engine oil pressure – check 29

Engine/transmission – oil change and filter renewal 8
Evaporative emission control (EVAP) system – check 23
Front forks – oil change 38
Fuel hoses – renewal 35
Fuel system – check 9
Headlight aim – check and adjustment 15
Idle speed – check and adjustment 2
Nuts and bolts – tightness check 19
Pulse secondary air injection system (PAIR) – check 21
Sidestand/centrestand – check 16
Sidestand, centrestand, lever pivots and cables – lubrication 7
Spark plugs – gap check and adjustment 5
Spark plugs – renewal 6
Steering head bearings – freeplay check and adjustment 18
Steering head bearings – re-greasing 31
Suspension – check 17
Swingarm and suspension linkage bearings – lubrication 32
Throttle and choke cables – check 11
Valve clearances – check and adjustment 26
Wheels and tyres – general check 20
Wheel bearings – check 30

Degrees of difficulty

Easy, suitable for novice with little experience	Fairly easy, suitable for beginner with some experience	Fairly difficult, suitable for competent DIY mechanic	Difficult, suitable for experienced DIY mechanic	Very difficult, suitable for expert DIY or professional

Specifications

Engine

Cylinder numbering .... 1 to 4 from left to right
Spark plugs
  Type
    V, W, X and Y (1997 to 2000) models .... NGK CR9EHVX-9
    1 (2001) models onward .... NGK IMR9A-9H, or DENSO IUH27D
  Electrode gap .... 0.8 to 0.9 mm
Engine idle speed
  V and W (1997 and 1998) models
    US, Swiss and Austrian market models .... 1100 ± 100 rpm
    All other market models .... 1000 ± 100 rpm
  X and Y (1999 and 2000) models .... 1100 ± 50 rpm
  1 (2001) models onward .... 1100 ± 100 rpm
Carburettor synchronisation – max. difference between carburettors .. 20 mm Hg
Valve clearances (COLD engine)
  Intake valves .... 0.13 to 0.19 mm
  Exhaust valves .... 0.19 to 0.25 mm
Cylinder compression .... 185 psi (12.8 Bar)
Oil pressure (at pressure switch, with engine warm) .... 71 psi (5.0 Bar) @ 5400 rpm, oil @ 80°C

Miscellaneous
Drive chain slack . . . . 25 to 35 mm
Throttle cable freeplay . . . . 2 to 6 mm
Tyre pressures (cold) . . . . see *Daily (pre-ride) checks*

Recommended lubricants and fluids
Engine/transmission oil type . . . . API grade SE, SF or SG motor oil
Engine/transmission oil viscosity . . . . SAE 10W40
Engine/transmission oil capacity
    Oil change . . . . 3.8 litres
    Oil and filter change . . . . 3.9 litres
    Following engine overhaul – dry engine, new filter . . . . 4.6 litres
Coolant type . . . . 50% distilled water, 50% corrosion inhibited ethylene glycol anti-freeze

Coolant capacity
    Radiator and engine . . . . 3.2 litres
    Reservoir . . . . 1.1 litres
Brake fluid . . . . DOT 4
Clutch fluid . . . . DOT 4
Front forks . . . . see Chapter 6 Specifications
Drive chain . . . . SAE 80 or 90 gear oil or chain lubricant suitable for O-ring chains
Steering head bearings . . . . multi-purpose grease
Swingarm pivot bearings . . . . multi-purpose grease
Suspension linkage bearings . . . . multi-purpose grease
Bearing seal lips . . . . multi-purpose grease
Gearchange lever/rear brake pedal pivots . . . . multi-purpose grease
Front brake lever pivot and piston tip . . . . silicone grease
Clutch lever pivot and piston tip . . . . silicone grease
Cables . . . . cable lubricant or engine oil
Sidestand and centrestand pivots . . . . molybdenum disulphide grease
Throttle grip . . . . multi-purpose grease or dry film lubricant

Torque settings
Rear axle nut . . . . 93 Nm
Spark plugs . . . . 12 Nm
Engine/transmission oil drain plug . . . . 29 Nm
Engine/transmission oil filter . . . . 10 Nm
Steering head bearing adjuster nut . . . . 25 Nm
Steering stem nut . . . . 103 Nm
Top yoke fork clamp bolts . . . . 23 Nm
Timing inspection cap . . . . 18 Nm

Maintenance schedule

Note: *The daily (pre-ride) checks outlined in the owner's manual covers those items which should be inspected on a daily basis. Always perform the pre-ride inspection at every maintenance interval (in addition to the procedures listed). The intervals listed below are the intervals recommended by the manufacturer for each particular operation during the model years covered in this manual. Your owner's manual may have different intervals for your model.*

Daily (pre-ride)
☐ See *'Daily (pre-ride) checks'* at the beginning of this manual.

After the initial 600 miles (1000 km)
Note: *This check is usually performed by a Honda dealer after the first 600 miles (1000 km) from new. Thereafter, maintenance is carried out according to the following intervals of the schedule.*

Every 500 miles (800 km) – US models
☐ Check, adjust and lubricate the drive chain (Section 1)

Every 600 miles (1000 km) – European models
- [ ] Check, adjust and lubricate the drive chain (Section 1)

Every 4000 miles (6000 km) or 6 months (whichever comes sooner)
- [ ] Check and adjust the idle speed (Section 2)
- [ ] Check the brake pads (Section 3)
- [ ] Check the clutch (Section 4)
- [ ] Check the spark plugs – US V, W, X and Y (1997 to 2000) models (Section 5)

Every 8000 miles (12,000 km) or 12 months (whichever comes sooner)
Carry out all the items under the 4000 mile (6000 km) check, plus the following
- [ ] Check the spark plugs – European V, W, X and Y (1997 to 2000) models (Section 5)
- [ ] Renew the spark plugs – US V, W, X and Y (1997 to 2000) models (Section 6)
- [ ] Lubricate the clutch/gearshift/brake lever/brake pedal/sidestand and centrestand pivots, and the throttle and choke cables (Section 7)
- [ ] Renew the engine oil and filter (Section 8)
- [ ] Check the fuel system and hoses (Section 9)
- [ ] Check the battery terminals (Section 10)
- [ ] Check and adjust the throttle and choke cables (Section 11)
- [ ] Check/adjust the carburettor synchronisation – V and W models (Section 12)
- [ ] Check the cooling system (Section 13)
- [ ] Check the brake system and brake light switch operation (Section 14)
- [ ] Check and adjust the headlight aim (Section 15)
- [ ] Check the sidestand and centrestand (Section 16)
- [ ] Check the suspension (Section 17)
- [ ] Check and adjust the steering head bearings (Section 18)
- [ ] Check the tightness of all nuts, bolts and fasteners (Section 19)
- [ ] Check the condition of the wheels and tyres (Section 20)
- [ ] Check the pulse secondary air injection (PAIR) system (Section 21)

Every 12,000 miles (18,000 km) or 18 months (whichever comes first)
Carry out all the items under the 4000 mile (6000 km) check, plus the following
- [ ] Renew the air filter element (Section 22)
- [ ] Check the evaporative emission control (EVAP) system hoses – California models (Section 23)
- [ ] Change the brake fluid (Section 24) at this mileage interval or every two years
- [ ] Change the clutch fluid (Section 25) at this mileage interval or every two years

Every 16,000 miles (24,000 km) or two years (whichever comes sooner)
Carry out all the items under the 8000 mile (12,000 km) check, plus the following
- [ ] Check and adjust the valve clearances (Section 26)
- [ ] Renew the spark plugs – European V, W, X and Y (1997 to 2000) models (Section 5)
- [ ] Check the spark plugs – 1 (2001) models onward (Section 5)

Every 24,000 miles (36,000 km) or two years (whichever comes sooner)
Carry out all the items under the 12,000 mile (18,000 km) and 8000 mile (12,000 km) checks, plus the following
- [ ] Change the coolant (Section 27)

Every 32,000 miles (48,000 km)
- [ ] Renew the spark plugs – 1 (2001) models onward (Section 5)

Non-scheduled maintenance
- [ ] Check the cylinder compression (Section 28)
- [ ] Check the engine oil pressure (Section 29)
- [ ] Check the wheel bearings (Section 30)
- [ ] Re-grease the steering head bearings (Section 31)
- [ ] Re-grease the swingarm and suspension linkage bearings (Section 32)
- [ ] Renew the brake master cylinder and caliper seals (Section 33)
- [ ] Renew the brake hoses (Section 34)
- [ ] Renew the fuel hoses (Section 35)
- [ ] Renew the clutch hose (Section 36)
- [ ] Renew the clutch master and slave cylinder seals (Section 37)
- [ ] Change the front fork oil (Section 38)

Component locations – right-hand side

1 Rear brake fluid reservoir
2 Coolant reservoir
3 Front brake fluid reservoir

4 Cooling system pressure
   cap
5 Engine oil filter

6 Engine oil drain plug
7 Engine oil filler cap
8 Engine oil level dipstick

9 Rear brake pedal height
   adjuster

Component locations – left-hand side

1 Clutch fluid reservoir	3 Air filter	6 Drive chain adjuster	9 DCBS secondary master
2 Steering head bearing	4 Fuel filter	7 Idle speed adjuster	cylinder
adjuster	5 Battery	8 Coolant drain plug	

1 This Chapter is designed to help the home mechanic maintain his/her motorcycle for safety, economy, long life and peak performance.

2 Deciding where to start or plug into the routine maintenance schedule depends on several factors. If your motorcycle has been maintained according to the warranty standards, you may want to pick up routine maintenance as it coincides with the next mileage or calendar interval. If you have owned the machine for some time but have never performed any maintenance on it, then you may want to start at the nearest interval and include some additional procedures to ensure that nothing important is overlooked. If you have just had a major engine overhaul, then you may want to start the maintenance routine from the beginning. If you have a used machine and have no knowledge of its history or maintenance record, you may desire to combine all the checks into one large service initially and then settle into the maintenance schedule prescribed.

3 Before beginning any maintenance or repair, the machine should be cleaned thoroughly, especially around the oil filter, spark plugs, valve covers, body panels, carburettors, etc. Cleaning will help ensure that dirt does not contaminate the engine and will allow you to detect wear and damage that could otherwise easily go unnoticed.

4 Certain maintenance information is sometimes printed on decals attached to the motorcycle. If the information on the decals differs from that included here, use the information on the decal.

Every 500 miles (800 km) – US models, every 600 miles (1000 km) – European models

> **1 Drive chain and sprockets –** check, adjustment, cleaning and lubrication

Check

1 A neglected drive chain won't last long and can quickly damage the sprockets. Routine chain adjustment and lubrication isn't difficult and will ensure maximum chain and sprocket life.

2 To check the chain, place the bike on its centrestand and shift the transmission into neutral. Make sure the ignition switch is OFF.

3 Push up on the bottom run of the chain and measure the slack midway between the two sprockets, then compare your measurement to that listed in this Chapter's Specifications **(see illustration)**. As the chain stretches with wear, adjustment will periodically be necessary (see below). Since the chain will rarely wear evenly, rotate the rear wheel so that another section of chain can be checked; do this several times to check the entire length of chain.

4 In some cases where lubrication has been neglected, corrosion and galling may cause the links to bind and kink, which effectively shortens the chain's length. Such links should be thoroughly cleaned and worked free. If the chain is tight between the sprockets, rusty or kinked, it's time to replace it with a new one. If you find a tight area, mark it with felt pen or paint, and repeat the measurement after the bike has been ridden. If the chain's still tight in the same area, it may be damaged or worn. Because a tight or kinked chain can damage the transmission bearings, it's a good idea to replace it with a new one.

5 Check the entire length of the chain for damaged rollers, loose links and pins, and missing O-rings and replace it with a new one if damage is found. **Note:** *Never install a new chain on old sprockets, and never use the old chain if you install new sprockets – replace the chain and sprockets as a set.*

6 Remove the front sprocket cover (see Chapter 6). Check the teeth on the front sprocket and the rear sprocket for wear **(see illustration)**.

7 Inspect the drive chain slider on the front of the swingarm for excessive wear and damage. There are wear limit arrows marked on the front of the slider. Replace it with a new one if it has worn down to the lines or the tips of the arrows (see Chapter 6).

Adjustment

8 Place the machine on its centrestand and rotate the rear wheel until the chain is positioned with the tightest point at the centre of its bottom run, then place the machine on its sidestand.

9 Slacken the axle nut **(see illustration)**.

10 Turn the adjuster bolt on each side of the swingarm evenly until the amount of freeplay specified at the beginning of the Chapter is obtained at the centre of the bottom run of the chain **(see illustration)**. Following adjustment, check that each chain adjustment marker is in the same position in relation to the mark on

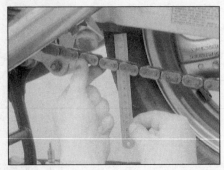

1.3 Push up on the chain and measure the slack

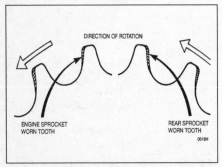

1.6 Check the sprockets in the areas indicated to see if they are worn excessively

1.9 Slacken the axle nut (arrowed)

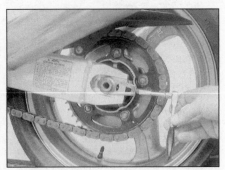

1.10a Turn each adjuster by an equal amount . . .

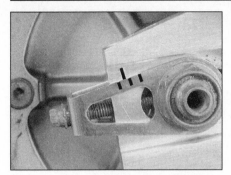

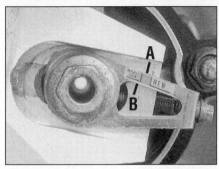

1.10b . . . then check the alignment marks as described

1.12 When the index line (A) meets the red zone (B), replace the chain with a new one

1.13 Tighten the axle nut to the specified torque

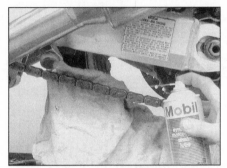

1.15 Apply the lubricant to the overlap in the sideplates

the swingarm **(see illustration)**. It is important the index line on the swingarm aligns with the same notch on each adjuster; if not, the rear wheel will be out of alignment with the front. If the line is difficult to see, use the rear edge of the swingarm as an index instead.

11 If there is a discrepancy in the chain adjuster positions, adjust one of them so that its position is exactly the same as the other. Check the chain freeplay as described above and readjust if necessary.

12 Also check the alignment of the wear decal on the left-hand adjustment marker with

the index line on the swingarm **(see illustration)**. When the index line meets the red REPLACE CHAIN zone, the drive chain has stretched excessively and must be replaced with a new one.

13 Counter-hold the axle head and tighten the axle nut to the torque setting specified at the beginning of the Chapter **(see illustration)**. Recheck the adjustment, then place the machine on its centrestand and spin the wheel to make sure it runs freely.

Cleaning and lubrication

14 If required, wash the chain in paraffin (kerosene) or a suitable non-flammable or high flash-point solvent that will not damage the O-rings, then wipe it off and allow it to dry, using compressed air if available. If the chain is excessively dirty it should be removed from the machine and allowed to soak in the paraffin or solvent (see Chapter 6).
Caution: Don't use petrol (gasoline), an unsuitable solvent or other cleaning fluids which might damage the internal sealing properties of the chain. Don't use high-pressure water to clean the chain. The entire process shouldn't take longer than ten minutes, otherwise the O-rings could be damaged.

15 For routine lubrication, the best time to lubricate the chain is after the motorcycle has been ridden. When the chain is warm, the lubricant will penetrate the joints between the sideplates better than when cold. **Note:** *Honda specifies SAE 80 to SAE 90 gear oil or an aerosol chain lube that it is suitable for O-ring or X-ring (sealed) chains; do not use any other chain lubricants – the solvents could damage the chain's sealing rings.* Apply the oil to the area where the sideplates overlap – not the middle of the rollers **(see illustration)**.

> **HAYNES HINT**
> *Apply the lubricant to the top of the lower chain run, so centrifugal force will work the oil into the chain when the bike is moving. After applying the lubricant, let it soak in a few minutes before wiping off any excess.*

> ⚠ *Warning: Take care not to get any lubricant on the tyres or brake system components. If any of the lubricant inadvertently contacts them, clean it off thoroughly using a suitable solvent before riding the machine.*

Every 4000 miles (6000 km) or 6 months

2 Idle speed –
check and adjustment

1 The idle speed should be checked and adjusted before and after the carburettors or throttle bodies are synchronised (balanced), after checking the valve clearances, and when it is obviously too high or too low. Before adjusting the idle speed, make sure the valve clearances and spark plug gaps are correct, and the air filter is clean. Also, turn the handlebars from side-to-side and check the idle speed does not change as you do. If it does, the throttle cables may not be adjusted or routed correctly, or may be worn out. This

is a dangerous condition that can cause loss of control of the bike. Be sure to correct this problem before proceeding.
2 The engine should be at normal operating temperature, which is usually reached after 10 to 15 minutes of stop-and-go riding. Place the motorcycle on its sidestand, and make sure the transmission is in neutral.
3 The idle speed adjuster is located on the left-hand side of the machine, between the frame and the fairing side panel **(see illustration)**. With the engine idling, adjust the speed by turning the adjuster screw until the idle speed listed in this Chapter's Specifications is obtained. Turn the screw clockwise to increase idle speed, and anti-clockwise to decrease it.
4 Snap the throttle open and shut a few

times, then recheck the idle speed. If necessary, repeat the adjustment procedure.
5 If a smooth, steady idle can't be achieved,

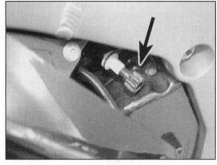

2.3 Idle speed adjuster (arrowed)

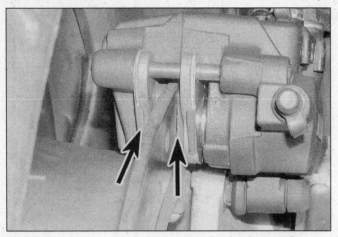

3.1a Location of brake pad wear indicators (arrowed) – pads in situ

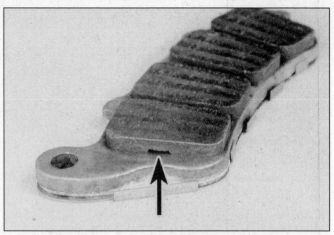

3.1b Brake pad wear indicator (arrowed) – pad removed

the fuel/air mixture may be incorrect (see Chapter 4) or the carburettors or throttle bodies may need synchronising. Also check the intake manifold rubbers for cracks or a loose clamp which will cause an air leak, resulting in a weak mixture. On fuel injected (X (1999) models onward), if this does not solve the problem, check the starter valve (see Chapter 4).

3 Brake pads – wear check

1 Each brake pad has wear indicators in the form of cutouts in the friction material. The wear indicators should be plainly visible by looking at the edges of the friction material from the best vantage point (from below the caliper on the front brake and from behind the caliper on the rear brake), although an accumulation of road dirt and brake dust could make them difficult to see **(see illustrations)**. If the indicators aren't visible, then the amount of friction material remaining should be, and it will be obvious when the pads need replacing. Honda do not specify a minimum thickness for the friction material, but anything less than 1 mm should be considered worn. **Note:** *Some after-market pads may use different indicators to those on the original equipment.*

2 If the pads are worn to or beyond the wear indicator (i.e. the beginning of the cutout) or there is little friction material remaining, they must be replaced with new ones, though it is advisable to replace the pads before they become this worn. If the pads are dirty or if you are in doubt as to the amount of friction material remaining, remove them for inspection (see Chapter 7). If the pads are excessively worn, check the brake discs (see Chapter 7).

3 Refer to Chapter 7 for details of pad replacement.

4 Clutch – check and adjustment

1 All models are fitted with an hydraulic clutch, which requires no adjustment.
2 Check the fluid level in the reservoir (see *Daily (pre-ride) checks).*
3 Inspect the hose and its connections for signs of fluid leakage, cracking, deterioration and wear. The clutch fluid should be changed every two years (see Section 25), and the hose replaced with a new one either if damaged or deteriorated, or every few years irrespective of condition (see Section 36). The master and slave cylinder seals should be changed every few years, or if leakage from them is evident (see Section 37).
4 Check the operation of the clutch. If there is evidence of air in the system (spongy feel to the lever, difficulty in engaging gear, drag when in gear), bleed the clutch (see Chapter 2). If the lever feels stiff or sticky, overhaul the release mechanism (see Chapter 2).
5 The clutch lever has a span adjuster which alters the distance of the lever from the handlebar. Each setting is identified by a notch in the adjuster which aligns with the arrow on the lever bracket. Turn the adjuster ring until the setting which best suits the rider is obtained **(see illustration)**.

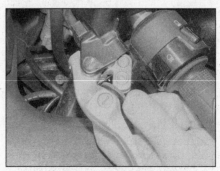

4.5 Adjusting the clutch lever span

5 Spark plug gaps – check and adjustment

Note: *Refer to the Maintenance schedule for the correct servicing interval for your model.*

Conventional spark plugs – V to Y (1997 to 2000) models

1 Make sure your spark plug socket is the correct size before attempting to remove the plugs – a suitable one is supplied in the motorcycle's tool kit which is stored under the seat.
2 It is possible to access the spark plugs from the front, but access is restricted. It does however mean there is no need to remove the fuel tank. For best access using this method, and to prevent the possibility of damaging any bodywork, remove both the fairing side panels and the fairing (see Chapter 8). Otherwise, remove only the fairing side panels, the cockpit trim panels and the fuel tank trim panels (see Chapter 8). On V and W (1997 and 1998) models, remove the trim panels from around the oil cooler hoses and release the hoses from the guides. On X (1999) models onward, unscrew the bolts securing the oil cooler to the frame, but leave it attached to the radiator (see Chapter 2) – there is no need to detach the oil hoses. On all models, displace the radiator from its mounts and move it away as much as possible (see Chapter 3) – there is no need to detach any hoses, but disconnect the wiring connector. If access is still too restricted for you, drain the coolant (see Section 27), and remove the oil cooler and/or radiator as required. The alternative and easier method is to remove the fuel tank and the air filter housing (see Chapter 4), and to access the plugs from the top.
3 Clean the area around the plug caps to prevent any dirt falling into the spark plug channels.
4 Check that the cylinder location is marked

5.4a Remove the spark plug cap

5.4b Unscrew the spark plug using the tool provided in the kit or a suitable alternative

on each plug lead, then pull the cap off each spark plug **(see illustration)**. Clean the area around the base of the plugs to prevent any dirt falling into the engine. Using either the plug removing tool supplied in the bike's toolkit or a deep socket type wrench, unscrew the plugs from the cylinder head **(see illustration)**. Lay each plug out in relation to its cylinder; if any plug shows up a problem it will then be easy to identify the troublesome cylinder.

5 Inspect the electrodes for wear. Both the centre and side electrodes should have square edges and the side electrodes should be of uniform thickness. Look for excessive

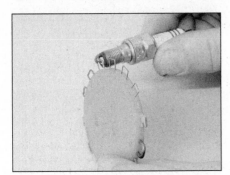

5.8a Using a wire type gauge to measure the spark plug electrode gap

deposits and evidence of a cracked or chipped insulator around the centre electrode. Compare your spark plugs to the colour spark plug reading chart at the end of this manual. Check the threads, the washer and the ceramic insulator body for cracks and other damage.

6 If the electrodes are not excessively worn, if no cracks or chips are visible in the insulator, and if the deposits can be easily removed with a wire brush, the plugs can be re-gapped and re-used. If in doubt concerning the condition of the plugs, replace them with new ones, as the expense is minimal.

7 Cleaning spark plugs by sandblasting is permitted, provided you blow out the plugs with compressed air and clean them with a high flash-point solvent afterwards.

8 Before installing the plugs, make sure they are the correct type and heat range and check the gap between the electrodes **(see illustrations)**. Compare the gap to that specified and adjust as necessary. If the gap must be adjusted, bend the side electrodes only and be very careful not to chip or crack the insulator nose **(see illustration)**. Make sure the washer is in place before installing each plug.

9 Since the cylinder head is made of aluminium, which is soft and easily damaged,

thread the plugs into the heads turning the tool by hand **(see illustration)**. Once the plugs are finger-tight, the job can be finished with a spanner on the tool supplied or a socket drive **(see illustration 5.4b)**. If new plugs are being used, tighten them by 1/2 a turn after the washer has seated. If the old plugs are being reused, tighten them by 1/8 to 1/4 turn after they have seated. If a torque wrench can be applied, tighten the spark plugs to the torque setting specified at the beginning of the Chapter. Otherwise tighten them according the instructions on the box. Do not over-tighten them.

HAYNES HiNT *As the plugs are quite recessed, slip a short length of hose over the end of the plug to use as a tool to thread it into place. The hose will grip the plug well enough to turn it, but will start to slip if the plug begins to cross-thread in the hole – this will prevent damaged threads.*

10 Reconnect the spark plug caps, making sure they are securely connected to the correct cylinder **(see illustration 5.4a)**. Install all other components previously removed.

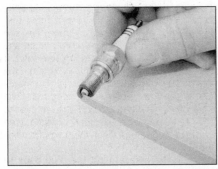

5.8b Using a feeler gauge to measure the spark plug electrode gap (conventional plug only)

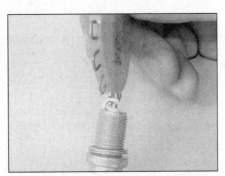

5.8c Adjust the electrode gap by bending the side electrode only (conventional plug only)

5.9 Thread the plug as far as possible turning the tool by hand

Iridium spark plugs – 1 (2001) models onward

11 Refer to Steps 1 to 4 above to remove the spark plugs from the engine.

12 Iridium spark plugs have much better anti-oxidation and anti-corrosion qualities than conventional plugs and thus do not require such frequent maintenance.

13 At the specified interval check the condition of the electrodes, referring to the spark plug reading chart at the end of this manual if signs of contamination are evident. Contaminated plugs should be renewed and not cleaned using conventional methods.

14 Examine the pointed iridium-tipped centre electrode; if the tip has rounded off, the plug is worn. Measure the gap between the two electrodes with a wire type gauge (see illustration 5.8a) – do not use blade type feeler gauges because the iridium tip might become damaged. The gap should be as given in the Specifications at the beginning of this chapter; if the electrodes have worn beyond this figure the plug must be renewed. Do not bend the outer electrode to adjust the gap.

15 Check the threads, the washer and the ceramic insulator body for cracks and other damage.

16 Install the plugs as described in Steps 9 and 10 above. Note that Honda advise that the specified iridium plugs must be fitted to this model – do not substitute with conventional plugs.

> **HAYNES HiNT** *Stripped plug threads in the cylinder head can be repaired with a Heli-Coil insert – see 'Tools and Workshop Tips' in the Reference section.*

Every 8000 miles (12,000 km) or 12 months

Carry out all the items under the 4000 mile (6000 km) check, plus the following:

6 Spark plugs – renewal
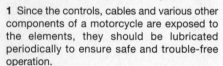

Note: *Refer to the Maintenance schedule for the correct renewal interval for your model.*

1 Remove the old spark plugs as described in Section 5 and install new ones.

7 Stands, lever pivots and cables – lubrication

1 Since the controls, cables and various other components of a motorcycle are exposed to the elements, they should be lubricated periodically to ensure safe and trouble-free operation.

2 The footrests, clutch and brake levers, brake pedal, gearchange lever and linkage, sidestand and centrestand pivots should be lubricated frequently. In order for the lubricant to be applied where it will do the most good, the component should be disassembled. The lubricant recommended by Honda for each application is listed at the beginning of the Chapter. If chain or cable lubricant is being used, it can be applied to the pivot joint gaps and will usually work its way into the areas where friction occurs, so less disassembly of the component is needed (however it is always better to do so and clean off all dirt and old lubricant first). If motor oil or light grease is being used, apply it sparingly as it may attract dirt (which could cause the controls to bind or wear at an accelerated rate). **Note:** *One of the best lubricants for the control lever pivots is a dry-film lubricant (available from many sources by different names).*

3 To lubricate the cables, disconnect the relevant cable at its upper end, then lubricate it with a pressure adapter and aerosol lubricant, or if one is not available, using the set-up shown **(see illustrations)**. See Chapter 4 for the choke and throttle cable removal procedures.

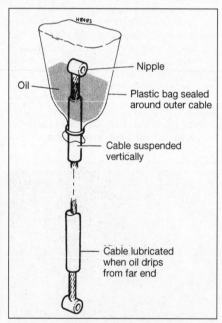

8 Engine oil and oil filter – change

⚠️ *Warning: Be careful when draining the oil, as the exhaust pipes, the engine, and the oil itself can cause severe burns.*

1 Consistent routine oil and filter changes are the single most important maintenance procedure you can perform on a motorcycle. The oil not only lubricates the internal parts of the engine, transmission and clutch, but it also acts as a coolant, a cleaner, a sealant, and a protectant. Because of these demands, the oil takes a terrific amount of abuse and should be replaced often with new oil of the recommended grade and type. Saving a little money on the difference in cost between a good oil and a cheap oil won't pay off if the engine is damaged. The oil filter should be changed with every oil change.

2 Before changing the oil, warm up the engine so the oil will drain easily. Put the motorcycle on its centrestand. Remove the fairing side panels (see Chapter 8).

3 Position a clean drain tray below the engine. Unscrew the oil filler cap from the clutch cover to vent the crankcase and to act as a reminder that there is no oil in the engine **(see illustration)**.

7.3a Lubricating a cable with a pressure lubricator. Make sure the tool seals around the inner cable

7.3b Lubricating a cable with a makeshift funnel and motor oil

8.3 Unscrew the oil filler cap . . .

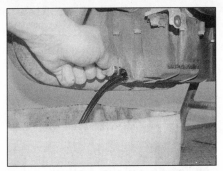

8.4 . . . and the oil drain plug and allow the oil to completely drain

8.5a Install the drain plug, using a new sealing washer if necessary, . . .

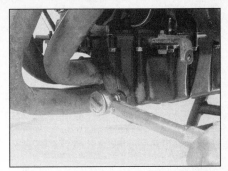

8.5b . . . and tighten it to the specified torque setting

4 Unscrew the oil drain plug from the front of the engine and allow the oil to flow into the drain tray **(see illustration)**. Check the condition of the sealing washer on the drain plug and replace it with a new one if it is damaged or worn – it is advisable to use a new one whatever the condition of the old one.

5 When the oil has completely drained, fit the plug to the sump, using a new sealing washer if necessary, and tighten it to the torque setting specified at the beginning of the Chapter **(see illustrations)**. Avoid overtightening, as it is quite easy to damage the threads in the sump.

6 Now place the drain tray below the oil filter. Unscrew the oil filter using a filter removing strap or chain-wrench and tip any residual oil into the drain tray **(see illustrations)**. A filter socket can be used if it is not too bulky, but there is not much clearance between the filter

and exhaust downpipes and not all aftermarket ones will fit (using the Honda special tool (pt. no. 07HAA-PJ70100) will guarantee a fit).

7 Ensure the crankcase is clean and free from dirt, then smear clean engine oil onto the rubber seal on the new filter and thread it onto the engine **(see illustrations)**. Tighten it to the specified torque setting using the filter socket if available (and if your torque wrench is not too bulky), or tighten the filter as tight as possible by hand, or by the number of turns specified on the filter itself or its packaging. **Note:** *Do not use a strap or chain filter removing tool to tighten the filter as you will damage it.*

8 Refill the engine to the proper level using the recommended type and amount of oil (see *Daily (pre-ride) checks)*. With the motorcycle vertical, the oil level should lie between the upper and lower level lines on the dipstick (see *Daily (pre-ride) checks)*. Install the filler

cap **(see illustration 7.3)**. Start the engine and let it run for two or three minutes (make sure that the oil pressure light extinguishes after a few seconds). Shut it off, wait a few minutes, then check the oil level. If necessary, add more oil to bring the level up to the upper level line. Check around the drain plug and the oil filter for leaks. A leak around the drain plug probably means a new washer is needed. A leak around the filter probably means it is not tight enough. Install the fairing side panels (see Chapter 8).

> **HAYNES HiNT** *Saving a little money on the difference between good and cheap oils won't pay off if the engine is damaged as a result.*

9 The old oil drained from the engine cannot be re-used and should be disposed of properly. Check with your local refuse disposal company, disposal facility or environmental agency to see whether they will accept the used oil for recycling. Don't pour used oil into drains or onto the ground.

8.6a Unscrew the filter using a filter removing tool . . .

8.6b . . . and allow the oil to drain

> **HAYNES HiNT** *Check the old oil carefully – if it is very metallic coloured, then the engine is experiencing wear from break-in (new engine) or from insufficient lubrication. If there are flakes or chips of metal in the oil, then something is drastically wrong internally and the engine will have to be disassembled for inspection and repair. If there are pieces of fibre-like material in the oil, the clutch is experiencing excessive wear and should be checked.*

8.7a Smear clean oil onto the seal . . .

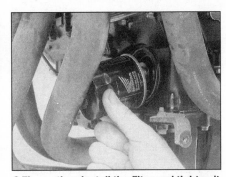

8.7b . . . then install the filter and tighten it as described

OIL CARE
FOLLOW THE CODE

OIL BANK LINE
0800 66 33 66
www.oilbankline.org.uk

Note: It is antisocial and illegal to dump oil down the drain. To find the location of your local oil recycling bank, call this number free.

9 Fuel system – check

Warning: Petrol (gasoline) is extremely flammable, so take extra precautions when you work on any part of the fuel system. Don't smoke or allow open flames or bare light bulbs near the work area, and don't work in a garage where a natural gas-type appliance is present. If you spill any fuel on your skin, rinse it off immediately with soap and water. When you perform any kind of work on the fuel system, wear safety glasses and have a fire extinguisher suitable for a Class B type fire (flammable liquids) on hand.

Check – carburettor models (V and W, 1997 and 1998 models)

1 Raise the fuel tank (see Chapter 4) and check the tank, the fuel tap and the fuel hoses for signs of leakage, deterioration or damage; in particular check that there is no leakage from the fuel hoses. Also check the vacuum hose to the fuel tap. Renew any hoses which are cracked or have deteriorated.

2 If the fuel tap is leaking, tighten the assembly screws (see Chapter 4). If leakage persists undo the screws and disassemble the tap, noting how the components fit (see Chapter 4). Inspect and clean all components and rebuild the tap. If leakage persists, replace the whole tap with a new one – individual components are not available. If the carburettor gaskets are leaking, the carburettors should be disassembled and rebuilt using new gaskets and seals (see Chapter 4).

Check – fuel injected models (X (1999) models onward)

3 Raise the fuel tank (see Chapter 4) and check the tank and the fuel hoses for signs of leakage, deterioration or damage. Also check for signs of fuel leakage between the injectors, the fuel rail and the throttle bodies. If necessary, remove the injectors and replace the O-rings and seals (see Chapter 4).

Filter cleaning

4 Cleaning or replacement of the fuel filter is advised after a particularly high mileage has been covered. It is also necessary if fuel starvation is suspected, or if the filter looks clogged or dirty. Honda do not specify a replacement interval – fuel is so clean now that this may not always be necessary. Check the condition of the inside of your tank – if it is old and there is evidence of rust, remove, drain and clean the tank and tap (see Chapter 4), and fit a new filter afterwards.

5 On carburettor models, a fuel strainer is fitted in the tank and is held in place by the fuel tap. Remove the fuel tank and the fuel tap (see Chapter 4). Withdraw the gauze strainer and discard the O-ring. Clean off all traces of dirt and fuel sediment. Check the gauze for holes. If any are found, a new strainer must be fitted. Replace O-ring with a new one, then fit the strainer into the tank and install the tap (see Chapter 4).

6 On fuel injection models, an in-line fuel filter is fitted alongside the fuel pump inside the fuel tank. To replace the filter, remove the fuel pump assembly from the tank (see Chapter 4). Undo the clamp screw and release the filter from its holder, noting which way round it fits **(see illustration)**. Have a rag handy to soak up any residual fuel, then release the clamps and disconnect the hoses from the filter, noting which fits where. Discard the filter. Install the new filter, making sure it is the correct way round, and secure it with the clamp. Fit the hoses to the unions on the filter and secure them with the clamps. A fuel strainer is fitted in the base of the fuel pump assembly housing. It is basically a wad of coarse steel wool. Check that there are no large particles of dirt caught in it and clean it through using petrol if necessary. If it is clogged with debris, replace it with a new wad. Install the fuel pump assembly (see Chapter 4). Start the engine and check that there are no leaks.

10 Battery – check

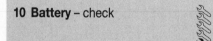

1 All models covered in this manual are fitted with a sealed MF (maintenance free) battery. **Note:** *Do not attempt to remove the battery* caps to check the electrolyte level or battery specific gravity. Removal will damage the caps, resulting in electrolyte leakage and battery damage. All that should be done is to check that the terminals are clean and tight and that the casing is not damaged or leaking. See Chapter 9 for further details.

2 If the machine is not in regular use, disconnect the battery and give it a refresher charge every month to six weeks (see Chapter 9).

11 Throttle and choke cables – check

Throttle cables

1 Make sure the throttle grip rotates smoothly and freely from fully closed to fully open with the front wheel turned at various angles. The grip should return automatically from fully open to fully closed when released.

2 If the throttle sticks, this is probably due to a cable fault. Remove the cables (see Chapter 4) and lubricate them (see Section 7). Install the cables, making sure they are correctly routed. If this fails to improve the operation of the throttle, the cables must be replaced with new ones. Note that in very rare cases the fault could lie in the carburettors or throttle bodies (according to model) rather than the cables, necessitating their removal and inspection of the throttle linkage (see Chapter 4).

3 With the throttle operating smoothly, check for a small amount of freeplay in the cables, measured in terms of the amount of twistgrip rotation before the throttle opens, and compare the amount to that listed in this Chapter's Specifications **(see illustration)**. If it's incorrect, adjust the cables to correct it as follows.

4 Freeplay adjustments can be made using the adjuster in the accelerator cable where it leaves the throttle/switch housing on the handlebar. Loosen the locknut and turn the adjuster in or out as required until the specified amount of freeplay is obtained (see this Chapter's Specifications), then retighten the locknut **(see illustration)**.

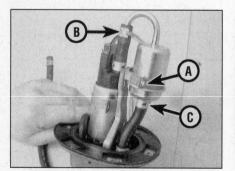

9.6 Undo the screw (A) and release the clamp, then detach the hoses (B and C)

11.3 Throttle cable freeplay is measured in terms of twistgrip rotation

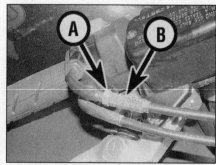

11.4 Throttle cable adjuster locknut (A) and adjuster (B) – twistgrip end

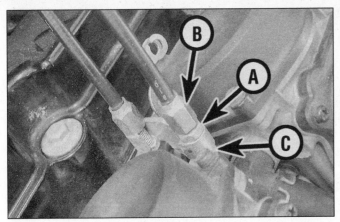
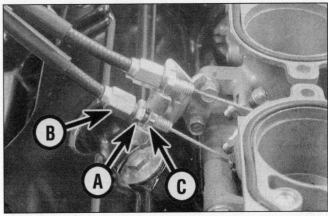

11.5a Throttle cable adjuster locknut (A), adjuster (B) and lower nut (C) – carburettor end

11.5b Throttle cable adjuster locknut (A), adjuster (B) and lower nut (C) – throttle body end

5 If the adjuster has reached its limit of adjustment, reset it so that the freeplay is at a maximum, then remove the fuel tank and air filter housing (see Chapter 4) and adjust the cable at the carburettor/throttle body end. The adjuster is on the upper cable in the bracket on carburettor models, and on the lower cable on fuel injection models. Slacken the adjuster locknut, then screw the adjuster in or out as required, making sure the lower nut remains captive in the bracket, thereby threading itself along the adjuster as you turn it, until the specified amount of freeplay is obtained, then tighten the locknut (see illustrations). Further adjustments can now be made at the throttle end. If the cable cannot be adjusted as specified, replace it with a new one (see Chapter 4).

⚠ **Warning: Turn the handlebars all the way through their travel with the engine idling. Idle speed should not change. If it does, the cables may be routed incorrectly. Correct this condition before riding the bike.**

6 Check that the throttle twistgrip operates smoothly and snaps shut quickly when released.

Choke cable (carburettor models)

7 If the choke does not operate smoothly this is probably due to a cable fault. Remove the cable (see Chapter 4) and lubricate it (see Section 7). Check that the inner cable slides freely and easily in the outer cable. If not, replace the cable with a new one. With the cable removed, make sure the choke lever is able to slide freely in the switch housing. Install the cable, routing it so it takes the smoothest route possible.
8 If this fails to improve the operation of the choke, the fault could lie in the carburettors rather than the cable, necessitating the removal of the carburettors and inspection of the choke plungers and the linkage between them (see Chapter 4).

12 Carburettors – synchronisation (V and W models)

⚠ **Warning: Petrol (gasoline) is extremely flammable, so take extra precautions when you work on any part of the fuel system. Don't smoke or allow open flames or bare light bulbs near the work area, and don't work in a garage where a natural gas-type appliance is present. If you spill any fuel on your skin, rinse it off immediately with soap and water. When you perform any kind of work on the fuel** system, wear safety glasses and have a fire extinguisher suitable for a Class B type fire (flammable liquids) on hand.

⚠ **Warning: Take great care not to burn your hand on the hot engine unit when accessing the gauge take-off points on the intake manifolds. Do not allow exhaust gases to build up in the work area; either perform the check outside or use an exhaust gas extraction system.**

1 Carburettor synchronisation is simply the process of adjusting the carburettors so they pass the same amount of fuel/air mixture to each cylinder. This is done by measuring the vacuum produced in each intake duct. Carburettors that are out of synchronisation will cause increased fuel consumption, increased engine temperature, less than ideal throttle response and higher vibration levels. Before synchronising the carburettors, make sure the valve clearances are properly set.
2 To properly synchronise the carburettors, you will need a set of vacuum gauges or calibrated tubes to indicate engine vacuum. The equipment used should be suitable for a four cylinder engine and come complete with the necessary adapters and hoses to fit the take-off points. **Note:** *Because of the nature of the synchronisation procedure and the need for special instruments, most owners leave the task to a Honda dealer.*
3 Start the engine and let it run until it reaches normal operating temperature.

⚠ **Warning: The engine and carburettors will be hot. With the restricted access to the screws, great care must be taken not to burn yourself while synchronising the carburettors.**

4 Remove the fuel tank (see Chapter 4). Remove the blanking screws or caps or detach the vacuum hose(s) from the vacuum take-off points on the engine, noting what fits where (arrangement varies between models) **(see illustrations)**. Thread in suitable adapter pieces where blanking screws have been removed **(see illustration 12.13b)**.

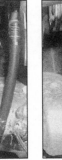

12.4a Vacuum take-off points (arrowed) – cylinders 1 and 2

12.4b Vacuum take-off points (arrowed) – cylinders 3 and 4

5 Connect the vacuum gauge hoses to the adapters or take-off points **(see illustration 12.14)**. Make sure they are a good fit because any air leaks will result in false readings. Obtain a suitable petrol container to act as a remote fuel tank and connect it to the carburettor fuel hoses using suitable hoses and adapters.

6 Start the engine and adjust the idle speed (see Section 2). If using vacuum gauges fitted with damping adjustment, set this so that the needle flutter is just eliminated but so that they can still respond to small changes in pressure.

7 The vacuum reading for each cylinder should be the same. If the vacuum readings vary, adjust the carburettors by turning the synchronising screws situated in the throttle linkage between the carburettors until the readings are the same **(see illustration)**. **Note:** *Do not press hard on the screw whilst adjusting it, otherwise a false reading will be obtained.* The No. 3 carburettor is the base carburettor to which all other carburettors should be matched. First synchronise the No. 4 carburettor to the No. 3 using the synchronising screw situated between them. Now synchronise Nos. 1 and. 2 carburettors using the synchronising screw between them. Now synchronise Nos. 1 and 2 to Nos. 3 and 4 using the centre synchronising screw.

8 When the carburettors are synchronised, open and close the throttle quickly to settle the linkage, and recheck the gauge readings, readjusting if necessary.

9 When the adjustment is complete, recheck the vacuum readings, then adjust the idle speed by turning the throttle stop screw (see Section 2) until the idle speed listed in this Chapter's Specifications is obtained. Stop the engine.

10 Remove the vacuum gauges and any adapters, then install the blanking screws or caps to their original positions and reconnect the hose(s) previously detached. Install the fuel tank (see Chapter 4).

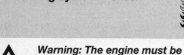

13 Cooling system – check

Warning: The engine must be cool before beginning this procedure.

1 Check the coolant level (see *Daily (pre-ride) checks*).

2 Remove the fairing side panels (see Chapter 8). Check the entire cooling system for evidence of leakage. Examine each rubber coolant hose along its entire length. Look for cracks, abrasions and other damage. Squeeze each hose at various points. They should feel firm, yet pliable, and return to their original shape when released. If they are dried out or hard, replace them with new ones.

3 Check for evidence of leaks at each cooling system joint and around the pump on the left-

12.7 Adjust the carburettors using the synchronisation screws (arrowed) until the gauge readings are the same

hand side of the engine. Tighten the hose clips carefully to prevent future leaks. If the pump is leaking, check that the cover bolts are tight. If they are, replace the O-ring in the cover with a new one (see Chapter 3).

4 To prevent leakage of coolant from the cooling system to the lubrication system and vice versa, two seals are fitted on the pump shaft. On the bottom of the pump housing there is a drain hole. If either seal fails, the drain allows the coolant or oil to escape and prevents them mixing. The seal on the water pump side is of the mechanical type which bears on the rear face of the impeller. The second seal, which is mounted behind the mechanical seal is of the normal feathered lip type. If on inspection the drain shows signs of coolant leakage, remove the pump and replace it with a new one – it comes as an assembly. Refer to Chapter 3 for details.

5 Check the radiator for leaks and other damage. Leaks in the radiator leave tell-tale scale deposits or coolant stains on the outside of the core below the leak. If leaks are noted, remove the radiator (see Chapter 3) and have it repaired or replace it with a new one.

Caution: Do not use a liquid leak stopping compound to try to repair leaks.

6 Check the radiator fins for mud, dirt and insects, which may impede the flow of air through the radiator. If the fins are dirty, remove the radiator (see Chapter 3) and clean it using water or low pressure compressed air directed through the fins from the inner side of the radiator. If the fins are bent or distorted, straighten them carefully with a screwdriver. If the air flow is restricted by bent or damaged fins over more than 20% of the radiator's surface area, replace the radiator with a new one.

7 Check the oil cooler and its pipes/hoses in a similar manner to the Steps above.

8 Remove the pressure cap from the radiator filler neck by turning it anti-clockwise until it reaches a stop **(see illustration)**. If you hear a hissing sound (indicating there is still pressure in the system), wait until it stops. Now press down on the cap and continue turning it until it can be removed. Check the condition of the coolant in the system. If it is rust-coloured or if

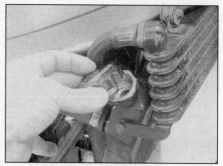

13.8 Remove the pressure cap as described

accumulations of scale are visible, drain and flush the system and refill it with new coolant (See Section 27). Check the cap seal for cracks and other damage. If in doubt about the pressure cap's condition, have it tested by a Honda dealer or replace it with a new one. Install the cap by turning it clockwise until it reaches the first stop then push down on it and continue turning until it can turn no further.

9 Check the antifreeze content of the coolant with an antifreeze hydrometer. Sometimes coolant looks like it's in good condition, but might be too weak to offer adequate protection. If the hydrometer indicates a weak mixture, drain, flush and refill the system (see Section 27).

10 Start the engine and let it reach normal operating temperature, then check for leaks again. As the coolant temperature increases, the electric fan (mounted on the back of the radiator) should come on automatically and the temperature should begin to drop. If it does not, refer to Chapter 3 and check the fan and fan circuit carefully.

11 If the coolant level is consistently low, and no evidence of leaks can be found, have the entire system pressure checked by a Honda dealer.

14 Brake system – check

General check

1 A routine general check of the brake system will ensure that any problems are discovered and remedied before the rider's safety is jeopardised.

2 Check the brake lever and pedal for loose connections, improper or rough action, excessive play, bends, and other damage. Replace any damaged parts with new ones (see Chapter 7).

3 Make sure all brake component fasteners are tight. Check the brake pads for wear (see Section 3) and make sure the fluid level in the reservoirs is correct (see *Daily (pre-ride) checks*). Look for leaks at the hose and pipe

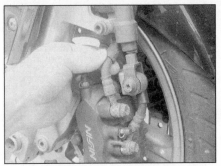

14.3 Flex the hoses and check for cracks, bulges and leaking fluid. Also check the pipes and all connections for leaks

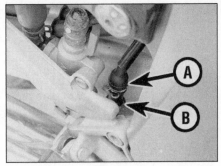

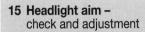

14.5 Hold the rear brake light switch body (A) and turn the adjuster ring (B) as required

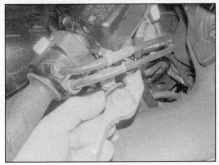

14.6 Adjusting the front brake lever span

connections and check for cracks in the hoses and pipes **(see illustration)**. If the lever or pedal is spongy, bleed the brakes (see Chapter 7).

4 Make sure the brake light operates when the front brake lever is pulled in. The front brake light switch, mounted on the underside of the master cylinder, is not adjustable. If it fails to operate properly, check it (see Chapter 9).

5 Make sure the brake light is activated just before the rear brake takes effect. If adjustment is necessary, hold the switch and turn the adjuster ring on the switch body until the brake light is activated when required **(see illustration)**. The switch is mounted on the inside of the rider's right-hand footrest bracket, just ahead of the master cylinder. If the brake light comes on too late, turn the ring clockwise. If the brake light comes on too soon or is permanently on, turn the ring anti-clockwise. If the switch doesn't operate the brake light, check it (see Chapter 9).

6 The front brake lever has a span adjuster which alters the distance of the lever from the handlebar **(see illustration)**. Each setting is identified by a notch in the adjuster which aligns with the arrow on the lever. Turn the adjuster ring until the setting which best suits the rider is obtained.

7 The height of the rear brake pedal can be adjusted to suit the rider's preference. Slacken the clevis locknut on the master cylinder pushrod, then turn the pushrod using

a spanner on the hex at the top of the rod until the pedal is at the desired height **(see illustration)**. On completion tighten the locknut securely. Adjust the rear brake light switch after adjusting the pedal height (see Step 5). Note that Honda specify a standard pedal height, achieved by setting the distance between the eye in the clevis and the master cylinder lower mounting bolt hole at 64 to 66 mm.

DCBS (Dual Combined Brake System) check

8 With the machine on its centrestand, and while an assistant spins the rear wheel by hand, pull the left-hand front brake caliper up so that the secondary master cylinder pushrod is activated, and check that the rear wheel is locked by the brake. If the wheel can be turned, the DCBS system is faulty and must be checked (see Chapter 7). Also check that the linkage between the left-hand caliper and the secondary master cylinder pushrod moves smoothly and freely.

9 Place a jack under the sump, with a piece of wood between them to spread the load, and raise the front wheel off the ground. Make sure the jack is not located either on the fairing, the exhaust or the oil filter. Press the rear brake pedal down and check that the front wheel is locked by the brake. If the wheel can be turned, the DCBS system is faulty and must be checked (see Chapter 7).

15 Headlight aim – check and adjustment

Note: *An improperly adjusted headlight may cause problems for oncoming traffic or provide poor, unsafe illumination of the road ahead. Before adjusting the headlight aim, be sure to consult with local traffic laws and regulations – for UK models refer to MOT Test Checks in the Reference section.*

1 The headlight beam can adjusted both horizontally and vertically. Before making any adjustment, check that the tyre pressures are correct and the suspension is adjusted as required. Make any adjustments to the headlight aim with the machine on level ground, with the fuel tank half full and with an assistant sitting on the seat. If the bike is usually ridden with a passenger on the back, have a second assistant to do this.

2 Vertical adjustment is made by turning the adjuster knob on the top left corner of the headlight unit **(see illustration)**. Remove the left-hand cockpit trim panel to access the knob (see Chapter 8). Turn it clockwise to move the beam up, and anti-clockwise to move it down.

3 Horizontal adjustment is made by turning the adjuster knob on the bottom right corner of the headlight unit **(see illustration 15.2)**. Remove the right-hand cockpit trim panel to access the knob (see Chapter 8). Turn it clockwise to move the beam to the right, and anti-clockwise to move it to the left.

16 Sidestand and centrestand – check

1 Check the stand springs for damage and distortion. The springs must be capable of retracting the stands fully and holding them retracted when the motorcycle is in use. If a spring is sagged or broken it must be replaced with a new one.

2 Lubricate the stand pivots regularly (see Section 7).

14.7 Slacken the locknut (A) and turn the pushrod using the hex (B) to adjust pedal height

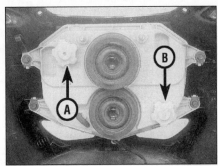

15.2 Headlight beam vertical adjustment knob (A), horizontal adjustment knob (B)

17.7a Checking for play in the swingarm bearings

17.7b Checking for play in the rear shock mountings and suspension linkage bearings

18.4 Checking for play in the steering head bearings

3 Check the stands and their mounts for bends and cracks. Stands can often be repaired by welding.
4 Check the operation of the sidestand switch by shifting the transmission into neutral, retracting the stand and starting the engine. Pull in the clutch lever and select a gear. Extend the sidestand. The engine should stop as the sidestand is extended. If the sidestand switch does not operate as described, check its circuit (see Chapter 9).

17 Suspension – check

1 The suspension components must be maintained in top operating condition to ensure rider safety. Loose, worn or damaged suspension parts decrease the motorcycle's stability and control.

Front suspension

2 While standing alongside the motorcycle, apply the front brake and push on the handlebars to compress the forks several times. See if they move up-and-down smoothly without binding. If binding is felt, the forks should be disassembled and inspected (see Chapter 6).
3 Inspect the area around the dust seal for signs of oil leakage, then carefully lever up the dust seal using a flat-bladed screwdriver and inspect the area around the fork seal. If leakage is evident, the seals must be replaced with new ones (see Chapter 6).
4 Check the tightness of all suspension nuts and bolts to be sure none have worked loose.

Rear suspension

5 Inspect the rear shock for fluid leakage and tightness of its mountings. If leakage is found, the shock should be replaced with a new one (see Chapter 6).
6 With the aid of an assistant to support the bike, compress the rear suspension several times. It should move up and down freely without binding. If any binding is felt, the worn or faulty component must be identified and

checked (see Chapter 6). The problem could be due to either the shock absorber, the suspension linkage components or the swingarm components.
7 Support the motorcycle on its centrestand so that the rear wheel is off the ground. Grab the swingarm and rock it from side to side – there should be no discernible movement at the rear **(see illustration)**. If there's a little movement or a slight clicking can be heard, inspect the tightness of all the rear suspension mounting bolts and nuts, referring to the torque settings specified at the beginning of Chapter 6, and re-check for movement. Next, grasp the top of the rear wheel and pull it upwards – there should be no discernible freeplay before the shock absorber begins to compress **(see illustration)**. Any freeplay felt in either check indicates worn bearings in the suspension linkage or swingarm, or worn shock absorber mountings. The worn components must be replaced with new ones(see Chapter 6).
8 To make an accurate assessment of the swingarm bearings, remove the rear wheel (see Chapter 7) and the bolt securing the suspension linkage assembly to the swingarm (see Chapter 6). Grasp the rear of the swingarm with one hand and place your other hand at the junction of the swingarm and the frame. Try to move the rear of the swingarm from side-to-side. Any wear (play) in the bearings should be felt as movement between the swingarm and the frame at the front. If there is any play the swingarm will be felt to move forward and backward at the front (not from side-to-side). Next, move the swingarm up and down through its full travel. It should move freely, without any binding or rough spots. If there is any play in the swingarm or if it does not move freely, remove the bearings for inspection (see Chapter 6).

18 Steering head bearings – freeplay check and adjustment

1 This motorcycle is equipped with caged ball steering head bearings which can become

dented, rough or loose during normal use of the machine. In extreme cases, worn or loose steering head bearings can cause steering wobble – a condition that is potentially dangerous.

Check

2 Support the motorcycle on its centrestand. Raise the front wheel off the ground either by having an assistant push down on the rear or by placing a support under the engine.
3 Point the front wheel straight-ahead and slowly move the handlebars from side-to-side. Any dents or roughness in the bearing races will be felt and the bars will not move smoothly and freely. Again point the wheel straight ahead, then tap the front of the wheel to one side. The wheel should 'fall' under its own weight to the limit of its lock, indicating that the bearings are not too tight. Check for similar movement to the other side. If the steering doesn't move freely through its entire lock, and it's not due to the resistance of cables or hoses, then the bearings should be adjusted as described below.
4 Next, grasp the bottom of the forks and try to move them forward and backward **(see illustration)**. Any looseness in the steering head bearings will be felt as front-to-rear movement of the forks. If play is felt in the bearings, adjust the steering head as described below.

 HAYNES HINT *Freeplay in the fork due to worn fork bushes can be misinterpreted for steering head bearing play – do not confuse the two.*

Adjustment

5 Remove the fuel tank (see Chapter 4) and the fairing (see Chapter 8). This will prevent the possibility of damage should a tool slip.
6 Displace the handlebars from the top yoke (see Chapter 6). Support them so the brake and clutch master cylinders are upright to prevent the possibility of fluid leakage. There is no need to remove assemblies from the handlebars, or to disconnect any cables, hoses or wiring.

18.7 Slacken the fork clamp bolt (arrowed) on each side

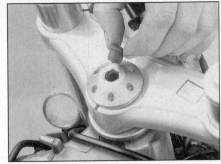

18.8a Pull the cap out of the nut ...

18.8b ... then unscrew the nut

7 Slacken the fork clamp bolts in the top yoke **(see illustration)**.
8 Remove the rubber blanking cap from the steering stem nut **(see illustration)**. Unscrew the nut using a hex key and remove the washer **(see illustration)**.
9 Gently ease the top yoke up off the fork tubes and position it clear of the head bearings, using a rag to protect other components **(see illustration)**.
10 Bend the lockwasher tabs out of the notches in the locknut **(see illustration)**. Unscrew the locknut using either your fingers (it shouldn't be tight), a C-spanner or a suitable drift located in one of the notches **(see illustration)**. Remove the lockwasher, bending up the remaining tabs to release it from the adjuster nut if necessary **(see illustration)**.

Inspect the tabs for cracks or signs of fatigue. If there are any, discard the lockwasher and use a new one; otherwise the old one can be re-used, but note that Honda do recommend using a new one as a matter of course.
11 Using either the C-spanner or drift, slacken the adjuster nut slightly until pressure is just released, then tighten it until all freeplay is removed, yet the steering is able to move freely **(see illustration)**. The object is to set the adjuster nut so that the bearings are under a very light loading, just enough to remove any freeplay. If the correct tools are available, tighten the adjuster nut to the torque setting specified at the beginning of the Chapter. Now turn the steering from lock-to-lock five times and recheck the adjustment or torque setting. If the bearings cannot be correctly

adjusted, disassemble the steering head and check the bearings and races (see Chapter 6). *Caution: Take great care not to apply excessive pressure because this will cause premature failure of the bearings.*
12 With the bearings correctly adjusted, install the lockwasher, using a new one if the tabs are weakened or cracked, onto the adjuster nut and fit two tabs into the slots in the adjuster nut **(see illustration 18.10c)**.
13 Hold the adjuster nut to prevent it from moving, then install the locknut and tighten it finger-tight **(see illustration 18.10b)**. Tighten the locknut further (but no more than 90∞) until its notches align with the remaining lockwasher tabs. Secure the locknut in position by bending up the lock washer tabs into its notches **(see illustration)**.

18.9 Gently ease the yoke up off the forks

18.10a Bend down the tabs securing the locknut ...

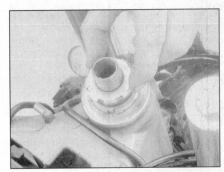

18.10b ... then unscrew the locknut ...

18.10c ... and remove the lockwasher

18.11 Adjust the bearings as described using either a C-spanner or a drift

18.13 Bend the tabs up into the notches in the locknut

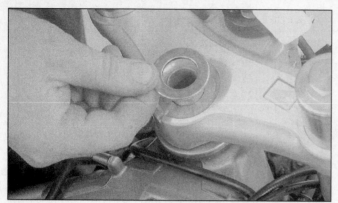

18.14a Install the washer . . .

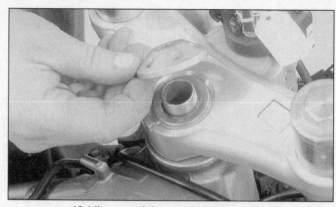

18.14b . . . and the steering stem nut . . .

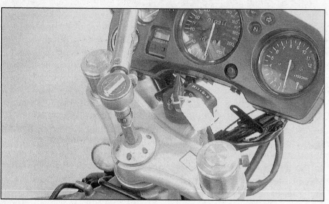

18.14c . . . then tighten the nut . . .

18.14d . . . and the fork clamp bolts to the specified torque

14 Fit the top yoke onto the steering stem **(see illustration 18.9)**. Install the nut, not forgetting the washer, and tighten it to the torque setting specified at the beginning of the Chapter **(see illustrations)**. Now tighten both the fork clamp bolts to the specified torque **(see illustration)**.
15 Check the bearing adjustment as described above and re-adjust if necessary.
16 Install the handlebars (see Chapter 6), the fuel tank (see Chapter 4) and the fairing (see Chapter 8). Fit the blanking cap into the stem nut **(see illustration 18.8a)**.

19 Nuts and bolts – tightness check

1 Since vibration of the machine tends to loosen fasteners, all nuts, bolts, screws, etc. should be periodically checked for proper tightness.
2 Pay particular attention to the following:
Lever and pedal bolts
Footrest and stand bolts
Engine mounting bolts
Shock absorber and suspension linkage bolts and swingarm pivot bolts
Handlebar clamp bolts

Front axle bolt and axle clamp bolts
Front fork clamp bolts (top and bottom yoke)
Rear axle nut
Brake caliper mounting bolts
Brake hose banjo bolts and caliper bleed valves
Brake disc bolts
Exhaust system bolts/nuts
3 If a torque wrench is available, use it along with the torque specifications at the beginning of this and other Chapters.

20 Wheels and tyres – general check

Tyres

1 Check the tyre condition and tread depth thoroughly – see *Daily (pre-ride) checks*.

Wheels

2 Cast wheels are virtually maintenance free, but they should be kept clean and checked periodically for cracks and other damage. Also check the wheel runout and alignment (see Chapter 7). Never attempt to repair damaged cast wheels; they must be replaced with new ones. Check the valve rubber for

signs of damage or deterioration and have it replaced if necessary. Also, make sure the valve stem cap is in place and tight.

21 Pulse secondary air injection (PAIR) system – check

Note: *This system is fitted to UK market X (1999) models onward, and all US, Swiss and Austrian models.*
1 Remove the air filter housing (see Chapter 4). Visually inspect the hoses between the reed valves on the valve cover and the PAIR control valve above it, and between the control valve and the air filter housing, for kinks and splits and any other damage or deterioration **(see illustration 12.13c)**. On US V and W (1997 and 1998) models, similarly check the vacuum hose between the control valve and its take-off point on the engine near the carburettors. Make sure that all hoses are securely connected with a clamp on each end. Replace any hoses that are damaged or deteriorated.
2 See Chapter 4 for further information and tests on the system. Note that on California models there is an emission control system hose routing diagram on a label stuck to the top of the air filter housing.

Every 12,000 miles (18,000 km) or 18 months

Carry out all the items under the 4000 mile (6000 km) check, plus the following:

22 Air filter – renewal

Caution: If the machine is continually ridden in wet or dusty conditions, the filter should be replaced more frequently.

1 Remove the fuel tank (see Chapter 4). On fuel injection models, disconnect the IAT (intake air temperature) sensor wiring connector **(see illustration)**.

2 Undo the screws securing the air filter housing cover and remove it **(see illustrations)**. Remove the element from the housing, noting how it fits, and discard it **(see illustration)**.

3 Fit the new filter element into the housing, making sure it is properly seated, then install the cover **(see illustration)**. On fuel injection models, connect the IAT (intake air temperature) sensor wiring connector **(see illustration 22.1)**.

4 Install the fuel tank (see Chapter 4).

5 To clean the filter in between replacement intervals, tap it on a hard surface to dislodge any dirt and use compressed air to clear the element, directing the air in the opposite way to normal flow **(see illustration)**. Do not use any solvents or cleaning agents on the element as it is pre-treated with a dust adhesive. If the machine is constantly used in dirty or dusty conditions the filter should be replaced at more frequent intervals than specified.

23 Evaporative emission control (EVAP) system – check

Note: *This system is fitted to California models.*

1 Remove the fuel tank (see Chapter 4). Visually inspect all the system hoses between the fuel tank, the purge control and solenoid valves, and the canister for kinks and splits and any other damage or deterioration. Make sure that the hoses are securely connected with a clamp on each end. Replace any hoses that are damaged or deteriorated.

2 Check the EVAP canister and the two valves for cracks or other damage.

3 See Chapter 4 for further information and tests on the system. Note that there is an emission control system hose routing diagram on a label stuck to the top of the air filter housing.

24 Brakes – fluid change

1 The brake fluid should be changed at this interval or every two years. It should also be changed whenever a master cylinder or caliper overhaul is carried out.

2 Refer to the brake bleeding section in Chapter 7, noting that all old fluid must be pumped from the fluid reservoir and hydraulic lines before filling with new fluid.

> **HAYNES HiNT**
> *Old brake fluid is invariably much darker in colour than new fluid, making it easy to see when all old fluid has been expelled from the system.*

25 Clutch – fluid change

1 The clutch fluid should be changed at this interval or every two years. It should also be changed whenever a master or slave cylinder overhaul is carried out.

2 Refer to the clutch bleeding section in Chapter 2, noting that all old fluid must be pumped from the fluid reservoir and hydraulic lines before filling with new fluid.

> **HAYNES HiNT**
> *Old brake fluid is invariably much darker in colour than new fluid, making it easy to see when all old fluid has been expelled from the system.*

22.1 Disconnect the IAT sensor wiring connector – X (1999) models onward

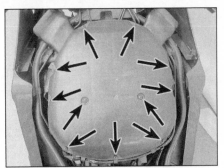

22.2a Air filter cover screws (arrowed) – V and W (1997 and 1998) models

22.2b Air filter cover screws (arrowed) – X (1999) models onward

22.2c Remove the element from the housing, noting how it fits

22.3 Install the new element then fit the cover

22.5 Direct the air in the opposite direction of normal flow

Every 16,000 miles (24,000 km) or two years

Carry out all the items under the 8000 mile (12,000 km) check, plus the following:

26 Valve clearances – check and adjustment

1 The engine must be completely cool for this maintenance procedure, so let the machine stand overnight before beginning.
2 Remove the spark plugs (see Section 5).
3 Remove the valve cover (see Chapter 2).
4 Make a chart or sketch of all valve positions so that a note of each clearance can be made against the relevant valve.
5 Unscrew the timing inspection cap from the right-hand crankcase cover **(see illustration)**. To check the valve clearances the engine must be turned so that the valve being checked is closed. The engine can be turned using a suitable spanner or socket on the timing rotor bolt and turning it in a clockwise direction only **(see illustration 26.6a)**. Alternatively, place the motorcycle on its centrestand so that the rear wheel is off the ground, select a high gear and rotate the rear wheel by hand in its normal direction of rotation.
6 Turn the engine until the line next to the 'T' mark on the timing rotor aligns with the static timing mark, which is a notch in the inspection hole rim, and the IN and EX marks on the intake

and exhaust camshaft sprockets respectively are facing away from each other and are flush with the cylinder head top surface **(see illustrations)**. If the marks are facing towards each other, rotate the engine clockwise one full turn until the line next to the 'T' mark again aligns with the static timing mark. The sprocket marks will now be facing away.
7 With the engine in this position, check the clearances on the Nos. 1 and 3 cylinder inlet valves. Insert a feeler gauge of the same thickness as the correct valve clearance (see Specifications) between the camshaft lobe and the follower of each valve and check that it is a firm sliding fit – you should feel a slight drag when the you pull the gauge out. If not, use the feeler gauges to obtain the exact clearance. Record the measured clearance on the chart.
8 Now rotate the engine 180° clockwise until the index line on the timing rotor is at the top **(see illustration)**. With the engine in this position, check the clearances on the Nos. 2 and 4 cylinder exhaust valves using the method described in Step 7.
9 Now rotate the engine 180° clockwise until the line next to the 'T' mark aligns with the static timing mark **(see illustration 26.6a)**. With the engine in this position, check the clearances on the Nos. 2 and 4 cylinder inlet valves using the method described in Step 7.
10 Now rotate the engine 180° clockwise until the index line on the timing rotor is at the

top **(see illustration 26.8)**. With the engine in this position, check the clearances on the Nos. 1 and 3 cylinder exhaust valves using the method described in Step 7.
11 When all clearances have been measured and charted, identify whether the clearance on any valve falls outside the specified range. If any do, the shim must be replaced with one of a thickness which will restore the correct clearance.
12 Shim replacement requires removal of the camshafts (see Chapter 2). There is no need to remove both camshafts if shims from only one side of the cylinder need replacing. Place rags over the spark plug holes and the cam chain tunnel to prevent a shim from dropping into the engine on removal.
13 With the camshaft removed, remove the cam follower of the valve in question, then retrieve the shim from the inside of the follower **(see illustrations)**. The follower is best removed with a magnet or using the suction created by a valve lapping tool, but long nosed pliers can be used with care. If the shim is not in the follower, pick it out of the top of the valve spring retainer using either a magnet, a small screwdriver with a dab of grease on it (the shim will stick to the grease), or a screwdriver and a pair of pliers **(see illustration 27.16)**. Do not allow the shim to fall into the engine.
14 A size mark should be stamped on one face of the shim – a shim marked 175 is 1.75 mm

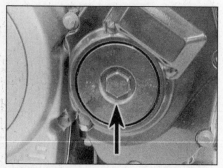
26.5 Remove the timing inspection cap (arrowed)

26.6a Turn the engine until the line next to the T mark aligns with the notch . . .

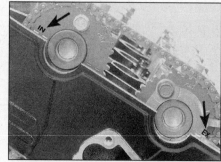
26.6b . . . and the camshaft sprocket marks are as shown

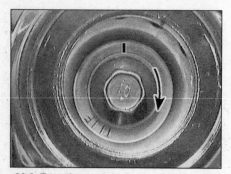
26.8 Turn the engine clockwise 180° until the index line is at the top

26.13a Carefully lift out the follower using a valve lapping tool or a magnet . . .

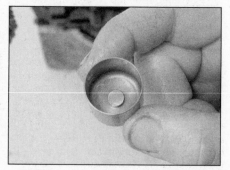
26.13b . . . and retrieve the shim from inside it

thick. If the mark is not visible the shim thickness will have to be measured using a micrometer. It is recommended that the shim is measured anyway to check that it has not worn.

15 Calculate the required replacement shim by using the formula $a = b - c + d$, where a is the required shim size, b is the measured valve clearance, c is the specified valve clearance, and d is the existing shim thickness. For example:

> The measured clearance of an inlet valve is 0.20 mm, so b = 0.20.
> The specified clearance range for an inlet valve is 0.13 to 0.19 mm, the mid-point being 0.16 mm, so c = 0.16.
> The thickness of the existing shim is 2.200 mm, so d = 2.2.
> Therefore, the required replacement shim a = 0.20 – 0.16 + 2.2 (a = 2.24 mm)

Note: *If the required replacement shim is greater than 2.800 mm (the largest available), the valve is probably not seating correctly due to a build-up of carbon deposits and should be checked and cleaned or resurfaced as required (see Chapter 2).*

16 Shims are available in 0.025 mm increments from 1.200 mm to 2.800 mm. Obtain the replacement shim, then lubricate it with molybdenum disulphide oil (a 50/50 mixture of molybdenum disulphide grease and engine oil) and fit it into the recess in the top of the valve spring retainer with the size mark facing up **(see illustration)**.

26.16 Install the shim using a magnet or a screwdriver with a dab of grease . . .

26.17 . . . then install the follower

17 Check that the shim is correctly seated, then lubricate the follower with molybdenum disulphide oil and install it onto the valve, making sure it fits squarely in its bore **(see illustration)**. Repeat the process for any other valves until the clearances are correct, then install the camshafts (see Chapter 2).

18 Rotate the crankshaft several turns to seat the new shim(s), then check the clearances again.

19 Install all disturbed components in a reverse of the removal sequence. Install the timing inspection cap using a new O-ring if required, and smear the O-ring and the cap threads with grease **(see illustration)**. Tighten the cap to the torque setting specified at the beginning of the Chapter.

20 Check and adjust the idle speed (see Section 2).

26.19 Fit the cap using a new O-ring and smear it and the threads with grease

Every 24,000 miles (36,000 km) or two years

Carry out all the items under the 12,000 mile (18,000 km) and 8000 mile (12,000 km) checks, plus the following:

27 Cooling system – draining, flushing and refilling

⚠ *Warning: Allow the engine to cool completely before performing this maintenance operation. Also, don't allow antifreeze to come into contact with your skin or the painted surfaces of the motorcycle. Rinse off spills immediately with plenty of water. Antifreeze is highly toxic if ingested. Never leave antifreeze lying around in an open container or in puddles on the floor; children and pets are attracted by its sweet smell and may drink it. Check with local authorities (councils) about disposing of antifreeze. Many communities have collection centres which will see that antifreeze is disposed of safely. Antifreeze is also combustible, so don't store it near open flames.*

Draining

1 Remove the seat and the fairing side panels (see Chapter 8).

2 Remove the pressure cap from the top of the radiator by turning it anti-clockwise until it reaches a stop **(see illustration 13.8)**. If you hear a hissing sound (indicating there is still pressure in the system), wait until it stops. Now press down on the cap and continue turning the cap until it can be removed. Also remove the coolant reservoir cap.

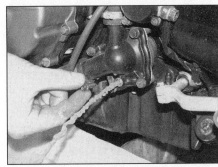

27.3 Unscrew the drain plug and allow the coolant to drain

3 Position a suitable container beneath the water pump on the left-hand side of the engine. Unscrew the drain plug and allow the coolant to completely drain from the system **(see illustration)**. Retain the old sealing washer for use during flushing.

4 Now position the container beneath the front of the engine on the left-hand side. Unscrew the cylinder drain plug and allow the coolant to completely drain from the cylinder jacket **(see illustration)**. Retain the

27.4 Remove the drain plug (arrowed) and drain the cylinder jacket

27.5 Detach the top hose from the filler neck and drain the reservoir

old sealing washer for use during flushing.

5 Place the container on the right-hand side of the engine. Disconnect the reservoir hose (the top hose) from the radiator filler neck, then place it below the level of the reservoir and allow it to drain into the container **(see illustration)**. When the reservoir is empty, fit the hose back onto the filler neck.

Flushing

6 Flush the system with clean tap water by inserting a garden hose in the radiator filler neck. Allow the water to run through the system until it is clear and flows out cleanly. If the radiator is extremely corroded, remove it

(see Chapter 3) and have it cleaned by a specialist.

7 Clean the drain holes in the water pump and cylinder bock then install the drain plugs using the old sealing washers.

8 Fill the cooling system with clean water mixed with a flushing compound. Make sure the flushing compound is compatible with aluminium components, and follow the manufacturer's instructions carefully. Fit the radiator cap.

9 Start the engine and allow it to reach normal operating temperature. Let it run for about ten minutes.

10 Stop the engine. Let it cool for a while, then cover the pressure cap with a heavy rag and turn it anti-clockwise to the first stop, releasing any pressure that may be present in the system. Once the hissing stops, push down on the cap and remove it completely.

11 Drain the system once again.

12 Fill the system with clean water and repeat the procedure in Steps 6 to 10.

Refilling

13 Fit new sealing washers onto the drain plugs and tighten them securely.

14 Fill the system with the proper coolant mixture (see this Chapter's Specifications). **Note:** *Pour the coolant in slowly to minimise the amount of air entering the system.*

15 When the system is full (all the way up to the base of the radiator filler neck), start the engine and allow it to idle for 2 to 3 minutes. Flick the throttle twistgrip part open 3 or 4 times, so that the engine speed rises to approximately 4000 – 5000 rpm, then stop the engine. This process will bleed any trapped air bubbles from the system.

16 If necessary, top up the coolant level to the base of the upper radiator filler neck and install the pressure cap. Also top up the coolant reservoir to the UPPER level mark (see *Daily (pre-ride) checks*).

17 Start the engine and allow it to reach normal operating temperature, then shut it off. Let the engine cool then remove the pressure cap as described in Step 2. Check that the coolant level is still up to the base of the upper radiator filler neck. If it's low, add the specified mixture until it reaches the base of the filler neck. Refit the cap.

18 Check the coolant level in the reservoir and top up if necessary.

19 Check the system for leaks. Install the seat and the fairing side panels (see Chapter 8).

20 Do not dispose of the old coolant by pouring it down the drain. Instead pour it into a heavy plastic container, cap it tightly and take it into an authorised disposal site or service station – see *Warning* at the beginning of this Section.

Non-scheduled maintenance

28 Cylinder compression – check

1 Among other things, poor engine performance may be caused by leaking valves, incorrect valve clearances, a leaking head gasket, or worn pistons, rings and/or cylinder walls. A cylinder compression check will help pinpoint these conditions and can also indicate the presence of excessive carbon deposits in the cylinder heads.

2 The only tools required are a compression gauge and a spark plug wrench. A compression gauge with a threaded end for the spark plug hole is preferable to the type which requires hand pressure to maintain a tight seal. Depending on the outcome of the initial test, a squirt-type oil can may also be needed.

3 Make sure the valve clearances are correctly set (see Section 26) and that the cylinder head nuts are tightened to the correct torque setting (see Chapter 2).

4 Refer to *Fault Finding Equipment* in the Reference section for details of the compression test. Refer to the specifications at the beginning of the Chapter for compression figures.

29 Engine – oil pressure check

1 The oil pressure warning light should come on when the ignition (main) switch is turned ON and extinguish a few seconds after the engine is started – this serves as a check that the warning light bulb is sound. If the oil pressure light comes on whilst the engine is running, low oil pressure is indicated – stop the engine immediately and carry out an oil level check (see *Daily (pre-ride) checks*).

2 An oil pressure check must be carried out if the warning light comes on when the engine is running yet the oil level is good (Step 1). It can also provide useful information about the condition of the engine's lubrication system.

3 To check the oil pressure, a suitable gauge and adapter (which screws into the crankcase) will be needed. Honda provide a gauge and adapter (part Nos. 07506-3000000 and 07510 4220100) for this purpose, or one can be obtained commercially.

4 Warm the engine up to normal operating temperature then stop it.

5 Remove the oil pressure switch (see Chapter 9) and screw the adapter into the crankcase threads. Connect the oil pressure gauge to the adapter.

6 Start the engine and briefly increase the

engine speed to 5400 rpm whilst watching the gauge reading. The oil pressure should be similar to that given in the Specifications at the start of this Chapter.

7 If the pressure is significantly lower than the standard, either the pressure relief valve is stuck open, the oil pump or its drive mechanism is faulty, the oil strainer or filter is blocked, or there is other engine damage. Also make sure the correct grade oil is being used. Begin diagnosis by checking the oil filter, strainer and relief valve, then the oil pump (see Chapter 2). If those items check out okay, chances are the bearing oil clearances are excessive and the engine needs to be overhauled.

8 If the pressure is too high, either an oil passage is clogged, the relief valve is stuck closed or the wrong grade of oil is being used.

9 Stop the engine and unscrew the gauge and adapter from the crankcase.

10 Install the oil pressure switch (see Chapter 9). Check the oil level (see *Daily (pre-ride) checks*).

30 Wheel bearings – check

1 Wheel bearings will wear over a period of time and result in handling problems.

30.2 Checking for play in the wheel bearings

2 Support the motorcycle upright using an auxiliary stand so that the wheel being checked is off the ground Check for any play in the bearings by pushing and pulling the wheel against the axle **(see illustration)**. Also spin the wheel and check that it rotates smoothly.

3 If any play is detected in the hub, or if the wheel does not rotate smoothly (and this is not due to brake or transmission drag), the wheel bearings must be removed and inspected for wear or damage (see Chapter 7).

31 Steering head bearings – re-greasing

1 Over a period of time the grease will harden or may be washed out of the bearings by incorrect use of jet washes.

2 Disassemble the steering head for re-greasing of the bearings. Refer to Chapter 6 for details.

32 Swingarm and suspension linkage bearings – re-greasing

1 Over a period of time the grease will harden or dirt will penetrate the bearings due to failed seals.

2 The suspension is not equipped with grease nipples. Remove the swingarm and suspension linkage as described in Chapter 6 for greasing of the bearings.

33 Brake caliper and master cylinder seals – renewal

1 Brake seals will deteriorate over a period of time and lose their effectiveness, leading to sticking operation or fluid loss, or allowing the ingress of air and dirt. Refer to Chapter 7 and dismantle the components for seal renewal.

34 Brake hoses – renewal

1 The hoses will in time deteriorate with age and should be renewed regardless of their apparent condition. Refer to Chapter 7 and disconnect the brake hoses from the master cylinders and calipers. Always replace the banjo union sealing washers with new ones.

2 Check the condition of the brake pipes, in particular looking for creases and dents, and replace them as necessary if damage is found.

35 Fuel hoses – renewal

> ⚠ *Warning: Petrol (gasoline) is extremely flammable, so take extra precautions when you work on any part of the fuel system. Don't smoke or allow open flames or bare light bulbs near the work area, and don't work in a garage where a natural gas-type appliance is present. If you spill any fuel on your skin, rinse it off immediately with soap and water. When you perform any kind of work on the fuel system, wear safety glasses and have a fire extinguisher suitable for a Class B type fire (flammable liquids) on hand.*

1 The fuel system hoses should be renewed at the first signs of cracking or hardening. This includes all the vent and drain hoses, and the vacuum hoses.

2 Remove the fuel tank (see Chapter 4). Disconnect the fuel hoses from the fuel tank and the carburettors or throttle bodies, noting the routing of each hose and where it connects (see Chapter 4 if required). It is

advisable to make a sketch of the various hoses before removing them to ensure they are correctly installed.

3 Secure each new hose to its unions using new clamps or sealing washers, according to model. Refer to Chapter 4 for torque settings for the fuel delivery and return hose fasteners on fuel injected models. Run the engine and check for leaks before taking the machine out on the road.

36 Clutch hose – renewal

1 The hose will in time deteriorate with age and should be renewed regardless of its apparent condition.

2 Refer to Chapter 2 and disconnect the hose from the master and slave cylinders. Always replace the banjo union sealing washers with new ones.

37 Clutch master and slave cylinder seals – renewal

1 The seals will deteriorate over a period of time and lose their effectiveness, leading to sticking operation or fluid loss, or allowing the ingress of air and dirt. Refer to Chapter 2 and dismantle the components for seal renewal.

38 Front forks – oil change

1 Fork oil degrades over a period of time and loses its damping qualities. Refer to Chapter 6 for front fork removal, oil draining and refilling, following the relevant steps. The forks do not need to be completely disassembled.

2 Remove the forks from the machine (see Chapter 6, Section 6).

3 Working on one fork leg at a time, refer to steps 5 to 8 of Chapter 6, Section 7, and drain the oil from the fork leg. Fill with the specified amount and type of fork oil (see Chapter 6 Specifications) and reassembly the fork (see Steps 27 to 30).

4 Install the forks.

Chapter 2
Engine, clutch and transmission

Contents

Degrees of difficulty

Easy, suitable for novice with little experience		Fairly easy, suitable for beginner with some experience		Fairly difficult, suitable for competent DIY mechanic		Difficult, suitable for experienced DIY mechanic		Very difficult, suitable for expert DIY or professional	

Specifications

General

Type	Four-stroke in-line four
Capacity	1137 cc
Bore	79.0 mm
Stroke	58.0 mm
Compression ratio	11.0 to 1
Cylinder numbering	1 to 4 from left to right
Cooling system	Liquid cooled
Clutch	Wet multi-plate
Transmission	Six-speed constant mesh
Final drive	Chain

Camshafts and followers

Inlet lobe height
  V and W (1997 and 1998) models
    Standard . . . . 38.54 to 38.78 mm
    Service limit (min) . . . . 38.24 mm
  X (1999) models onward
    Standard . . . . 38.42 to 38.50 mm
    Service limit (min) . . . . 38.12 mm
Exhaust lobe height
  V and W (1997 and 1998) models
    Standard . . . . 38.30 to 38.54 mm
    Service limit (min) . . . . 38.00 mm
  X (1999) models onward
    Standard . . . . 38.38 to 38.46 mm
    Service limit (min) . . . . 38.08 mm
Oil clearance
  V and W (1997 and 1998) models
    Standard . . . . 0.020 to 0.062 mm
    Service limit (max) . . . . 0.10 mm
  X (1999) models onward
    Standard . . . . 0.020 to 0.074 mm
    Service limit (max) . . . . 0.10 mm
Runout (max) . . . . 0.05 mm
Camshaft follower diameter
  Standard . . . . 25.978 to 25.993 mm
  Service limit (min) . . . . 25.97 mm
Camshaft follower bore diameter
  Standard . . . . 26.010 to 26.026 mm
  Service limit (min) . . . . 26.04 mm

Cylinder head

Warpage (max) . . . . 0.10 mm

Valves, guides and springs

Valve clearances . . . . See Chapter 1
Inlet valve
  Stem diameter
    Standard . . . . 4.975 to 4.990 mm
    Service limit (min) . . . . 4.965 mm
  Guide bore diameter
    Standard . . . . 5.000 to 5.012 mm
    Service limit (max) . . . . 5.040 mm
  Stem-to-guide clearance . . . . 0.010 to 0.037 mm
  Seat width
    Standard . . . . 0.90 to 1.10 mm
    Service limit (max) . . . . 1.50 mm
  Valve guide height above cylinder head . . . . 16.3 to 16.5 mm
Exhaust valve
  Stem diameter
    Standard . . . . 4.960 to 4.975 mm
    Service limit (min) . . . . 4.950 mm
  Guide bore diameter
    Standard . . . . 5.000 to 5.012 mm
    Service limit (max) . . . . 5.040 mm
  Stem-to-guide clearance . . . . 0.025 to 0.052 mm
  Seat width
    Standard . . . . 0.90 to 1.10 mm
    Service limit (max) . . . . 1.50 mm
  Valve guide height above cylinder head . . . . 16.3 to 16.5 mm
Valve spring free length (inlet and exhaust)
  Inner spring
    Standard . . . . 37.4 mm
    Service limit (min) . . . . 35.4 mm
  Outer spring
    Standard . . . . 40.6 mm
    Service limit (min) . . . . 38.6 mm

Starter clutch

Starter driven gear hub OD
    Standard . . . .   51.699 to 51.718 mm
    Service limit (min) . . . .   51.684 mm

Clutch

Friction plates
    V and W (1997 and 1998) models   9
    X (1999) models onward   7
Plain plates
    V and W (1997 and 1998) models   8
    X (1999) models onward   6
Friction plate thickness
    Standard . . . .   3.72 to 3.88 mm
    Service limit (min) . . . .   3.5 mm
Plain plate warpage (max) . . . .   0.3 mm
Spring free length
    V and W (1997 and 1998) models
        Standard . . . .   53.1 mm
        Service limit (min) . . . .   50.1 mm
    X (1999) models onward
        Standard . . . .   57.4 mm
        Service limit (min) . . . .   56.2 mm
Clutch guide OD
    Standard . . . .   34.975 to 34.991 mm
    Service limit (min) . . . .   34.965 mm
Clutch guide ID
    Standard . . . .   28.000 to 28.021 mm
    Service limit (max) . . . .   28.031 mm
Input shaft OD at clutch guide
    Standard . . . .   27.980 to 27.993 mm
    Service limit (max) . . . .   27.970 mm

Clutch release mechanism

Master cylinder bore diameter
    V and W (1997 and 1998) models
        Standard . . . .   14.000 to 14.043 mm
        Service limit (max) . . . .   14.06 mm
    X (1999) models onward
        Standard . . . .   12.700 to 12.743 mm
        Service limit (max) . . . .   12.76 mm
Master cylinder piston diameter
    V and W (1997 and 1998) models
        Standard . . . .   13.957 to 13.984 mm
        Service limit (min) . . . .   13.94 mm
    X (1999) models onward
        Standard . . . .   12.657 to 12.684 mm
        Service limit (min) . . . .   12.65 mm
Clutch fluid . . . .   DOT 4

Lubrication system

Oil pressure . . . .   see Chapter 1
Oil pump (engine and cooler circuits)
    Inner rotor tip-to-outer rotor clearance
        Standard . . . .   0.15 mm
        Service limit (max) . . . .   0.20 mm
    Outer rotor-to-body clearance
        Standard . . . .   0.15 to 0.21 mm
        Service limit (max) . . . .   0.35 mm
    Rotor endfloat
        Standard . . . .   0.04 to 0.09 mm
        Service limit (max) . . . .   0.12 mm

Cylinder bores

Bore
  Standard . . . . 79.000 to 79.015 mm
  Service limit (max) . . . . 79.100 mm
Warpage (max) . . . . 0.05 mm
Ovality (out-of-round) (max) . . . . 0.10 mm
Taper (max) . . . . 0.10 mm
Cylinder compression . . . . see Chapter 1

Pistons

Piston diameter (measured 15 mm up from skirt, at 90° to piston pin axis)
  Standard . . . . 78.970 to 78.990 mm
  Service limit (min) . . . . 78.90 mm
Piston-to-bore clearance
  Standard pistons . . . . 0.010 to 0.045 mm
  Oversize (+ 0.50) pistons (following rebore) . . . . 0.015 to 0.050 mm
Piston pin diameter
  Standard . . . . 18.994 to 19.000 mm
  Service limit (min) . . . . 18.984 mm
Piston pin bore diameter in piston
  Standard . . . . 19.002 to 19.008 mm
  Service limit (max) . . . . 19.03 mm
Piston pin-to-piston pin bore clearance . . . . 0.002 to 0.014 mm

Piston rings

Ring end gap (installed)
  Top ring
    Standard . . . . 0.20 to 0.35 mm
    Service limit (max) . . . . 0.50 mm
  Second ring
    Standard . . . . 0.40 to 0.55 mm
    Service limit (max) . . . . 0.70 mm
  Oil ring side-rail
    Standard . . . . 0.20 to 0.80 mm
    Service limit (max) . . . . 1.0 mm
Ring-to-groove clearance
  Top ring
    Standard . . . . 0.030 to 0.065 mm
    Service limit (max) . . . . 0.08 mm
  Second ring
    Standard . . . . 0.015 to 0.045 mm
    Service limit (max) . . . . 0.06 mm

Connecting rods

Small-end internal diameter
  Standard . . . . 19.030 to 19.051 mm
  Service limit (max) . . . . 19.061 mm
Small-end-to-piston pin clearance . . . . 0.030 to 0.057 mm
Big-end side clearance
  Standard . . . . 0.05 to 0.20 mm
  Service limit (max) . . . . 0.3 mm
Big-end oil clearance
  Standard . . . . 0.030 to 0.052 mm
  Service limit (max) . . . . 0.062 mm

Crankshaft and bearings

Main bearing oil clearance
  Standard . . . . 0.017 to 0.035 mm
  Service limit (max) . . . . 0.045 mm
Runout (max) . . . . 0.30 mm

Transmission

Gear ratios (no. of teeth)	
Primary reduction	1.571 to 1 (88/56T)
Final reduction	
European models	2.588 to 1 (44/17T)
US and Canadian models	2.647 to 1 (45/17T)
1st gear	2.769 to 1 (36/13T)
2nd gear	2.000 to 1 (32/16T)
3rd gear	1.579 to 1 (30/19T)
4th gear	1.333 to 1 (28/21T)
5th gear	1.167 to 1 (28/24T)
6th gear	1.042 to 1 (25/24T)
Input shaft 5th and 6th gears ID	
Standard	31.000 to 31.025 mm
Service limit (max)	31.04 mm
Input shaft 5th and 6th gears bush OD	
Standard	30.950 to 30.975 mm
Service limit (min)	30.93 mm
Input shaft 5th and 6th gears gear-to-bush clearance	
Standard	0.020 to 0.070 mm
Service limit (max)	0.10 mm
Input shaft 5th gear bush ID	
Standard	27.985 to 28.006 mm
Service limit (max)	28.02 mm
Input shaft OD at 5th gear bush point	
Standard	27.967 to 27.980 mm
Service limit (min)	27.957 mm
Input shaft-to-bush clearance at 5th gear bush point	
Standard	0.005 to 0.039 mm
Service limit (max)	0.08 mm
Output shaft 2nd, 3rd and 4th gears ID	
Standard	33.000 to 33.025 mm
Service limit (max)	33.04 mm
Output shaft 2nd gear bush OD	
Standard	32.955 to 32.980 mm
Service limit (min)	32.93 mm
Output shaft 3rd and 4th gears bush OD	
Standard	32.950 to 32.975 mm
Service limit (min)	32.93 mm
Output shaft 2nd gear gear-to-bush clearance	
Standard	0.020 to 0.070 mm
Service limit (max)	0.11 mm
Output shaft 3rd and 4th gears gear-to-bush clearance	
Standard	0.025 to 0.075 mm
Service limit (max)	0.11 mm
Output shaft 2nd gear bush ID	
Standard	29.985 to 30.006 mm
Service limit (max)	30.02 mm
Output shaft OD at 2nd gear bush point	
Standard	29.967 to 29.980 mm
Service limit (min)	29.957 mm
Output shaft-to-bushing clearance at 2nd gear bush point	
Standard	0.005 to 0.039 mm
Service limit (max)	0.08 mm

Selector drum and forks

Selector fork end thickness	
Standard	5.93 to 6.00 mm
Service limit (min)	5.90 mm
Selector fork bore ID	
Standard	12.000 to 12.021 mm
Service limit (max)	12.03 mm
Selector fork shaft OD	
Standard	11.957 to 11.968 mm
Service limit (min)	11.95 mm

Torque settings

Balancer idle gear shaft stopper bolt	12 Nm
Balancer shaft holder mounting bolt	27 Nm
Balancer shaft holder pinch bolt	12 Nm
Balancer timing inspection cap	7 Nm
Cam chain guide blade bolts	12 Nm
Cam chain tensioner cap bolt	12 Nm
Cam chain tensioner blade nut	12 Nm
Cam chain tensioner mounting bolts	
V and W (1997 and 1998) models	12 Nm
X (1999) models onward	10 Nm
Camshaft holder bolts	12 Nm
Camshaft sprocket bolts	20 Nm
Clutch cover bolts	12 Nm
Clutch hose banjo bolt	34 Nm
Clutch master cylinder clamp bolts	12 Nm
Clutch nut	127 Nm
Clutch release cylinder bleed valve	6 Nm
Clutch release cylinder bolts	10 Nm
Clutch spring bolts	12 Nm
Connecting rod nuts	41 Nm
Crankcase breather separator bolts	12 Nm
Crankcase lower half 9 mm bolts	37 Nm
Crankcase lower half 10 mm bolt	39 Nm
Crankcase lower 6 mm bolts	12 Nm
Crankcase lower half 7 mm bolts	18 Nm
Crankcase upper half 8 mm bolts	25 Nm
Cylinder head 6 mm bolts	10 Nm
Cylinder head 10 mm bolts	
V and W (1997 and 1998) models	67 Nm
X (1999) models onward	69 Nm
Engine mountings	
Adjuster bolts	11 Nm
Adjuster bolt locknuts	54 Nm
Rear mounting bolt nuts	64 Nm
Front mounting bolts	
V and W (1997 and 1998) models	39 Nm
X (1999) models onward	40 Nm
Oil pipe bolts	12 Nm
Oil return pipe retainer bolt	12 Nm
Oil strainer/pipe retainer plate nut	12 Nm
Oil pump assembly long bolt	13 Nm
Oil pump driven sprocket bolt	15 Nm
PAIR system reed valve cover bolts	10 Nm
Selector drum cam bolt	23 Nm
Selector drum retainer plate bolts	12 Nm
Sidestand bracket bolts	54 Nm
Starter clutch bolts	16 Nm
Stopper arm bolt	12 Nm
Timing inspection cap	18 Nm
Timing rotor bolt	59 Nm
Timing rotor cover bolts	12 Nm
Valve cover bolts	10 Nm

1 General information

The engine/transmission unit is a liquid-cooled in-line four cylinder. The sixteen valves are operated by double overhead camshafts which are chain driven off the right-hand end of the crankshaft. The engine/transmission is a unit assembly constructed from aluminium alloy. The crankcase divides horizontally.

The crankcase incorporates a wet sump, pressure-fed lubrication system which uses a dual circuit oil pump that is chain-driven off the back of the clutch. One circuit supplies the engine and transmission, the other circuits sends oil to a cooler mounted on the front of the engine. Each circuit has a dual rotor trochoidal pump. The system has an oil filter, an oil pressure switch, and two pressure relief valves. The main relief valve is in the feed to the oil filter, the second valve is in the feed to the oil cooler.

The alternator is on the left-hand end of the crankshaft and has the starter clutch mounted behind it. The water pump is on the left-hand side of the engine, and its drive shaft is keyed to the oil pump drive shaft. The pulse generator and ignition timing rotor are on the right-hand end of the crankshaft.

Power from the crankshaft is routed to the transmission via the clutch. The clutch is of the wet, multi-plate type and is gear-driven off the crankshaft. The clutch is operated hydraulically. The transmission is a six-speed constant-mesh unit. Final drive to the rear wheel is by chain and sprockets.

2 Operations possible with the engine in the frame

The components and assemblies listed below can be removed without having to remove the engine/transmission assembly from the frame. If however, a number of areas require attention at the same time, removal of the engine is recommended.

Valve cover
Cam chain tensioner and blades
Camshafts and cam chain
Ignition timing rotor and pulse generator
Clutch
Gearchange mechanism
Alternator
Oil filter and oil cooler
Oil sump, oil pump, oil strainer and oil pressure relief valves
Starter motor
Starter clutch
Water pump
Selector drum and forks (though much easier with engine removed)
Front balancer shaft

3 Operations requiring engine removal

It is necessary to remove the engine/transmission assembly from the frame to gain access to the following components.
Cylinder head
Pistons, piston rings and cylinder bores
Transmission shafts
Crankshaft and bearings
Connecting rods and bearings
Rear balancer shaft

4 Major engine repair – general note

1 It is not always easy to determine when or if an engine should be completely overhauled, as a number of factors must be considered.
2 High mileage is not necessarily an indication that an overhaul is needed, while low mileage, on the other hand, does not preclude the need for an overhaul. Frequency of servicing is probably the single most important consideration. An engine that has regular and frequent oil and filter changes, as well as other required maintenance, will most likely give many miles of reliable service. Conversely, a neglected engine, or one which has not been run in properly, may require an overhaul very early in its life.
3 Exhaust smoke and excessive oil consumption are both indications that piston rings and/or valve guides are in need of attention, although make sure that the fault is not due to oil leakage.
4 If the engine is making obvious knocking or rumbling noises, the connecting rods and/or main bearings are probably at fault.
5 Loss of power, rough running, excessive valve train noise and high fuel consumption rates may also point to the need for an overhaul, especially if they are all present at the same time. If a complete tune-up does not remedy the situation, major mechanical work is the only solution.
6 An engine overhaul generally involves restoring the internal parts to the specifications of a new engine. The piston rings and main and connecting rod bearings are usually replaced and the cylinder walls honed or, if necessary, re-bored, during a major overhaul. Generally the valve seats are re-ground, since they are usually in less than perfect condition at this point. The end result should be a like new engine that will give as many trouble-free miles as the original.
7 Before beginning the engine overhaul, read through the related procedures to familiarise yourself with the scope and requirements of the job. Overhauling an engine is not all that difficult, but it is time consuming. Plan on the motorcycle being tied up for a minimum of two weeks. Check on the availability of parts

and make sure that any necessary special tools, equipment and supplies are obtained in advance.
8 Most work can be done with typical workshop hand tools, although a number of precision measuring tools are required for inspecting parts to determine if they must be replaced. Often a dealer will handle the inspection of parts and offer advice concerning reconditioning and replacement. As a general rule, time is the primary cost of an overhaul so it does not pay to install worn or substandard parts.
9 As a final note, to ensure maximum life and minimum trouble from a rebuilt engine, everything must be assembled with care in a spotlessly clean environment.

5 Engine – removal and installation

Caution: The engine is very heavy. Engine removal and installation should be carried out with the aid of at least one assistant; personal injury or damage could occur if the engine falls or is dropped.

Removal

1 Support the bike on its centrestand, making sure it is on level ground. Work can be made easier by raising the machine to a suitable working height on an hydraulic ramp or a suitable platform. Make sure the motorcycle is secure and will not topple over (see *Tools and Workshop Tips* in the Reference section).
2 Remove the seat, seat cowling, fairing and fairing side panels (see Chapter 8). Remove the fairing side panel brackets on each front corner of the engine if required. Note how they fit and which fits where.
3 If the engine is dirty, particularly around its mountings, wash it thoroughly. This will make work much easier and rule out the possibility

On all models a peg spanner is required to slacken and tighten the adjuster bolt locknuts on two of the engine mounting bolts. If the Honda service tool (Part no 07VMA-MAT0100) is not available, a suitable one will have to fabricated out of a piece of steel tubing, or an old 22 mm socket

5.11 Pull back the cover and remove the nut securing the starter motor lead

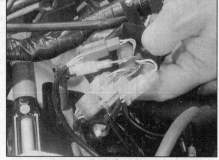

5.12 Disconnect the relevant wiring connectors in the boot (fuel injected model shown)

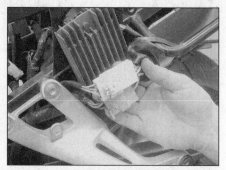

5.13 Disconnect the wiring connector with the three yellow wires

of caked on lumps of dirt falling into some vital component.
4 Drain the engine oil and the cooling system (see Chapter 1).
5 Remove the fuel tank and the air filter housing (see Chapter 4).
6 Remove the radiator along with its hoses (see Chapter 3). It is advisable to remove the lower radiator bracket from the engine (it is secured by a single bolt) to prevent the possibility of damaging the front mudguard when manoeuvring the engine out of the frame.
7 Remove the oil cooler along with its pipes/hoses (see Section 7).
8 Remove the exhaust system (see Chapter 4).
9 Remove the carburettors or throttle bodies (according to model) (see Chapter 4). Plug the engine inlet manifolds with clean rag.

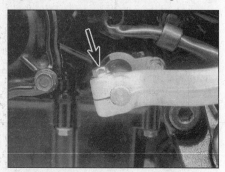

5.16 Note the alignment of the punch mark, then remove the bolt (arrowed) and slide the arm off the shaft

10 Disconnect the negative (–ve) lead from the battery, and remove it if required (see Chapter 9). Feed the lead through to the engine and coil it on the crankcase.
11 If required, remove the starter motor (see Chapter 9). Otherwise, pull back the rubber cover on the starter motor terminal, then unscrew the nut and disconnect the lead **(see illustration)**.
12 Disconnect the ignition pulse generator, sidestand switch, speed sensor and engine sub-harness wiring connectors – they are housed inside the rubber boot above the crankcase **(see illustration)**. The sub-harness feeds the oil pressure switch, neutral switch and coolant temperature sender, and on fuel injection models the knock sensor. On V and W (1997 and 1998) models also disconnect the alternator wiring connector, also inside the boot. On fuel injection models also disconnect the camshaft pulse generator wiring connector, also inside the boot. Release the wiring from any clips or ties, noting its routing, and feed it through to its source so that it does not impede engine removal.
13 On X (1999) models onward disconnect the alternator wiring connector, which is inside the rubber boot next to the regulator/rectifier **(see illustration)**. Release the wiring from any clips or ties and feed it through to the engine, noting its routing.
14 On US V and W (1997 and 1998) models, and on all X (1999) models onward, remove the PAIR system solenoid valve and hoses (see Chapter 4).

15 Disconnect the HT leads from the spark plugs and remove the ignition coils. If the leads don't have their cylinder identity marked on them, label each one to ensure correct reconnection.
16 Unscrew the gearchange lever pinch bolt and slide the lever off the shaft, noting how the punch mark on the shaft aligns with the slot in the lever **(see illustration)**.
17 Remove the front sprocket (see Chapter 6).
18 Unscrew the two bolts securing the sidestand bracket to the frame and remove the sidestand assembly **(see illustration)**.
19 At this point, position an hydraulic or mechanical jack under the engine with a block of wood between the jack head and sump. Make sure the jack is centrally positioned so the engine will not topple in any direction when the last mounting bolt is removed. Raise the jack to take the weight of the engine, but make sure it is not lifting the bike and taking the weight of that as well. The idea is to support the engine so that there is no pressure on any of the mounting bolts once they have been slackened, so they can be easily withdrawn.
20 Unscrew the nuts on the left-hand ends of the upper and lower rear engine mounting bolts **(see illustration)**. Slacken the adjuster bolt locknuts on the right-hand ends of the upper and lower rear engine mounting bolts using a suitable peg spanner (see **Tool Tip** on previous page) **(see illustration)**. The locknuts can remain loose on the adjuster

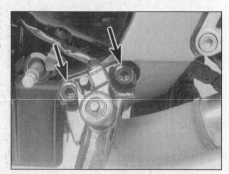

5.18 Unscrew the two bolts (arrowed) and remove the sidestand assembly

5.20a Unscrew the nuts on the rear mounting bolts

5.20b Slacken the locknuts and remove them if required . . .

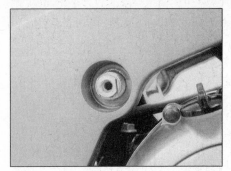

5.20c . . . then back off the adjuster bolts using a hex key in the mounting bolt head

5.21 Unscrew the front right-hand bolt and remove the spacer

5.22 Unscrew the front left-hand bolts (arrowed)

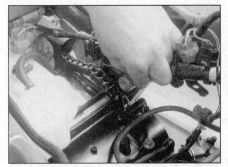

5.24a Withdraw the upper rear mounting bolt, collecting the left-hand spacer . . .

5.24b . . . and the right-hand spacer

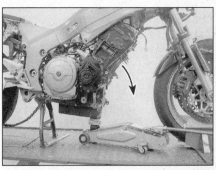

5.24c Lower the jack and allow the engine to pivot forwards on the lower rear mounting bolt

bolts, or they can be removed if required. Partially unscrew the adjuster bolts using an Allen key in the mounting bolt head, which engages with the adjuster bolt, until the adjuster is flush with the inside of the frame **(see illustration)**.

21 Unscrew and remove the front mounting bolt on the right-hand side, noting the washer, and remove the spacer from between the engine and frame **(see illustration)**.

22 Unscrew and remove the front mounting bolts on the left-hand side **(see illustration)**.

23 Check that the engine is properly supported by the jack.

24 The engine can now be removed from the frame (see **Caution** above). Check that all wiring, cables and hoses are well clear, then withdraw the upper rear mounting bolt and remove the two spacers **(see illustrations)**. Carefully lower the jack, allowing the engine to pivot on the lower rear mounting bolt, until the jack is fully retracted **(see illustration)**. Support the engine and remove the lower mounting bolt, then manoeuvre the engine from the frame and lift it away **(see illustration)**. If required, remove the adjuster bolts from the frame **(see illustration)**.

Installation

25 If removed, thread the adjuster bolts into the frame until they are flush with the inside **(see illustration 5.24e)**.

26 Manoeuvre the engine into position under the frame and lift it onto the jack. Manoeuvre the engine to align the lower rear mounting bolt holes then install the bolt from the right-hand side and engage its head in the adjuster bolt so they are locked together **(see illustration 5.24d)**. Raise the jack, allowing the engine to pivot on the lower mounting bolt, until the other mounting bolt holes align,

5.24d Withdraw the lower rear bolt (arrowed) and remove the engine

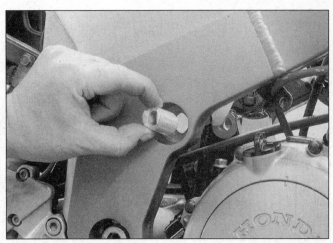

5.24e Thread the adjuster bolts out of the frame if required

5.27a Tighten the upper and lower adjuster bolts (arrowed) . . .

5.27b . . . using a hex key in the mounting bolt head

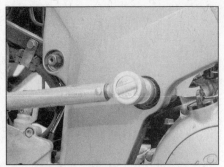

5.28 Tighten the locknuts using the special tool or peg spanner described

then install the upper rear mounting bolt from the right-hand side, not forgetting the two spacers that fit between the engine and frame on each side **(see illustrations 5.24b and a)**. Make sure the coolant reservoir locating bracket does not get caught between the right-hand spacer and the engine. Install the front mounting bolts on each side loosely, not forgetting to fit the spacer between the engine and the frame, and the washer on the bolt, on the right-hand front mounting **(see illustrations 5.22 and 5.21)**. Make sure no wires, cables or hoses become trapped between the engine and the frame. Tighten the mounting bolts in the order described below.

27 Tighten the lower and upper rear adjuster bolts to the specified torque using an Allen key in the mounting bolt head **(see illustrations)**.

28 If removed, thread the locknuts onto the adjuster bolts **(see illustration 5.20b)**. Tighten the locknuts to the specified torque setting using the peg spanner (see **Tool Tip** above) **(see illustration)**. It is advisable to make a reference mark between the adjuster bolt and the frame to make sure that it does not turn as the locknut is being tightened.

29 Fit the nuts onto the left-hand ends of the rear mounting bolts, then counter-hold the bolts and tighten the nuts to the specified torque setting **(see illustration 5.20a)**.

30 Tighten the front mounting bolts on each side to the specified torque setting **(see illustration)**.

31 The remainder of the installation

procedure is the reverse of removal, noting the following points:

a) If removed, tighten the sidestand bracket bolts to the specified torque setting **(see illustration 5.18)**.

b) Use new gaskets on the exhaust pipe connections.

c) Align the punch mark on the gearchange shaft with the slit in the lever when fitting the lever onto the shaft, and tighten the pinch bolt securely **(see illustration 5.16)**.

d) Make sure all wires, cables and hoses are correctly routed and connected, and secured by any clips or ties.

e) Refill the engine with oil and coolant (see Chapter 1).

f) Adjust the throttle cable freeplay.

g) Adjust the drive chain (see Chapter 1).

h) Start the engine and check that there are no oil or coolant leaks. Adjust the idle speed (see Chapter 1).

---

6 Engine disassembly and reassembly – general information

Disassembly

1 Before disassembling the engine, thoroughly clean and degrease its external surfaces. This will prevent contamination of the engine internals, and will also make working a lot easier and cleaner. A high flash-

point solvent, such as paraffin (kerosene) can be used, or better still, a proprietary engine degreaser. Use old paintbrushes and toothbrushes to work the solvent into the various recesses of the engine casings. Take care to exclude solvent or water from the electrical components and inlet and exhaust ports.

 Warning: The use of petrol (gasoline) as a cleaning agent should be avoided because of the risk of fire.

2 When clean and dry, position the engine on the workbench, leaving suitable clear area for working. Gather a selection of small containers, plastic bags and some labels so that parts can be grouped together in an easily identifiable manner. Also get some paper and a pen so that notes can be taken. You will also need a supply of clean rag, which should be as absorbent as possible.

3 Before commencing work, read through the appropriate section so that some idea of the necessary procedure can be gained. When removing components note that great force is seldom required, unless specified (checking the specified torque setting of the particular bolt being removed will indicate how tight it is, and therefore how much force should be needed). In many cases, a component's reluctance to be removed is indicative of an incorrect approach or removal method – if in any doubt, re-check with the text.

4 An engine support stand made from short lengths of 2 x 4 inch wood bolted together into a rectangle will help support the engine **(see illustration)**. The perimeter of the mount should be just big enough to accommodate the sump within it so that the engine rests on its crankcase. Alternatively place individual blocks under the crankcase as required to ensure the engine is stable.

5 When disassembling the engine, keep 'mated' parts together (including gears, cylinder bores, pistons, connecting rods, valves, etc. that have been in contact with each other during engine operation). These 'mated' parts must be reused or replaced as an assembly.

6 A complete engine / transmission disassembly should be done in the following

5.30 Tighten the front bolts to the specified torque

6.4 An engine support made from pieces of 2 x 4 inch wood

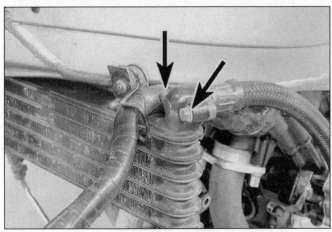

7.3 Unscrew the bolts (arrowed) and detach the hose from each side of the cooler

7.4 Unscrew the bolts (arrowed) and detach the guides and pipes from the engine

general order with reference to the appropriate Sections.

Remove the valve cover
Remove the camshafts
Remove the cylinder head
Remove the clutch
Remove the alternator/starter clutch (see Chapter 9)
Remove the starter motor (see Chapter 9)
Remove the gearchange mechanism
Remove the cam chain and blades
Remove the oil sump
Remove the oil pump
Remove the selector drum and forks
Separate the crankcase halves
Remove the connecting rods and pistons
Remove the crankshaft
Remove the transmission shafts
Remove the balancer shafts

Reassembly

7 Reassembly is accomplished by reversing the general disassembly sequence.

7 Oil cooler and pipes – removal, inspection and installation

Note: *The oil cooler can be removed with the engine in the frame. If the engine has been removed, ignore the steps which do not apply.*

Removal

1 Remove the fairing side panels and the fairing (see Chapter 8). On X (1999) models onward, also remove the trim panels on the air ducts, or for better access the air ducts themselves.
2 Drain the engine oil (see Chapter 1).
3 To remove the cooler without its feed and return pipes, unscrew the bolts securing the hose unions to the cooler and detach the hoses **(see illustration)**. Discard the O-rings as new ones must be used. Now unscrew the cooler mounting bolts (two on V and W (1997

and 1998) models, four on X (1999) models onward), noting the collars, and the wiring loom guide with the top left bolt on X (1999) models onward, and remove the cooler.
4 To remove the cooler with its feed and return pipes, unscrew the bolts securing each pipe guide and union to the crankcase and detach the pipes from the engine **(see illustration)**. Discard the O-rings as new ones must be used. Do not separate the pipes from the guides. Now unscrew the cooler mounting bolts (two on V and W (1997 and 1998) models, four on X (1999) models onward), noting the collars, and the wiring loom guide with the top left bolt on X (1999) models onward, and remove the cooler and hoses/pipes.
5 To remove the hoses/pipes but leave the cooler in place, unscrew the bolts securing the hose unions to the cooler **(see illustration 7.3)**, then unscrew the bolts securing the pipe guides and unions to the crankcase **(see illustration 7.4)**, then detach the pipes/hoses from the engine and cooler and remove them. Discard the union O-rings as new ones must be used.

Inspection

6 Check the cooler fins for mud, dirt and insects, which may impede the flow of air

7.7 Use a new O-ring on each hose and pipe union

through the radiator. If the fins are dirty, clean the cooler using water or low pressure compressed air directed through the fins from the inner side of the radiator. If the fins are bent or distorted, straighten them carefully with a screwdriver. If the air flow is restricted by bent or damaged fins over more than 20% of the cooler's surface area, replace the cooler with a new one.

Installation

7 Installation is the reverse of removal, noting the following:
a) *Always use new O-rings on the pipe and hose unions and smear them with clean oil (see illustration).*
b) *Check the condition of the cooler mounting grommets and replace them if they are damaged or deteriorated.*
c) *Fill the engine with oil (see Chapter 1).*

8 Valve cover – removal and installation

Note: *The valve cover can be removed with the engine in the frame. If the engine has been removed, ignore the steps which do not apply.*

Removal

1 On V and W (1997 and 1998) models, remove the carburettors (see Chapter 4). On X (1999) models onward, remove the air filter housing (see Chapter 4), then unscrew the two bolts securing the throttle cable bracket to the throttle bodies and detach the cable ends from the throttle cam, noting how they fit.
2 On US V and W (1997 and 1998) models, and on all X (1999) models onward, remove the PAIR system solenoid valve and hoses, and the reed valve covers (see Chapter 4). The reed valves themselves can remain in their housings, but take care not to damage them or let them drop out.

8.5a Unscrew the bolts (arrowed) . . .

8.5b . . . and remove the cover

3 Release the crankcase breather hose clamp and detach the hose from its union on the valve cover.

4 Pull the spark plug caps off the plugs and secure them clear of the cover.

5 Unscrew the valve cover bolts and lift the cover off the cylinder head **(see illustrations)**. If it is stuck, do not try to lever it off with a screwdriver. Tap it gently around the sides with a rubber hammer or block of wood to dislodge it. Note the rubber washers fitted in the cover and remove them if they are loose **(see illustration 8.11a)**. The rubber gasket is normally glued into the groove in the cover, and is best left there if it is reusable. If the gasket is in any way damaged,

deformed or deteriorated, remove it and use a new one.

6 On US V and W (1997 and 1998) models, and on all X (1999) models onward, note the PAIR system joint pieces that link the air passages between the valve cover and cylinder head and remove them with their O-rings for safekeeping if required, taking great care not to drop them in the engine **(see illustration)**.

7 If required, unscrew the bolts securing the crankcase breather system separator and remove it from the valve cover **(see illustration)**. Discard the gasket as a new one must be used. Clean out the breather chamber and aperture.

Installation

8 If removed, install the breather separator using a new gasket **(see illustration 8.7)**. Apply a suitable non-permanent thread locking compound to the bolts and tighten them to the torque setting specified at the beginning of the Chapter.

9 On US V and W (1997 and 1998) models, and on all X (1999) models onward, if removed, install the PAIR system joint pieces with their O-rings, using new ones if the old ones are damaged, deformed or deteriorated **(see illustration 8.6)**.

10 Examine the valve cover gasket for signs of damage or deterioration and replace it with new one if necessary. If a new one is used, clean all traces of the old glue from the groove in the cover and clean it and the cylinder head mating surface with solvent. Fit the new gasket into the groove, using a suitable glue, sealant or grease to hold it in place **(see illustration)**. Also apply a suitable sealant to the cutouts in the cylinder head **(see illustration)**.

11 Position the valve cover on the cylinder head, making sure the gasket stays in place **(see illustration 8.5b)**. If removed, fit the rubber washers into the cover, using new ones if required, and making sure they are installed with the "UP" mark facing up **(see illustration)**. Install the cover bolts and tighten them to the specified torque setting,

8.6 Remove the PAIR system joint pieces (arrowed) and their O-rings if required

8.7 Crankcase breather separator bolts (arrowed)

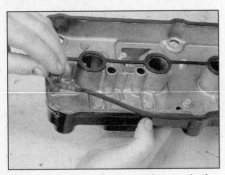

8.10a Make sure the gasket locates in the groove and stays there

8.10b Apply a sealant to the cutouts in the cylinder head (arrowed)

8.11a Make sure the UP mark on the washers faces up . . .

8.11b ... then install the bolts and tighten them to the specified torque

9.2 Unscrew the cap bolt (arrowed) and remove the washer

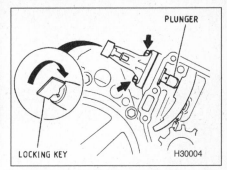

9.3a Honda locking key in position with tensioner plunger retracted. Tensioner mounting bolts arrowed

tightening the outer rear bolts (marked by a triangle on the cover) first **(see illustration)**.
12 Install the remaining components in the reverse order of removal. On US V and W (1997 and 1998) models, and on all X (1999) models onward, tighten the PAIR system reed valve cover bolts to the specified torque setting.

9 Cam chain tensioner – removal and installation

Note: *The cam chain tensioner can be removed with the engine in the frame. If the engine has been removed, ignore the steps which do not apply.*

Removal

1 Remove the right-hand fairing side panel (see Chapter 8).
2 Unscrew the tensioner cap bolt and remove the sealing washer **(see illustration)**.
3 If the Honda tensioner locking key is available, insert it in the end of the tensioner so that it engages the slotted plunger and turn it clockwise until the plunger is fully retracted, then push the key into the slots in the end of the tensioner body to lock it **(see illustration)**.

Unscrew the tensioner mounting bolts and withdraw the tensioner from the engine. If the Honda tool is not available, a home-made equivalent can be easily made out of a piece of 1 mm steel plate cut to the dimensions shown **(see illustration)**.
4 If a locking key is not available, first slacken the tensioner mounting bolts slightly **(see illustration)**. Insert a small flat-bladed screwdriver in the end of the tensioner so that it engages the slotted plunger. Turn the screwdriver clockwise until the plunger is fully retracted and hold it in this position while unscrewing the tensioner mounting bolts **(see illustration)**. Withdraw the tensioner from the engine, then release the screwdriver – the plunger will spring back out once the screwdriver is removed, but can be easily reset on installation.
5 Discard the gasket as a new one must be used on installation. Do not dismantle the tensioner.

Installation

6 Check that the plunger moves smoothly when wound into the tensioner and springs back out freely when released **(see illustration 9.8a)**. Ensure the tensioner and cylinder block surfaces are clean and dry.

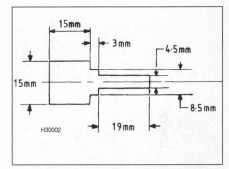

9.3b A copy of Honda's locking key can be made using 1 mm thick steel cut to the dimensions shown

7 If the locking key described above is being used, insert it in the end of the tensioner so that it engages the slotted plunger and turn it clockwise until the plunger is fully retracted, then push the key into the slotted end of the tensioner body to lock it in this position **(see illustrations 9.3a and b)**. Install the tensioner and tighten the bolts to the torque setting specified at the beginning of the Chapter. Remove the key, then install the tensioner cap bolt with a new sealing washer and tighten it to the specified torque **(see illustration 9.8d)**.
8 If the key is not available, insert a small flat-

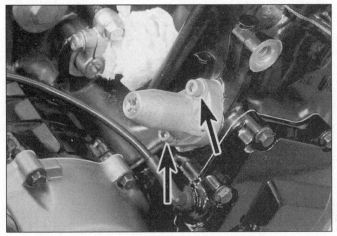

9.4a Slacken the mounting bolts (arrowed) slightly . . .

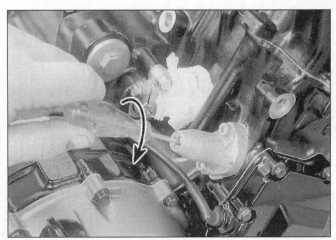

9.4b ... then insert the screwdriver, retract the tensioner and unscrew the mounting bolts

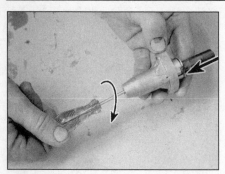

9.8a Insert the screwdriver and retract the plunger . . .

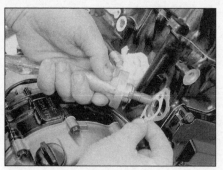

9.8b . . . then install the tensioner using a new gasket . . .

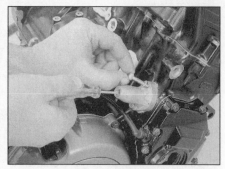

9.8c . . . and fit and tighten the mounting bolts

9.8d Install the cap bolt using a new sealing washer

10.2 Remove the timing inspection cap (arrowed)

bladed screwdriver in the end of the tensioner so that it engages the slotted plunger (see illustration). Turn the screwdriver clockwise until the plunger is fully retracted and hold it in this position whilst the tensioner is installed. Fit a new gasket onto the tensioner body, then install the tensioner and its mounting bolts and tighten them to the specified torque (see illustrations). Release and remove the screwdriver, then install the tensioner end bolt with a new sealing washer and tighten it securely (see illustration).

9 Install the remaining components.

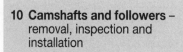

10 Camshafts and followers –
removal, inspection and
installation

Note: *The camshafts can be removed with the engine in the frame. Place clean rags over the spark plug holes and the cam chain tunnel to prevent any component from dropping into the engine.*

Removal

1 Remove the valve cover (see Section 8). On X (1999) models onward, remove the cam pulse generator (see Chapter 4).

2 Unscrew the timing inspection cap from the right-hand crankcase cover (see illustration). The engine must be turned so that the No. 1

piston is at TDC (top dead centre) on its compression stroke. The engine can be turned using a suitable spanner or socket on the timing rotor bolt and turning it in a clockwise direction only. Alternatively, place the motorcycle on its centrestand so that the rear wheel is off the ground, select a high gear and rotate the rear wheel by hand in its normal direction of rotation (removing the spark plugs first will make this a lot easier – see Chapter 1).

3 Turn the engine until the line next to the 'T' mark on the timing rotor aligns with the static timing mark, which is a notch in the inspection hole rim, and the IN and EX marks on the intake and exhaust camshaft sprockets respectively are facing away from each other and are flush with the cylinder head top surface (see illustrations and 10.21). If the marks are facing towards each other, rotate the engine clockwise one full turn until the line next to the 'T' mark again aligns with the static timing mark. The sprocket marks will now be facing away.

4 Either remove the cam chain tensioner (see Section 9), or if you prefer, obtain or fabricate the tensioner locking tool, then retract and lock the tensioner plunger using the tool as described in Section 9, Steps 2 and 3. Also unscrew the bolts securing the top cam chain guide and remove it (see illustration).

5 Before disturbing the camshaft holders,

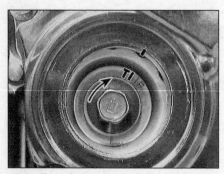

10.3a Turn the engine until the line next to the T mark aligns with the notch . . .

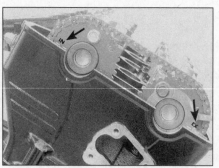

10.3b . . . and the camshaft sprocket marks are as shown

10.4 Unscrew the bolts (arrowed) and remove the guide

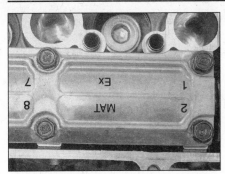

10.5 Note the markings on the holders and the tightening sequence numbers for the holder bolts

10.6a Unscrew and remove the ten holder bolts . . .

10.6b . . . and remove the holder

check for identification markings. The intake camshaft holder is marked IN and the exhaust camshaft holder is marked EX **(see illustration)**. These markings ensure that the holders can be matched up to their original locations on installation. If no markings are visible, mark your own using a felt pen. Also note the numbers marked on each holder, adjacent to each bolt. These numbers denote the **tightening** sequence for the holder bolts.

6 If both camshafts are being removed, remove the intake camshaft first. Unscrew the camshaft holder bolts for the camshaft being worked on, slackening them evenly and a little at a time in a **reverse** of the tightening sequence marked on the holder **(see illustration)**. Remove the bolts and lift off the camshaft holders, noting how they fit **(see illustration)**. Retrieve the dowels from either the holder or the cylinder head if they are loose.

7 Carefully lift the camshaft off the head and disengage the sprocket from the chain **(see illustration)**. The camshafts are marked for identification. The intake camshaft is marked IN and the exhaust camshaft is marked EX **(see illustration)**. If the marks aren't clear make your own as the camshafts must be installed in their original location. While the camshafts are out, don't allow the cam chain to go slack and do not rotate the crankshaft – the chain may drop down and bind between

the crankshaft and case, which could damage these components. Wire the chain to another component or secure it using a rod of some sort to prevent it from dropping.

8 If the followers and shims are being removed from the cylinder head, obtain a container which is divided into sixteen compartments, and label each compartment with the location of a valve, i.e. intake or exhaust camshaft, left or right valve. If a container is not available, use labelled plastic bags (egg cartons also do very well!). Remove the cam follower of the valve in question, then retrieve the shim from the inside of the follower **(see illustrations)**. The follower is best removed with a magnet or using the suction created by a valve lapping tool, but long nosed pliers can be used with care. If the shim is not in the follower, pick it out of the top of the valve spring retainer using either a magnet, a small screwdriver with a dab of grease on it (the shim will stick to the grease), or a screwdriver and a pair of pliers **(see illustration 10.24a)**. Do not allow the shim to fall into the engine.

9 The sprockets can be separated from the camshafts if required by removing the two bolts that hold them. Both sprockets are identical and are therefore interchangeable, but mark them according to their camshaft so they can be installed in their original position. Also make alignment marks between the

sprocket and the camshaft so that the sprocket can be installed the correct way round to avoid confusion when setting up the timing. Alternatively, make a drawing of each camshaft showing the positions of the lobes relative to the marks on the sprocket. On X (1999) models onward, also note the alignment and fitting of the cam pulse generator rotor on the exhaust camshaft.

Inspection

10 Inspect the bearing surfaces of the camshaft holders and cylinder head and the corresponding journals on the camshafts. Look for score marks, deep scratches and evidence of spalling (a pitted appearance). Check the oil passages for clogging.

10.7a Lift out the camshaft and disengage the chain from the sprocket

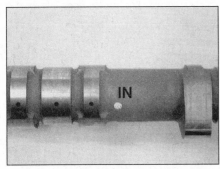

10.7b Note the identity mark on each camshaft

10.8a Carefully lift out the follower using a valve lapping tool or a magnet . . .

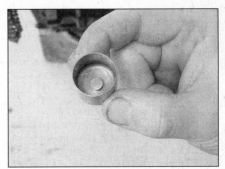

10.8b . . . and retrieve the shim from inside it

10.11 Measure the height of the camshaft lobes with a micrometer

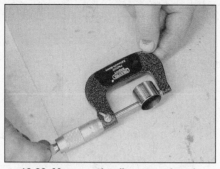

10.20 Measure the diameter of each follower

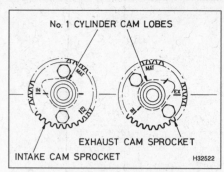

10.21 Camshaft and sprocket alignment

11 Check the camshaft lobes for heat discoloration (blue appearance), score marks, chipped areas, flat spots and spalling. Measure the height of each lobe with a micrometer (see illustration) and compare the results to the minimum height listed in this Chapter's Specifications. If damage is noted or wear is excessive, the camshaft must be replaced with a new one.

12 Check the amount of camshaft runout by supporting each end on V-blocks, and measuring any runout using a dial gauge. If the runout exceeds the specified limit the camshaft must be replaced with a new one.

HAYNES HiNT Refer to Tools and Workshop Tips in the Reference section for details of how to read a micrometer and dial gauge.

13 Next, check the camshaft journal oil clearances. Check each camshaft in turn rather than at the same time. Clean the camshaft and the bearing surfaces in the cylinder head and camshaft holder with a clean lint-free cloth, then lay the camshaft in its correct location in the cylinder head (see Step 7).

14 Cut some strips of Plastigauge and lay one piece on each journal, parallel with the camshaft centreline. Make sure the camshaft holder dowels are installed (see illustration 10.26a). Lay the holder in its correct place in the case (see Step 5) (see illustration 10.26b). Install all the holder bolts and tighten them evenly and a little at a time in the correct numerical sequence (see Step 5) to the torque setting specified at the beginning of the Chapter. Whilst tightening the bolts, make sure the holder is being pulled squarely down and is not binding on the dowels. While doing this, don't let the camshaft rotate, or the Plastigauge will be disturbed and you will have to start again.

15 Now unscrew the bolts evenly and a little at a time in a **reverse** of the numerical sequence and carefully lift off the camshaft holder.

16 To determine the oil clearance, compare the crushed Plastigauge (at its widest point)

on each journal to the scale printed on the Plastigauge container. Compare the results to this Chapter's Specifications. If the oil clearance is greater than specified, replace the camshaft with a new one and recheck the clearance. If the clearance is still too great, also replace the cylinder head and holder with new ones.

HAYNES HiNT Before replacing the camshafts, cylinder head or holders because of damage, check with local machine shops specialising in motorcycle engine work. In the case of the camshafts, it may be possible for cam lobes to be welded, reground and hardened, at a cost far lower than that of a new camshaft. If the bearing surfaces in the case or holders are damaged, it may be possible for them to be bored out to accept bearing inserts. Due to the cost of new components it is recommended that all options be explored before condemning them as trash!

17 Except in cases of oil starvation, the cam chain should wear very little. If the chain has stretched excessively, which makes it difficult to maintain proper tension, or if it is stiff or the links are binding or kinking, replace it with a new one. Refer to Section 11 for replacement.

18 Check the sprockets for wear, cracks and other damage. If the sprockets are worn, the cam chain is also worn, and so probably is the sprocket on the crankshaft. If severe wear is apparent, the entire engine should be disassembled for inspection.

19 Inspect the cam chain guides and tensioner blade (see Section 11).

20 Inspect the outer surface of each cam follower for evidence of scoring or other damage. If a follower is in poor condition, it is probable that the bore in the cylinder head in which it works is also damaged. Check for clearance between each follower and its bore. Measure the outer diameter of each follower and the inner diameter of its bore and compare the results to the Specifications (see illustration). If any follower is worn beyond its service limit replace it with a new one. If any

bore is worn beyond its limit, is seriously out-of-round or tapered, replace the cylinder head with a new one.

Installation

21 If separated, fit the sprockets onto the camshafts, on X (1999) models onward not forgetting to fit the camshaft pulse generator rotor with the exhaust camshaft sprocket. Make sure they are installed the correct way round and in their original location as identified by the marks made on removal (Step 9), and the accompanying illustration (see illustration). Apply a suitable non-permanent thread locking compound to the sprocket bolts and tighten them to the torque setting specified at the beginning of the Chapter. If you find it difficult to hold the camshaft while tightening the bolts, tighten them as much as possible now, then fully tighten them after the camshaft has been installed, when the timing rotor bolt can be used to counter-hold it.

22 If removed, lubricate each shim and its follower with molybdenum disulphide oil (a 50/50 mixture of molybdenum disulphide grease and engine oil). Fit each shim into its recess in the top of the valve spring retainer with the size mark facing up, making sure it is correctly seated (see illustration). Note: It is most important that the shims and followers are returned to their original valves otherwise the valve clearances will be inaccurate. Install each follower, making sure it fits squarely in its bore (see illustration 10.9b).

23 Make sure the bearing surfaces on the

10.22a Install the shim using a magnet or a screwdriver with a dab of grease . . .

10.22b . . . then install the follower

10.26a Install the exhaust camshaft as described . . .

10.26b . . . then fit the holder

camshafts and in the holders and cylinder head are clean, then apply molybdenum disulphide oil (a 50/50 mixture of molybdenum disulphide grease and engine oil) to each of them. Also apply it to the camshaft lobes.

24 The camshafts and holders must be installed in their correct location according to their identification marks (see Steps 7 and 5).

25 Check that the line next to the 'T' mark on the timing rotor aligns with the notch in the inspection hole rim **(see illustration 10.3a)**. If both camshafts have been removed, install the exhaust camshaft first, then the intake.

26 Lay the exhaust camshaft (marked EX) onto the head with the EX mark on the sprocket facing forward and level with the cylinder head **(see illustration 10.21)**. Fit the cam chain around the sprocket as you install the camshaft, pulling up on the chain to remove all slack in the front run between the crankshaft and the camshaft **(see illustration)**. Fit the exhaust camshaft holder dowels into the head or holder if removed, then install the holder (marked EX) and tighten its bolts finger-tight **(see illustration and 10.6a)**. Now tighten them evenly and a little at a time in the correct numerical sequence (see Step 5) to the torque setting specified at the beginning of the Chapter. Whilst tightening the bolts, make sure the holder is being pulled squarely down and is not binding on the dowels.

27 Lay the intake camshaft (marked IN) onto the head with the IN mark on the sprocket facing back and level with the cylinder head **(see illustration 10.21)**. Fit the cam chain

around the sprocket as you install the camshaft, pulling on it to remove all slack from between the two camshaft sprockets **(see illustration 10.7a)**. Any slack in the chain must lie in the rear run of the chain between the intake camshaft and the crankshaft so that it is later taken up by the tensioner. Fit the intake camshaft holder dowels into the head or holder if removed, then install the holder (marked IN) and tighten its bolts finger-tight **(see illustration 10.6b and a)**. Now tighten them evenly and a little at a time in the correct numerical sequence (see Step 5) to the torque setting specified at the beginning of the Chapter. Whilst tightening the bolts, make sure the holder is being pulled squarely down and is not binding on the dowels.

Caution: The holders are likely to break if they are not tightened down evenly and squarely.

28 If the tensioner locking tool was used to retract and hold the tensioner plunger, remove it to release the plunger. If the tensioner was removed, use a piece of wooden dowel to press on the back of the cam chain tensioner blade via the tensioner bore in the cylinder block to ensure that any slack in the cam chain is taken up and transferred to the rear run of the chain (where it will later be taken up by the tensioner). At this point check that all the timing marks are still in **exact** alignment as described in Step 3. Note that it is easy to be slightly out (one tooth on the sprocket) without the marks appearing drastically out of alignment. If the marks are out, verify which sprocket is misaligned, then

either reinstall the tensioner locking tool and retract the plunger, or remove the wooden dowel. Unscrew the sprocket's bolts and slide it off the camshaft, then disengage it from the chain. Move the camshaft round as required, then fit the sprocket back onto the chain and onto the camshaft, and check the marks again. With everything correctly aligned, apply a suitable non-permanent thread locking compound to the sprocket bolts and tighten them to the torque setting specified at the beginning of the Chapter.

Caution: If the marks are not aligned exactly as described, the valve timing will be incorrect and the valves may strike the pistons, causing extensive damage to the engine.

29 Install the top cam chain guide and tighten its bolts securely **(see illustration)**. Either install the cam chain tensioner (see Section 9), or remove the tensioner locking tool, according to the method you used earlier. Turn the engine clockwise through two full turns and check again that all the timing marks still align (see Step 3).

30 Check the valve clearances and adjust them if necessary (see Chapter 1).

31 Install the timing inspection cap using a new O-ring if required, and smear the O-ring and the cap threads with grease **(see illustration)**. Tighten the cap to the torque setting specified at the beginning of the Chapter.

32 Install the valve cover (see Section 8). On X (1999) models onward, install the camshaft pulse generator (see Chapter 4).

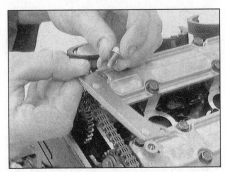

10.29 Install the top cam chain guide

10.31 Fit the cap using a new O-ring and smear it and the threads with grease

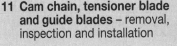

11 Cam chain, tensioner blade and guide blades – removal, inspection and installation

Note: *The cam chain and its blades can be removed with the engine in the frame. If the engine has been removed, ignore the steps which do not apply.*

Removal

Cam chain

1 Remove the camshafts (see Section 10).
2 Remove the timing rotor (see Section 22).

11.4a Slip the cam chain off the sprocket and draw it out of the engine

11.4b Remove the sprocket if required, noting the wide spline

securing the top cam chain guide and remove it **(see illustration 10.4)**. Note that the tensioner should be installed or reset (as applicable) after the guide has been refitted.

Inspection

Cam chain

12 Check the chain for binding, kinks and any obvious damage and replace it with a new one if necessary. Check the camshaft and crankshaft sprocket teeth for wear and renew the cam chain, camshaft sprockets and crankshaft as a set if necessary.

Tensioner and guide blades

13 Check the sliding surface and edges of the blades for excessive wear, deep grooves, cracking and other obvious damage, and replace them with new ones if necessary.

Installation

14 Installation of the chain and blades is the reverse of removal. Tighten the blade nut and guide bolts to the torque setting specified at the beginning of the Chapter.

11.6a Unscrew the nut (arrowed) and remove the washer . . .

11.6b . . . then draw the blade out of the top

3 Remove the front guide blade (see below).
4 Draw the cam chain off the crankshaft sprocket and out of the engine **(see illustration)**. If required, slide the sprocket off the end of the crankshaft, noting the wide spline that means it can only be installed in one position – mark the outer face of the sprocket with a dab or paint as a reference to fitting it the correct way around on installation **(see illustration)**.

Tensioner blade

5 Remove the intake camshaft (see Section 10).
6 Unscrew the domed nut securing the blade to the back of the cam chain tunnel and draw the blade out of the engine **(see illustrations)**. Check the condition of the sealing washer and

replace it with a new one if it is damaged or deformed.

Front guide blade

7 Remove the exhaust camshaft (see Section 10). If the cylinder head is being removed, proceed with that now and continue this procedure afterwards, otherwise carry on.
8 Remove the pulse generator/timing rotor cover (see Section 22).
9 Unscrew the pivot bolt securing the blade to the crankcase and draw the blade out of the engine **(see illustrations)**.

Top guide blade

10 Remove the valve cover (see Section 8).
11 It is advisable to release the cam chain tension or remove the tensioner (see Section 9) beforehand. Unscrew the bolts

12 Cylinder head – removal and installation

Caution: *The engine must be completely cool before beginning this procedure or the cylinder head may become warped.*
Note: *To remove the cylinder head, the engine must be removed from the frame.*

Removal

1 Remove the engine from the frame (see Section 5).
2 Remove the camshafts, followers and shims (see Section 10).
3 Remove the cam chain tensioner blade (see Section 11).
4 Disconnect the coolant temperature sensor wiring connector **(see illustration)**. If required, remove the thermostat housing (see Chapter 3).
5 The cylinder head is secured by two 6 mm

11.9a Unscrew the pivot bolt (arrowed) . . .

11.9b . . . and draw the blade out of the top

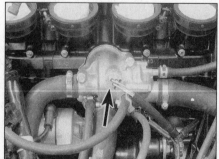

12.4 Disconnect the wiring connector from the sensor (arrowed)

12.5 Cylinder head 6 mm bolts (B) and 10 mm bolts (A)

12.6 Lift the head up off the block

bolts and ten 10 mm bolts **(see illustration)**. First unscrew and remove the 6 mm bolts. Now unscrew and remove the 10 mm bolts, slackening them evenly and a little at a time in a criss-cross pattern working from the outside to the middle until they are all loose.

6 Hold the cam chain up and pull the cylinder head up off the block, then pass the cam chain down through the tunnel **(see illustration)**. Do not let the chain fall into the crankcase – secure it with a piece of wire or metal bar to prevent it from doing so. If the head is stuck, tap around the joint faces with a soft-faced mallet. Do not attempt to free the head by inserting a screwdriver between the head and block mating surfaces – you'll damage them.

7 Remove the old cylinder head gasket and discard it as a new one must be used. If they are loose, remove the dowels from the crankcase or the underside of the cylinder head **(see illustration 12.11)**.

8 Check the cylinder head gasket and the mating surfaces on the cylinder head and crankcase for signs of leakage, which could indicate warpage. Refer to Section 14 and check the flatness of the cylinder head.

9 Clean all traces of old gasket material from the cylinder head and crankcase. If a scraper is used, take care not to scratch or gouge the soft aluminium. Be careful not to let any of the

gasket material fall into the crankcase, the cylinder bore or the oil and coolant passages.

Installation

10 Lubricate the cylinder bore with engine oil. If removed, fit the dowels into the crankcase **(see illustration 12.11)**.

11 Ensure both cylinder head and crankcase mating surfaces are clean, then lay the new head gasket over the cam chain and guide blade and onto the crankcase, locating it over the dowels and making sure all the holes are correctly aligned **(see illustration)**. Never re-use the old gasket.

12 Carefully fit the cylinder head onto the block, making sure it locates correctly onto the dowels **(see illustration 12.6)**. Feed the cam chain up through the tunnel as you install the head, then secure it in place with a piece of wire to prevent it from falling back down.

13 Apply some molybdenum disulphide oil (a 50/50 mixture of molybdenum disulphide grease and engine oil) to the threads and the underside of the heads of the ten 10 mm bolts. Install the 10 mm and the 6 mm bolts and tighten them all finger-tight **(see illustrations)**. Now tighten the 10 mm bolts evenly and a little at a time in a criss-cross pattern working from the middle to the outside to the torque setting specified at the beginning of the Chapter **(see illustration)**.

Now tighten the 6 mm bolts to the specified torque.

14 Install the remaining components in a reverse of their removal sequence, referring to the relevant Sections or Chapters (see Steps 1 to 4).

13 Valves/valve seats/valve guides – servicing

1 Because of the complex nature of this job and the special tools and equipment required, most owners leave servicing of the valves, valve seats and valve guides to a professional.

12.11 Install the dowels (arrowed) then lay the new gasket on the block

12.13a Install the 10 mm bolts with their washers . . .

12.13b . . . and the 6 mm bolts . . .

12.13c . . . and tighten them as described to the specified torque

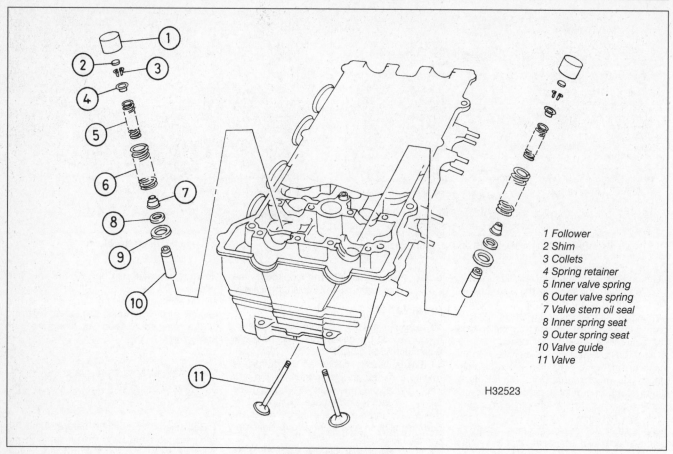

1 Follower
2 Shim
3 Collets
4 Spring retainer
5 Inner valve spring
6 Outer valve spring
7 Valve stem oil seal
8 Inner spring seat
9 Outer spring seat
10 Valve guide
11 Valve

H32523

14.3 Valve components

However, you can make an initial assessment of whether the valves are seating correctly, and therefore sealing, by pouring a small amount of solvent into each of the valve ports. If the solvent leaks past any valve into the combustion chamber area the valve is not seating correctly and sealing.

2 You can also remove the valves from the cylinder head, clean the components, check them for wear to assess the extent of the work needed, and, unless a valve service is required, grind in the valves (see Section 14). The head can then be reassembled.

3 A dealer service department will remove the valves and springs, replace the valves and guides, recut the valve seats, check and replace the valve springs, spring retainers and collets (as necessary), replace the valve stem seals with new ones and reassemble the valve components.

4 After the valve service has been performed, the head will be in like-new condition. When the head is returned, be sure to clean it again very thoroughly before installation on the engine to remove any metal particles or abrasive grit that may still be present from the valve service operations. Use compressed air, if available, to blow out all the holes and passages.

14 Cylinder head and valves – disassembly, inspection and reassembly

1 As mentioned in the previous section, valve overhaul should be left to a Honda dealer. However, disassembly, cleaning and inspection of the valves and related components can be done (if the necessary special tools are available) by the home mechanic. This way no expense is incurred if the inspection reveals that overhaul is not required at this time.

2 To disassemble the valve components without the risk of damaging them, a valve spring compressor is absolutely essential. Make sure it is suitable for motorcycle work.

Disassembly

3 Before proceeding, arrange to label and store the valves along with their related components in such a way that they can be returned to their original locations without getting mixed up **(see illustration)**. A good way to do this is to use the same container as the followers and shims are stored in (see Section 10), or to obtain a separate container which is divided into sixteen compartments, and label each compartment with the location of a valve, i.e. intake or exhaust camshaft, left

or right valve. If a container is not available, use labelled plastic bags (egg cartons also do very well!).

4 Clean all traces of old gasket material from the cylinder head. If a scraper is used, take care not to scratch or gouge the soft aluminium. Refer to Tools and Workshop Tips for details of gasket removal methods.

5 Compress the valve spring on the first valve

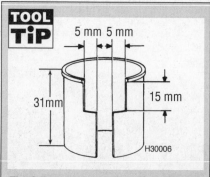

TOOL TiP

5 mm 5 mm

31mm

15 mm

H30006

The follower bore in the cylinder head can be protected from scratches by the valve spring compressor by fabricating a shield from a 35 mm film canister. Cut the canister to the dimensions shown.

14.5a Compressing the valve springs using a valve spring compressor

14.5b Make sure the compressor locates correctly both on the bottom of the valve . . .

14.5c . . . and on the top of the spring retainer

with a spring compressor, making sure it is correctly located onto each end of the valve assembly **(see illustrations)**. On the underside of the head make sure the plate on the compressor only contacts the valve and not the soft aluminium of the head – if the plate is too big for the valve, use a spacer between them. Do not compress the springs any more than is absolutely necessary. Remove the collets, using either needle-nose pliers, tweezers, a magnet or a screwdriver with a dab of grease on it **(see illustration)**. Carefully release the valve spring compressor and remove the spring retainer, noting which way up it fits, and the outer and inner springs from the top of the head, and the valve from the underside of the head **(see illustrations 14.28c, b and a)**. If the valve binds in the guide (won't pull through), push it back into the head and deburr the area around the collet groove with a very fine file or whetstone **(see illustration)**.

6 Once the valve has been removed and labelled, pull the valve stem seal off the top of the valve guide with pliers and discard it (the old seals should never be reused) **(see illustration)**. Now remove the inner and outer spring seats **(see illustrations 14.25b and a)**. The seats are difficult to get hold of, so either use a small magnet or turn the head upside down and tip them out, taking care not to let them lose themselves.

7 Repeat the procedure for the remaining valves. Remember to keep the parts for each valve together and in order so they can be reinstalled in the same location.

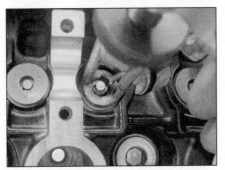

14.5d Remove the collets with needle-nose pliers, tweezers, a magnet or a screwdriver with a dab of grease on it

8 Next, clean the cylinder head with solvent and dry it thoroughly. Compressed air will speed the drying process and ensure that all holes and recessed areas are clean.

9 Clean all of the valve springs, collets, retainers and spring seats with solvent and dry them thoroughly. Do the parts from one valve at a time so they don't get mixed up.

10 Scrape off any deposits that may have formed on the valve, then use a motorised wire brush to remove deposits from the valve heads and stems. Again, make sure the valves do not get mixed up.

Inspection

11 Inspect the head very carefully for cracks and other damage. If cracks are found, a new head will be required. Check the camshaft bearing surfaces for wear and evidence of

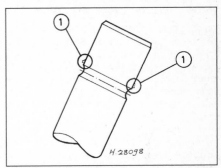

14.5e If the valve stem won't pull through the guide, deburr the area above the collet groove (1)

seizure. Check the camshafts and holders for wear as well (see Section 10).

12 Using a precision straight-edge and a feeler gauge set to the warpage limit listed in the specifications at the beginning of the Chapter, check the head gasket mating surface for warpage. Refer to *Tools and Workshop Tips* in the Reference section for details of how to use the straight-edge.

13 Examine the valve seats in the combustion chamber. If they are pitted, cracked or burned, the head will require work beyond the scope of the home mechanic. Measure the valve seat width and compare it to this Chapter's Specifications **(see illustration)**. If it exceeds the service limit, or if it varies around its circumference, valve overhaul is required.

14 Measure the valve stem diameter **(see illustration)**. Clean the valve guides using a

14.6 Pull the seal off the valve stem

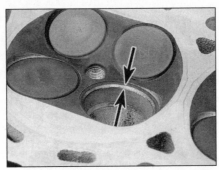

14.13 Measure the valve seat width with a ruler (or for greater precision use a vernier caliper)

14.14a Measure the valve stem diameter with a micrometer

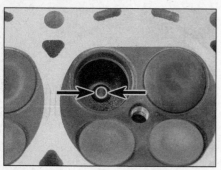

14.14b Insert a small bore gauge into the valve guide and expand it so there's a slight drag when it's pulled out, then measure the bore gauge with a micrometer

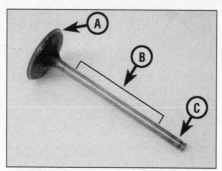

14.15 Check the valve face (A), stem (B) and collet groove (C) for signs of wear and damage

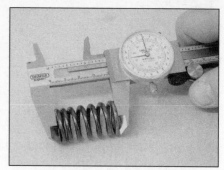

14.17a Measure the free length of the valve springs

guide reamer to remove any carbon build-up, then measure the inside diameters of the guides (at both ends and in the centre of the guide) with a small bore gauge, and measure the gauge with a micrometer **(see illustration)**. Measure the guides at the ends and at the centre to determine if they are worn in a bell-mouth pattern (more wear at the ends). Subtract the stem diameter from the valve guide diameter to obtain the valve stem-to-guide clearance. If the stem-to-guide clearance is greater than listed in this Chapter's Specifications, renew whichever components are worn beyond their specification limits. If the valve guide is within specifications, but is worn unevenly, it should be renewed.

15 Carefully inspect each valve face, stem

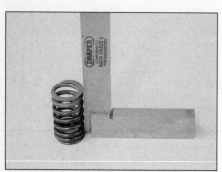

14.17b Check the valve springs for squareness

and collet groove area for cracks, pits and burned spots **(see illustration)**.

16 Rotate the valve and check for any obvious indication that it is bent, in which case it must be replaced with a new one. Check the end of the stem for pitting and excessive wear. The presence of any of the above conditions indicates the need for valve servicing. The stem end can be ground down, provided that the amount of stem above the collet groove after grinding is sufficient.

17 Check the end of each valve spring for wear and pitting. Measure the spring free lengths and compare them to the specifications **(see illustration)**. If any spring is shorter than specified it has sagged and must be replaced with a new one. Also place the spring upright on a flat surface and check it for bend by placing a ruler against it **(see illustration)**. If the bend in any spring is excessive, it must be replaced with a new one.

18 Check the spring retainers and collets for obvious wear and cracks. Any questionable parts should not be reused, as extensive damage will occur in the event of failure during engine operation.

19 If the inspection indicates that no overhaul work is required, the valve components can be reinstalled in the head.

Reassembly

20 Unless a valve service has been performed, before installing the valves in the

head they should be ground in (lapped) to ensure a positive seal between the valves and seats. This procedure requires coarse and fine valve grinding compound and a valve grinding tool. If a grinding tool is not available, a piece of rubber or plastic hose can be slipped over the valve stem (after the valve has been installed in the guide) and used to turn the valve.

21 Apply a small amount of coarse grinding compound to the valve face and some molybdenum disulphide oil (a 50/50 mixture of molybdenum disulphide grease and engine oil) to the valve stem, then slip the valve into the guide **(see illustration)**. **Note:** *Make sure each valve is installed in its correct guide and be careful not to get any grinding compound on the valve stem.*

22 Attach the grinding tool (or hose) to the valve and rotate the tool between the palms of your hands. Use a back-and-forth motion (as though rubbing your hands together) rather than a circular motion (i.e. so that the valve rotates alternately clockwise and anti-clockwise rather than in one direction only) **(see illustration)**. Lift the valve off the seat and turn it at regular intervals to distribute the grinding compound properly. Continue the grinding procedure until the valve face and seat contact area is of uniform width and unbroken around the entire circumference of the valve face and seat **(see illustration and 14.13)**.

23 Carefully remove the valve from the guide

14.21 Apply the lapping compound very sparingly, in small dabs, to the valve face only

14.22a Rotate the valve grinding tool back and forth between the palms of your hands

14.22b The valve face and seat should show a uniform unbroken ring and the seat should be the specified width all the way round

14.25a Fit the outer spring seat . . .

14.25b . . . followed by the inner spring seat

14.26a Fit a new valve stem seal . . .

and wipe off all traces of grinding compound, making sure none gets in the guide. Use solvent to clean the valve and wipe the seat area thoroughly with a solvent soaked cloth.

24 Repeat the procedure with fine valve grinding compound, then repeat the entire procedure for the remaining valves.

25 Working on one valve at a time, lay the outer spring seat in place in the cylinder head, then the inner, making sure they fit correctly **(see illustrations)**.

26 Using a stem seal fitting tool or an appropriate size deep socket, fit a new valve stem seal onto the guide, using the tool or socket to push the seal over the end of the valve guide until it is felt to clip into place **(see illustrations)**. Don't twist or cock the seal, or it will not seal properly against the valve stem. Also, don't remove it again or it will be damaged.

27 Coat the valve stem with molybdenum disulphide oil (a 50/50 mixture of molybdenum disulphide grease and engine oil), then install it into its guide, rotating it slowly to avoid damaging the seal **(see illustration)**. Check that the valve moves up and down freely in the guide.

28 Next, install the inner and outer springs, with the closer-wound coils facing down into the cylinder head, followed by the spring retainer, with its shouldered side facing down so that it fits into the top of the inner spring **(see illustrations)**.

29 Compress the valve spring with a spring compressor *(see Tool Tip)*, making sure it is correctly located onto each end of the valve assembly **(see illustrations 14.5a, b and c)**. On the underside of the head make sure the plate on the compressor only contacts the valve and not the soft aluminium of the head –

if the plate is too big for the valve, use a spacer between them. Do not compress the springs any more than is necessary to slip the collets into place. Apply a small amount of grease to the collets to help hold them in place. Locate each collet in turn into the groove in the valve stem, then carefully release the compressor, making sure the collets seat and lock as you do **(see illustration 14.5d)**. Check that the collets are securely locked in the retaining groove.

30 Support the cylinder head on blocks so the valves can't contact the workbench top, then very gently tap the top of the valve stem with a brass drift **(see illustration)**. This will help seat the collets in the groove. If you don't have a brass drift, fit the shim into its recess in the top of the valve spring retainer and use a soft-faced hammer and a piece of wood as an interface

14.26b . . . using the special tool shown or a deep socket to press it squarely into place

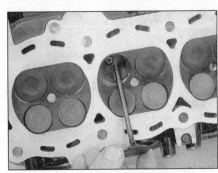

14.27 Lubricate the stem and slide the valve into its correct location

14.28a Fit the inner valve spring . . .

14.28b . . . and the outer valve spring, with their closer wound coils facing down . . .

14.28c . . . then fit the spring retainer

14.30 Tap the top of the valve stem to fully seat the collets

15.3 Check the starter clutch as described – it should turn freely anticlockwise

15.4 Draw the gear out of the clutch

15.6b Unscrew the bolts and remove the sprag assembly

 HAYNES HiNT *Check for proper sealing of the valves by pouring a small amount of solvent into each of the valve ports. If the solvent leaks past any valve into the combustion chamber area the valve grinding operation on that valve should be repeated.*

31 Repeat the procedure for the remaining valves. Remember to keep the parts for each valve together and separate from the other valves so they can be reinstalled in the same location. After the cylinder head and camshafts have been installed, check and adjust the valve clearances as required (see Chapter 1).

15 Starter clutch – check, removal, inspection and installation

Note: *The starter clutch can be removed with the engine in the frame. If the engine has been removed, ignore the steps which do not apply.*

Check

1 The operation of the starter clutch can be checked while it is in situ. Remove the starter motor (see Chapter 9). Check that the idle/reduction gear is able to rotate freely clockwise as you look at it via the starter motor aperture, but locks when rotated anti-clockwise. If not, the starter clutch is faulty and should be removed for inspection.

Removal

2 Remove the alternator – the starter clutch is mounted on the back of it (see Chapter 9). If the starter driven gear does not come away with the starter clutch, slide it off the crankshaft.

Inspection

3 With the alternator rotor face down on a workbench, check that the starter driven gear rotates freely in an anti-clockwise direction and locks against the rotor in a clockwise direction **(see illustration)**. If it doesn't, the starter clutch should be dismantled for further investigation.

4 Withdraw the starter driven gear from the starter clutch **(see illustration)**. If the gear appears stuck, rotate it anti-clockwise as you withdraw it to free it from the starter clutch.
5 Check the condition of the sprags inside the clutch body and the corresponding surface on the driven gear hub **(see illustration 15.4)**. If they are damaged, marked or flattened at any point, they should be replaced with new ones. Measure the outside diameter of the hub and check that it has not worn beyond the service limit specified. To remove the sprag assembly, hold the rotor using a holding strap and unscrew the six bolts inside the rotor **(see illustration)**. Separate the sprag assembly from the rotor, noting which was round the sprag is fitted. Install the new assembly in a reverse sequence. Apply clean engine oil to the sprags. Apply a suitable non-permanent thread locking compound to the bolts and tighten them to the torque setting specified at the beginning of the Chapter.
6 Check the needle roller bearing on the crankshaft and the bearing surfaces in the starter driven gear hub and on the crankshaft. If the bearing surfaces show signs of excessive wear or the bearing itself is worn or damaged, they should be replaced with new ones.
7 Check the teeth of the starter idle/reduction gear and the corresponding teeth of the starter driven gear and starter motor drive shaft. Replace the gears and/or starter motor if worn or chipped teeth are discovered on related gears. Also check the idle/reduction gear shaft for damage, and check that the

16.2 Unscrew the bolts (arrowed) and remove the cover

gear is not a loose fit on the shaft. Replace the shaft with a new one if necessary.

Installation

8 Lubricate the needle roller bearing on the crankshaft with clean engine oil. Lubricate the outside of the starter driven gear hub with clean engine oil, then fit the gear into the clutch, rotating it anti-clockwise as you do so to spread the sprags and allow the hub to enter.
9 Install the alternator (see Chapter 9).

16 Clutch – removal, inspection and installation

Note 1: *The clutch can be removed with the engine in the frame. If the engine has been removed, ignore the steps which don't apply.*
Note 2: *The clutch nut must be discarded and a new one used on installation – it is best to obtain the nut in advance.*

Removal

1 Remove the right-hand fairing side panel (see Chapter 8). Drain the engine oil (see Chapter 1).
2 Working evenly in a criss-cross pattern, unscrew the clutch cover bolts **(see illustration)**. Remove the cover, being prepared to catch any residual oil. Discard the gasket as a new one must be used.
3 Working in a criss-cross pattern, gradually slacken the clutch spring bolts until spring pressure is released **(see illustration)**. To

16.3a Unscrew the pressure plate bolts (arrowed) and remove the springs

16.3b Withdraw the pushrod from the engine, noting which way round it fits

16.5a Unstake the nut . . .

16.5b . . . then unscrew it as described and remove the washers

prevent the assembly from turning, cover it with a rag and hold it securely – the bolts are not very tight. If available, have an assistant to hold the clutch while you unscrew the bolts. Remove the bolts and springs, then remove the clutch pressure plate **(see illustrations 16.26b and a)**. Remove the pushrod end-piece from either the back of the pressure plate or the end of the shaft **(see illustration 16.25b)**. If required also withdraw the pushrod from inside the shaft – you may need a magnet or magnetised screwdriver to draw it out **(see illustration 16.25a)**. Otherwise, remove the front sprocket cover (see Chapter 6), then withdraw the pushrod from the left-hand side **(see illustration)**. Note the differences in the ends of the pushrod and which way round it fits.

4 Remove the clutch friction and plain plates, noting how they fit and keeping them in the same order as you remove them **(see illustrations 16.)**. Note how the tabs on the outer friction plate locate in the shallow slots in the housing, while the rest sit in the deep

slots. On V and W (1997 and 1998) models, the innermost plain and friction plates are secured by a wire retainer which is part of the anti-judder mechanism – if required, remove the retainer, the plain plate, the friction plate, the anti-judder spring and the spring seat, noting carefully how they fit, and that the wire retainer should be discarded as Honda specify to use a new one if the assembly is disturbed. Also note that the friction plate has a larger internal diameter than the others to accommodate the spring and spring seat. On X (1999) models onward, the anti-judder mechanism has not been fitted, but note that the outer and inner friction plates have blue coloured tabs, while the others are brown – if the colours are difficult to identify, just make sure you keep the plates in the correct order as the blue-coded plates must be fitted first and last.

5 The clutch nut is staked against the input shaft. Unstake the nut using a screwdriver, a punch, or a suitable grinding tool – take care not to damage the threads on the end of the

shaft **(see illustration)**. To remove the clutch nut, the input shaft must be locked. This can be done in several ways. If the engine is in the frame, engage 6th gear and have an assistant hold the rear brake on hard with the rear tyre in firm contact with the ground. Alternatively, the Honda service tool (Pt. No. 07724-0050002), or a similar commercially available or home-made tool **(see Tool tip)**, can be used to stop the clutch centre from turning whilst the nut is slackened **(see illustration)**. Unscrew the nut and remove the spring washer and the thrust washer from the input shaft **(see illustration 16.22c and b)**. Discard the nut as a new one must be used on installation.

6 Remove the clutch centre and the thrust washer from the shaft **(see illustrations 16.23a and 16.22)**.

7 To remove the clutch housing it is necessary to align the primary drive sub-gear teeth with the main gear. To do this, locate a suitable screwdriver or rod in the holes in the gears and twist against spring tension to align their teeth **(see illustration)**. Slide the clutch housing off the shaft, noting that you may have to prevent the guide in the centre of the housing from sliding with it by pressing on its rim using a very small screwdriver **(see illustration 16.21b)**. If the guide slides with the housing, it brings the oil pump drive chain with it which could distort the chain. Note how the holes in the back of the housing engage with the pins on the oil pump drive sprocket.

8 If required, unscrew the oil pump driven sprocket bolt and remove the driven sprocket,

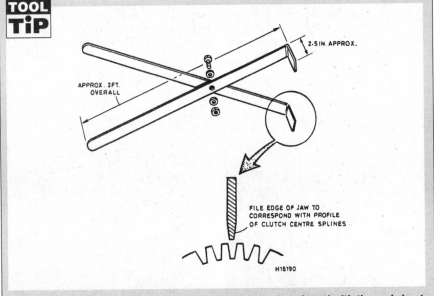

TOOL TiP

2·5 IN. APPROX.

APPROX. 2FT. OVERALL

FILE EDGE OF JAW TO CORRESPOND WITH PROFILE OF CLUTCH CENTRE SPLINES

H16190

A clutch centre holding tool can be made using two strips of steel with the ends bent over and filed, with a bolt in the middle to create the scissor effect

16.7 Align the main and sub-gear teeth as shown and draw the housing off the shaft

16.8a Unscrew the oil pump sprocket bolt (arrowed) . . .

16.8b . . . locking the sprocket as shown to prevent it turning

the chain and the drive sprocket **(see illustrations and 16.20a)**. Lock the sprocket to prevent it from turning whilst slackening the bolt by locating a rod between the one of the holes in the sprocket and the crankcase **(see Tool Tip)**. Also remove the clutch housing guide from the input shaft **(see illustration 16.19)**.

Inspection

9 After an extended period of service the clutch friction plates will wear and promote clutch slip. Measure the thickness of each friction plate using a vernier caliper **(see illustration)**. If any plate has worn to or

beyond the service limits given in the Specifications at the beginning of the Chapter, the friction plates must be renewed as a set. Also, if any of the plates smell burnt or are glazed, they must be renewed as a set.
10 The plain plates should not show any signs of excess heating (bluing). Check for warpage using a flat surface and feeler gauges **(see illustration)**. If any plate exceeds the maximum permissible amount of warpage, or shows signs of bluing, all plain plates must be renewed as a set.
11 Measure the free length of each clutch spring using a vernier caliper **(see illustration)**. If any spring is below the service limit specified, renew all the springs as a set. On V and W (1997 and 1998) models, also check the anti-judder spring and spring seat for damage or distortion and replace them with new ones if necessary.
12 Inspect the clutch assembly for burrs and indentations on the edges of the protruding tabs of the friction plates and/or slots in the edge of the housing with which they engage. Similarly check for wear between the inner tongues of the plain plates and the slots in the clutch centre. Wear of this nature will cause clutch drag and slow disengagement during gear changes as the plates will snag when the pressure plate is lifted. With care a small

amount of wear can be corrected by dressing with a fine file, but if this is excessive the worn components should be renewed.
13 Inspect the clutch housing guide bearing surface and the needle roller bearing in the clutch housing. If there are any signs of wear, pitting or other damage the affected parts must be renewed. The bearing is a press fit in the housing – refer to *Tools and Workshop Tips* in the Reference Section for details on bearing removal and installation. When removing the old bearing, note carefully how it sits in the centre (i.e. what it is flush with), and install the new bearing so that it sits in exactly the same place, and so the marked end will be facing out when the clutch is installed.
14 Check the pressure plate and its bearing for signs of wear or damage and roughness **(see illustration)**. Check that the bearing outer race is a tight fit in the centre of the lifter, and that the inner race rotates freely without any rough spots. Check the pushrod end piece for signs of wear or damage. Replace any parts necessary with new ones.
15 Withdraw the pushrod and check that it is straight by rolling it on a flat surface – if it is bent, replace it with a new one **(see illustration 16.3b)**. Remove the front sprocket cover (see Chapter 6) and check the pushrod oil seal in the left-hand side of the crankcase

16.9 Measuring clutch friction plate thickness

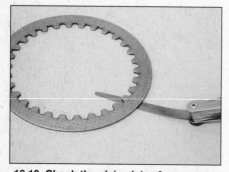

16.10 Check the plain plates for warpage

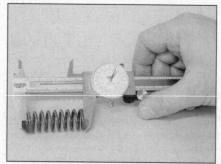

16.11 Measure the free length of the springs as shown

16.14 Check the bearing in the pressure plate

16.15 Check the clutch pushrod oil seal (arrowed) for leakage

16.19 Slide the guide onto the shaft

16.20a Slide the drive sprocket onto the shaft, then fit the chain and the driven sprocket

16.20b Locate the drive sprocket over the guide and the driven sprocket onto the pump shaft . . . .

16.20c . . . . then install the bolt . . .

16.20d . . . and tighten it to the specified torque

for signs of leakage and replace it if necessary **(see illustration)**. To replace it, lever out the old seal using a screwdriver. Apply grease to the lips of the new seal, then press or drive it squarely into place.

16 Using a vernier caliper, measure the internal and external diameter of the clutch housing guide, and the external diameter of the input shaft where the guide sits. Compare the measurements to the specifications at the beginning of the Chapter and renew any components that are worn beyond their service limit. Also check all the above components for signs of damage or scoring, and renew if necessary.

17 Check the teeth of the primary driven gear on the back of the clutch housing and the corresponding teeth of the primary drive gear on the crankshaft. Renew the clutch housing and/or crankshaft if worn or chipped teeth are discovered.

Installation

18 Remove all traces of old gasket from the crankcase and clutch cover surfaces.
19 If removed, smear the inside and outside of the clutch housing guide with molybdenum disulphide oil (a 50/50 mixture of molybdenum disulphide grease and engine oil), then slide the guide onto the input shaft

with the flanged end inwards **(see illustration)**.
20 Slide the oil pump drive sprocket onto the shaft, making sure the pins face out, and slip the chain around the sprocket **(see illustrations)**. Engage the driven sprocket with the chain, making sure the OUT mark faces out, then locate the sprocket on the oil pump **(see illustration)**. Apply a suitable non-permanent thread locking compound to the sprocket bolt and tighten it to the torque setting specified at the beginning of the chapter (see *Tool Tip*), not forgetting its washer **(see illustrations)**.

> **TOOL TIP** *Insert a screwdriver or drift through one of the holes in the sprocket and lock it against the crankcase to prevent the sprocket from turning whilst tightening the bolt.*

21 To install the clutch housing it is necessary to align the primary drive sub-gear teeth with the main gear using the method employed on removal (see Step 7). Slide the clutch housing over the housing guide on the input shaft, making sure that the pins on the oil pump drive sprocket locate in the holes in the rear of the housing (make sure they can't turn independently) **(see illustrations)**.

16.21a Locate the pins on the drive sprocket in the holes in the back of the clutch housing (arrowed) . . .

16.21b . . . and align the main and sub-gear teeth as shown

16.22 Fit the thrust washer . . .

16.23a . . . and the clutch centre

16.23b Fit the thrust washer . . .

16.23c . . . and the spring washer, with the OUT mark facing out

16.23d Fit a new clutch nut . . .

16.23e . . . and tighten it to the specified torque

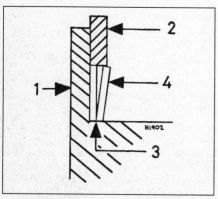

16.23f Stake the nut against the detent in the shaft end

16.24 Anti-judder spring installation details (V and W models)

1 Clutch centre
2 Inner friction plate
3 Spring seat
4 Anti-judder spring

22 Slide the thrust washer onto the shaft (see illustration).

23 Slide the clutch centre onto the shaft splines (see illustration), then install the thrust washer and the spring washer with its OUT mark facing out (see illustrations). Install the new clutch nut and, using the method employed on removal to lock the input shaft (see Step 5), tighten the nut to the torque setting specified at the beginning of the Chapter (see illustrations). Stake the collar of the nut into the indent on the end of the shaft (see illustration).

24 On V and W (1997 and 1998) models, if removed, fit the anti-judder spring seat into the clutch centre, then fit the spring so that the outer edge is raised and facing outwards (see illustration). Now fit the innermost friction plate (the one with the larger internal diameter) over the spring and spring seat,

then fit the plain plate. Secure them with a new wire retainer, making sure it locates correctly in its groove.

25 Coat each clutch plate with engine oil prior to installation, then build up the plates as follows: on V and W (1997 and 1998) models first fit a friction plate, then a plain plate, then alternate friction and plain plates until all are installed, making sure the outermost friction plate is installed with its tabs fitting into the shallow slots in the housing. On X (1999) models onward, first fit the innermost friction plate with the blue coded tab, then fit a plain plate, then alternate brown-coded friction plates and plain plates until all except the outermost blue-coded friction plate is installed, then fit that with its tabs fitting into the shallow slots in the housing (see illustrations).

26 Lubricate the pressure plate bearing, the

16.25a On X models onwards, fit a blue-tabbed friction plate first . . .

16.25b . . . then a plain plate . . .

16.25c . . . then alternate between brown-tabbed friction plates and plain plates until they are all installed (and finishing with a plain plate) . . .

16.25d . . . then fit the second blue-tabbed friction plate, locating its tabs into the shallow slots in the housing

16.26 Install the pushrod end-piece

pushrod end-piece and the pushrod with molybdenum disulphide oil (a 50/50 mixture of molybdenum disulphide grease and engine oil). Note the differences in the end sections of the clutch pushrod – the longer end section faces the left-hand side of the engine (towards the release mechanism), the shorter end section faces the right-hand side (towards the clutch). Slide the pushrod into the shaft – if the sprocket cover has been removed it can be inserted from the left-hand side **(see illustration 16.3b)**. Fit the pushrod end-piece into the shaft **(see illustration)**.

27 Fit the pressure plate onto the clutch, engaging the protrusions on its inner rim in the slots in the inside of the clutch centre **(see illustration)**. Install the springs and the bolts and tighten them evenly in a criss-cross sequence to the specified torque setting **(see illustration)**. Counter-hold the clutch housing to prevent it turning when tightening the spring bolts.

28 Apply a smear of a suitable sealant 10 to 15 mm either side of the crankcase joints on the mating surface with the clutch cover. Install the clutch cover using a new gasket and tighten its bolts evenly in a criss-cross pattern to the specified torque setting **(see illustrations)**. If removed, install the front sprocket cover (see Chapter 6).

29 Fill the engine with oil (see Chapter 1).

16.27a Fit the pressure plate . . .

16.27b . . . then install the springs and tighten the bolts as described

16.28a Fit a new gasket (the sealant will hold it in place) . . .

16.28b . . . then install the cover

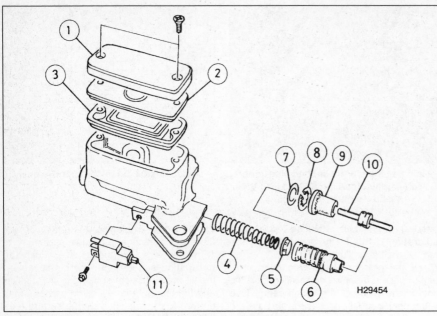

17.3 Clutch master cylinder assembly

1 Reservoir cover
2 Diaphragm plate
3 Rubber diaphragm
4 Spring
5 Primary cup (V and W)
  (1997 and 1998) models

6 Piston assembly (includes
  the seal on V and W (1997
  and 1998) models, and the
  seal and primary cup on X
  (1999) models onward

7 Washer
8 Circlip
9 Rubber boot
10 Pushrod
11 Clutch switch

17 Clutch release mechanism – removal, overhaul and installation

Warning: Hydraulic fluid can harm your eyes and damage painted surfaces, so use extreme caution when handling and pouring it and cover surrounding surfaces with rag.

1 All models have an hydraulic clutch release mechanism consisting of a master cylinder and a release (or slave) cylinder, linked by a hydraulic hose.

Master cylinder

2 If the master cylinder is leaking fluid, or if the clutch does not work properly when the lever is applied, and bleeding the system does not help (see below), and the hydraulic hoses are all in good condition, then master cylinder overhaul is recommended.

3 Before disassembling the master cylinder, read through the entire procedure and make sure that you have the correct rebuild kit (see illustration). Also, you will need some new DOT 4 hydraulic brake and clutch fluid, some clean rags and internal circlip pliers.
Note: *To prevent damage to the paint from spilled brake fluid, always cover the fuel tank and fairing when working on the master cylinder.*

Caution: Disassembly, overhaul and reassembly of the master cylinder must be done in a spotlessly clean work area to avoid contamination and possible failure of the hydraulic system components.

Removal

Note: *If the master cylinder is being displaced from the handlebar and not being removed completely or overhauled, follow Steps 5 and 8 only.*

4 Support the motorcycle on its centre-stand. Slacken the reservoir cap screws, then lightly tighten them again. Turn the handlebars to full right lock so that the top of the reservoir is level.
5 Disconnect the clutch switch wiring connectors (see illustration). If required, remove the clutch switch (see Chapter 9).
6 If the master cylinder is being overhauled, remove the clutch lever (see Chapter 6). If it is just being displaced it can remain in situ.
7 If the master cylinder is being completely removed or overhauled, unscrew the clutch hose banjo bolt and separate the hose from the master cylinder, noting its alignment (see illustration). Discard the sealing washers as they must be replaced with new ones. Wrap the end of the hose in a clean rag and suspend in an upright position or bend down carefully and place the open end in a clean container. The objective is to prevent excessive loss of brake fluid, fluid spills and system contamination. If the master cylinder is just being displaced and not completely removed or overhauled, do not disconnect the brake hose.
8 Unscrew the master cylinder clamp bolts, noting how the UP mark faces up and the top mating surfaces of the clamp align with the punch mark on the handlebar, then lift the master cylinder away from the handlebar (see illustration).

Overhaul

9 Remove the reservoir cap and lift off the diaphragm plate and the rubber diaphragm (see illustration 17.3). Drain the brake fluid from the reservoir into a suitable container. Wipe any remaining fluid out of the reservoir with a clean rag.
10 Draw the pushrod out of the master cylinder, noting how it locates in the rubber boot – the boot may come away with the pushrod.
11 If it didn't come with the pushrod, remove the rubber boot from the end of the piston in the cylinder.

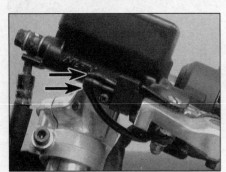

17.5 Clutch switch wiring connectors (arrowed)

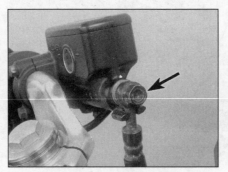

17.7 Clutch hose banjo bolt (arrowed)

17.8 Master cylinder clamp bolts (arrowed)

17.28 Clutch hose banjo bolt (arrowed)

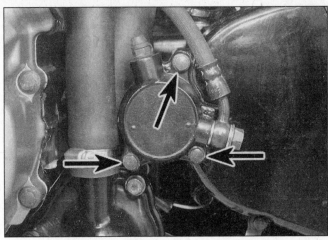

17.29 Release cylinder mounting bolts (arrowed)

12 Using circlip pliers, remove the circlip, then slide out the washer, piston assembly, primary cup and spring, noting how they fit. Lay the parts out in the proper order and way round to prevent confusion during reassembly.

13 Clean all parts with clean brake/clutch fluid. If compressed air is available, use it to dry the parts thoroughly (make sure it's filtered and unlubricated).

Caution: Do not, under any circumstances, use a petroleum-based solvent to clean the parts.

14 Check the master cylinder bore for corrosion, scratches, nicks and score marks. If the necessary measuring equipment is available, compare the dimensions of the piston and bore to those given in the Specifications Section of this Chapter. If damage or wear is evident, the master cylinder must be replaced with a new one. If the master cylinder is in poor condition, then the release cylinder should be checked as well. Check that the fluid inlet and outlet ports in the master cylinder are clear.

15 The dust boot, circlip, washer, piston assembly, primary cup and spring are included in the rebuild kit. Use all of the new parts, regardless of the apparent condition of the old ones. If the seal is not already on the piston, fit it according to the layout of the old one. Lubricate the piston assembly and primary cup with clean brake/clutch fluid.

16 Fit the spring into the master cylinder so that its narrow end faces out. On V and W (1997 and 1998) models, slip the primary cup into the bore with the cupped side innermost and locate it against the spring, making sure the lips do not turn inside out.

17 Fit the piston assembly into the master cylinder, making sure it is the correct way round. Fit the washer onto the end of the piston. Depress the piston and install the new circlip, making sure that it locates in the groove.

18 Apply some silicone grease to the inside of the rubber boot and to the pushrod. Fit the boot over the pushrod, locating the narrow rim of the boot into the groove. Install the

pushrod, making sure the wide rim of the boot locates correctly in the groove in the end of the master cylinder.

19 Fit the pushrod into the end of the master cylinder, making sure the rubber boot locates in the groove.

20 Inspect the reservoir cover rubber diaphragm and renew it if it is damaged or deteriorated.

Installation

21 Locate the master cylinder on the handlebar and fit the clamp with its UP mark facing up, aligning the top mating surfaces of the clamp with the punch mark on the handlebar **(see illustration 17.8)**. Tighten the upper bolt first, then the lower bolt, to the torque setting specified at the beginning of the Chapter.

22 If detached, connect the clutch hose to the master cylinder, using new sealing washers on each side of the union, and aligning the hose as noted on removal **(see illustration 17.7)**. Tighten the banjo bolt to the specified torque setting.

23 If removed, install the clutch switch (see Chapter 9). Otherwise, connect the clutch switch wiring connectors **(see illustration 17.5)**.

24 If removed, install the clutch lever (see Chapter 6).

25 Fill the fluid reservoir with new DOT 4 brake/clutch fluid as described in *Daily (pre-ride) checks*. Refer below and bleed the air from the system.

26 Fit the rubber diaphragm, making sure it is correctly seated, the diaphragm plate and the cover onto the master cylinder reservoir, and tighten the cover screws securely but not overtight.

27 Check the operation of the clutch before riding the motorcycle.

Release cylinder

Removal

28 For best access, remove the left-hand fairing side panel (see Chapter 8). If the release cylinder is just being displaced and not

completely removed or overhauled, do not disconnect the clutch hose. Otherwise, unscrew the clutch hose banjo bolt and separate the hose from the release cylinder, noting its alignment **(see illustration)**. Plug the hose end or wrap a plastic bag around it to minimise fluid loss and prevent dirt entering the system. Discard the sealing washers as new ones must be used on installation. **Note:** *If you're planning to overhaul the release cylinder and don't have a source of compressed air to blow out the piston, just loosen the banjo bolt at this stage and retighten it lightly. The hydraulic system can then be used to force the piston out of the body once the cylinder has been unbolted. Disconnect the hose once the piston has been sufficiently displaced.*

29 Unscrew the three bolts securing the release cylinder to the sprocket cover and remove the cylinder **(see illustration)**. Remove the gasket and discard it. Retrieve the two dowels if they are loose. If required, withdraw the pushrod, noting which way round it fits. Do not operate the clutch lever with the release cylinder removed.

HAYNES HiNT

If the release cylinder is not being disassembled, the piston can be prevented from creeping out of the release cylinder by restraining it with a couple of cable ties passed through the mounting bolt holes.

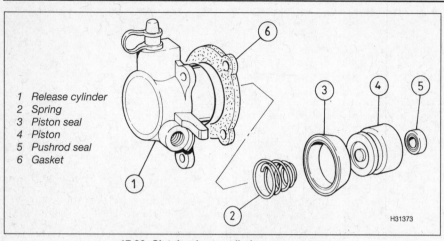

1 Release cylinder
2 Spring
3 Piston seal
4 Piston
5 Pushrod seal
6 Gasket

H31373

17.30 Clutch release cylinder components

Overhaul

30 Have a supply of clean rags on hand, then pump the clutch lever to expel the piston under hydraulic pressure **(see illustration)**. If the hose has already been detached, use a jet of compressed air directed into the fluid inlet to expel the piston.

 Warning: Use only low air pressure, otherwise the piston may be forcibly expelled and cause damage or injury. Wrap the cylinder in a rag before applying the air.

31 Remove the spring from the piston.
32 Using a plastic or wooden tool, remove the piston seal from the groove in the piston. Also remove the pushrod seal from the front of the piston by levering it out with a screwdriver. Discard both seals as new ones must be used.
33 Clean the piston and release cylinder bore with clean hydraulic fluid.
Caution: Do not, under any circumstances, use a petroleum-based solvent to clean hydraulic parts.
34 Inspect the piston and release cylinder bore for signs of corrosion, nicks and burrs and loss of plating. If surface defects are found, the piston and cylinder should be replaced with new ones. If the release cylinder is in poor condition the master cylinder should also be overhauled (see above).

35 Check that the pushrod is straight by rolling it on a flat surface – if it is bent, replace it with a new one. Check the pushrod oil seal in the crankcase for signs of leakage and replace it with a new one if necessary – lever out the old seal with a flat bladed screwdriver and press or drive the new one into place.
36 Lubricate the new piston seal with clean hydraulic fluid and fit it into the groove in the piston so that its narrow end butts against the rim of the piston. Fit the narrow end of the spring over the lug on the inner end of the piston. Smear a new pushrod seal with grease and press it into the outer end of the piston with its marked side facing out. Lubricate the piston and seal with clean hydraulic fluid and insert the assembly into the cylinder, making sure the spring stays in place on the piston. Use your thumbs to press it fully in.

Installation

37 If removed, lubricate the pushrod with molybdenum disulphide oil (a 50/50 mixture of molybdenum disulphide grease and engine oil). Note the differences in the end sections of the clutch pushrod – the longer end section faces the left-hand side of the engine (towards the release mechanism), the shorter end section faces the right-hand side (towards the clutch). Slide the pushrod into the sprocket cover and through the engine. Wipe the outer end of the pushrod clean and smear some silicon grease onto it.

38 Fit the dowels into the sprocket cover if removed, then fit a new gasket onto the dowels **(see illustration)**. Remove the cable ties if used, then install the release cylinder and tighten the bolts to the torque setting specified at the beginning of the Chapter **(see illustration)**.
39 If the hydraulic hose was disconnected, use a new sealing washer on each side of the banjo union. Position the union as noted on removal and tighten the banjo bolt to the specified torque setting **(see illustration 17.28)**.
40 Slacken the master cylinder reservoir cover screws, then remove the cover, diaphragm plate and diaphragm **(see illustration 17.3)**. Fill the reservoir with new hydraulic fluid (see *Daily (pre-ride) checks*) and bleed the system as described below. Check for fluid leaks.

Clutch bleeding

41 Bleeding the clutch is simply the process of removing all the air bubbles from the master cylinder, the hydraulic hose and the release cylinder. Bleeding is necessary whenever a clutch system hydraulic connection is loosened, when a component or hose is replaced, or when the master cylinder or release cylinder is overhauled. Leaks in the system may also allow air to enter, but leaking clutch fluid will reveal their presence and warn you of the need for repair.
42 To bleed the clutch, you will need some new DOT 4 brake and clutch fluid, a length of clear vinyl or plastic tubing, a small container partially filled with clean fluid, a supply of clean rags and a spanner to fit the bleed valve. Note that there are commercially available bleeding kits of various sorts that enable the job to be done much more easily than the manual method described. When using such a tool, follow the manufacturer's instructions.
43 Cover the fuel tank and other painted components to prevent damage in the event that fluid is spilled.
44 Support the motorcycle on its centre-stand, and turn the handlebars to full right lock so that the top of the reservoir is level. Access to the cover screws is partially restricted by the windshield, so if a short or angled screwdriver is not available, slacken the screws before turning the handlebars, but do not remove the cover, diaphragm plate and diaphragm until the reservoir is level.
45 Slowly pump the clutch lever a few times until no air bubbles can be seen floating up from the bottom of the reservoir. Doing this bleeds air from the master cylinder end of the hose. Note that it is sometimes possible for air to become trapped in the top of the union between the hose and the master cylinder, which is the natural high point of the system with the handlebars in the normal position. If this is the case, and you will know because you will be unable to bleed the clutch successfully, displace the master cylinder

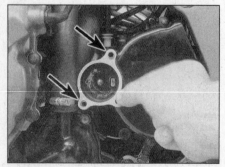

17.38a Locate the new gasket onto the dowels (arrowed) . . .

17.38b . . . then fit the release cylinder

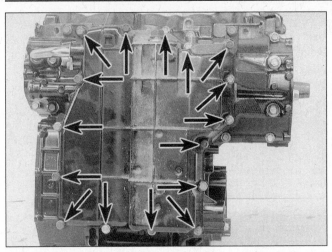

18.3a Unscrew the bolts (arrowed) and remove the sump . . .

18.3b . . . pulling the oil pipe out of the crankcase (arrow)

from the handlebar (see above) and hold it up so that the union is no longer the high point, and this will allow the bubbles of air to climb to the reservoir.

Caution: Do not pump the lever too quickly as fluid could spurt out of the reservoir and onto a painted component.

46 Pull the dust cap off the bleed valve on the release cylinder and attach one end of the clear tubing to the valve. Submerge the other end in the fluid in the container. Check the fluid level in the reservoir. Do not allow it to drop below the lower mark during the bleeding process.

47 Pump the clutch lever slowly three or four times and hold it in against the handlebar, then open the bleed valve. When the valve is opened, fluid will flow out of the release cylinder into the clear tubing.

48 When the fluid stops flowing, tighten the bleed valve, then release the lever gradually. Repeat the process until no air bubbles are visible in the fluid leaving the release cylinder and the clutch action feels smooth and progressive. If the system is being bled for a fluid change, repeat until the new clean fluid can be seen emerging – the colour difference between old and new fluid is fairly obvious. On completion, tighten the bleed valve to the

torque setting specified at the beginning of the Chapter.

49 Ensure that the reservoir level is above the lower mark, then fit the rubber diaphragm, making sure it is correctly seated, the diaphragm plate and the cover onto the master cylinder reservoir, and tighten the cover screws securely but not overtight. Wipe up any spilled fluid and check that there are no leaks from the system when activated. Refit the dust cap over the bleed valve.

50 If removed, install the left-hand fairing side panel (see Chapter 8).

18 Oil sump, oil strainer and pressure relief valve – removal, inspection and installation

Note: *The oil sump, strainer and pressure relief valve can be removed with the engine in the frame. If the engine has been removed, ignore the steps which don't apply.*

Removal

1 Drain the engine oil (see Chapter 1).

2 While the oil is draining, remove the exhaust system (see Chapter 4).

3 Unscrew the sump bolts, slackening them evenly in a criss-cross sequence to prevent distortion **(see illustration)**. Remove the sump, drawing the oil return pipe from the crankcase as you do **(see illustration)**. Discard the O-ring as a new one must be used. If required, remove the bolt securing the pipe retainer and draw the pipe out of the sump **(see illustrations 18.13b and a)**. Discard the O-ring.

4 To remove the oil strainer from the oil pump, unscrew the nut securing the strainer/oil pipe retaining plate and remove it, noting how it fits **(see illustration)**. Pull the strainer out of the pump, noting how it locates around the stud and the lug on the pump **(see illustration)**. Remove the rubber seal and discard it as a new one must be used.

5 To remove the oil pipes, first (and if not already done) unscrew the nut securing the strainer/oil pipe retaining plate and remove it, noting how it fits **(see illustration 18.4a)**. Unscrew the pipe retaining bolts and pull the pipes out of the pump and crankcase **(see illustration)**. Discard the O-ring as a new ones must be used.

6 To remove the pressure relief valve, pull it

18.4a Unscrew the nut (arrowed) and remove the plate . . .

18.4b . . . then pull out the strainer

18.5 Unscrew the bolts (arrowed) and remove the pipes

18.6 Pull the relief valve out of its socket

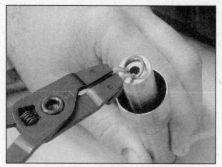

18.9a Remove the circlip . . .

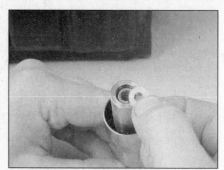

18.9b . . . and the spring seat . . .

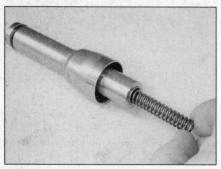

18.9c . . . then draw out the spring . . .

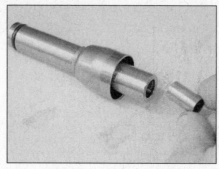

18.9d . . . and the plunger

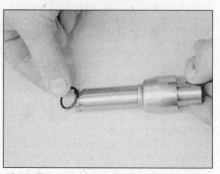

18.10 Fit a new O-ring onto the relief valve body

out of its socket in the crankcase – it is a push-fit **(see illustration)**. Discard the O-ring as a new one must be used.

Inspection

7 Remove all traces of sealant from the sump and crankcase mating surfaces, and clean the inside of the sump with solvent. Blow through all the oil pipes and passages with compressed air if available.

8 Clean the oil strainer in solvent and remove any debris caught in the mesh. If the strainer gauze is damaged, replace the strainer with a new one.

9 Push the relief valve plunger into the valve body and check that it moves smoothly and

freely against spring pressure. If not, remove the circlip, noting that it is under spring pressure, then remove the spring seat, spring and plunger **(see illustrations)**. Clean all components in solvent, then check the plunger and the valve body for evidence of scoring, wear and any other damage. If any is found, replace the relief valve with a new one – individual components are not available. Otherwise, coat the plunger with oil and fit it closed end first back into the valve and recheck the movement. If it is good, install the spring and spring seat and secure them with the circlip.

Installation

10 Fit a new O-ring onto the relief valve and

smear it with clean oil, then push the valve into its socket in the sump **(see illustration and 18.6)**.
11 Fit new O-rings onto the oil pipes and smear them with clean oil. Press the pipes into the pump and crankcase, making sure they seat correctly **(see illustration)**. Apply a suitable non-permanent thread locking compound to the pipe bolt threads and tighten them to the torque setting specified at the beginning of the Chapter **(see illustration 18.5)**. If the strainer has not been removed, fit the strainer/oil pipe retaining plate, then apply the threadlock to the nut and tighten it to the specified torque **(see illustration 18.12c)**.
12 Fit a new rubber seal into the strainer orifice in the oil pump **(see illustration)**. Do

18.11 Fit a new O-ring onto each end the pipes, then press them into their bores and secure them with the bolts

18.12a Fit the rubber seal into the pump . . .

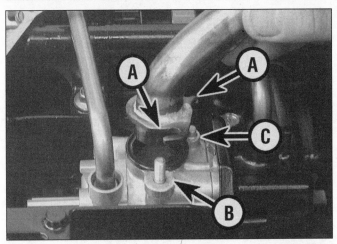

18.12b . . . then install the strainer, aligning the cutouts (A) with the stud (B) and lug (C)

18.12c Fit the retaining plate and secure it with the nut

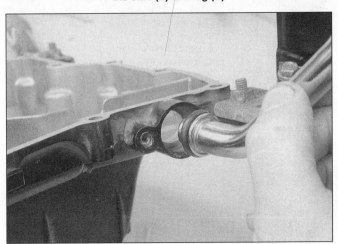

18.13a Fit the pipe using a new O-ring . . .

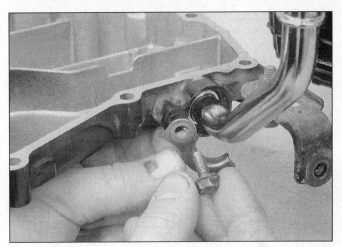

18.13b . . . and secure it with the retainer

not fit it onto the strainer as it will distort when the strainer is fitted onto the pump. Fit the strainer onto the pump, locating the small cutout in the strainer base over the lug on the pump **(see illustration)**. Fit the strainer/oil pipe retaining plate, then apply a suitable non-permanent thread locking compound to the nut and tighten it to the specified torque setting **(see illustration)**.

13 If the oil return pipe was removed from the sump, fit a new O-ring and smear it with clean oil. Fit the pipe into the sump, then secure it with the retainer and tighten the bolt to the specified torque setting **(see illustrations)**. Fit a new O-ring onto the crankcase end of the pipe and smear it with oil.

14 Clean the mating surfaces of the sump and crankcase with solvent. Apply a suitable sealant (such as Three Bond 1207B) to the sump mating surface. Position the sump onto the crankcase, making sure the oil pie enters its bore in the crankcase, and install the bolts finger-tight **(see illustrations 18.3b and a)**. Tighten the bolts evenly and a little at a time in

a criss-cross pattern, starting with the front right-hand and rear left-hand corner bolts.

15 Install the exhaust system, but do not yet fit the fairing side panels (see Chapter 4).

16 Fill the engine with the correct type and quantity of oil as described in Chapter 1. Start the engine and check that there are no leaks around the sump.

17 Install the fairing side panels (see Chapter 8).

19 Oil pump – removal, inspection and installation

Note: *The oil pump can be removed with the engine in the frame. If the engine has been removed, ignore the steps which don't apply.*

Removal

1 Remove the sump, the oil strainer, and the right – hand oil pipe (see Section 18).

2 Remove the clutch, along with the oil pump drive and driven sprockets (see Section 16).

3 Unscrew the three bolts securing the pump to the crankcase, then remove the pump, noting how it fits **(see illustration)**. If the dowels remain in the crankcase, remove them for safekeeping if they are loose. It is quite likely that they will remain in the pump as they are long dowels that locate the inner cover on the pump body as well as locating the pump on the crankcase.

19.3 Unscrew the bolts (arrowed) and remove the pump

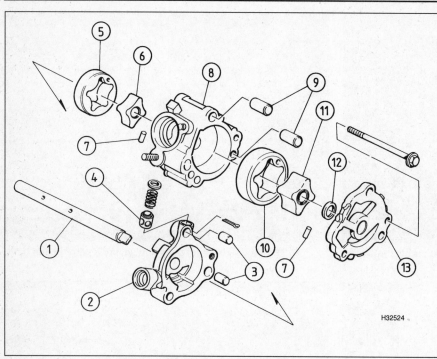

19.4a Oil pump assembly

1 Pump shaft
2 Outer cover
3 Dowels
4 Pressure relief valve
5 Cooler outer rotor

6 Cooler inner rotor
7 Drive pins
8 Main body
9 Dowels

10 Main outer rotor
11 Main inner rotor
12 Thrust washer
13 Inner cover

Inspection

Note: *When removing the rotors from the oil pump, note the punch mark in each outer rotor and which way it faces as the rotors must be installed the same way round so that mated surfaces continue to run together.*

4 Unscrew the single bolt securing the covers to the pump body, then remove the outer (cooling circuit) cover (the outer rotor may come with it) **(see illustrations)**. Remove the cover dowels if they are loose **(see illustration)**. Remove the outer and inner rotors, noting which way round they fit and how the inner rotor locates over the drive pin **(see illustration)**. Withdraw the drive pin from the shaft **(see illustration)**.

5 Remove the long dowels from the inner cover if they are loose (and if they didn't stay in the crankcase) **(see illustration)**. Remove the inner (feed circuit) cover, then remove the thrust washer from the drive shaft **(see illustrations)**. Withdraw the shaft from the pump and remove the drive pin, noting how it fits **(see illustration)**. Remove the inner and outer rotors, noting which way round they fit **(see illustrations)**.

6 Clean all the components in solvent.

7 Inspect the pump body and rotors for scoring and wear. If any damage, scoring or uneven or excessive wear is evident, replace the pump with a new one (individual components are not available).

8 Fit the feed circuit inner and outer rotors

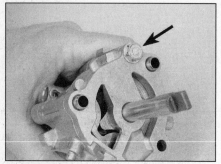

19.4b Unscrew the bolt (arrowed) . . .

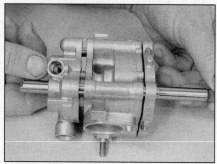

19.4c . . . and remove the outer cover . . .

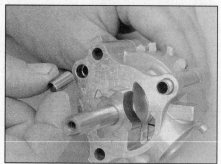

19.4d . . . and the dowels

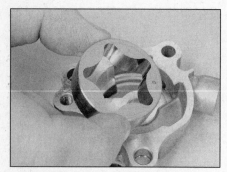

19.4e Remove the cooler outer rotor . . .

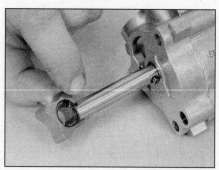

19.4f . . . and the inner rotor, noting how it fits . . .

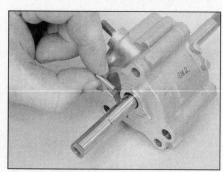

19.4g . . . and the drive pin

19.5a Remove the long dowels . . .

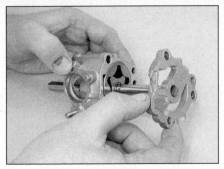

19.5b . . . and the inner cover

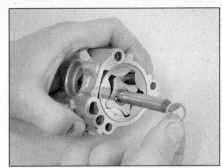

19.5c Remove the thrust washer . . .

into the pump body, and the cooling circuit rotors into the outer cover. Measure the clearance between the inner rotor tip and the outer rotor with a feeler gauge and compare it to the service limit listed in the specifications at the beginning of the Chapter (see illustration). If the clearance measured is greater than the maximum listed, replace the pump with a new one.

9 Measure the clearance between the outer rotor and the pump body with a feeler gauge and compare it to the maximum clearance listed in the specifications at the beginning of the Chapter (see illustration). If the clearance measured is greater than the maximum listed, replace the pump with a new one.

10 Lay a straight-edge across the rotors and the pump body and, using a feeler gauge, measure the rotor end-float (the gap between the rotors and the straight-edge (see illustration). If the clearance measured is greater than the maximum listed, replace the pump with a new one.

11 Check the pump drive chain and drive and driven sprockets for wear or damage, and renew them as a set if necessary.

12 Withdraw the split pin securing the cooling circuit pressure relief valve, noting that it is under spring pressure, then remove the spring seat, spring and plunger, noting which way round it fits (see illustrations). Clean all components in solvent, then check the plunger and the valve body for evidence of

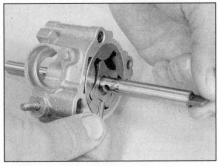

19.5d . . . then withdraw the shaft and remove the drive pin

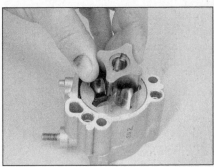

19.5e Remove the main inner rotor . . .

19.5f . . . and the outer rotor

19.8 Measure the inner rotor tip-to-outer rotor clearance as shown (inner cover shown removed for clarity)

19.9 Measure the outer rotor-to-body clearance as shown

19.10 Measure the rotor end-float as shown

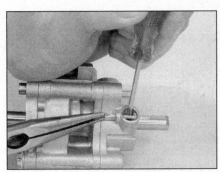

19.12a Remove the split pin . . .

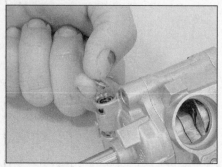

19.12b ... the spring seat ...

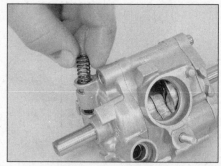

19.12c ... the spring ...

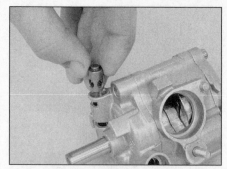

19.12d ... and the plunger

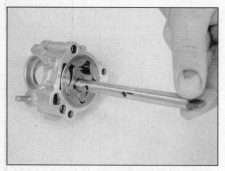

19.14a Slide the shaft through the pump
as described

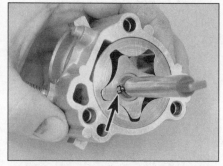

19.14b Locate the drive pin ends into the
cutouts in the inner rotor (arrow)

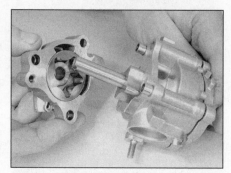

19.15a Fit the outer rotor and cover onto
the inner rotor and dowels

scoring, wear and any other damage. If any is found, replace the oil pump with a new one – individual components are not available. Otherwise, coat the plunger with oil and fit it back into the valve with its shouldered end facing out. Check that it moves smoothly and freely in the bore. If it is good, install the spring and spring seat and secure them with the circlip.

13 If the pump is good, make sure all the components are clean, then lubricate them with new engine oil.

14 Fit the feed circuit outer rotor into the pump body with the punch mark facing the same way as noted on removal (see **Note** and Step 4) **(see illustration 19.5f)**. Fit the inner rotor into the outer rotor with the cutouts in the inner rotor facing out **(see illus-**

tration 19.5e). Slide the drive shaft through the inner rotor and pump body, making sure the end with the driven sprocket bolt hole goes through to the cooling circuit side and the tabbed end remains on the feed circuit side **(see illustration)**. Slide the feed circuit drive pin into its hole in the driveshaft **(see illustration 19.5d)**, and locate it into the cutouts in the inner rotor **(see illustration)**. Slide the thrust washer onto the shaft so it covers the drive pin **(see illustration 19.5c)**. Slide the inner cover onto the pump, then fit the long dowels through the cover and into the pump **(see illustration 19.5b and a)**.

15 Fit the cooling circuit drive pin into the hole in the driveshaft **(see illustration 19.4g)**, then slide the inner rotor onto the shaft so that the cutouts on the inside of the rotor locate

over the ends of the drive pin **(see illustration 19.4f)**. Fit the outer rotor into the cover with the punch mark facing the same way as noted on removal **(see illustration 19.4e)**. Fit the dowels into the body if removed **(see illustration 19.4d)**, then slide the outer cover and rotor down the shaft and locate them over the inner rotor and onto the dowels **(see illustration and 19.4c)**. Install the single bolt from the feed circuit side and tighten it to the torque setting specified at the beginning of the Chapter **(see illustration)**.

16 Rotate the pump shaft by hand and check it turns the rotors smoothly and freely.

Installation

17 Pour some oil into the pump and rotate the shaft to distribute it **(see illustration)**.

19.15b Install the long bolt and tighten it to the specified torque

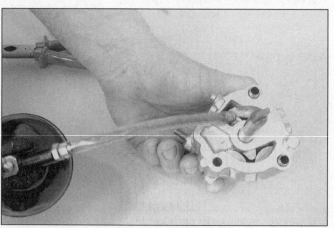

19.17 Prime the pump ...

19.18a . . . then install it as described . . .

19.18b . . . and secure it with the bolts

18 Manoeuvre the pump into position and rotate the drive shaft to align the tab on the end with the slot in the water pump shaft. Install the pump, making sure the dowels locate correctly, and the shafts engage **(see illustration)**. Fit the mounting bolts and tighten them securely **(see illustration)**.
19 Install the pump drive and driven sprockets and chain, and the clutch (see Section 16).
20 Install the oil pipe, strainer and sump (see Section 18).

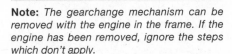

20 Gearchange mechanism – removal, inspection and installation

Note: *The gearchange mechanism can be removed with the engine in the frame. If the engine has been removed, ignore the steps which don't apply.*

Removal

1 Make sure the transmission is in neutral. Remove the clutch (see Section 16). There is no need to remove the oil pump drive and driven sprockets and chain. Block the holes into the sump with clean rag to prevent anything falling in.

20.4 Withdraw the shaft/arm assembly, noting how it fits

2 Unscrew the gearchange lever pinch bolt and slide the lever off the shaft, noting how the punch mark on the shaft aligns with the slot in the lever **(see illustration 5.16)**.
3 Wrap a single layer of thin insulating tape around the gearchange shaft splines to protect the oil seal lips as the shaft is removed.
4 Note how the gearchange shaft centralising spring ends fit on each side of the locating pin in the casing, and how the pawls on the selector arm locate onto the pins on the end of the selector drum **(see illustration 20.10)**. Grasp the end of the shaft and withdraw the shaft/arm assembly **(see illustration)**. Retrieve the washer from the crankcase if it didn't come with the shaft.
5 If required, note how the stopper arm spring ends locate and how the roller on the arm locates in the neutral detent on the selector drum cam, then unscrew the stopper arm bolt and remove the arm, the washer and the spring, noting how they fit **(see illustration)**.

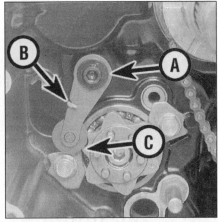

20.5 Unscrew the bolt (A) and remove the arm, noting how the spring ends (B) locate, and how the roller sits in the neutral detent (C)

Inspection

6 Check the selector arm for cracks, distortion and wear of its pawls, and check for any corresponding wear on the pins on the selector drum cam. Also check the stopper arm roller and the detents in the selector drum cam for any wear or damage, and make sure the roller turns freely. Replace any components that are worn or damaged with new ones. Remove the selector drum cam by unscrewing the bolt in its centre **(see illustration)**. Note the locating pin in the end of the drum and remove it for safekeeping if required. On installation, locate the pin in the cutout in the back of the cam. Apply a suitable non-permanent thread locking compound to the cam bolt and tighten it to the torque setting specified at the beginning of the Chapter.
7 Inspect the shaft centralising spring and the stopper arm return spring for fatigue, wear or damage. If any is found, they must be replaced with new ones. Also check that the centralising spring locating pin in the crankcase is securely tightened. If it is loose, remove it and apply a non-permanent thread locking compound to its threads, then tighten it securely.
8 Check the gearchange shaft for straightness and damage to the splines. If the

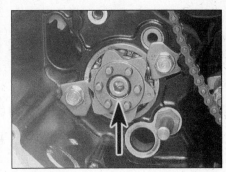

20.6 Selector drum cam bolt (arrowed)

20.8a Check the seal (arrowed) as described

20.8b Unscrew the bolt and remove the retainer . . .

20.8c . . . then lever out the seal

shaft is bent you can attempt to straighten it, but if the splines are damaged the shaft must be replaced with a new one. Also check the condition of the shaft oil seal in the left-hand side of the crankcase **(see illustration)**. If it is damaged, deteriorated or shows signs of leakage it must be replaced with a new one. Unscrew the bolt securing the seal retainer plate and remove the plate **(see illustration)**. Lever out the old seal with a screwdriver **(see illustration)**. With the seal removed, check the condition of the needle bearing, and replace that with a new one as well if necessary **(see illustration)**. Fit the new bearing and press or drive the new seal squarely into place, with its lip facing inward, using a seal driver or suitable socket **(see**

illustration). Fit the retainer plate and tighten its bolt securely.

Installation

9 If removed, locate the stopper arm return spring over the lug on the crankcase **(see illustration)**. Fit the bolt through the stopper arm, then fit the washer onto the bolt **(see illustration)**. Install the arm, locating the roller onto the neutral detent on the selector drum and making sure the spring ends are positioned correctly **(see illustration 20.5)**. Tighten the bolt to the torque setting specified at the beginning of the Chapter. Check that the arm and spring ends are correctly positioned.
10 Check that the shaft centralising spring is

properly positioned and slide the washer onto the shaft if removed **(see illustration)**. Apply some grease to the lips of the gearchange shaft oil seal in the left-hand side of the crankcase. Slide the shaft into place and push it all the way through the case until the splined end comes out the other side **(see illustration 20.4)**. Locate the selector arm pawls onto the pins on the selector drum and the centralising spring ends onto each side of the locating pin **(see illustration)**.
11 Remove the rag that was blocking the sump, then install the clutch (see Section 16).
12 Slide the gearchange lever onto the shaft, aligning the punch mark on the shaft with the slit in the lever **(see illustration 5.16)**. Install the pinch bolt and tighten it securely.

20.8d Remove and check the bearing

20.8e Press or drive the new seal into place

20.9a Locate the spring . . .

20.9b . . . then install the stopper arm

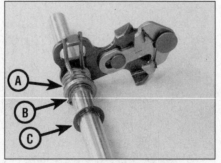

20.10a Make sure the centralising spring (A), circlip (B) and washer (C) are correctly installed

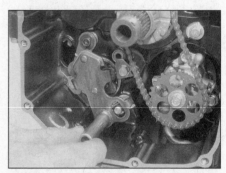

20.10b Locate the selector arm as shown

21 Selector drum and forks – removal, inspection and installation

Note: *The selector drum and forks can be removed and installed with the crankcases joined and the engine in the frame. Having said that, it is much easier if the engine is removed so that you don't have to work upside down. If the crankcases are being separated anyway, remove the selector drum and forks afterwards as it is slightly easier.*

Removal

1 The selector drum and forks are located in the lower crankcase half. If required, remove the engine (see Section 5) and, again if required, separate the crankcase halves (see Section 22). Otherwise, just remove the sump, and to improve access the oil strainer (see Section 18).

2 If not already done, remove the gearchange mechanism (see Section 20).

3 Before removing the selector forks, note that each fork carries an identification letter. The right-hand fork has an "R", the centre fork a "C", and the left-hand fork an "L". The right-hand and centre forks have their letter facing to the right-hand side, and the left-hand fork has its letter facing to the left. If no letters are visible, mark them yourself using a felt pen.

4 Unscrew the bolts securing the selector drum bearing retainer plates and remove the plates, noting how they fit **(see illustration)**.

5 If the crankcases have been separated, support the selector forks and withdraw the shaft from the casing, then remove the forks. Withdraw the selector drum from the right-hand side of the engine.

6 If the crankcases have not been separated, withdraw the selector fork shaft from the casing, then pivot each fork out of its track in the selector drum **(see illustration)**. Withdraw the selector drum from the right-hand side of the engine **(see illustration)**. Remove the selector forks, noting how they locate in the groove in their pinion **(see illustration)**.

7 Once removed from the case, slide the forks back onto the shaft in their correct order and way round.

Inspection

8 Inspect the selector forks for any signs of wear or damage, especially around the fork ends where they engage with the groove in the pinion. Check that each fork fits correctly in its pinion groove. Check closely to see if the forks are bent. If the forks are in any way damaged they must be replaced with new ones.

9 Measure the thickness of the fork ends and compare the readings to the specifications **(see illustration)**. Replace the forks with new ones if they are worn beyond their specifications.

10 Check that the forks fit correctly on their shaft. They should move freely with a light fit but no appreciable freeplay. Measure the

internal diameter of the fork bores and the corresponding diameter of the fork shaft **(see illustration)**. Replace the forks and/or shaft with new ones if they are worn beyond their specifications. Check that the fork shaft holes in the casing are neither worn nor damaged.

11 Check the selector fork shaft for trueness by rolling it along a flat surface. A bent rod will cause difficulty in selecting gears and make the gearshift action heavy. Replace the shaft with a new one if it is bent.

12 Inspect the selector drum grooves and selector fork guide pins for signs of wear or damage. If either component shows signs of wear or damage the fork(s) and drum must be replaced with new ones.

13 Check that the selector drum bearing rotates freely and has no sign of freeplay between it and the casing. To fit a new bearing, remove the selector drum cam by unscrewing the bolt in its centre. Note the locating pin in the end of the drum and remove it for safekeeping if required. Remove the old bearing and fit a new one (see *Tools and Workshop Tips* in the Reference Section if necessary). Install the selector drum cam, locating the pin in the cutout in the back of the cam. Apply a suitable non-permanent thread locking compound to the cam bolt and tighten it to the torque setting specified at the beginning of the Chapter.

Installation

14 If the crankcases have been separated,

21.4 Unscrew the bolts (arrowed) and remove the plates

21.6a Withdraw the shaft and displace the forks from the selector drum . . .

21.6b . . . then remove the selector drum

21.6c Remove the selector forks (arrowed), noting how and which way round they fit

21.9 Measure the fork end thickness . . .

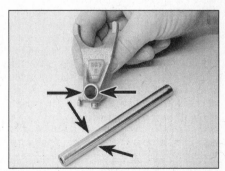

21.10 . . . the fork bore ID and the fork shaft OD

21.15a Install each fork in turn . . .

21.15b . . . making sure each locates correctly . . .

21.15c . . . in the groove in its pinion

21.15d Position the drum so the neutral contact (B) is against the neutral switch contact (A)

21.15e Slide the shaft through each fork in turn . . .

21.15f . . . locating the guide pins in the drum grooves (arrow)

slide the selector drum into position in the crankcase. Make sure the drum end locates into its bore in the casing, and position it so that the neutral contact is against the neutral switch. Lubricate the selector fork shaft with clean engine oil and slide it into the crankcase, through each fork in turn (making sure they are correctly positioned – see Step 3), and into its bore, locating the guide pin on the end of each fork into its groove in the drum.

15 If the crankcases have not been separated, install the selector forks, locating each in the groove of its pinion, making sure they are fitted in the correct order and way round (see Step 3) **(see illustrations)**. Position they forks so they will not get in the way of the selector drum when sliding it in **(see illustration 21.6c)**. Slide the selector drum into position in the crankcase, making sure the drum end locates into its bore in the casing **(see illustration 21.6b)**. Position the drum so that the neutral contact is against the neutral switch **(see illustration)**. Lubricate the selector fork shaft with clean engine oil and slide it into the crankcase **(see illustration 21.6a)**, through each fork in turn, and into its bore, locating the guide pin on the end of each fork into its groove in the drum **(see illustrations)**.

16 Clean the threads of the selector drum retainer plate bolts, then apply a suitable non-permanent thread locking compound. Install the plates, locating them as shown with their

OUT markings facing outwards, and tighten the bolts securely **(see illustration 21.4)**.

17 Install any remaining components according to your removal procedure.

22 Timing rotor –
removal and installation

Note: The timing rotor can be removed with the engine in the frame. If the engine has been removed, ignore the steps which don't apply.

Removal

1 Remove the right-hand fairing side panel (see Chapter 8). If you want to move the timing rotor cover away from the machine, raise the fuel tank (see Chapter 4), then trace the ignition pulse generator wiring from the cover and disconnect it at the red 2-pin connector inside the rubber boot **(see illustration 5.12)**. Release the wiring from any clips or ties and feed it through to the cover, noting its routing.

2 Working evenly in a criss-cross pattern, unscrew the timing rotor cover bolts **(see illustration)**. Remove the cover, being prepared to catch any residual oil. Discard the gasket as a new one must be used. Remove the dowels if they are loose.

3 To remove the timing rotor bolt, the crankshaft must be prevented from turning. If

the engine is in the frame, engage 6th gear and have an assistant hold the rear brake on hard with the rear tyre in firm contact with the ground. If the engine has been removed, remove the alternator cover (see Chapter 9) and use a rotor holding strap to counter-hold the alternator rotor while slackening the bolt. The alternator bolt is tighter than the timing rotor bolt so there is no danger of the wrong one coming undone.

4 Remove the bolt and its washer, then slide the timing rotor off the end of the crankshaft,

22.2 Unscrew the bolts (arrowed) and remove the cover

22.4 Unscrew the bolt (arrowed) and remove the timing rotor

22.5 Align the wide spline on the crankshaft with that in the rotor (arrow) . . .

22.6a . . . then install the oiled bolt . . .

22.6b . . . and tighten it to the specified torque

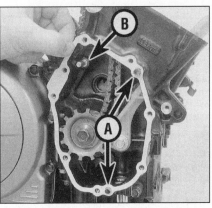

22.7a Install the dowels (A), and check that the plug (B) is in situ, then fit a new gasket onto the dowels . . .

22.7b . . . and install the cover

noting how it locates over a wide spline so that it can only be fitted in one position **(see illustration)**.

Installation

5 Slide the timing rotor onto the end of the crankshaft, aligning the wide splines **(see illustration)**.
6 Apply some engine oil to the threads and the underside of the head on the bolt. Install the bolt with its washer and tighten it to the torque setting specified at the beginning of the Chapter using the same method as on removal to prevent the crankshaft turning **(see illustrations)**.
7 Apply a smear of a suitable sealant 10 to 15 mm either side of the crankcase joints on the mating surface with the timing rotor cover. Fit the cover dowels into the crankcase if removed, and check that the sealing plug is installed **(see illustration)**. Install the cover using a new gasket, making sure they locate correctly onto the dowels **(see illustration)**. Apply the sealant to the threads of the bolts that fit into the upper rear holes that are marked with a triangle. Tighten the bolts evenly in a criss-cross pattern to the specified torque setting. If disconnected, reconnect the ignition pulse generator wiring connector.

23 Front balancer shaft – removal, inspection, bearing selection, installation, and adjustment

Note: *The front balancer shaft can be*

removed with the engine in the frame. If the engine has been removed, ignore the steps which don't apply.

Removal

1 Remove the sump (see Section 18).
2 Unscrew the timing inspection cap from the right-hand crankcase cover **(see illustration 10.2)**. The engine must be turned so that the No. 1 piston is at TDC (top dead centre). The engine can be turned using a suitable spanner or socket on the timing rotor bolt and turning it in a clockwise direction only. Alternatively, place the motorcycle on its centrestand so that the rear

23.3 Check that the notches (arrowed) are aligned

wheel is off the ground, select a high gear and rotate the rear wheel by hand in its normal direction of rotation (removing the spark plugs first will make this a lot easier – see Chapter 1).
3 Turn the engine until the line next to the 'T' mark on the timing rotor aligns with the static timing mark, which is a notch in the inspection hole rim **(see illustration 10.3a)**. At this point the notch in the balancer should align with the mark on the crankcase **(see illustration)**.
4 Make an alignment mark on the shaft holder with the punch mark on the end of the balancer shaft – this will give a good indication as to the starting point for the backlash setting when the shaft is installed **(see illustration)**. Slacken the balancer shaft holder pinch bolt, then unscrew the holder

23.4a Make an alignment mark between the end of the shaft and the holder as an installation aid

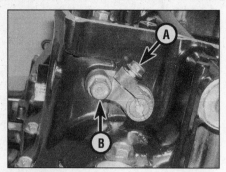

23.4b Slacken the holder pinch bolt (A) then unscrew the mounting bolt (B) and slide the holder off the shaft

23.5 Turn the shaft so its punch mark faces down

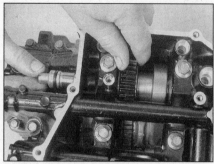

23.6 Withdraw the shaft and remove the gear/weight

mounting bolt and slide the holder off the shaft **(see illustration)**.

5 Turn the shaft until the punch mark on its end is facing down – if the shaft is not in this position it cannot be withdrawn as the offset on it will stop it from doing so (the shaft provides an eccentric adjustment to allow the backlash between the balancer gear and its drive gear on the crankshaft to be optimised to reduce noise) **(see illustration)**.

6 Support the balancer gear/weight assembly, then withdraw the shaft and remove the gear/weight **(see illustration)**. If the shaft is difficult to withdraw, turn it slightly either way to free it. Discard the shaft O-ring as a new one must be used.

Inspection

7 Inspect the teeth on the gear for signs of wear or damage, and replace it with a new one if necessary. If damage is found, check the teeth on the drive gear on the crankshaft. The gear/weight can be disassembled if required – all components are available individually.

8 Remove the washer from each end of the gear/weight, noting which fits where **(see illustration)**. Slide the shaft back into the gear/weight and check that it runs freely and smoothly in the bearings. If there is any evidence of wear on the shaft, or it is a sloppy fit in the bearings, and the bearings are good, replace the shaft with a new one. If the shaft does not run smoothly and freely, or if there is any wear or damage evident, replace them

with new ones. Note that all components are matched by size and should be replaced either as a set, or by matching them using the coded markings (see Steps 9 and 10).

9 Separate the weight from the gear **(see illustration)**. Check the condition of the rubber damper assembly in the gear for damage, deformation and deterioration, and replace them with new ones if necessary.

Bearing selection

10 Replacement bearings for the balancer are supplied on a selected fit basis. Code letters and numbers stamped on the components are used to identify the correct replacement bearings. The balancer gear/weight size code letters (there are two because there are two bearings, the right-hand one for the gear end and the left-hand one for the weight end) are marked on the balancer web and will be either an A, a B or a C **(see illustration)**. The shaft size code number or colour is marked on the shaft and will be either a 1 or blue, a 2 or black, or a 3 or red.

11 A range of bearings are available. To select the correct bearing colour code, using

the table below cross-refer the gear and weight size code (marked on the balancer web – the right-hand marking is for the gear size, the left-hand marking is for the weight size) with the shaft size code (marked on the shaft – if it is difficult to see you will have to measure the shaft diameter at the bearing points using a Vernier caliper, or preferably a micrometer). For example, if the balancer gear size is B, and the shaft size is 3, then the bearing required for the gear end of the shaft is B – Blue. The colour is marked on the bearing.

Installation

12 Fit a new O-ring onto the balancer shaft and smear it with clean oil. Check that the crankshaft is still positioned so that the No. 1 piston is at TDC (see Step 3). Position the balancer gear/weight assembly in the crankcase so that the notch in the balancer aligns with the mark on the crankcase, then slide the shaft in with the punch mark on its end facing down **(see illustration 23.6)**. If the shaft is difficult to insert, turn it slightly either way to free it.

Balancer gear/ weight ID codes	Balancer shaft OD code		
	1 or Blue 17.996 to 18.000 mm	2 or Black 17.991 to 17.996 mm	3 or Red 17.987 to 17.991 mm
A – 26.996 to 27.000 mm	C – White	B – Blue	A – Red
B – 26.991 to 26.996 mm	D – Green	C – White	B – Blue
C – 26.987 to 26.991 mm	E – Yellow	D – Green	C – White

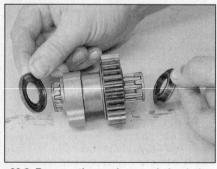

23.8 Remove the washers and check the bearings as described

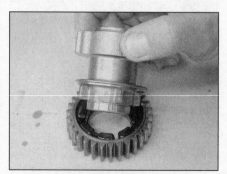

23.9 Separate the weight from the gear and check the rubber dampers

23.10 The size codes for selecting new bearings are marked on the gear and shaft

23.13a Install the holder and secure it with the mounting bolt

23.13b Turn the shaft to align it as before then temporarily tighten the pinch bolt

13 Fit the holder onto the end of the shaft and tighten its mounting bolt to the torque setting specified at the beginning of Chapter **(see illustration)**. Turn the shaft using a screwdriver until the punch mark aligns with the backlash setting mark made earlier on the holder **(see illustration)**. Temporarily tighten the shaft pinch bolt.
14 Carry out the static backlash adjustment procedure (see below).
15 Turn the engine clockwise through 360° (one full turn) and check that the crankshaft and balancer marks still align (see Step 12). Install the sump (see Section 18).
16 Install the timing inspection cap using a new O-ring if required, and smear the O-ring and the cap threads with grease **(see illustration 10.31)**. Tighten the cap to the torque setting specified at the beginning of the Chapter.
17 Carry out the dynamic backlash adjustment procedure (see below).

Backlash adjustment

Note: *A backlash adjustment is provided so that the gears mesh at their optimum point for quiet running with minimal wear. If the amount of backlash is too great, the shafts will clatter. If the gears are running tight, they will whine, and wear very quickly. At the optimum point the gears will run very quietly – it is easy to tell the difference with the engine running. Adjustment is possible due to the offset on the shaft which allows eccentric movement of the balancer gear in relation to its drive gear when the shaft is turned. The static adjustment procedure allows the backlash to be set up in*

24.3 Remove the sealing plug and discard its O-ring

roughly the optimum position, but the dynamic procedure should always be carried out as well to fine tune the setting. The static procedure need only be carried out if the shaft has been removed and reinstalled. If the shaft has not been removed, the dynamic procedure can be carried out on its own. If, having carried out the backlash adjustment, there is still noise from the engine, carry out the rear balancer idle gear and rear balancer shaft adjustment procedure as well (see Section 33).

Static adjustment

Note: *This procedure must be carried out when the engine is cold.*
18 Slacken the balancer shaft holder pinch bolt **(see illustration 23.4b)**.
19 Turn the shaft slightly anti-clockwise, then turn it clockwise until resistance is felt – at this point backlash between the gears has been eliminated **(see illustration 23.13b)**. Now turn the shaft anti-clockwise one graduation as marked on the holder, then temporarily tighten the pinch bolt.
20 Now carry out the dynamic adjustment procedure (see below).

Dynamic adjustment

Note: *This procedure must be carried out when the engine is warm.*
21 Remove the right-hand fairing side panel

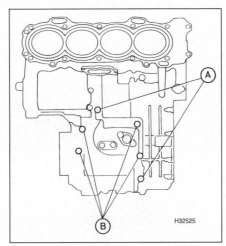

24.4 Upper crankcase 8 mm bolts – without washers (A), with washers (B)

(see Chapter 8). Start the engine and allow it to warm up, then let it idle.
22 Slacken the balancer shaft holder pinch bolt **(see illustration 23.4b)**.
23 Turn the shaft clockwise until the gears begin to whine, then turn it slowly anti-clockwise until the whine disappears, but not so much that the whine is replaced by a clatter **(see illustration 23.13b)**. The optimum point is when the gears run at their quietest. Rev the engine and check that there is no unwanted noise at varying speeds.
24 On completion, tighten the pinch bolt to the torque setting specified at the beginning of the Chapter. Install the right-hand fairing side panel (see Chapter 8).

24 Crankcase halves – separation and reassembly

Note: *To separate the crankcase halves, the engine must be removed from the frame.*

Separation

1 To access the pistons, connecting rods, crankshaft, bearings, and transmission shafts, the crankcase must be split into two parts. The selector drum and forks can be removed and installed with the crankcases joined.
2 To enable the crankcases to be separated, the engine must be removed from the frame (see Section 5). Before the crankcases can be separated the following components must be removed:
a) Valve cover (Section 8).
b) Camshafts (Section 10).
c) Cylinder head (Section 12) – see Note.
d) Alternator/starter clutch (Chapter 9).
e) Clutch (Section 16).
f) Cam chain and blades (Section 11) – see Note.
g) Gearchange mechanism (Section 20) – see Note.
h) Oil sump, oil pipes, strainer and pressure relief valve (Section 18).
i) Oil pump (Section 19).
j) Front balancer shaft (Section 23).
k) Starter motor (Chapter 9) – see Note.
Note: *If the crankcases are being separated in order to remove the crankshaft or transmission shafts, the cylinder head can remain in situ. However, if removal of the connecting rod assemblies is intended, full disassembly of the top-end is necessary. The gearchange mechanism can remain in situ unless the selector drum and forks are being removed.*
3 Remove the sealing plug from the right-hand side of the upper crankcase – it is a push-fit **(see illustration)**. Discard the O-ring as a new one must be used.
4 Unscrew the six 8 mm upper crankcase bolts **(see illustration)**. Unscrew the bolts evenly, a little at a time and in a criss-cross sequence until they are finger-tight, then remove them. Note the sealing washers fitted

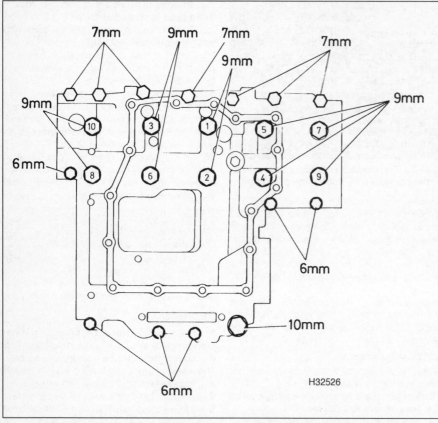

24.6 Lower crankcase 6 mm bolts, 7 mm bolts, 10 mm bolt, and 9 mm bolts

to four of the bolts. **Note:** *As each bolt is removed, store it in its relative position in a cardboard template of the crankcase halves. This will ensure all bolts are installed in the correct location on reassembly.*

5 Turn the engine upside down.

6 Unscrew the six 6 mm, the seven 7 mm and one 10 mm lower crankcase bolts **(see illustration)**. Now unscrew the ten 9 mm main bearing bolts evenly, a little at a time and in a criss-cross sequence in a **REVERSE** of the tightening sequence shown (i.e. starting from the outside and working to the centre) until they are finger-tight, then remove them. **Note:** *As each bolt is removed, store it in its relative position in a cardboard template of the crankcase halves. This will ensure all bolts are installed in the correct location on reassembly.*

7 Carefully lift the lower crankcase half off the upper half, using a soft-faced hammer to tap around the joint to initially separate the halves if necessary **(see illustration)**. **Note:** *If the halves do not separate easily, make sure all fasteners have been removed. Do not try and separate the halves by levering against the crankcase mating surfaces as they are easily scored and will leak oil in the future if damaged.* The lower crankcase half will come away with the gearchange mechanism (if not already removed) and the selector drum and forks, leaving the crankshaft and transmission shafts in the upper crankcase half.

8 Remove the three locating dowels from the crankcase if they are loose (they could be in either crankcase half), and the two oil orifices, noting how they fit **(see illustration)**.

9 Refer to Sections 23 to 31 for the removal and installation of the components housed within the crankcases.

Reassembly

10 Remove all traces of sealant from the crankcase mating surfaces.

11 Ensure that all components and their bearings are in place in the upper and lower crankcase halves. If the transmission shafts have not been removed, check the condition of the output shaft oil seal on the left-hand end of the shaft and the clutch pushrod oil seal on the left-hand end of the input shaft and replace them if they are damaged or deteriorated – it is good practice to renew these seals as a matter of course when the crankcases are separated **(see illustration)**.

12 Generously lubricate the crankshaft and transmission shafts, particularly around the bearings, with clean engine oil, then use a rag soaked in high flash-point solvent to wipe over the mating surfaces of both crankcase halves to remove all traces of oil.

13 If removed, install the three locating dowels and the two oil orifices in the upper crankcase half **(see illustration 24.8)**. Make sure the orifices are installed the correct way round **(see illustration)**.

14 Apply a small amount of suitable sealant

24.7 Carefully separate the crankcase halves

24.8 Remove the dowels (A) if they are loose, and the oil orifices (B)

24.11 Check the output shaft seal (A) and the pushrod seal (B)

24.13 Install the oil orifices as shown

to the outer mating surface of the lower crankcase half as shown **(see illustration)**. *Caution: Do not apply an excessive amount of sealant as it will ooze out when the case halves are assembled and may obstruct oil passages. Do not apply the sealant on or too close to any of the bearing inserts or surfaces.*

15 Check again that all components are in position, particularly that the bearing shells are still correctly located in the lower crankcase half. Carefully fit the lower crankcase half down onto the upper crankcase half, making sure the dowels all locate correctly into the lower crankcase half **(see illustration 24.7)**. If the selector drum and forks are installed, make sure each selector fork locates correctly in the groove in its pinion.

16 Check that the lower crankcase half is correctly seated. **Note:** *The crankcase halves should fit together without being forced. If the casings are not correctly seated, remove the lower crankcase half and investigate the problem. Do not attempt to pull them together using the crankcase bolts as the casing will crack and be ruined.*

17 Clean the threads of the ten 9 mm (main bearing) lower crankcase bolts. Apply some oil to the threads and the underside of the heads of the bolts and insert them in their original locations **(see illustration 24.6)**. Secure all bolts finger-tight at first, then tighten them evenly and a little at a time in the correct tightening sequence shown to the torque setting specified at the beginning of the Chapter.

18 Clean the threads of the six 6 mm, seven 7 mm and one 10 mm lower crankcase bolts and insert them in their original locations **(see illustration 24.6)**. Secure all bolts finger-tight at first, then tighten them evenly and a little at a time in a criss-cross sequence, starting with the 10 mm bolt, to the torque settings specified at the beginning of the Chapter.

19 Turn the engine over. Clean the threads of the six 8 mm upper crankcase bolts and insert them in their original locations not forgetting the sealing washers fitted to the four bolts that locate in the holes marked by a triangle **(see illustration 24.4)**. Use new washers if the old ones are damaged or deformed. Secure all bolts finger-tight at first, then tighten them evenly a little at a time in a criss-cross sequence to the torque settings specified at the beginning of the Chapter.

20 With all crankcase fasteners tightened, check that the crankshaft and transmission shafts rotate smoothly and easily. Check that the transmission shafts rotate freely and independently in neutral, then, if it is installed, rotate the selector drum by hand and select each gear in turn whilst rotating the input shaft (you will have to temporarily fit the gearchange lever onto the shaft to do this). Check that all gears can be selected and that the shafts rotate freely in every gear. If there are any signs of undue stiffness, tight or rough spots, or of any other problem, the fault must be rectified before proceeding further.

21 Fit a new O-ring onto the sealing plug and fit it into the right-hand side of the upper crankcase – it is a push-fit **(see illustration 24.3)**.

22 Install all other removed assemblies in a reverse of the sequence given in Step 2.

25 Crankcase halves and cylinder bores – inspection and servicing

Crankcase halves

1 After the crankcases have been separated, remove the crankshaft, connecting rods and pistons, transmission shafts, selector drum and forks (if not already done), rear balancer shaft, neutral switch, oil pressure switch, speed sensor and knock sensor (where fitted), referring to the relevant Sections of this Chapter, to Chapter 9 for the oil pressure and neutral switches, and to Chapter 4 for the speed and knock sensors. If there are any other components or assemblies that have not been removed as part of your strip-down procedure, for example the cam chain tensioner (if the locking tool was used when removing the camshaft), the starter motor, the water pump or the coolant union, remove these as well, referring to the relevant Chapter.

2 Clean the crankcases thoroughly with new solvent and dry them with compressed air. Blow out all oil passages with compressed air.

3 Remove all traces of old gasket sealant from the mating surfaces. Clean up minor damage to the surfaces with a fine sharpening stone or grindstone.

Caution: Be very careful not to nick or gouge the crankcase mating surfaces or oil leaks will result. Check both crankcase halves very carefully for cracks and other damage.

4 Small cracks or holes in aluminium castings can be repaired with an epoxy resin adhesive as a temporary measure. Permanent repairs can only be done by argon-arc welding, and only a specialist in this process is in a position to advise on the economy or practical aspect of such a repair. If any damage is found that can't be repaired, replace the crankcase halves as a set.

5 Damaged threads can be economically reclaimed using a diamond section wire insert, for example of the Heli-Coil type (though there are other makes), which is easily fitted after drilling and re-tapping the affected thread.

6 Sheared studs or screws can usually be removed with extractors, which consist of a tapered, left-hand thread screw of very hard steel. These are inserted into a pre-drilled hole in the stud, and usually succeed in dislodging the most stubborn stud or screw. If a stud has sheared above its bore line, it can be removed using a conventional stud extractor which avoids the need for drilling.

 Refer to Tools and Workshop Tips for details of installing a thread insert and using screw extractors.

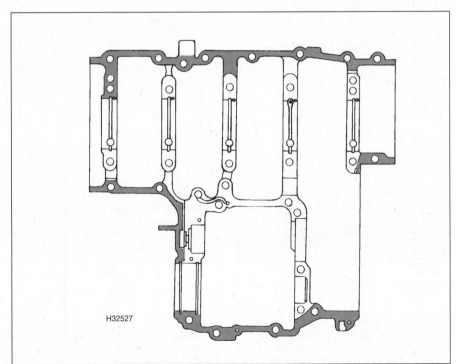

H32527

24.14 Apply sealant to the shaded areas of the lower crankcase half

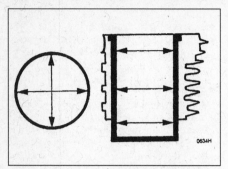

25.11 Measure each cylinder bore in the directions shown with a telescoping gauge, then measure the gauge with a micrometer

7 Install all components and assemblies, referring to the relevant Sections of this and the other Chapters, before reassembling the crankcase halves.

Cylinder bores

8 Do not attempt to separate the cylinder liners from the cylinder block.
9 Check the cylinder walls carefully for scratches and score marks.
10 Using a precision straight-edge and a feeler gauge set to the warpage limit listed in the specifications at the beginning of the Chapter, check the block gasket mating surface for warpage. Refer to *Tools and Workshop Tips* in the Reference section for details of how to use the straight-edge. If warpage is excessive the crankcases must be replaced with new ones.
11 Using telescoping gauges and a micrometer (see *Tools and Workshop Tips*), check the dimensions of each cylinder to assess the amount of wear, taper and ovality. Measure near the top (but below the level of the top piston ring at TDC), centre and bottom (but above the level of the oil ring at BDC) of the bore, both parallel to and across the crankshaft axis (see illustration). Compare the results to the specifications at the beginning of the Chapter. If the cylinders are worn, oval or tapered beyond the service limit they can be rebored, an oversize (+ 0.50) set of pistons and rings and available. Note that the piston-to-bore clearance for the oversize piston is slightly greater than that for the standard piston (see Specifications) – the person carrying out the rebore must be aware of this.
12 If the precision measuring tools are not available, take the crankcases to a Honda dealer or specialist motorcycle repair shop for assessment and advice.
13 If the cylinder bores are in good condition and the piston-to-bore clearance is within specifications (see Section 28), the cylinders should be honed (de-glazed). To perform this operation you will need the proper size flexible hone with fine stones, or a bottle-brush type hone, plenty of light oil or honing oil, some clean rags and an electric drill motor.
14 Hold the block sideways (so that the bores are horizontal rather than vertical) in a vice with

soft jaws or cushioned with wooden blocks. Mount the hone in the drill motor, compress the stones and insert the hone into the cylinder. Thoroughly lubricate the cylinder, then turn on the drill and move the hone up and down in the cylinder at a pace which produces a fine cross-hatch pattern on the cylinder wall with the lines intersecting at an angle of approximately 60°. Be sure to use plenty of lubricant and do not take off any more material than is necessary to produce the desired effect. Do not withdraw the hone from the cylinder while it is still turning. Switch off the drill and continue to move it up and down in the cylinder until it has stopped turning, then compress the stones and withdraw the hone. Wipe the oil from the cylinder and repeat the procedure on the other cylinders. Remember, do not take too much material from the cylinder wall.
15 Wash the bores thoroughly with warm soapy water to remove all traces of the abrasive grit produced during the honing operation. Be sure to run a brush through the stud holes and flush them with running water. After rinsing, dry the cylinders thoroughly and apply a thin coat of light, rust-preventative oil to all machined surfaces.
16 If you do not have the equipment or desire to perform the honing operation, take the crankcase to a Honda dealer or specialist motorcycle repair shop.

26 Main and connecting rod bearings – general information

1 Even though main and connecting rod bearings are generally replaced with new ones during the engine overhaul, the old bearings should be retained for close examination as they may reveal valuable information about the condition of the engine.
2 Bearing failure can occur for many reasons: a of lack of lubrication, the presence of dirt or other foreign particles, overloading the engine, and corrosion. Regardless of the cause of bearing failure, it must be corrected before the engine is reassembled to prevent it from happening again.
3 When examining the main or connecting rod bearings, remove them from their journal and lay them out on a clean surface in the same general position as their location in the crankcase or on the crankshaft. This will enable you to match any noted bearing problems with the corresponding journal.
4 Dirt and other foreign particles get into the engine in a variety of ways. It may be left in the engine during assembly or it may pass through filters or breathers. It may get into the oil and from there into the bearings. Metal chips from machining operations and normal engine wear are often present. Abrasives are sometimes left in engine components after reconditioning operations, especially when parts are not thoroughly cleaned using the proper methods. Whatever the source, these foreign objects often end up imbedded in the

soft bearing material and are easily recognised. Large particles will not imbed in the bearing and will score or gouge the bearing and journal. The best prevention for this is to clean all parts thoroughly and keep everything spotlessly clean during engine reassembly. Frequent and regular oil and filter changes are also recommended.
5 Lack of lubrication or lubrication breakdown has a number of interrelated causes. Excessive heat (which thins the oil), overloading (which squeezes the oil from the bearing face) and oil leakage or throw off (from excessive bearing clearances, worn oil pump or high engine speeds) all contribute to lubrication breakdown. Blocked oil passages will also starve a bearing and destroy it. When lack of lubrication is the cause of bearing failure, the bearing material is wiped or extruded from the steel backing of the bearing. Temperatures may increase to the point where the steel backing and the journal turn blue from overheating.

 HAYNES HiNT *Refer to Tools and Workshop Tips for bearing fault finding.*

6 Riding habits can have a definite effect on bearing life. Full throttle low speed operation, or labouring the engine, puts very high loads on bearings, which tend to squeeze out the oil film. These loads cause the bearings to flex, which produces fine cracks in the bearing face (fatigue failure). Eventually the bearing material will loosen in pieces and tear away from the steel backing. Short trip riding leads to corrosion of bearings, as insufficient engine heat is produced to drive off the condensed water and corrosive gases produced. These products collect in the engine oil, forming acid and sludge. As the oil is carried to the engine bearings, the acid attacks and corrodes the bearing material.
7 Incorrect bearing installation during engine assembly will lead to bearing failure as well. Tight fitting bearings which leave insufficient bearing oil clearances result in oil starvation. Dirt or foreign particles trapped behind a bearing insert result in high spots on the bearing which lead to failure.
8 To avoid bearing problems, clean all parts thoroughly before reassembly, double check all bearing clearance measurements and lubricate the new bearings with clean engine oil during installation.

27 Connecting rods and bearings – removal, inspection and installation

Note: *To remove the connecting rods the engine must be removed from the frame and the crankcases separated.*

Removal

1 Remove the engine from the frame (see Section 5) and separate the crankcase halves (see Section 24).

27.2 Measure the connecting rod side clearance using a feeler gauge

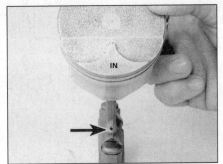

27.3 Note the various markings as described, and the oil hole (arrowed)

27.5 Withdraw the piston and connecting rod assembly from the top of the cylinder

2 Before removing the rods from the crankshaft, measure the side clearance with a feeler gauge as shown (see illustration). If the clearance is greater than the service limit listed in this Chapter's Specifications, replace the rods with new ones. If the clearance is still excessive, replace the crankshaft with a new one.

3 Using paint or a felt marker pen, mark the relevant cylinder identity on each connecting rod and cap. Mark across the cap-to-connecting rod join and note which side of the rod faces the front of the engine to ensure that the cap and rod are fitted the correct way around on reassembly. Note that the number already across the rod and cap indicates rod size grade (see illustration 27.21b). The piston crown is marked IN and this mark faces the intake side of the cylinder, and the oil hole in the big-end of the connecting rod should face the same way, to the back of the engine (intake side) (see illustration).

4 Remove the crankshaft (see Section 30).

5 Raise the crankcase onto wooden blocks to provide room for the connecting rod/piston assemblies to be removed from the top of the bore. Alternatively turn the crankcase on its side, but remove the transmission shafts first otherwise they will fall out (see Section 31). Push each piston/connecting rod assembly up and remove it from the top of the bore making sure the connecting rod does not mark the cylinder walls (see illustration). Keep the rod, cap, bolts, and (if they are to be

reused) the bearing shells together in their correct positions to ensure correct installation.

> **HAYNES HiNT** *To ease removal of the pistons, carefully remove any ridge of carbon built up on the top of each cylinder bore using a scraper. If there is a pronounced wear ridge, remove it using a ridge reamer.*

Caution: Do not try to remove the piston/connecting rod from the bottom of the cylinder bore. The piston will not pass the crankcase main bearing webs. If the piston is pulled right to the bottom of the bore the oil control ring will expand and lock the piston in position. If this happens it is likely the ring will be broken.

6 Immediately install the relevant bearing shells (if removed), bearing cap, and bolts on each piston/connecting rod assembly so that they are all kept together as a matched set.

7 Remove the pistons from the connecting rods if required (see Section 28).

Inspection

8 Check the connecting rods for cracks and other obvious damage.

9 Apply clean engine oil to the piston pin, insert it into the connecting rod small-end and check for any freeplay between the two (see

illustration). Measure the pin external diameter and the small-end bore diameter, then calculate the difference to obtain the small-end-to-piston pin clearance (see illustrations). Compare the result to the specifications at the beginning of the Chapter. If the clearance is greater than specified, renew the components that are worn beyond their specified limits.

10 Refer to Section 26 and examine the connecting rod bearing shells. If they are scored, badly scuffed, corroded, or appear to have seized, new shells must be installed. Always replace the shells in the connecting rods as a set. If they are badly damaged, check the corresponding crankpin. Evidence of extreme heat, such as discoloration, indicates that lubrication failure has occurred. Be sure to thoroughly check the oil pump and pressure regulator as well as all oil holes and passages before reassembling the engine.

11 Have the rods checked for twist and bend by a Honda dealer if you are in doubt about their straightness.

Oil clearance check

12 Whether new bearing shells are being fitted or the original ones are being re-used, the connecting rod bearing oil clearance should be checked prior to reassembly. Check the clearance on one rod at a time.

13 Clean the backs of the bearing shells and the bearing housings in both the connecting rod and cap.

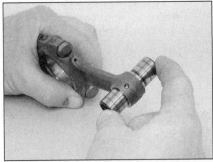

27.9a Slip the piston pin into the rod's small-end and rock it back and forth to check for looseness

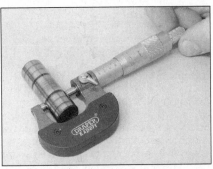

27.9b Measure the external diameter of the pin . . .

27.9c . . . and the internal diameter of the connecting rod small-end

27.14a Fit each shell into its housing . . .

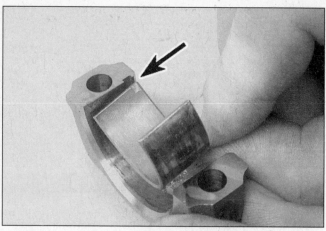

27.14b . . . making sure each tab locates in its notch (arrow)

14 Press the bearing shells into their housings, making sure the tab on each shell engages the notch in the connecting rod/cap and the oil holes align **(see illustrations)**. Make sure the bearings are fitted in the correct location and take care not to touch any shell's bearing surface with your fingers. Lay the crankshaft in the upper crankcase half, making sure it is the correct way round and that all the main bearing shells are installed (see Section 30).

15 Cut a length of the appropriate size Plastigauge (it should be slightly shorter than the width of the crankpin). Place a strand of Plastigauge on the (cleaned) crankpin journal, making sure it is not over the oil hole. Pull the connecting rod onto the crankpin and fit the cap onto the rod **(see illustrations 30.27 and 30.2b)**. Make sure the cap is fitted the correct way around so the previously made markings align, and that the rod is facing the right way (see Step 3). Apply some clean oil to the threads and under the heads of the connecting rod nuts. Install the nuts and tighten them evenly and alternately, in two or three stages, to the torque setting specified at the beginning of the Chapter, all the time ensuring that the connecting rod does not rotate on the crankshaft **(see illustrations 30.2b and 30.28)**. It is highly advisable to have an assistant to hold the crankshaft down in the crankcase while tightening the nuts as it could jump out.

16 Slacken the nuts and remove the connecting rod cap, again taking great care not to rotate the rod or crankshaft. Compare the width of the crushed Plastigauge on the crankpin to the scale printed on the Plastigauge envelope to obtain the connecting rod bearing oil clearance. Compare the reading to the specifications at the beginning of the Chapter.

17 On completion carefully scrape away all traces of the Plastigauge material from the crankpin and bearing shells using a fingernail or other object which is unlikely to score the shells.

18 If the clearance is within the range listed in this Chapter's Specifications and the bearings are in perfect condition, they can be reused. If the clearance is beyond the service limit, replace the bearing shells with new ones (see Steps 21 and 22). Check the oil clearance once again (the new shells may be thick enough to bring bearing clearance within the specified range). Always replace all of the shells at the same time.

19 If the clearance is still greater than the service limit listed in this Chapter's Specifications, the crankpin is worn and the crankshaft should be replaced with a new one.

20 Repeat the oil clearance check for the other connecting rods.

Bearing shell selection

21 Replacement bearing shells for the big-end bearings are supplied on a selected fit basis. Code letters and numbers stamped on the connecting rod and crankshaft are used to identify the correct replacement bearings. The crankpin journal size letters are stamped on the outside of the left-hand crankshaft web, and will be either an A or a B **(see illustration)**. The first letter, after the L, is for the No. 1 cylinder connecting rod (left-hand journal), and the letters correspond consecutively for each cylinder. The connecting rod size code number is marked across the flat face of the connecting rod and cap and will be either a 1 or a 2 **(see illustration)**.

22 A range of bearing shells is available. To select the correct bearing shell colour code for a particular big-end, use the table below and cross-refer the crankpin journal size letter (stamped on the web) with the connecting rod size number (stamped on the rod). For example, if the crankpin size is B, and the connecting rod size is 1, then the bearing required is green. The colour is marked on the side of the shell.

Installation

23 Fit the pistons onto the connecting rods (see Section 28).

24 Clean the backs of the bearing shells and the bearing housings in both cap and rod. If new shells are being fitted, ensure that all

Crankpin journal code	Connecting rod code	
	1 – (43.000 to 43.008 mm)	2 – (43.008 to 43.016 mm)
A – (39.995 to 40.003 mm)	C – Yellow	B – Green
B – (39.987 to 39.995 mm)	B – Green	A – Brown

27.21a Crankpin journal size letters (bottom row). Top row is for main bearings

27.21b Connecting rod size number

27.25a Carefully feed each ring into the bore

27.25b Clamp the rings in position by tightening the bands on the compressor . . .

27.25c . . . then push the piston into its bore

traces of the protective grease are cleaned off using paraffin (kerosene). Wipe the shells, cap and rod dry with a clean lint free cloth. Install the bearing shells in the connecting rods and caps, making sure the tab on each shell engages the notch in the connecting rod/cap and the oil holes align **(see illustration 27.14a and b)**. Lubricate the shells with molybdenum disulphide oil (a 50/50 mixture of molybdenum disulphide grease and clean engine oil).

25 Lubricate the pistons, rings and cylinder bore with clean engine oil. Insert the piston/connecting rod assembly into the top of its bore, taking care not to allow the connecting rod to mark the bore **(see illustration 27.5)**. Make sure the "IN" mark on the piston crown is on the intake side of the bore and the connecting rod is the right way round (see Step 3), then carefully compress and feed each piston ring into the bore until the piston crown is flush with the top of the bore **(see illustration)**. If available, a piston ring compressor makes installation a lot easier **(see illustrations)**.

26 Install the crankshaft (see Section 30).

27 Reassemble the crankcase halves (see Section 24).

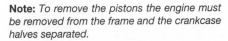

28 Pistons – removal, inspection and installation

Note: *To remove the pistons the engine must be removed from the frame and the crankcase halves separated.*

Removal

1 Remove the connecting rods (see Section 27).

2 Before removing the piston from the connecting rod, use a sharp scriber or felt marker pen to write the cylinder identity on the crown of each piston (or on the inside of the skirt if the piston is dirty and going to be cleaned). Each piston crown should already be marked IN and this mark faces the intake side of the cylinder (the same way as the oil hole in the big-end of the connecting rod), though these marks are likely to be invisible until the piston is cleaned.

3 Carefully prise out the circlip on one side of

the piston using needle-nose pliers or a small flat-bladed screwdriver inserted into the notch **(see illustration)**. Push the piston pin out from the other side to free the piston from the connecting rod **(see illustration)**. Remove the other circlip and discard them as new ones must be used. When the piston has been removed, install its pin back into its bore so that related parts do not get mixed up.

> **HAYNES HINT**
> *If a piston pin is a tight fit in the piston bosses, soak a rag in boiling water then wring it out and wrap it around the piston – this will expand the alloy piston sufficiently to release its grip on the pin. If the piston pin is particularly stubborn, extract it using a drawbolt tool, but be careful to protect the piston's working surfaces.*

Inspection

4 Using your thumbs or a piston ring removal and installation tool, carefully remove the rings from the pistons **(see illustrations 29.12, 11, and 9c, b and a)**. Do not nick or gouge the pistons in the process. Carefully note which way up each ring fits and in which groove as they must be installed in their original positions if being re-used. The upper surface of the top ring is marked with the letter R at one end, and the second (middle) ring is marked RN. The top and middle rings can also be identified by the fact that the top

ring is narrower in width than the second (middle) ring.

5 Scrape all traces of carbon from the tops of the pistons. A hand-held wire brush or a piece of fine emery cloth can be used once most of the deposits have been scraped away. Do not, under any circumstances, use a wire brush mounted in a drill motor to remove deposits from the pistons; the piston material is soft and will be eroded away by the wire brush.

6 Use a piston ring groove cleaning tool to remove any carbon deposits from the ring grooves. If a tool is not available, a piece broken off an old ring will do the job. Be very careful to remove only the carbon deposits. Do not remove any metal and do not nick or gouge the sides of the ring grooves.

7 Once the deposits have been removed, clean the pistons with solvent and dry them thoroughly. If the identification previously marked on the piston is cleaned off, be sure to re-mark it with the correct identity. Make sure the oil return holes below the oil ring groove are clear.

8 Carefully inspect each piston for cracks around the skirt, at the pin bosses and at the ring lands. Normal piston wear appears as even, vertical wear on the thrust surfaces of the piston and slight looseness of the top ring in its groove. If the skirt is scored or scuffed, the engine may have been suffering from overheating and/or abnormal combustion, which caused excessively high operating temperatures. The oil pump should be checked thoroughly. Also check that the circlip grooves are not damaged.

28.3a Prise out the circlip . . .

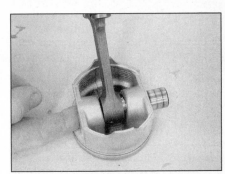

28.3b . . . then push out the pin and remove the piston

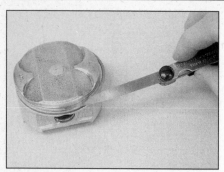

28.10 Measure the piston ring-to-groove clearance with a feeler gauge

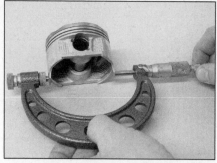

28.11 Measure the piston diameter with a micrometer at the specified distance from the bottom of the skirt

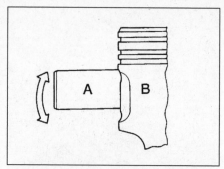

28.12a Slip the pin (A) into the piston (B) and try to rock it back and forth. If it's loose, replace the piston and pin

9 A hole in the piston crown, an extreme to be sure, is an indication that abnormal combustion (pre-ignition) was occurring. Burned areas at the edge of the piston crown are usually evidence of spark knock (detonation). If any of the above problems exist, the causes must be corrected or the damage will occur again.

10 Measure the piston ring-to-groove clearance by laying each piston ring in its groove and slipping a feeler gauge in beside it **(see illustration)**. Make sure you have the correct ring for the groove (see Step 5). Check the clearance at three or four locations around the groove. If the clearance is greater than specified, renew both the piston and rings as a set. If new rings are being used, measure the clearance using the new rings. If the clearance is greater than that specified, the piston is worn and must be replaced with a new one.

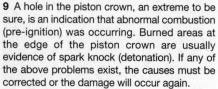

28.12b Measure the internal diameter of the bore in the piston

11 Check the piston-to-bore clearance by measuring the bore (see Section 25) and the piston diameter. Make sure each piston is matched to its correct cylinder. Measure the piston 15.0 mm up from the bottom of the skirt and at 90° to the piston pin axis **(see illustration)**. Subtract the piston diameter from the bore diameter to obtain the clearance. If it is greater than the specified figure, the piston must be replaced with a new one (assuming the bore itself is within limits).

12 Apply clean engine oil to the piston pin, insert it into the piston and check for any freeplay between the two **(see illustration)**. Measure the pin external diameter **(see illustration 27.9b)**, and the pin bore in the piston **(see illustration)**. Calculate the difference to obtain the piston pin-to-piston pin bore clearance. Compare the result to the specifications at the beginning of the Chapter. If the clearance is greater than specified, replace the components that are worn beyond their specified limits. If not already done (see Section 27), repeat the measurements between the pin and the connecting rod small-end **(see illustration 27.9c)**.

Installation

13 Inspect and install the piston rings (see Section 29).

14 Lubricate the piston pin, the piston pin bore and the connecting rod small-end bore with molybdenum disulphide oil (a 50/50 mixture of molybdenum disulphide grease and clean engine oil).

15 When installing the pistons onto the connecting rods, make sure the IN mark on

the piston crown faces the same way as the oil hole in the big-end of the connecting rod **(see illustration 27.3)**.

16 Install a **new** circlip in one side of the piston (do not re-use old circlips) **(see illustration)**. Line up the piston on its correct connecting rod, and insert the piston pin from the other side **(see illustration)**. Secure the pin with the other **new** circlip **(see illustration)**. When installing the circlips, compress them only just enough to fit them in the piston, and make sure they are properly seated in their grooves with the open end away from the removal notch.

17 Install the connecting rods (see Section 27) and reassemble the crankcase halves (see Section 24).

29 Piston rings – inspection and installation

1 It is good practice to renew the piston rings when an engine is being overhauled. Before installing the new rings, check the end gaps with the rings installed in the bore, as follows.

2 Lay out the pistons and the new ring sets so the rings will be matched with the same piston and bore during the end gap measurement procedure and engine assembly.

3 To measure the installed ring end gap, insert the top ring into the top of the bore and square it up with the bore walls by pushing it in with the top of the piston. The ring should be about 20 mm below the top edge of the

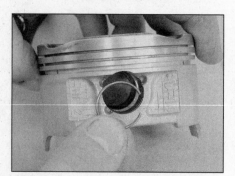

28.16a Fit a new circlip into one side ...

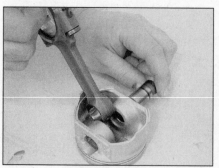

28.16b ... then fit the connecting rod and slide in the pin ...

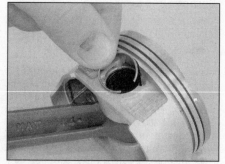

28.16c ... and fit the other new circlip

29.3 Measuring piston ring installed end gap

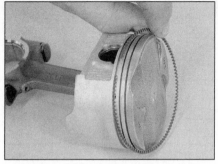

29.8a Install the oil ring expander in its groove . . .

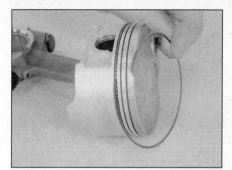

29.8b . . . then fit the lower side rail . . .

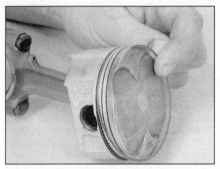

29.8c . . . and the upper side rail on each side of it.

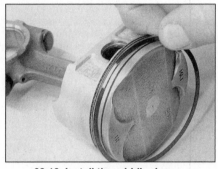

29.10 Install the middle ring . . .

29.11 . . . and the top ring as described

bore. Slip a feeler gauge between the ends of the ring and compare the measurement to the specifications at the beginning of the Chapter (see illustration).

4 If the gap is larger or smaller than specified, double check to make sure that you have the correct rings before proceeding.

5 Excess end gap is not critical unless it exceeds the service limit. Again, double-check to make sure you have the correct rings for your engine and check that the bore is not worn (see Section 25).

6 Repeat the procedure for each ring that will be installed in the bore. Remember to keep the rings, pistons and bores matched up.

7 Once the ring end gaps have been checked/corrected, the rings can be installed on the pistons (see illustration 29.12).

8 Install the oil control ring (lowest on the piston) first. It is composed of three separate components, namely the expander and the upper and lower side rails. Slip the expander into the groove, making sure the ends don't overlap, then install the lower side rail (see illustrations). Do not use a piston ring installation tool on the side rails as they may be damaged. Instead, place one end of the side rail into the groove between the expander and the ring land. Hold it firmly in place and slide a finger around the piston while pushing the rail into the groove. Next, install the upper side rail in the same manner (see illustration). Check that the ends of the expander have not overlapped.

9 After the three oil ring components have been installed, check to make sure that both the upper and lower side rails can be turned smoothly in the ring groove.

10 The upper surface of each compression ring is marked with the letter R at one end. The rings can also be identified by the fact that the top ring is narrower in width than the second (middle) ring and has a different profile. Install the second (middle) compression ring next. Make sure that the identification letter near the end gap is facing up. Fit the ring into the middle groove in the piston (see illustration). Do not expand the ring any more than is necessary to

slide it into place. To avoid breaking the ring, use a piston ring installation tool.

11 Finally, install the top ring in the same manner into the top groove in the piston (see illustration). Make sure the identification letter near the end gap is facing up.

12 Once the rings are correctly installed, check they move freely without snagging and stagger their end gaps as shown (see illustration).

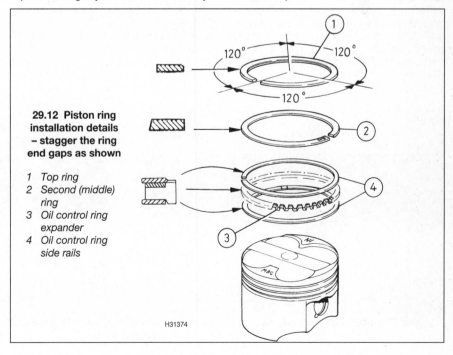

29.12 Piston ring installation details – stagger the ring end gaps as shown

1 Top ring
2 Second (middle) ring
3 Oil control ring expander
4 Oil control ring side rails

H31374

30.2a Unscrew the nuts . . .

30.2b . . . and remove the connecting rod caps

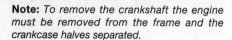

30 Crankshaft and main bearings – removal, inspection and installation

Note: *To remove the crankshaft the engine must be removed from the frame and the crankcase halves separated.*

Removal

1 Remove the engine from the frame (see Section 5) and separate the crankcase halves (see Section 24).

2 Using paint or a felt marker pen, mark the relevant cylinder identity on each connecting rod and cap. Mark across the cap-to-connecting rod join and note which side of the cap faces the front of the engine to ensure that they are fitted the correct way around onto the correct rod on reassembly. Note that the number already across the rod and cap indicates rod size grade **(see illustration 27.21b)**. Unscrew the connecting rod cap nuts and separate the caps from the crankpin **(see illustrations)**. **Note:** *If no work is to be carried out on the piston/connecting rod assemblies there is no need to remove them from the bores, but push them up to the top of the bores so that the bottom ends are clear of the crankshaft If you do remove them, refer to Section 27.*

3 Lift the crankshaft out of the upper crankcase half, taking care not to dislodge the main bearing shells **(see illustration)**.

4 The main bearing shells can be removed from the crankcase halves by pushing their centres to the side, then lifting them out, or by carefully levering them out using a small screwdriver **(see illustration)**. Keep the shells in order.

Inspection

5 Clean the crankshaft with solvent, squirting it under pressure through all the oil passages. If available, blow the crank dry with compressed air, and also blow through the oil passages. Check the primary drive gear and its sub-gear, and the balancer shaft drive gear for wear or damage. If any of the teeth are excessively worn, chipped or broken, the crankshaft must be replaced with a new one. If wear or damage is found, also inspect the primary driven gear on the back of the clutch housing and the balancer shafts (see Sections 16, 23 and 33).

6 Check the springs between the primary drive gear and its sub-gear. To separate the sub-gear from the main gear, remove the large circlip, the plain washer and the sprung washer, noting which way round they fit. Discard the circlip as a new one must be used. Lever out the springs, noting how they fit, and remove the sub-gear, noting how one

of its holes aligns with the hole in the main gear – mark this alignment as an aid to installation. When fitting the sub-gear back on, apply some molybdenum disulphide oil (a 50/50 mixture of molybdenum disulphide grease and clean engine oil) to the contact areas between the main gear, the sub gear, the sprung washer and the plain washer. Fit the sprung washer so that its convex side faces outwards (inner rim is raised off the sub-gear and facing out), and fit the new circlip with its large tab on the right as you look at it, and with the chamfered edge on the inside. Align the ends so that they are at a right-angle to the cutouts in the end of the crankshaft.

7 Refer to Section 26 and examine the main bearing shells. If they are scored, badly scuffed or appear to have been seized, new bearings must be installed. Always replace the main bearings as a set. If they are badly damaged, check the corresponding crankshaft journals. Evidence of extreme heat, such as discoloration, indicates that lubrication failure has occurred. Be sure to thoroughly check the oil pump and pressure regulator as well as all oil holes and passages before reassembling the engine.

8 Give the crankshaft journals a close visual examination, paying particular attention where damaged bearings have been discovered. If the journals are scored or pitted in any way a new crankshaft will be required. Note that undersizes are not available, precluding the option of re-grinding the crankshaft.

9 Place the crankshaft on V-blocks and check the runout at the main bearing journals using a dial gauge. Compare the reading to the maximum specified at the beginning of the Chapter. If the runout exceeds the limit, the crankshaft must be replaced.

Oil clearance check

10 Whether new bearing shells are being fitted or the original ones are being re-used, the main bearing oil clearance should be checked before the engine is reassembled. Main bearing oil clearance is measured with a product known as Plastigauge.

30.3 Lift the crankshaft out of the crankcase . . .

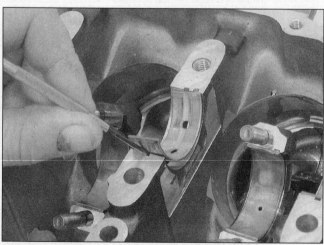

30.4 . . . and remove the shells if required

11 Clean the backs of the bearing shells and the bearing housings in both crankcase halves.
12 Press the bearing shells into their cutouts, ensuring that the tab on each shell engages in the notch in the crankcase **(see illustration 30.24)**. Make sure the bearings are fitted in the correct locations and take care not to touch any shell's bearing surface with your fingers.
13 Ensure the shells and crankshaft are clean and dry. Lay the crankshaft in position in the upper crankcase **(see illustration 30.3)**. Install the three crankcase dowels if removed **(see illustration 24.8)**.
14 Cut five lengths of the appropriate size Plastigauge (they should be slightly shorter than the width of the crankshaft journals). Place a strand of Plastigauge on each (cleaned) journal, avoiding the oil hole. Make sure the crankshaft is not rotated.
15 Carefully fit the lower crankcase half onto the upper half **(see illustration 24.7)**. Check that the lower half is correctly seated. **Note:** *Do not tighten the crankcase bolts if the casing is not correctly seated.* Clean the threads of the ten 9 mm (main bearing) lower crankcase bolts. Apply some oil to the threads and the underside of the heads of the bolts and insert them in their original locations. Secure all bolts finger-tight at first, then tighten them evenly and a little at a time in the correct tightening sequence shown to the torque setting specified at the beginning of the Chapter **(see illustration 24.6)**. Make sure that the crankshaft is not rotated as the bolts are tightened.
16 Slacken each bolt evenly a little at a time in a reverse of the tightening sequence until they are all finger-tight, then remove the bolts. Carefully lift off the lower crankcase half, making sure the Plastigauge is not disturbed.
17 Compare the width of the crushed Plastigauge on each crankshaft journal to the scale printed on the Plastigauge envelope to obtain the main bearing oil clearance. Compare the reading to the specifications at the beginning of the Chapter.
18 On completion carefully scrape away all traces of the Plastigauge material from the crankshaft journal and bearing shells; use a fingernail or other object which is unlikely to score them.

19 If the oil clearance falls into the specified range, no bearing shell replacement is required (provided they are in good condition). If the clearance is beyond the service limit, refer to the marks on the case and the marks on the crankshaft and select new bearing shells (see Steps 21 and 22). Install the new shells and check the oil clearance once again (the new shells may bring bearing clearance within the specified range). Always replace all of the shells at the same time.
20 If the clearance is still greater than the service limit listed in this Chapter's Specifications (even with replacement shells), the crankshaft journal is worn and the crankshaft should be replaced with a new one.

Main bearing shell selection

21 Code letters and numbers stamped on the crankshaft and crankcase are used to identify the correct replacement bearings. The crankshaft main bearing journal size numbers are stamped on the outside of the left-hand crankshaft web and will be either a 1, a 2 or a 3 **(see illustration 27.21a)**. The first letter, after the L, is for the left-hand journal, and the numbers correspond consecutively for each journal. The corresponding main bearing housing size letters are stamped into the left-hand side of the upper crankcase half and will be either an A, a B or a C **(see illustration)**. The left-hand letter corresponds to the left-hand journal, and run consecutively from left to right.
22 A range of bearing shells is available. To select the correct bearing for a particular journal, use the table below and cross-refer the main bearing journal size number (stamped on the crank web) with the main bearing housing size letter (stamped on the crankcase) to determine the colour code of the bearing required. For example, if the

30.21 Main bearing housing codes

journal code is 3, and the housing code is A, then the bearing required is Green. The colour is marked on the side of the shell.

Installation

23 Clean the backs of the bearing shells and the bearing cut-outs in both crankcase halves. If new shells are being fitted, ensure that all traces of the protective grease are cleaned off using paraffin (kerosene). Wipe the shells and crankcase halves dry with a lint-free cloth. Make sure all the oil passages and holes are clear, and blow them through with compressed air if it is available.
24 Press the bearing shells into their locations. Make sure the tab on each shell engages in the notch in the casing **(see illustration)**. Make sure the bearings are fitted in the correct locations and take care not to touch any shell's bearing surface with your fingers. Lubricate each shell with molybdenum disulphide oil (a 50/50 mixture of molybdenum disulphide grease and clean engine oil).
25 If the rear balancer shaft and its idle gear were removed, and you have installed the balancer gear/weight but not yet the idle gear,

Main bearing journal code	Main bearing housing code		
	A – (43.000 to 43.006 mm)	B – (43.006 to 43.012 mm)	C – (43.012 to 43.018 mm)
1 – (40.000 to 40.003 mm)	E – Pink	D – Yellow	C – Green
2 – (39.994 to 40.000 mm)	D – Yellow	C – Green	B – Brown
3 – (39.988 to 39.994 mm)	C – Green	B – Brown	A – Black

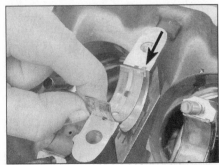

30.24 Fit the shells, locating the tabs in the notches (arrow)

30.25a Align the balancer gear tooth mark with the projection on the crankcase . . .

30.25b . . . and the marks on the primary drive sub-gear with the crankcase mating surface

30.27 Pull the connecting rod onto the crankpin and fit the cap

30.28 Tighten the cap nuts as described to the specified torque

31.1 Remove the pushrod oil seal, noting how it locates

position the balancer gear/weight so that the index line on one of its teeth aligns with the rear edge of the projection in the gear/weight housing, visible via the inspection aperture (see illustration). Lower the crankshaft into position in the upper crankcase (see illustration 30.3), making sure all bearings remain in place, and that it is positioned with the index lines on the outside of the primary drive sub-gear parallel with the crankcase mating surface (see illustration). Now install the balancer idle gear (see Section 33).

26 If the rear balancer shaft and its idle gear were not removed, unscrew the balancer timing inspection cap from the upper crankcase half (see illustration 33.5). Position the balancer gear/weight so that the index line on one of its teeth aligns with the rear edge of the projection in the gear/weight housing, visible via the inspection aperture (see illustration 30.25a). Lower the crankshaft into position in the upper crankcase, making sure all bearings remain in place, and that it is positioned with the index lines on the outside of the primary drive sub-gear parallel with the crankcase mating surface (see illustration 30.25b). Make sure that as you engage the balancer drive gear on the crankshaft with the idle gear, and seat the crankshaft in its bearings, the alignment marks between the balancer gear/weight and the projection in the housing, and between the primary drive sub-gear and the crankcase

remain in alignment as described. If the idle gear turns as you fit the crankshaft the marks will misalign and you will have to remove and reinstall the crankshaft.

27 Lubricate the crankpin with molybdenum disulphide oil (a 50/50 mixture of molybdenum disulphide grease and clean engine oil). Pull the connecting rod onto the crankpin and fit the cap onto the rod (see illustration and 30.2b). Make sure the cap is fitted the correct way around so the previously made markings align, and that the rod is facing the right way (see Step 2 and Section 27).

28 Apply some clean oil to the threads and under the heads of the connecting rod nuts. Install the nuts (see illustration 30.2a) and tighten them evenly and alternately, in two or three stages, to the torque setting specified at the beginning of the Chapter (see illustration). It is highly advisable to have an assistant to hold the crankshaft down in the crankcase while tightening the bolts as it could jump out.

29 Check that the crankshaft is free to rotate easily, then install the other connecting rods in the same way. Check to make sure that all components have been returned to their original locations using the marks made on disassembly. Re-check the rear balancer timing marks.

30 Check that the rods rotate smoothly and freely on the crankpin. If there are any signs of roughness or tightness, remove the rods and

re-check the bearing clearance. Sometimes tapping the bottom of the connecting rod cap will relieve tightness, but if in doubt, recheck the clearances.

31 Reassemble the crankcase halves (see Section 24).

31 Transmission shafts and bearings – removal and installation

Note: To remove the transmission shafts the engine must be removed from the frame and the crankcases separated.

Removal

1 Remove the engine from the frame (see Section 5) and separate the crankcase halves (see Section 24). Remove the clutch pushrod oil seal (see illustration).

2 Unscrew the two bolts securing the transmission input shaft bearing retainer plate to the right-hand side of the crankcase and remove the plate (see illustration).

3 Lift the output shaft and input shaft out of the casing, noting their relative positions and how they fit together (see illustrations). If they are stuck, use a soft-faced hammer and gently tap on the ends of the shafts to free them. Remove the needle bearing dowels – if they are not in their holes in the crankcase, remove them from the bearings themselves

31.2 Unscrew the bolts (arrowed) and remove the plate

31.3a Remove the output shaft . . .

31.3b . . . and the input shaft

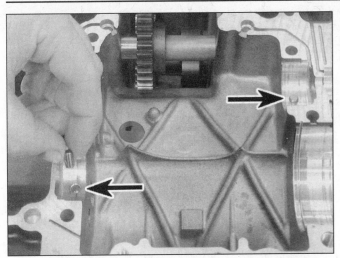

31.3c Remove the bearing dowels from their holes (arrows)

31.6 Lubricate the end of the shaft and fit the oil seal

on the shafts **(see illustration)**. If necessary, the input shaft and output shaft can be disassembled and inspected for wear or damage (see Section 32).

4 Referring to *Tools and Workshop Tips* (Section 5) in the Reference Section, check the bearings on the transmission shafts. Replace the bearings if necessary, noting that the output shaft left-hand bearing is not available separately from the shaft. Also check the condition of the output shaft oil seal and clutch pushrod oil seal and renew them if worn or damaged.

Installation

5 Fit the needle bearing dowels into their holes in the crankcase **(see illustration 31.3c)**.

6 Lubricate the left-hand end of the output shaft with clean oil and slide the new oil seal on so that its stamped markings face outwards **(see illustration)**. Smear the seal lips with oil.

7 Lower the input shaft into position in the upper crankcase, making sure the hole in the needle bearing outer race engages correctly with the dowel **(see illustration 31.3b)**.

8 Lower the output shaft into position in the upper crankcase **(see illustration 31.3a)**, making sure the ring retainer on the ball bearing engages correctly with the groove in the bearing housing, the locating pin sits in the cutout in the crankcase, and the hole in the needle bearing outer race engages correctly with the dowel **(see illustration)**. Also ensure that the oil seal lip locates in the crankcase groove.

Caution: If the ring retainer or dowel do not locate correctly, the crankcase halves will not seat properly.

9 Make sure both transmission shafts are correctly seated and their related pinions are correctly engaged **(see illustration)**. Fit a new clutch pushrod oil seal into its seat so that the seal's stamped markings face outwards **(see illustration 31.1)**.

10 Fit the input shaft bearing retainer plate onto the right-hand side of the crankcase, then apply a non-permanent thread locking compound to its bolts and tighten them securely **(see illustration 31.2)**.

11 Position the gears in the neutral position and check the shafts are free to rotate easily and independently (i.e. the input shaft can turn whilst the output shaft is held stationary) before proceeding further.

12 Reassemble the crankcase halves (see Section 24).

32 Transmission shafts – disassembly, inspection and reassembly

1 Remove the transmission shafts from the crankcase (see Section 31). Always disassemble the transmission shafts

31.8 Make sure the ring retainer (A) and the bearing pin (B) locate correctly as shown

31.9 Make sure the shafts are correctly installed and engaged as shown

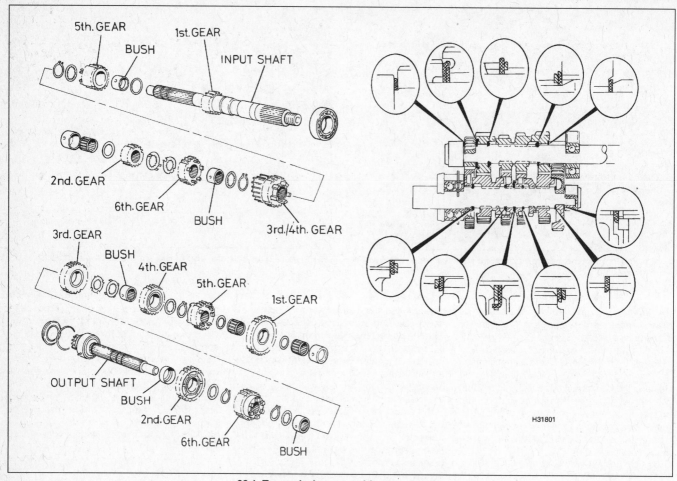

32.1 Transmission assembly components

separately to avoid mixing up the components **(see illustration)**.

Input shaft disassembly

When disassembling the transmission shafts, place the parts on a long rod or thread a wire through them to keep them in order and facing the proper direction.

2 Slide the needle bearing outer race and bearing off the left-hand end of the shaft, followed by the thrust washer and the 2nd gear pinion **(see illustrations 32.20d, c, b and a)**.
3 Slide the tabbed lockwasher off the shaft, then turn the slotted splined washer to offset the splines and slide it off the shaft, noting how they fit together **(see illustrations 32.19c and a)**. Slide the sixth gear pinion and its bush off the shaft, followed by the splined washer **(see illustrations 32.18c, b and a)**.
4 Remove the circlip securing the combined 3rd/4th gear pinion, then slide the pinion off the shaft **(see illustrations 32.17b and a)**.

5 Remove the circlip securing the 5th gear pinion, then slide the splined washer, the pinion and its bush, and the thrust washer off the shaft **(see illustrations 32.16e, d, c, b and a)**. The 1st gear pinion is integral with the shaft **(see illustration 32.15)**.
6 If required, remove the caged ball bearing from the right-hand end of the shaft, referring to *Tools and Workshop Tips* (Section 5) in the Reference Section **(see illustration 32.15)**.

Input shaft inspection

7 Wash all of the components in clean solvent and dry them off.
8 Check the gear teeth for cracking, chipping, pitting and other obvious wear or damage. Any pinion that is damaged as such must be replaced.
9 Inspect the dogs and the dog holes in the gears for cracks, chips, and excessive wear especially in the form of rounded edges. Make sure mating gears engage properly. Replace the paired gears as a set if necessary.
10 Check for signs of scoring or bluing on the pinions, bushes and shaft. This could be caused by overheating due to inadequate lubrication. Check that all the oil holes and

passages are clear. Replace any damaged pinions or bushes.
11 Check that each pinion moves freely on the shaft or bush but without undue freeplay. Check that each bush moves freely on the shaft but without undue freeplay. If the necessary equipment is available the individual components can be measured and the results compared with the specifications at the beginning of this Chapter.
12 The shaft is unlikely to sustain damage unless the engine has seized, placing an unusually high loading on the transmission, or the machine has covered a very high mileage. Check the surface of the shaft, especially where a pinion turns on it, and replace the shaft if it has scored or picked up, or if there are any cracks. Damage of any kind can only be cured by replacement.
13 Check the washers and circlips and replace any that are bent or appear weakened or worn. Use new ones if in any doubt. Note that it is good practice to renew all circlips when overhauling gearshafts.

Input shaft reassembly

14 During reassembly, apply molybdenum disulphide oil (a 50/50 mixture of molybdenum

32.15 Fit the bearing onto the shaft as shown

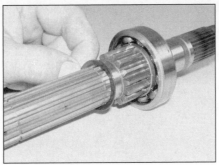

32.16a Slide the thrust washer . . .

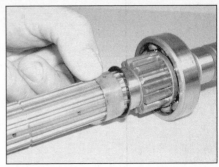

32.16b . . . the 5th gear pinion bush . . .

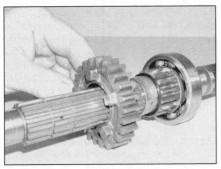

32.16c . . . the 5th gear pinion . . .

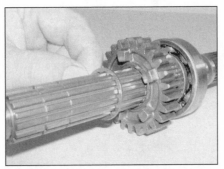

32.16d . . . and the splined washer onto the shaft . . .

32.16e . . . and secure them with the circlip, making sure it locates properly in its groove

disulphide grease and clean engine oil) to the mating surfaces of the shaft, pinions and bushes. When installing the circlips, do not expand their ends any further than is necessary. Install the stamped circlips and washers so that their chamfered side faces the pinion it secures (see illustration 32.1).
15 If removed, fit the caged ball bearing onto the right-hand end of the shaft, referring to

Tools and Workshop Tips (Section 5) in the Reference Section (see illustration).
16 Slide the thrust washer onto the left-hand end of the shaft, followed by the 5th gear pinion bush, aligning the oil hole in the bush with the hole in the shaft (see illustrations). Fit the 5th gear pinion with its dogs facing away from the integral 1st gear (see illustration). Slide the splined washer onto the shaft, then fit the circlip, making sure that

it locates correctly in the groove in the shaft (see illustrations).
17 Slide the combined 3rd/4th gear pinion onto the shaft with the larger 4th gear pinion facing the 5th gear pinion (see illustration). Fit the circlip, making sure it is locates correctly in its groove in the shaft (see illustration).
18 Slide the splined washer onto the shaft, followed by the 6th gear pinion bush, aligning

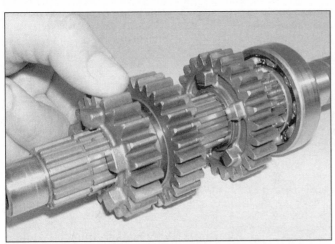

32.17a Slide the combined 3rd/4th gear pinion onto the shaft . . .

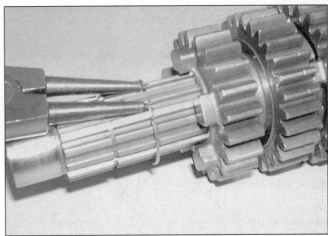

32.17b . . . and secure it with the circlip

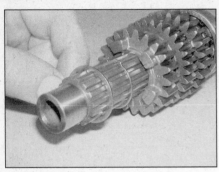

32.18a Slide the splined washer . . .

32.18b . . . the 6th gear pinion bush . . .

32.18c . . . and the 6th gear pinion onto the shaft

32.19a Slide on the slotted splined washer . . .

32.19b . . . and locate it as shown . . .

the oil hole in the bush with the hole in the shaft, and the 6th gear pinion, making sure its dogs face the 3rd/4th gear pinion **(see illustrations)**.
19 Slide the slotted splined washer onto the shaft and locate it in its groove, then turn it in the groove so that the splines on the washer align with the splines on the shaft and secure the washer in the groove **(see illustrations)**. Slide the tabbed lockwasher onto the shaft, so that the tabs locate into the slots in the outer rim of the splined washer **(see illustrations)**.
20 Slide the 2nd gear pinion and the thrust washer onto the end of the shaft, then fit the needle roller bearing and its outer race over the end of the shaft **(see illustrations)**.

32.19c . . . then slide on the tabbed lockwasher . . .

32.19d . . . and locate it as shown

32.20a Slide the 2nd gear pinion . . .

32.20b . . . the thrust washer . . .

32.20c . . . the needle bearing . . .

32.20d . . . and the bearing outer race onto the shaft

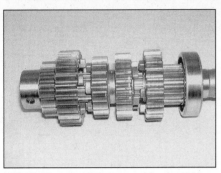

32.21 The complete assembly should be as shown

32.31a Slide the 2nd gear pinion bush . . .

32.31b . . . the 2nd gear pinion . . .

32.31c . . . and the splined washer onto the shaft . . .

32.31d . . . and secure them with the circlip . . .

32.31e . . . making sure it locates in the groove

21 Check that all components have been correctly installed (see illustration).

Output shaft disassembly

22 Slide the needle bearing outer race and bearing off the right-hand end of the shaft (see illustration 32.37d).
23 Slide the thrust washer off the shaft, followed by the 1st gear pinion and its needle roller bearing, the thrust washer and the 5th gear pinion (see illustrations 32.37c, b and a, and 32.36b and a).
24 Remove the circlip securing the 4th gear pinion, then slide the splined washer, the pinion and its splined bush off the shaft (see illustrations 32.35d, c, b and a).
25 Slide the tabbed lockwasher off the shaft, then turn the slotted splined washer to offset the splines and slide it off the shaft, noting how they fit together (see illustrations 32.34c, b and a).
26 Slide the 3rd gear pinion and its splined bush, followed by the splined washer, off the shaft (see illustrations 32.33c, b and a).
27 Remove the circlip securing the 6th gear pinion, then slide the pinion off the shaft (see illustrations 32.32b and a).
28 Remove the circlip securing the 2nd gear pinion, then slide the splined washer, the

pinion and its bush off the shaft (see illustrations 32.31e, c, b and a).

Output shaft inspection

29 Refer to Steps 7 to 13 above.

Output shaft reassembly

30 During reassembly, apply engine oil to the mating surfaces of the shaft, pinions and bushes. When installing the circlips, do not expand the ends any further than is necessary. Install the stamped circlips and washers so that their chamfered side faces the pinion it secures (see illustration 32.1).
31 Slide the 2nd gear pinion bush onto the

32.32a Slide the 6th gear pinion onto the shaft . . .

shaft, aligning the oil hole in the bush with the hole in the shaft, then slide on the 2nd gear pinion so that its dished side faces away from the shaft bearings. Install the splined washer, then fit the circlip, making sure it is locates correctly in its groove in the shaft (see illustrations).
32 Slide the 6th gear pinion with its selector fork groove facing away from the 2nd gear pinion, then fit the circlip, making sure it is locates correctly in its groove in the shaft (see illustrations).
33 Slide the splined washer and the 3rd gear pinion bush onto the shaft, making sure the oil hole in the bush aligns with the hole in the

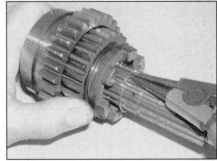

32.32b . . . and secure it with the circlip

32.33a Slide the splined washer . . .

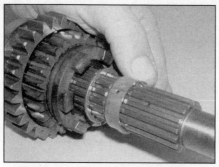

32.33b . . . the 3rd gear pinion bush . . .

32.33c . . . and the 3rd gear pinion onto the shaft

32.34a Slide the slotted splined washer onto the shaft . . .

32.34b . . . and locate it as shown

shaft. Slide on the 3rd gear pinion so that its dished side faces the 6th gear pinion (see illustrations).

34 Slide the slotted splined washer onto the shaft and locate it in its groove, then turn it in the groove so that the splines on the washer align with the splines on the shaft and secure the washer in the groove (see illustrations). Slide the lockwasher onto the shaft, so that the tabs on the lockwasher locate into the slots in the outer rim of the spline washer (see illustration).

35 Slide the 4th gear pinion bush onto the shaft, making sure the oil hole in the bush aligns with the hole in the shaft. Install the 4th gear pinion so that its dished side faces away from the 3rd gear pinion. Install the splined washer, then fit the circlip, making sure it is locates correctly in its groove in the shaft (see illustrations).

36 Slide the 5th gear pinion onto the shaft with its selector fork groove facing the 4th gear pinion, followed by the thrust washer (see illustrations).

37 Slide the 1st gear pinion needle roller bearing onto the shaft. Install the 1st gear pinion so that its dished side faces the 5th gear pinion and its flat surface is facing outwards. Install the thrust washer, then fit the needle roller bearing and its outer race over the end of the shaft (see illustrations).

38 Check that all components have been correctly installed (see illustration).

32.34c Slide the lockwasher onto the shaft and locate it as shown

32.35a Slide the 4th gear pinion bush . . .

32.35b . . . the 4th gear pinion . . .

32.35c . . . and the splined washer onto the shaft . . .

32.35d . . . and secure them with the circlip

32.36a Slide the 5th gear pinion . . .

32.36b . . . and the thrust washer onto the shaft

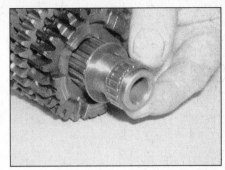

32.37a Slide the needle bearing . . .

33 Rear balancer shaft – removal, inspection, bearing selection, installation, and adjustment

Note: *To remove the rear balancer shaft the engine must be removed from the frame and the crankcases separated..*

Removal

1 Remove the engine from the frame (see Section 5) and separate the crankcase halves (see Section 24). Remove the crankshaft (see Section 30) and the transmission shafts (see Section 31).

2 Make an alignment mark on the balancer idle gear shaft holder with the punch mark on the end of the balancer idle gear shaft – this will give a good indication as to the starting point for the backlash setting when the shaft is installed **(see illustration)**. Slacken the shaft holder pinch bolt, then unscrew the holder mounting bolt and slide the holder off the shaft **(see illustration)**. Also unscrew the shaft stopper bolt **(see illustration)**.

3 Turn the shaft using a screwdriver in the slot until the punch mark on its end is facing up – if the shaft is not in this position it cannot be withdrawn as the offset on it will stop it from doing so (the shaft provides an eccentric adjustment to allow the backlash between the

32.37b . . . the 1st gear pinion . . .

32.37c . . . and the thrust washer onto the shaft . . .

32.37d . . . then fit the needle bearing on the end of the shaft

32.38 The assembled shaft should be as shown

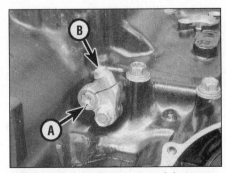

33.2a Make an alignment mark between the end of the shaft and the holder as an installation aid (A), then slacken the pinch bolt (B)

33.2b Unscrew the mounting bolt and slide the holder off the shaft

33.2c Unscrew the shaft stopper bolt (arrowed)

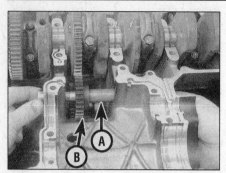

33.4 Withdraw the shaft and remove the spacer (A) and the gear (B)

33.5 Remove the inspection cap

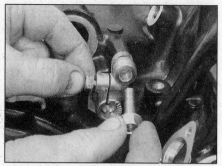

33.6 Make an alignment mark between the end of the shaft and the holder, then slacken the pinch bolt, unscrew the mounting bolt and slide the holder off the shaft

balancer gear and its drive gear on the crankshaft to be optimised to reduce noise).

4 Support the balancer idle gear, then withdraw the shaft and remove the spacer and the gear **(see illustration)**. If the shaft is difficult to withdraw, turn it slightly either way to free it. Discard the shaft O-ring as a new one must be used.

5 Unscrew the balancer timing inspection cap from the upper crankcase half **(see illustration)**.

6 Make an alignment mark on the rear balancer shaft holder with the punch mark on the end of the balancer shaft – this will give a good indication as to the starting point for the backlash setting when the shaft is installed **(see illustration)**. Slacken the balancer shaft holder pinch bolt, then unscrew the holder mounting bolt and slide the holder off the shaft.

7 Turn the shaft until the punch mark on its end is facing down – if the shaft is not in this position it cannot be withdrawn as the offset on it will stop it from doing so (the shaft provides an eccentric adjustment to allow the backlash between the balancer gear and its drive gear on the crankshaft to be optimised to reduce noise).

8 Support the balancer idle gear/weight assembly, then withdraw the shaft and remove the gear/weight **(see illustration)**. If the shaft is difficult to withdraw, turn it slightly either way to free it. Discard the shaft O-ring as a new one must be used.

Inspection

9 Inspect the teeth on the balancer and idle gears for signs of wear or damage, and replace them with new ones if necessary. If damage is found, check the teeth on the drive gear on the crankshaft. The balancer/weight can be disassembled if required – all components are available individually.

10 Remove the washer from each end of the gear/weight, noting which fits where **(see illustration 23.8)**. Slide the shaft back into the gear/weight and check that it runs freely and smoothly in the bearings. If there is any evidence of wear on the shaft, or it is a sloppy fit in the bearings, and the bearings are good, replace the shaft with a new one. If the shaft does not run smoothly and freely, or if there is any wear or damage evident, replace them

with new ones. Note that all components are matched by size and should be replaced either as a set, or by matching them using the coded markings (see Steps 13 and 14).

11 Separate the gear from the weight **(see illustration 23.9)**. Check the condition of the rubber damper assembly in the gear for damage, deformation and deterioration, and replace them with new ones if necessary.

12 Check the condition of the bearing in the idle gear and replace it with a new one if necessary – it is secured by a circlip, and will probably need to be driven out **(see illustration)**. Refer to *Tools and Workshop Tips* in the Reference Section for more information on bearing checks, and removal and installation methods.

Bearing selection

13 Replacement bearings for the balancer gear/weight are supplied on a selected fit basis. Code letters and numbers stamped on the components are used to identify the correct replacement bearings. The balancer gear/weight size code letters (there are two because there are two bearings, the right-hand

one for the gear end and the left-hand one for the weight end) are marked on the balancer web and will be either an A, a B or a C **(see illustration 23.10)**. The shaft size code number or colour is marked on the shaft and will be either a 1 or blue, a 2 or black, or a 3 or red.

14 A range of bearings are available. To select the correct bearing colour code, using the table below cross-refer the gear and weight size code (marked on the balancer web – the right-hand marking is for the gear size, the left-hand marking is for the weight size) with the shaft size code (marked on the shaft – if it is difficult to see you will have to measure the shaft diameter at the bearing points using a Vernier caliper, or preferably a micrometer). For example, if the balancer gear size is B, and the shaft size is 3, then the bearing required for the gear end of the shaft is B – Blue. The colour is marked on the bearing.

Installation

15 Fit a new O-ring onto the balancer gear/weight shaft and smear it with clean oil **(see illustration)**. Position the balancer

	Balancer shaft OD code		
Balancer gear/ weight ID codes	1 or Blue 17.996 to 18.000 mm	2 or Black 17.991 to 17.996 mm	3 or Red 17.987 to 17.991 mm
A – 26.996 to 27.000 mm	C – White	B – Blue	A – Red
B – 26.991 to 26.996 mm	D – Green	C – White	B – Blue
C – 26.987 to 26.991 mm	E – Yellow	D – Green	C – White

33.12 Check the bearing and renew it if necessary – it is held by a circlip

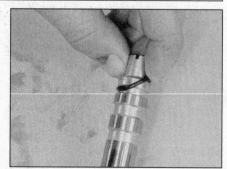

33.15 Fit a new O-ring onto the balancer gear/weight shaft

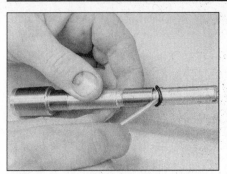

33.18a Fit a new O-ring onto the idle gear shaft

33.18b Locate the gear then slide the shaft through it . . .

33.18c . . . and the spacer . . .

gear/weight assembly in the crankcase so that the index line on one of its teeth aligns with the rear edge of the projection in the gear/weight housing, visible via the inspection aperture **(see illustration 30.25a)**, then slide the shaft in with the punch mark on its end facing down **(see illustration 33.8)**. If the shaft is difficult to insert, turn it slightly either way to free it.

16 Turn the crankcase over or onto its side. Fit the holder onto the end of the shaft and tighten its mounting bolt to the torque setting specified at the beginning of the Chapter **(see illustration 33.6)**. Turn the shaft using a screwdriver until the punch mark aligns with the backlash setting mark made earlier on the holder. Temporarily tighten the shaft pinch bolt.

17 Install the crankshaft (see Section 30). Make sure the crankshaft and balancer gear/weight are aligned as described in Step 25 of that Section.

18 Fit a new O-ring onto the balancer idle gear shaft and smear it with clean oil **(see illustration)**. Position the balancer idle gear in the crankcase with its shouldered side facing the left-hand side of the engine and mesh it with the balancer gear and the drive gear on the crankshaft **(see illustration)**. Slide the shaft in with the punch mark on its end facing down. Once the shaft has located in the gear, position the spacer between the gear and crankcase and slide the shaft all the way in **(see illustrations)**. Check that the balancer gear/weight and crankshaft marks are still aligned. If not, partially withdraw the shaft to

allow the idle gear to be slide out of mesh with the balancer gear and the crankshaft. Turn the balancer gear and/or crankshaft as required until all marks are aligned, then engage the idle gear again and slide the shaft through. If the shaft is difficult to insert, turn it slightly either way to free it.

19 Fit the holder onto the end of the shaft and tighten its mounting bolt to the torque setting specified at the beginning of the Chapter **(see illustration 33.2b)**. Turn the shaft using a screwdriver until the punch mark aligns with the backlash setting mark made earlier on the holder **(see illustration)**. Temporarily tighten the shaft pinch bolt. Apply a suitable non-permanent thread locking compound to the shaft stopper bolt threads, then install the bolt with its washer and tighten it to the specified torque setting **(see illustration)**.

20 Carry out the static backlash adjustment procedure (see below).

21 Turn the crankshaft through 360∞ (one full turn) and check that the crankshaft and balancer marks still align. If the connecting rods have not yet been fitted onto the crankshaft but they are located in the cylinder bores, make sure the rod bolts do not come into contact with the crankpin as you turn the crankshaft as the journal could be scratched. Install the transmission shafts (see Section 31).

22 Install the balancer timing inspection cap using a new O-ring if required, and smear the O-ring and the cap threads with grease **(see illustration 33.5)**. Tighten the cap to the

torque setting specified at the beginning of the Chapter.

23 Carry out the dynamic backlash adjustment procedure (see below).

Backlash adjustment

Note: *A backlash adjustment is provided so that the gears mesh at their optimum point for quiet running with minimal wear. If the amount of backlash is too great, the shafts will clatter. If the gears are running tight, they will whine, and wear very quickly. At the optimum point the gears will run very quietly – it is easy to tell the difference with the engine running. Adjustment is possible due to the offset on the shaft which allows eccentric movement of the balancer gear in relation to its drive gear when the shaft is turned. The static adjustment procedure allows the backlash to be set up in roughly the optimum position, but the dynamic procedure should always be carried out as well to fine tune the setting. The static procedure need only be carried out if the shaft has been removed and reinstalled. If the shaft has not been removed, the dynamic procedure can be carried out on its own. If, having carried out the backlash adjustment, there is still noise from the engine, carry out the front balancer shaft adjustment procedure as well (see Section 23).*

Static adjustment

Note: *This procedure must be carried out when the engine is cold.*

24 Slacken the balancer idle gear shaft holder pinch bolt **(see illustration 33.19a)**.

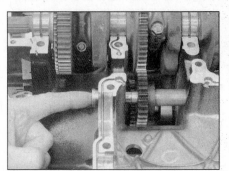

33.18d . . . and push it all the way in

33.19a Turn the shaft to align it as before then temporarily tighten the pinch bolt

33.19b Secure the shaft with the stopper bolt

33.26 Slacken the holder pinch bolt (A) and turn the shaft (B) as described

25 Turn the shaft slightly clockwise, then turn it anti clockwise until resistance is felt – at this point backlash between the gears has been eliminated. Now turn the shaft anti-clockwise one graduation as marked on the holder, then temporarily tighten the pinch bolt.

26 Now slacken the balancer shaft holder pinch bolt **(see illustration)**.

27 Turn the shaft slightly clockwise, then turn it anti clockwise until resistance is felt – at this point backlash between the gears has been eliminated. Now turn the shaft anti-clockwise one graduation as marked on the holder, then temporarily tighten the pinch bolt.

28 Now carry out the dynamic adjustment procedure (see below).

Dynamic adjustment

Note: *This procedure must be carried out when the engine is warm.*

29 Remove the right-hand fairing side panel (see Chapter 8). Start the engine and allow it to warm up, then let it idle.

30 Slacken the balancer idle gear shaft holder pinch bolt **(see illustration 33.19a)**.

31 Turn the shaft anti-clockwise until the gears begin to whine, then turn it slowly

clockwise until the whine disappears, but not so much that the whine is replaced by a clatter. The optimum point is when the gears run at their quietest. Rev the engine and check that there is no unwanted noise at varying speeds.

32 Now slacken the balancer shaft holder pinch bolt **(see illustration 33.26)**.

33 Turn the shaft anti-clockwise until the gears begin to whine, then turn it slowly clockwise until the whine disappears, but not so much that the whine is replaced by a clatter. The optimum point is when the gears run at their quietest. Rev the engine and check that there is no unwanted noise at varying speeds.

34 On completion, tighten the pinch bolts to the torque setting specified at the beginning of the Chapter. Install the right-hand fairing side panel (see Chapter 8).

34 Initial start-up after overhaul

1 Make sure the engine oil and coolant levels are correct (see *Daily (pre-ride) checks*). Make sure there is fuel in the tank.

2 Turn the engine kill switch to the ON position and shift the gearbox into neutral. Turn the ignition ON. On V and W (1997 and 1998) models set the choke enough to encourage the bike to start, but not so much as to allow it to race.

3 Start the engine and allow it to run at a moderately fast idle until it reaches operating temperature.

 Warning: If the oil pressure warning light doesn't go off, or it comes on while the engine is running, stop the engine immediately.

4 Check carefully for oil and coolant leaks and make sure the transmission and controls, especially the brakes, function properly before road testing the machine. Refer to Section 35 for the recommended running-in procedure.

5 Upon completion of the road test, and after the engine has cooled down completely, recheck the valve clearances (see Chapter 1) and check the engine oil and coolant levels (see *Daily (pre-ride) checks*).

35 Recommended running-in procedure

1 Treat the machine gently for the first few miles to make sure oil has circulated throughout the engine and any new parts installed have started to seat.

2 Even greater care is necessary if new pistons/rings or a new crankcase/bores have been fitted, and the bike will have to be run in as when new. This means greater use of the transmission and a restraining hand on the throttle until at least 600 miles (1000 km) have been covered. There's no point in keeping to any set speed limit – the main idea is to keep from labouring the engine and to gradually increase performance up to the 600 mile (1000 km) mark. Experience is the best guide, since it's easy to tell when an engine is running freely. The following maximum engine speed limitations, which Honda provide for new motorcycles, can be used as a guide.

3 If a lubrication failure is suspected, stop the engine immediately and try to find the cause. If an engine is run without oil, even for a short period of time, severe damage will occur.

Running-in guide to engine speeds

Up to 600 miles (1000 km)	5000 rpm max	Vary throttle position/speed
600 to 1000 miles (1000 to 1600 km)	7000 rpm max	Vary throttle position/speed. Use full throttle for short bursts
Over 1000 miles (1600 km)	10,800 rpm max	Do not exceed tachometer red line

Chapter 3
Cooling system

Contents

Degrees of difficulty

| Easy, suitable for novice with little experience | | Fairly easy, suitable for beginner with some experience | | Fairly difficult, suitable for competent DIY mechanic | | Difficult, suitable for experienced DIY mechanic | | Very difficult, suitable for expert DIY or professional | |

Specifications

Coolant

Mixture type and capacity .... see Chapter 1

Cooling fan switch – V, W, X and Y (1997 to 2000) models

Switch closes (fan ON) .... 98 to 102°C
Switch opens (fan OFF) .... 93 to 97°C

Coolant temperature sensor

V and W (1997 and 1998) models
  Resistance @ 20°C .... 45 to 60 ohms
X and Y (1999 and 2000) models
  Resistance @ 80°C .... 47.5 to 56.8 K-ohms
  Resistance @ 120°C .... 14.9 to 17.3 K-ohms
1 (2001) model onward
  Resistance @ 80°C .... 2.1 to 2.6 K-ohms
  Resistance @ 120°C .... 0.62 to 0.76 K-ohms

Thermostat

UK V (1997) models
  Opening temperature .... 69 to 73°C
  Fully open .... 85°C
  Valve lift .... 8 mm (min)
All other models
  Opening temperature .... 80 to 84°C
  Fully open .... 95°C
  Valve lift .... 8 mm (min)

Radiator

Cap valve opening pressure .... 16 to 20 psi (1.1 to 1.4 Bar)

Torque settings

Cooling fan blade nut .... 2 Nm
Cooling fan motor nuts .... 18 Nm
Fan switch – V, W, X and Y (1997 to 2000) models .... 18 Nm
Water pump bolts .... 13 Nm

1 General information

The cooling system uses a water/antifreeze coolant to carry away excess heat from the engine and maintain as constant a temperature as possible. The cylinders are surrounded by a water jacket from which the heated coolant is circulated by thermosyphonic action in conjunction with a water pump, which is driven by the oil pump. The hot coolant passes upwards to the thermostat and through to the radiator. The coolant then flows across the core of the radiator, then to the water pump and back to the engine where the cycle is repeated.

A thermostat is fitted in the system to prevent the coolant flowing through the radiator when the engine is cold, therefore accelerating the speed at which the engine reaches normal operating temperature. A coolant temperature sensor mounted in the thermostat housing transmits information to the temperature gauge on the instrument panel, and on fuel-injected models to the ECM (electronic control module).

A cooling fan is fitted to the back of the radiator to aid cooling in extreme conditions by drawing extra air through; on V, W, X and Y (1997 to 2000) models a thermostatically-controlled switch fitted to the left-hand side of the radiator triggers the operation of the fan motor. On 1 (2001) models onward, the fan motor is triggered by a signal from the ECM, which receives information on coolant temperature from the thermo sensor.

The complete cooling system is partially sealed and pressurised, the pressure being controlled by a valve contained in the spring-loaded radiator cap. By pressurising the coolant the boiling point is raised, preventing premature boiling in adverse conditions. The overflow pipe from the system is connected to a reservoir into which excess coolant is expelled under pressure. The discharged coolant automatically returns to the radiator by the vacuum created when the engine cools.

 Warning: Do not remove the pressure cap from the radiator when the engine is hot. Scalding hot coolant and steam may be blown out under pressure, which could cause serious injury. When the engine has cooled, place a thick rag, like a towel, over the pressure cap; slowly rotate the cap anti-clockwise to the first stop. This procedure allows any residual pressure to escape. When the steam has stopped escaping, press down on the cap while turning it anti-clockwise and remove it. Do not allow antifreeze to come in contact with your skin or painted surfaces of the motorcycle. Rinse off any spills immediately with plenty of water. Antifreeze is highly toxic if ingested. Never leave antifreeze lying around in an open container or in puddles on the floor; children and pets are attracted by its sweet smell and may drink it. Check with the local authorities about disposing of used antifreeze. Many communities will have collection centres which will see that antifreeze is disposed of safely.

Caution: At all times use the specified type of antifreeze, and always mix it with distilled water in the correct proportion. The antifreeze contains corrosion inhibitors which are essential to avoid damage to the cooling system. A lack of these inhibitors could lead to a build-up of corrosion which would block the coolant passages, resulting in overheating and severe engine damage. Distilled water must be used as opposed to tap water to avoid a build-up of scale which would also block the passages.

2 Radiator pressure cap – check

1 If problems such as overheating or loss of coolant occur, check the entire system as described in Chapter 1. The radiator cap opening pressure should be checked by a Honda dealer with the special tester required to do the job. If the cap is defective, replace it with a new one.

3 Cooling fan and fan switch – check and replacement

Cooling fan
Check

1 If the engine is overheating and the cooling fan isn't coming on, first check the cooling fan circuit fuse (see Chapter 9). On V, W, X and Y (1997 to 2000) models, then check the fan switch as described below. On 1 (2001) models onward, check the fan relay as described below, then the coolant temperature sensor (see Section 4).
2 If the fan does not come on (and the fan switch or relay and sensor are good), the fault lies in either the cooling fan motor or the relevant wiring. Test all the wiring and connections as described in Chapter 9, following the relevant Wiring Diagram. Disconnect the fan wiring connector (see Step 3) and check that there is battery voltage at the black/blue wire terminal on the loom side of the connector with the ignition ON. If not, check the wiring. On 1 (2001) models onward, if everything appears to be in good working order after all tests have been made, bear in mind that the ECM (electronic control module) could be faulty.
3 To test the cooling fan motor, remove the left-hand fairing side panel (see Chapter 8). Disconnect the fan wiring connector and on V, W, X and Y (1997 to 2000) models the fan switch wiring connector **(see illustrations)**. Using a 12 volt battery and two jumper wires with suitable connectors, connect the battery positive (+ve) lead to the black/blue wire terminal on the fan side of the wiring connector, and the battery negative (–ve) lead

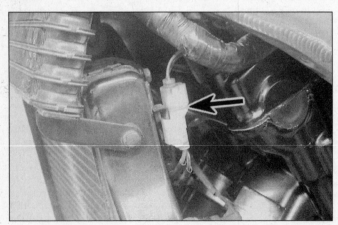
3.3a Disconnect the fan wiring connector (arrowed) . . .

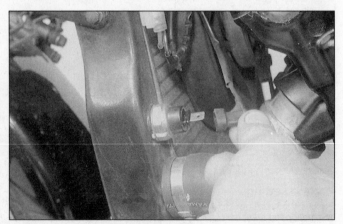
3.3b . . . and the fan switch wiring connector (V, W, X and Y) models

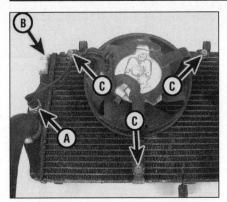

3.5 Disconnect the switch connector (A) and release the connector (B) from its lug, then undo the bolts (C) and remove the fan assembly

to the fan switch wiring connector on V, W, X and Y (1997 to 2000) models, and to the black wire terminal on 1 (2001) models onward. Once connected the fan should operate. If it does not, and the wiring is all good, then the fan motor is faulty. Individual components are available for the fan assembly.

Replacement

⚠️ *Warning: The engine must be completely cool before carrying out this procedure.*

4 Remove the radiator (see Section 6).
5 Disconnect the wiring connector from the fan switch **(see illustration)**. Free the fan

wiring connector from its lug on the radiator and all the wiring from any clamps.
6 Undo the three screws securing the fan assembly to the radiator, noting that one screw also secures the earth (ground) wire **(see illustration 3.5)**.
7 Unscrew the fan blade nut and remove the blade. Undo the three nuts on the front of the fan motor securing it to the bracket and separate them.
8 Installation is the reverse of removal. Apply a suitable non-permanent thread locking compound on the fan blade nut and tighten it to the torque setting specified at the beginning of the Chapter. Also tighten the fan motor nuts to the specified torque. Do not forget to attach the earth (ground) cable to the radiator.
9 Install the radiator (see Section 7).

Cooling fan switch – V, W, X and Y (1997 to 2000) models

Check

10 If the engine is overheating and the cooling fan isn't coming on, first check the cooling fan circuit fuse (see Chapter 9). If the fuse is blown, check the fan circuit for a short to earth (see the wiring diagrams at the end of this book).
11 If the fuse is good, remove the left-hand fairing side panel (see Chapter 8). Disconnect the wiring connector from the fan switch on the radiator **(see illustration 3.3b)**. Using a jumper wire if necessary, connect the wire to

earth (ground). The fan should come on. If it does, the fan switch is defective and must be replaced with a new one. If it does not come on, check for battery voltage at the switch wiring connector with the ignition ON. If voltage is present, test the fan motor itself (see Step 3). If there is no voltage, check the wiring and connectors for a fault or break.
12 If the fan is on the whole time, disconnect the wiring connector. The fan should stop. If it does, the switch is defective and must be replaced. If it doesn't, check the wiring between the switch and the fan for a short to earth, and the fan itself.
13 If the fan works but is suspected of cutting in at the wrong temperature, a more comprehensive test of the switch can be made as follows.
14 Remove the switch (see Steps 16 to 19). Fill a small heatproof container with oil and place it on a stove. Connect the positive (+ve) probe of an ohmmeter to the terminal of the switch and the negative (–ve) probe to the switch body, and using some wire or other support suspend the switch in the oil so that just the sensing portion and the threads are submerged **(see illustration 4.13)**. Also place a thermometer capable of reading temperatures up to 110°C in the coolant so that its bulb is close to the switch. **Note:** *None of the components should be allowed to directly touch the container.*
15 Initially the ohmmeter reading should be very high indicating that the switch is open (OFF). Heat the oil, stirring it gently.

⚠️ *Warning: This must be done very carefully to avoid the risk of personal injury.*

When the temperature reaches around 98 to 102°C the meter reading should drop to around zero ohms, indicating that the switch has closed (ON). Now turn the heat off. As the temperature falls below 93 to 97°C the meter reading should show infinite (very high) resistance, indicating that the switch has opened (OFF). If the meter readings obtained are different, or they are obtained at different temperatures, then the switch is faulty and must be replaced with a new one.

Replacement

⚠️ *Warning: The engine must be completely cool before carrying out this procedure.*

16 Drain the cooling system (see Chapter 1).
17 Disconnect the wiring connector from the fan switch on the left-hand side of the radiator **(see illustration 3.3b)**. Unscrew the switch and withdraw it from the radiator. Discard the O-ring as a new one must be used.
18 Install the switch using a new O-ring and tighten it to the torque setting specified at the beginning of the Chapter. Take care not to overtighten the switch as the radiator could be damaged.
19 Reconnect the switch wiring and refill the cooling system (see Chapter 1).

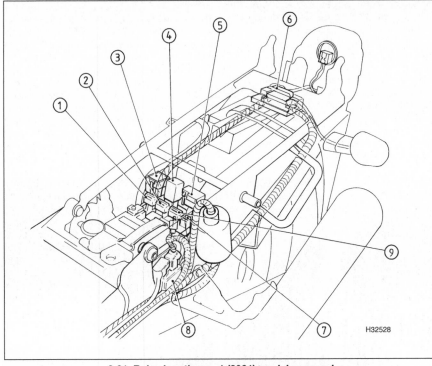

3.21 Relay locations – 1 (2001) models onward

1 Cooling fan relay
2 Engine stop relay
3 Bank angle sensor
4 Turn signal relay
5 Fusebox
6 ECM
7 Headlight relay
8 Starter relay
9 Fuel cut-off relay

H32528

Cooling fan relay – 1 (2001) models onward

Check

20 If the engine is overheating and the cooling fan isn't coming on, first check the cooling fan circuit fuse (see Chapter 9). If the fuse is blown, check the fan circuit for a short to earth (see the wiring diagrams at the end of this book).

21 If the fuse is good, remove the seat (see Chapter 8). Displace the cooling fan relay and disconnect its wiring connector – the relay is on the right-hand end of the row of four relays **(see illustration)**. Set a multimeter to the ohms x 1 scale and connect it across the relay's black and green wire terminals. There should be no continuity (infinite resistance). Using a fully-charged 12 volt battery and two insulated jumper wires, connect the positive (+ve) terminal of the battery to the black/white wire terminal on the relay, and the negative (–ve) terminal to the green/blue wire terminal on the relay. At this point the relay should be heard to click and the multimeter read 0 ohms (continuity). If this is the case the relay is proved good. If the relay does not click when battery voltage is applied and still indicates no continuity (infinite resistance) across its terminals, it is faulty and must be replaced with a new one.

22 If the relay is good, check for battery voltage at the black/white wire with the ignition switch ON. If there is no voltage, check the wiring, referring to the relevant Wiring Diagram at the end of Chapter 9. If voltage is present, check that there is continuity to earth in the green wire with the ignition switch OFF. If there is no continuity, check the wiring. Also check the wiring between the relay and the ECM (electronic control module), and between the relay and the fan motor wiring connector on the radiator (see the *wiring diagrams* at the end of this book) – there should be continuity in all wires.

23 If the fan is on the whole time, disconnect the relay wiring connector. The fan should stop. If it does, the relay is defective and must be replaced. If it doesn't, check the wiring between the relay and the fan for a short to earth, and the fan itself.

24 If the fan works but is suspected of cutting in at the wrong temperature, check the thermo sensor (see Section 4).

Replacement

⚠ *Warning: The engine must be completely cool before carrying out this procedure.*

25 Remove the seat (see Chapter 8).
26 Displace the cooling fan relay and disconnect its wiring connector – the relay is on the right-hand end of the row of four relays **(see illustration 3.21)**. Remove the relay from its rubber sleeve.
27 Installation is the reverse of removal.

---

4 Coolant temperature gauge and sensor – check and replacement

Coolant temperature gauge – V, W, X and Y (1997 to 2000) models

Check

1 The circuit consists of the sensor mounted in the thermostat housing and the gauge assembly mounted in the instrument cluster. If the system malfunctions check first that the battery is fully charged and that the fuses are all good.

2 If the gauge is not working, remove the fuel tank (see Chapter 4). Disconnect the wiring connector from the sensor and turn the ignition switch ON **(see illustration)**. The temperature gauge needle should be on the 'C' on the gauge. Using a jumper wire attached to the wiring connector terminal, earth the sensor wire on the engine – on X and Y (1999 and 2000) models with a three-pin connector, attach the jumper wire to the green/blue wire terminal in the connector. The needle should swing immediately over to the 'H' on the gauge.

Caution: Do not earth the wire for any longer than is necessary to take the reading, or the gauge may be damaged.

If the needle moves as described above, the gauge is proven good, however the sensor is

proven defective and must be replaced with a new one.

3 If the needle movement is still faulty, or if it does not move at all, the fault lies in the wiring or the gauge itself. Remove the fairing (see Chapter 8).

4 Check for continuity in the wire between the temperature sensor and the temperature gauge green/blue wire terminal on the back of the instrument cluster. If there is no continuity, locate the break in the wire and repair it or replace it with a new one. Also check for battery voltage at the sensor end of the wire, using the green/blue wire terminal on X and Y models. If voltage is present, the gauge is faulty and must be replaced with a new one (see Chapter 9).

5 If no voltage is present, check for battery voltage between the black/brown (+) and green/blue (-) wire terminals on the temperature gauge with the ignition ON. If no voltage is present, check for voltage at the black/brown wire terminal. If there is none, there is a fault in that wire. If voltage is present, replace the gauge with a new one (see Chapter 9). Otherwise check all the wiring, particularly for continuity to earth in the green/black wire, referring to the *Wiring Diagrams* at the end of Chapter 9.

Replacement

6 See Chapter 9.

Coolant temperature gauge – 1 (2001) models onward

Check

7 The coolant temperature gauge is part of the instrument cluster LCD unit and is operated by the fuel injection system thermo sensor (see Chapters 4 and 9). If the system malfunctions check first that the battery is fully charged and that the fuses are all good.

8 If the gauge is not working, or flashes 122 – 132°C when the engine is cold, raise or remove the fuel tank (see Chapter 4). Ensure the ignition is switched off then disconnect the wiring connector from the sensor, which is mounted in the thermostat housing **(see illustration 4.2)**. Turn the ignition switch on; the gauge should display —°C. If it doesn't, check the green/blue wire between the sensor connector and the instrument cluster for continuity. If there is no continuity, or there is continuity to earth (ground), trace the fault in the wire and repair it. If there is continuity, the gauge is faulty and must be replaced with a new one. If the display is as it should be, check the thermo sensor (see below). Turn the ignition switch off again.

9 If the gauge is not working, or displays —°C when the engine is warm, raise or remove the fuel tank (see Chapter 4). Ensure the ignition is switched off then disconnect the wiring connector from the sensor, which is mounted in the thermostat housing **(see illustration 4.2)**. Earth (ground) the green/blue terminal of the sensor wiring connector. Turn the ignition switch on again; the gauge should

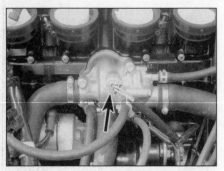

4.2 Disconnect the wiring connector (arrowed) from the sensor – X (1999) models onward shown

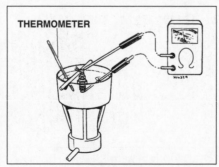

4.13 Temperature gauge sensor testing set-up

display 132°C which flashes continually. If the gauge performs as described, the thermo sensor is proven defective and must be renewed. If the temperature gauge display does not perform as expected, the fault lies in the wiring or the gauge itself. Check all the relevant wiring and wiring connectors (see Chapter 9). If all appears to be well, the instrument cluster LCD unit or printed circuit board is defective and must be renewed (see Chapter 9).

Caution: Do not leave the ignition switched on for any longer than is necessary to take the reading, or the gauge may be damaged.

Replacement

10 The temperature gauge is part of the instrument cluster LCD unit (see Chapter 9).

Coolant temperature sensor

Check

11 Drain the cooling system (see Chapter 1). The sensor is mounted in the thermostat housing.

12 Remove the sensor (see Steps 15 to 18 below).

13 Fill a small heatproof container with oil and place it on a stove. Using an ohmmeter, connect the positive (+ve) probe of the meter to the terminal on the sensor, on X (1999) models onward using the green/blue wire terminal, and the negative (–ve) probe to the body of the sensor. Using some wire or other support suspend the sensor in the oil so that just the sensing head and the threads are submerged, with the head a minimum of 40 mm above the bottom of the container. Also place a thermometer capable of reading temperatures up to 130°C in the oil so that its bulb is close to the sensor **(see illustration)**. *Note: None of the components should be allowed to directly touch the container.*

14 Begin to heat the oil, stirring it gently.

 Warning: This must be done very carefully to avoid the risk of personal injury.

When the temperature reaches around 80°C, turn the heat down and maintain the temperature steady for three minutes. The meter reading should be as specified at the

beginning of the Chapter. Turn the heat on again. When the temperature reaches around 120°C, again turn the heat down and maintain it for three minutes. The meter reading should again be as specified at the beginning of the Chapter. If the meter readings obtained are different by a margin of 10% or more, then the sensor is faulty and must be replaced with a new one.

Replacement

 Warning: The engine must be completely cool before carrying out this procedure.

15 Drain the cooling system (see Chapter 1). The sensor is mounted in the thermostat housing.

16 Disconnect the sensor wiring connector **(see illustration 4.2)**. Unscrew the sensor and remove it from the thermostat housing.

17 On V and W (1997 and 1998) models, apply a smear of sealant to the threads of the new sensor, making sure none gets on the head. On X (1999) models onward, fit a new sealing washer onto the sensor. Install the sensor and tighten it securely. Connect the sensor wiring.

18 Refill the cooling system (see Chapter 1).

5 Thermostat and housing – removal, check and installation

Removal

Note: *From the W (1998) model onward the complete thermostat housing can be removed without removing the thermostat itself – ignore the points in Step 3 relating to cover and thermostat removal.*

 Warning: The engine must be completely cool before carrying out this procedure.

1 The thermostat is automatic in operation and should give many years service without requiring attention. In the event of a failure, the valve will probably jam open, in which case the engine will take much longer than normal to warm up. Conversely, if the valve

jams shut, the coolant will be unable to circulate and the engine will overheat. Neither condition is acceptable, and the fault must be investigated promptly.

2 Drain the cooling system (see Chapter 1). Remove the fuel tank (see Chapter 4). The thermostat housing is on the back of the engine in the middle.

3 On V (1997) models, if you are removing the housing from the engine rather than just the thermostat from the housing, slacken the clamps securing the hoses to the housing and detach them, noting which fits where. Also disconnect the coolant temperature sensor wiring connector. Unscrew the two bolts securing the cover and separate it from the housing. Withdraw the thermostat, noting how it fits. Discard the cover O-ring as a new one must be used. If required, pull the housing off the engine. Discard the O-ring.

4 On W (1998) models onward, to remove the thermostat, unscrew the three bolts securing the cover and separate it from the housing **(see illustration)**. Withdraw the thermostat, noting how it fits **(see illustration)**. Where fitted, discard the cover O-ring as a new one must be used. To remove the thermostat housing, disconnect the temperature gauge sensor or thermo sensor wiring connector **(see illustration 4.2)**. Slacken the clamps securing all the hoses to the cover and housing and detach them, noting which fits where **(see illustration)**. Unscrew the bolts securing the housing to the engine and remove the housing. Discard the O-ring.

Check

5 Examine the thermostat visually before carrying out the test. If it remains in the open position at room temperature, it should be replaced with a new one. Check the condition of the rubber seal around the thermostat and replace it with a new one if it is damaged, deformed or deteriorated.

6 Suspend the thermostat by a piece of wire in a container of cold water. Place a thermometer capable of reading temperatures up to 110°C in the water so that the bulb is

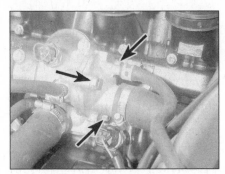

5.4a Unscrew the bolts (arrowed) and detach the cover . . .

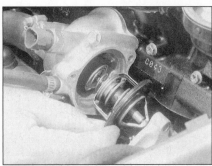

5.4b . . . and withdraw the thermostat from the housing

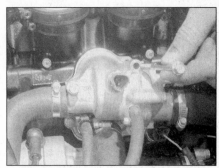

5.4c Detach the hoses from the housing then unscrew the mounting bolts

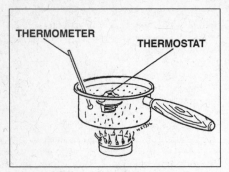

5.6 Thermostat testing set-up

5.9a Install the thermostat with the hole at the top . . .

5.9b . . . then fit the cover and install the bolts

5.9c Install the housing using a new O-ring

close to the thermostat **(see illustration)**. Heat the water, noting the temperature when the thermostat opens, and compare the result with the specifications given at the beginning of the Chapter. Also check the amount the valve opens after it has been heated for a few minutes and compare the measurement to the specifications. If the readings obtained differ from those given, the thermostat is faulty and must be replaced with a new one.

7 In the event of thermostat failure, as an emergency measure only, it can be removed and the machine used without it (this is better than leaving a permanently closed thermostat in, but if it is permanently open, you might as well leave it in). **Note:** *Take care when starting the engine from cold as it will take much longer than usual to warm up.* Ensure that a new unit is installed as soon as possible.

Installation

8 On V (1997) models, if the housing was removed, fit a new O-ring into the groove, using a dab of grease to keep it in place if required, then locate it on the engine. To install the thermostat, fit it with the hole facing up and locate the ribs in the grooves. Fit a new O-ring onto the cover, using a dab of grease to keep it in place if required. Fit the cover onto the housing, then install the bolts and tighten them securely.

9 On W (1998) models onward, to install the thermostat, fit it with the hole facing up and locate the ribs in the grooves **(see illustration)**. Where fitted, install a new O-ring onto the cover, using a dab of grease to keep it in place if. Fit the cover onto the housing, then install the bolts and tighten them

securely **(see illustration)**. To install the thermostat housing, fit a new O-ring into the groove, using a dab of grease to keep it in place if required **(see illustration)**. Fit the housing and tighten the bolts securely **(see illustration 5.4c)**. Attach the hoses to their unions on the cover and housing and tighten the clamps **(see illustration 4.2)**. Connect the temperature gauge sensor or thermo sensor wiring connector **(see illustration 4.2)**.

10 Refill the cooling system (see Chapter 1).

11 Install the fuel tank (see Chapter 4).

6 Radiator – removal and installation

Removal

⚠️ *Warning: The engine must be completely cool before carrying out this procedure.*

Note: *If the radiator is being removed as part of the engine removal procedure, detach the hoses from their unions on the engine rather than on the radiator and remove the radiator with the hoses attached to it. Note the routing of the hoses.*

1 Drain the cooling system (see Chapter 1).

2 Disconnect the fan wiring connector **(see illustration 3.3a)**.

3 Slacken the clamps securing the hoses to the radiator and detach them, noting which fits where **(see illustrations)**.

4 On V and W (1997 and 1998) models, release the air guide plate hooks from the oil cooler hoses. Free the lower mounting bracket lug from the grommet on the radiator. Unscrew the radiator mounting bolt, then lower the left-hand side slightly and draw it to the right to free the top grommet from its lug, and remove it.

5 On X (1999) models onward, unscrew the two oil cooler bolts that thread into the radiator, then pivot the oil cooler forwards **(see illustration 6.3b)**. Unscrew the radiator mounting bolt, then draw it to the left to free the top and bottom grommets from the lugs and remove it **(see illustration)**. Note the

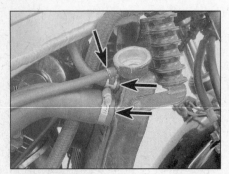

6.3a Detach the three hoses (arrowed) from the right-hand side of the radiator . . .

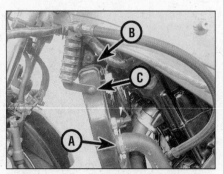

6.3b . . . and the single hose (A) from the left-hand side. Radiator mounting bolt (B), oil cooler bolt (C)

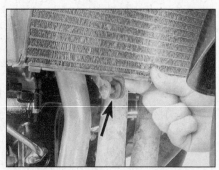

6.5 Draw the radiator to the left to free the grommets from the lugs (bottom one arrowed)

7.5 Slacken the clamps (arrowed) and detach the hoses from the pump

7.6a Water pump cover and mounting bolts (arrowed)

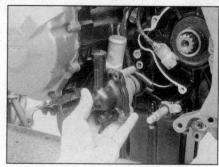

7.6b Draw the pump out of the engine

arrangement of the collars and rubber grommets.

6 If necessary, remove the cooling fan and its switch (except 1 models) from the radiator (see Section 3).Check the radiator for signs of damage and clear any dirt or debris that might obstruct air flow and inhibit cooling. If the radiator fins are badly damaged or broken the radiator must be replaced with a new one. Also check the rubber mounting grommets, and renew them if necessary.

Installation

7 Installation is the reverse of removal, noting the following.
a) Make sure the rubber grommets fit correctly onto the locating lugs.
b) Make sure the collars and washers are correctly installed with the mounting bolt.
c) Make sure that the fan wiring is correctly connected.
d) Ensure the coolant hoses are in good condition (see Chapter 1), and are securely retained by their clamps, using new ones if necessary.
e) On completion refill the cooling system as described in Chapter 1.

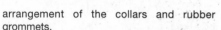

7   Water pump – check, removal and installation

Check

1 The water pump is located on the lower left-hand side of the engine. Visually check the area around the pump for signs of leakage.

2 To prevent leakage of water from the cooling system to the lubrication system and vice versa, two seals are fitted on the pump shaft. On the bottom of the pump housing there is also a drain hole. If either seal fails, the drain allows the coolant or oil to escape and prevents them mixing.

3 The seal on the water pump side is of the mechanical type which bears on the rear face of the impeller. The second seal, which is mounted behind the mechanical seal, is of the normal feathered lip type. If on inspection the drain shows signs of leakage, remove the pump and replace it with a new one – it comes as an assembly.

Removal

4 Drain the coolant (see Chapter 1).

5 Slacken the clamps securing the coolant hoses to the pump cover and housing and detach the hoses, noting which fits where **(see illustration)**.

6 The pump can be removed complete by unscrewing the top and bottom bolts that secure it to the crankcase, leaving the left and right bolts securing the cover untouched **(see illustration)**. To remove the cover, unscrew all the bolts. Note the position of each bolt as they are different lengths. Carefully draw the pump from the crankcase, noting how it fits **(see illustration)**. It may be necessary to lever it out to overcome the O-ring on the pump body. Remove the O-ring from the rear of the pump body and discard it as a new one must be used. If the cover has been removed, discard its O-ring.

7 Wiggle the water pump impeller back-and-forth and in-and-out **(see illustration)**. If there is excessive movement, replace the pump with a new one. Also check for corrosion or a build-up of scale in the pump body and clean or replace the pump as necessary.

Installation

8 Apply a smear of grease to the new pump body O-ring and fit it into the groove in the body **(see illustration)**. Slide the pump into the crankcase, aligning the slot in the impeller shaft with the tab on the oil pump shaft **(see illustration)**.

9 If the cover was removed, smear the new O-ring with grease and fit it into its groove in the cover, then fit the cover onto the pump **(see illustration)**.

7.7 Check the pump impeller as described

7.8a Fit a new O-ring onto the pump body . . .

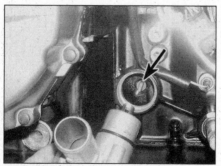

7.8b . . . and align the slot in the shaft with the tab on the oil pump shaft (arrowed)

7.9 Install the cover using a new O-ring

8.4a Water inlet union bolts (arrowed)

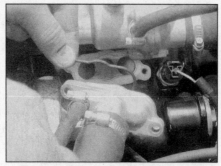

8.4b Discard the O-ring and use a new
one on installation

10 Clean any corrosion off the long bolts and apply a smear of copper grease to their threads to prevent further corrosion. The short bolts have specially formed end threads designed to cut through any corrosion that has built up via the open ends of their bores, but it is best to clean them up any way and apply some copper grease. Install the bolts and tighten them to the torque setting specified at the beginning of the Chapter – the long bolts are for the top and bottom holes and the short bolts are for the left and right holes **(see illustration 7.6a)**.

11 Fit the coolant hoses onto the pump housing and cover and secure them with their clamps **(see illustrations 7.5)**.

12 Refill the cooling system (see Chapter 1).

8 Coolant hoses and unions – removal and installation

Removal

1 Before removing a hose, drain the coolant (see Chapter 1).

2 Use a screwdriver to slacken the larger-bore hose clamps, then slide them back along the hose and clear of the union spigot. The smaller-bore hoses are secured by spring clamps which can be expanded by squeezing their ears together with pliers.

Caution: The radiator unions are fragile. Do not use excessive force when attempting to remove the hoses.

3 If a hose proves stubborn, release it by rotating it on its union before working it off. If all else fails, cut the hose with a sharp knife. Whilst this means replacing the hose, it is preferable to buying a new radiator.

4 The inlet union to the cylinder block can be removed by unscrewing its bolts **(see illustration)**. If the union is removed, the O-ring must be replaced with a new one **(see illustration)**. The outlet from the cylinder head goes into the thermostat housing, which is covered in Section 5.

Installation

5 Slide the clamps onto the hose and then work the hose on to its union.

> **HAYNES HiNT**
> *If the hose is difficult to push on its union, soften it by soaking it in very hot water, or alternatively a little soapy water on the union can be used as a lubricant.*

6 Rotate the hose on its unions to settle it in position before sliding the clamps into place and tightening them securely.

7 If the inlet union to the cylinder block has been removed, fit a new O-ring into the groove, using a dab of grease to hold it in place if necessary **(see illustration 8.4b)**. Install the union and tighten the mounting bolts securely **(see illustration 8.4a)**.

Chapter 4
Fuel and exhaust systems

Contents

Degrees of difficulty

Easy, suitable for novice with little experience		Fairly easy, suitable for beginner with some experience		Fairly difficult, suitable for competent DIY mechanic		Difficult, suitable for experienced DIY mechanic		Very difficult, suitable for expert DIY or professional	

Specifications

Fuel
Grade
   UK market .... Unleaded, minimum 91 RON (Research Octane Number)
   US market .... Unleaded, minimum pump octane number 86
Fuel tank capacity (including reserve)
   V and W (1997 and 1998) models .... 22.0 litres
   X (1999) models onward .... 24.0 litres

Carburettors – V and W (1997 and 1998) models

Type	Keihin CV
Size (throttle bore)	42 mm
Pilot screw base setting (turns out)	
UK and general European market models	$2\frac{1}{4}$
German market models	$2\frac{1}{8}$
French market models	$2\frac{1}{2}$
Swiss and Northern European market models	$2\frac{3}{8}$
Austrian market models	$2\frac{5}{8}$
US 49-state and Canadian market models	$2\frac{3}{4}$
US California market models	$2\frac{1}{2}$
Float height	13.7 mm
Idle speed	see Chapter 1
Pilot jet	42
Main jet	
UK models	
Nos. 1 and 4 cylinder carburettors	142
Nos. 2 and 3 cylinder carburettors	145
US models	
Nos. 1 and 4 cylinder carburettors	140
Nos. 2 and 3 cylinder carburettors	142
Jet needle	
UK models	J5FZ
US 49 State/Canada models	J5FZ
California models	J5FU

Fuel injection system – X (1999) models onward

Throttle bore diameter	36 mm
Idle speed	see Chapter 1
Fuel pressure at specified idle speed*	
X and Y (1999 and 2000) models	43 psi (3.0 Bar)
1 (2001) models onward	50 psi (3.5 Bar)
Minimum fuel flow rate	220 cc every 10 seconds

Fuel pressure regulator vacuum hose disconnected and plugged

Fuel injection system test data – X (1999) models onward

Note: *Values given are only accurate at 20°C (68°F)*

Cam pulse generator minimum peak voltage output	0.7 volts
Ignition pulse generator minimum peak voltage output	0.7 volts
Coolant temperature sensor resistance	2.2 to 2.7 K-ohms
Fuel injector resistance	13.0 to 14.4 K-ohms
Intake air temperature sensor resistance	1 to 4 K-ohms
Throttle body synchronisation – max. difference between bodies	20 mm Hg
Pulse secondary air (PAIR) control valve resistance	20 to 24 ohms
Evaporative emission control (EVAP) system control	
valve – California models	30 to 34 ohms

Fuel gauge sender unit resistance

Full position	4 to 10 ohms
Empty position	81 to 91 ohms

Pulse secondary air (PAIR) system

Control valve resistance – X (1999) models onward	20 to 24 ohms

Torque settings

Cam pulse generator mounting plate bolts – X (1999) models onward	12 Nm
Exhaust downpipe nuts	20 Nm
Fast idle system wax unit screws	5 Nm
Fuel pressure regulator nut – X (1999) models onward	27 Nm
Fuel pressure release bolt – X (1999) models onward	15 Nm
Fuel rail nuts – X (1999) models onward	10 Nm
Fuel supply hose banjo union nut and bolt – X (1999) models onward	22 Nm
Knock sensor	31 Nm
Timing rotor cover bolts	12 Nm
Silencer clamp bolts	17 Nm
Silencer mounting nuts	26 Nm

1 General information and precautions

General information

On V and W (1997 and 1998) carburettor models, the fuel supply system consists of the fuel tank, strainer, fuel tap, fuel hoses, carburettors, and control cables. The fuel tap is semi-automatic in that it has both a manually operated valve and a vacuum operated valve. The manual valve need only be closed when the fuel tank is removed. With the manual valve open, the automatic valve opens by a vacuum acting on a diaphragm when the engine is turned. If the manual valve is closed, the diaphragm valve will not bypass it when the engine is turned.

On X (1999) fuel-injection models onward, the fuel supply system consists of the fuel tank, fuel pump, filter, fuel hoses, throttle bodies, injectors, and control cables. There is no fuel tap – the fuel pump is switched on and off with the engine and supplies the fuel. The fuel flows to the fuel rail on the throttle body assembly, and this acts as a reservoir for the fuel injectors, controlled by a pressure relief valve which directs excess fuel back to the fuel tank. There is an injector for each cylinder, and these inject fuel into the throttle bodies where it mixes with the air before passing to the intake ducts. The injectors are operated by the Electronic Control Module (ECM) using the information obtained from the various sensors it monitors (refer to the relevant Sections for more information on the operation of the fuel injection system).

All models have a fuel gauge in the instrument cluster which is actuated by a level sensor inside the fuel tank, and this is backed up by a low fuel level warning light in the gauge which comes on when there is approximately four litres of fuel left (assuming the bike is upright).

The carburettors used on V and W (1997 and 1998) models are CV types. There is a carburettor for each cylinder. For cold starting, a choke lever is mounted in the left-hand switch housing on the handlebar.

Air is drawn into the carburettors or throttle bodies via an air filter which is housed under the fuel tank.

The exhaust system is a four-into-two design.

Many of the fuel system service procedures are considered routine maintenance items and for that reason are covered in Chapter 1.

Precautions

![warning triangle] **Warning: Petrol (gasoline) is extremely flammable, so take extra precautions when you work on any part of the fuel system. Always remove the battery (see Chapter 9). Don't smoke or allow open flames or bare light bulbs near the work area, and don't work in a garage where a natural gas-type appliance is present. If you spill any fuel on your skin, rinse it off immediately with soap and water. When you perform any kind of work on the fuel system, wear safety glasses and have a fire extinguisher suitable for a class B type fire (flammable liquids) on hand.**

Always perform service procedures in a well-ventilated area to prevent a build-up of fumes.

Never work in a building containing a gas appliance with a pilot light, or any other form of naked flame. Ensure that there are no naked light bulbs or any sources of flame or sparks nearby.

Do not smoke (or allow anyone else to smoke) while in the vicinity of petrol (gasoline) or of components containing it. Remember the possible presence of vapour from these sources and move well clear before smoking.

Check all electrical equipment belonging to the house, garage or workshop where work is being undertaken (see the Safety first! section of this manual). Remember that certain electrical appliances such as drills, cutters etc. create sparks in the normal course of operation and must not be used near petrol (gasoline) or any component containing it. Again, remember the possible presence of fumes before using electrical equipment.

Always mop up any spilt fuel and safely dispose of the rag used.

Any stored fuel that is drained off during servicing work must be kept in sealed containers that are suitable for holding petrol (gasoline), and clearly marked as such; the containers themselves should be kept in a safe place. Note that this last point applies equally to the fuel tank if it is removed from the machine; also remember to keep its filler cap closed at all times.

Read the Safety first! section of this manual carefully before starting work.

On X (1999) fuel-injection models onward, residual pressure will remain in the fuel feed hose and fuel rail assembly long after the motorcycle was last used. Before disconnecting any fuel line, ensure the ignition is switched off then depressurise the fuel system (see Section 2). It is vital that no dirt or debris is not allowed to enter the fuel tank or the fuel rail assembly whilst the fuel pipes are disconnected. Any foreign matter in the fuel system components could result in injector damage/malfunction. Ensure the ignition is switched off before disconnecting or reconnecting any fuel injection system wiring connector. If a connector is disconnected or reconnected with the ignition switched on, the engine control module (ECM) may be damaged.

2 Fuel tank and fuel tap – removal and installation

![warning triangle] **Warning: Refer to the precautions given in Section 1 before starting work.**

Fuel tank – V and W (1997 and 1998) models

Removal

1 Make sure the fuel cap is secure. Remove the seat (see Chapter 8).

2 To raise the rear of the tank, first disconnect the fuel level sender wiring connector, then remove the rear mounting bolts **(see illustrations 2.14a and b)**. Pull the rear of each tank trim panel away from the tank to release the lugs from the grommets **(see illustration 2.14c)**. Get the rear wheel axle spanner and its extension handle from the toolkit. Lift the rear of the tank and fit the extension handle between it and the cutout in the tank bracket, then slot the spanner through the cutout in the tank and into the handle **(see illustrations 2.14d and e)**. Note that the tank can be raised higher by using a longer prop if there is not enough access, but always make sure that the prop is secure at each end so that there is no danger of the tank dropping.

3 To remove the tank, first raise it as described above. Turn the fuel tap OFF **(see illustration)**. Disconnect the fuel hoses and vacuum hose from the tap, noting which fits where. Also disconnect the breather and overflow hoses from their unions on the tank, again noting which fits where. Remove the prop and lower the tank, then draw it back and carefully lift it off the frame, noting how the front mounting lug rubbers locate **(see illustration 2.15e and f)**. Take care not to lose the lug rubbers.

4 Check all the tank rubbers for signs of damage or deterioration and replace them with new ones if necessary.

Installation

5 Installation is the reverse of removal. Check that the tank mounting rubbers are fitted and in good condition. Make sure all the hoses are securely connected. Start the engine and

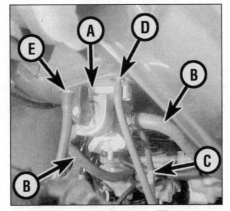

2.3 Fuel tap (A), fuel hoses (B), vacuum hose (C), breather hose (D) and overflow hose (E)

2.8 Fuel tap mounting bolts (arrowed)

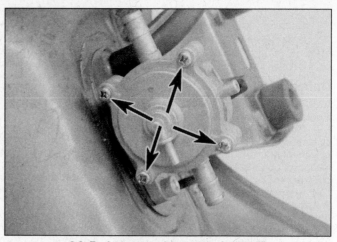

2.9 Fuel tap assembly screws (arrowed)

check that there is no sign of fuel leakage. Do not forget to turn the fuel tap ON before lowering and securing the rear of the tank (see illustration 2.3).

Fuel tap – V and W (1997 and 1998) models

Removal

6 If the tap is faulty, it can be disassembled and inspected. The most likely problem is a hole or split in the diaphragm. Before removing and dismantling the tap, check that the vacuum hose is securely attached at both ends, and that there are no splits or cracks in the hose. If in doubt, attach a spare hose to the vacuum union on the tap and apply a vacuum to the hose. If fuel does not flow through the tap (make sure it is turned ON), remove it and disassemble it to check the diaphragm. No individual components are available for the tap (except the strainer), so if it is faulty an new one must be installed.

7 Remove the fuel tank as described above. Connect drain hoses to the fuel hose unions (or connect a single hose to one union and block the other using a suitable plug) and insert the end(s) in a container suitable that is large enough for storing the petrol. Turn the fuel tap to the ON position, then attach a suitable hose to the vacuum union and apply a vacuum to allow the tank to drain.

8 Unscrew the two bolts securing the tap and withdraw it from the tank (see illustration). Withdraw the strainer as well and discard its O-ring as a new one should be used.

9 If the fuel tap has been leaking, tightening the assembly screws may help (see illustration). Slacken all the screws a little first, then tighten them evenly a little at a time to ensure the cover seats properly on the tap body. If leakage persists, the tap should be replaced with a new one, however nothing is lost by dismantling it for further inspection. Undo the screws and disassemble the tap, noting how the components fit. Inspect all

components for wear or damage. Hold the diaphragm up to a light to check for splits or holes. According to Honda's parts fiche, individual components are not available for the tap (except the strainer and O-ring), however their manual suggests that a new diaphragm, holder, spring and cover are available as a set. When assembling the tap, the air vent pipe in the diaphragm holder and the vacuum hose union on the cover must point down (i.e. away from the tank).

10 Clean the strainer to remove all traces of dirt and fuel sediment and check it for holes. If any are found, replace it with a new one.

Installation

11 Fit a new O-ring onto the strainer and insert it in the tank. Install the fuel tap, making sure it locates correctly over the strainer, and tighten the bolts (see illustration 2.8).

12 Install the fuel tank (see above).

Fuel tank – X (1999) models onward

Removal

Note: Due to the arrangement of the fuel delivery and return system, which has no manual tap and no self sealing valves on the hoses, removing the tank involves a certain amount of unavoidable fuel spillage, which is

obviously dangerous. Refer to the precautions given in Section 1 before starting work, and have plenty of rag on hand to mop up fuel spills. Once the fuel hoses have been disconnected their ends should be blocked to prevent the tank from draining itself – a nut and bolt with sealing washers, or a suitably tight section of hose, can be used to block the supply hose banjo eye.

Once the tank has been removed, store it upside down, resting it on some soft rag to prevent damaging the paintwork, and make sure the hose ends are above the level of the tank. Try to time the removal procedure with a near empty tank, which makes it much easier to lift, and means less fuel will be spilt in the event of something not going quite according to plan! To avoid unnecessary spillage, the best thing to do is to completely drain the tank before removing it. Obtain a suitable container for storing the petrol, and release the fuel pressure first, then drain the tank via the fuel return hose, disconnecting it from the fuel rail rather than the tank (see below).

13 Make sure the fuel cap is secure. Remove the seat (see Chapter 8).

14 To raise the rear of the tank, first disconnect the fuel level sensor wiring connector, then remove the rear mounting bolts (see illustrations). Pull the rear of each

2.14a Disconnect the wiring connector . . .

2.14b . . . then unscrew the two bolts (arrowed)

2.14c Carefully release the trim panels from the tank, then raise it at the back . . .

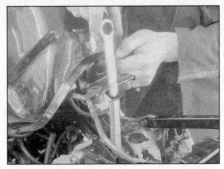

2.14d and locate the tools as described and shown . . .

2.14e . . . to form a prop

tank trim panel away from the tank to release the lugs from the grommets (see illustration). Get the rear wheel axle spanner and its extension handle from the toolkit. Lift the rear of the tank and fit the extension handle between it and the cutout in the tank bracket, then slot the spanner through the cutout in the tank and into the handle (see illustrations). Note that the tank can be raised higher by using a longer prop if there is not enough access, but always make sure that the prop is secure at each end so that there is no danger of the tank dropping.

15 To remove the tank, the fuel pressure must first be released and the residual fuel in the supply line drained off. Raise the tank as described above. Remove the battery (see Chapter 9). Disconnect the fuel pump wiring connector (see illustration). Place a rag and a suitable container for catching the residual fuel under the fuel supply hose union, then slowly slacken the pressure release bolt in the centre of the union (not the union bolt itself) until you hear a hissing sound (see illustration). At this point the fuel will spray out, so be ready with the rag to prevent it doing so. After the initial pressure has been reduced the bolt can be slackened a little further to allow the residual fuel to flow out. Once the pressure has been released, tighten

the bolt. As mentioned above (see Note), it is best to now fully drain the tank. To do this, place some fresh rag under the right-hand end of the fuel rail and position a suitable container very close by so that the return hose end can be placed in it. Release the clamp securing the return hose to the fuel rail, then detach it and place it immediately into the container, and allow the tank to drain (see illustration). Now place some fresh rag under the left-hand end of the fuel rail, then unscrew the nut securing the banjo union and draw it off the fuel rail, noting its alignment and the sealing washers, and being prepared for some more residual fuel (see illustration). Fit the

2.15a Disconnect the pump wiring connector (arrowed)

2.15b Pressure release bolt (A), breather hose (B) and overflow hose (C)

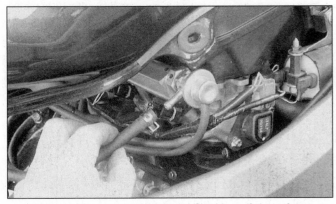

2.15c Disconnect the fuel return hose from the regulator

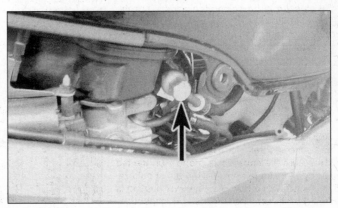

2.15d Unscrew the nut (arrowed) and detach the feed hose, noting the washers

2.15e Carefully remove the tank . . .

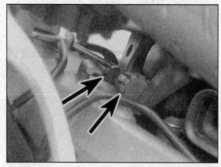

2.15f . . . noting how the rubbers (arrowed)
locate

from the tank union, again use new sealing washers, then fit the neck of the hose between the lugs and tighten the bolt to the specified torque.

18 Make sure the return hose clamps are in good condition and use new ones if they have deformed or weakened. Check that the tank mounting rubbers are fitted and in good condition. Make sure all the hoses are securely connected. Start the engine and check that there is no sign of fuel leakage.

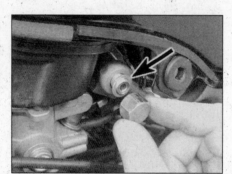

2.17a Fit a new sealing washer (arrowed),
then the feed hose . . .

2.17b . . . followed by another sealing
washer (arrowed) and the nut

nut back onto the fuel rail stud. If you haven't drained the tank, block the banjo eye on the end of the hose using a nut, bolt (M12 x 30 mm, 1.75 pitch) and the sealing washers, or a short length of the correct width hose, and block the end of the return hose using a suitable bolt or plug (using a hose clamp is not that successful as the hose is quite stiff and therefore difficult to seal, and there is always the possibility of cracking it, though a pair of long-nose mole grips with a large socket over each nose section might work – see *Tools and Workshop Tips* (Section 9) in the Reference Section). Disconnect the breather and overflow hoses from their unions on the tank, noting which fits where **(see illustration 2.15b)**. Remove the prop and lower the tank, then draw it back and carefully lift it off the frame, noting how the front

mounting lug rubbers locate **(see illustrations)**. If there is fuel in the tank, place it upside down on some clean soft rag. Take care not to lose the lug rubbers.

16 Check all the tank rubbers for signs of damage or deterioration and replace them with new ones if necessary.

Installation

17 Installation is the reverse of removal. Before installing the tank, unscrew the pressure release bolt again **(see illustration 2.15b)**, then fit a new sealing washer and tighten the bolt to the torque setting specified at the beginning of the Chapter. Use new sealing washers on each side of the supply hose banjo union and tighten the union nut to the specified torque **(see illustrations)**. If the supply hose was removed

3 Fuel tank –
cleaning and repair

1 All repairs to the fuel tank should be carried out by a professional who has experience in this critical and potentially dangerous work. Even after cleaning and flushing of the fuel system, explosive fumes can remain and ignite during repair of the tank.

2 If the fuel tank is removed from the bike, it should not be placed in an area where sparks or open flames could ignite the fumes coming out of the tank. Be especially careful inside garages where a natural gas-type appliance is located, because the pilot light could cause an explosion.

4 Air filter housing –
removal and installation

Removal

1 Remove the fuel tank (see Section 2).

2 Displace the ignition coil from each side of the air filter housing by unscrewing its nuts on V and W (1997 and 1998) models, or bolt on X (1999) models onward **(see illustrations)**. On V and W (1997 and 1998) models, free the wiring from the clips on the rim of the housing **(see illustration)**.

3 Release the clamp securing the crankcase breather hose to the housing and detach the

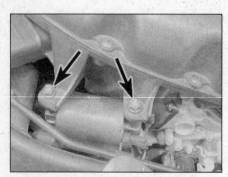

4.2a Coil mounting nuts (arrowed) –
V and W (1997 and 1998) models

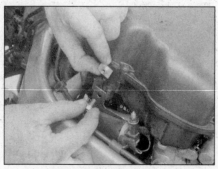

4.2b Coil mounting bolt and captive nut –
X, Y and 1 (1999 to 2001) models

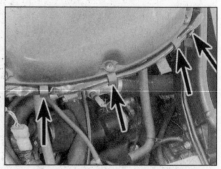

4.2c On V and W (1997 and 1998) models,
release the wiring from the clips (arrowed)

4.3a Disconnect the crankcase breather hose . . .

4.3b . . . the PAIR system hose (where fitted) . . .

4.3c . . . and the carburettor breather hose (carburettor models)

hose **(see illustration)**. On UK X (1999) models onward, and all US, Swiss and Austrian models, also detach the PAIR system hose **(see illustration)**. On V and W (1997 and 1998) models, detach the carburettor breather hose from the housing **(see illustration)**. Note that if any of the hoses are difficult to pull off their unions while the housing is still in situ, detach them after it has been lifted slightly off the carburettors or throttle bodies. On California models, displace the EVAP system purge control valve and solenoid valve from the rear of the housing.

4 On V and W (1997 and 1998) models, undo the clamp screws securing the filter housing to the carburettors **(see illustration)**. Lift the

housing up off the carburettors and remove it **(see illustration 4.3c)**.

5 On X (1999) models onward, remove the air filter (see Chapter 1). Undo the air funnel/filter housing mounting screws and remove the funnels, noting which fits where **(see illustrations)**. Lift the housing up off the throttle bodies, releasing the air ducts at the front as you do, and remove it **(see illustration)**.

Installation

6 Installation is the reverse of removal. On X (1999) models onward, check the condition of the throttle body O-rings and use new ones if they are in any way damaged or deteriorated **(see illustration)**. Fit the longer air intake

funnels above the middle (Nos. 2 and 3) throttle bodies (each funnel pair is marked L or R to denote which side it fits on) **(see illustration 4.5b)**. On all models check the condition of the various hoses and their clamps and use new ones if they are in any way damaged or deteriorated.

5 Fuel/air mixture adjustment – general information

Note: *This information only applies to carburettor-equipped engines, the V and W (1997 and 1998) models.*

4.4 Slacken the clamps (arrowed) and ease the housing off the carburettors

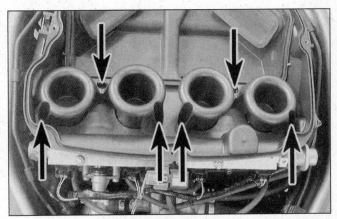

4.5a Undo the screws . . .

4.5b . . . and remove the funnels . . .

4.5c . . . and the housing

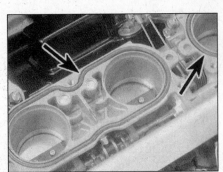

4.6 Replace the throttle body O-rings (arrowed) with new ones if necessary

Adjustment

1 If the engine runs extremely rough at idle or continually stalls, and if a carburettor overhaul does not cure the problem (and it definitely is a carburation problem – see Section 6), the pilot screws may require adjustment. It is worth noting at this point that unless you have the experience to carry this out on a multi-cylinder machine it is best to entrust the task to a motorcycle dealer, tuner or fuel systems specialist. Note that you will need a long thin flexible drive screwdriver with an angled end to access the pilot screws **(see illustration 8.11)**.

2 Before adjusting the pilot screws, warm the engine up to normal working temperature. Stop the engine and remove the tank (see Section 2). Screw in all four pilot screws until they seat lightly, then back them out to the number of turns specified (see this Chapter's Specifications). This is the base position for adjustment.

3 Arrange a temporary fuel supply using an auxiliary tank and some hosing. Start the engine and reset the idle speed to the correct level (see Chapter 1). Working on the carburettor for cylinder no. 3 first, turn the pilot screw by a small amount either side of the base position to find the point at which the highest consistent idle speed is obtained. Now do the same for the other three cylinders. Blip the throttle open a couple of times, then readjust the idle speed to the specified figure.

4 Turn the pilot screw on cylinder no. 3 carburettor in so that the idle speed drops by 50 rpm, then readjust the idle speed. Now turn the pilot screw in again so that the idle speed drops by 50 rpm, then turn the screw out by the following amount:

Swiss and Northern European
  market models . . . . ½ turn
US 49-state and Canadian
  market models . . . . ¾ turn
All other market models . . . . .1 turn

5 Repeat Step 4 on cylinder nos. 1, 2 and 4 carburettors.

Note: *For US models that will be used continuously above an altitude of 2000m, the pilot screws should be set 3/4 turn in from their standard position.*

Restrictions

6 Due to the increased emphasis on controlling exhaust emissions in certain world markets, regulations have been formulated which prevent adjustment of the air/fuel mixture. On such models the pilot screw positions are pre-set at the factory and in some cases have a limiter cap fitted to prevent tampering. Where adjustment is possible, it can only be made in conjunction with an exhaust gas analyser to ensure that the machine does not exceed the emissions regulations.

6 Carburettor overhaul – general information

Note: *This information only applies to the V and W (1997 and 1998) models.*

1 Poor engine performance, hesitation, hard starting, stalling, flooding and backfiring are all signs that major carburettor maintenance may be required.

2 Keep in mind that many so-called carburettor problems are really not carburettor problems at all, but mechanical problems within the engine or ignition system malfunctions. Try to establish for certain that the carburettors are in need of maintenance before beginning a major overhaul.

3 Check the fuel tap and strainer, the fuel and vacuum hoses, the intake manifold joint clamps, the air filter, the ignition system, the spark plugs and carburettor synchronisation before assuming that a carburettor overhaul is required.

4 Most carburettor problems are caused by dirt particles, varnish and other deposits which build up in and block the fuel and air passages. Also, in time, gaskets and O-rings

shrink or deteriorate and cause fuel and air leaks which lead to poor performance.

5 When overhauling the carburettors, disassemble them completely and clean the parts thoroughly with a carburettor cleaning solvent and dry them with filtered, unlubricated compressed air. Blow through the fuel and air passages with compressed air to force out any dirt that may have been loosened but not removed by the solvent. Once the cleaning process is complete, reassemble the carburettor using new gaskets and O-rings.

6 Before disassembling the carburettors, make sure you have all necessary O-rings and other parts, some carburettor cleaner, a supply of clean rags, some means of blowing out the carburettor passages and a clean place to work. It is recommended that only one carburettor be overhauled at a time to avoid mixing up parts.

7 Carburettors – removal and installation

Note: *This information only applies to the V and W (1997 and 1998) models.*

 Warning: Refer to the precautions given in Section 1 before starting work.

Removal

1 Remove the fuel tank and the air filter housing (see Sections 2 and 4).

2 Detach the throttle and choke cables from the carburettors (see Sections 20 and 21). There is no need to detach them from the handlebar end as well.

3 Disconnect the throttle position sensor wiring connector **(see illustration)**.

4 On California models, Swiss and Austrian models, disconnect the air cut-off valve hose from the right-hand end of the carburettors.

5 Release the idle speed adjuster from its holder and feed it through to the base of the carburettors **(see illustration)**.

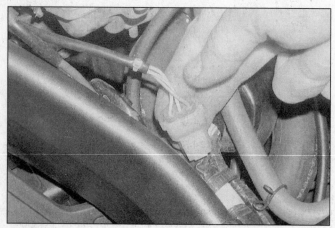

7.3 Disconnect the throttle position sensor wiring connector

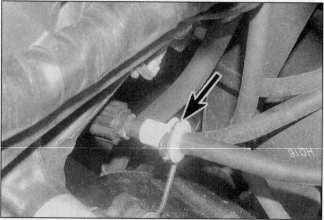

7.5 Release the idle speed adjuster from its holder (arrowed)

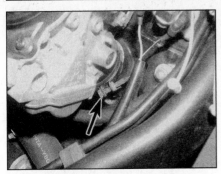

7.6a Slacken the lower clamp screw (arrowed) on each carburettor . . .

7.6b . . . and ease the carburettors up off the cylinder head

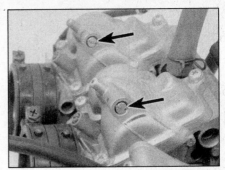

7.7 Carburettor drain screws (arrowed)

6 Fully slacken the lower clamps on the cylinder head intake manifold rubbers **(see illustration)**. Ease the carburettors up off the intakes, noting that they are quite a tight fit, and remove them along with the manifold rubbers **(see illustration)**. **Note:** *Keep the carburettors upright to prevent fuel spillage from the float chambers and the possibility of the piston diaphragms being damaged.* **Caution: Stuff clean rag into each cylinder head intake after removing the** *carburettors to prevent anything from falling in.*

7 Place a suitable container below the float chambers, then slacken the drain screw on each chamber in turn and drain all the fuel from the carburettors **(see illustration)**. Discard the drain screw O-rings as new ones must be used. Once all the fuel has been drained, fit the new O-rings and tighten the drain screws securely.

8 If necessary, slacken the clamps securing the manifold rubbers to the carburettors and remove them, noting which way up and round they fit.

Installation

9 Installation is the reverse of removal, noting the following.

a) *Check for cracks or splits in the cylinder head intake manifold rubbers and the various hoses, and replace them with new ones if necessary.*

b) *If removed, make sure the manifold rubbers are installed with the CARB UP marking facing up and towards the carburettor, aligning the slotted tab on the side with the projection on the carburettor, and that they are full engaged. Tighten the clamps so that the gap between the clamp ends is 11 to 13 mm.*

c) *Make sure the manifold rubbers are fully engaged with the cylinder head when the carburettors are installed and the clamps are securely tightened.*

d) *Make sure all hoses are correctly routed and secured and not trapped or kinked.*

e) *Check the operation of the throttle and choke cables and adjust them as necessary (see Chapter 1).*

f) *Check idle speed and carburettor synchronisation and adjust as necessary (see Chapter 1).*

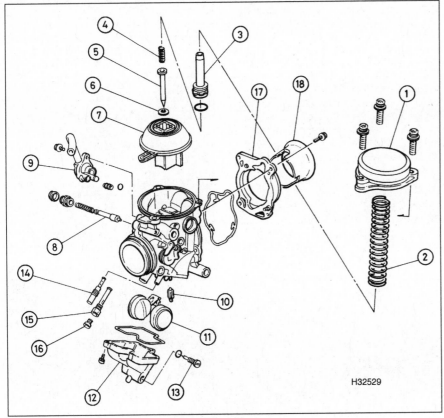

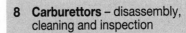

8.1 Carburettor components

1 Top cover	7 Diaphragm/piston	13 Drain screw
2 Spring	8 Choke valve	14 Pilot jet
3 Jet needle holder	9 Air cut-off valve	15 Needle jet holder
4 Spring	10 Float needle valve	16 Main jet
5 Jet needle	11 Float	17 Air funnel holder
6 Washer	12 Float chamber	18 Air funnel

H32529

8 Carburettors – disassembly, cleaning and inspection

Note: *This information only applies to the V and W (1997 and 1998) models.*

⚠️ **Warning: Refer to the precautions given in Section 1 before starting work.**

Disassembly

1 Remove the carburettors from the machine (see Section 7) **(see illustration)**. **Note:** *Do not separate the carburettors unless absolutely necessary; each carburettor can be dismantled sufficiently for all normal cleaning and adjustments while joined together. Dismantle each carburettor separately to avoid interchanging parts.*

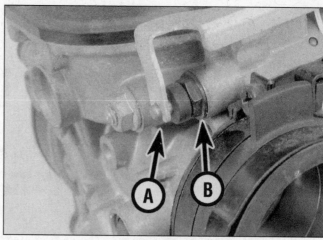

8.2a Release the return spring (A), then undo the screws (B)

8.2b Note how the bar locates onto each choke plunger end (A). Choke plunger nut (B)

2 Release the end of the choke linkage bar return spring from the bar, noting how it locates **(see illustration)**. Remove the screws securing the bar to the carburettors, noting the plastic washers. Lift off the bar, noting how it fits, and remove the collars and return spring, noting how the other end locates **(see illustration)**. Unscrew the choke plunger nut, using a pair of thin nosed pliers if access is too restricted for a spanner, and withdraw the plunger assembly from the carburettor body.
3 Unscrew and remove the top cover retaining screws **(see illustration)**. Lift off the

cover and remove the spring from inside the piston **(see illustration)**.
4 Carefully peel the diaphragm away from its sealing groove in the carburettor and withdraw the diaphragm and piston assembly **(see illustration)**.
Caution: Do not use a sharp instrument to displace the diaphragm as it is easily damaged.
5 Thread a 4 mm screw into the top of the needle holder (one of the top cover retaining screws is ideal), then grasp the screw head using a pair of pliers and carefully draw the

holder out of the piston **(see illustrations)**. Note the spring in the base of the needle holder – it should stay in place, but take care not to lose it. Push the needle up from the bottom of the piston and withdraw it from the top together with the washer **(see illustration)**. **Note:** *The jet needle fitted as standard is fixed and does not provide a means of height adjustment. The item shown in the photograph is part of an aftermarket tuning kit and provides a means of adjustment by repositioning the E-clip in the jet needle grooves.*

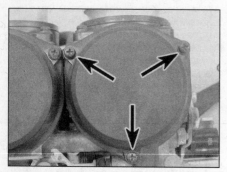

8.3a Undo the screws (arrowed) . . .

8.3b . . . and remove the cover and spring

8.4 Peel the diaphragm off the carburettor and withdraw the diaphragm and piston assembly

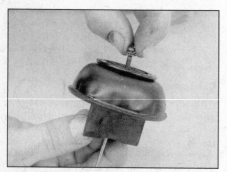

8.5a Thread the bolt into the holder . . .

8.5b . . . and draw it out of the piston

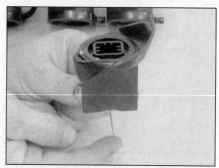

8.5c Push the needle up from the bottom and withdraw it from the top

8.6 Remove the screws (arrowed) and lift off the chamber

8.7 Remove the pilot jet (arrowed) . . .

8.8 . . . the main jet (arrowed) . . .

6 Remove the screws securing the float chamber to the base of the carburettor and remove it **(see illustration)**. Remove the rubber gasket and discard it as a new one must be used.

7 Unscrew and remove the pilot jet **(see illustration)**.

8 Unscrew and remove the main jet from the base of the needle jet holder **(see illustration)**.

9 Unscrew and remove the needle jet holder **(see illustration)**.

10 Displace the float pin using a small screwdriver and withdraw it from the pivot **(see illustration)**. Remove the float, then slide the float needle valve off, noting how it fits **(see illustrations 10.2b and a)**.

11 The pilot screw can be removed if required, but note that its setting will be disturbed (see *Haynes Hint*). Where fitted, remove the pilot screw cap – it is probably sealed in place and will need to be prised out. Unscrew and remove the pilot screw along with its spring, washer and O-ring **(see illustration)**. Discard the O-ring as a new one must be used.

HAYNES HINT *To record the pilot screw's current setting, turn the screw it in until it seats lightly, counting the number of turns necessary to achieve this, then fully unscrew it. On installation, the screw is simply backed out the number of turns you've recorded.*

12 Do not remove the throttle position sensor unnecessarily. If you do need to remove it, refer to Chapter 5.

13 Undo the screws securing the air intake funnel assembly and remove it, noting how they fit **(see illustration 10.11)**. Separate the funnel from its holder if required by twisting it to free the tabs, noting how it fits. Discard the O-ring if it is in any way damaged, deformed or deteriorated.

Cleaning

Caution: Use only a petroleum based solvent for carburettor cleaning. Don't use caustic cleaners.

14 Submerge the metal components in the solvent for approximately thirty minutes (or longer, if the directions recommend it).

15 After the carburettor has soaked long enough for the cleaner to loosen and dissolve most of the varnish and other deposits, use a nylon-bristled brush to remove the stubborn deposits. Rinse it again, then dry it with compressed air.

16 Use a jet of compressed air to blow out all of the fuel and air passages in the main and upper body, not forgetting the air jets in the carburettor intake.

Caution: Never clean the jets or passages with a piece of wire or a drill bit, as they will be enlarged, causing the fuel and air metering rates to be upset.

Inspection

17 Check the operation of the choke plunger

assembly. If it doesn't move smoothly, inspect the needle on the end of the plunger, the plunger shaft, the spring and the plunger linkage bar **(see illustration 8.1)**. Replace any component that is worn, damaged or bent – individual parts are not available.

18 If removed from the carburettor, check the tapered portion of the pilot screw and the spring and O-ring for wear or damage. Replace them with new ones if necessary.

19 Check the carburettor body, float chamber and top cover for cracks, distorted sealing surfaces and other damage. If any defects are found, replace the faulty component, although replacement of the entire carburettor will probably be necessary (check with a Honda dealer on the availability of separate components).

20 Check the piston diaphragm for splits, holes and general deterioration. Holding it up to a light will help to reveal problems of this nature.

21 Insert the piston in the carburettor body and check that it moves up-and-down smoothly. Check the surface of the piston for wear. If it's worn excessively or doesn't move smoothly in the guide, renew the components as necessary.

22 Check the jet needle for straightness by rolling it on a flat surface such as a piece of glass. Replace it with a new one if it's bent or if the tip is worn.

23 Check the tip of the float needle valve and the valve seat. If either has grooves or scratches in it, or is in any way worn, they

8.9 . . . and the needle jet holder (arrowed)

8.10 Displace the float pin (arrowed) and remove the float assembly

8.11 If required, remove the pilot screw (arrowed) along with its O-ring, washer and spring

should be renewed as a set. Gently push down on the rod on the top of the needle valve then release it – if it doesn't spring back, replace the valve with a new one.

24 Operate the throttle shaft to make sure the throttle butterfly valve opens and closes smoothly. If it doesn't, cleaning the throttle linkage may help. Otherwise, replace the carburettor with a new one.

25 Check the float for damage. This will usually be apparent by the presence of fuel inside the float. If the float is damaged, it must be replaced with a new one.

26 On California, Swiss and Austrian models, to remove the air cut-off valves, the carburettors must be separated (see Section 9). Remove the screw securing the cut-off valve and separate it from the carburettor. Remove the air jet and O-rings. Check the condition of the O-rings and discard them if

they are damaged, deformed or deteriorated. To check the valve, apply a vacuum to the hose attached to the valve cover. With the vacuum applied, air should not be able to flow between the ports in the valve. With no vacuum applied, air should be able to flow. If the valve does not behave as described, replace it with a new one.

9 Carburettors – separation and joining

Note: *This information only applies to the V and W (1997 and 1998) models.*

⚠️ *Warning: Refer to the precautions given in Section 1 before starting work.*

Separation

1 The carburettors do not need to be separated for normal overhaul. If you need to separate them (to replace a carburettor body, for example), refer to the following procedure **(see illustration)**. If required, first remove the manifold rubbers (see Section 7, Step 8), and the air intake funnels (see Section 8, Step 13).

2 Remove the carburettors from the machine (see Section 7). Mark the body of each carburettor with its cylinder number to ensure that it is positioned correctly on reassembly.

3 Remove the screws securing the choke linkage bar to the carburettors, noting the plastic washers **(see illustration 8.2a)**. Lift off the bar, noting how it fits, and remove the collars and return spring, noting how the ends locate **(see illustration 8.2b)**.

4 Make a note or sketch of the arrangement

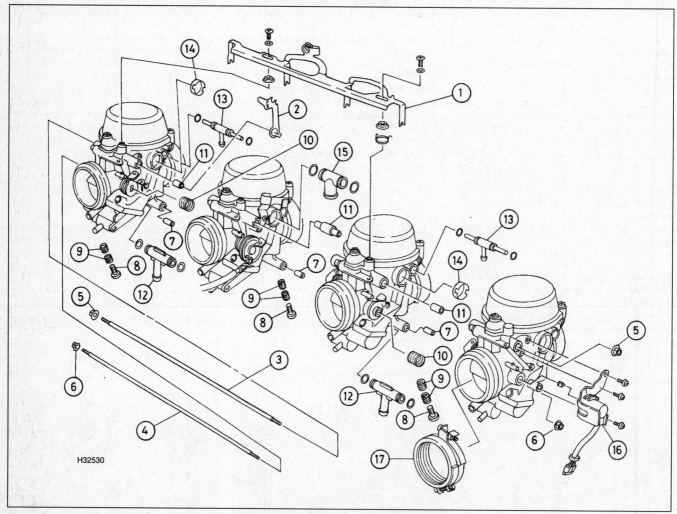

H32530

9.1 Carburettor assembly

1 Choke linkage bar
2 Choke cable bracket
3 Upper connecting bolt (6 mm)
4 Lower connecting bolt (5 mm)
5 Upper connecting bolt nuts
6 Lower connecting bolt nuts
7 Lower connecting bolt dowels
8 Synchronising screws
9 Synchronising screw springs
10 Throttle shaft springs
11 Upper connecting bolt dowels
12 Fuel joints
13 Air vent joints
14 Air joints
15 Air joint
16 Throttle position sensor
17 Intake joint

9.4a Note the positions of the various hoses . . .

9.4b . . . before detaching them

of the fuel hoses, the air vent hoses and the breather hoses, and mark them according to their union **(see illustrations)**. If required, release the clamps securing the hoses and carefully pull them off.

5 Remove the throttle position sensor (see Chapter 5).

6 Make a note of how the throttle return springs, linkage assembly and carburettor synchronisation springs are arranged to ensure that they are fitted correctly on reassembly **(see illustrations)**. Also note the arrangement of the various hose unions, joint pieces and collars, and of the cable brackets **(see illustration 9.1)**.

7 Evenly unscrew the nuts from one end of the long connecting bolts which hold the carburettors together **(see illustration)**. Withdraw the two bolts from the other end of the carburettors.

8 Carefully separate carburettor Nos. 1 and 2 from Nos. 3 and 4, so they are in two pairs. Retrieve the synchronisation spring, the dowels (noting which fits where) and the breather hose T-piece and its O-rings as they are separated.

9 Separate carburettors 1 and 2 by gently pulling them apart. Retrieve the throttle linkage spring, synchronisation spring, both

dowels, air vent T-piece, fuel T-piece and breather joint. Carry out the same procedure to separate carburettors. 3 and 4, noting the choke cable guide.

Joining

10 Assembly is the reverse of the disassembly procedure, noting the following.

a) *Use new O-rings on all the T-piece unions* **(see illustration 9.1)**.

b) *The carburettor joining bolts are different diameter; the front (engine side) bolt is 6 mm, whereas the rear (intake side) bolt is 5 mm diameter. Similarly, the dowels between each carburettor are sized accordingly. Tighten the nuts evenly to the specified torque setting, ensuring correct alignment of the carburettors, and that no more than 3 mm of bolt thread extends from the outer face of any nut.*

c) *If the manifold rubbers were removed, make sure they are installed with the CARB UP marking facing up and towards the carburettor, aligning the slotted tab on the side with the projection on the carburettor, and that they are full engaged. Tighten the clamps so that the gap between the clamp ends is 11 to 13 mm.*

d) *Check the operation of both the choke and throttle linkages ensuring that both*

operate smoothly and return quickly under spring pressure before installing the carburettors on the machine.

e) *Check carburettor synchronisation (see Chapter 1).*

10 Carburettors – reassembly and float height check

Note: *This information only applies to the V and W (1997 and 1998) models.*

⚠️ **Warning: Refer to the precautions given in Section 1 before proceeding.**

Note: *When reassembling the carburettors, be sure to use the new O-rings, gaskets and other parts supplied in the rebuild kit. Do not overtighten the carburettor jets and screws as they are easily damaged.*

1 Install the pilot screw (if removed) along with its spring, washer and O-ring, turning it in until it seats lightly **(see illustration 8.11)**. Now, turn the screw out the number of turns previously recorded on disassembly. Where removed, fit a new cap on the screw, applying a little bonding agent to hold it in position.

2 Slide the float needle valve onto the float, then position the float assembly in the

9.6a Note the arrangement of the throttle linkage . . .

9.6b . . . and the synchronisation springs and screws

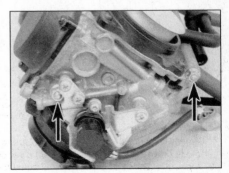

9.7 Unscrew the nuts (arrowed) and withdraw the connecting bolts

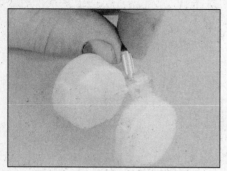

10.2a Fit the needle valve into the holder . . .

10.2b . . . then fit the float assembly, making sure the valve enters the seat (arrow) . . .

10.2c . . . and secure it with the pin

carburettor, making the needle valve locates in its seat, and install the pin, making sure it is secure **(see illustrations)**.

3 Install the needle jet holder **(see illustration)**. Screw the main jet into the end of the needle jet holder **(see illustration)**.

4 Install the pilot jet **(see illustration)**.

5 To check the float height, hold the carburettor so the float hangs down, then tilt it back until the needle valve is just seated, but not so far that the needle's spring-loaded tip is compressed. Measure the distance between the gasket face (with the gasket removed) and the bottom of the float with an accurate ruler **(see illustration)**. The correct setting should be as given in the

Specifications at the beginning of the Chapter. If it is incorrect, replace the float and needle valve with new ones – the float height is not adjustable.

6 With the float height checked, fit a new rubber gasket onto the float chamber, making sure it is seated properly in its groove, then fit the chamber onto the carburettor and tighten the screws securely **(see illustration)**.

7 Insert the jet needle into the piston, making sure the washer does not fall off **(see illustration)**. Fit a new O-ring into the groove in the needle holder and smear it with oil. Check that the spring is in the base of the needle holder, or install it if removed. Align the tabs on the holder with the slots in the piston

and insert the holder, pushing it down until the O-ring is felt to locate in its groove **(see illustration 8.5b)**. Remove the bolt used on removal from the holder, if not already done **(see illustration 8.5a)**.

8 Turn the diaphragm inside out so that its rim faces down **(see illustration 8.5a)**. Insert the piston assembly into the carburettor, ensuring the needle is correctly aligned with the needle jet **(see illustration 8.4)**. Keep a finger on the bottom of the piston to keep it raised (inserting your finger via the air intake) so the diaphragm stays inside out – this will prevent the rim popping out of the groove. Align the loop on the diaphragm rim with its groove in the carburettor body, then press the

10.3a Install the needle jet holder . . .

10.3b . . . the main jet . . .

10.4 . . . and the pilot jet

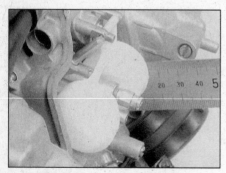

10.5 Measuring the float height

10.6 Fit a new O-ring (arrowed) and install the float chamber

10.7 Insert the jet needle into the piston

10.8 Press the diaphragm rim into the groove, making sure the loop (arrowed) locates correctly

10.9 Fit the spring into the cover then install the cover as described

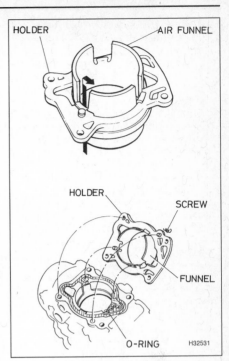

10.11 Air funnel installation

diaphragm outer edge into its groove, making sure it is correctly seated **(see illustration)**.

9 Keeping the piston raised, fit the spring, locating it over the needle holder **(see illustration 8.3b)**. Fit the top cover onto the carburettor, locating the top of the spring inside the raised section in the cover **(see illustration)**. Align the protrusion on the cover with the loop on the diaphragm. Make sure the diaphragm rim stays seated in its groove and does not get pinched by the cover, then install the cover screws and tighten them securely. You can now let the piston drop.

10 Fit the choke plunger assembly into the carburettor body and tighten the nut to secure it. Fit the return spring over its lug, and fit the plastic collars. Fit the choke linkage bar onto the plungers, making sure the slots locate correctly behind the nipple on the end of each choke plunger **(see illustration 8.2b)**. Fit the plastic washers and secure the linkage bar in place with the screws **(see illustration 8.2a)**. Hook up the linkage bar return spring.

11 If the air intake funnels were removed, use new O-rings if necessary and fit them into the groove in the intake side of each carburettor **(see illustration)**. Fit the air funnel into the holder and rotate it so that its tabs are locked in place. Align the cutouts in the air funnel with the corresponding raised lands on the intake bore, and fit the pins on the holder into the holes in the carburettor body. Tighten the four screws securely.

12 If removed, install the throttle position sensor (See Chapter 5).

13 Install the carburettors (see Section 7).

11 Fuel injection system – general information

Note: *This information only applies to X (1999) models onward.*

1 Honda's PGM-FI system has an electronic control module (ECM) that operates both the injection and ignition systems **(see illustration)**. The fuel injection side of the system is covered in this Chapter; refer to Chapter 5 for information on the ignition system.

2 The fuel pump, contained in the fuel tank, pumps fuel to the fuel rail on the throttle body assembly, via a filter. Fuel supply pressure is controlled by the pressure regulator which keeps the pressure in the fuel rail constant, returning excess fuel to the tank via the return hose. The fuel rail acts as a reservoir for the four injectors (one for each cylinder) which are operated by the Engine Control Module (ECM).

3 The engine control module (ECM) monitors signals from the following sensors.

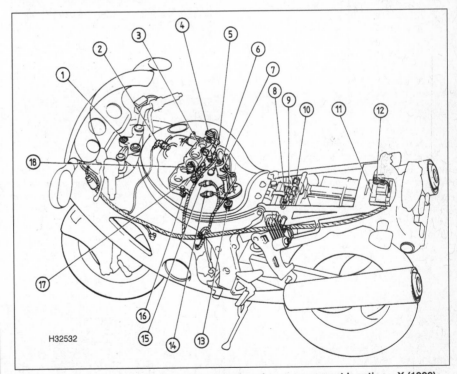

11.1 Fuel injection and engine management systems component location – X (1999) models onwards

1 Ignition (main) switch and immobiliser receiver
2 PAIR solenoid valve
3 Cam pulse generator
4 Throttle position sensor
5 Fuel pressure regulator
6 Fuel pump
7 Ignition pulse generator

8 Fuel cut-off relay
9 Engine stop relay
10 Bank angle sensor
11 ECM
12 Atmospheric pressure (BARO) sensor (X and Y models)
13 Speed sensor

14 Knock sensor
15 Coolant temperature sensor
16 Fuel injectors
17 Manifold absolute pressure (MAP) sensor
18 Intake air temperature (IAT) sensor

a) *Throttle position sensor – informs the ECM of the throttle position, and the rate of throttle opening or closing.*

b) *Coolant temperature sensor – informs the ECM of engine temperature. It also actuates the temperature gauge (see Chapter 3).*

c) *Manifold absolute pressure (MAP) sensor – informs the ECM of the engine load by monitoring the pressure in the throttle body inlet tracts.*

d) *Intake air temperature (IAT) sensor – informs the ECM of the temperature of the air entering the throttle body.*

e) *Cam pulse generator – informs the ECM of engine speed and camshaft position.*

f) *Ignition pulse generator – informs the ECM of engine speed and crankshaft position.*

g) *Atmospheric (barometric) pressure (BARO) sensor – informs the ECM of the atmospheric (barometric) pressure the motorcycle is operating in. Fitted to X and Y (1999 and 2000) models only.*

h) *Speed sensor – informs the ECM of the speed of the motorcycle (see Chapter 9).*

i) *Knock sensor – senses any abnormal vibration in the combustion chamber caused by knocking, a combustion problem that can be caused by low grade fuel. Based on the information received the ECM advances or retards the ignition to control the problem.*

j) *Oxygen sensor (only on models with catalytic converter – German and Swiss X and Y models, and all 1 models) – informs the ECM of the oxygen content of the exhaust gases.*

4 All the information from the sensors is analysed by the ECM, and from that it determines the appropriate ignition and fuelling requirements of the engine. The ECM controls the fuel injector by varying its pulse width – the length of time the injector is held open – to provide more or less fuel, as appropriate. The mixture strength (fuel/air ratio) is also constantly varied by the ECM, to provide the best setting for cold starting, warm-up, idle, cruising, and acceleration. Due to the layout of the engine, the fuelling needs for each cylinder are slightly different and the ECM is programmed to compensate for this; the injection system is fully sequential, with each injector receiving its own operating signal from the ECM.

5 Cold starting and warm up idle speeds are controlled by an 'automatic fast idle system', which basically takes the place of a manual choke lever. A heat sensitive wax-filled unit that has engine coolant circulating around it actuates the starter valve arrangement in the throttle body assembly via a linkage rod. When the coolant is cold the wax unit is contracted and the starter valves are open. As the coolant heats up the wax expands, closing the starter valves. The starter valves allow additional air to bypass the throttle valves when the throttle is closed, and this increases the engine idle speed.

6 If there is an abnormality in any of the readings obtained from any sensor, the ECM enters its back-up mode. In this event, the ECM ignores the abnormal sensor signal, and assumes a pre-programmed value which will allow the engine to continue running (albeit at reduced efficiency). If the ECM enters this back-up mode, or when any faults occur, the FI warning light in the instrument cluster will come on, and the relevant fault code will be stored in the ECM memory. The fault can be identified using the fault codes which can be accessed using the self-diagnosis function (see Section 12). However if there are certain faults detected in the injectors or the cam or ignition pulse generators, the back-up mode becomes ineffective and the ECM will not allow the engine to run at all. Note that European models have an immobiliser system (HISS – Honda Ignition Security System) which will not allow the engine to be started unless the correct key is used. A fault in this system should not be confused with a fuel injection system fault. The immobiliser system has its own fault-diagnosis function (see Chapter 5).

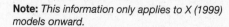

12 Fuel injection system – fault diagnosis and checking

Note: *This information only applies to X (1999) models onward.*

Fault diagnosis

1 If the fuel injection system (FI) warning light on the instrument cluster illuminates when the motorcycle is running, a fault has occurred in the fuel injection/ignition system. The engine control module (ECM) will store the relevant fault code in its memory and this code can be read as follows using the self-diagnostic mode of the ECM. While the engine is running and the motorcycle is being used, the FI light will come on and stay on. When the motorcycle is on its sidestand and the engine is running below 5000 rpm, the FI light will flash, the pattern of the flashes indicating the code for the fault the ECM has identified.

2 If the engine can be started, place the motorcycle on its sidestand then start the engine and allow it to idle. Whilst the engine is idling, observe the FI warning light on the instrument cluster.

3 If the engine cannot be started, or to check for any stored fault codes even though the FI light has not illuminated, remove the seat (see Chapter 8) to gain access to the fuel injection system service check wiring connector, which is a white 3-pin (2 wire) single sided connector inside the rubber boot close to the taillight. Ensure the ignition is switched OFF then bridge the outer terminals of the service check connector with an auxiliary wire **(see illustration)**. With the terminals connected, make sure the kill switch is in the RUN position then turn the ignition ON and observe the FI warning light. If there are no stored fault codes, the FI light will come on and stay on. If there are stored fault codes, the FI light will flash.

4 The fuel injection system warning light uses long (1.3 second) and short (0.5 second) flashes to give out the fault code. A long flash is used to indicate the first digit of a double digit fault code (i.e. 10 and above). If a single digit fault code is being displayed (i.e. 0 – 9), there will be a number of short flashes equivalent to the code being displayed. For example, two long (1.3 sec) flashes followed by five short (0.5 sec) flashes indicates the fault code number 25. If there is more than one fault code, there will be a gap before the other codes are revealed (the codes will be revealed in order, starting with the lowest and finishing with the highest). Once all codes have been revealed, the ECM will continuously run through the code(s) stored in its memory, revealing each one in turn with a short gap between them.

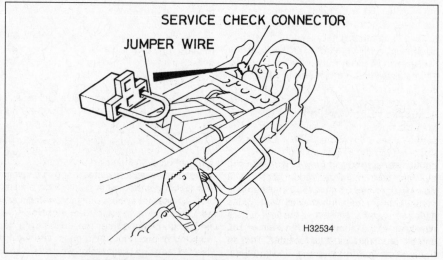

SERVICE CHECK CONNECTOR

JUMPER WIRE

H32534

12.3 Bridge between the outer terminals of the connector

Fault code (No. of flashes)	Symptoms	Possible cause
0 – no code (warning light constantly on)	Engine does not start	Blown fuse (main, engine stop or fuel pump) Faulty power supply to ECM Faulty engine stop relay Faulty engine stop switch/open circuit on switch earth (ground) wire Faulty ignition switch Faulty bank angle sensor Faulty ECM
0 – no code (warning light constantly on)	Engine runs normally	Short circuit in warning light wiring Short circuit in service check connector wiring Faulty ECM
0 – no code (warning light off)	Engine runs normally	Blown warning light bulb Open circuit in warning light wiring Faulty ECM
1	Engine runs normally	Faulty MAP sensor or wiring
2	Engine runs normally	Faulty MAP sensor/vacuum hose
7	Engine difficult to start at low temperatures	Faulty coolant temperature sensor or wiring
8	Poor throttle response	Faulty throttle position sensor or wiring
9	Engine runs normally	Faulty intake air temperature sensor or wiring
10 – (X and Y (1999 and 2000) models only)	Engine runs poorly at high altitude	Faulty atmospheric (barometric) pressure sensor or wiring
11	Engine operates normally	Faulty speed sensor or wiring
12	Engine does not start	Faulty No. 1 injector or wiring
13	Engine does not start	Faulty No. 2 injector or wiring
14	Engine does not start	Faulty No. 3 injector or wiring
15	Engine does not start	Faulty No. 4 injector or wiring
18	Engine does not start	Faulty cam pulse generator or wiring
19	Engine does not start	Faulty ignition pulse generator or wiring
20	Engine operates normally	Faulty EPROM in ECM
25	Engine operates normally	Faulty knock sensor or wiring
The following codes are only applicable to models with catalytic converter		
21	Engine operates normally	Faulty oxygen sensor
23	Engine operates normally	Faulty oxygen sensor heating element
Once all the codes have been revealed, switch off the ignition and (where necessary) remove the auxiliary wire from the service check connector. Identify the fault using the table above, then refer below on for checking procedures.		

5 Once the fault has been identified and corrected, it will be necessary to reset the system by removing the fault code from the ECM memory. To do this, ensure the ignition is switched OFF then bridge the terminals of the service check connector (see Step 3) **(see illustration 12.3)**. Turn the ignition switch ON then disconnect the auxiliary wire from the service check connector. When the wire is disconnected the FI light should come on for about five seconds, during which time the auxiliary wire must be reconnected. The warning light should start to flash when it is reconnected, indicating that all fault codes have been erased. However if the light flashes twenty times the memory has not been erased and the procedure must be repeated. Turn off the ignition then remove the auxiliary wire. Check the operation of the warning light (in some cases it may be necessary to repeat the erasing procedure more than once) then install the seat.

Checking

6 While some of the sensors can be checked using home equipment, there are others which can only be tested using the Honda special electronic diagnostic test pin box which can be plugged into the system. If a fault appears, use the diagnostic function and fault code system described above to work out which component is faulty. First ensure that the relevant system wiring connectors are securely connected and free of corrosion – poor connections are the cause of the majority of problems. Also check the wiring itself for any obvious faults or breaks, and use a continuity tester to check the wiring between its connectors, referring to the *Wiring Diagrams* at the end of Chapter 9. Next refer to Section 13 to see if there are any other specific checks that can be made on that particular component. If this fails to reveal the cause of the problem, the motorcycle should be taken to a suitably-equipped Honda dealer for testing. They will have access to the test pin box which should locate the fault quickly and simply.

7 Also ensure that the fault is not due to poor maintenance – i.e., check that the air filter element is clean, that the spark plugs are in good condition and correctly gapped, that the valve clearances are correctly adjusted, that the cylinder compression pressures are correct, and the ignition timing is correct (refer to Chapters 1, 2, 4 and 5). It is also worth removing the sensor(s) in question (see

Section 13) and checking that the sensing portion is clean and not obstructed by anything. Where there is a vacuum hose to a sensor, make sure it is securely connected at both ends and has no cracks or splits.

13 Fuel injection system components – check, removal and installation

Note: *This information only applies to X (1999) models onward.*
Caution: Ensure the ignition is switched off before disconnecting/reconnecting any fuel injection system wiring connector. If a connector is disconnected/reconnected with the ignition switched on the engine control module (ECM) could be damaged.

Fuel injectors

 Warning: Refer to the precautions given in Section 1 before starting work.

Check

1 Remove the air filter housing (see Section 7).
2 If the engine runs, start it and allow it to idle. Check the operation of each injector using a stethoscope or sounding rod; an injector will emit a 'clicking' noise when functioning **(see illustration)**. If any injector is silent, either the injector or its wiring harness are faulty. **Note:** *Reconnect the wiring connector to the intake air temperature sensor (on the air filter housing cover) to prevent the ECM detecting a fault while making the check.*
3 If the engine does not run, disconnect the

wiring connectors from the injectors **(see illustration)**. Connect an ohmmeter across the terminals of each injector and measure its resistance. Compare the readings obtained for each injector to that given in the Specifications. Also check that there is no continuity to earth on the black/white wire terminal on the injector. If the resistance of any injector differs greatly from that specified, or there is continuity to earth, the injector should be renewed. Also check for battery voltage at the black/white wire terminal in the wiring connector. If there is no voltage, check the wiring.

Removal

4 Remove the air filter housing (see Section 7). If required, remove the throttle bodies (see Section 14) – this is not essential, but will make the job less fiddly **(see illustration 15.3a)**.
5 If the throttle bodies are in situ, disconnect the wiring connectors from the injectors **(see illustration 13.3)**. Disconnect the vacuum hose from the fuel pressure regulator **(see illustration)**. Displace the MAP sensor from the fuel rail by removing its screw **(see illustration)**.
6 Counter-hold the hex on the base of the fuel rail mounting studs, then unscrew the nuts **(see illustration)**. Carefully lift off the fuel rail assembly – the injectors will probably come away with the fuel rail, but could stay in the throttle body **(see illustration 13.10)**.
7 Remove the injectors from either the fuel rail or throttle body assembly **(see illustration)**. Note the correct fitted position of the O-ring, rubber spacer and seal on each injector; the O-ring and seal must be renewed, but the spacer can be reused as long as it is not damaged, deformed or deteriorated.

Installation

8 Lubricate the new seals, spacers and O-rings with a smear of engine oil. Slide the spacer onto the top of each injector, then fit a new O-ring into the groove **(see illustration)**.
9 Ease the injectors into position in the fuel rail, taking care not to damage the O-rings **(see illustration 13.7)**. Make sure the injector wiring connector sockets are all positioned so

13.2 Using a stethoscope to check the fuel injectors

13.3 Disconnect the wiring connector from the injector and measure the resistance between the injector terminals

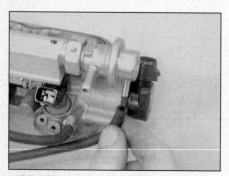
13.5a Disconnect the vacuum hose from the pressure regulator . . .

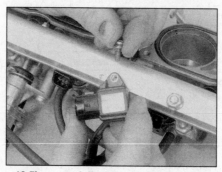
13.5b . . . and displace the MAP sensor

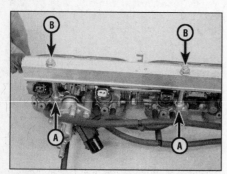
13.6 Counter-hold each stud using the hex (A) at its base and unscrew the nuts (B)

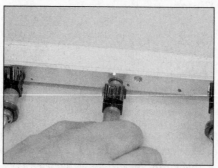
13.7 Pull each injector out of the fuel rail or throttle body as appropriate

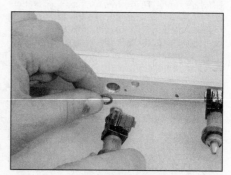
13.8 Fit a new O-ring into the groove in the top of each injector

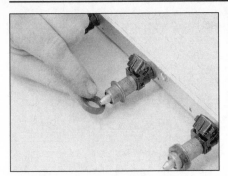

13.9 Fit a new seal onto the bottom of each injector

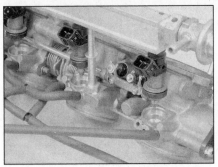

13.10a Install the fuel rail, making sure the injectors seat correctly . . .

13.10b . . . then fit the nuts and tighten them to the specified torque

they will point to the rear when the fuel rail is installed. Fit the seals onto the bottom of the injectors **(see illustration)**.

10 Install the fuel rail assembly, making sure each injector enters its throttle body and the seals stay in place and seat correctly **(see illustration)**. Fit the fuel rail nuts and tighten them to the torque setting specified at the beginning of the Chapter, counter-holding the base hex as before **(see illustration and 13.6)**.

11 Connect the vacuum tube and fit the MAP sensor **(see illustrations 13.5a and b)**. Install the throttle bodies if removed, or reconnect the injector wiring connectors **(see illustration 13.3)**.

Fuel pressure regulator

 Warning: Refer to the precautions given in Section 1 before starting work.

Check

12 Check the fuel flow rate and pressure (see Section 17).

Removal

13 Remove the fuel tank and air filter housing (see Sections 2 and 4). Remove the fuel injectors (see above).

14 Make alignment marks between the regulator and fuel rail. Clamp the rail in a vice using a rag to protect it.

15 Unscrew the regulator nut and remove the regulator from the end of the fuel rail. Note the joint piece between the regulator and the fuel rail and remove it. Discard its O-rings as new ones must be used.

13.18 Disconnect the throttle position sensor wiring connector

Installation

16 Fit new O-rings on to the joint piece. Fit the joint piece and the regulator, aligning it as marked, and tighten the nut to the torque setting specified at the beginning of the Chapter.

17 Install the fuel injectors and fuel rail (see above), then install the air filter housing and fuel tank (see Sections 2 and 4).

Throttle position sensor

Check

18 The throttle position sensor operation can only be checked using the Honda diagnostic test pin box (see Section 10). Its power supply can be checked as follows. Remove the air filter housing (see Section 4). Disconnect the wiring connector from the sensor **(see illustration)**. Connect the positive (+) lead of a voltmeter to the yellow/red terminal of the sensor wiring connector, then connect the negative (–) lead to a good earth. Turn the ignition switch ON and check that a voltage of 4.75 to 5.25 volts is present. If it isn't, there is a fault in the yellow/red wire or the ECM. Now connect the negative lead to the green/orange terminal of the connector and check that the same voltage is present. If it isn't, there is a fault in the green/orange wire or the ECM. If there is voltage, check for continuity to earth in the red/yellow wire. If there is, trace the fault in the wire and repair it. If there isn't, and the sensor is proven good by the Honda tester, then the ECM is faulty.

13.20 The coolant temperature sensor (arrowed) screws into the thermostat housing

Removal and installation

19 The throttle position sensor is an integral part of the throttle body assembly and is not available separately. If the sensor is faulty, the complete throttle body assembly will have to be renewed.

Coolant temperature sensor

Note: *The sensor also operates the coolant temperature gauge (see Chapter 3).*

Check

20 Remove the fuel tank (See Section 2). The sensor is mounted in the thermostat housing on the back of the engine **(see illustration)**.

21 Disconnect the wiring connector from the sensor. With the engine cold, connect an ohmmeter across the sensor pink and green/orange terminals and measure its resistance. Compare the reading obtained to that given in the Specifications noting that the specified value is only valid at 20°C (68°F); the sensor resistance will increase at lower temperatures and decrease at higher temperatures. If the resistance reading differs greatly from that specified, the sensor is probably faulty.

22 If the sensor appears to be functioning correctly, check its power supply. Connect the positive (+) lead of a voltmeter to the pink terminal of the sensor wiring connector, then connect the negative (–) lead to a good earth. Turn the ignition switch ON and check that a voltage of 4.75 to 5.25 volts is present. If it isn't, there is a fault in the pink wire or the ECM. Now connect the negative lead to the green/orange terminal of the connector and check that the same voltage is present. If it isn't, there is a fault in the green/orange wire or the ECM. If there is voltage, the ECM is probably faulty.

Removal

 Warning: The engine must be completely cool before carrying out this procedure.

23 Drain the cooling system (see Chapter 1). Remove the fuel tank (See Section 2). The sensor is mounted in the thermostat housing **(see illustration 13.20)**.

24 Disconnect the sensor wiring connector.

Unscrew the sensor and remove it from the housing. Discard the sealing washer.

Installation

25 Fit a new sealing washer onto the sensor. Install the sensor in the thermostat housing and tighten it securely. Connect the sensor wiring.
26 Install the fuel tank (see Chapter 4) and refill the cooling system (see Chapter 1).

Manifold absolute pressure (MAP) sensor

Check

27 The MAP sensor can only be checked using the Honda diagnostic test pin box (see Sections 11 and 12). However you can raise the fuel tank (see Section 2) and make sure that the vacuum hose to it is securely fixed at both ends, and has no cracks or splits. The sensor is mounted on the fuel rail **(see illustration 13.29)**.

Removal

28 Raise or remove the fuel tank (see Section 2).
29 Disconnect the wiring connector and vacuum hose from the MAP sensor, which is mounted on the fuel rail **(see illustration)**. Undo the retaining screw and remove the sensor.

Installation

30 Installation is the reverse of removal.

Intake air temperature (IAT) sensor

Check

31 Raise or remove the fuel tank (see Section 2). The sensor is mounted in the rear of the air filter housing. Disconnect its wiring connector **(see illustration)**.
32 With the sensor cold, connect an ohmmeter across the sensor terminals and measure its resistance. Compare the reading obtained to that given in the Specifications noting that the specified value is only valid at 20°C (68°F); the sensor resistance will increase at lower temperatures and decrease at higher temperatures. If the resistance reading differs greatly from that specified, the sensor is probably faulty.
33 If the sensor appears to be functioning correctly, check its power supply. Connect the positive (+) lead of a voltmeter to the grey/blue terminal of the sensor wiring connector, then connect the negative (–) lead to a good earth. Turn the ignition switch ON and check that a voltage of 4.75 to 5.25 volts is present. If it isn't, there is a fault in the grey/blue wire or the ECM. Now connect the negative lead to the green/orange terminal of the connector and check that the same voltage is present. If it isn't, there is a fault in the green/orange wire or the ECM. If there is voltage, the ECM is probably faulty.

13.29 Disconnect the wiring connector and the vacuum tube from the MAP sensor

Removal

34 Raise or remove the fuel tank (see Section 2). The sensor is mounted in the rear of the air filter housing.
35 Disconnect the sensor wiring connector **(see illustration 13.31)**. Undo the retaining screws and remove the sensor from the housing.

Installation

36 Installation is the reverse of removal.

Cam pulse generator

Check

37 Raise or remove the fuel tank (see Section 2).
38 Trace the wiring back from the sensor, which is on the right-hand end of the cylinder head, to its white 2-pin wiring connector inside the rubber boot above the crankcase and disconnect it **(see illustration)**. Perform the following check(s).
39 Using an ohmmeter check for continuity between each of the connector terminals and earth (ground). If there is continuity between either of the connector terminals and earth (ground) then the cam pulse generator is faulty.
40 Connect the positive (+) lead of a voltmeter and peak voltage adapter arrangement* to the white/yellow terminal of the cam pulse generator connector and the negative (–) lead to the grey terminal of the

13.38 Disconnect the cam pulse generator wiring connector

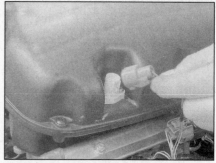

13.31 Disconnect the IAT sensor wiring connector

connector. Turn the engine over on the starter motor and note the voltage reading obtained. If this reading is below the specified minimum, the cam pulse generator is faulty. *Note: Honda specify their own Imrie diagnostic tester (model 625), or the peak voltage adapter (Pt. No. 07HGJ-0020100) with an aftermarket digital multimeter having an impedance of 10 M-ohm/DCV minimum for this test.*
41 If the cam pulse generator functions correctly then the fault must be in the wiring harness or the ECM, and can be located by a Honda dealer with the test pin box.

Removal

42 Remove the right-hand fairing side panel (see Chapter 8). Raise or remove the fuel tank (see Section 2).
43 Trace the wiring back from the sensor, which is on the right-hand end of the cylinder head, to its white 2-pin wiring connector inside the rubber boot above the crankcase and disconnect it **(see illustration 13.38)**. Feed the wiring through to the pulse generator, noting its routing.
44 Unscrew the three bolts securing the cam pulse generator mounting plate to the cylinder head and draw it off **(see illustrations)**. Discard the gasket, and the sealing washers if they are damaged or deformed. Note the locating pins and remove them for safekeeping if they are loose.
45 Unscrew the two bolts securing the pulse

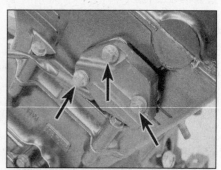

13.44 Unscrew the bolts (arrowed) and draw the sensor assembly out of the engine

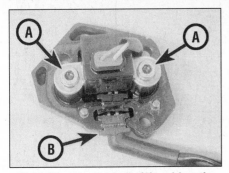

13.45 Unscrew the bolts (A) and free the wiring grommet (B)

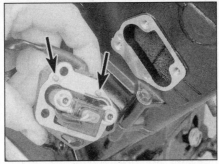

13.47a Fit the locating pins (arrowed) and a new gasket . . .

13.47b . . . then install the sensor

13.47c Use new sealing washers if necessary

generator, then free the wiring grommet **(see illustration)**.

Installation

46 Fit the pulse generator onto the mounting plate and tighten its bolts securely **(see illustration 13.45)**. Apply a suitable sealant to the wiring grommet and fit it into its cutout.

47 Fit the locating pins into the mounting plate if removed, then fit a new gasket **(see illustration)**. Install the sensor mounting plate and secure it with the bolts, using new sealing washers if necessary, and tighten them to the torque setting specified at the beginning of the Chapter **(see illustrations)**.

48 Feed the wiring back to the connector and reconnect it **(see illustration 13.38)**. Install the fairing side panel and the fuel tank.

Ignition pulse generator

Check

49 Raise or remove the fuel tank (see Section 2).

50 Trace the wiring back from the sensor, which is mounted in the timing rotor cover on the right-hand side of the engine, to its red 2-pin wiring connector inside the rubber boot above the crankcase and disconnect it **(see illustration)**. Perform the following check(s).

51 Using an ohmmeter check for continuity between each of the connector terminals and earth (ground). If there is continuity between either of the connector terminals and earth (ground) then the ignition pulse generator is faulty.

52 Connect the positive (+) lead of a

voltmeter and peak voltage adapter arrangement* to the yellow terminal of the ignition pulse generator connector and the negative (–) lead to the white/yellow terminal of the connector. Turn the engine over on the starter motor and note the voltage reading obtained. If this reading is below the specified minimum, the ignition pulse generator is faulty. ***Note:** Honda specify their own Imrie diagnostic tester (model 625), or the peak voltage adapter (Pt. No. 07HGJ-0020100) with an aftermarket digital multimeter having an impedance of 10 M-ohm/DCV minimum for this test.*

53 If the cam pulse generator functions correctly then the fault must be in the wiring harness or the ECM, and can be located by a Honda dealer with the test pin box.

Removal

54 Remove the right-hand fairing side panel (see Chapter 8). Raise or remove the fuel tank (see Section 2).

55 Trace the wiring back from the sensor, which is mounted in the timing rotor cover on the right-hand side of the engine, to its red 2-pin wiring connector inside the rubber boot above the crankcase and disconnect it **(see illustration 13.50)**.

56 Working evenly in a criss-cross pattern,

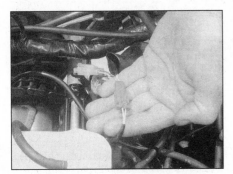

13.50 Disconnect the ignition pulse generator wiring connector

13.56 Unscrew the bolts (arrowed) and remove the cover

unscrew the timing rotor cover bolts **(see illustration)**. Remove the cover, being prepared to catch any residual oil. Discard the gasket as a new one must be used. Remove the dowels if they are loose.

57 Undo the sensor mounting bolts, then free the wiring grommet from the cover and remove the sensor **(see illustration)**.

Installation

58 Remove all traces of sealant from the sensor wiring grommet and timing rotor cover and apply a smear of fresh sealant to the grommet.

59 Locate the grommet and sensor correctly in the cover and tighten the bolts securely **(see illustration 13.57)**.

60 Apply a smear of a suitable sealant 10 to 15 mm either side of the crankcase joints on the mating surface with the timing rotor cover.

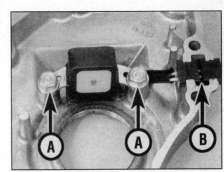

13.57 Unscrew the bolts (A) and free the wiring grommet (B)

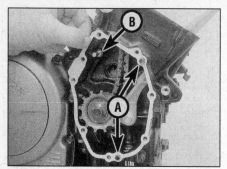

13.60a Install the dowels (A), and check that the plug (B) is in situ, then fit a new gasket onto the dowels . . .

13.60b . . . and install the cover

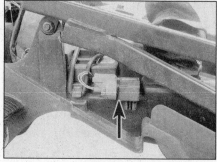

13.61 Atmospheric pressure sensor (arrowed)

Fit the cover dowels into the crankcase if removed, and check that the sealing plug is installed, then fit a new gasket **(see illustration)**. Install the cover, making sure it locates correctly onto the dowels **(see illustration)**. Apply the sealant to the threads of the bolts that fit into the upper rear holes that are marked with a triangle. Tighten the bolts evenly in a criss-cross pattern to the specified torque setting.

Atmospheric (barometric) pressure (BARO) sensor – X and Y (1999 and 2000) models only

Check

61 Remove the seat cowling (see Chapter 8). The sensor is mounted on the rear of the sub-frame on the right-hand side **(see illustration)**. Disconnect its wiring connector.
62 The sensor can only be checked using the Honda diagnostic test pin box (see Section 10). Its power supply can be checked as follows. Connect the positive (+) lead of a voltmeter to the yellow/red terminal of the sensor wiring connector, then connect the negative (–) lead to a good earth. Turn the ignition switch ON and check that a voltage of 4.75 to 5.25 volts is present. If it isn't, there is a fault in the yellow/red wire or the ECM. Now connect the negative lead to the green/orange terminal of the connector and check that the same voltage is present. If it isn't, there is a fault in the green/orange wire or the ECM. Now connect the positive lead to the light green/black terminal of the connector and check that the same voltage is present. If it

isn't, there is a fault in the light green/black wire or the ECM. If there is voltage, and the sensor is proven good by the Honda tester, then the ECM is faulty.

Removal

63 Remove the seat cowling (see Chapter 8). The sensor is mounted on the rear of the sub-frame on the right-hand side **(see illustration 13.61)**.
64 Disconnect the wiring connector then undo the retaining screw and remove the sensor.

Installation

65 Installation is the reverse of removal.

Speed sensor

66 See Chapter 9, Section 16.

Bank angle sensor

Check

67 Position the motorcycle on its centrestand and remove the seat (see Chapter 8). The bank angle sensor is mounted behind the battery **(see illustration)**.
68 With the ignition switch on, connect the negative (–) lead of a voltmeter to the green terminal of the bank angle sensor connector (the connector must still be connected). Connect the voltmeter positive (+) lead first to

the white terminal and check that battery voltage (approximately 12 volts) is present then connect it to the red/white terminal and check that between 0 to 1 volt is present.
69 Switch the ignition off then remove the retaining screws and free the bank angle sensor from its mounting. Hold the sensor horizontal and switch the ignition on; the engine stop relay (located behind the battery) should click. Slowly tilt the sensor to the left whilst listening to the engine stop relay; once the sensor reaches an angle of approximately 60° the relay should be heard to click (indicating power supply is open). Switch the ignition off and return the sensor to the horizontal, then switch the ignition back on again (engine stop relay should click again) and tilt the sensor to the right. The engine stop relay should be heard to click again once the sensor reaches an angle of around 60°.
70 If voltage readings/relay performance are not as given, then it is likely the bank angle sensor is faulty.

Removal

71 Remove the seat (see Chapter 8). The bank angle sensor is mounted behind the battery **(see illustration 13.67)**.
72 Disconnect the bank angle sensor wiring connector then slacken and remove the retaining screws and remove the sensor from its mounting.

Installation

73 Installation is the reverse of removal. Make sure the sensor is fitted with its `UP' mark facing upwards.

Engine stop relay

Check

74 Remove the relay (see below).
75 Connect an ohmmeter across the black/white and red/white terminals of the relay. Using a battery and auxiliary wires, connect the battery positive (+) terminal to the red/orange terminal of the relay and the negative (–) terminal to the black terminal of the relay and note the meter reading obtained. If the relay is operating correctly there should be continuity (zero resistance) when the battery is connected and no continuity (infinite

13.67 Bank angle sensor (arrowed)

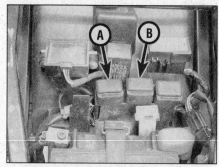

13.76 Engine stop relay (A), fuel cut-off relay (B) – note that while on X and Y (1999 and 2000) models (shown) the relay mount on the right-hand side of the bike is empty, on 1 (2001) models it holds the cooling fan relay – do not confuse them

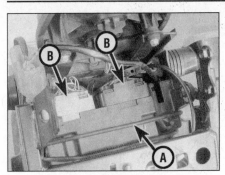

13.86 The ECM (A) and its wiring connectors (B)

13.91a Disconnect the knock sensor wiring connector . . .

13.91b . . . then unscrew and remove it

resistance) when the battery is disconnected. If this is not the case, renew the relay.

Removal

76 Remove the seat (see Chapter 8). The engine stop relay is located behind the battery (see illustration).
77 Free the relay from its mounting, then disconnect the wiring connector and remove the relay from the motorcycle.

Installation

78 Installation is the reverse of removal.

Fuel cut-off relay

Check

79 Remove the relay (see below).
80 Connect an ohmmeter across the black/white and brown terminals of the relay. Using a battery and auxiliary wires, connect the battery positive (+) terminal to the brown/black terminal of the relay and the negative (–) terminal to the black/white terminal of the relay and note the meter reading obtained. If the relay is operating correctly there should be continuity (zero resistance) when the battery is connected and no continuity (infinite resistance) when the battery is disconnected. If this is not the case, renew the relay.

Removal

81 Remove the seat (see Chapter 8). The fuel cut-off relay is behind the battery (see illustration 13.76).
82 Free the relay from its mounting, then disconnect the wiring connector and remove the relay from the motorcycle.

Installation

83 Installation is the reverse of removal.

Engine control module (ECM)

Check

84 The engine control module (ECM) can only be checked using the Honda diagnostic test pin box.

Removal

85 Remove the seat (see Chapter 8) and disconnect the battery negative (–) terminal.

86 Release the ECM retaining strap and lift the ECM off the rear mudguard (see illustrations).
87 Ensure the ignition is switched off, then disconnect the wiring connectors and remove the ECM.

Installation

88 Installation is the reverse of removal.

Knock sensor

Check

89 The knock sensor can only be checked using the Honda diagnostic test pin box (see Sections 11 and 12).

Removal

90 Raise or remove the fuel tank (see Section 2).
91 Disconnect the wiring connector from the sensor, which is threaded into the engine next to the thermostat housing (see illustration). Unscrew and remove the sensor.

Installation

92 Installation is the reverse of removal. Tighten the sensor to the torque setting specified at the beginning of the Chapter.

Oxygen sensor – models with catalytic converter

Check

93 The operation of the oxygen sensor can only be checked using the Honda diagnostic test pin box (see Section 10).

Removal

Note: The oxygen sensor is delicate and will not work if it is dropped or knocked, if its power supply is disrupted, or if any cleaning materials are used on it. Ensure the exhaust system is cold before proceeding.
94 Remove the right-hand fairing side panel (see Chapter 8).
95 Trace the wiring back from the sensor to the wiring connector and disconnect it.
96 Unscrew the oxygen sensor and remove it from the exhaust front pipe.

Installation

97 Installation is the reverse of removal.

14 Throttle body assembly – removal and installation

Note: This information only applies to X (1999) models onward.

⚠ Warning: Refer to the precautions given in Section 1 before starting work.

Removal

1 Remove the fuel tank and the air filter housing (Sections 2 and 4).
2 On X and Y (1999 and 2000) models, disconnect the wiring connector from each fuel injector (see illustration and 13.3). Disconnect the throttle position sensor wiring connector (see illustration 13.18). Disconnect the MAP sensor wiring connector (see illustration 13.29). On 1 (2001) models onward, the throttle body sub-harness can be disconnected from the main wiring harness at the 14-pin block connector, rather than disconnecting the wiring from the individual components.
3 On California models, disconnect the EVAP system solenoid valve vacuum hose from the five-way hose joint on the throttle body assembly.
4 Release the idle speed adjuster from its

14.2 Disconnect the fuel injector wiring connectors (arrowed)

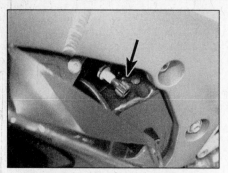

14.4 Release the idle speed adjuster (arrowed) from its holder

14.5 Unscrew the throttle cable bracket bolts (arrowed) then free the cable ends from the cam

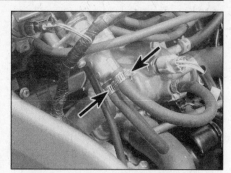

14.6 Slacken the clamps (arrowed) and detach the hoses from the wax unit

14.7a Slacken the throttle body clamp screws . . .

14.7b . . . and ease them up and out of the intake rubbers

holder and feed it through to the base of the carburettors **(see illustration)**.

5 Remove the bolts securing the throttle cable bracket to the throttle body **(see illustration)**. Free both inner cables from the throttle cam. Note that if access is too restricted, this can be done after the throttle bodies have been displaced.

Caution: Do not snap the throttle cam/valves from fully open to fully closed once the cables have been disconnected because this can lead to engine idle speed problems.

6 Slacken the clamps securing the coolant hoses to the fast idle system wax unit **(see illustration)**. Detach the hoses and plug the

ends to prevent loss of coolant.

7 Slacken the four retaining clips securing the throttle body assembly to the intake rubbers, noting which way they face **(see illustration)**. Ease the throttle body assembly out of the rubbers and remove it **(see illustration)**. If you find the lower clamps (securing the rubbers to the cylinder head) easier to access, slacken these and remove the throttle bodies with the rubbers attached.

8 Whilst the throttle body assembly is removed, tape over or plug the intake rubbers to prevent dirt/debris from entering the intake ports. If the intake rubbers shown signs of damage or deterioration they must be renewed. Note their orientation and how the

clamps locate and are positioned before removing them.

Caution: The throttle body assembly must be treated as a sealed unit. With the exception of the fast idle system wax unit screws, NEVER loosen any of the white-painted nuts/bolts/screws on the assembly as these are pre-set at the factory to ensure correct synchronisation of the throttle valves and idle circuit. Only remove the yellow painted nuts/bolts/screws if any procedure directs it. The only components on the assembly which are serviceable are the starter valves (see Section 14) and the various vacuum hoses.

Caution: NEVER use a solvent-based carburettor cleaner to clean the throttle body assembly. The throttle bores are covered with a molybdenum coating which could be removed by the cleaner.

Installation

9 Prior to installation, check the throttle body vacuum hoses for signs of damage or deterioration and renew any suspect hoses **(see illustrations)**.

10 Remove the tape/plugs from the intakes and make sure the intake rubber retaining clip screws are correctly positioned as noted on removal.

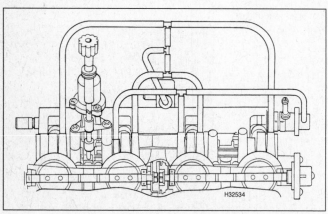

14.9a Vacuum hose location and routing – X and Y (1999 and 2000) models

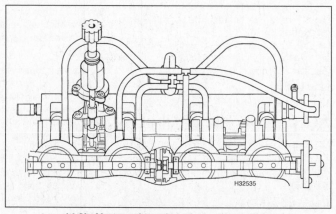

14.9b Vacuum hose location and routing – 1 (2001) models onward

14.14 Connect the hoses to the wax unit and secure them with the clamps

11 Lubricate the rubbers with a light smear of engine oil to ease installation then rest the throttle body assembly in position.

12 Connect the throttle inner cables to the cam, then fit the cable bracket to the throttle body and securely tighten its bolts **(see illustration 14.5)**. This can be done after the throttle bodies have been installed if required.

13 Ease the throttle body assembly into the intake rubbers (or ease the rubbers onto the intake manifolds if that is the way they were removed) **(see illustration 14.7b)**. Ensure each body is fully engaged, then tighten all the retaining clips so that the gap between the ends of each clip is 11 to 13 mm **(see illustration 14.7a)**.

14 Fit the coolant hoses onto the wax unit and tighten the clamps securely **(see illustration)**.

15 Connect the injector, throttle position sensor and MAP sensor wiring connectors, making sure they are all secure **(see illustrations 13.2 and 13.3, 13.18 and 13.29)**.

16 On California models, connect the EVAP system solenoid valve vacuum hose to the five-way hose joint on the throttle body assembly.

17 Fit the idle speed adjuster into its holder **(see illustration 14.4)**.

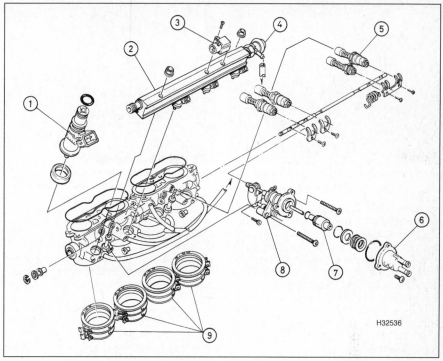

15.3a First idle system starter valve and wax unit assembly

1 Fuel injector	4 Fuel pressure regulator	7 Wax element
2 Fuel rail	5 Starter valve	8 Fast idle unit body
3 MAP sensor	6 Fast idle unit cover	9 Intake joints

18 Install the air filter housing and the fuel tank (Sections 4 and 2).

15 Starter valves – removal, installation and synchronisation

Note: *This information only applies to X (1999) models onward.*

⚠ **Warning: Refer to the precautions given in Section 1 before starting work.**

Removal

1 Remove the throttle body assembly (see Section 14).

2 If required for improved access, remove the fuel injectors (see Section 13).

3 Screw each starter valve adjustment nut in until it seats lightly and note the amount of turns needed to do so on a piece of paper **(see illustrations)**. Only three of the four valves are adjustable – the valve for the No. 3 cylinder throttle body is the base and is pre-set and is not adjustable.

15.3b Screw the Nos. 1 and 2 cylinder starter valve nuts (arrowed) . . .

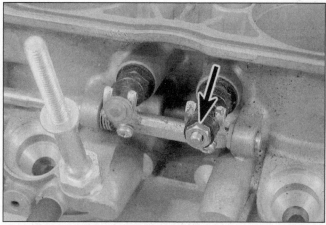

15.3c . . . and the No. 4 cylinder valve nut (arrowed) in as described

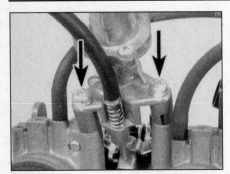

15.4 Undo the screws (arrowed) and pivot the wax unit up

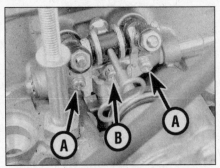

15.5 Nos. 1 and 2 starter valve arm screws (A), wax unit pivot bracket screw (B)

15.6 Nos. 3 and 4 starter valve arm screws (arrowed)

4 Undo the two screws securing the fast idle system wax unit to the throttle body assembly and pivot it up (see illustration).

5 Undo the screws securing the arms for the Nos.1 and 2 starter valves and remove the arms, noting how they fit (see illustration). From the XX-5 (2005) model onward, a double arm secures the starter valves.

6 Undo the two screws securing the double arm for the Nos. 3 and 4 starter valves to the shaft and remove the arm, noting how it fits (see illustration).

7 Undo the screw securing the wax unit pivot bracket to the shaft (see illustration 15.5). Remove the E-clip and washer securing the left-hand end of the shaft and draw it out from the right-hand end, noting how it passes through the pivot bracket and how the return spring fits (see illustration). Remove the wax unit. Note the collar in each of the bores that the shaft runs in and remove them for safekeeping if they are loose.

8 Unscrew the starter valve base nuts and remove the four valves from the throttle body, keeping them in their correct fitted order (see illustration).

9 Check all components for wear and damage and renew as necessary.

Installation

10 Clean the starter valves and throttle body passages using compressed air only. Do not use a carburettor cleaner or any other solvent.

11 Install each starter valve in its original location. Tighten the valve base nuts then check that each valve moves smoothly and easily in its bore by pulling on the valve end, and that it closes fully under spring pressure (see illustration 15.8).

12 Fit the collars into the shaft bores if removed. Position the fast idle system wax unit on the throttle body assembly in its 'pivoted up' position that was used on removal (see Step 4). Slide the shaft in from the right-hand end, fitting the return spring as you do and making sure the shaft passes through the wax unit pivot bracket. Make sure the collars stay in place. Slide the shaft fully in and secure it with the washer and E-clip, making sure it locates correctly in its groove (see illustration 15.7). Install the pivot bracket screw (see illustration 15.5).

13 Locate the arms for the Nos. 1 and 2 starter valves on the shaft and under the valve ends and secure them with the screws (see illustration 15.5). Make sure the arm ends engage correctly with the valves.

14 Locate the double arm for the Nos. 3 and 4 starter valves on the shaft and under the valve ends and secure it with the screws (see illustration 15.6). Make sure the arm ends engage correctly with the valves. Locate the return spring end onto the arm, and make sure the other end is correctly located against the throttle body. Check the operation of the starter valve shaft before continuing; it should move smoothly and easily, drawing all the valves out as it turns, and return to the fully closed position under pressure of the return springs.

15 Locate the wax unit on its mounts and tighten the screws (to the torque setting specified at the beginning of the Chapter if you have the correct tools) (see illustration 15.4).

16 Turn the starter valve adjustment nuts in until they seat lightly then back each one out by the exact number of turns noted prior to removal (see illustrations 15.3a and b).

17 Fit the fuel injectors if removed (see Section 13) and install the throttle body assembly (Section 14). On completion check the starter valve synchronisation (see below).

Synchronisation

18 Starter valve synchronisation is simply the process of adjusting the valves so they pass the same amount of air to each cylinder on cold start and warm-up. This is done by measuring the vacuum produced in each intake duct. Starter valves that are out of synchronisation will result in uneven idling when cold starting and warming the engine. Before synchronising the starter valves, make sure the valve clearances are properly set.

15.7 Remove the E-clip and washer (arrowed) from the end of the shaft, then withdraw the shaft

15.8 Unscrew the starter valves using the base nuts (arrowed) and remove them

15.20a Remove the blanking bolts (arrowed) . . .

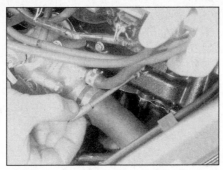

15.20b . . . and thread in suitable adapters

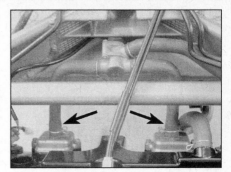

15.20c Detach the hoses (arrowed) and fit blanking caps to the unions

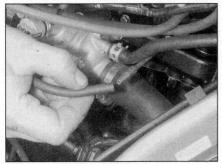

15.21 Connect the vacuum gauge hoses to the adapters

15.23a Adjust the starter valves using the synchronisation screws (arrowed) . . .

15.23b . . . until the gauge readings are the same

19 To properly synchronise the starter valves, you will need a set of vacuum gauges or calibrated tubes to indicate engine vacuum. The equipment used should be suitable for a four cylinder engine and come complete with the necessary adapters and hoses to fit the take-off points. **Note:** *Because of the nature of the synchronisation procedure and the need for special instruments, most owners leave the task to a Honda dealer.*

20 Remove the fuel tank and the air filter housing (see Sections 2 and 4). Remove the blanking screws from the cylinder take-off points and thread in suitable adapter pieces **(see illustrations)**. Detach the air hoses from the PAIR system reed valve cover unions on the valve cover and fit blanking caps in their place **(see illustration)**.

21 Connect the vacuum gauge hoses to the adapters **(see illustration)**. Make sure they are a good fit because any air leaks will result in false readings. Reinstall the air filter housing and the fuel tank, but leave the tank raised at the rear (see Section 2).

22 Start the engine and adjust the idle speed (see Chapter 1). If using vacuum gauges fitted with damping adjustment, set this so that the needle flutter is just eliminated but so that they can still respond to small changes in pressure.

23 The vacuum readings for the Nos. 1, 2 and 4 cylinders should be the same as the No. 3 cylinder. The No. 3 starter valve is the base to which all the others should be matched, and cannot itself be adjusted. If the vacuum readings vary, adjust each starter valve as

required by turning the synchronising nut on the end of the valve, until the readings are the same **(see illustrations)**. **Note:** *Do not press hard on the nut whilst adjusting it, otherwise a false reading will be obtained.*

24 When the adjustment is complete, recheck the vacuum readings, then adjust the idle speed by turning the throttle stop screw (see Chapter 1) until the correct idle speed. Stop the engine.

25 Remove the vacuum gauges and adapters, then install the blanking screws. Remove the blanking caps from the PAIR system unions on the valve cover and reconnect the PAIR system hoses.

---

16 Fast idle system wax unit – removal, inspection and installation

Note: *This information only applies to X (1999) models onward.*

⚠ *Warning: Refer to the precautions given in Section 1 before starting work.*

Removal

1 Remove the wax unit by following Steps 1 to 7 in Section 15 **(see illustration 15.3a)**.

Inspection

2 Undo the three screws securing the wax unit cover and remove it **(see illustration)**. Discard the O-ring as a new one must be used. Remove the spring, spring seat and wax

element from the body (or in reverse order from the cover, depending where they are). Discard the wax element O-rings.

3 Visually inspect all components for signs of wear and damage and renew them as required.

4 The wax element expands with heat. If you suspect it is not working correctly, place it first in a cold place and check that it is fully retracted. Now gently heat it using a hairdryer or equivalent and check that it expands.

5 Check that the pushrod moves smoothly in and out of the body.

6 Check the spring for fatigue and distortion.

Installation

7 Install the wax unit by following Steps 12 to 18 in Section 15.

16.2 Wax unit cover screws (arrowed)

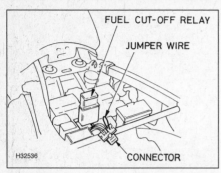

17.3 Bridge the relay terminals as shown

17.4a Fuel return hose union (arrowed)

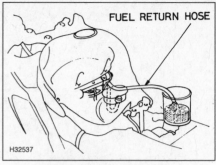

17.4b Fuel flow rate check

17 Fuel supply system – flow rate and pressure check

Note: *This information only applies to X (1999) models onward.*

 Warning: Refer to the precautions given in Section 1 before starting work.

1 If there is thought to be a problem with the fuel supply system, the fuel flow rate and fuel pressure can be checked as follows.

Fuel flow rate check

2 Raise and support the fuel tank (see Section 2).

3 Ensure the ignition is switched off then disconnect the wiring connector from the fuel cut-off relay (located behind the battery – see Section 13) **(see illustration 13.76)**. Using an auxiliary wire, bridge the brown and black/white wiring terminals of the connector **(see illustration)**.

4 Position a wad of rag and a suitable container for fuel beneath the fuel return hose union on the fuel tank and have ready a suitable plug to block the union. Working quickly to minimise fuel loss, disconnect the return hose from the tank and plug the tank union **(see illustration)**. Place the end of the return hose into the container and mop up all spilt fuel **(see illustration)**.

5 Turn on the ignition switch for exactly 10 seconds, catching all the fuel expelled from the return hose in the container, and then turn off the ignition switch. Measure the amount of fuel collected and compare this to the minimum fuel flow amount given in the Specifications.

6 If fuel flow is below the specified minimum there is a problem in the fuel supply system. Likely causes are.

a) Blocked/restricted fuel feed or return hose.
b) Blocked fuel filter.
c) Faulty fuel pressure regulator.
d) Faulty fuel pump.

7 On completion, reconnect the return hose to the fuel tank and secure it in position with the retaining clip **(see illustration 17.4)**.

8 Remove the bridging wire from the fuel cut-off relay and reconnect the wiring connector. Start the engine and check that there is no sign of fuel leakage. If all is well, lower the tank back into position (see Section 2) then install the seat (see Chapter 8).

Fuel pressure check

Note: *A pressure gauge will be required for this check. Honda specify the use of their gauge (Pt. No. 07406-0040002). If another gauge is used an adapter may be needed to thread into the union bolt, depending on the size of the gauge hose connector. A new sealing washer for the pressure release bolt will also be required.*

9 Raise and support the fuel tank (see Section 2) then disconnect the battery negative (–) terminal.

10 Disconnect the vacuum hose from the fuel pressure regulator and plug the hose end **(see illustration)**.

11 Place a rag and a suitable container for catching the residual fuel under the fuel supply hose union, then slowly slacken the pressure release bolt in the centre of the union (not the union bolt itself) until you hear a hissing sound **(see illustration 17.11A)**. At this point the fuel will spray out, so be ready with the rag to prevent it doing so. After the initial pressure has been reduced the bolt can be slackened a little further to allow the residual fuel to flow out.

12 Remove the pressure release bolt and its sealing washer and replace it with the pressure gauge, using the sealing washer if it doesn't have its own, and working quickly to minimise

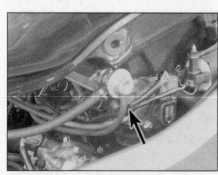

17.10 Disconnect the vacuum hose (arrowed) from the pressure regulator

fuel spillage **(see illustration 17.11B)**. Securely tighten the gauge to ensure there are no fuel leaks. Mop up any spilt fuel.

13 Connect the battery negative (–) lead then start the engine and allow it to idle at the specified speed. Note the pressure present in

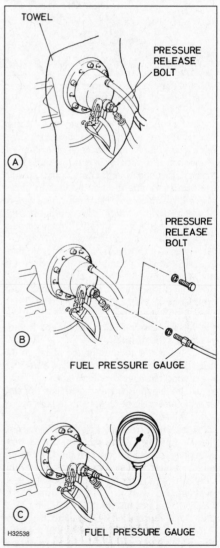

17.11 Fuel pressure check sequence

the fuel system by reading the gauge, then turn the engine off **(see illustration 17.11C)**. Compare the reading obtained to that given in the Specifications.

14 If the fuel pressure is higher than specified, likely causes are.
 a) *Blocked/restricted fuel feed or return hose.*
 b) *Faulty fuel pressure regulator.*
 c) *Faulty fuel pump (although this is unlikely).*

15 If the fuel pressure is lower than specified, likely causes are.
 a) *Leaking fuel hose union/injector.*
 b) *Blocked fuel filter.*
 c) *Faulty fuel pressure regulator.*
 d) *Faulty fuel pump.*

16 On completion, disconnect the battery negative (–) lead again. Remove the fuel gauge and sealing washer, then quickly install the pressure release bolt using a new sealing washer and tighten it to the torque setting specified at the beginning of the Chapter **(see illustration 17.11B)**. Reconnect the vacuum hose to the fuel pressure regulator **(see illustration 17.10)**. Reconnect the battery then start the engine and check that there is no sign of fuel leakage. If all is well, lower the tank back into position (see Section 2).

18 Fuel pump – check, removal and installation

Note: *This information only applies to X (1999) models onward.*

 Warning: Refer to the precautions given in Section 1 before starting work.

Check

1 The fuel pump is located inside the fuel tank. The fuel pump runs for a few seconds when the ignition is switched ON, to pressurise the fuel system, and then cuts out until the engine is started. If the pump is thought to be faulty, first check the fuses (see Chapter 9). If they are in good condition proceed as follows.
2 Raise and support the fuel tank (see Section 2).
3 Ensure the ignition is switched OFF then

18.3 Disconnect the fuel pump wiring connector (arrowed)

disconnect the fuel pump wiring connector **(see illustration)**. Connect the positive (+) lead of a voltmeter to the brown terminal of the connector and the negative (–) lead to the green terminal of the connector. Switch the ignition ON whilst noting the reading obtained on the meter.
4 If battery voltage is present for a few seconds, the fuel pump circuit is operating correctly and the fuel pump is proven to be faulty.
5 If no reading is obtained, check the fuel pump circuit wiring for continuity and make sure all the connectors are free from corrosion and are securely connected. Repair/replace the wiring as necessary and clean the connectors using electrical contact cleaner. If this fails to reveal the fault, check the following components.
 a) *Engine stop switch (see Chapter 9).*
 b) *Fuel cut-off relay (see Section 13).*
 c) *Engine stop relay (see Section 13).*
 d) *Bank angle sensor (see Section 13).*
 e) *Engine control module (ECM) (see Section 13).*

Removal

6 Remove the fuel tank (see Section 2).
7 With the fuel tank supported upside-down, unscrew the fuel pump mounting plate nuts **(see illustration)**. Carefully remove the pump assembly from the tank along with the mounting plate seal **(see illustration 18.15)**. Discard the seal – a new seal must be used on installation **(see illustration 18.14)**.

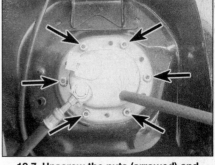
18.7 Unscrew the nuts (arrowed) and carefully withdraw the pump assembly from the tank

8 To remove the pump from its mounting plate, first disconnect the wiring connector from the pump **(see illustration)**.
9 Release the fuel hose clamp and detach the hose from the pump **(see illustration 18.8)**.
10 Undo the retaining clamp screw, noting the earth (ground) lead, and remove the clamp **(see illustration 18.8)**. Remove the pump, noting how it fits. Check the wire strainer in the base of the pump housing for signs of dirt/damage and clean/renew (as necessary).

Installation

11 If removed, fit the pump into its housing, then secure it with the clamp and tighten the screw, not forgetting to attach the earth wire **(see illustration 18.8)**.
12 Reconnect the pump wiring connector **(see illustration 18.8)**.
13 Reconnect the fuel hose to the pump and secure it with the clamp **(see illustration 18.8)**.
14 Ensure the mounting plate and tank surfaces are clean and dry, then fit the new seal onto the plate making sure its locating pins are all located correctly in the plate holes **(see illustration)**.
15 Manoeuvre the pump assembly into the tank, and seat it in position **(see illustration)**.
16 Fit the nuts and tighten them by hand **(see illustration 18.7)**. Now tighten them evenly and in a criss-cross pattern to the torque setting specified at the beginning of the Chapter.
17 Install the fuel tank (see Section 2).

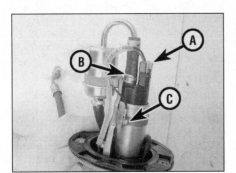
18.8 Wiring connector (A), fuel hose (B), clamp screw and earth lead (C)

18.14 Fit a new seal, locating the pegs in the holes

8.15 Carefully fit the pump assembly into the tank

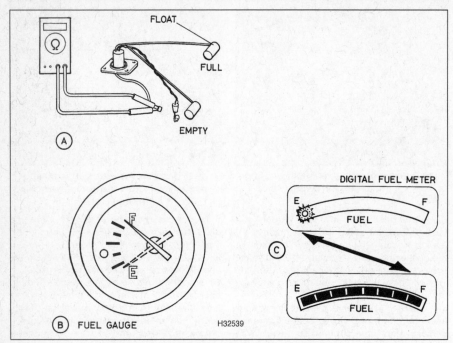

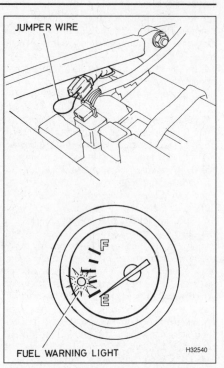

19.2 Fuel gauge and sender unit test procedure

*Move the float arm up and down and check that the meter and gauges perform as described –
see Text procedure*

**19.4 Bridge the terminals as described
and shown and check the light comes on**

19 Fuel gauge, warning light and sender unit – check and replacement

Check

1 Remove the fuel gauge sender unit (see below). Connect an ohmmeter across the sender unit grey/black and green/black wire terminals then check the resistance reading whilst moving the float arm slowly from the full to empty position and back again **(see illustration 19.2A)**. Compare the readings obtained to those given in the Specifications. Not only should the full and empty readings be as specified but the value should change evenly and progressively as the float arm is moved. If not the sender unit is faulty and should be renewed.
2 If the sender unit functions correctly, connect it to the wiring connector then switch

the ignition ON. Move the float arm up and down again and check that the operation of the gauge corresponds to the movement of the arm **(see illustration 19.2 parts A and B)**. On 1 (2001) models onward, check that when the arm is in the empty position, the last indicator on the LCD display flashes **(see illustration 19.2 parts A and C)**. If the gauge does not function correctly, switch off the ignition and remove the fairing (see Chapter 8).
3 Disconnect the wiring connectors from the instrument cluster and fuel gauge sender unit. Use an ohmmeter to check for continuity in the grey/black and green/black wires between the cluster and sender unit wiring, using the relevant *Wiring Diagram* at the end of Chapter 9 to make sure you have the correct instrument cluster connector. Also check for continuity to earth (ground) in the green/black wire. If continuity (zero resistance) is not present, repair/replace the wiring harness. If

continuity exists, then the gauge is probably faulty, but note that it could be the instrument cluster printed circuit board.
4 On V, W, X and Y (1997 to 2000) models, if the warning light does not come on, disconnect the fuel sender unit wiring connector and bridge between the brown/black and green/black wire terminals on the connector using a jumper wire **(see illustration)**. Turn the ignition switch ON – the warning light should come on. If it does, replace the sender unit with a new one. If it doesn't, check for continuity in the brown/black and green/black wires between the cluster and sender unit wiring, using the relevant *Wiring Diagram* at the end of Chapter 9 to make sure you have the correct instrument cluster connector. Also check for continuity to earth (ground) in the green/black wire. If continuity (zero resistance) is not present, repair/replace the wiring harness. If continuity exists, then the gauge warning light is probably faulty, but note that it could be the instrument cluster printed circuit board. If the light is faulty, the gauge must be renewed as the light is integral with it.

Replacement

5 See Chapter 9 for replacement of the fuel gauge.
6 To replace the sender unit, remove the fuel tank and drain it (see Section 2).
7 Either free the wiring from the clip on the tank and feed it through to the sender, or detach the wiring connectors from the terminals on the sender unit base and free the wiring from the clip **(see illustrations)**.

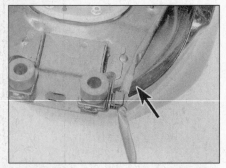

**19.7a Either free the wiring from its clip
(arrowed) and feed it to the sender . . .**

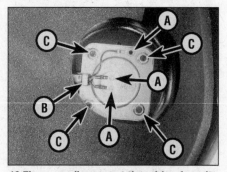

**19.7b . . . or disconnect the wiring from its
terminals (A) and free it from the clip (B).
Sender unit retaining nuts (C)**

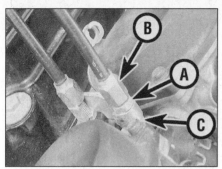

20.2 Slacken the locknut (A), then unscrew the adjuster (B) until the captive nut (C) is free of its lug, then slip the cable out of the bracket and detach the end from the carburettor

Unscrew the nuts securing the sender and draw it out of the tank, taking care not to bend the float arm. Discard the O-ring.

8 Fit a new O-ring onto the sender and install it in the tank. Tighten the nuts securely. Connect and secure the wiring according to your removal procedure.

9 Install the tank (see Section 2), and check carefully for leaks before using the bike.

20 Throttle cables – removal and installation

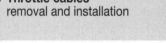

⚠️ **Warning: Refer to the precautions given in Section 1 before proceeding.**

Removal

1 Remove the fuel tank and the air filter housing (see Sections 2 and 4). Mark each cable according to its location.

2 On V and W (1997 and 1998) models, slacken the opening (top) cable adjuster locknut and thread it fully up, then unscrew the adjuster until the captive nut is free (you may not need to do this if there is already enough clearance to release the captive nut from the bracket – it depends on the setting of the adjuster), then slip the cable out of the bracket and detach the inner cable nipple from the throttle cam on the carburettors **(see illustration)**. Now unscrew the closing

20.3a Free the upper (closing) cable from the bracket as described . . .

20.3c Free the lower (opening) cable from the bracket as described . . .

(bottom) cable hex until the captive nut is free, then slip the cable out of the bracket and detach the inner cable nipple from the cam. Withdraw the cables from the machine noting their correct routing.

3 On X (1999) models onward, unscrew the closing (top) cable hex until the captive nut is free, then slip the cable out of the bracket and detach the inner cable nipple from the throttle body cam **(see illustration)**. Now slacken the opening (bottom) cable adjuster locknut and thread it fully up, then unscrew the adjuster until the captive nut is free (you may not need to do this if there is already enough clearance to release the captive nut from the bracket – it depends on the setting of the adjuster), then slip the cable out of the bracket and detach the inner cable nipple from the cam **(see illustrations)**. Withdraw the cables from the machine noting their correct routing.

20.3b . . . and slip the end out of the cam (arrowed)

20.3d . . . and slip the end out of the cam (arrowed)

4 Slacken the cable elbow nuts at the switch housing, then remove the housing screws and separate the halves **(see illustrations)**. Detach the cable nipples from the twistgrip. Detach the upper housing half from the handlebar, then fully unscrew the closing (bottom) cable elbow nut and remove the cable from the housing. Thread the housing off the opening (top) cable elbow and withdraw the cable. Mark each cable to ensure it is connected correctly on installation.

Installation

5 Fit the opening cable elbow into the top socket of the upper half of the switch housing and thread the housing onto it as far as it will go without becoming tight on the bottom of the threads – the elbow must stay loose so that it aligns itself – then thread the nut onto

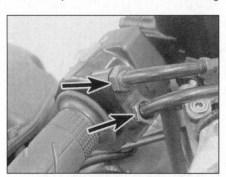

20.4a Slacken the elbow nuts (arrowed) . . .

20.4b . . . then remove the screws . . .

20.4c . . . and separate the housing halves

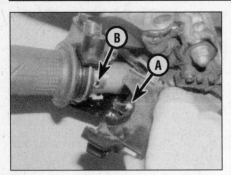

20.5 Locate the pin (A) in the hole (B)

21.2a Release the outer cable from its holder using a screwdriver . . .

21.2b . . . then free the inner cable end from its socket on the choke linkage bar

the elbow, again not so that it is tight. Fit the closing cable into the bottom socket and tighten the nut finger-tight. Fit the upper half of the housing onto the handlebar, then lubricate the cable nipples with multi-purpose grease and fit them into the twistgrip. Fit the bottom half of the housing onto the handlebar, making sure the pin locates in the hole in the bottom of the handlebar, then install the screws and tighten them securely **(see illustration and 20.4b)**. Now tighten both cable elbow nuts **(see illustration 20.4a)**.

6 Feed the cables through to the carburettors or throttle bodies, making sure they are correctly routed. The cables must not interfere with any other component and should not be kinked or bent sharply.

7 On V and W (1997 and 1998) models, lubricate the closing cable nipple with multi-purpose grease and fit it into the carburettor throttle cam. Fit the cable into the lower bracket, locating the bottom nut against the lug so that it is captive **(see illustration 11.2c)**, then thread the hex into the nut until it is tight **(see illustration 20.2)**. Lubricate the opening cable nipple with multi-purpose grease and fit it into the carburettor throttle cam. Fit the opening cable adjuster into the upper bracket, locating the nut against the lug so that it is captive, then thread the locknut down the adjuster, but do not yet tighten it **(see illustration 20.2)**. Thread the adjuster in or out until the

specified amount of cable freeplay is obtained (see Chapter 1). Tighten the locknut against the bracket.

8 On X (1999) models onward, lubricate the opening cable nipple with multi-purpose grease and fit it into the throttle body cam **(see illustration 20.3d)**. Fit the opening cable adjuster into the lower bracket, locating the bottom nut against the lug so that it is captive, then thread the top nut down the adjuster, but do not yet tighten it **(see illustration 20.3c)**. Thread the adjuster in or out until the specified amount of cable freeplay is obtained (see Chapter 1). Tighten the locknut against the bracket. Lubricate the closing cable nipple with multi-purpose grease and fit it into the throttle body cam **(see illustration 20.3b)**. Fit the cable into the upper bracket, locating the nut against the lug so that it is captive **(see illustration 20.3a)**, then thread the hex into the nut until it is tight.

9 Operate the throttle to check that it opens and closes freely.

10 Check and adjust the throttle cable freeplay if required (see Chapter 1). Turn the handlebars back and forth to make sure the cable doesn't cause the steering to bind.

11 Install the air filter housing and the fuel tank (see Sections 4 and 2).

12 Start the engine and check that the idle speed does not rise as the handlebars are turned. If it does, the throttle cable is routed incorrectly. Correct the problem before riding the motorcycle.

21 Choke cable (V and W (1997 and 1998) models) – removal and installation

Removal

1 Remove the fuel tank and the air filter housing (see Sections 2 and 4).

2 Release the outer cable from its holder using a screwdriver, then free the inner cable end from its socket on the choke linkage bar **(see illustrations)**.

3 Remove the left-hand switch housing screws and separate the halves from the handlebar, noting how the choke lever locates in the housing **(see illustration)**. Free the cable end from the choke lever. Withdraw the cable from the machine noting its routing.

Installation

4 Installation is the reverse of removal. Make sure the cable is correctly routed – it must not interfere with any other component and should not be kinked or bent sharply. Check the operation of the cable (see Chapter 1).

22 Exhaust system – removal and installation

⚠ **Warning: If the engine has been running the exhaust system will be very hot. Allow the system to cool before carrying out any work.**

Removal

Silencers

1 Slacken the clamp bolts securing the silencer in the downpipe assembly **(see illustration)**.

HAYNES HiNT *Exhaust system clamp bolts tend to become corroded and seized. It is advisable to spray them with WD40 or a similar product before attempting to slacken them.*

21.3 Undo the screws (arrowed) and separate the switch housing

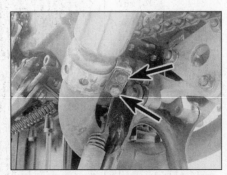

22.1 Slacken the clamp bolts (arrowed)

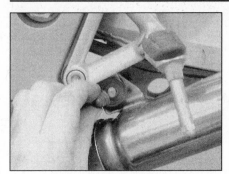

22.2a Unscrew the nut . . .

22.2b . . . and remove the collar

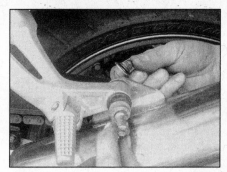

22.3a Unscrew the nut and withdraw the bolt . . .

22.3b . . . and remove the silencer as described

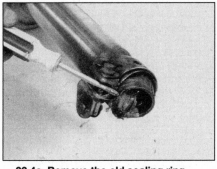

22.4a Remove the old sealing ring . . .

22.4b . . . and fit a new one

2 Unscrew the nut and remove the collar securing the front of the silencer **(see illustrations)**.

3 Unscrew the nut and remove the bolt and washers securing the rear of the silencer **(see illustration)**. Twist the silencer to release the front mounting stud from its grommet, then withdraw the silencer from the downpipe assembly and remove it – if removing the right-hand silencer, twist it anti-clockwise; if removing the left-hand silencer, twist it clockwise **(see illustration)**.

4 Note the arrangement of the washers, collars and rubbers on the silencer mountings. Fit new rubbers if the old ones are damaged, deformed or deteriorated. Check the condition of the sealing ring between the silencer and downpipe assembly and replace it with a new one if it is damaged or deformed **(see illustrations)**. Honda recommend always using a new one, but they can be difficult to remove, and unless they are damaged they are re-usable. It is too easy to damage a new one trying to install it to make it worthwhile destroying a good one that is already installed.

Downpipe assembly

5 Remove the fairing side panels (see Chapter 8).

6 Remove the radiator (see Chapter 3). **Note:** *Though it is possible to remove the downpipe assembly with the radiator just displaced from its mountings rather than removed altogether, there is always the possibility of damaging it when unscrewing or tightening the nuts or when manoeuvring the downpipes. As radiators are fairly fragile and easily damaged, and don't take long to remove, it is best to do so.*

7 Remove the silencers (see above). Where a catalytic converter is fitted, disconnect the oxygen sensor wiring (see Section 13).

8 Unscrew the nut and withdraw the bolt securing the rear of the downpipe assembly, noting the washer and the collar **(see illustration)**.

9 Unscrew the nuts securing the header pipes to the cylinder head **(see illustration)**.

22.8 Downpipe assembly rear mounting bolt (arrowed)

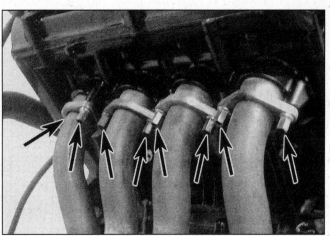

22.9a Unscrew the nuts (arrowed) . . .

22.9b . . . and draw off the flanges . . .

22.9c . . . then manoeuvre the downpipe assembly out of the head

22.10 Use new sealing rings in each port

Draw the flanges off the studs and manoeuvre the downpipe assembly out of the head and remove it **(see illustrations)**. Remove the gasket from each port in the cylinder head and discard them as new ones must be used **(see illustration 22.10a)**.

Installation

10 Installation is the reverse of removal, noting the following:

a) *Use a new gasket in each cylinder head port **(see illustration)**. Replace any damaged, deformed or deteriorated mounting rubbers with new ones.*

b) *Use new sealing rings between the downpipe assembly and the silencers if required, bearing in mind the information in Step 4 above **(see illustrations 22.4a and b)**.*

c) *Apply a smear of copper grease to the clamp bolts to prevent them from seizing up.*

d) *Leave all fasteners loose until the entire system has been installed, making alignment of the various sections easier. Tighten the silencer mountings last.*

e) *Tighten the front downpipe nuts, the silencer clamp bolts and the silencer mounting nuts to the torque settings specified at the beginning of the Chapter.*

f) *Run the engine and check the system for leaks.*

23 Pulse secondary air (PAIR) system components – general information

General information

Note: *This system is fitted to UK market X (1999) models onward, and all US, Swiss and Austrian models.*

1 To reduce the amount of unburned hydrocarbons released in the exhaust gases, a pulse secondary air (PAIR) system is fitted. The system consists of the control valve (mounted under the front of the air filter housing), the reed valves (fitted in the valve cover) and the hoses linking them **(see illustrations)**. The control valve is actuated by the engine vacuum on US V and W (1997 and 1998) models, and electronically by the ECM on all other models.

2 Under certain operating conditions, the vacuum or a signal from the ECM (according to model) opens up the PAIR control valve which then allows filtered air to be drawn through the reed valves and cylinder head passages and into the exhaust ports. The air mixes with the exhaust gases, causing any unburned particles of the fuel in the mixture to be burnt in the exhaust port/pipes. This process changes a considerable amount of hydrocarbons and carbon monoxide into relatively harmless carbon dioxide and water. The reed valves in the valve cover are fitted to prevent the flow of exhaust gases back up the cylinder head passages and into the air filter housing.

Testing

Control valve

3 Remove the valve from the motorcycle (see below).

4 Check the operation of the control valve by blowing through the air filter housing hose union; air should flow freely through the reed valve hose unions. On US V and W (1997 and 1998) models now apply a vacuum to the vacuum hose and repeat the check; no air should now flow through the valve if it is functioning correctly. On X (1999) models onward, now connect battery voltage (12 volts) across the valve terminals and repeat the check; no air should now flow through the valve if it is functioning correctly.

5 On X (1999) models onward, if an ohmmeter is available, check the resistance of the control valve windings by connecting an ohmmeter between its connector terminals and compare the reading obtained to that given in the Specifications. Renew the valve if faulty.

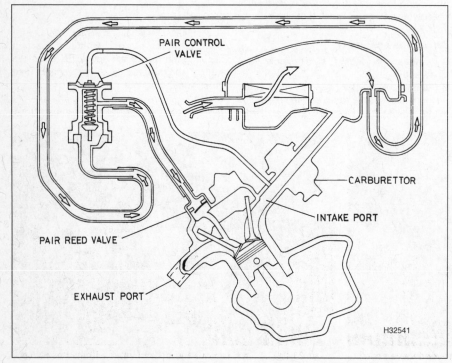

PAIR CONTROL VALVE

CARBURETTOR

INTAKE PORT

PAIR REED VALVE

EXHAUST PORT

H32541

23.1a PAIR system – US market V and W (1997 and 1998) models

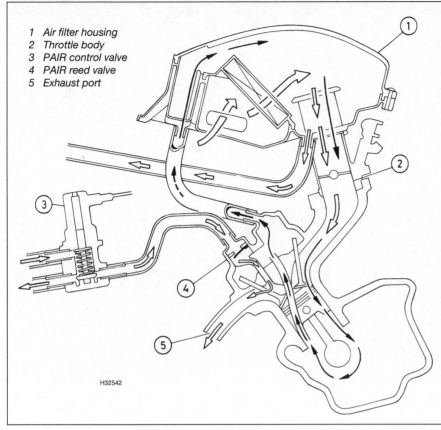

1 Air filter housing
2 Throttle body
3 PAIR control valve
4 PAIR reed valve
5 Exhaust port

H32542

23.1b PAIR system – X (1999) models onward

23.9 Disconnect the control valve wiring connector

10 Release the clamps securing the reed valve hoses and disconnect them, then remove the control valve from the motorcycle **(see illustrations)**.

11 Installation is the reverse of removal. Note that on California models there is an emission control system hose routing diagram on a label stuck to the top of the air filter housing.

Reed valves

12 It is possible to access the reed valves from the front, but access is restricted. It does however mean there is no need to remove the fuel tank. For best access using this method, and to prevent the possibility of damaging any bodywork, remove both the fairing side panels and the fairing (see Chapter 8). Otherwise, remove only the fairing side panels, the cockpit trim panels and the fuel tank trim panels (see Chapter 8). On V and W (1997 and 1998) models, remove the trim panels from around the oil cooler hoses and release the hoses from the guides. On X (1999) models onward, unscrew the bolts securing the oil cooler to the frame, but leave it attached to the radiator (see Chapter 2) – there is no need to detach the oil hoses. On all models, displace the radiator from its mounts and move it away as much as possible (see Chapter 3) – there is no need to detach any hoses, but disconnect the wiring connector. If access is still too restricted for you, drain the

Reed valves

6 Disconnect the reed valve hoses from the control valve (see below).

7 Check each valve by blowing and sucking on the hose end. Air should flow through the hose only when blown down it and not when sucked back up. If this is not the case the reed valve is faulty, but before buying new components it is worth disassembling the valve (see below) and checking whether the problem is caused by a build-up of carbon

deposits, which can be scraped off and cleaned up.

Removal and installation

Control valve

8 Remove the air filter housing (see Section 4).

9 On US V and W (1997 and 1998) models, disconnect the vacuum hose from the valve. On X (1999) models onward, disconnect the wiring connector **(see illustration)**.

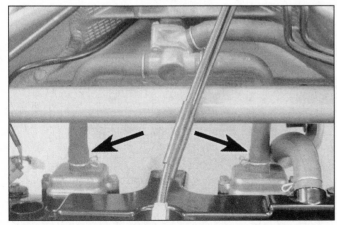

23.10a Detach the hoses (arrowed) from the reed valve cover unions . . .

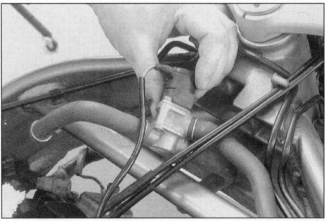

23.10b . . . and remove the control valve with its hoses

coolant (see Section 27), and remove the oil cooler and/or radiator as required. The alternative and easier method is to remove the fuel tank and the air filter housing (see Chapter 4), and the ignition coils (see Chapter 5), and to access the valves from the top.

13 To remove either valve, first release the clamp and detach the air hose from its union **(see illustration 23.10a)**. Unscrew the bolts securing the reed valve cover and remove the cover **(see illustrations)**. Remove the reed valve and the base plate, noting which way around they are fitted **(see illustrations)**.

14 Installation is the reverse of removal. Scrape away any carbon deposits from the reed seating surfaces and from around the reed holder. Make sure the reed valve components are correctly fitted.

23.13a Unscrew the bolts . . .

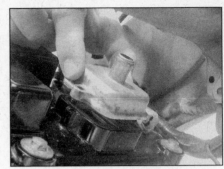
23.13b . . . and remove the cover . . .

24 Evaporative emission control (EVAP) system components – general information

General information

1 To minimise the escape into the atmosphere of fuel vapour from the tank, and on V and W (1997 and 1998) models the carburettors, an evaporative emissions control system is fitted to all California models **(see illustrations)**. The fuel tank filler cap is

23.13c . . . then remove the reed valve . . .

23.13d . . . and its base plate

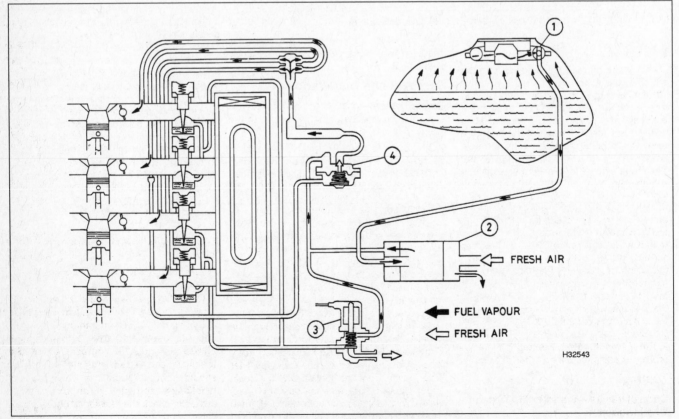

24.1a EVAP system – V and W (1997 and 1998) models

1 Fuel tank filler neck   2 Canister   3 Carburettor air vent valve   4 Purge control valve

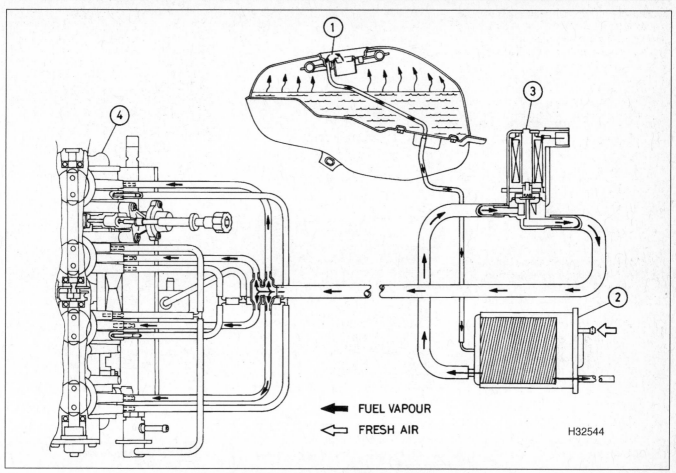

24.1b EVAP system – X (1999) models onward

1 Fuel tank filler neck   2 Canister   3 Purge control valve   4 Throttle body

sealed and a charcoal canister is mounted under the fuel tank. The canister collects the fuel vapours generated when the motorcycle is parked and stores them until they can be cleared from the canister, via the control valve(s), into the throttle body inlet tracts to be burned by the engine during normal combustion. On V and W (1997 and 1998) models, the system control valves are opened and closed by the vacuum created in the inlet tracts when the engine is running. Vapour from the fuel tank is controlled by the purge control valve, while vapour from the carburettors is controlled by the CAV (carburettor air vent) valve. On X (1999) models onward, the purge control valve for the fuel tank vapour is opened and closed by the engine control module (ECM). There is no CAV valve.

2 The valves should be tested if there is a problem starting the engine when it is hot.

Testing

Control valves – V and W (1997 and 1998) models

3 Remove the relevant valve from the motorcycle (see below).

4 Check the operation of the purge control valve by connecting an auxiliary hose to the vacuum hose union and applying a vacuum of 250 mm Hg. Check that the valve is able to hold the vacuum once it is applied. Now blow through the inlet (canister hose) union; air should flow freely through the valve and out the outlet hose (carburettor hose) union. Disconnect the vacuum hose – no air should now flow through the valve. Now connect the auxiliary hose to the outlet hose (carburettor hose) union and apply a vacuum of 250 mm Hg. Check that the valve is able to hold the vacuum once it is applied. Renew the valve if it doesn't perform as described.

5 To check the operation of the CAV control valve reconnect its wiring connector. With the ignition switch OFF, blow through the inlet (carburettor hose) union; air should flow freely through the valve and out the outlet (canister hose) union. Turn the ignition ON, and again blow through the inlet (carburettor hose) union; air should now flow freely through the valve and out the open (unhosed) union, and not out of the outlet (canister hose) union. If the valve doesn't perform as described,

disconnect its wiring connector and check for battery voltage using a multimeter across the connector terminals (positive lead to the black/brown wire terminal, negative lead to the green wire terminal) with the ignition ON. If voltage is present, the valve is faulty. If no voltage is present, check the wiring for faults and repair or renew as necessary, then check the operation of the valve again.

Control valve – X (1999) models onward

6 Remove the valve from the motorcycle (see below).

7 Check the operation of the control valve by blowing through the inlet (canister hose) union; air should not flow through the valve and out the outlet hose union. Connect battery voltage (12 volts) across the valve terminals and repeat the check; now air should flow through the valve if it is functioning correctly. If an ohmmeter is available, check the resistance of the control valve windings and compare the reading obtained to that given in the Specifications. Renew the valve if faulty. If it behaves as described, check for battery voltage using a multimeter across the wiring connector terminals with the ignition ON

Charcoal canister

8 No testing of the canister is possible, if it is thought to be faulty it must be renewed.

Removal and installation

Control valves – V and W (1997 and 1998) models

9 To replace the purge control valve, remove the fuel tank (see Section 2). Disconnect the hoses from the valve, noting which fits where, then release the valve from its mounting.

10 To replace the CAV valve, remove the fuel tank (see Section 2). Disconnect the hoses from the valve, noting which fits where, then disconnect the wiring connector and release the valve from its mounting.

11 Installation is the reverse of removal.

Control valve – X (1999) models onward

12 Remove the fuel tank (see Section 2).

13 Disconnect the hoses from the valve, noting which fits where, then disconnect the wiring connector. Unscrew the mounting bolts and remove the valve.

14 Installation is the reverse of removal.

Charcoal canister

15 Remove the fuel tank (see Section 2).

16 Unscrew the canister bracket mounting bolts and displace the canister, then disconnect the hoses, noting which fits where.

17 Installation is the reverse of removal.

25 Catalytic converter – general information

Note: *A catalytic converter is fitted to German and Swiss market models from 1999 (X model) and most other markets from the 2001 (1 model) onward.*

General information

1 A catalytic converter is incorporated in the exhaust downpipe pipe assembly to minimise the level of exhaust pollutants released into the atmosphere.

2 The catalytic converter consists of a canister containing a fine mesh impregnated with a catalyst material, over which the hot exhaust gases pass. The catalyst speeds up the oxidation of harmful carbon monoxide, unburned hydrocarbons and soot, effectively reducing the quantity of harmful products released into the atmosphere via the exhaust gases.

3 The catalytic converter is of the closed-loop type with exhaust gas oxygen content information being fed back to the fuel injection system engine control module (ECM) by the oxygen sensor. There is a sensor which is screwed into the downpipe assembly, just in front of the catalytic converter.

4 The oxygen sensor contains a heating element which is controlled by the ECM. When the engine is cold, the ECM switches on the heating element which warms the exhaust gases as they pass over the sensor. This brings the catalytic converter quickly up to its normal operating temperature and decreases the level of exhaust pollutants emitted whilst the engine warms up. Once the engine is sufficiently warmed up, the ECM switches off the heating element.

5 Refer to Section 22 for information and exhaust downpipe assembly (which incorporates the catalytic converter) removal and installation, and Section 13 for oxygen sensor removal and installation information.

Precautions

6 The catalytic converter is a reliable and simple device which needs no maintenance in itself, but there are some facts of which an owner should be aware if the converter is to function properly for its full service life.

a) *DO NOT use leaded or lead replacement petrol (gasoline) – the additives will coat the precious metals, reducing their converting efficiency and will eventually destroy the catalytic converter.*

b) *Always keep the ignition and fuel systems well-maintained in accordance with the manufacturer's schedule – if the fuel/air mixture is suspected of being incorrect have it checked on an exhaust gas analyser.*

c) *If the engine develops a misfire, do not ride the bike at all (or at least as little as possible) until the fault is cured.*

d) *DO NOT use fuel or engine oil additives – these may contain substances harmful to the catalytic converter.*

e) *DO NOT continue to use the bike if the engine burns oil to the extent of leaving a visible trail of blue smoke.*

f) *Remember that the catalytic converter is FRAGILE – do not strike it with tools during servicing work.*

Chapter 5
Ignition system

Contents

Degrees of difficulty

| Easy, suitable for novice with little experience | | Fairly easy, suitable for beginner with some experience | | Fairly difficult, suitable for competent DIY mechanic | | Difficult, suitable for experienced DIY mechanic | | Very difficult, suitable for expert DIY or professional | |

Specifications

General information
Cylinder numbering . . . .   1 to 4 from left to right
Spark plugs . . . .   See Chapter 1

Ignition timing
V and W (1997 and 1998) models . . . .   9° BTDC ('F' mark) at idle
X (1999) models onward . . . .   12° BTDC ('F' mark) at idle

Ignition HT coils
Primary winding resistance . . . .   2.4 to 2.8 ohms @ 20°C
Secondary winding resistance . . . .   32.0 to 34.0 K-ohms @ 20°C
Plug cap resistance . . . .   approx. 5 K-ohms
Initial voltage (see text) . . . .   Battery voltage (approximately 12 volts)
Minimum peak voltage (see text) . . . .   100 volts

Ignition pulse generator – V and W (1997 and 1998) models
Minimum peak voltage (see text) . . . .   0.7 volts
Note: *The ignition pulse generator for X (1999) models onward is covered in Chapter 4 under fuel injection system components*

Throttle position sensor – V and W (1997 and 1998) models
Input voltage (see text) . . . .   4.5 to 5.5 volts
Output voltage . . . .   see text
Note: *The throttle position sensor for X (1999) models onward is covered in Chapter 4 under fuel injection system components*

Torque settings
Timing inspection cap . . . .   18 Nm
Timing rotor cover bolts . . . .   12 Nm

1 General information

All models are fitted with a fully transistorised electronic ignition system, which due to its lack of mechanical parts is totally maintenance free.

On V and W (1997 and 1998) models, the system comprises the timing rotor, ignition pulse generator, throttle position sensor, ignition control unit, and ignition HT coils (refer to the wiring diagrams at the end of Chapter 9 for details).

On X (1999) models onward, the system is basically the same, but control is integrated into the fuel injection system electronic control module (ECM), and the ignition pulse generator and throttle position sensor have dual roles in providing information for both the ignition and the fuelling side of the engine. All the system components for these models are therefore covered in Chapter 4. However the ignition side of the system basically operates in the same way.

The ignition timing rotor, which is on the right-hand end of the crankshaft, has triggers which magnetically actuate the pulse generator coil as the crankshaft rotates. The pulse generator coil sends a signal to the ignition control unit or ECM which then supplies the ignition HT coils with the power necessary to produce a spark at the plugs. A throttle position sensor also supplies the control unit with information that is used in determining the optimum firing point for all conditions. The system incorporates an electronic advance system controlled by the signals from the pulse generator coil and the sensors.

The system uses two HT coils, one for Nos. 1 and 4 cylinders, the other for Nos. 2 and 3. The coils are mounted on each side of the air filter housing.

The system incorporates a safety interlock circuit which will cut the ignition if the sidestand is extended whilst the engine is running and in gear, or if a gear is selected whilst the engine is running and the sidestand is down. It also prevents the engine from being started if the sidestand is down and the engine is in gear. The engine can be started with the sidestand up when it is in gear as long as the clutch lever is pulled in.

European market X (1999) models onward are equipped with Honda's HISS immobiliser system which will not allow the engine to be started unless the correct key is used. The immobiliser system has its own fault-diagnosis function.

Because of their nature, the individual ignition system components can be checked but not repaired. If ignition system troubles occur, and the faulty component can be isolated, the only cure for the problem is to replace the part with a new one. Keep in mind that most electrical parts, once purchased, cannot be returned. To avoid unnecessary expense, make very sure the faulty component has been positively identified before buying a replacement part.

Note that there is no provision for adjusting the ignition timing on these models.

2 Ignition system – check

⚠️ *Warning: The energy levels in electronic systems can be very high. On no account should the ignition be switched on whilst the plugs or plug caps are being held. Shocks from the HT circuit can be most unpleasant. Secondly, it is vital that the engine is not turned over or run with any of the plug caps removed, and that the plugs are soundly earthed (grounded) when the system is checked for sparking. The ignition system components can be seriously damaged if the HT circuit becomes isolated.*

1 As no means of adjustment is available, any failure of the system can be traced to failure of a system component or a simple wiring fault. Of the two possibilities, the latter is by far the most likely. In the event of failure, check the system in a logical fashion, as described below.

2 Working on one HT lead at a time, disconnect the lead from its spark plug – to access them refer to Chapter 1, Section 5. Connect the lead to a spare spark plug that is known to be good and lay the plug against the cylinder head with the threads contacting it **(see illustration)**. If necessary, hold the spark plug with an insulated tool.

⚠️ *Warning: Do not remove any of the spark plugs from the engine to perform this check – atomised fuel being pumped out of the open spark plug hole could ignite, causing severe injury! Make sure the plugs are securely held against the engine – if they are not earthed when the engine is turned over, the ignition control unit could be damaged.*

3 Having observed the above precautions, check that the kill switch is in the RUN position and the transmission is in neutral, then turn the ignition switch ON and turn the engine over on the starter motor. If the system is in good condition a regular, fat blue spark should be evident at the plug electrode. If the spark appears thin or yellowish, or is non-existent, further investigation will be necessary. Turn the ignition OFF and repeat the check for each lead.

4 The ignition system must be able to produce a spark which is capable of jumping a particular size gap. Honda do not provide a specification, but a healthy system should produce a spark capable of jumping at least 6 mm. A simple testing tool can be made to test the minimum gap across which the spark will jump (see **Tool Tip**).

5 Connect one of the spark plug HT leads from one coil to the protruding electrode on the test tool, and clip the tool to a good earth (ground) on the engine or frame **(see illustration)**. Check that the kill switch is in the RUN position, turn the ignition switch ON and turn the engine over on the starter motor. If the system is in good condition a regular, fat blue spark should be seen to jump the gap

2.2 Ground (earth) the spark plug and operate the starter – bright blue sparks should be visible

TOOL TiP

A simple spark gap testing tool can be made from a block of wood, a large alligator clip and two nails, one of which is fashioned so that a spark plug cap or bare HT lead end can be connected to its end. Make sure the gap between the two nail ends is the same as specified

2.5 Connect the tester as shown – when the starter is operated sparks should jump between the nails

between the nail ends. Repeat the test for the other lead and coil. If the test results are good the entire ignition system can be considered good. If the spark appears thin or yellowish, or is non-existent, further investigation will be necessary.

6 Ignition faults can be divided into two categories, namely those where the ignition system has failed completely, and those which are due to a partial failure. The likely faults are listed below, starting with the most probable source of failure. Work through the list systematically, referring to the subsequent sections for full details of the necessary checks and tests. **Note:** *Before checking the following items ensure that the battery is fully charged and that all fuses are in good condition.*

  a) *Loose, corroded or damaged wiring connections, broken or shorted wiring between any of the component parts of the ignition system (see Chapter 9).*
  b) *Faulty HT lead or spark plug cap, faulty spark plug, dirty, worn or corroded plug electrodes, or incorrect gap between electrodes.*
  c) *Faulty ignition (main) switch or engine kill switch (see Chapter 9).*
  d) *Faulty neutral, clutch or sidestand switch (see Chapter 9).*
  e) *Faulty ignition pulse generator or damaged trigger on timing rotor.*
  f) *Faulty ignition HT coil(s) (see Section 3).*
  g) *Faulty throttle position sensor.*
  h) *Faulty ignition control unit or ECM.*

7 If working on a V or W (1997 or 1998) models refer to the following sections of this Chapter for ignition pulse generator, throttle position sensor and ignition control unit tests.

8 If working on an X (1999) model onwards, refer to Sections 12 and 13 of Chapter 4 for testing details.

---

3 Ignition HT coils – check, removal and installation

Check

1 Remove the fuel tank (see Chapter 4). Check the coils visually for loose or damaged terminals, cracks and other damage.

2 Remove the seat (see Chapter 8). Disconnect the battery negative (–ve) lead.

3 Remove the air filter housing (see Chapter 4). Disconnect the primary circuit wiring connectors from the coil being tested **(see illustration)**. Also disconnect the relevant HT leads from their spark plugs **(see illustration)**. Mark the locations of all wires and leads before disconnecting them. Remove the coil.

4 Set an ohmmeter or multimeter to the ohms x 1 scale and measure the resistance between the primary circuit terminals on the coil **(see illustration)**. This will give a resistance reading of the primary windings of the coil and

3.3a Disconnect the primary circuit wiring connectors (arrowed) from the coil . . .

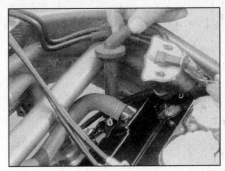

3.3b . . . and the spark plug caps from the plugs

should be consistent with the value given in the Specifications at the beginning of the Chapter.

5 To check the condition of the secondary windings, set the meter to the K-ohm scale. Connect one meter probe to one spark plug cap and the other probe to the other cap **(see illustration)**. If the reading obtained is not within the range shown in the Specifications, unscrew the cap from the end of the HT lead and repeat the measurement. If the reading is now approximately 5 K-ohms less than that specified, then one or both caps could be faulty. To test the caps, measure their resistance, which should be around 5 K-ohms. If the caps are good, separate the lead from the coil by unscrewing its retainer, and check the lead for continuity (zero resistance). If there is no continuity (i.e. a very high resistance), the lead is faulty. If the coil reading is still outside the specified range, it is likely that the coil is defective. To confirm this, the coil must be tested as described below using the specified equipment, or by a Honda dealer.

6 Honda specify their own Imrie diagnostic tester (model 625), or the peak voltage adapter (Pt. No. 07HGJ-0020100) with an aftermarket digital multimeter having an impedance of 10 M-ohm/DCV minimum, for a complete test. If this equipment is available, connect the positive (+) lead of the voltmeter and peak voltage adapter arrangement to the yellow/blue (Nos. 1 and 3 cylinder coil) or blue/yellow (Nos. 2 and 4 cylinder coil) wire

terminal on the coil, with the wiring connector still securely connected, and connect the negative (–) lead to a suitable earth (ground) point.

7 Check that the kill switch is in the RUN position and the transmission is in neutral, then turn the ignition switch ON. Note the initial voltage reading on the meter, then turn the engine over on the starter motor and note the ignition coil peak voltage reading on the meter. Once both readings have been noted, turn the ignition switch off and disconnect the meter.

8 If the initial voltage reading is not as expected or the peak voltage readings are lower than the specified minimum then a fault is present somewhere else in the ignition system circuit (see Section 2); note that the peak voltage readings for each coil can be different but each one must exceed the specified minimum.

9 If the initial and peak voltage readings are as specified and the plug does not spark, then the ignition HT coil, HT lead or plug cap are faulty (the plug caps and leads are available separately). In order to determine conclusively that an ignition coil is defective, it should be tested by a Honda dealer. If the coil is confirmed to be faulty, it must be renewed; the coil is a sealed unit and cannot therefore be repaired.

Removal

10 The coils are mounted one on each side of the air filter housing. To remove the coils

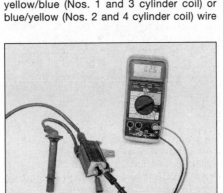

3.4 To test the coil primary resistance, connect the multimeter leads between the primary circuit terminals

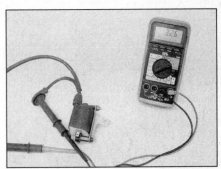

3.5 To test the coil secondary resistance, connect the multimeter leads between the spark plug caps

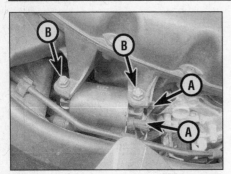

3.11a Primary circuit connectors (A) and mounting nuts (B) – V and W models

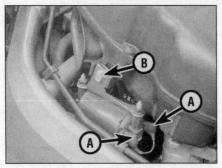

3.11b Primary circuit connectors (A) and mounting bolt (B) – X (1999) models onward

3.11c Note the captive nut on the air filter housing

with their HT leads and spark plug caps, remove the air filter housing (see Chapter 4), then disconnect the primary circuit wiring connectors from the coils and pull the caps off the spark plugs, noting which leads and wires fit where **(see illustrations 3.3a and b)**. The coils can now be removed. Note the spacers fitted on the coil mounting. On X (1999) models onward, separate the coils from their mounting brackets if required. Note the spacers fitted on the coil mounting.

11 To remove the coils by themselves, i.e. without their HT leads, remove the fuel tank (see Chapter 4), then unscrew the HT lead retainers and draw the leads out of the coils, noting which fits where. Also disconnect the primary circuit wiring connectors, again noting which fits where **(see illustrations)**. Unscrew the coil mounting nuts or bolt (according to model) and remove the coil. On X (1999) models onward, note the bolt's captive nut in the air filter housing and remove it for safekeeping if required, and separate the coils from their mounting brackets if required **(see illustration)**. Note the spacers fitted on the coil mounting.

Installation

12 Installation is the reverse of removal. Make sure the wiring connectors and HT leads are securely connected – the yellow/blue and blue/yellow primary circuit wire connectors are for the positive terminals on the coils, the black/white wire connectors are for the negative terminals.

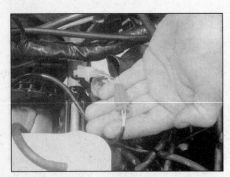

4.2 Ignition pulse generator wiring connector

---

4   Ignition pulse generator (V and W (1997 and 1998) models) – check, removal and installation

Check

1 Raise or remove the fuel tank (see Chapter 4).
2 Trace the wiring back from the sensor, which is mounted in the timing rotor cover on the right-hand side of the engine, to its red 2-pin wiring connector inside the rubber boot above the crankcase and disconnect it **(see illustration)**. Perform the following check(s).
3 Using an ohmmeter check for continuity between each of the connector terminals and earth (ground). If there is continuity between either of the connector terminals and earth (ground) then the pulse generator coil is faulty.
4 Honda specify their own Imrie diagnostic tester (model 625), or the peak voltage adapter (Pt. No. 07HGJ-0020100) with an aftermarket digital multimeter having an impedance of 10 M-ohm/DCV minimum, for a complete test. If this equipment is available, connect the positive (+) lead of the voltmeter and peak voltage adapter arrangement to the yellow terminal of the pulse generator coil connector and the negative (–) lead to the

4.8 Unscrew the bolts (arrowed) and remove the cover

---

white/yellow terminal of the connector. Turn the engine over on the starter motor and note the voltage reading obtained. If this reading is below the specified minimum, the pulse generator coil is faulty.
5 If the pulse generator coil functions correctly then the fault must be in the wiring harness or the ECM, and can be located by a Honda dealer with the test pin box.

Removal

6 Remove the right-hand fairing side panel (see Chapter 8). Raise or remove the fuel tank (see Chapter 4).
7 Trace the wiring back from the sensor, which is mounted in the timing rotor cover on the right-hand side of the engine, to its red 2-pin wiring connector inside the rubber boot above the crankcase and disconnect it **(see illustration 4.2)**.
8 Working evenly in a criss-cross pattern, unscrew the timing rotor cover bolts **(see illustration)**. Remove the cover, being prepared to catch any residual oil. Discard the gasket as a new one must be used. Remove the dowels if they are loose.
9 Undo the sensor mounting bolts, then free the wiring grommet from the cover and remove the sensor **(see illustration)**.

Installation

10 Remove all traces of sealant from the sensor wiring grommet and timing rotor cover and apply a smear of fresh sealant to the grommet.

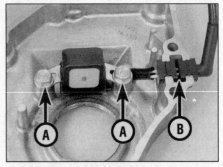

4.9 Unscrew the bolts (A) and free the grommet (B)

11 Locate the grommet and sensor correctly in the cover and tighten the bolts securely **(see illustration 4.9)**.

12 Apply a smear of a suitable sealant 10 to 15 mm either side of the crankcase joints on the mating surface with the timing rotor cover. Fit the cover dowels into the crankcase if removed, and check that the sealing plug is installed, then fit a new gasket **(see illustration)**. Install the cover, making sure it locates correctly onto the dowels **(see illustration)**. Apply the sealant to the threads of the bolts that fit into the upper rear holes that are marked with a triangle. Tighten the bolts evenly in a criss-cross pattern to the specified torque setting.

5 Ignition control unit (V and W (1997 and 1998) models) – check, removal and installation

Check

1 If the tests shown in the preceding Sections have failed to isolate the cause of an ignition fault, it is possible that the ignition control unit is faulty. No test details are available with which the unit can be tested on home workshop equipment. Take the machine to a Honda dealer for testing.

Removal

2 Remove the seat (see Chapter 8) and disconnect the battery negative (–) lead. The control unit is mounted on the rear mudguard at the back, ahead of the taillight unit.

3 Lift the ignition control unit with its rubber sleeve off the sleeve's mounting lugs, then disconnect the wiring connector and remove the unit.

Installation

4 Installation is the reverse of removal. Make sure the wiring connector is correctly and securely connected.

4.12a Install the dowels (A), and check that the plug (B) is in situ, then fit a new gasket onto the dowels . . .

6 Ignition timing – general information and check

General information

1 Since no provision exists for adjusting the ignition timing and since no component is subject to mechanical wear, there is no need for regular checks; only if investigating a fault such as a loss of power or a misfire, should the ignition timing be checked.

2 The ignition timing is checked dynamically (engine running) using a stroboscopic lamp. The inexpensive neon lamps should be adequate in theory, but in practice may produce a pulse of such low intensity that the timing mark remains indistinct. If possible, one of the more precise xenon tube lamps should be used, powered by an external source of the appropriate voltage. **Note:** *Do not use the machine's own battery as an incorrect reading may result from stray impulses within the machine's electrical system.*

4.12b . . . and install the cover

Check

3 Warm the engine up to normal operating temperature then stop it. Remove the right-hand fairing side panel (see Chapter 8).

4 Unscrew the timing inspection cap from the left-hand crankcase cover **(see illustration)**. Discard the O-ring as a new one must be used.

5 The timing mark on the rotor which indicates the firing point at idle speed for the No. 1 cylinder is an 'F' mark **(see illustration)**. The static timing mark with which this should align is the index line on the crankcase cover.

> **HAYNES HINT** *The timing marks can be highlighted with white paint to make them more visible under the stroboscope light.*

6 Connect the timing light to the No. 1 cylinder HT lead as described in the manufacturer's instructions.

7 Start the engine and aim the light at the static timing mark.

8 With the machine idling, the timing mark 'F' should align with the static timing mark.

6.4 Unscrew the timing inspection cap (arrowed)

6.5 'F' mark and static timing mark

6.11 Install the cap using a new O-ring

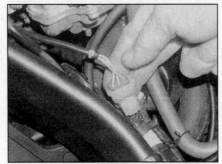

7.2 Disconnect the sensor wiring connector

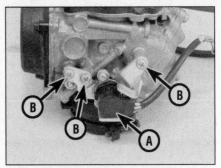

7.9 Throttle position sensor (A) and its mounting screws (B)

9 Slowly increase the engine speed whilst observing the timing mark. The timing mark should start to move anti-clockwise at approximately 1500 rpm, increasing in relation to the engine speed until it reaches full advance (no identification mark).

10 As already stated, there is no means of adjustment of the ignition timing on these machines. If the ignition timing is incorrect, or suspected of being incorrect, one of the ignition system components is at fault, and the system must be tested as described in the preceding Sections of this Chapter.

11 When the check is complete, Install the timing inspection cap using a new O-ring, and smear it and the cap threads with grease **(see illustration)**. Tighten the cap to the torque settings specified at the beginning of the Chapter.

7 Throttle position sensor (V and W (1997 and 1998) models) – check and replacement

1 The throttle position sensor (TPS) is mounted on the right-hand side of the rear cylinder carburettor and is keyed to the throttle shaft. The sensor provides the ignition control unit with information on throttle position and rate of opening or closing. To test the sensor a special wiring harness adapter (Part No. 07GMJ-ML80100) is required. If this is not available, take the machine to a Honda dealer for testing. If the tool is available, test the sensor as follows:

Check

2 Raise or remove the fuel tank (see Chapter 4). Disconnect the sensor's wiring connector and connect the harness adapter between the two halves of the connector **(see illustration)**.

3 To check the input voltage to the sensor, connect the positive (+) lead of a voltmeter to the red crocodile clip on the adapter, and the negative (–) lead to the green clip. Turn the ignition switch ON and check that a voltage of 4.5 to 5.5 volts is present. If it isn't, there is a fault in the wiring or the ignition control unit. If the voltage measured is within the range, note the exact reading on a piece of paper.

4 To check the output voltage with the throttle fully open, connect the meter positive lead to the white clip, leaving the negative lead on the green clip. Turn the ignition ON and open the throttle fully. Note the reading down on a piece of paper. Now multiply the input voltage recorded in Step 3 by 0.824 and record the result. The open throttle output voltage measured must be within 10% of the number just calculated.

5 To check the output voltage with the throttle fully closed, leave the meter still connected as above. Turn the throttle stop screw (idle speed adjuster) fully out, counting and recording the number of turns as you do (this is so it can be returned to its original setting on completion of the checks). Record the meter reading with the throttle fully closed on a piece of paper. Now multiply the input voltage recorded in Step 3 by 0.1 and record the result. The closed throttle output voltage measured must be within 10% of the number just calculated.

6 Now check that the voltage rises smoothly and gradually, and corresponding to the movement of the throttle, by slowly opening the throttle from fully closed to fully open and back to fully closed.

7 Remove the harness adapter. If all the readings and values were as specified, use a multimeter set to resistance or a continuity tester, and check for continuity between the terminals on the wiring loom side of the sensor wiring connector and the corresponding terminals on the ignition control unit connector, referring to the *Wiring Diagrams* at the end of Chapter 9 (first disconnect the ICU connector). There should be continuity between each terminal. If not, this is probably due to a damaged or broken wire between the connectors; pinched or broken wires can usually be repaired. Also check the connectors for loose or corroded terminals, and check the sensor itself for cracks and other damage. If the wiring and connectors are good, check the adjustment of the sensor as described below.

8 If the readings and values were not as specified, and the wiring is good, the sensor or the ignition control unit could be faulty. Take them to a Honda dealer for further testing. If the sensor is confirmed to be faulty, it must be replaced with a new one; it is a sealed unit and cannot therefore be repaired.

Replacement

9 Remove the carburettors (see Chapter 4). The throttle sensor is mounted on the right-hand end of the carburettor assembly **(see illustration)**.

10 Undo the screws and remove the sensor, noting how it keys onto the end of the throttle shaft.

11 Install the sensor, locating the tab on the throttle shaft in the cutouts on the inside of the sensor, and tighten the screws securely.

8 Immobiliser (HISS) system

General information

1 Honda's HISS (Honda Ignition Security System) is fitted to European market X (1999) models onwards. The system will only allow the machine to be started if the correct registered key is used to turn the ignition ON. The system consists of a transponder which is part of the ignition key, a receiver which is fitted around the ignition switch, and the electronic control module (ECM).

2 When the ignition is switched ON, the ECM sends power through the receiver to the transponder. The transponder sends a coded signal back through the receiver to the ECM. If the signal sent by the transponder matches the signal stored in the ECM memory, the immobiliser indicator light in the tachometer (marked by a key symbol) comes on for two seconds, then goes out, and the ECM allows the engine to be started. If the key code signal is not recognised, or if there is a fault in the system, the indicator light stays on. If the light stays on, refer to the fault diagnosis and troubleshooting Sections below. Likewise if the light does not come on at all.

3 The ECM can store the codes for up to four registered keys. They keys should be kept separately (i.e. not on the same key-ring) as the proximity of another key to the one being used in the switch can lead to the signal from it being jammed, and the bike will not start. The key has a built in transponder which can be damaged if the key is dropped or knocked,

gets too hot, is too close to a magnetic object, or is submerged in water for too long. If all the keys are lost, the ECM must be replaced with a new one, so always make sure you have at least one spare key. If a new key is obtained, it must be registered into the system before the bike can be started.

Key registration procedure

To register a new key

Note: *To do this you will need the Honda special tool (Part No. 07XMZ-MBW0100) which is a wiring loom adapter that plugs into the ignition pulse generator wiring connector. If this tool is not available, registration must be carried at a Honda dealer with the special tool.*

4 Obtain a new key from a Honda dealer, then have it cut to match the original key.
5 Raise or remove the fuel tank (see Chapter 4), then disconnect the red 2-pin ignition pulse generator wiring connector which is inside the rubber boot. Connect the special tool wiring connector to the ECM side of the connector, then connect the red coloured clip of the tool to the battery positive (+ve) terminal and the green coloured clip to the battery negative (-ve) terminal.
6 Turn the ignition switch ON using your original key. The immobiliser indicator light should come on and stay on (if it starts to flash after ten seconds, then there is a fault in the system, which will have gone into fault diagnosis, and the pattern of the flashes it emits should be matched with the fault code (see below)). Now disconnect the red clip from the battery positive terminal and leave it disconnected for at least two seconds, then reconnect it. The indicator should now come on for two seconds, then begin to flash repeatedly four times. This indicates that the system is in registration mode. At this point the registrations of all keys except the one in the switch will have been cancelled, so if you have another spare apart from the new one you want to register, this will also have to registered.
7 Turn the ignition OFF and remove the original key, placing it well away from the receiver.
8 Insert the new key into the switch and turn it ON. The indicator should now come on for two seconds, then begin to flash repeatedly four times. This indicates that the system has registered the new key. Turn the ignition OFF and remove the key.
9 To register any other spare keys that will have been cancelled, repeat Step 8. Up to four keys can be registered.
10 On completion turn the ignition OFF, then remove the special tool and reconnect the ignition pulse generator wiring connector. Now turn the ignition ON using any of the registered keys to return the system to normal mode.
11 Check that all registered keys can start the motorcycle.

To register new keys with a new ignition switch

Note: *To do this you will need the Honda special tool (Part No. 07XMZ-MBW0100)*

which is a wiring loom adapter that plugs into the ignition pulse generator wiring connector. If this tool is not available, registration must be carried at a Honda dealer with the special tool.

12 Obtain a new switch and two (or more if you want) new keys (which I presume come with the switch).
13 Remove the faulty switch (see Chapter 9), but retain the receiver to fit with the new switch.
14 Raise or remove the fuel tank (see Chapter 4), then disconnect the red 2-pin ignition pulse generator wiring connector which is inside the rubber boot. Connect the special tool wiring connector to the ECM side of the connector, then connect the red coloured clip of the tool to the battery positive (+ve) terminal and the green coloured clip to the battery negative (-ve) terminal.
15 Place one of the original registered keys for the faulty switch next to the receiver.
16 Connect the new ignition switch to its connector in the wiring loom, but keep it away from the receiver. Turn the new switch ON with one of the new keys. The immobiliser indicator light should come on and stay on, which means the ECM recognises the old key that is next to the receiver (if it starts to flash after ten seconds, then there is a fault in the system, which will have gone into fault diagnosis, and the pattern of the flashes it emits should be matched with the fault code (see below)). Now disconnect the red clip from the battery positive terminal and leave it disconnected for at least two seconds, then reconnect it. The indicator should now come on for two seconds, then begin to flash repeatedly four times. This indicates that the system is in registration mode. At this point the registrations of all keys except the one near the receiver will have been cancelled.
17 Turn the ignition OFF and remove the new key.
18 Install the new ignition switch, then fit the receiver onto it (see Chapter 9).
19 Insert the new key into the switch and turn it ON. The indicator should now come on for two seconds, then begin to flash repeatedly four times. This indicates that the system has registered the new key. Turn the ignition OFF and disconnect the red clip of the special tool from the battery positive terminal.
20 Turn the ignition ON using the newly registered key. The indicator light should come on for two seconds, then go off.
21 Turn the ignition OFF and reconnect the red clip to the battery positive terminal.
22 Turn the ignition ON using the newly registered key. The indicator light should come on and stay on. Now disconnect the red clip from the battery positive terminal and leave it disconnected for at least two seconds, then reconnect it. The indicator should now come on for two seconds, then begin to flash repeatedly four times. This indicates that the system is in registration mode. At this point the registrations of all old keys (for the faulty switch) are cancelled.

23 Turn the ignition OFF and remove the key, placing it well away from the receiver.
24 Insert the second new unregistered key and turn the ignition ON. The indicator should now come on for two seconds, then begin to flash repeatedly four times. This indicates that the system has registered the second new key. Turn the ignition OFF and remove the key.
25 To register any other new spare keys, repeat Step 24. Up to four keys can be registered.
26 On completion turn the ignition OFF, then remove the special tool and reconnect the ignition pulse generator wiring connector. Now turn the ignition ON using any of the registered keys to return the system to normal mode.
27 Check that all newly registered keys can start the motorcycle.

To register new keys with a new ECM (electronic control module)

28 Obtain a new ECM along with two (or more if you want) new keys. Install the ECM (see Chapter 4). Have the keys cut to match the original key for your ignition switch.
29 Insert a new key into the switch and turn it ON. The indicator should now come on for two seconds, then begin to flash repeatedly four times. This indicates that the system has registered the new key. If the indicator stays on for ten seconds then starts to flash, then there is a fault in the system, which will have gone into fault diagnosis, and the pattern of the flashes it emits should be matched with the fault code (see below)).
30 Turn the ignition OFF and remove the key.
31 Insert the second new key and turn the ignition ON. The indicator should now come on for two seconds, then begin to flash repeatedly four times. This indicates that the system has registered the second new key.
32 Turn the ignition OFF and remove the key.
33 The new ECM will only register two new keys at this stage. If you have a third key that you want to register, refer to Steps 4 to 10 to register it, noting that you will need the special tool mentioned therein.
34 Check that both newly registered keys can start the motorcycle.

Fault diagnosis

Note: *To enter the fault diagnosis mode of the system you will need the Honda special tool (Part No. 07XMZ-MBW0100) which is a wiring loom adapter that plugs into the ignition pulse generator wiring connector. If this tool is not available, fault diagnosis must be carried at a Honda dealer with the special tool.*

35 There are two fault diagnosis modes, one for if there is a fault during normal use, and one for a fault that occurs when registering a new key. Make sure you refer to the correct table below when matching the fault code pattern.
36 If the indicator light has come on and stayed on during normal use, raise or remove the fuel tank (see Chapter 4). Disconnect the red 2-pin ignition pulse generator wiring connector which is inside the rubber boot.

Connect the special tool wiring connector to the ECM side of the connector, then connect the red coloured clip of the tool to the battery positive (+ve) terminal and the green coloured clip to the battery negative (-ve) terminal.

37 Turn the ignition switch ON. The indicator light in the tachometer will come on for ten seconds, then start to flash. This means it has entered diagnostic mode, and the pattern of the flashes indicates the fault that has occurred. The pattern repeats continuously. Match the pattern with the fault codes below, making sure you refer to the relevant table. If the indicator stays on after ten seconds and does not flash, then there is no fault logged in the system.

Troubleshooting procedure

Indicator light does not come on when ignition switched ON

38 Check the fuses (see Chapter 9).
39 If the fuses are good, check whether the neutral and oil pressure warning lights have come on.
40 If the lights have not come on, remove the fairing (see Chapter 8). Disconnect the immobiliser indicator black 2-pin wiring connector and the instrument cluster blue 10-pin connector. Using a voltmeter, connect the positive (+ve) probe to the black/brown wire terminal on the loom side of the indicator connector and the negative (-ve) probe to the green wire terminal on the loom side of the instrument cluster connector. With the ignition ON there should be battery voltage. If voltage is present, the indicator unit is faulty and must be replaced with a new one (see Chapter 9). If there is no voltage, check for continuity in the wiring, referring to the *Wiring Diagrams* at the end of Chapter 9. The green wire goes to earth (ground).
41 If the lights have come on, remove the seat (see Chapter 8). Disconnect the ECM 22-pin black wiring connector. Using a voltmeter, connect the positive (+ve) probe to the white/red wire terminal on the loom side of the indicator connector and the negative (-ve) probe to earth (ground). Turn the ignition ON – there should be battery voltage.
42 If there was no voltage, using a voltmeter, connect the positive (+ve) probe to the white/red wire terminal on the loom side of the indicator connector and the negative (-ve) probe to the green wire terminal on the loom side of the instrument cluster connector. Turn the ignition ON – there should be no voltage for two seconds, then there should be battery voltage. If there is no voltage after two seconds, check for continuity in the wiring, referring to the *Wiring Diagrams* at the end of Chapter 9. The green wire goes to earth (ground). If no voltage is present, the indicator unit is faulty and must be replaced with a new one (see Chapter 9). If there is voltage, check for continuity in the white/red wire between the indicator unit and the ECM.
43 If there is voltage in Step 41, disconnect the ECM 22-pin black wiring connector. Using a voltmeter, connect the positive (+ve) probe to the black/white wire terminal on the loom side of the

Table 1: If fault is indicated during normal use

Flash pattern	Fault	Solution
Two short, one long, one short	Faulty ECM	Install new ECM
Two short, two long	Faulty receiver or wiring	Follow Troubleshooting procedure below
One long, three short	Signal jammed by other key	Place other key well away from receiver
One long, two short, one long	Signal jammed by other key	Place other key well away from receiver

Table 2: If fault is indicated during key registration

Flash pattern	Fault	Solution
One short, one long, one short, one long	Key already registered	Use a new or cancelled key
Two short, two long	Faulty receiver or wiring	Follow Troubleshooting procedure below
One short, one long, two short	Key already registered on old ECM	Use a new key

ECM connector and the negative (-ve) probe to earth (ground). Turn the ignition ON – there should be battery voltage. If there is no voltage, check for continuity in the black/white wire, referring to the *Wiring Diagrams* at the end of Chapter 9. If voltage is present, check for continuity to earth (ground) in the green wire. If the wiring is good, check the ECM connector for loose, damaged or corroded terminals. If the connector is good, then the ECM could be faulty, and should be checked by a Honda dealer.

Indicator light stays on when ignition switched ON

44 Check that none of the other registered keys are close to the receiver. If they are, remove them and try the ignition again.
45 Turn the ignition ON with a spare key and check the indicator light, which should come on for two seconds, then go out. If it does, the first key is faulty. If it doesn't, perform the fault diagnosis procedure described above. If a fault code is displayed, use the appropriate table to determine the fault and the solution.
46 If no fault code is displayed, or the system does not go into fault diagnosis mode, remove the seat (see Chapter 8). Disconnect the ECM 22-pin black wiring connector. Using a voltmeter, connect the positive (+ve) probe to the white/red wire terminal on the loom side of the indicator connector and the negative (-ve) probe to earth (ground). Turn the ignition ON – there should be battery voltage. If there is no voltage, check for continuity in the white/red wire between the ECM and the indicator unit.
47 If there is voltage, check for continuity in the yellow and white/yellow wires between the ECM and the ignition pulse generator, referring to the *Wiring Diagrams* at the end of Chapter 9. If there is no continuity, trace the fault and repair or replace the wiring as necessary. If there is continuity, the ECM could be faulty and should be taken to a Honda dealer for assessment.

Fault code indicated by flash pattern

48 If the 'two short, two long' flash pattern

has been indicated during the fault diagnosis procedure, remove the fairing (see Chapter 8). Trace the wiring from the receiver on the ignition switch and disconnect it at the 4-pin white connector. Using a voltmeter, connect the positive (+ve) probe to the yellow/red wire terminal on the loom side of the receiver connector and the negative (-ve) probe to earth (ground). Turn the ignition ON – there should be approximately 5 volts present. If there is no voltage, check for continuity in the yellow/red wire between the ECM and the receiver, and repair or replace the wiring if there is no continuity.
49 If there is 5 volts present, check for continuity to earth (ground) in the green/orange wire, and repair or replace the wiring if there is no continuity.
50 If the wiring is good, using a voltmeter, connect the positive (+ve) probe to the pink wire terminal on the loom side of the receiver connector and the negative (-ve) probe to earth (ground). Turn the ignition ON – there should be approximately 5 volts present. If there is, the receiver is faulty.
51 If there is no voltage, check for continuity in the orange/blue and pink wires between the ECM and the receiver, and repair or replace the wiring if there is no continuity between the connectors, or if there is continuity in either to earth (ground). If the wiring is good, the receiver is faulty.

Replacement

52 To replace the receiver, remove the fairing (see Chapter 8). Trace the wiring from the receiver on the ignition switch and disconnect it at the 4-pin white connector. Undo the screws securing the receiver around the ignition switch and remove the receiver, noting how it fits. If you don't have the correct tools to easily access the screws, follow the procedure for removing the top yoke in the ignition switch replacement Section in Chapter 9.
53 To replace the ECM, see Chapter 4.

Chapter 6
Frame, suspension and final drive

Contents

Degrees of difficulty

Easy, suitable for novice with little experience		**Fairly easy,** suitable for beginner with some experience		**Fairly difficult,** suitable for competent DIY mechanic		**Difficult,** suitable for experienced DIY mechanic		**Very difficult,** suitable for expert DIY or professional	

Specifications

Front forks

Fork oil type . . . . Pro-Honda SS8 suspension fluid or 10W fork oil
Fork oil capacity
   V and W (1997 and 1998) models . . . . 486 ± 2.5 cc
   X (1999) models onward . . . . 483 ± 2.5 cc
Fork oil level*
   V and W (1997 and 1998) models . . . . 154 mm
   X (1999) models onward . . . . 142 mm
Fork spring free length (min)
   V and W (1997 and 1998) models
      Standard . . . . 237.9 mm
      Service limit . . . . 233.1 mm
   X (1999) models onward
      Standard . . . . 232.9 mm
      Service limit . . . . 228.2 mm
Fork tube runout limit . . . . 0.2 mm
*Oil level is measured from the top of the tube with the fork spring removed and the leg fully compressed.

Final drive

Drive chain slack and lubricant	see Chapter 1
Drive chain	
Type	DID 50ZVS or RK 50LFOZ1
Length	110 links
Joining link pin projection from side plate (unstaked)	
DID type chain	1.15 to 1.55 mm
RK type chain	1.20 to 1.40 mm
Joining link staked ends diameter	
DID type chain	5.50 to 5.80 mm
RK type chain	5.55 to 5.85 mm
Sprocket sizes	
Front (engine) sprocket	17T
Rear (wheel) sprocket	
European models	44T
US and Canadian models	45T

Torque settings

Bottom yoke fork clamp bolts	49 Nm
Brake hose holder bolt (left-hand fork)	12 Nm
Brake pipe joint (right-hand fork)	12 Nm
Centrestand pivot bolts	54 Nm
Clutch master cylinder clamp bolts	12 Nm
Delay valve mounting bolts	12 Nm
Footrest bracket mounting bolts	26 Nm
Fork damper cartridge bolt	20 Nm
Fork top bolt	23 Nm
Front brake master cylinder clamp bolts	12 Nm
Front sprocket bolt	54 Nm
Handlebar clamp bolts	26 Nm
Handlebar end-weight screws	10 Nm
Rear sprocket nuts	108 Nm
Shock absorber mounting bolt nuts	42 Nm
Silencer mounting nut	26 Nm
Sidestand bracket mounting bolts	54 Nm
Sidestand pivot bolt	10 Nm
Sidestand pivot bolt nut	29 Nm
Steering head bearing adjuster nut (see text)	25 Nm
Steering stem nut	103 Nm
Suspension linkage bolt nuts	
Linkage arm to frame	59 Nm
Linkage arm to linkage plate	42 Nm
Linkage plate to swingarm	42 Nm
Swingarm brake hose guide bolts	12 Nm
Swingarm drive chain slider bolts	9 Nm
Swingarm pivot adjuster bolt	15 Nm
Swingarm pivot adjuster bolt locknut	64 Nm
Swingarm pivot bolt nut	93 Nm
Top yoke fork clamp bolts	23 Nm

1 General information

All models have a box-section twin-spar aluminium frame which uses the engine as a stressed member.

Front suspension is by a pair of oil-damped telescopic forks. The forks have a cartridge damper but are not adjustable.

At the rear, a box-section aluminium swingarm acts on a single shock absorber via a three-way linkage. The shock absorber is adjustable for rebound damping.

The drive to the rear wheel is by chain and sprockets.

2 Frame – inspection and repair

1 The frame should not require attention unless accident damage has occurred. In most cases, frame replacement is the only satisfactory remedy for such damage. A few frame specialists have the jigs and other equipment necessary for straightening the frame to the required standard of accuracy, but even then there is no simple way of assessing to what extent the frame may have been over stressed.

2 After the machine has accumulated a lot of miles, the frame should be examined closely for signs of cracking or splitting at the welded joints. Loose engine mount bolts can cause ovaling or fracturing of the mounting tabs. Minor damage can often be repaired by welding, depending on the extent and nature of the damage.

3 Remember that a frame which is out of alignment will cause handling problems. If misalignment is suspected as the result of an accident, it will be necessary to strip the machine completely so the frame can be thoroughly checked.

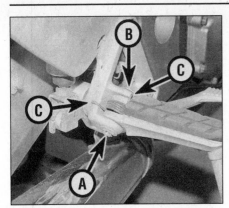

3.1a Remove the circlip and washer (A) and withdraw the pivot pin (B), noting the return spring ends (C) – front footrest

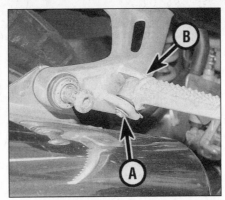

3.1b Remove the circlip and washer (A) and withdraw the pivot pin (B) – rear footrest

bolts and the silencer nut to the torque setting specified at the beginning of the Chapter.
d) *Check the operation of the rear brake light switch (see Chapter 1).*

Gearchange lever

Removal

10 Unscrew the gearchange lever pinch bolt and slide the lever off the shaft, noting how the punch mark on the shaft aligns with the slit in the lever clamp **(see illustration)**. If you can't see the mark, make you own.

Installation

11 Slide the lever onto the shaft, aligning the slit in the clamp with punch mark on the end of the shaft, and tighten the clamp bolt securely. Note that for personal preference the lever can be moved around the shaft to give a lower or higher lever height – the alignment punch mark is meant as a guide for its setting only.

---

3 Footrests, brake pedal and gearchange lever – removal and installation

Footrests

Removal

1 Remove the split pin and washer from the bottom of the footrest pivot pin, then withdraw the pivot pin and remove the footrest **(see illustrations)**. On the front footrests, note the fitting of the return spring. On the rear footrests, note the fitting of the detent plate, ball and spring, and take care not to lose the ball and spring when removing the footrest.
2 The rider's footrest rubbers can be renewed if required by removing the bolt(s) on the underside of the footrest. Note the fitting of the mounting plate for the rubber.

Installation

3 Installation is the reverse of removal.

Brake pedal

Removal

4 Unscrew the nut securing the front of the

silencer to the footrest bracket and remove the collar **(see illustration)**.
5 Unscrew the footrest bracket mounting bolts and displace the bracket so that you can access the back of it **(see illustration 3.4)**. Make sure you do not strain the brake hose.
6 Unhook the brake pedal return spring and the brake light switch spring from the hook on the pedal **(see illustration)**.
7 Remove the split pin from the clevis pin securing the brake pedal to the master cylinder pushrod **(see illustration 3.6)**. Remove the clevis pin and separate the pedal from the pushrod.
8 Remove the circlip and washer securing the brake pedal on its pivot and slide it off **(see illustration 3.6)**.

Installation

9 Installation is the reverse of removal, noting the following:
a) *Apply molybdenum disulphide oil to the brake pedal pivot.*
b) *Use a new split pin on the clevis pin securing the brake pedal to the master cylinder pushrod.*
c) *Tighten the footrest bracket mounting*

---

4 Sidestand and centrestand – removal and installation

Sidestand

Removal

1 The sidestand is attached to a bracket on the frame. Springs anchored between them ensure the stand is held in the retracted or extended position. Support the bike on the centrestand.
2 To remove the sidestand without its bracket, first displace the sidestand switch (see Chapter 9). There is no need to disconnect its wiring connector or remove it completely, just let it hang from its wiring. Unhook the stand springs, then unscrew the nut on the inside of the pivot bolt **(see**

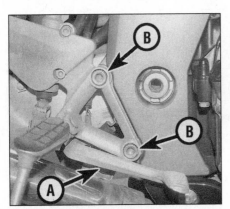

3.4 Unscrew the nut (A) and remove the collar, then unscrew the bolts (B) and displace the bracket

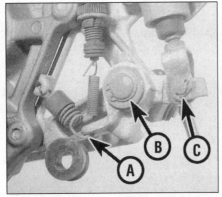

3.6 Unhook the springs (A), remove the split pin (C) and detach the pushrod, then remove the circlip (B) and slide off the pedal

3.10 Unscrew the bolt (arrowed) and slide off the lever, noting the alignment of the punch mark with the slit

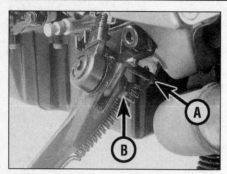

4.2 Unhook the spring ends (A), then unscrew the nut (B)

4.3a Disconnect the wiring connector . . .

4.3b . . . then unscrew the bolts (arrowed) and remove the sidestand assembly

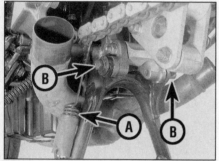

4.8 Unhook the springs (A), then unscrew the pivot bolts (B)

illustration). Unscrew the pivot bolt and remove the stand.

3 To remove the complete sidestand assembly, raise or remove the fuel tank (see Chapter 4). Trace the wiring from the sidestand switch and disconnect it at the green 2-pin wiring connector inside the rubber boot (see illustration). Release the wiring from any clips or guides, noting its routing. Unscrew the two sidestand bracket mounting bolts and remove the stand assembly (see illustration).

Installation

4 If the stand itself has been separated from

its bracket, apply grease to the pivot bolt shank and tighten the bolt and nut to the torque settings specified at the beginning of the Chapter (see illustration 4.2). Reconnect the springs and check that they hold the stand securely up when not in use – an accident is almost certain to occur if the stand extends while the machine is in motion.

5 If the sidestand bracket has been removed, tighten its mounting bolts to the specified torque setting (see illustration 4.3b). Make sure the sidestand switch wiring is correctly routed and secured by any clips or guides (see illustration 4.3a).

6 Check the operation of the sidestand switch (see Chapter 1).

Centrestand

Removal

7 The centrestand is attached to the frame. Springs anchored between them ensure the stand is held in the retracted or extended position. Support the bike on the sidestand.

8 Unhook the stand springs, then unscrew the pivot bolts (see illustration). Remove the stand, noting the collars and on the right-hand mount the spring washer that fit between the stand and the frame mounts.

Installation

9 Apply grease to the pivot bolt shanks and the collars and tighten the bolts to the torque setting specified at the beginning of the Chapter (see illustration 4.8). Reconnect the springs and check that they hold the stand securely up when not in use – an accident could occur if the stand extends while the machine is in motion.

5 Handlebars and levers – removal and installation

Right handlebar removal

Note: *The handlebar can be displaced from the top yoke without having to remove the individual assemblies from it – follow Step 4 only.*

1 Disconnect the wires from the brake light switch (see illustration). Unscrew the two master cylinder assembly clamp bolts and position the assembly clear of the handlebar, making sure no strain is placed on the hydraulic hose (see illustration). Keep the master cylinder reservoir upright to prevent possible fluid leakage.

5.1a Disconnect the wiring connectors (arrowed)

5.1b Unscrew the master cylinder clamp bolts (arrowed) and displace the assembly

5.2a Undo the screws (arrowed) . . .

5.2b . . . and displace the switch housing

5.4a Remove the snap-ring . . .

2 Unscrew the two handlebar switch housing screws and separate the halves **(see illustration)**. If required, free the throttle cable ends from the throttle pulley, creating slack in the cable as necessary using the adjusters (see Chapter 1). To avoid having to do this, note that the throttle pulley can be slid off the end of the handlebar with the cables still attached after the handlebar has been displaced from the fork (see Step 5).
3 Unscrew the handlebar end-weight retaining screw, then remove the weight from the end of the handlebar **(see illustration 5.8)**. If the throttle cables have been detached, slide the twistgrip off the handlebar.
4 Prise the snap-ring from the top of the fork using a small screwdriver inserted in the slit in the handlebar clamp **(see illustration)**.

Slacken the handlebar clamp bolt, then ease the handlebar up and off the fork **(see illustrations)**.
5 If required, unscrew the handlebar end-weight retaining screw, then remove the weight from the end of the handlebar and slide off the twistgrip.

Left handlebar removal

Note: *The handlebar can be displaced from the top yoke without having to remove the individual assemblies from it – follow Step 9 only.*
6 Disconnect the wires from the clutch switch **(see illustration)**. Unscrew the two master cylinder assembly clamp bolts and position the assembly clear of the handlebar, making sure no strain is placed on the hydraulic hose **(see illustration)**. Keep the master cylinder

reservoir upright to prevent possible fluid leakage.
7 Unscrew the two handlebar switch housing screws and separate the halves, noting how the choke lever or blanking plug (according to model) locates in the housing **(see illustration)**. On V and W (1997 and 1998) models, free the choke cable end from the lever.
8 If required, unscrew the handlebar end-weight retaining screw, then remove the weight from the end of the handlebar and slide off the grip **(see illustration)**. If the grip has been glued on, you will probably have to slit it with a knife to remove it. Also slide the choke lever or blanking plug (according to models) off the handlebar.
9 Prise the snap-ring from the top of the fork using a small screwdriver inserted in the slit in

5.4b . . . then slacken the clamp bolt (arrowed) . . .

5.4c . . . and slide the handlebar up and off the fork

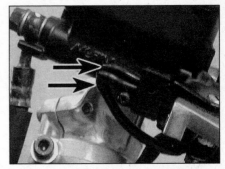

5.6a Disconnect the wiring connectors (arrowed)

5.6b Unscrew the master cylinder clamp bolts (arrowed) and displace the assembly

5.7 Undo the screws (arrowed) and displace the switch housing

5.8 Handlebar end-weight screw (arrowed)

5.9a Remove the snap-ring, then slacken
the clamp bolt (arrowed) . . .

5.9b . . . and slide the handlebar up and off
the fork

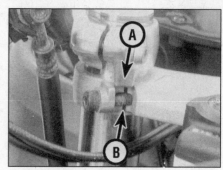

5.10a Locate the lug (A) in the slot (B)

the handlebar clamp **(see illustration)**.
Slacken the handlebar clamp bolt, then ease
the handlebar up and off the fork **(see
illustrations)**.

Handlebar installation

10 Installation is the reverse of removal,
noting the following.

a) *When installing the right handlebar, apply
some grease to it. If the throttle cables
were not detached, slide the throttle
twistgrip and cable housing assembly
onto the handlebar before fitting the
handlebar onto the fork.*

b) *When installing the left handlebar, if
removed do not forget to slide the choke
lever or blanking plug (according to
model) onto the handlebar before fitting
the grip or the switch housing.*

c) *When fitting the handlebars onto the
forks, locate the lug on the bottom of
each handlebar clamp in the slot in the
yoke, so that the handlebars are set in the
correct position (see illustration).*

d) *Refer to the Specifications at the
beginning of the Chapter and tighten the
handlebar clamp bolts to the specified
torque setting (see illustration 5.4b). Fit
the snap-ring into its groove (see
illustration 5.4a).*

e) *Make sure the front brake and clutch
master cylinder assembly clamps are
installed with the UP mark facing up, and*

with the clamp mating surfaces aligned
with the punch mark on the top of the
handlebar. Tighten the master cylinder
clamp bolts to the specified torque
setting, tightening the top bolt first **(see
illustration 5.1b)**.

f) *Make sure the pin in the lower half of
each switch housing locates in its hole in
the handlebar (see illustration). Tighten
the front housing screw first, then the rear
(see illustration 5.2a).*

g) *When installing the handlebar end-
weights, align the boss with the groove on
the inner weight inside the handlebar. Use
new end-weight retaining screws and
tighten them to the specified torque
setting. If new grips are being fitted,
secure them using a suitable adhesive.*

h) *Do not forget to reconnect the front brake
light switch and clutch switch wiring
connectors (see illustrations 5.1a and
5.6a).*

Lever removal

11 To remove the brake lever, undo the lever
pivot screw locknut, then undo the pivot
screw and remove the lever **(see illustration)**.
12 To remove the clutch lever, undo the lever
pivot screw locknut, then undo the pivot
screw and remove the lever **(see illustration)**.
Note how the pushrod end locates into the
hole in the swivel-piece.

Lever installation

13 Installation is the reverse of removal.
Apply silicone grease to the pushrod tip and
to its socket in the brake lever or swivel-piece
in the clutch lever. Apply lithium or
molybdenum grease to the pivot bolt shafts
and the contact areas between the lever and
its bracket. Apply a spray lubricant such as
WD40, or a dry-film teflon lubricant to the
lever span adjuster mechanism.

6 Forks –
  removal and installation

Removal

*Caution: Although not strictly necessary,
before removing the forks it is
recommended that the fairing and fairing
panels are removed (see Chapter 8). This
will prevent accidental damage to the
paintwork.*
1 Displace the handlebars and tie them up
using cable ties, making sure no strain is
placed on the master cylinder hoses (see
Section 5). There is no need to detach or
disconnect anything from the handlebars.
2 Remove the front wheel (see Chapter 7).
Unscrew the bolt securing the front brake
hose holder to the left-hand fork, and the bolt

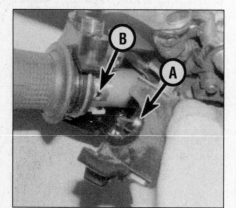

5.10b Locate the pin (A) in the hole (B)

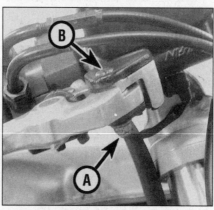

5.11 Undo the nut (A), then undo the pivot
screw (B) and remove the lever

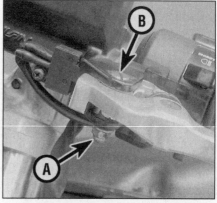

5.12 Undo the nut (A), then undo the pivot
screw (B) and remove the lever

6.2a Unscrew the brake hose holder bolt (arrowed) on the left-hand fork . . .

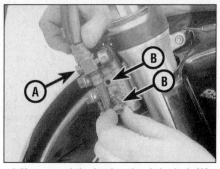

6.2b . . . and the brake pipe joint bolt (A) and delay valve bolts (B) on the right-hand fork

6.4a Slacken the fork clamp bolt (arrowed) in the top yoke . . .

securing the brake pipe joint and the bolts securing the delay valve to the right-hand fork **(see illustrations)**. Displace the whole assembly off the forks. **Note:** *These components should be displaced from both forks even if only one fork is being removed to prevent the possibility of bending one of the brake pipes.*

3 Remove the front mudguard (see Chapter 8).
4 Working on one fork at a time, slacken the fork clamp bolt in the top yoke **(see illustration)**. If the fork is to be disassembled, or if the fork oil is being changed, it is advisable to slacken the fork top bolt at this stage **(see illustration)**. Note the amount of protrusion of the fork above the top yoke.
5 Slacken the fork clamp bolt in the bottom yoke, and remove the fork by twisting it and pulling it downwards **(see illustrations)**.

 HAYNES HiNT *If the fork legs are seized in the yokes, spray the area with penetrating oil and allow time for it to soak in before trying again.*

Installation

6 Remove all traces of corrosion from the fork tube and the yokes. Slide the fork up through the bottom yoke and into the top yoke, making sure all cables, hoses and wiring are

routed on the correct side of the fork **(see illustration 6.5b)**.
7 Set the amount of protrusion of the fork tube above the top yoke at 39 mm, noting that the measurement is from the top surface of the top yoke to the top edge of the fork tube, and not the top of the fork top bolt **(see illustration)**. Make sure it is the same on both sides.
8 Tighten the fork clamp bolt in the bottom yoke to the torque setting specified at the beginning of the Chapter **(see illustration)**. If the fork has been dismantled or if the fork oil was changed, tighten the fork top bolt to the specified torque setting **(see illustration)**. Now tighten the

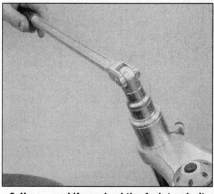

6.4b . . . and if required the fork top bolt

6.5a Slacken the fork clamp bolt (arrowed) in the bottom yoke . . .

6.5b . . . and draw the fork down and out of the yokes

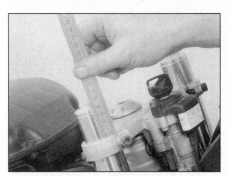

6.7 Set the fork height as shown, making sure it is the same on both sides

6.8a Tighten the bottom yoke clamp bolt . . .

6.8b . . . the fork top bolt (if loose) . . .

6.8c ... and the top yoke clamp bolt to the specified torque settings

fork clamp bolt in the top yoke **(see illustration)**.

9 Install the front mudguard (see Chapter 8), the front wheel (see Chapter 7), and the handlebars (see Section 5). Fit the brake hose holder onto the left-hand fork and the delay valve and brake pipe joint on to the right-hand fork and tighten their bolts to the specified torque setting **(see illustration 6.2a or b)**.

10 Check the operation of the front forks and brakes before taking the machine out on the road.

7 Forks – disassembly, inspection and reassembly

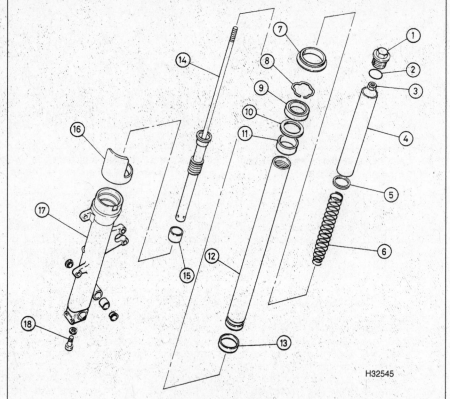

7.1 Front fork components

1 Top bolt	7 Dust seal	13 Lower bush
2 O-ring	8 Retaining clip	14 Damper cartridge
3 Nut	9 Oil seal	15 Seat
4 Spacer	10 Washer	16 Protector
5 Spring seat	11 Top bush	17 Slider
6 Spring	12 Fork tube	18 Damper cartridge bolt

Disassembly

1 Remove the forks (see Section 6). Always dismantle the fork legs separately to avoid interchanging parts and thus causing an accelerated rate of wear. Store all components in separate, clearly marked containers **(see illustration)**.

2 Prise the protector off the top of the fork slider – there are three points around its base that a screwdriver can be inserted, but take care not to scratch the fork **(see illustration)**.

3 Before dismantling the fork, it is advisable to slacken the damper cartridge bolt now so that there is less chance of the damper rotating with it (due to the pressure of the

spring). Compress the fork tube in the slider so that the spring exerts maximum pressure on the damper head, then have an assistant slacken the bolt in the base of the fork slider **(see illustration)**.

4 If the fork top bolt was not slackened with the fork in situ, carefully clamp the fork tube in a vice equipped with soft jaws, taking care not to overtighten or score its surface, and slacken the top bolt **(see illustration 6.4b)**.

5 Unscrew the fork top bolt from the top of the fork tube **(see illustration)**. The bolt will remain threaded on the damper rod.

6 Carefully clamp the fork slider in a vice and slide the fork tube down into the slider a little way (wrap a rag around the top of the tube to minimise oil spillage) while, with the aid of an assistant if necessary, keeping the damper rod fully extended. Counter-hold the nut on the rod and thread the fork top bolt off **(see**

7.2 Remove the protector as described

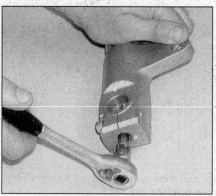

7.3 Slacken the damper rod bolt

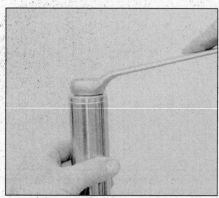

7.5 Unscrew the top bolt ...

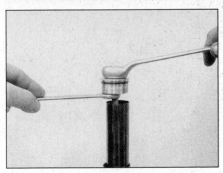

7.6 ... then counter-hold the nut and thread the top bolt off the rod

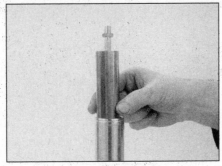

7.7a Remove the spacer ...

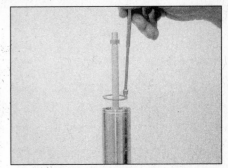

7.7b ... the spring seat ...

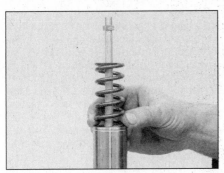

7.7c ... and the spring

7.11 Prise out the dust seal using a flat bladed screwdriver

7.12 Prise out the retaining clip using a flat bladed screwdriver

illustration). Thread the nut fully down the rod.

7 Remove the spacer, the spring seat and the spring **(see illustrations)**.

8 Invert the fork leg over a suitable container and pump the fork and damper rod vigorously to expel as much fork oil as possible.

9 Remove the previously slackened damper rod bolt and its copper sealing washer from the bottom of the slider **(see illustration 7.3)**. Discard the sealing washer as a new one must be used.

10 Withdraw the damper cartridge from inside the fork tube **(see illustration 7.22a)**. The damper seat may come away with it and

be on the bottom of the cartridge – if it doesn't, it can be removed later.

11 Carefully prise out the dust seal from the top of the slider to gain access to the oil seal retaining clip **(see illustration)**. Discard the dust seal as a new one must be used.

12 Carefully remove the retaining clip, taking care not to scratch the surface of the tube **(see illustration)**.

13 To separate the tube from the slider it is necessary to displace the oil seal and top bush. The bottom bush does not pass through the top bush, and this can be used to good effect. Push the tube gently inwards until it stops against the damper rod seat.

Take care not to do this forcibly or the seat may be damaged. Now pull the tube sharply outwards until the bottom bush strikes the top bush. Repeat this operation until the top bush and seal are tapped out of the slider **(see illustration)**.

14 With the tube removed, slide off the oil seal, washer and top bush, noting which way up they fit **(see illustration)**. Discard the oil seal as a new one must be used.

Caution: Do not remove the bottom bush from the tube unless it is to be replaced.

15 If it didn't come out with the damper, tip the damper seat out of the slider, noting which way up it fits.

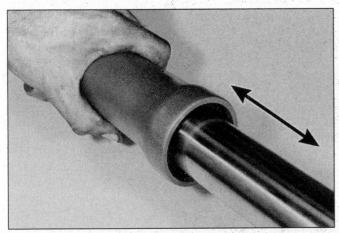

7.13 To separate the fork tube from the slider, pull them apart firmly several times – the slide hammer effect will displace the oil seal and bush

7.14 The oil seal (1), washer (2), top bush (3) and bottom bush (4) will come out with the fork tube

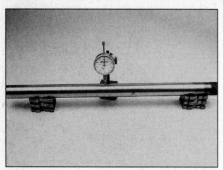

7.17 Check the fork tube for runout using V-blocks and a dial gauge

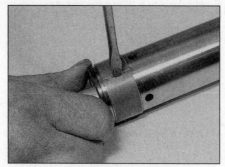

7.19 Prise off the bottom bush using a flat bladed screwdriver

7.21 Slide the tube into the slider

Inspection

16 Clean all parts in solvent and blow them dry with compressed air, if available. Check the fork tube for score marks, scratches, flaking of the chrome finish and excessive or abnormal wear. Look for dents in the tube and replace the tube in both forks if any are found. Check the fork seal seat for nicks, gouges and scratches. If damage is evident, leaks will occur. Also check the oil seal washer for damage or distortion and replace it if necessary.

17 Check the fork tube for runout using V-blocks and a dial gauge **(see illustration)**. If the amount of runout exceeds the service limit specified, the tube should be replaced.

⚠️ *Warning: If the tube is bent or exceeds the runout limit, it should not be straightened; replace it with a new one.*

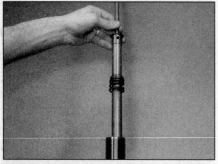

7.22a Slide the damper rod into the tube

18 Check the spring for cracks and other damage. Measure the spring free length and compare the measurement to the specifications at the beginning of the Chapter. If it is defective or sagged below the service limit, replace the springs in both forks with new ones. Never replace only one spring. Also check the rebound spring on the damper cartridge.

19 Examine the working surfaces of the two bushes; if worn or scuffed they must be replaced. To remove the bottom bush from the fork tube, prise it apart at the slit using a flat-bladed screwdriver and slide it off **(see illustration)**. Make sure the new one seats properly.

20 Check the damper cartridge assembly for damage and wear, and replace it if necessary. Holding the outside of the damper, pump the rod in and out. If it does not move smoothly the damper must be replaced with a new one.

Reassembly

21 Oil the fork tube and bottom bush with the specified fork oil and insert the tube into the slider **(see illustration)**.

22 Fit the seat onto the bottom of the damper cartridge. With the fork horizontal (to prevent the seat dropping off), slide the damper cartridge into the fork tube until it seats on the bottom of the slider **(see**

illustration). Fit a new copper sealing washer onto the damper rod bolt and apply a few drops of a suitable non-permanent thread locking compound **(see illustration)**. Fit the bolt into the bottom of the slider and tighten it to the specified torque setting. If the damper cartridge rotates inside the tube as you tighten the bolt, wait until the fork is fully reassembled and tighten it then (the pressure of the spring on the cartridge will prevent it from turning).

23 Push the fork tube fully into the slider, then oil the top bush and slide it down over the tube **(see illustration)**. Press the bush squarely into its recess in the slider as far as possible, then install the oil seal washer with its flat side facing up **(see illustration)**. Use either the Honda service tool (Pt. Nos. 07947-KA50100 and 07947-KA40200) or a suitable piece of tubing to tap the bush fully into place; the tubing must be slightly larger in diameter than the fork tube and slightly smaller in diameter than the bush recess in the slider. Take care not to scratch the fork tube during this operation; it is best to make sure that the fork tube is pushed fully into the slider so that any accidental scratching is confined to the area above the oil seal.

24 When the bush is seated fully and squarely in its recess in the slider, (remove the washer to check, wipe the recess clean, then reinstall the washer), install the new oil seal **(see illustration)**.

7.22b Apply a thread locking compound to the damper rod bolt and use a new sealing washer

7.23a Install the top bush . . .

7.23b . . . followed by the washer

7.24 Make sure the oil seal is the correct way up

7.25 Install the retaining clip . . .

7.26 . . . followed by the dust seal

HAYNES HiNT *Wrap some insulating tape around the snap-ring groove in the top of the fork tube – this will prevent the possibility of damage to the oil seal lips as it is slid down the tube.*

Smear the seal's lips with fork oil and slide it over the tube so that its markings face upwards, and drive the seal into place as described in Step 23 until the retaining clip groove is visible above it.

HAYNES HiNT *Place the old oil seal on top of the new one to protect it when driving the seal into place.*

25 Once the seal is correctly seated, fit the retaining clip, making sure it is correctly located in its groove **(see illustration)**.
26 Lubricate the lips of the new dust seal then slide it down the fork tube and press it into position **(see illustration)**.
27 Slowly pour in the specified quantity of the specified grade of fork oil and pump the fork and damper rod at least ten times each to distribute it evenly **(see illustration)**. Fully compress the fork tube and damper rod into the slider and measure the oil level, and make any adjustment by adding more or tipping some out until it is at the level specified at the beginning of the Chapter **(see illustration)**.
28 Clamp the slider in a vice via the brake

caliper mounting lugs, taking care not to overtighten and damage them. Pull the fork tube and damper rod out of the slider as far as possible, then install the spring with its closer-wound coils at the bottom **(see illustration 7.7c)**. Install the spring seat **(see illustration)**. Install the spacer **(see illustration 7.7a)**.
29 Fit a new O-ring onto the fork top bolt. Make sure the damper rod nut is at the base of the threads on the rod. Thread the top bolt onto the rod until it seats **(see illustration)**, then counter-hold the top bolt and tighten the nut up against it **(see illustration 7.6)**.
30 Withdraw the tube fully from the slider and carefully screw the top bolt into it, making sure it does not cross-thread **(see illustration)**. **Note:** *The top bolt can be tightened to the specified torque setting at*

this stage if the tube is held between the padded jaws of a vice, but do not risk distorting the tube by doing so. A better method is to tighten the top bolt when the fork leg is being installed and is securely held in the bottom yoke.
31 If the damper cartridge bolt requires tightening (see Step 22), clamp the fork slider between the padded jaws of a vice and have an assistant compress the tube into the slider so that maximum spring pressure is placed on the damper rod head – tighten the damper rod bolt to the specified torque setting **(see illustration 7.3)**.
32 Remove the insulating tape from around the circlip groove in the fork tube. Fit the fork protector onto the top of the slider **(see illustration 7.2)**.
33 Install the forks (see Section 6).

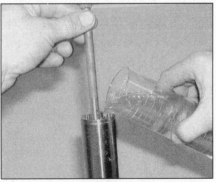

7.27a Pour the oil into the top of the tube while pumping the damper rod

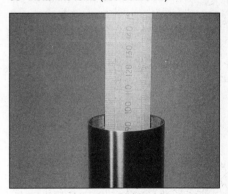

7.27b Measure the oil level with the fork held vertical

7.28 Install the spring seat

7.29 Thread the top bolt onto the rod

7.30 Thread the top bolt into the slider

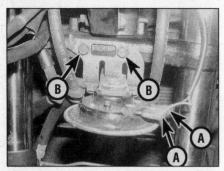

8.2 Disconnect the wiring connectors (A), then unscrew the bolts (B) and displace the bracket

8.3 The wiring connectors are inside the boot (arrowed)

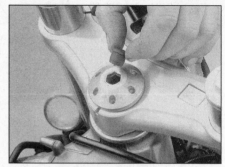

8.4a Remove the plug . . .

8 Steering stem – removal and installation

Removal

1 Remove the fuel tank (see Chapter 4) and the fairing (see Chapter 8). This will prevent the possibility of damage should a tool slip. Also remove the front forks (see Section 6).
2 Disconnect the horn wiring connectors **(see illustration)**. Unscrew the bolts securing the front brake hose and horn mounting bracket to the bottom yoke and displace it. Take care not to strain or knock the brake hoses when removing the steering stem.
3 If the top yoke is being removed from the bike rather than just being displaced, trace the

wiring from the ignition switch, and the immobiliser receiver (where fitted), and disconnect it/them at the white connector(s) inside the rubber boot in front of the instrument cluster **(see illustration)**.
4 Pull the rubber cap out of the steering stem nut, then unscrew the nut using a hex key and remove the washer **(see illustrations)**. Lift the top yoke up off the steering stem and position it clear, using a rag to protect the tank or other components if it is only being displaced **(see illustration)**.
5 Bend down the tabs on the steering stem lockwasher to release it from the locknut, then unscrew and remove the locknut using either your fingers (it shouldn't be tight) or a suitable C-spanner or a drift located in one of the notches **(see illustration)**. Remove the lockwasher, bending up the remaining tabs to

release it from the adjuster nut if necessary **(see illustration)**. Inspect the tabs for cracks or signs of fatigue. If there are any, discard the lockwasher and use a new one; otherwise the old one can be reused.
6 Supporting the bottom yoke, unscrew the adjuster nut using either a C-spanner, a peg-spanner or socket, or a drift located in one of the notches **(see illustrations 8.10d and c)**. Remove the adjuster nut and the bearing cover from the steering stem **(see illustration)**.
7 Gently lower the bottom yoke and steering stem out of the frame **(see illustration)**.
8 Remove the inner race and bearing from the top of the steering head **(see illustrations 8.10b and a)**. Remove the bearing from the base of the steering stem **(see illustration 8.9)**. Remove all traces of old grease from the bearings and races and

8.4b . . . then unscrew the nut and remove the washer . . .

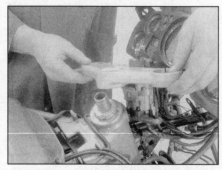

8.4c . . . and lift off the top yoke

8.5a Unscrew the locknut . . .

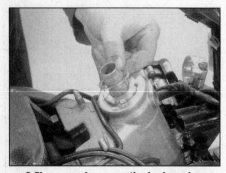

8.5b . . . and remove the lockwasher

8.6 Unscrew and remove the adjuster nut

8.7 Draw the bottom yoke/steering stem out of the steering head

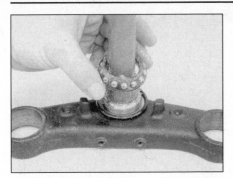

8.9 Fit the lower bearing onto the steering stem

8.10a Fit the upper bearing . . .

8.10b . . . its inner race . . .

check them for wear or damage as described in Section 9. **Note:** *Do not attempt to remove the races from the steering head or the steering stem unless they are to be replaced with new ones.*

Installation

9 Smear a liberal quantity of multi-purpose grease onto the bearing races. Also work some grease well into both the upper and lower bearings. Fit the lower bearing onto the steering stem **(see illustration)**.

10 Carefully lift the steering stem/bottom yoke up through the steering head **(see illustration 8.7)**. Fit the upper bearing and its inner race into the top of the steering head, then install the bearing cover **(see illustrations)**. Apply some clean engine oil to the adjuster nut and thread the nut on the steering stem **(see illustration)**.

11 If the correct tools are available, tighten the adjuster nut to the torque setting specified at the beginning of the Chapter, then turn the steering stem through its full lock four or five times and re-tighten the adjuster nut to the specified setting. Ensure that the steering stem is able to move freely from lock to lock following adjustment – if necessary reset the bearing adjustment as described in Chapter 1.

12 If the correct tools are not available, tighten the nut using a C-spanner or drift so that bearing play is eliminated, but the steering stem is able to move freely from lock

to lock – refer to the procedure in Chapter 1 for details **(see illustration)**.

Caution: Take great care not to apply excessive pressure because this will cause premature failure of the bearings.

13 When the bearings are correctly adjusted, install the lockwasher, using a new one if the tabs are weakened or cracked, onto the adjuster nut and fit the two bent tabs into the slots in the adjuster nut **(see illustration 8.5b)**. Install the locknut and tighten it finger-tight, then tighten it further (to a maximum of 90°) until the remaining tabs on the lockwasher align with the slots in the locknut **(see illustration 8.5a)**. Hold the adjuster nut to prevent it from moving if necessary. Secure the locknut in position by bending up the other lockwasher tabs into its notches **(see illustration)**.

14 Fit the top yoke onto the steering stem **(see illustration 8.4c)**, then install the washer and steering stem nut and tighten it finger-tight **(see illustration 8.4b)**. Temporarily install one of the forks to align the top and bottom yokes, and secure it by tightening the bottom yoke clamp bolt only. Now tighten the steering stem nut to the torque setting specified at the beginning of the Chapter **(see illustration)**. Fit the rubber cap into the nut **(see illustration 8.4a)**.

15 Install the remaining components in a reverse of the removal procedure, referring to the relevant Sections or Chapters, and to the torque settings specified at the beginning of the Chapter.

16 Carry out a check of the steering head bearing freeplay as described in Chapter 1, and if necessary re-adjust.

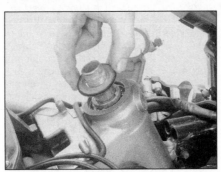

8.10c . . . the bearing cover . . .

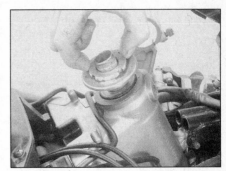

8.10d . . . and the adjuster nut

8.12 Tighten the adjuster nut as described

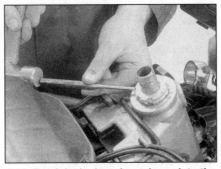

8.13 Bend the lockwasher tabs up into the notches in the lockwasher

8.14 Tighten the steering stem nut to the specified torque

9.4a Drive the bearing races out with a brass drift . . .

9 Steering head bearings –
inspection and replacement

Inspection

1 Remove the steering stem (see Section 8).
2 Remove all traces of old grease from the bearings and races and check them for wear or damage.
3 The outer races should be polished and free from indentations. Inspect the bearing rollers for signs of wear, damage or discoloration, and examine the roller retainer cage for signs of cracks or splits. If there are any signs of wear on any of the above components both upper and lower bearing assemblies must be renewed as a set. Only remove the outer races in the steering head and the lower bearing inner race on the steering stem if they need to be replaced – do not re-use them once they have been removed.

Replacement

4 The outer races are an interference fit in the steering head and can be tapped from position with a suitable drift **(see illustrations)**. Tap firmly and evenly around each race to ensure that it is driven out squarely. It may prove advantageous to curve the end of the drift slightly to improve access.
5 Alternatively, the races can be removed using a slide-hammer type bearing extractor; these can often be hired from tool shops.

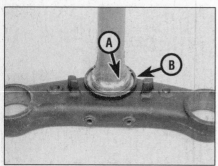

9.7a Lower bearing inner race (A) and dust seal (B)

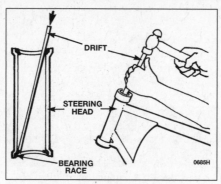

9.4b . . . locating it as shown

6 The new outer races can be pressed into the head using a drawbolt arrangement **(see illustration)**, or by using a large diameter tubular drift. Ensure that the drawbolt washer or drift (as applicable) bears only on the outer edge of the race and does not contact the working surface. Alternatively, have the races installed by a Honda dealer equipped with the bearing race installation tools.

> **HAYNES HINT**
> *Installation of new bearing outer races is made much easier if the races are left overnight in the freezer. This causes them to contract slightly making them a looser fit. Alternatively, use a freeze spray.*

7 The lower bearing inner race should only be removed from the steering stem if a new one is being fitted. To remove the race, use two screwdrivers placed on opposite sides to work it free, using blocks of wood to improve leverage and protect the yoke, or tap under it using a cold chisel **(see illustration)**. If the steering stem is placed on its side on a hard surface, thread a suitable nut onto the top to prevent the threads being damaged. If the race is firmly in place it will be necessary to use a puller, or in extreme circumstances to split the race using an angle grinder **(see**

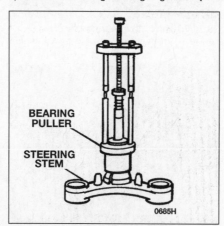

9.7b Remove the lower bearing race using a puller if necessary

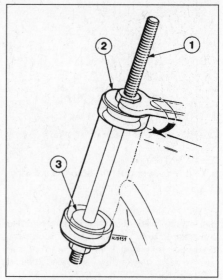

9.6 Drawbolt arrangement for fitting steering stem bearing races

1 Long bolt or threaded bar
2 Thick washer
3 Guide for lower race

illustration). Take the steering stem to a Honda dealer if required.
8 Remove the dust seal from the bottom of the stem and replace it with a new one **(see illustration 9.7a)**. Smear the new one with grease.
9 Fit the new lower race onto the steering stem. A length of tubing with an internal diameter slightly larger than the steering stem will be needed to tap the new race into position **(see illustration)**.
10 Install the steering stem (see Section 8).

10 Rear shock absorber –
removal, inspection and installation

> ⚠ **Warning: Do not attempt to disassemble this shock absorber. It is nitrogen-charged under high pressure. Improper**

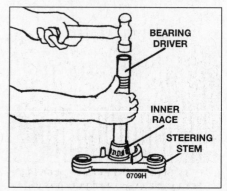

9.9 Drive the new bearing on using a suitable bearing driver or a length of pipe

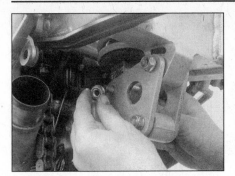

10.3 Unscrew the nut and withdraw the lower mounting bolt

10.4a Unscrew the nut and withdraw the upper mounting bolt . . .

10.4b . . . and remove the shock absorber from the top

disassembly could result in serious injury. Instead, take the shock to a dealer service department with the proper equipment to do the job.

Removal

1 Support the motorcycle on its centrestand. Position a support under the rear wheel so that it does not drop when the shock absorber is removed, but also making sure that the weight of the machine is off the rear suspension so that the shock is not compressed.
2 Remove the fuel tank (see Chapter 4). For best access, remove the exhaust silencers (see Chapter 4).
3 Unscrew the nut and withdraw the bolt securing the bottom of the shock absorber to the linkage plates **(see illustration)**.
4 Unscrew the nut on the shock absorber upper mounting bolt **(see illustration)**. Withdraw the bolt, noting how its right-hand end supports the coolant reservoir, and manoeuvre the shock out of the top of the frame **(see illustration)**.

Inspection

5 Inspect the shock absorber for obvious physical damage and oil leakage, and the coil spring for looseness, cracks or signs of fatigue.
6 Inspect the pivot hardware at the top and bottom of the shock for wear or damage.
7 Check the condition of the grease seals in

10.10 Tighten the bolts to the specified torque

the bottom mount and replace them with new ones if they are damaged, deformed or deteriorated. Lever out the old ones using a flat bladed screwdriver and press the new ones squarely into place.
8 With the dust seals removed, check the condition of the bearing and replace it with a new one if necessary. Refer to *Tools and Workshop Tips* in the Reference Section for more information on bearing checks and replacement methods.
9 With the exception of the bottom pivot hardware, individual components are not available for the shock absorber. If it is worn or damaged, it must be replaced with a new one.

Installation

10 Installation is the reverse of removal. Apply multi-purpose grease to the shock

absorber and linkage arm/plate pivot points. Install the shock absorber with the rebound damping adjuster (on the bottom of the shock) facing the left-hand side. Install the bolts and nuts finger-tight only until all components are in position, not forgetting to locate the coolant reservoir on the top bolt, then tighten them to the torque settings specified at the beginning of the Chapter.

11 Rear suspension linkage – removal, inspection and installation

Removal

1 Support the motorcycle on its centrestand. Position a support under the rear wheel so that it does not drop when the shock absorber lower mounting bolt is removed, but also making sure that the weight of the machine is off the rear suspension so that the shock is not compressed.
2 For best access, remove the exhaust silencers (see Chapter 4).
3 Unscrew the nuts and withdraw the bolts securing the linkage plates to the shock absorber **(see illustration and 10.3)** and the swingarm **(see illustration)**
4 Unscrew the nut and withdraw the bolt securing the linkage arm to the linkage plates and remove the plates, noting which way round they fit **(see illustration)**.
5 Unscrew the nut and withdraw bolt securing the linkage arm to the frame and

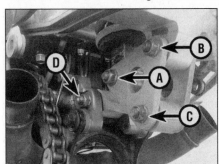

11.3a Shock lower mounting bolt (A), linkage plates-to-swingarm bolt (B), linkage arm-to-plates bolt (C), linkage arm-to-bracket bolt (D)

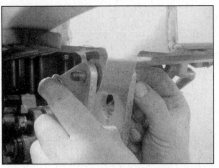

11.3b Remove the linkage plates-to-swingarm bolt

11.4 Remove the linkage arm-to-plates bolt and remove the plates

11.5 Remove the linkage arm-to-bracket bolt and remove the arm

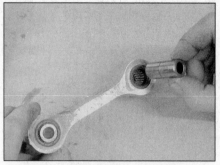

11.6a Withdraw the spacers . . .

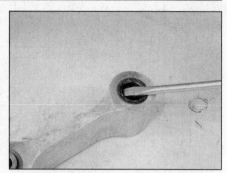

11.6b . . . and lever out the grease seals

remove the arm, noting which way round it fits (see illustration).

Inspection

6 Withdraw the spacers from the linkage arm and swingarm, noting any difference in sizes, then lever out the grease seals (see illustrations). Thoroughly clean all components, removing all traces of dirt, corrosion and grease (see illustration).

7 Inspect all components closely, looking for obvious signs of wear such as heavy scoring, or for damage such as cracks or distortion. Slip each spacer back into its bearing and check that there is not an excessive amount of freeplay between the two components. Renew any components as required.

8 Check the condition of the needle roller bearings. Refer to *Tools and Workshop Tips* (Section 5) in the Reference section for more information on bearings. If the linkage plate bearings in the swingarm need to be renewed, remove the swingarm (see Section 13).

9 Worn bearings can be drifted out of their bores, but note that removal will destroy them; new bearings should be obtained before work commences. The new bearings should be pressed or drawn into their bores rather than driven into position. In the absence of a press, a suitable drawbolt tool can be made up as described in *Tools and Workshop Tips* in the Reference section. Set the bearings centrally in their bores.

10 Check the condition of the grease seals and renew them if they are damaged, deformed or deteriorated. Lubricate the

needle bearings, spacers and seals with multi-purpose grease.

11 Press the seals squarely into place. Install the spacers.

Installation

12 Installation is the reverse of removal. Apply multi-purpose grease to the pivot points. Install the linkage plates with the arrow before the FR mark pointing to the front (see illustration 11.4). Install the bolts and nuts finger-tight only until all components are in position, then tighten the nuts to the torque settings specified at the beginning of the Chapter.

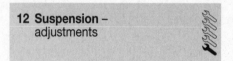

12 Suspension – adjustments

Front forks

1 The front forks are not adjustable.

Rear shock absorber

2 The shock absorber is adjustable for rebound damping.

3 Damping adjustment is made by turning the adjuster on the bottom of the shock absorber using a flat-bladed screwdriver (see illustration). To increase the damping (make the suspension harder), turn the adjuster clockwise. To decrease the damping (make the suspension softer), turn the adjuster anti-clockwise.

4 To set the standard position, turn the adjuster clockwise until it stops, then turn it anti clockwise approximately 1 turn until the

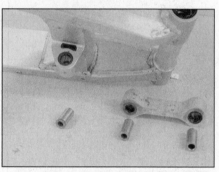

11.6c Clean and check the linkage pivot components as described

punch mark on the adjuster aligns with the index mark on the shock absorber.

13 Swingarm – removal and installation

Removal

1 For best access, remove the silencers (see Chapter 4). Remove the rear wheel (see Chapter 7).

2 Unscrew the bolt securing each rear brake hose guide to the swingarm (see illustration). Displace the rear brake caliper and bracket assembly from the swingarm (there is no need to disconnect the brake hoses), noting how it locates, and tie it to the frame, making sure no strain is placed on the hoses (see illustration).

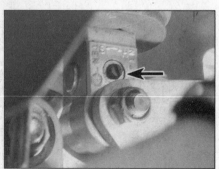

12.3 Rear shock absorber rebound damping adjuster (arrowed)

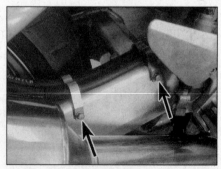

13.2a Unscrew the brake hose guide bolts (arrowed)

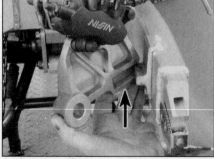

13.2b Detach the caliper assembly from the swingarm and tie it to the frame, noting how the slot in the bracket locates onto the lug on the swingarm (arrow)

13.3 Unscrew the bolts (arrowed) and remove the chain guard

13.5 Unscrew the nut (arrowed)

13.6a Slacken the locknut (arrowed) . . .

13.6b . . . using the special tool if available

13.7 Unscrew the adjuster bolt using a hex key in the pivot bolt head

13.8a Withdraw the pivot bolt and remove the swingarm

3 Unscrew the bolts securing the chain guard to the swingarm and remove the guard, noting how it locates **(see illustration)**.
4 Unscrew the nuts and withdraw the bolts securing the suspension linkage plates to the shock absorber and the swingarm **(see illustrations 10.3 and 11.3b)**. Swing the linkage assembly down so it is out of the way.
5 Unscrew the nut on the left-hand end of the swingarm pivot bolt **(see illustration)**.
6 Slacken the locknut on the adjuster bolt on the right-hand end of the pivot bolt – you do not have to thread it fully off the adjuster unless you want to **(see illustration)**. The locknut requires a Honda service tool, Pt. No. 07908-4690003, which is a special wrench **(see illustration)**. The locknut can be unscrewed using a suitable peg spanner, but

there is no alternative to the use of this tool to achieve the correct torque setting in the tightening procedure (see Step 16); if you do not have access to it, you can tighten the locknut using a normal peg spanner, but it should be later tightened by a Honda dealer with the special tool to ensure the correct torque setting is achieved.
7 The swingarm pivot bolt fits and locks into the head of the adjuster bolt (actually a threaded sleeve). Using an Allen key in the pivot bolt, slacken and partially unscrew the adjuster bolt so that its inner end is clear of the swingarm, i.e. flush with or just inset from the inside of the frame **(see illustration)**.
8 With the adjuster bolt clear, support the swingarm and withdraw the pivot bolt **(see illustration)**. Manoeuvre the swingarm clear

of the shock absorber and out of the frame. Remove the adjuster bolt and locknut if required **(see illustration)**.
9 Remove the chain slider from the swingarm if necessary, noting the collars that fit with the bolts. If it is badly worn or damaged, it should be replaced with a new one – there are some wear limit arrows on the front **(see illustration)**. Inspect all pivot components for wear or damage as described in Section 14.

Installation

10 Remove the collar from the left-hand side of the swingarm pivot and withdraw the spacer **(see illustrations)**. Clean of all old grease, then lubricate the grease seals, bearings, collar, spacer, and the pivot bolt with multi-purpose grease. Insert the spacer,

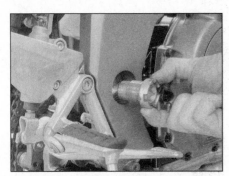

13.8b Remove the adjuster bolt and locknut if required

13.9 Renew the chain slider if it has worn to the tips of the arrows

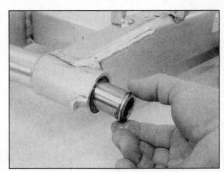

13.10a Remove the collar . . .

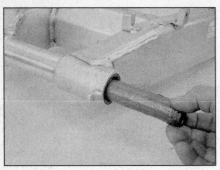

13.10b . . . and withdraw the spacer

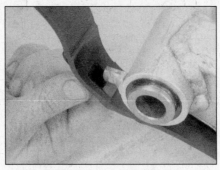

13.11a Locate the cutout in the front over the lug on the swingarm . . .

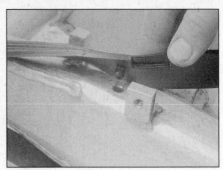

13.11b . . . and the pegs in the holes

then fit the collar. Similarly clean and lubricate the suspension linkage plate to swingarm pivot components.

11 If removed, install the slider, making sure it locates correctly **(see illustrations)**. Apply a suitable non-permanent thread locking compound to the chain slider mounting bolts, then fit them with their collars and tighten them to the torque setting specified at the beginning of the Chapter.

12 If removed, thread the adjuster bolt a little way into the frame, making sure it does not protrude from the inside **(see illustration 13.8b)**.

13 Offer up the swingarm and have an assistant hold it in place **(see illustration)**. Make sure the drive chain is looped over the front of the swingarm. Slide the pivot bolt through the adjuster bolt and swingarm, and engage the head of the pivot bolt in the adjuster bolt so they are locked together **(see illustration 13.8a)**. Tighten the adjuster bolt to the torque setting specified at the beginning of the Chapter by turning the pivot bolt using a suitable Allen key **(see illustration)**.

14 Thread the pivot bolt nut finger-tight onto the left-hand end of the bolt **(see illustration)**.

15 Install the adjuster bolt locknut (if removed) and tighten it as much as possible by hand **(see illustration)**. Tighten the locknut further using the service tool as described in Step 6, using an Allen key applied through its middle to counter-hold the pivot bolt and adjuster bolt and prevent them from turning.

Then, using a torque wrench fitted in the hole in the arm of the service tool, tighten the locknut to the specified torque setting **(see illustration)**. **Note:** *The specified torque setting takes into account the extra leverage provided by the offset in the service tool and cannot be duplicated without it.*

16 Tighten the pivot bolt nut to the specified torque setting, again using an Allen key to counter-hold the pivot bolt and adjuster bolt and prevent them from turning **(see illustration)**.

17 Align the rear suspension linkage plates with the swingarm and the shock absorber, then install the bolts and tighten the nuts to the specified torque setting **(see illustration 11.3b and 10.3)**.

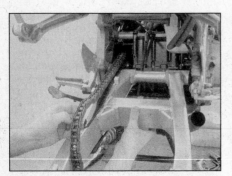

13.13a Install the swingarm, making sure the chain is correctly positioned

13.13b Tighten the adjuster bolt to the specified torque

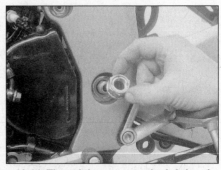

13.14 Thread the nut onto the left-hand end of the bolt

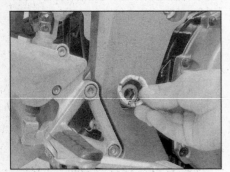

13.15a Install the locknut . . .

13.15b . . . and tighten it to the specified torque as described

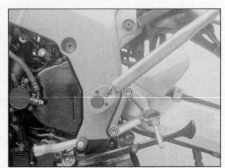

13.16 Tighten the pivot bolt nut to the specified torque

13.18 Make sure the chain guard locates correctly over the lug (arrow)

18 Install the chain guard, making sure it locates correctly, and tighten the bolts securely (see illustration and 13.3).
19 Fit the rear brake caliper and bracket assembly onto the swingarm, locating the slot in the bracket onto the lug on the swingarm (see illustration 13.2b). Fit the brake hose guides and tighten their bolts to the specified torque setting (see illustration 13.2a).
20 Install the rear wheel (see Chapter 7). If removed, install the silencers (see Chapter 4).
21 Check and adjust the drive chain slack (see Chapter 1). Check the operation of the rear suspension before taking the machine on the road.

14 Swingarm – inspection, bearing check and replacement

Inspection

1 Remove the swingarm (see Section 13).
2 Thoroughly clean the swingarm, removing all traces of dirt, corrosion and grease.
3 Inspect the swingarm closely, looking for obvious signs of wear such as heavy scoring, and cracks or distortion due to accident damage. Any damaged or worn component must be replaced.
4 Check the swingarm pivot bolt for straightness by rolling it on a flat surface such as a piece of plate glass (first wipe off all old grease and remove any corrosion using fine emery cloth). If the equipment is available,

place the axle in V-blocks and measure the runout using a dial indicator. If the axle is bent or the runout exceeds the limit specified, replace it.

Bearing check and replacement

5 Remove the collar from the left-hand side of the swingarm pivot and withdraw the spacer (see illustrations 13.10a and b). Lever out the grease seal from each side of the pivot (see illustration).
6 Refer to *Tools and Workshop Tips (Section 5)* in the Reference section and check the bearings – there are two caged ball bearings in the right-hand side of the pivot, and a needle bearing in the left-hand side. Clean them and inspect them for wear or damage. If the bearings do not run smoothly and freely or if there is excessive freeplay, they must be replaced with new ones – refer to the Reference Section for removal and installation methods. The caged ball bearings in the right-hand side are held by a circlip (see illustration). The needle bearing in the left-hand side of the swingarm must be replaced with a new one if it is removed – it cannot be reused (see illustration).
7 Check the condition of the grease seals and replace them if they are damaged, deformed or deteriorated.
8 Lubricate the bearings with multi-purpose grease, then fit the grease seals. Insert the central bearing spacer, then fit the collar into the left-hand side (see illustrations 13.10b and a).

15 Drive chain – removal, cleaning and installation

Removal

Note: *The original equipment drive chain fitted to these models has a staked-type master (joining) link which can be disassembled using either Honda service tool, Pt. No. 07HMH-MR10103 for UK models, or 07HMH-MR1010B for US models, or one of several commercially-available drive chain cutting/staking tools. Such chains can be recognised by the master link*

side plate's identification marks (and usually its different colour), as well as by the staked ends of the link's two pins which look as if they have been deeply centre-punched, instead of peened over as with all the other pins.

> ⚠ *Warning: NEVER install a drive chain which uses a clip-type master (split) link. Use ONLY the correct service tools to secure the staked-type of master link – if you do not have access to such tools, have the chain replaced by a dealer service department or bike repair shop to be sure of having it securely installed.*

1 Place the motorcycle on its centrestand. Locate the joining link in a suitable position to work on by rotating the back wheel. Slacken the drive chain as described in Chapter 1.
2 Unscrew the bolts securing the chain guard to the swingarm and remove the guard, noting how it locates (see illustration 13.3).
3 Remove the front sprocket cover (see Section 16).
4 Split the chain at the joining link using the chain cutter, following carefully the manufacturer's operating instructions (see also Section 8 in *Tools and Workshop Tips* in the Reference Section). Remove the chain from the bike, noting its routing around the swingarm.

Cleaning

5 Soak the chain in kerosene (paraffin) for approximately five or six minutes, then clean it using a soft brush.
Caution: Don't use gasoline (petrol), solvent or other cleaning fluids which might damage its internal sealing properties. Don't use high-pressure water. Remove the chain, wipe it off, then blow dry it with compressed air immediately. The entire process shouldn't take longer than ten minutes – if it does, the O-rings in the chain rollers could be damaged.

Installation

> ⚠ *Warning: NEVER install a drive chain which uses a clip-type master (split) link. If you do not have access to a chain riveting tool, have the chain fitted by a dealer service department.*

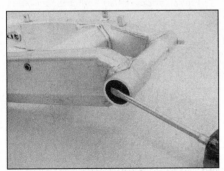

14.5 Lever out the grease seals

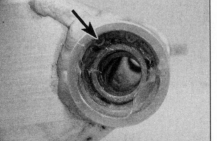

14.6a There are two caged ball bearings in the right-hand side, secured by a circlip (arrowed) . . .

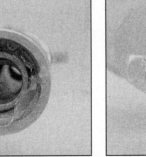

14.6b . . . and a needle bearing in the left-hand side

16.1 Unscrew the remaining bolts (arrowed) and remove the cover

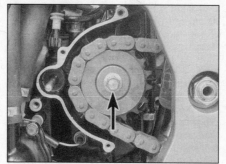

16.6 Unscrew the bolt (arrowed) and remove the washer

16.7 Draw the sprocket off the shaft and disengage the chain

6 Fit the drive chain around the swingarm and sprockets, leaving the two ends in a convenient position to work on.

7 Refer to Section 8 in *Tools and Workshop Tips* in the Reference Section. Install the new joining link from the inside with the four O-rings correctly located between the link plate and side plate. Install the new side plate with its identification marks facing out. Measure the amount that the joining link pins project from the side plate and check they are within the measurements specified at the beginning of the Chapter. Stake the new link using the drive chain cutting/staking tool, following carefully the instructions of both the chain manufacturer and the tool manufacturer. DO NOT re-use old joining link components.

8 After staking, check the joining link and staking for any signs of cracking. If there is any evidence of cracking, the joining link,

O-rings and side plate must be replaced. Measure the diameter of the staked ends in two directions and check that it is evenly staked and within the measurements specified at the beginning of the Chapter.

9 Install the sprocket cover (see Section 16).

10 Install the chain guard, making sure it locates correctly, and tighten the bolts securely **(see illustrations 13.18 and 13.3)**.

11 On completion, adjust and lubricate the chain following the procedures described in Chapter 1.

Caution: Use only the recommended lubricant.

16 Sprockets – check and replacement

Check

1 Displace the clutch release cylinder (see Chapter 2) – there is no need to disconnect the hose. Unscrew the bolts securing the front sprocket cover, noting the wiring clamp, and remove the cover **(see illustration)**. Remove the dowels and the guide plate if they are loose.

2 Check the wear pattern on both sprockets (see Chapter 1, Section 1). If the sprocket teeth are worn excessively, replace the chain and both sprockets as a set. Whenever the sprockets are inspected, the drive chain should be inspected also (see Chapter 1). If you are renewing the chain, renew the sprockets as well.

3 Adjust and lubricate the chain following the procedures described in Chapter 1.

Caution: Use only the recommended lubricant.

Replacement

Front sprocket

4 Displace the clutch release cylinder (see Chapter 2) – there is no need to disconnect the hose. Unscrew the bolts securing the front sprocket cover, noting the wiring clamp, and position the cover aside **(see illustration 16.1)**. Remove the dowels and the guide plate if they are loose.

5 Slacken the drive chain as described in Chapter 1.

6 Have an assistant apply the rear brake, then unscrew the sprocket bolt and remove the washer **(see illustration)**.

7 Slide the sprocket and chain off the shaft and slip the sprocket out of the chain **(see illustration)**.

8 Engage the new sprocket with the chain, making sure the "530" mark (on original equipment, or the marked side on aftermarket equipment) is facing out, and slide it on the shaft **(see illustration)**. Take up the slack in the chain.

9 Install the sprocket bolt with its washer and tighten it to the torque setting specified at the beginning of the Chapter, using the rear brake to prevent the sprocket turning **(see illustrations)**.

10 Fit the dowels and guide plate if removed **(see illustration)**. Install the sprocket cover

16.8 Fit the new sprocket into the chain and slide it on the shaft

16.9a Install the bolt with its washer . . .

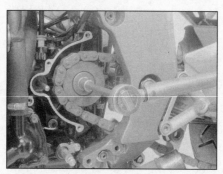

16.9b . . . and tighten it to the specified torque

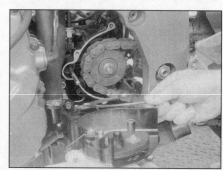

16.10a Fit the dowels and guide plate . . .

16.10b . . . and install the cover

16.12 Rear sprocket nuts (arrowed)

17.2 Lift the sprocket coupling out of the wheel

and tighten its bolts, then install the clutch release cylinder (see Chapter 2) **(see illustration)**. Adjust and lubricate the chain following the procedures described in Chapter 1.

Rear sprocket

11 Remove the rear wheel (see Chapter 7).
12 Unscrew the nuts securing the sprocket to the hub assembly **(see illustration)**. Remove the sprocket, noting which way round it fits.
13 Install the sprocket onto the hub with the stamped mark facing out. Tighten the nuts evenly and in a criss-cross sequence to the torque setting specified at the beginning of the Chapter.
14 Install the rear wheel (see Chapter 7).

17 Rear sprocket coupling/rubber dampers – check and replacement

1 Remove the rear wheel (see Chapter 7).
Caution: Do not lay the wheel down on the disc as it could become warped. Lay the

wheel on wooden blocks so that the disc is off the ground.
2 Lift the sprocket coupling away from the wheel leaving the rubber dampers in position **(see illustration)**. Note the spacer inside the coupling – it should be a tight fit but remove it if it is likely to drop out. Check the coupling for cracks or any obvious signs of damage. Also check the sprocket studs for wear or damage.
3 Lift the rubber damper segments from the wheel and check them for cracks, hardening

and general deterioration **(see illustration)**. Renew them as a set if necessary.
4 Check the condition of the hub O-ring and replace it with a new one if it is damaged, deformed or deteriorated **(see illustration)**.
5 Checking and replacement procedures for the sprocket coupling bearing are described in Chapter 7.
6 Installation is the reverse of removal. Make sure the spacer is still correctly installed in the coupling, or install it if it was removed.
7 Install the rear wheel (see Chapter 7).

17.3 Check the rubber dampers . . .

17.4 . . . and the O-ring (arrowed)

Chapter 7
Brakes, wheels and tyres

Contents

Degrees of difficulty

Easy, suitable for novice with little experience	**Fairly easy,** suitable for beginner with some experience	**Fairly difficult,** suitable for competent DIY mechanic	**Difficult,** suitable for experienced DIY mechanic	**Very difficult,** suitable for expert DIY or professional

Specifications

Front brakes

Brake fluid type	DOT 4
Caliper bore ID	
Left caliper upper piston	
Standard	25.400 to 25.450 mm
Service limit	25.460 mm
Left caliper centre and lower pistons	
Standard	22.650 to 22.700 mm
Service limit	22.710 mm
Right caliper upper piston	
Standard	27.000 to 27.050 mm
Service limit	27.060 mm
Right caliper centre piston	
Standard	22.650 to 22.700 mm
Service limit	22.710 mm
Right caliper lower piston	
Standard	25.400 to 25.450 mm
Service limit	25.460 mm

Front brakes (continued)

Caliper piston OD
  Left caliper upper piston
    Standard . . . . 25.318 to 25.368 mm
    Service limit . . . . 25.310 mm
  Left caliper centre and lower pistons
    Standard . . . . 22.585 to 22.618 mm
    Service limit . . . . 22.560 mm
  Right caliper upper piston
    Standard . . . . 26.916 to 26.968 mm
    Service limit . . . . 26.910 mm
  Right caliper centre piston
    Standard . . . . 22.585 to 22.618 mm
    Service limit . . . . 22.560 mm
  Right caliper lower piston
    Standard . . . . 25.318 to 25.368 mm
    Service limit . . . . 25.310 mm
Master cylinder bore ID
  Standard . . . . 12.700 to 12.743 mm
  Service limit . . . . 12.760 mm
Master cylinder piston OD
  Standard . . . . 12.657 to 12.684 mm
  Service limit . . . . 12.650 mm
Secondary master cylinder bore ID
  Standard . . . . 14.000 to 14.043 mm
  Service limit . . . . 14.055 mm
Secondary master cylinder piston OD
  Standard . . . . 13.957 to 13.984 mm
  Service limit . . . . 13.945 mm
Disc minimum thickness
  Standard . . . . 5.0 mm
  Service limit . . . . 4.0 mm
Disc maximum runout . . . . 0.3 mm

Rear brake

Brake fluid type . . . . DOT 4
Caliper bore ID
  Outer pistons
    Standard . . . . 22.650 to 22.700 mm
    Service limit . . . . 22.710 mm
  Centre piston
    Standard . . . . 25.400 to 25.450 mm
    Service limit . . . . 25.460 mm
Caliper piston OD
  Outer pistons
    Standard . . . . 22.585 to 22.618 mm
    Service limit . . . . 22.560 mm
  Centre piston
    Standard . . . . 25.318 to 25.368 mm
    Service limit . . . . 25.310 mm
Master cylinder bore ID
  Standard . . . . 17.460 to 17.503 mm
  Service limit . . . . 17.515 mm
Master cylinder piston OD
  Standard . . . . 17.417 to 17.444 mm
  Service limit . . . . 17.405 mm
Disc minimum thickness
  Standard . . . . 5.0 mm
  Service limit . . . . 4.0 mm
Disc maximum runout . . . . 0.3 mm

Wheels

Maximum wheel runout (front and rear)
  Axial (side-to-side) . . . . 2.0 mm
  Radial (out-of-round) . . . . 2.0 mm
Maximum axle runout (front and rear) . . . . 0.20 mm

Tyres

Tyre pressures . . . . see *Daily (pre-ride)* checks
Tyre sizes*
    Front 120/70-ZR17 58W
    Rear 180/55-ZR17 73W
Refer to the owners handbook or the tyre information label on the chain guard for approved tyre brands.

Torque settings

Brake caliper bleed valves	6 Nm
Brake caliper body joining bolts	32 Nm
Brake disc bolts	
Front	20 Nm
Rear	42 Nm
Brake hose banjo bolts	34 Nm
Brake hose holder bolt (left-hand fork)	12 Nm
Brake pad retaining pins	18 Nm
Brake pipe joining nuts	17 Nm
Brake pipe joint mounting bolt (right-hand fork)	12 Nm
Delay valve mounting bolts	12 Nm
Footrest bracket mounting bolts	26 Nm
Front axle bolt	59 Nm
Front axle clamp bolts	22 Nm
Front brake caliper mounting bolts	
Right-hand caliper	31 Nm
Left-hand caliper	
Caliper bracket lower pivot bolt	31 Nm
Caliper bracket/secondary master cylinder joining/pivot bolt	25 Nm
Front master cylinder clamp bolts	12 Nm
Proportional control valve mounting bolts	12 Nm
Rear axle nut	93 Nm
Rear master cylinder mounting bolts	12 Nm
Secondary master cylinder mounting bolts	31 Nm
Silencer mounting nut	26 Nm

1 General information

All models covered in this manual are fitted with cast alloy wheels designed for tubeless tyres only. Both front and rear brakes are hydraulically operated disc brakes. The machine is fitted with Honda's Dual Combined Braking System (DCBS), where the front and rear brakes are applied simultaneously – the system may be known as LBS (linked braking system) is certain markets.

Each front brake is operated by a three-piston sliding caliper. The upper and lower piston of each caliper are hydraulically linked to the front master cylinder and the centre pistons are linked to the rear master cylinder. The right side caliper is fixed to the fork slider but the left side caliper is mounted onto a bracket which is allowed to pivot on the left fork slider. This mounting bracket incorporates the secondary master cylinder which is actuated by the torque action of the front left caliper and is connected to the outer pistons of the rear brake caliper, via the proportional control valve.

The rear brake is also operated by a three-piston sliding caliper. The centre piston of the caliper is linked to the rear master cylinder and the outer pistons to the secondary master cylinder (via the proportional control valve). The rear master cylinder is also connected to the centre piston of each front brake caliper, via a delay valve. The system operates as follows.

Front brake operation

When the front brake lever is applied, hydraulic pressure from the front master cylinder is applied to the upper and lower pistons of each front brake caliper (as in a conventional braking system) **(see illustration 1a)**. As the calipers grip the discs, the torque causes the left side caliper mounting bracket to pivot around its lower mounting. The forward motion of the mounting bracket transfers this force to the secondary master

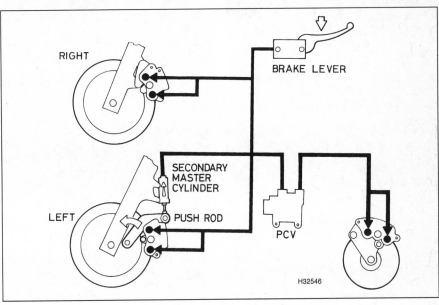

1a Front brake lever operation

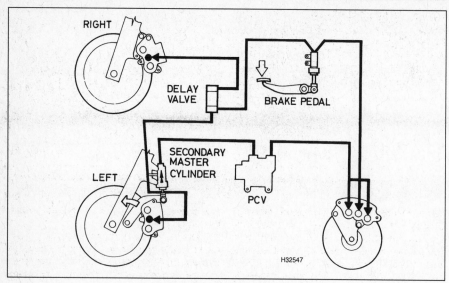

1b Rear brake pedal operation

cylinder pushrod which then hydraulically applies the outer pistons of the rear brake caliper via a proportional control valve, which regulates the pressure to prevent the rear wheel locking under extreme braking.

Rear brake operation

When the rear brake pedal is applied, hydraulic pressure from the master cylinder is applied to the centre piston of the rear brake caliper (as in a conventional braking system) and also to the centre piston of each front

brake caliper **(see illustration 1b)**. The torque reaction of the front left caliper on the secondary master cylinder applies the outer pistons of the rear caliper, via the proportional control valve.

A delay valve is incorporated in the hydraulic supply to the front brake calipers. The valve allows hydraulic pressure to act immediately only on the left side caliper centre piston and isolates the right side caliper. Only when the pressure in the hydraulic system rises above a preset amount does the delay

valve open and also apply the right side caliper centre piston. The action of the delay valve prevents the front forks 'diving' when the rear brake is applied hard and ensures a more natural feel to the braking system.

Caution: Disc brake components rarely require disassembly. Do not disassemble components unless absolutely necessary. If a hydraulic brake line is loosened, the entire system must be disassembled, drained, cleaned and then properly filled and bled upon reassembly. Do not use solvents on internal brake components. Solvents will cause the seals to swell and distort. Use only clean brake fluid or denatured alcohol for cleaning. Use care when working with brake fluid as it can injure your eyes and it will damage painted surfaces and plastic parts.

2 Brake pads – replacement

⚠️ *Warning: The dust created by the brake system may contain asbestos, which is harmful to your health. Never blow it out with compressed air and don't inhale any of it. An approved filtering mask should be worn when working on the brakes.*

1 To allow for the increased friction material thickness of new pads, push the brake caliper against the disc so that the pistons are forced back into the caliper **(see illustration)**. It may be necessary to remove the master cylinder reservoir cover or cap and diaphragm (remove the seat cowling to access the rear reservoir – see Chapter 8) and siphon out some fluid – do not siphon brake fluid by mouth because it is poisonous. If the pistons are difficult to push back, attach a length of clear hose to the bleed valve and place the open end in a suitable container, then open the valve and try again. Take great care not to draw any air into the system. If in doubt, bleed the brakes afterwards (see Section 10).

2 Unscrew the pad retaining pin plug and the pad retaining pin, then withdraw the pin and remove the pads **(see illustrations)**. Press the pads up against the pad spring to ease

2.1 Push the caliper against the disc to force the pistons in

2.2a Front calipers – unscrew the pad pin plug . . .

2.2b . . . and the pad pin . . .

2.2c . . . and remove the pads

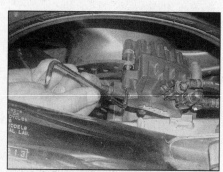

2.2d Rear caliper – unscrew the pad pin plug . . .

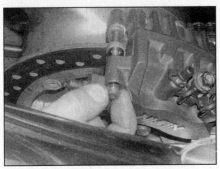

2.2e . . . and the pad pin . . .

2.2f . . . and remove the pads

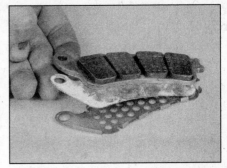

2.6 Check that the shim and lining are properly fitted

removal of the pin if necessary. Note that unless a very short or angled screwdriver is available, it is necessary to remove the right-hand silencer to access the rear caliper pad pin plug (see Chapter 4).

3 Inspect the surface of each pad for contamination and check whether the friction material has worn beyond its service limit (see Chapter 1, Section 3). If either pad is worn to or beyond the service limit, is fouled with oil or grease, or is heavily scored or damaged by dirt and debris, both sets of pads must be renewed as a set. Note that it is extremely difficult to effectively degrease the friction material; if the pads are contaminated in any way new ones must be fitted.

4 If the pads are in good condition clean them carefully, using a fine wire brush which is completely free of oil and grease to remove all

traces of road dirt and corrosion. Using a pointed instrument, clean out the grooves in the friction material and dig out any embedded particles of foreign matter. Any areas of glazing may be removed using emery cloth. Spray with a dedicated brake cleaner to remove any dust. It is also worth spraying the inside of the caliper to remove any dust there, and also to spray the discs.

5 Check the condition of the brake disc (see Section 4).

6 Remove all traces of corrosion from the pad pin and check that it is not bent or damaged. Note that the original pads come with a shim, and a lining that sits between the shim and the back of the pad – check they are properly fitted (see illustration). Smear the pin, the back of the pads and the leading and trailing edges of the backing material with copper-

based grease, making sure that none gets on the friction material.

7 Make sure the pad spring is correctly positioned in the caliper. Insert the pads so that the friction material faces the disc, then press the pads up against the spring and slide the pad retaining pin through (see illustrations). Make sure the pin passes through the hole in each pad, and the pads locate correctly (see illustrations). Tighten the pad retaining pin to the torque setting specified at the beginning of the Chapter. Install the pad pin plug.

8 Top up the master cylinder reservoir if necessary (see Daily (pre-ride) checks).

9 Operate the brake lever or pedal several times to bring the pads into contact with the disc. Check the operation of the brake before riding the motorcycle.

2.7a Front calipers – install the pads . . .

2.7b . . . and push them up against the pad spring to align the holes when installing the pad pin

2.7c Rear caliper – install the pads . . .

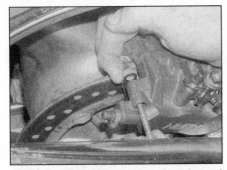

2.7d . . . and push them up against the pad spring to align the holes when installing the pad pin

2.7e Make sure the end of each pad (front shown) . . .

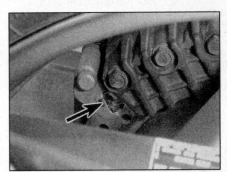

2.7f . . . locates correctly against the guide in the bracket (rear shown)

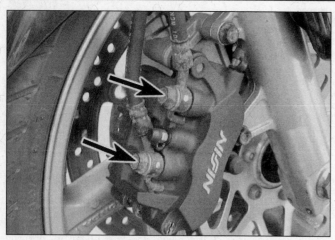

3.1a Brake hose banjo bolts – right-hand caliper

3.1b Brake hose banjo bolts – left-hand caliper

3 Front brake calipers – removal, overhaul and installation

Warning: If a caliper indicates the need for an overhaul (usually due to leaking fluid or sticky operation), all old brake fluid should be flushed from the system. Also, the dust created by the brake system may contain asbestos, which is harmful to your health. Never blow it out with compressed air and don't inhale any of it. An approved filtering mask should be worn when working on the brakes. Do not, under any

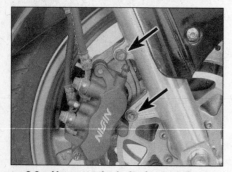

3.3a Unscrew the bolts (arrowed) . . .

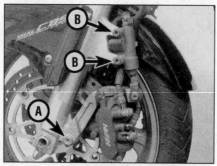

3.3b . . . and slide the caliper off the disc

circumstances, use petroleum-based solvents to clean brake parts. Use clean brake fluid, brake cleaner or denatured alcohol only.

Note: Honda recommend using new mounting bolts and caliper body joining bolts when the old ones are removed. This is because the bolts are pre-treated with a locking compound. It is possible, however, to clean up the old bolts and reinstall them using a suitable non-permanent thread locking compound that is commercially available.

Removal

1 If the calipers are just being displaced and not completely removed or overhauled, do not disconnect the brake hoses. If the calipers are being completely removed or overhauled, remove the brake hose banjo bolts and detach the hoses, noting their alignment with the caliper, and which hose fits where **(see illustrations)**. Plug the hose ends or wrap a plastic bag tightly around to minimise fluid loss and prevent dirt entering the system. Discard the sealing washers as new ones must be used on installation. **Note:** If you are planning to overhaul the caliper and don't have a source of compressed air to blow out the pistons, just loosen the banjo bolts at this stage and retighten them lightly. The bike's hydraulic system can then be used to force the pistons

out of the body once the pads have been removed. Disconnect the hoses once the pistons have been sufficiently displaced.

2 If the calipers are being overhauled, remove the brake pads (see Section 2).

3 To remove or displace the right-hand caliper, unscrew the mounting bolts and slide it off the disc **(see illustration)**.

4 To displace the left-hand caliper assembly, unscrew the caliper bracket pivot bolt and the secondary master cylinder mounting bolts and draw the whole assembly away, leaving the master cylinder connected to the caliper bracket **(see illustration)**. Note how the lower mounting bolt and the collar in the bracket act as the pivot for the caliper to activate the secondary master cylinder.

5 To remove the left-hand caliper, unscrew the caliper bracket pivot bolt and the bracket/secondary master cylinder joining/pivot bolt and slide the caliper off the disc **(see illustration)**. Note how the lower mounting bolt acts as the pivot for the caliper to activate the secondary master cylinder, and that the upper mounting bolt secures the secondary master cylinder pushrod.

Overhaul

6 Separate the caliper from the bracket by sliding them apart, noting how they locate **(see illustration 7.5a)**. If required, remove the

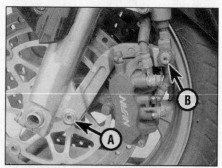

3.4 Unscrew the bracket pivot bolt (A) and the master cylinder bolts (B)

3.5 Unscrew the bracket pivot bolt (A) and the bracket/master cylinder joining bolt (B)

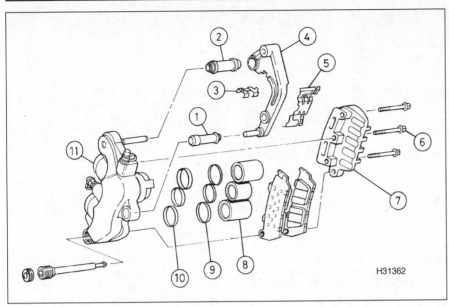

3.7 Front right-hand caliper assembly – the left-hand caliper is similar

1 Slider pin rubber boot
2 Slider pin rubber boot
3 Pad guide
4 Caliper bracket
5 Pad spring
6 Caliper body joining
  bolts
7 Inner body
8 Pistons
9 Dust seals
10 Piston seals
11 Main body

pad spring from the caliper and the guide from the bracket, noting how they fit (see illustrations 7.5b and c).

7 Clean the exterior of the caliper with denatured alcohol or brake system cleaner (see illustration).

8 Unscrew the joining bolts securing the caliper inner body to the main body and separate them (see illustration 7.7). Discard the bolts as Honda specify new ones should be used (see Note at top).

9 Remove the pistons from the caliper body, either by pumping them out by operating the brake lever and pedal until they are displaced, or by forcing them out using compressed air (see illustration 7.8). Mark each piston head and caliper body with a felt marker to ensure that the pistons can be matched to their original bores on reassembly. If the compressed air method is used, place the caliper piston-side down either on a piece of wood or a wad of rag, then use compressed air directed into the fluid inlets to force the pistons out of the body. Use only low pressure to ease the pistons out and make sure the pistons are displaced at the same time. If the air pressure is too high and the pistons are forced out, the caliper and/or pistons, or even you, may be damaged.

 Warning: Never place your fingers in front of the pistons in an attempt to catch or protect them when applying compressed air, as serious injury could result.
Caution: Do not try to remove the pistons by levering them out, or by using pliers or any other grips.

10 Using a wooden or plastic tool, remove the dust seals from the caliper bores. Discard them as new ones must be used on installation. If a metal tool is being used, take great care not to damage the caliper bores.

11 Remove and discard the piston seals in the same way.

12 Clean the pistons and bores with clean brake fluid of the specified type. If compressed air is available, use it to dry the parts thoroughly (make sure it's filtered and unlubricated).

Caution: Do not, under any circumstances, use a petroleum-based solvent to clean brake parts.

13 Inspect the caliper bores and pistons for signs of corrosion, nicks and burrs and loss of plating. If surface defects are present, the caliper assembly must be renewed. If the necessary measuring equipment is available, compare the dimensions of the caliper bores and piston diameters to those specified at the beginning of the Chapter, and install a new caliper or pistons if necessary. If the caliper is in bad shape the master cylinder should also be checked.

14 Lubricate the new piston seals with clean brake fluid and fit them into their grooves in the caliper bores. Note that different sizes of bore and piston are used (see Specifications), and care must therefore be taken to ensure that the correct size seals are fitted to the correct bores. The same applies when fitting the new dust seals and pistons.

15 Lubricate the new dust seals with silicone grease and fit them into their grooves in the caliper bores.

16 Lubricate the pistons with clean brake

fluid and fit them closed-end first into the caliper bores (see illustration 7.8). Using your thumbs, push the pistons all the way in, making sure they enter the bore squarely.

17 If you are using the old caliper inner body mounting bolts (see Note at top), clean them up and apply a suitable non-permanent thread locking compound to the threads. Otherwise use the specified new bolts that are pre-coated with a thread-lock. Fit the inner body on to the caliper and tighten the bolts to the torque setting specified at the beginning of the Chapter (see illustration 7.7).

18 If removed, fit the pad spring into the caliper and the guide onto the bracket (see illustration 7.5b and c).

19 Remove the slider pin rubber boots from the caliper and the bracket (see illustration 7.18a). Clean off all traces of corrosion and hardened grease from the boots and pins. Renew the rubber boots if they are damaged, deformed or deteriorated. Apply a smear of silicone based grease to the slider pins and boots. Fit the boots into their bores, then slide the caliper back onto the bracket (see illustration 7.18b). Check that the caliper slides freely on the pins.

Installation

20 If the caliper has not been overhauled, and if not already done, separate the caliper from the bracket by sliding them apart, noting how they locate (see illustration 7.5a). Remove the slider pin rubber boots from the caliper and the bracket (see illustration 7.18a). Clean off all traces of corrosion and hardened grease from the boots and pins. Renew the rubber boots if they are damaged, deformed or deteriorated. Check that the pad spring in the caliper and the guide on the bracket are securely in place (see illustration 7.18b). Apply a smear of silicone based grease to the slider pins and boots. Fit the boots into their bores, then slide the caliper back onto the bracket. Check that the caliper slides freely on the pins.

21 When working on the left-hand caliper, remove the collar from the lower mounting point on the front fork, then lever out the grease seals and check the condition of the needle bearings in the pivot (see illustration). Clean and regrease them. Refer to Tools and

3.21 Withdraw the collar, then check, clean and grease the bearings

3.24 Install the left-hand caliper according to your removal procedure

4.2 Set up a dial gauge with the probe contacting the brake disc, then rotate the wheel to check for runout

Workshop Tips in the Reference Section and check the condition of the bearings, and replace them with new ones if necessary. Also check the condition of the grease seals and renew them if they are damaged, deformed or deteriorated. Apply grease to the caliper bracket pivot bolt and its collar. If the caliper was separated from the secondary master cylinder, also clean and regrease the bolt that joins them and the collar in the pivot.

22 If you are using the old mounting bolts (see **Note** at top), clean them up and apply a suitable non-permanent thread locking compound to the threads. Otherwise use the specified new bolts that are pre-coated with a thread-lock.

23 Slide the caliper assembly onto the disc, making sure the pads sit squarely on either side **(see illustration 3.3b)**.

24 When installing the left-hand caliper, locate the bottom of the bracket over the pivot point on the fork **(see illustration)**. If the caliper was removed by itself, locate the secondary master cylinder pushrod on to the pivot point on the top of the bracket **(see illustration 3.5)**. If the caliper and master cylinder were removed as an assembly, locate the master cylinder on its bracket **(see illustration 3.4)**.

25 Tighten the bolts to the torque settings specified at the beginning of the Chapter.

26 If detached, connect the brake hoses to the caliper, using new sealing washers on

each side of the fittings. Align the hoses as noted on removal **(see illustration 3.1a or b)**. Tighten the banjo bolts to the torque setting specified at the beginning of the Chapter.

27 Fill the master cylinder reservoir with DOT 4 brake fluid (see *Daily (pre-ride) checks*) and bleed the hydraulic system as described in Section 10.

28 Check for leaks and thoroughly test the operation of the brakes before riding the motorcycle on the road.

4 Brake discs (front and rear) – inspection, removal and installation

Note: *Honda recommend using new disc mounting bolts when the old ones are removed. This is because the bolts are pre-treated with a locking compound. It is possible, however, to clean up the old bolts and reinstall them using a suitable non-permanent thread locking compound that is commercially available.*

Inspection

1 Visually inspect the surface of the disc for score marks and other damage. Light scratches are normal after use and won't affect brake operation, but deep grooves and heavy score marks will reduce braking efficiency and accelerate pad wear. If a disc is

badly grooved it must be machined or replaced with a new one.

2 To check disc runout, position the bike on its centrestand. When checking the front wheel, support the bike so that the wheel is raised off the ground, taking care to support the bike in such a way as to not damage anything. Mount a dial gauge to a fork leg or on the swingarm, according to wheel, with the plunger on the gauge touching the surface of the disc about 10 mm (1/2 in) from the outer edge **(see illustration)**. Rotate the wheel and watch the indicator needle, comparing the reading with the limit listed in the Specifications at the beginning of the Chapter. If the runout is greater than the service limit, check the wheel bearings for play (see Chapter 1). If the bearings are worn, replace them with new ones (see Section 15) and repeat this check. It is also worth removing the disc (see below) and checking for built-up corrosion (see Step 6) as this will cause runout. If the runout is still excessive, it will have to be replaced with a new one, although machining by an engineer may be possible.

3 The disc must not be machined or allowed to wear down to a thickness less than the service limit as listed in this Chapter's Specifications and as marked on the disc itself **(see illustrations)**. Check the thickness of the disc using a micrometer **(see illustration)**. If the thickness of the disc is less than the service limit, it must be replaced with a new one.

4.3a Front disc minimum thickness markings

4.3b Rear disc minimum thickness markings

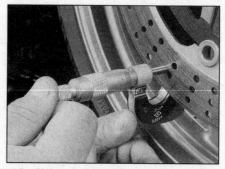

4.3c Using a micrometer to measure disc thickness

4.5a Front disc bolts (arrowed)

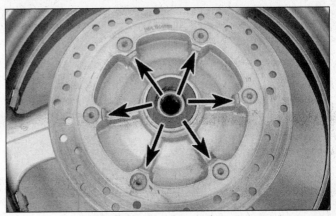

4.5b Rear disc bolts (arrowed)

Removal

4 Remove the wheel (see Section 13 or 14). *Caution: Do not lay the wheel down and allow it to rest on the disc – the disc could become warped. Set the wheel on wood blocks so the disc doesn't support the weight of the wheel.*

5 Mark the relationship of the disc to the wheel, so it can be installed in the same position. Unscrew the disc retaining bolts, loosening them a little at a time in a criss-cross pattern to avoid distorting the disc, then remove the disc from the wheel **(see illustrations)**.

Installation

6 Before installing the disc, make sure there is no dirt or corrosion where the disc seats on the hub, particularly right in the angle of the seat, as this will not allow the disc to sit flat when it is bolted down and it will appear to be warped when checked or when using the brake.

7 Install the disc on the wheel, making sure the directional arrow is on the outside and pointing in the direction of normal (i.e. forward) rotation. Align the previously applied matchmarks (if you're reinstalling the original disc).

8 Apply a suitable non-permanent thread locking compound to the bolts, using new ones if required (see **Note** at top) and tighten them evenly in a criss-cross pattern to the

torque setting specified at the beginning of the Chapter **(see illustration 7.5a or b)**. Clean off all grease from the brake disc(s) using acetone or brake system cleaner. If a new brake disc has been installed, remove any protective coating from its working surfaces.

9 Install the wheel (see Section 13 or 14).

10 Operate the brake lever and pedal several times to bring the pads into contact with the disc. Check the operation of the brakes carefully before riding the bike.

5 Front brake master cylinder – removal, overhaul and installation

1 If the master cylinder is leaking fluid, or if the lever does not produce a firm feel when the brake is applied, and bleeding the brakes does not help (see Section 10), and the hydraulic hoses, pipes and unions are all in good condition, then master cylinder overhaul is recommended.

2 Before disassembling the master cylinder, read through the entire procedure and make sure that you have the correct rebuild kit. Also, you will need some new DOT 4 brake fluid, some clean rags and internal circlip pliers. **Note:** *To prevent damage to the paint from spilled brake fluid, always cover the fuel tank when working on the master cylinder.*
Caution: Disassembly, overhaul and

reassembly of the brake master cylinder must be done in a spotlessly clean work area to avoid contamination and possible failure of the brake hydraulic system components.

Removal

Note: *If the master cylinder is being displaced from the handlebar and not being removed completely or overhauled, follow Steps 4 and 7 only.*

3 Loosen, but do not remove, the screws holding the reservoir cover in place.

4 Disconnect the electrical connectors from the brake light switch **(see illustration)**.

5 Remove the front brake lever (see Chapter 6).

6 Unscrew the brake hose banjo bolt and separate the hose from the master cylinder, noting its alignment **(see illustration)**. Discard the two sealing washers as they must be replaced with new ones. Wrap the end of the hose in a clean rag and suspend it in an upright position or bend it down carefully and place the open end in a clean container. The objective is to prevent excessive loss of brake fluid, fluid spills and system contamination.

7 Unscrew the master cylinder clamp bolts, then lift the master cylinder and reservoir away from the handlebar, noting how the top mating surfaces of the clamp align with the punch mark on the top of the handlebar **(see illustration)**.

5.4 Disconnect the brake light switch wiring connectors (arrowed)

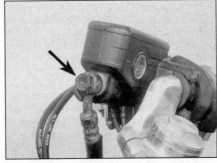

5.6 Note the alignment of the hose before removing the banjo bolt (arrowed)

5.7 Unscrew the clamp bolts (arrowed) and remove the master cylinder assembly

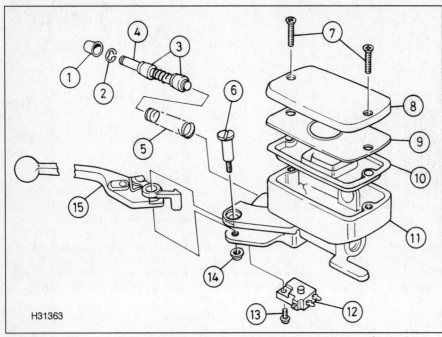

H31363

5.10 Front brake master cylinder assembly

1 Dust boot	6 Pivot screw	11 Master cylinder/reservoir
2 Circlip	7 Screws	body
3 Piston assembly	8 Reservoir cover	12 Brake light switch
4 Pushrod	9 Diaphragm plate	13 Screw
5 Spring	10 Diaphragm	14 Nut
		15 Brake lever

Caution: Do not tip the master cylinder upside down or brake fluid will run out.

8 Remove the reservoir cover, diaphragm plate and rubber diaphragm. Drain the brake fluid from the reservoir into a suitable container. Wipe any remaining fluid out of the reservoir with a clean rag.

9 Undo the brake light switch screw and remove the switch, noting how it fits.

Overhaul

10 Remove the pushrod, noting how it locates in the rubber boot. Carefully remove the dust boot from the end of the piston, noting how it locates **(see illustration)**.

11 Using circlip pliers, remove the circlip and slide out the piston assembly and the spring, noting how they fit. If they are difficult to remove, apply low pressure compressed air to the fluid outlet. Lay the parts out in order as you remove them to prevent confusion during reassembly.

12 Clean all parts with clean brake fluid or denatured alcohol. If compressed air is available, use it to dry the parts thoroughly (make sure it's filtered and unlubricated).

Caution: Do not, under any circumstances, use a petroleum-based solvent to clean brake parts.

13 Check the master cylinder bore for corrosion, scratches, nicks and score marks. If the necessary measuring equipment is available, compare the dimensions of the piston and bore to those given in the Specifications

Section of this Chapter. If damage or wear is evident, the master cylinder must be replaced with a new one. If the master cylinder is in poor condition, then the calipers should be checked as well. Check that the fluid inlet and outlet ports in the master cylinder are clear.

14 The dust boot, circlip, piston assembly and spring are included in the rebuild kit. Use all of the new parts, regardless of the apparent condition of the old ones. If the cup and seal are not already on the piston, fit them according to the layout of the old ones.

15 Install the spring in the master cylinder so that its narrow end faces out.

16 Lubricate the piston assembly with clean brake fluid and fit it into the master cylinder, making sure it is the correct way round. Make sure the lips on the cup and seal do not turn inside out when they are slipped into the bore. Depress the piston and install the new circlip, making sure that it locates in the groove in the master cylinder.

17 Install the rubber dust boot, making sure the lip is seated correctly in the groove in the master cylinder. Smear the pushrod ends with silicone grease. Install the pushrod, locating the rubber boot around the groove in the middle.

18 Inspect the reservoir rubber diaphragm and renew it if it is damaged or deteriorated.

Installation

19 Locate the brake light switch on the underside of the master cylinder and secure it with the screw.

20 Attach the master cylinder to the handlebar and fit the clamp with its UP mark facing up **(see illustration 5.7)**. Align the top mating surfaces of the clamp with the punch mark on the top of the handlebar, then tighten the top bolt first, then the bottom bolt to the torque setting specified at the beginning of the Chapter.

21 Connect the brake hose to the master cylinder, using new sealing washers on each side of the union, and aligning the hose as noted on removal **(see illustration 5.6)**. Tighten the banjo bolt to the torque setting specified at the beginning of the Chapter.

22 Install the brake lever (see Chapter 6).

23 Connect the brake light switch wiring **(see illustration 5.4)**.

24 Fill the fluid reservoir with new DOT 4 brake fluid as described in *Daily (pre-ride) checks*. Refer to Section 10 of this Chapter and bleed the air from the system.

25 Fit the rubber diaphragm, making sure it is correctly seated, the diaphragm plate and the cover or cap onto the reservoir.

26 Check the operation of the front brake and brake light before riding the motorcycle.

---

6 Secondary master cylinder, delay valve and proportional control valve – overhaul

Secondary master cylinder

Removal

1 Before disassembling the master cylinder, read through the entire procedure and make sure that you have the correct rebuild kit. Also, you will need some new DOT 4 brake fluid, some clean rags and internal circlip pliers. **Note:** *To prevent damage to any paint from spilled brake fluid, always cover painted components when working on the master cylinder.*

Caution: Disassembly, overhaul and reassembly of the brake master cylinder must be done in a spotlessly clean work area to avoid contamination and possible failure of the brake hydraulic system components.

2 Unscrew the top brake hose banjo bolt, noting its alignment, and separate the hose from the master cylinder **(see illustration)**.

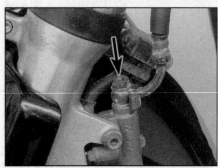

6.2 Secondary master cylinder hose top banjo bolt (arrowed)

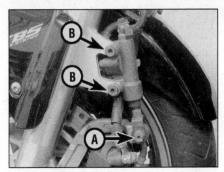

6.3 Unscrew the bracket/pushrod joining bolt (A), then unscrew the mounting bolts (B)

Plug the hose end or wrap a plastic bag tightly around it to minimise fluid loss and prevent dirt entering the system. Discard the sealing washers as new ones must be used on installation.

3 Unscrew the caliper bracket/secondary master cylinder joining/pivot bolt and the secondary master cylinder mounting bolts **(see illustration)**. Displace the master cylinder and twist it to access the brake hose joint banjo bolt on the front, then unscrew that, following the guidelines in Step 2.

Overhaul

4 Dislodge the rubber dust boot from the master cylinder to reveal the pushrod retaining circlip **(see illustration)**.

5 Depress the pushrod and, using circlip pliers, release the circlip. Slide out the pushrod, piston assembly and spring. If they are difficult to remove, apply low pressure compressed air to the fluid outlet. Lay the parts out in the proper order to prevent confusion during reassembly.

6 Clean all of the parts with clean brake fluid or denatured alcohol.

Caution: Do not, under any circumstances, use a petroleum-based solvent to clean brake parts. If compressed air is available, use it to dry the parts thoroughly (make sure it's filtered and unlubricated).

7 Check the master cylinder bore for corrosion, scratches, nicks and score marks. If the necessary measuring equipment is available, compare the dimensions of the piston and bore to those given in the Specifications Section of this Chapter. If damage is evident, the master cylinder must be replaced with a new one.

8 The dust boot, circlip, piston assembly and spring are included in the rebuild kit. Use all of the new parts, regardless of the apparent condition of the old ones. If the seal is not on the piston, fit it according to the position of the old one.

9 Lubricate the primary cup with clean brake fluid and fit it onto the narrow end of the spring, so that the coil fits over the lug on the inside of the cup. Install the spring and cup in the master cylinder, with the cup end facing out, making sure its lips do not turn inside out.

10 Lubricate the piston assembly with clean

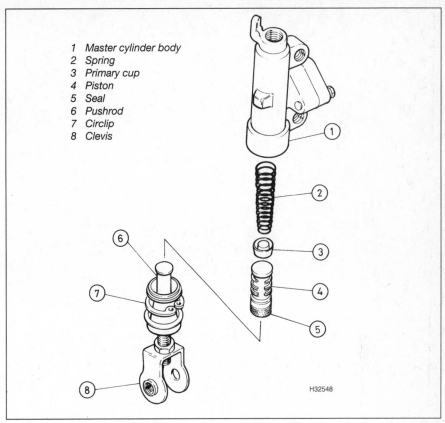

1 Master cylinder body
2 Spring
3 Primary cup
4 Piston
5 Seal
6 Pushrod
7 Circlip
8 Clevis

H32548

6.4 Secondary master cylinder assembly

hydraulic fluid and install it into the master cylinder, making sure it is the correct way round. Make sure the lips on the seal do not turn inside out when the piston is slipped into the bore.

11 Apply some silicone grease to the contact area between the pushrod and piston. Install the pushrod and depress it, then secure it with the circlip, making sure it is properly seated in the groove.

12 Locate the rubber dust boot in the groove.

13 Withdraw the collar from the pivot in the top of the brake caliper bracket. Clean off all traces of dirt, corrosion and old grease. Lubricate the collar and the pivot bolt with grease.

Installation

14 Connect the brake hose joint to the front of the master cylinder, using new sealing washers on each side of the banjo union. Ensure that the hose is positioned as noted on removal. Tighten the banjo bolt to the specified torque setting.

15 Install the master cylinder and tighten its mounting bolts to the specified torque setting **(see illustration 6.3)**. Locate the pushrod on to the pivot point on the top of the caliper bracket and tighten the joining/pivot bolt to the specified torque setting.

16 Connect the brake hose to the top of the master cylinder, using new sealing washers on each side of the banjo union **(see**

illustration 6.2). Ensure that the hose is positioned as noted on removal. Tighten the banjo bolt to the specified torque setting.

17 Bleed the system following the procedure in Section 10.

18 Check the operation of the brakes carefully before riding the motorcycle.

Delay valve and proportional control valve

Removal

19 The delay valve is mounted on the right-hand fork. Unscrew the two brake hose banjo bolts, noting the alignment of the hoses on the valve and which fits where, and separate the hoses from the valve **(see illustration)**. Plug

6.19a Brake hose banjo bolts (A), brake hose/pipe joint bolt (B), delay valve mounting bolts (C)

6.19b Brake pipe joining nut (arrowed)

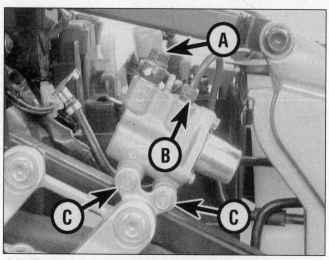

6.20 Brake hose banjo bolt (A), brake pipe joint nut (B), mounting bolts (C)

the hose ends or wrap a plastic bag tightly around them to minimise fluid loss and prevent dirt entering the system. Discard the sealing washers as new ones must be used on installation. Unscrew the bolt securing the brake hose/pipe joint to the right-hand fork and displace it to access the delay valve bolts. Also unscrew the brake pipe joining nut and detach the pipe from the valve, again plugging the end of the pipe (see illustration). Unscrew the delay valve mounting bolts and remove the valve.

20 The proportional control valve is mounted on the rear sub-frame on the right-hand side (see illustration). Remove the seat cowling for access (see Chapter 8). Unscrew the hose union banjo bolt and the pipe joint nut and separate the hose and pipe from the valve. Plug the ends or wrap a plastic bag tightly around them to minimise fluid loss and prevent dirt entering the system. Discard the union sealing washers as new ones must be used on installation. Unscrew the two bolts securing the valve and remove the valve.

Overhaul

21 Neither the delay valve nor the proportional control valve can be dismantled for overhaul, and no component parts are

available. If either valve fails, it must be replaced with a new one.

Installation

22 Installation is the reverse of removal. Use new sealing washers on each side of the banjo bolt unions. Tighten the banjo bolts, the pipe joining nut, the pipe joint mounting bolt, and the valve mounting bolts to the torque settings specified at the beginning of the Chapter. Bleed the hydraulic system as described in Section 10.

---

7 Rear brake caliper – removal, overhaul and installation 🔧

⚠️ **Warning: If a caliper indicates the need for an overhaul (usually due to leaking fluid or sticky operation), all old brake fluid should be flushed from the system. Also, the dust created by the brake system may contain asbestos, which is harmful to your health. Never blow it out with compressed air and don't inhale any of it. An approved filtering mask should be worn when working on the brakes. Do not, under any**

circumstances, use petroleum-based solvents to clean brake parts. Use clean brake fluid, brake cleaner or denatured alcohol only.

Note: *Honda recommend using new mounting bolts and caliper body joining bolts when the old ones are removed. This is because the bolts are pre-treated with a locking compound. It is possible, however, to clean up the old bolts and reinstall them using a suitable non-permanent thread locking compound that is commercially available.*

Removal

1 If the calipers are just being displaced and not completely removed or overhauled, do not disconnect the brake hoses. If the calipers are being completely removed or overhauled, remove the brake hose banjo bolts and detach the hoses, noting their alignment with the caliper, and which hose fits where (see illustration). Plug the hose ends or wrap a plastic bag tightly around to minimise fluid loss and prevent dirt entering the system. Discard the sealing washers as new ones must be used on installation. **Note:** *If you are planning to overhaul the caliper and don't have a source of compressed air to blow out the pistons, just loosen the banjo bolts at this stage and retighten them lightly. The bike's hydraulic system can then be used to force the pistons out of the body once the pads have been removed. Disconnect the hoses once the pistons have been sufficiently displaced.*

2 Remove the brake pads (see Section 2).

3 Remove the rear wheel (see Section 14).

4 Displace the caliper bracket from the swingarm, noting how it locates (see illustration).

Overhaul

5 Separate the caliper from the bracket by sliding them apart, noting how they locate (see

7.1 Brake hose banjo bolts (arrowed)

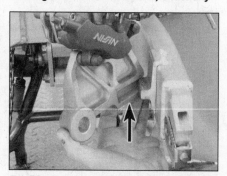

7.4 Displace the caliper/bracket assembly from the swingarm, noting how the slot in the bracket locates on the lug (arrow)

7.5a Separate the caliper and bracket by sliding them apart

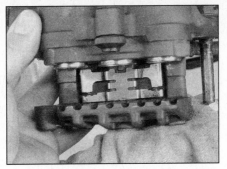

7.5b If required, remove the pad spring from the caliper . . .

7.5c . . . and the pad guide from the bracket, noting how they fit

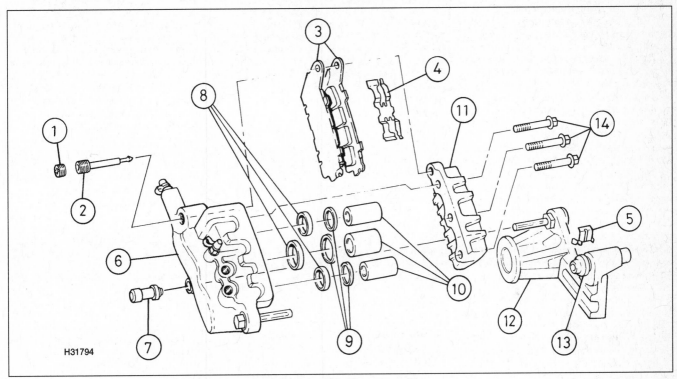

H31794

7.6 Rear brake caliper assembly

1 Plug	5 Pad guide	8 Piston seals	12 Caliper bracket
2 Pad retaining pin	6 Main body	9 Dust seals	13 Slider pin rubber boot
3 Brake pads	7 Slider pin rubber boot	10 Pistons	14 Caliper body joining bolts
4 Pad spring		11 Inner body	

illustration). If required, remove the pad spring from the caliper and the guide from the bracket, noting how they fit **(see illustrations)**.
6 Clean the exterior of the caliper with denatured alcohol or brake system cleaner **(see illustration)**.
7 Unscrew the joining bolts securing the caliper inner body to the main body and separate them **(see illustration)**. Discard the bolts as Honda specify new ones should be used (see **Note** at top).
8 Remove the pistons from the caliper body, either by pumping them out by operating the brake lever and pedal until the pistons are displaced, or by forcing them out using compressed air **(see illustration)**. Mark each

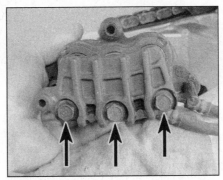

7.7 Caliper body joining bolts (arrowed)

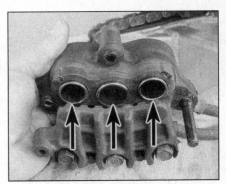

7.8 Displace the pistons (arrowed) as described

piston head and caliper body with a felt marker to ensure that the pistons can be matched to their original bores on reassembly. If the compressed air method is used, place the caliper piston-side down either on a piece of wood or a wad of rag, then use compressed air directed into the fluid inlets to force the pistons out of the body. Use only low pressure to ease the pistons out and make sure the pistons are displaced at the same time. If the air pressure is too high and the pistons are forced out, the caliper and/or pistons, or even you, may be damaged.

 Warning: Never place your fingers in front of the pistons in an attempt to catch or protect them when applying compressed air, as serious injury could result.
Caution: Do not try to remove the pistons by levering them out, or by using pliers or any other grips.

9 Using a wooden or plastic tool, remove the dust seals from the caliper bores. Discard them as new ones must be used on installation. If a metal tool is being used, take great care not to damage the caliper bores.
10 Remove and discard the piston seals in the same way.
11 Clean the pistons and bores with clean brake fluid of the specified type. If compressed air is available, use it to dry the parts thoroughly (make sure it's filtered and unlubricated).
Caution: Do not, under any circumstances, use a petroleum-based solvent to clean brake parts.
12 Inspect the caliper bores and pistons for signs of corrosion, nicks and burrs and loss of plating. If surface defects are present, the caliper assembly must be renewed. If the necessary measuring equipment is available, compare the dimensions of the caliper bores and piston diameters to those specified at the beginning of the Chapter, and install a new caliper or pistons if necessary. If the caliper is

in bad shape the master cylinder should also be checked.
13 Lubricate the new piston seals with clean brake fluid and fit them into their grooves in the caliper bores. Note that different sizes of bore and piston are used (see Specifications), and care must therefore be taken to ensure that the correct size seals are fitted to the correct bores. The same applies when fitting the new dust seals and pistons.
14 Lubricate the new dust seals with silicone grease and fit them into their grooves in the caliper bores.
15 Lubricate the pistons with clean brake fluid and fit them closed-end first into the caliper bores. Using your thumbs, push the pistons all the way in, making sure they enter the bore squarely **(see illustration 7.8)**.
16 If you are using the old caliper inner body mounting bolts (see **Note** at top), clean them up and apply a suitable non-permanent thread locking compound to the threads. Otherwise use the specified new bolts that are pre-coated with a thread-lock. Fit the inner body on to the caliper and tighten the bolts to the torque setting specified at the beginning of the Chapter **(see illustration 7.7)**.
17 If removed, fit the pad spring into the caliper and the guide onto the bracket **(see illustration 7.5b and c)**.
18 Remove the slider pin rubber boots from the caliper and the bracket **(see illustration)**. Clean off all traces of corrosion and hardened grease from the boots and pins. Renew the rubber boots if they are damaged, deformed or deteriorated. Apply a smear of silicone based grease to the slider pins and boots. Fit the boots into their bores, then slide the caliper back onto the bracket **(see illustration)**. Check that the caliper slides freely on the pins.

Installation

19 If the caliper has not been overhauled, and if not already done, separate the caliper from the bracket by sliding them apart, noting how they locate **(see illustration 7.5a)**. Remove the

slider pin rubber boots from the caliper and the bracket **(see illustration 7.18a)**. Clean off all traces of corrosion and hardened grease from the boots and pins. Renew the rubber boots if they are damaged, deformed or deteriorated. Check that the pad spring in the caliper and the guide on the bracket are securely in place **(see illustration 7.5b and c)**. Apply a smear of silicone based grease to the slider pins and boots. Fit the boots into their bores, then slide the caliper back onto the bracket **(see illustration 7.18b)**. Check that the caliper slides freely on the pins.
20 Locate the rear brake caliper and bracket assembly onto the swingarm **(see illustration 7.4)**.
21 Install the rear wheel (see Section 14).
22 Install the brake pads (see Section 2).
23 If detached, connect the brake hoses to the caliper, using new sealing washers on each side of the fittings. Align the hoses as noted on removal **(see illustration 7.1)**. Tighten the banjo bolts to the torque setting specified at the beginning of the Chapter.
24 Fill the master cylinder reservoir with DOT 4 brake fluid (see *Daily (pre-ride) checks*) and bleed the hydraulic system as described in Section 10.
25 Check for leaks and thoroughly test the operation of the brakes before riding the motorcycle on the road.

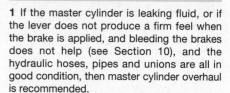
8 Rear brake master cylinder – removal, overhaul and installation

1 If the master cylinder is leaking fluid, or if the lever does not produce a firm feel when the brake is applied, and bleeding the brakes does not help (see Section 10), and the hydraulic hoses, pipes and unions are all in good condition, then master cylinder overhaul is recommended.
2 Before disassembling the master cylinder, read through the entire procedure and make sure that you have the correct rebuild kit.

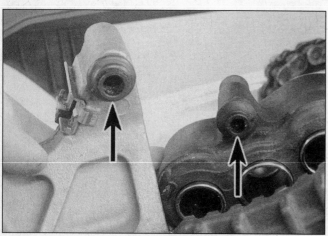
7.18a Remove the rubber boots (arrowed)

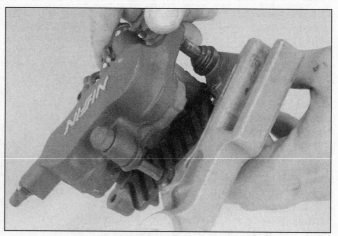
7.18b Slide the caliper back onto the bracket

Also, you will need some new DOT 4 brake fluid, some clean rags and internal circlip pliers. **Note:** *To prevent damage to the paint from spilled brake fluid, always cover the surrounding components when working on the master cylinder.*
Caution: Disassembly, overhaul and reassembly of the brake master cylinder must be done in a spotlessly clean work area to avoid contamination and possible failure of the brake hydraulic system components.

Removal

3 Remove the seat cowling (see Chapter 8). Unscrew the bolt securing the master cylinder reservoir **(see illustrations)**. Undo the reservoir cap and remove the diaphragm plate and diaphragm, then pour the fluid into a container. Separate the fluid reservoir hose from the elbow on the master cylinder by releasing the hose clamp **(see illustration)**.
4 Unscrew the brake hose banjo bolt and separate the hoses from the master cylinder, noting their alignment **(see illustration)**. Discard the sealing washers as they must be replaced with new ones. Wrap the ends of the hoses in a clean rag and suspend in an upright position, or bend down carefully and place the open end in a clean container. The objective is to prevent excessive loss of brake fluid, fluid spills and system contamination.
5 Remove the split pin from the clevis pin securing the brake pedal to the master cylinder pushrod **(see illustration)**. Remove the clevis pin and separate the pedal from the pushrod. If access is too restricted, unscrew the nut securing the front of the silencer to the footrest bracket and remove the collar, then unscrew the footrest bracket mounting bolts and displace the bracket so that you can access the back of it.
6 Unscrew the master cylinder mounting bolts and remove it from the footrest bracket **(see illustration)**.

Overhaul

7 If necessary, slacken the clevis locknut and remove the clevis from the pushrod, noting how far up it is threaded **(see illustration 8.3a)**.
8 Dislodge the rubber dust boot from the

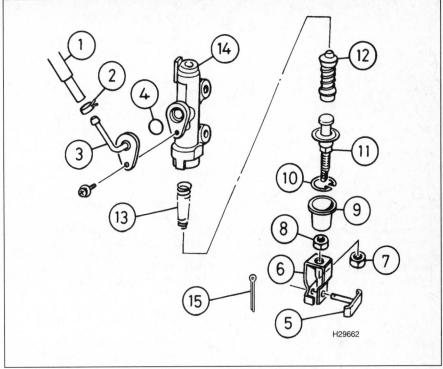

8.3a Rear brake master cylinder assembly

1 Reservoir hose	6 Clevis	11 Pushrod
2 Hose clamp	7 Clevis base nut	12 Piston assembly
3 Hose union	8 Locknut	13 Spring
4 O-ring	9 Rubber boot	14 Master cylinder body
5 Clevis pin	10 Circlip	15 Split pin

8.3b Unscrew the reservoir bolt (arrowed) and displace it

8.3c Release the clamp (arrowed) and detach the hose from the union

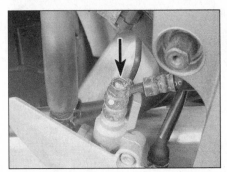

8.4 Brake hose banjo bolt (arrowed)

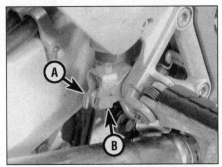

8.5 Remove the split pin (A) and withdraw the clevis pin (B)

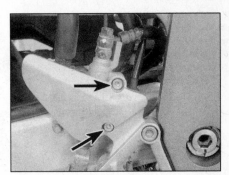

8.6 Rear master cylinder mounting bolts (arrowed)

base of the master cylinder to reveal the pushrod retaining circlip.

9 Depress the pushrod and, using circlip pliers, remove the circlip. Slide out the pushrod, piston assembly and spring. If they are difficult to remove, apply low pressure compressed air to the fluid outlet. Lay the parts out in the proper order to prevent confusion during reassembly.

10 If required, remove the screw securing the fluid reservoir hose union and detach it from the master cylinder. Discard the O-ring as a new one must be used. Inspect the reservoir hose for cracks or splits and replace with a new one if necessary.

11 Clean all of the parts with clean brake fluid or denatured alcohol.

Caution: Do not, under any circumstances, use a petroleum-based solvent to clean brake parts. If compressed air is available, use it to dry the parts thoroughly (make sure it's filtered and unlubricated).

12 Check the master cylinder bore for corrosion, scratches, nicks and score marks. If the necessary measuring equipment is available, compare the dimensions of the piston and bore to those given in the Specifications Section of this Chapter. If damage is evident, the master cylinder must be replaced with a new one. If the master cylinder is in poor condition, then the caliper should be checked as well.

13 The dust boot, circlip, piston assembly and spring are included in the rebuild kit. Use all of the new parts, regardless of the apparent condition of the old ones. If the seal is not on the piston, fit it according to the position of the old one.

14 Lubricate the primary cup with clean brake fluid and fit it onto the narrow end of the spring, so that the coil fits over the lug on the inside of the cup. Install the spring and cup in the master cylinder, with the cup end facing out, making sure its lips do not turn inside out.

15 Lubricate the piston assembly with clean hydraulic fluid and insert it in the master cylinder, making sure it is the correct way round. Make sure the lips on the seal do not turn inside out.

16 Install and depress the pushrod assembly, then install the new circlip, making sure it is properly seated in the groove.

17 Install the rubber dust boot, making sure it is seated properly in the groove.

18 If removed, fit a new O-ring to the fluid reservoir hose union, then install the union onto the master cylinder and secure it with its screw.

19 If removed, thread the clevis locknut and the clevis onto the master cylinder pushrod end. Set the clevis position as noted on removal. Honda specify the distance between the eye in the clevis and the lower mounting bolt hole should be 64.0 to 66.0 mm **(see illustration)**. Tighten the clevis locknut securely against the clevis.

Installation

20 Locate the master cylinder on the footrest bracket, then install the bolts and tighten them to the torque setting specified at the beginning of the Chapter **(see illustration 8.6)**. If the bracket has been displaced, tighten them finger-tight now and to the specified torque after it has been installed.

21 Align the brake pedal with the master cylinder pushrod clevis, then slide in the clevis pin and secure it using a new split pin **(see illustration 8.5)**.

22 If displaced, locate the footrest bracket and tighten the mounting bolts and the silencer nut to the torque settings specified at the beginning of the Chapter. If not already done, tighten the master cylinder bolts to the specified torque.

23 Connect the brake hoses to the master cylinder, using new sealing washers on each side of the unions. Align the hoses as noted on removal and tighten the banjo bolt to the specified torque setting **(see illustration 8.4)**.

24 Fit the fluid reservoir on its mount and secure it with its bolt **(see illustration 8.3b)**. Ensure that the hose is correctly routed then connect it to the union on the master cylinder and secure it with the clamp **(see illustration 8.3c)**. Check that the hose is secure and clamped at the reservoir end as well. If the clamps have weakened, use new ones.

25 Fill the fluid reservoir with new DOT 4 brake fluid (see *Daily (pre-ride) checks*) and bleed the system following the procedure in Section 10.

26 Check the operation of the brake carefully before riding the motorcycle.

9 Brake hoses, pipes and unions – inspection and replacement

Inspection

1 Brake hose and pipe condition should be checked regularly and the hoses replaced at the specified interval (see Chapter 1).

2 Twist and flex the rubber hoses while looking for cracks, bulges and seeping fluid **(see illustration)**. Check extra carefully around the areas where the hoses connect with the banjo fittings, as these are common areas for hose failure.

3 Inspect the metal brake pipes and the banjo union fittings connected to the brake hoses. If the fittings are rusted, scratched or cracked, replace them.

Replacement

4 The brake hoses have banjo union fittings on each end and the brake pipes have joining nuts **(see illustration 6.19b)**. Cover the surrounding area with plenty of rags and unscrew the banjo bolt or joining nut at each end of the hose or pipe, noting its alignment. Free the hose or pipe from any clips or guides and remove it. Discard the sealing washers on the hose banjo unions.

5 Position the new hose or pipe, making sure it isn't twisted or otherwise strained, and abut the tab on the hose union with the lug on the component casting, where present. Otherwise align the hose or pipe as noted on removal. Install the hose banjo bolts using new sealing washers on both sides of the unions. Tighten the banjo bolts and joining nuts to the torque settings specified at the beginning of this Chapter. Make sure the hoses and pipes are correctly aligned and routed clear of all moving components.

6 Flush the old brake fluid from the system, refill with new DOT 4 brake fluid (see *Daily (pre-ride) checks*) and bleed the air from the system (see Section 10). Check the operation of the brakes carefully before riding the motorcycle.

10 Brake system – bleeding

Note 1: *Honda specify the use of a vacuum-type brake bleeder to simplify the bleeding process. The bleeder is connected to the bleed valve, which is then opened, and is used to draw the air/fluid through the system and out of the bleed valve. Once all the air has been removed, the bleeder is removed and the brakes are then bled in the conventional way (described below) to complete the bleeding procedure. If you find that the conventional method of bleeding fails to remove the trapped air from the system, it will be necessary to obtain a vacuum-type brake*

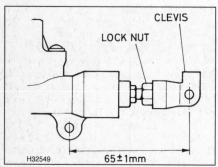
8.19 Set the position of the clevis as shown

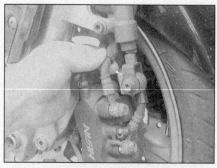
9.2 Flex the brake hoses and check for cracks, bulges and leaking fluid

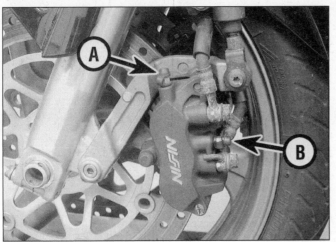

10.7 Left front caliper upper (A) and centre (B) bleed valves

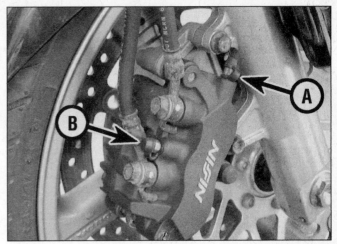

10.11 Right front caliper upper (A) and centre (B) bleed valves

bleeder kit from a motor accessory shop or entrust the work to a Honda dealer.

Note 2: *If using a vacuum-type brake bleeder, it may be found that air enters the caliper via the bleed valve threads as the valve is opened; if so, seal the threads with teflon tape. Also ensure that the tube which fits over the bleed valve head seals fully.*

1 Bleeding the brakes is simply the process of removing all the air bubbles from the brake fluid reservoirs, the hoses/pipes, the brake calipers and associated components. Bleeding is necessary whenever a brake system hydraulic connection is loosened, when a component or hose is renewed, or when the master cylinder or caliper is overhauled. Leaks in the system may also allow air to enter, but leaking brake fluid will reveal their presence and warn you of the need for repair.

2 To bleed the brakes using the conventional method, you will need some new DOT 4 brake fluid, a length of clear vinyl or plastic tubing, a small container partially filled with clean brake fluid, some rags and a spanner to fit the brake caliper bleed valves.

3 The dual combined braking system (CBS) can be split into two separate hydraulic circuits; the front brake lever circuit and the rear brake pedal circuit. The front brake lever circuit consists of the hoses and pipes linking the front master cylinder to the front brake calipers. The rear brake pedal circuit consists of the hoses and pipes linking the rear master cylinder to the rear caliper and delay valve, the hoses from the delay valve to the front brake calipers and secondary master cylinder and the hoses and pipe from the secondary master cylinder to the proportional control valve and rear brake caliper.

4 If bleeding is being carried out after a hose/pipe has been disconnected, identify which circuit the hose is part of, then carry out the relevant bleeding procedure described below **(see illustrations 1a and 1b)**.

Front brake lever hydraulic circuit

5 Cover the fuel tank and other painted components to prevent damage in the event that brake fluid is spilled.

6 Undo the retaining screws and remove the master cylinder reservoir cover, diaphragm plate and diaphragm and slowly pump the brake lever a few times, until no air bubbles can be seen floating up from the holes in the bottom of the reservoir. Doing this bleeds the air from the master cylinder end of the line. Loosely refit the reservoir cover.

7 Starting on the left side caliper, pull the dust cap off the **upper** bleed valve (the lower bleed valve is for the rear brake pedal circuit) **(see illustration)**. Attach one end of the clear vinyl or plastic tubing to the bleed valve and submerge the other end in the brake fluid in the container.

8 Remove the reservoir cover and check the fluid level. Do not allow the fluid level to drop below the lower mark during the bleeding process.

9 Carefully pump the brake lever three or four times and hold it in while opening the caliper bleed valve. When the valve is opened, brake fluid will flow out of the caliper into the clear tubing and the lever will move toward the handlebar.

10 Retighten the bleed valve, then release the brake lever gradually. Repeat the process until no air bubbles are visible in the brake fluid leaving the valve and the lever is firm when applied. Disconnect the bleeding equipment, then tighten the bleed valve to the specified torque and install the dust cap.

11 Repeat the procedure described in Paragraphs 7 to 10 on the right side front caliper, until all air is removed from the system and the brake lever feels firm again **(see illustration)**.

12 Top the fluid level up to the upper level mark (see *Daily (pre-ride) checks*) then install the diaphragm, diaphragm plate and reservoir cover assembly and securely tighten the retaining screws. Wipe up any spilled brake fluid and check the entire system for leaks.

 HAYNES HiNT *If it's not possible to produce a firm feel to the lever the fluid my be aerated. Let the brake fluid in the system stabilise for a few hours and then repeat the procedure when the tiny bubbles in the system have settled out. Failure to bleed satisfactorily after a reasonable repetition of the bleeding procedure may be due to worn master cylinder seals.*

Rear brake pedal hydraulic circuit

13 Remove the seat cowling (see Chapter 8) to gain access to the rear brake master cylinder fluid reservoir.

14 The brake pedal hydraulic circuit must always be bled in the following sequence.
 a) *Right side front brake caliper (centre) bleed valve.*
 b) *Left side front brake caliper (centre) bleed valve.*
 c) *Rear brake caliper centre bleed valve.*
 d) *Rear brake caliper outer (rear) bleed valve.*

15 Unscrew the fluid reservoir cover and lift out the diaphragm plate and diaphragm. Slowly pump the brake pedal a few times, until no air bubbles can be seen floating up from the holes in the bottom of the reservoir. Doing this bleeds the air from the master cylinder end of the line. Loosely refit the reservoir cover.

16 Starting with the right side front caliper **centre** bleed valve (the upper bleed valve is for the front brake lever pedal circuit), pull off the dust cap then attach one end of the clear vinyl or plastic tubing to the bleed valve **(see illustration 10.7)**. Submerge the other end of the tubing in the brake fluid in the container.

17 Check the fluid level. Do not allow the fluid level to drop below the lower mark during the bleeding process. If the fluid level is allowed to drop air will enter the hydraulic

10.22 Rear caliper centre bleed valve

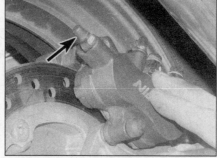

10.24 Rear caliper outer (rear) bleed valve (arrowed)

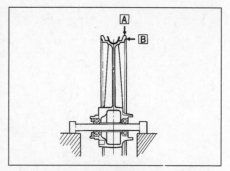

11.2 Check the wheel for radial (out-of-round) runout (A) and axial (side-to-side) runout (B)

circuit and the bleeding process will have to be restarted.

18 Carefully pump the brake pedal three or four times and hold it down while opening the bleed valve. When the valve is opened, brake fluid will flow out into the clear tubing and the pedal will move fully downwards.

19 Retighten the bleed valve, then release the brake pedal gradually. Repeat the process until no air bubbles are visible in the brake fluid leaving the valve. Disconnect the bleeding equipment, then tighten the bleed valve to the specified torque and install the dust cap.

20 Remove the dust cap from the left side front caliper **centre** bleed valve (the upper bleed valve is for the front brake lever pedal circuit). Attach one end of the clear vinyl or plastic tubing to the bleed valve and submerge the other end in the brake fluid in the container **(see illustration 10.11)**.

21 Repeat the procedure described in Paragraphs 17 to 19, until all air is removed from the left side front caliper.

22 Remove the dust cap from the rear caliper **centre** bleed valve **(see illustration)**. Attach one end of the clear vinyl or plastic tubing to the bleed valve and submerge the other end in the brake fluid in the container.

23 Repeat the procedure described in Paragraphs 17 to 19, until all air is removed.

24 Remove the dust cap from the rear caliper **outer (rear)** bleed valve **(see illustration)**. Attach one end of the clear vinyl or plastic tubing to the bleed valve and submerge the other end in the brake fluid in the container.

25 Repeat the procedure described in Paragraphs 17 to 19, until all air is removed.

26 The bleeding procedure is now complete and the brake pedal should feel firm.

> **HAYNES HINT** *If it's not possible to produce a firm feel to the pedal the fluid my be aerated. Let the brake fluid in the system stabilise for a few hours and then repeat the procedure when the tiny bubbles in the system have settled out. Failure to bleed the system satisfactorily (even with a vacuum-type brake bleeder) may be due to worn master cylinder seals.*

27 Top the fluid level up to the upper level mark (see *Daily (pre-ride) checks*) then install the diaphragm, diaphragm plate and reservoir cover assembly. Wipe up any spilled brake fluid.

28 Thoroughly test the operation of the brake before riding the motorcycle (see Chapter 1).

11 Wheels – inspection and repair

1 Position the motorcycle on its centrestand. When checking the front wheel, support the bike so that it is raised off the ground. Clean the wheels thoroughly to remove mud and dirt that may interfere with the inspection procedure or mask defects. Make a general check of the wheels (see Chapter 1) and tyres (see *Daily (pre-ride) checks*).

2 Attach a dial gauge to the fork slider or the swingarm and position its stem against the side of the rim **(see illustration)**. Spin the wheel slowly and check the axial (side-to-side) runout of the rim. In order to accurately check radial (out of round) runout with the dial gauge, the wheel would have to be removed from the machine, and the tyre from the wheel. With the axle clamped in a vice and the dial gauge positioned on the top of the rim, the wheel can be rotated to check the runout.

3 An easier, though slightly less accurate, method is to attach a stiff wire pointer to the fork slider or the swingarm and position the end a fraction of an inch from the wheel (where the wheel and tyre join). If the wheel is true, the distance from the pointer to the rim will be constant as the wheel is rotated. **Note:** *If wheel runout is excessive, check the wheel bearings and axle very carefully before replacing the wheel.*

4 Visually inspect the wheels for cracks, flat spots on the rim, and other damage. Look very closely for dents in the area where the tyre bead contacts the rim. Dents in this area may prevent complete sealing of the tyre against the rim, which leads to deflation of the tyre over a period of time. If damage is evident, or if runout in either direction is excessive, the wheel will have to be replaced with a new one. Never attempt to repair a damaged cast alloy wheel.

12 Wheels – alignment check

1 Misalignment of the wheels, which may be due to a cocked rear wheel or a bent frame or fork yokes, can cause strange and possibly serious handling problems. If the frame or yokes are at fault, repair by a frame specialist or replacement with new parts are the only alternatives.

2 To check the alignment you will need an assistant, a length of string or a perfectly straight piece of wood and a ruler. A plumb bob or other suitable weight will also be required.

3 Place the bike on the centrestand. Measure the width of both tyres at their widest points. Subtract the smaller measurement from the larger measurement, then divide the difference by two. The result is the amount of offset that should exist between the front and rear tyres on both sides.

4 If a string is used, have your assistant hold one end of it about halfway between the floor and the rear axle, touching the rear sidewall of the tyre.

5 Run the other end of the string forward and pull it tight so that it is roughly parallel to the floor **(see illustration)**. Slowly bring the string

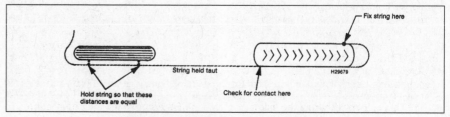

12.5 Wheel alignment check using string

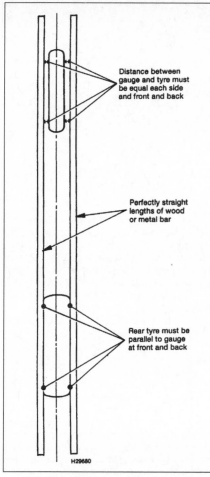

12.7 Wheel alignment check using a straight edge

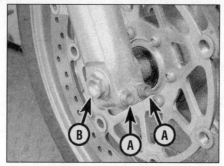

13.4 Slacken the axle clamp bolts (A), then unscrew the axle bolt (B)

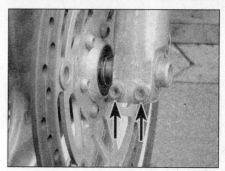

13.5a Slacken the axle clamp bolts (arrowed) . . .

into contact with the front sidewall of the rear tyre, then turn the front wheel until it is parallel with the string. Measure the distance from the front tyre sidewall to the string.

6 Repeat the procedure on the other side of the motorcycle. The distance from the front tyre sidewall to the string should be equal on both sides.

7 As previously mentioned, a perfectly straight length of wood or metal bar may be substituted for the string (see illustration). The procedure is the same.

8 If the distance between the string and tyre is greater on one side, or if the rear wheel appears to be cocked, refer to Chapter 1 and check that the chain adjuster markings are in the same position on each side of the swingarm.

9 If the front-to-back alignment is correct, the wheels still may be out of alignment vertically.

10 Using a plumb bob, or other suitable weight, and a length of string, check the rear wheel to make sure it is vertical. To do this, hold the string against the tyre upper sidewall and allow the weight to settle just off the floor. When the string touches both the upper and lower tyre sidewalls and is perfectly straight, the wheel is vertical. If it is not, place thin spacers under one leg of the stand until it is.

11 Once the rear wheel is vertical, check the front wheel in the same manner. If both wheels are not perfectly vertical, the frame and/or major suspension components are bent.

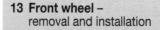

13 Front wheel – removal and installation

Removal

1 Position the motorcycle on its centrestand and support it under the crankcase so that the front wheel is off the ground. Always make sure the motorcycle is properly supported, and remove the fairing side panels to prevent

the possibility of damaging them if necessary (see Chapter 8).

2 Displace the right-hand brake caliper and the left-hand caliper/secondary master cylinder assembly (see Section 3). Support the calipers with a cable tie or a bungee cord so that no strain is placed on the hydraulic hoses. There is no need to disconnect the hoses from the calipers. Note: *Do not operate the front brake lever or the rear brake pedal, with the calipers removed.*

3 If required, remove the front mudguard (see Chapter 8). Whether you need to or not depends on how high the front wheel is off the ground. The mudguard extends round the wheel, meaning the wheel has to be lowered rather than drawn forward, so if the wheel is only just off the ground, you will need to remove it.

4 Slacken the axle clamp bolts on the bottom of the right-hand fork, then unscrew the axle bolt from the right-hand end of the axle (see illustration).

5 Slacken the axle clamp bolts on the bottom of the left-hand fork (see illustration). Support the wheel, then withdraw the axle from the left-hand side, using a screwdriver inserted through the holes in the end of the axle as a lever, and carefully lower the wheel (see illustration).

6 Remove the long wheel spacer from the right-hand side of the wheel and the short spacer from the left-hand side (see illustrations).

Caution: Don't lay the wheel down and allow it to rest on a disc – the disc could

13.5b . . . then withdraw the axle

13.6a Remove the long right-hand spacer . . .

13.6b . . . and the short left-hand spacer

13.11 Slide the axle in from the left . . .

13.12a . . . then install the axle bolt . . .

13.12b . . . and tighten it to the specified torque

become warped. Set the wheel on wood blocks so the disc doesn't support the weight of the wheel.

7 Check the axle for straightness by rolling it on a flat surface such as a piece of plate glass (first wipe off all old grease and remove any corrosion using fine emery cloth). If the equipment is available, place the axle in V-blocks and measure the runout using a dial gauge. If the axle is bent or the runout exceeds the limit specified, replace it with a new one.

8 Check the condition of the grease seals and wheel bearings (see Section 16).

Installation

9 Apply a smear of grease to the inside of the wheel spacers, and also to the outside where they fit into the wheel. Fit the long spacer into the right-hand side of the wheel and the short spacer into the left-hand side (see illustration 13.6a and b). Each side of the wheel can be identified using the directional arrow cast into one of the spokes near the rim. The arrow denotes the normal direction of rotation of the wheel.

10 Manoeuvre the wheel into position between the fork sliders, making sure the directional arrow is pointing in the normal direction of rotation. Apply a thin coat of grease to the axle.

11 Lift the wheel into place, making sure the spacers remain in position. Slide the axle in from the left-hand side (see illustration).

12 Install the axle bolt and tighten it to the torque setting specified at the beginning of the Chapter (see illustrations). Use a screwdriver inserted through the hole in the left-hand end of the axle to counter-hold it (see illustration 13.5b).

13 Tighten the axle clamp bolts on the bottom of the right-hand fork to the specified torque setting (see illustration 13.4).

14 Lower the front wheel to the ground, then install the brake calipers (see Section 3), and if removed, the front mudguard (see Chapter 8).

15 Apply the front brake a few times to bring the pads back into contact with the discs. Move the motorcycle off its stand, apply the front brake and pump the front forks a few times to settle all components in position. Now tighten the axle clamp bolts on the bottom of the left-hand fork to the specified torque (see illustration 13.5a).

16 Check for correct operation of the brakes before riding the motorcycle. Check that there is at least 0.7 mm clearance between each front brake disc and the caliper bracket – make the check using a feeler gauge.

14 Rear wheel – removal and installation

Removal

1 Place the motorcycle on its centrestand.

2 If required, remove the brake pads (see Section 2). Although this is not absolutely necessary, it was found that with the pads in place the disc has a tendency to dislodge them from their abutment with the front guide on the caliper bracket, and to drag the caliper bracket with it as the wheel is withdrawn.

3 Unscrew the axle nut and remove the washer (see illustration).

4 Support the wheel, then withdraw the axle from the left-hand side and lower the wheel to the ground (see illustration). Disengage the chain from the sprocket and remove the wheel from the swingarm (see illustration). If the axle is difficult to withdraw, either drift it through, making sure you don't damage the threads, or preferably create some slack in the chain (see Chapter 1).

5 Note how the caliper bracket locates against the swingarm, and support it so that it will not fall off. If required, displace the brake caliper bracket from the swingarm, noting how it fits, and tie it to the top of the frame, making sure no strain is placed on the hoses (see illustration 7.4).

Caution: Do not lay the wheel down and allow it to rest on the disc or the sprocket – they could become warped. Set the wheel on wood blocks so the disc or the sprocket doesn't support the weight of the wheel. Do not operate the brake pedal with the wheel removed.

6 Remove the spacer from each side of the

14.3 Unscrew the axle nut (arrowed) and remove the washer

14.4a Withdraw the axle . . .

14.4b . . . then lower the wheel to the ground and disengage the chain

14.6a Remove the spacer from the right-hand side . . .

14.6b . . . and from the left-hand side, noting which fits where

14.12a Install the washer and nut . . .

wheel for safekeeping, noting which fits where **(see illustrations)**.

7 Check the axle for straightness by rolling it on a flat surface such as a piece of plate glass (if the axle is corroded, first remove the corrosion with fine emery cloth). If the equipment is available, place the axle in V-blocks and check the runout using a dial indicator. If the axle is bent or the runout exceeds the limit specified at the beginning of the Chapter, replace it with a new one.

8 Check the condition of the grease seals and wheel bearings (see Section 16).

Installation

9 Apply a smear of grease to the inside of the wheel spacers, and also to the outside where they fit into the wheel. Fit the narrower spacer into the right-hand side of the wheel and the wider spacer into the left-hand side **(see illustration 14.6a and b)**. If displaced, locate the brake caliper bracket onto the swingarm **(see illustration 7.4)**.

10 Manoeuvre the wheel so that it is in between the ends of the swingarm. Apply a thin coat of grease to the axle. Make sure the brake caliper bracket is still correctly positioned against the swingarm.

11 Engage the drive chain with the sprocket and lift the wheel into position **(see illustration 14.4b)**. Make sure the spacers and caliper bracket remain correctly in place, and that the brake disc fits squarely into the caliper, and with the pads positioned correctly each side of the disc (if the pads were not previously removed). If there is not enough

slack in the chain to align the wheel with the swingarm and chain adjusters, slacken the adjuster bolts and tap the ends to move them up in the swingarm.

12 Install the axle from the left, making sure it passes through the chain adjusters and the caliper bracket **(see illustration 14.4a)**. Check that everything is correctly aligned. Fit the washer and nut, and tighten the nut to the torque setting specified at the beginning of the Chapter, counter-holding the axle head on the other side of the wheel to prevent it turning if necessary **(see illustrations)**. If the axle is difficult to install due to the tension of the chain, create some slack by turning the adjusters out, and readjust the tension before tightening the axle nut.

13 If removed, install the brake pads (see Section 2).

14 Operate the brake pedal several times to bring the pads into contact with the disc. Check the operation of the rear brake carefully before riding the bike.

15 Check the chain slack as described in Chapter 1 and adjust if necessary.

15 Wheel bearings – removal, inspection and installation

Front wheel bearings

Note: *Always replace the wheel bearings in pairs. Never replace the bearings individually.*

14.12b . . . and tighten it to the specified torque

Avoid using a high pressure cleaner on the wheel bearing area.

1 Remove the wheel, and if not already done remove the spacers from it (see Section 13).

2 Set the wheel on blocks so as not to allow the weight to rest on the brake disc.

3 Prise out the seal on each side of the wheel using a flat-bladed screwdriver, taking care not to damage the rim of the hub **(see illustration)**. Discard the seals as new ones should be used.

4 Using a metal rod (preferably a brass drift punch) inserted through the centre of the upper bearing, tap evenly around the inner race of the lower bearing to drive it from the hub **(see illustrations)**. The bearing spacer will also come out.

5 Lay the wheel on its other side so that the remaining bearing faces down. Remove the seal and drive the bearing out of the wheel using the same technique as above.

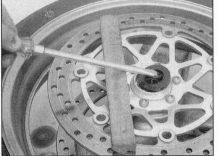

15.3 Lever out the grease seal on each side

15.4a Knock out the bearings using a drift . . .

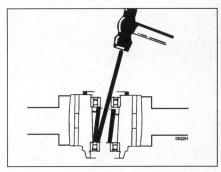

15.4b . . . locating it as shown

15.9 A socket can be used to drive in the bearing

15.11a Fit the grease seal and press or tap it into place . . .

15.11b . . . using a piece of wood ensures the seal sits flush with the rim

6 If the bearings are of the unsealed type or are only sealed on one side, clean them with a high flash-point solvent (one which won't leave any residue) and blow them dry with compressed air (don't let the bearings spin as you dry them). Apply a few drops of oil to the bearing. **Note:** *If the bearing is sealed on both sides don't attempt to clean it.*

 HAYNES HiNT *Refer to Tools and Workshop Tips (Section 5) for more information about bearings.*

7 Hold the outer race of the bearing and rotate the inner race – if the bearing doesn't turn smoothly, has rough spots or is noisy, replace it with a new one.
8 If the bearing is good and can be re-used,

15.13 Lift the sprocket coupling out of the wheel

wash it in solvent once again and dry it, then pack the bearing with grease.
9 Thoroughly clean the hub area of the wheel. Install one bearing into the recess in the hub, with the marked or sealed side facing outwards. Using the old bearing (if new ones are being fitted), a bearing driver or a socket large enough to contact the outer race of the bearing, drive it in until it's completely seated (see illustration).
10 Turn the wheel over and install the bearing spacer. If the inner side of the bearing is unsealed, pack grease into the bearing races. Drive the other bearing into place as described above.
11 Apply a smear of grease to the lips of the seals, then press them into the wheel. Gently drive them into place if necessary using a seal or bearing driver, a suitable socket or a flat piece of wood (see illustration). As the seals sit flush with the top surface of their housing, using a piece of wood as shown will automatically set them flush without the risk of setting them too deep and having to lever them out again (see illustration).
12 Clean off all grease from the brake discs using acetone or brake system cleaner then install the wheel (see Section 13).

Rear wheel bearings

13 Remove the rear wheel, and if not already done remove the spacers from it (see Section 14). Lift the sprocket coupling out of the wheel, noting how it fits and retrieve its shouldered spacer if it is loose (see illustration).

14 Set the wheel on blocks so as not to allow the weight of the wheel to rest on the brake disc.
15 Lever out the grease seal on the right-hand side of the wheel using a flat-bladed screwdriver, taking care not to damage the rim of the hub (see illustration). Discard the seal as a new one should be used.
16 Using a metal rod (preferably a brass drift punch) inserted through the centre of the right-hand bearing, tap evenly around the inner race of the left-hand bearing to drive it from the hub (see illustrations 15.4a and b). The bearing spacer will also come out.
17 Lay the wheel on its other side so that the remaining bearing faces down. Drive the bearing out of the wheel using the same technique as above.
18 Refer to Steps 6 to 8 above and check the bearings.
19 Thoroughly clean the hub area of the wheel. First install the right-hand bearing into its recess in the hub, with the marked or sealed side facing outwards. Using the old bearing (if new ones are being fitted), a bearing driver or a socket large enough to contact the outer race of the bearing, drive it in squarely until it's completely seated (see illustration).
20 Turn the wheel over and install the bearing spacer. Drive the left-hand side bearing into place as described above.
21 Check the condition of the hub O-ring and renew it if it is damaged, deformed or deteriorated (see illustration).
22 Apply a smear of grease to the lips of the

15.15 Lever out the grease seal

15.19 A socket can be used to drive in the bearing

15.21 Check the O-ring (arrowed) and fit a new one if necessary

15.25 Lever out the grease seal

15.26 Drive out the spacer . . .

15.27 . . . then drive out the bearing

new grease seal, and press it into the right-hand side of the wheel, using a seal or bearing driver, a suitable socket or a flat piece of wood to drive it into place if necessary **(see illustrations 15.11a and b)**. As the seal sits flush with the top surface of its housing, using a piece of wood as shown will automatically set it flush without the risk of setting it too deep and having to lever it out again.
23 Clean off all grease from the brake disc using acetone or brake system cleaner. Fit the sprocket coupling assembly onto the wheel ensuring that its shouldered spacer is in place **(see illustration 15.13)**, then install the wheel (see Section 14).

Sprocket coupling bearing

24 Remove the rear wheel, and if not already done remove the spacers from it (see Section 14). Lift the sprocket coupling out of the wheel, noting how it fits **(see illustration 15.13)**.
25 Using a flat-bladed screwdriver, lever out the grease seal from the outside of the coupling **(see illustration)**.
26 Remove the shouldered spacer from the inside of the coupling bearing, noting which way round it fits. The spacer could be a tight fit and may have to be driven out using a suitable socket or piece of tubing **(see**

illustration). Support the coupling on blocks of wood to do this.
27 Support the coupling on blocks of wood and drive the bearing out from the inside using a bearing driver or socket **(see illustration)**.
28 Refer to Steps 6 to 8 above and check the bearings.
29 Thoroughly clean the bearing recess then install the bearing into the coupling, with the marked or sealed side facing out. Using the old bearing (if a new one is being fitted), a bearing driver or a socket large enough to contact the outer race of the bearing, drive it in until it is completely seated **(see illustration)**.
30 Fit the shouldered spacer into the inside of the coupling, making sure it is the correct way round and fits squarely into the bearing. Drive it into place if it is tight, supporting the bearing on a suitable socket as you do to prevent it from being driven out at the same time **(see illustration)**.
31 Check the condition of the hub O-ring and replace it with a new one if it is damaged, deformed or deteriorated **(see illustration 15.21)**.
32 Apply a smear of grease to the lips of the new seal, and press it into the coupling, using a seal or bearing driver, a suitable socket or a

15.29 Drive in the new bearing

flat piece of wood to drive it into place if necessary **(see illustration)**. As the seal sits flush with the top surface of their housing, using a piece of wood as shown will automatically set it flush without the risk of setting it too deep and having to lever it out again.
33 Check the sprocket coupling/rubber dampers (see Chapter 6).
34 Clean off all grease from the brake disc using acetone or brake system cleaner. Fit the sprocket coupling into the wheel **(see illustration 15.13)**, then install the wheel (see Section 14).

15.30 Support the bearing as shown when driving in the spacer

15.32 Press or drive the seal into the coupling. Using a piece of wood as shown automatically sets the seal flush with the rim

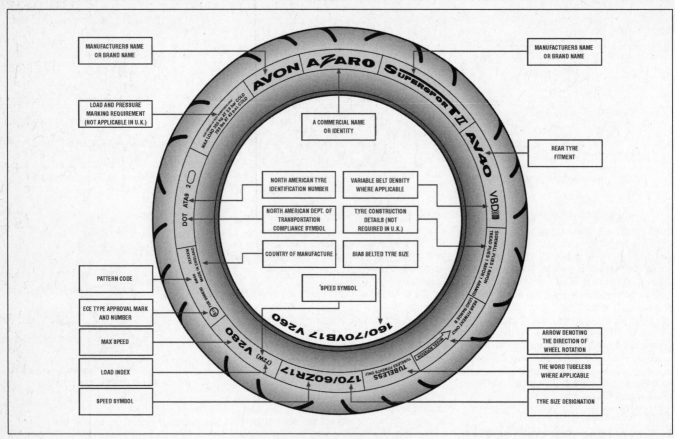

16.3 Common tyre sidewall markings

16 Tyres –
general information and fitting

General information

1 The wheels fitted to all models are designed to take tubeless tyres only. Tyre sizes are given in the Specifications at the beginning of this chapter.
2 Refer to the *Daily (pre-ride) checks* listed at the beginning of this manual for tyre maintenance.

Fitting new tyres

3 When selecting new tyres, refer to the tyre information label on the swingarm and the tyre options listed in the owners handbook. Ensure that front and rear tyre types are compatible, the correct size and correct speed rating; if necessary seek advice from a Honda dealer or tyre fitting specialist **(see illustration)**.
4 It is recommended that tyres are fitted by a motorcycle tyre specialist rather than

attempted in the home workshop. This is particularly relevant in the case of tubeless tyres because the force required to break the seal between the wheel rim and tyre bead is substantial, and is usually beyond the capabilities of an individual working with normal tyre levers. Additionally, the specialist will be able to balance the wheels after tyre fitting.
5 Note that punctured tubeless tyres can in some cases be repaired. Honda recommend that such repairs are carried out only by an authorised dealer.

Chapter 8
Bodywork

Contents

Degrees of difficulty

Easy, suitable for novice with little experience	**Fairly easy,** suitable for beginner with some experience	**Fairly difficult,** suitable for competent DIY mechanic	**Difficult,** suitable for experienced DIY mechanic	**Very difficult,** suitable for expert DIY or professional

1 General information

This Chapter covers the procedures necessary to remove and install the body parts. Since many service and repair operations on these motorcycles require the removal of the body parts, the procedures are grouped here and referred to from other Chapters.

In the case of damage to the body parts, it is usually necessary to remove the broken component and replace it with a new (or used) one. The material that the body panels are composed of doesn't lend itself to conventional repair techniques. There are however some shops that specialise in 'plastic welding', so it may be worthwhile seeking the advice of one of these specialists before consigning an expensive component to the bin.

When attempting to remove any body panel, first study it closely, noting any fasteners and associated fittings, to be sure of returning everything to its correct place on installation. In some cases the aid of an assistant will be required when removing panels, to help avoid the risk of damage to paintwork. Once the evident fasteners have been removed, try to withdraw the panel as described but DO NOT FORCE IT – if it will not release, check that all fasteners have been removed and try again. Where a panel engages another by means of tabs, be careful not to break the tab or its mating slot or to damage the paintwork. Remember that a few moments of patience at this stage will save you a lot of money in replacing broken fairing panels!

When installing a body panel, first study it closely, noting any fasteners and associated fittings removed with it, to be sure of returning everything to its correct place. Check that all fasteners are in good condition, including all trim nuts or clips and damping/rubber mounts; any of these must be replaced if faulty before the panel is reassembled. Check also that all mounting brackets are straight and repair or replace them if necessary before attempting to install the panel. Where assistance was required to remove a panel, make sure your assistant is on hand to install it. Tighten the fasteners securely, but be careful not to overtighten any of them or the panel may break (not always immediately) due to the uneven stress.

Where trim clips are used, to release them unscrew the centre of the clip, then pull the body of the clip out of the panel **(see illustration)**. When installing them, fit the body of the clip onto the panel then push the centre fully into the body. As they are made of plastic, the threads easily become worn and the centres may not unscrew, in which case lever the centre out of the body using a small screwdriver.

HAYNES HiNT *Note that a small amount of lubricant (liquid soap or similar) applied to the mounting rubber grommets of the seat cowling will assist the lugs to engage without the need for undue pressure.*

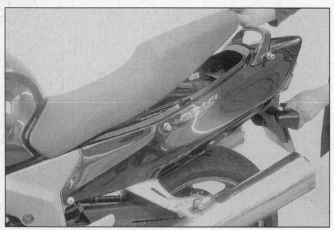

2.1 Unlock the seat, lift it up at the rear and draw it back

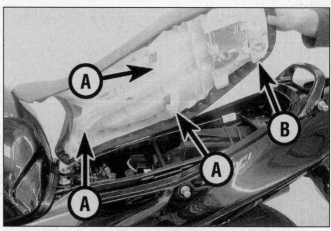

2.2 Make sure the tabs (A) and the latch hook (B) locate and engage correctly

2 Seat – removal and installation

Removal

1 Insert the ignition key into the seat lock located at the back on the left-hand side and turn it clockwise to unlock the seat **(see illustration)**. Remove the seat by drawing it back and up.

Installation

2 Installation is the reverse of removal. Locate the tab at the front under the tank bracket and the tabs in the middle under the bar across the sub-frame **(see illustration)**. Push the seat forward until it locates correctly, then push down on the rear to engage the latch.

3 Rear view mirrors – removal and installation

Removal

1 Pull back the rubber boot on the mirror stem.
2 On V and W (1997 and 1998) models, unscrew the two mounting bolts and displace the mirror, then draw out the turn signal wiring until the connector is accessible. Disconnect the wiring connector and remove the mirror along with the rubber insulator and the mounting plate, noting which way round they fit.
3 On X (1999) models onward, remove the windshield (see Section 4), then disconnect the turn signal wiring connector **(see illustration)**. Unscrew the two mounting bolts and remove the mirror along with the rubber insulator and the mounting plate, noting which way round they fit **(see illustration)**.
4 Remove the turn signal from the mirror if required (see Chapter 9).

Installation

5 Installation is the reverse of removal. Make sure the mounting plates are installed with the arrow next to the FR mark pointing forwards **(see illustration)**.

4 Fairing and body panels – removal and installation

Cockpit trim panels

1 Remove the trim clip from below the instrument cluster **(see illustration)**.
2 Remove the rearmost windshield nut and bolt **(see illustration)**.

3.3a Disconnect the wiring connector, then unscrew the bolts (arrowed) . . .

3.3b . . . and remove the mirror

3.5 Make sure the FR arrow points to the front

4.1 Cockpit trim panel trim clip (A) and bolt (B)

4.2 Remove the rearmost windshield nut and bolt

4.4 Carefully remove the panel, noting how it fits

4.7 The inner trim clip (arrowed) secures the panel to the frame

4.8a Release the panel from the tank and the side lug (arrowed) . . .

3 Unscrew the bolt securing the cockpit trim panel to the fuel tank trim panel **(see illustration 4.1)**.

4 Remove the panel, noting how it fits **(see illustration)**.

5 Installation is the reverse of removal.

Fuel tank trim panels

6 Remove the fairing side panel (see below) and the cockpit trim panel (see above).

7 Remove the two trim clips – there is one on the front outer corner, and one on the front inner section **(see illustration)**.

8 Pull the rear of the trim panel away from the fuel tank to release the peg from the grommet, then release the trim panel tab from around the side mounting lug and remove the panel **(see illustrations)**.

9 Installation is the reverse of removal.

Windshield

10 Remove the nut and bolt securing the windshield to the cockpit trim panel **(see illustration 4.2)**.

11 Undo the remaining screws securing the windshield and manoeuvre it carefully out of the fairing, noting how it fits **(see illustration)**.

12 Remove the threaded rubber collars from the fairing for safekeeping if they are loose.

13 Installation is the reverse of removal.

Fairing

Removal

14 Remove the cockpit trim panels and the fuel tank trim panels (see above).

15 Remove the windshield (see above).

16 Remove the rear view mirrors (see Section 3).

17 Remove the trim clip from the inside of the

fairing at the back, and if the centre panel was not removed when removing the fairing side panels, also remove the trim clip that joins them **(see illustration)**.

18 Carefully draw the fairing forward to release the pegs from the grommets on the fairing/instrument bracket **(see illustration)**. Disconnect the headlight and sidelight wiring connectors when accessible and release the wiring loom from the clip next to the headlight, then draw the fairing off the bike **(see illustrations)**.

19 If required, remove air duct(s). On V and W (1997 and 1998) models, the duct is are secured in the fairing by two trim clips. On X (1999) models onward, each duct is secured to the frame and the fairing side panel by trim clips and locates in the air filter housing.

4.8b . . . and remove it

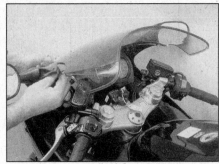

4.11 Carefully release the windshield from the fairing and remove it, noting how it fits

4.17 Release the rear trim clip (A), and the front one (B) if not already done

4.18a Draw the fairing forward to release the pegs from the grommets (arrowed) . . .

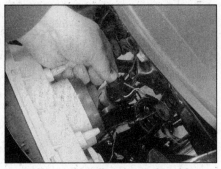

4.18b . . . then disconnect the wiring connectors . . .

4.18c . . . and remove the fairing

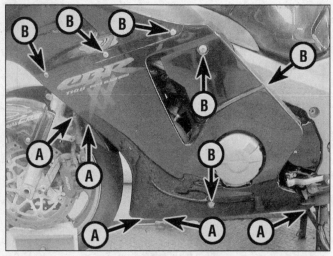

4.21 Remove the trim clips (A) and the bolts (B) - the right hand side is the same except a bolt replaces the lower rear trim clip

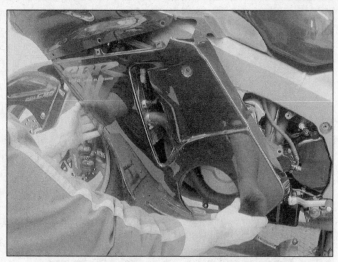

4.22 Carefully remove the panel, noting how it fits

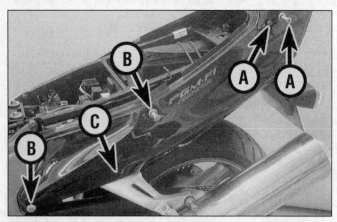

4.26 Unscrew the bolts (A) on each side and remove the grab-rail, then unscrew the other two bolts on each side (B), release the peg from the grommet (C) . . .

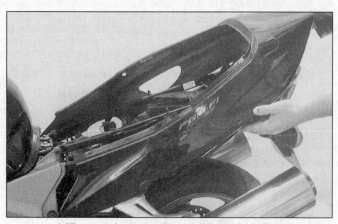

4.27 . . . and remove the cowling as described

Remove the headlight from the fairing if required (see Chapter 9).

Installation

20 Installation is the reverse of removal. Make sure the wiring connectors are correctly and securely connected.

Fairing side panels and centre panel

21 Remove the trim clips securing the side panel to the centre panel **(see illustration)**.
22 Unscrew the bolts securing the side panel to the fairing, the frame and centre panel **(see illustration 4.21)**. Carefully remove the panel, noting how it fits **(see illustration)**.
23 If required, release the trim clips securing the centre panel and remove it, noting how it locates.
24 Installation is the reverse of removal.

Seat cowling

25 Remove the seat (see Section 2).
26 Remove the cap from the grab-rail front

bolt **(see illustration)**. Unscrew the four bolts and remove the grabrail.
27 Remove the two remaining bolts on each side, then carefully pull each front side away to release the peg from its grommet **(see illustration 4.26)**. Draw the cowling back and off the bike **(see illustration)**.
28 Installation is the reverse of removal. The longer bungee-hook bolt fits at the rear.

5.1a Unscrew the two bolts (arrowed) on each side . . .

5 Front mudguard – removal and installation

1 Unscrew the four bolts securing the mudguard to the fork sliders and remove the mudguard, noting how it fits **(see illustrations)**.
2 Installation is the reverse of removal.

5.1b . . . and remove the mudguard

Chapter 9
Electrical system

Contents

Degrees of difficulty

Easy, suitable for novice with little experience		**Fairly easy,** suitable for beginner with some experience		**Fairly difficult,** suitable for competent DIY mechanic		**Difficult,** suitable for experienced DIY mechanic		**Very difficult,** suitable for expert DIY or professional	

Specifications

Battery

Capacity	12 V, 10 Ah
Voltage	
Fully charged	13.0 to 13.2 V
Uncharged	below 12.3 V
Charging rate	
Normal	0.9 A for 5 to 10 hrs
Quick	4.0 A for 0.5 hr
Current leakage	0.2 mA (max)

Alternator

Stator coil resistance
  V and W (1997 and 1998) models . . . .   0.22 to 0.26 ohms
  X (1999) models onward . . . .   0.1 to 1.0 ohms
Output
  V and W (1997 and 1998) models . . . .   0.39 kW @ 5000 rpm
  X (1999) models onward . . . .   0.46 kW @ 5000 rpm

Regulator/rectifier

Regulated voltage output . . . .   14.7 to 15.5 V @ 5000 rpm

Starter motor

Brush length
  Standard . . . .   12.0 to 13.0 mm
  Service limit (min) . . . .   4.5 mm

Instruments

Tachometer peak voltage (see Text) . . . .   10.5 V min.

Fuses

V and W (1997 and 1998) models
  Main . . . .   30 A
  Others . . . .   10 A x 5, 20 A x 1
X (1999) models onward
  Main . . . .   30 A
  PGM-FI (fuel injection system) . . . .   30 A
  Others . . . .   10 A x 5, 20 A x 1 (10 A x 4, 20 A x 2 later models)

Bulbs

Headlights . . . .   55/55 W halogen x 2
Sidelight . . . .   5.0 W
Brake/tail lights . . . .   21/5 W x 2
Turn signal lights
  European spec . . . .   21 W x 4
  US spec
    Front . . . .   32/3 cp x 2
    Rear . . . .   32 cp x 2
Instrument lights
  V, W, X and Y (1997 to 2000) models . . . .   1.7 W x 4
  1 (2001) models onward . . . .   1.4 W x 2
Turn signal indicator light
  V, W, X and Y (1997 to 2000) models . . . .   3.0 W x 2
  1 (2001) models onward . . . .   1.4 W x 2
High beam indicator light
  V, W, X and Y models . . . .   3.0 W
  1 (2001) models onward . . . .   LED
Neutral indicator light
  V, W, X and Y (1997 to 2000) models . . . .   3.0 W
  1 (2001) models onward . . . .   LED
Oil pressure indicator light
  V, W, X and Y (1997 to 2000) models . . . .   3.0 W
  1 (2001) models onward . . . .   LED
Sidestand indicator light (V and W (1997 and 1998) models) . . . .   3.0 W
PGM-FI indicator light
  X and Y (1999 and 2000) models . . . .   3.0 W
  1 (2001) models onward . . . .   LED
Immobiliser indicator light (European models) . . . .   LED

Torque settings

Alternator cover bolts . . . .   12 Nm
Alternator rotor bolt . . . .   103 Nm
Alternator stator bolts . . . .   12 Nm
Neutral switch . . . .   12 Nm
Oil pressure switch . . . .   12 Nm
Sidestand switch bolt . . . .   10 Nm
Steering stem nut . . . .   103 Nm
Top yoke fork clamp bolts . . . .   23 Nm

1 General information

All models have a 12-volt electrical system charged by a three-phase alternator with a separate regulator/rectifier.

The regulator maintains the charging system output within the specified range to prevent overcharging, and the rectifier converts the ac (alternating current) output of the alternator to dc (direct current) to power the lights and other components and to charge the battery. The alternator rotor is mounted on the left-hand end of the crankshaft.

The starter motor is mounted on the top of the crankcase behind the cylinders. The starting system includes the motor, the battery, the relay and the various wires and switches. If the engine kill switch is in the RUN position and the ignition (main) switch is ON, a starter interlock system prevents the engine from being started if the sidestand is down and the engine is in gear. The engine can be started with the sidestand up when it is in gear as long as the clutch lever is pulled in.

Note: *Keep in mind that electrical parts, once purchased, often cannot be returned. To avoid unnecessary expense, make very sure the faulty component has been positively identified before buying a replacement part.*

2 Electrical system – fault finding

⚠ *Warning: To prevent the risk of short circuits, the ignition (main) switch must always be OFF and the battery negative (–) terminal should be disconnected before any of the bike's other electrical components are disturbed. Don't forget to reconnect the terminal securely once work is finished or if battery power is needed for circuit testing.*

1 A typical electrical circuit consists of an electrical component, the switches, relays, etc. related to that component and the wiring and connectors that link the component to the battery and the frame. To aid in locating a problem in any electrical circuit, refer to the wiring diagrams at the end of this Chapter.

2 Before tackling any troublesome electrical circuit, first study the wiring diagram (see end of Chapter) thoroughly to get a complete picture of what makes up that individual circuit. Trouble spots, for instance, can often be narrowed down by noting if other components related to that circuit are operating properly or not. If several components or circuits fail at one time, chances are the fault lies in the fuse or earth (ground) connection, as several circuits often are routed through the same fuse and earth (ground) connections.

3 Electrical problems often stem from simple causes, such as loose or corroded connections or a blown fuse. Prior to any electrical fault finding, always visually check the condition of the fuse, wires and connections in the problem circuit. Intermittent failures can be especially frustrating, since you can't always duplicate the failure when it's convenient to test. In such situations, a good practice is to clean all connections in the affected circuit, whether or not they appear to be good. All of the connections and wires should also be wiggled to check for looseness which can cause intermittent failure.

4 If testing instruments are going to be utilised, use the wiring diagram to plan where you will make the necessary connections in order to accurately pinpoint the trouble spot.

5 The basic tools needed for electrical fault finding include a battery and bulb test circuit, a continuity tester, a test light, and a jumper wire. A multimeter capable of reading volts, ohms and amps is also very useful as an alternative to the above, and is necessary for performing more extensive tests and checks.

> **HAYNES HINT** *Refer to Fault Finding Equipment in the Reference section for details of how to use electrical test equipment.*

3 Battery – removal, installation, inspection and maintenance

Caution: Be extremely careful when handling or working around the battery. The electrolyte is very caustic and an explosive gas (hydrogen) is given off when the battery is charging.

Removal and installation

1 Remove the seat (see Chapter 8). Release the battery strap **(see illustration)**.

2 Unscrew the negative (–) terminal bolt first and disconnect the lead from the battery **(see illustration)**. Lift up the red insulating cover to access the positive (+) terminal, then unscrew

the bolt and disconnect the lead. Lift the battery from the bike **(see illustration)**.

3 On installation, clean the battery terminals and lead ends with a wire brush or knife and emery paper. Reconnect the leads, connecting the positive (+) terminal first.

> **HAYNES HINT** *Battery corrosion can be kept to a minimum by applying a layer of petroleum jelly to the terminals after the cables have been connected. There are also dedicated sprays commercially available.*

4 Fit the battery strap and install the seat (see Chapter 8).

Inspection and maintenance

5 The battery fitted to the models covered in this manual is of the maintenance free (sealed) type, therefore requiring no regular maintenance. However, the following checks should still be regularly performed.

6 Check the battery terminals and leads for tightness and corrosion. If corrosion is evident, unscrew the terminal screws and disconnect the leads from the battery, disconnecting the negative (–) terminal first, and clean the terminals and lead ends with a wire brush or knife and emery paper. Reconnect the leads, connecting the negative (–) terminal last, and apply a thin coat of petroleum jelly to the connections to slow further corrosion.

7 Keep the battery case clean to prevent

3.1 Release the battery strap

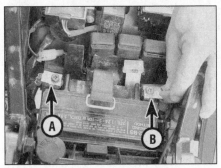

3.2a Disconnect the negative lead first (A), then the positive (B) . . .

3.2b . . . and remove the battery

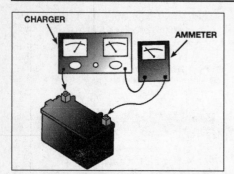

4.2 If the charger doesn't have ammeter built in, connect one in series as shown. DO NOT connect the ammeter between the battery terminals or it will be ruined

current leakage, which can discharge the battery over a period of time (especially when it sits unused). Wash the outside of the case with a solution of baking soda and water. Rinse the battery thoroughly, then dry it.

8 Look for cracks in the case and replace the battery with a new one if any are found. If acid has been spilled on the frame or battery box, neutralise it with a baking soda and water solution, dry it thoroughly, then touch up any damaged paint.

9 If the motorcycle sits unused for long periods of time, disconnect the cables from the battery terminals, negative (–) terminal first. Refer to Section 4 and charge the battery once every month to six weeks.

10 Check the condition of the battery by measuring the voltage present at the battery terminals. Connect the voltmeter positive (+)

probe to the battery positive (+) terminal, and the negative (–) probe to the battery negative (–) terminal. When fully charged there should be 13.0 to 13.2 volts present. If the voltage falls below 12.3 volts the battery must be removed, disconnecting the negative (–) terminal first, and recharged as described below in Section 4.

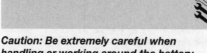

4 Battery – charging

Caution: Be extremely careful when handling or working around the battery. The electrolyte is very caustic and an explosive gas (hydrogen) is given off when the battery is charging.

1 Remove the battery (see Section 3). Connect the charger to the battery, making sure that the positive (+) lead on the charger is connected to the positive (+) terminal on the battery, and the negative (–) lead is connected to the negative (–) terminal.

2 Honda recommend that the battery is charged at the rate specified at the beginning of the Chapter. Exceeding this figure can cause the battery to overheat, buckling the plates and rendering it useless. Few owners will have access to an expensive current controlled charger, so if a normal domestic charger is used check that after a possible initial peak, the charge rate falls to a safe level **(see illustration)**. If the battery becomes hot during charging **stop**. Further charging will cause damage. **Note:** *In emergencies the*

battery can be charged at a higher rate of around 4.0 amps for a period of 0.5 hour. However, this is not recommended and the low amp charge is by far the safer method of charging the battery.

3 If the recharged battery discharges rapidly if left disconnected it is likely that an internal short caused by physical damage or sulphation has occurred. A new battery will be required. A sound item will tend to lose its charge at about 1% per day.

4 Install the battery (see Section 3).

5 If the motorcycle sits unused for long periods of time, charge the battery once every month to six weeks and leave it disconnected.

5 Fuses – check and replacement

1 The electrical system is protected by fuses of different ratings. All except the main fuse, and on X (1999) models onward the PGM-FI (fuel injection system) fuse are housed in the fusebox, which is located under the seat behind the bank of relays. The main fuse is integral with the starter relay, which is behind the seat cowling on the left-hand side of the bike. On X (1999) models onward, the PGM-FI fuse is located under the seat in front of the relay bank.

2 To access the fusebox fuses, remove the seat (see Chapter 8) and unclip the fusebox lid **(see illustrations)**. To access the main fuse, remove the seat cowling (see Chapter 8) and disconnect the starter relay wiring connector **(see illustration)**. To access the PGM-FI fuse, remove the seat (see Chapter 8) and unclip the fuseholder cap **(see illustration)**.

3 The fuses can be removed and checked visually. If you can't pull the fuse out with your fingertips, use a pair of suitable pliers. A blown fuse is easily identified by a break in the element **(see illustration)**. Each fuse is clearly marked with its rating and must only be replaced by a fuse of the correct rating. A spare fuse of each rating is housed in the fusebox, and a spare main/PGM-FI fuse is housed in the bottom of the rubber sleeve that holds the starter relay. If a spare fuse is used,

5.2a Unclip the lid . . .

5.2b . . . to access the fuses

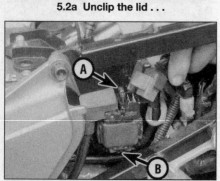

5.2c Disconnect the wiring connector to access the main fuse (A). The spare (B) is below

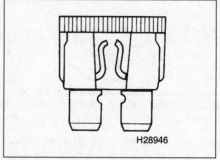

5.2d PGM-FI fuse (arrowed)

H28946

5.3 A blown fuse can be identified by a break in its element

always replace it so that a spare of each rating is carried on the bike at all times.

Warning: Never put in a fuse of a higher rating or bridge the terminals with any other substitute, however temporary it may be. Serious damage may be done to the circuit, or a fire may start.

4 If a fuse blows, be sure to check the wiring circuit very carefully for evidence of a short-circuit. Look for bare wires and chafed, melted or burned insulation. If the fuse is replaced before the cause is located, the new fuse will blow immediately.

5 Occasionally a fuse will blow or cause an open-circuit for no obvious reason. Corrosion of the fuse ends and fusebox terminals may occur and cause poor fuse contact. If this happens, remove the corrosion with a wire brush or emery paper, then spray the fuse end and terminals with electrical contact cleaner.

6 Lighting system – check

1 The battery provides power for operation of the headlight, tail light, brake light and instrument cluster lights. If none of the lights operate, always check battery voltage before proceeding. Low battery voltage indicates either a faulty battery or a defective charging system. Refer to Section 3 for battery checks and Sections 30 and 31 for charging system tests. Also, check the condition of the fuses. Note that if there is more than one problem at the same time, it is likely to be a fault relating to a multi-function component, such as one of the fuses governing more than one circuit, or the ignition switch. **Note:** *All US models and 2003-on Europe models have a hard-wired lighting system. Power to the dimmer switch is routed through the starter switch, thus enabling the lights to be turned off when the starter is operated.*

Headlight

2 If either or both headlight beams fail to work, first check the fuse (see Section 5), and then the bulb(s) (see Section 7). If they are good, use jumper wires to connect the bulb in question directly to the battery terminals. If the

light comes on, the problem lies in the wiring or connectors, the relay (HI beam only) or the switches in the circuit. Refer to Section 20 for the switch testing procedures, and also to the wiring diagrams at the end of this Chapter.

3 If the high beam does not work and the relay is suspected of being faulty, the easiest way to tell is to substitute it with another one, if available. Remove the seat to access the relays – it is mounted behind the battery **(see illustrations)**. If the beam then works, the faulty relay must be replaced with a new one. If a substitute is not available, remove the suspect one and test it as follows: set a multimeter to the ohms x 1 scale and connect it across the relay's blue/black and black/red wire terminals. There should be no continuity (infinite resistance). Using a fully-charged 12 volt battery and two insulated jumper wires, connect the positive (+) terminal of the battery to the blue wire terminal of the relay, and the negative (–) terminal to the green wire terminal. At this point the relay should be heard to click and the meter read 0 ohms (continuity). If this is the case the relay is good. If the relay does not click when battery voltage is applied and indicates no continuity (infinite resistance) across its terminals, it is faulty and must be replaced with a new one.

4 If the relay is good, check for battery voltage at the black/red wire terminal on the relay wiring connector with the ignition ON. If there is no voltage, check the wiring between the relay wiring connector and the ignition switch, via the fusebox, then check the switch itself (see Section 19). If voltage is present, check that there is continuity to the headlight wiring connector in the blue/black wire, and continuity to earth (ground) in the green wire from the headlight connector. Also check for battery voltage at the blue wire terminal on the relay wiring connector with the ignition ON, the light switch ON and the dimmer switch set to HI. If voltage is present, check for continuity to earth (ground) in the green wire from the relay wiring connector. Repair or renew the wiring or connectors as necessary.

5 If the low beam does not work, check for battery voltage at the blue/white wire terminal on the headlight wiring connector with the ignition ON, the light switch ON and the dimmer switch set to LO. If voltage is present, check for

continuity to earth (ground) in the green wire from the relay wiring connector. Repair or renew the wiring or connectors as necessary.

Tail light

6 If either or both tail lights fail to work, first check the fuse (see Section 5), and then the bulb(s) (see Section 9). If they are good, use jumper wires to connect the bulb in question directly to the battery terminals. If the light comes on, the problem lies in the wiring or connectors, or the switches in the circuit. Refer to Section 20 for the switch testing procedures, and also to the wiring diagrams at the end of this Chapter.

7 Check for battery voltage at the brown/white wire terminal on the tail light wiring connectors. If voltage is present, check for continuity to earth (ground) in the green wire from the wiring connector. If no voltage is indicated, check the wiring and connectors between the tail light and the ignition switch, via the fusebox, then check the switch itself (see Section 19).

Brake light

8 If either or both brake lights fail to work, first check the fuse (see Section 5), and then the bulb(s) (see Section 9). If they are good, use jumper wires to connect the bulb in question directly to the battery terminals. If the light comes on, the problem lies in the wiring or connectors, or the switches in the circuit.

9 Check for battery voltage at the green/yellow wire terminal on the tail light wiring connectors, first with the front brake lever on, then with the rear brake pedal on. If voltage is present with one brake on but not the other, then the switch or its wiring is faulty. If voltage is present in both cases, check for continuity to earth (ground) in the green wire from the wiring connectors. If no voltage is indicated, check the wiring and connectors between the brake light and the brake switches, the fusebox, and the ignition switch, then check the switches themselves (see Section 14 for the brake light switches and Section 19 for the ignition switch).

Instrument and warning lights

10 See Section 17 for instrument and warning light bulb replacement.

Turn signals

11 See Section 11 for turn signal circuit check.

7 Headlight bulb and sidelight bulb – replacement

Note: *The headlight bulbs are of the quartz-halogen type. Do not touch the bulb glass as skin acids will shorten the bulb's service life. If the bulb is accidentally touched, it should be wiped carefully when cold with a rag soaked in methylated spirit and dried before fitting.*

6.3a **Headlight relay (arrowed) – V and W (1997 and 1998) models**

6.3b **Headlight relay (arrowed) – X (1999) models onward**

7.2a Disconnect the wiring connector . . .

7.2b . . . and remove the dust cover

7.3a Release the clip . . .

 Warning: Allow the bulb time to cool before removing it if the headlight has just been on.

Headlight

1 Remove the cockpit trim panels (see Chapter 8).
2 Disconnect the relevant wiring connector from the back of the headlight and remove the rubber dust cover, noting how it fits **(see illustrations)**.
3 Release the bulb retaining clip, noting how it fits, then remove the bulb **(see illustrations)**.
4 Fit the new bulb, bearing in mind the information in the **Note** above. Make sure the tabs on the bulb fit correctly in the slots in the bulb housing, and secure it in position with the retaining clip.
5 Install the dust cover, making sure it is

correctly seated and with the 'TOP' mark at the top, and connect the wiring connector.
6 Check the operation of the headlight. Install the trim panels (see Chapter 8).

> **HAYNES HiNT** *Always use a paper towel or dry cloth when handling new bulbs to prevent injury if the bulb should break and to increase bulb life.*

Sidelight

7 Remove the access panel from the underside of the fairing **(see illustration)**.
8 Twist the bulbholder anti-clockwise and draw it out of its socket in the base of the headlight **(see illustration)**. Carefully pull the bulb out of the holder **(see illustration)**.
9 Fit the new bulb in the bulbholder, then

install the holder and turn it clockwise to secure it, Make sure it is correctly seated.
10 Check the operation of the sidelight. Install the access panel.

8 Headlight assembly – removal and installation

Removal

1 Remove the fairing (see Chapter 8). On V and W (1997 and 1998) models, remove the air duct from the fairing.
2 Undo the four bolts securing the headlight assembly to the fairing and remove the headlight, noting how it fits **(see illustration)**.

Installation

3 Installation is the reverse of removal. Make sure all the wiring is correctly connected and secured. Check the operation of the headlight and sidelight. Check the headlight aim (see Chapter 1).

9 Brake/tail light bulb and license plate bulb – replacement

Brake/tail light bulbs

V and W (1997 and 1998) models

1 Undo the screws securing the lens on the back of the tail light and remove it.

7.3b . . . and remove the bulb

7.7 Remove the access panel . . .

7.8a . . . then draw out the bulbholder . . .

7.8b . . . and remove the bulb

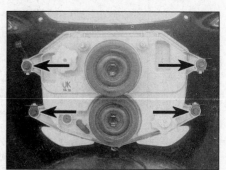
8.2 Headlight mounting bolts (arrowed)

9.5 Remove the bulbholder from the tail light . . .

9.6 . . . and pull the bulb from the holder

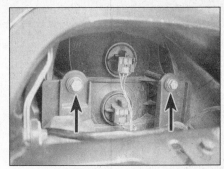

10.3 The tail light unit is secured by two nuts on X (1999) models onward

2 Push the bulb into the holder and twist it anti-clockwise to remove it. Check the socket terminals for corrosion and clean them if necessary. Line up the pins of the new bulb with the slots in the socket, then push the bulb in and turn it clockwise until it locks into place. **Note:** *The pins on the bulbs are offset so they can only be installed one way. It is a good idea to use a paper towel or dry cloth when handling the new bulb to prevent injury if it breaks, and to increase bulb life.*

3 Check the condition of the lens sealing ring and replace it with a new one if it is damaged, deformed or deteriorated. Fit the lens back onto the tail light and install the screws, taking care not to overtighten them as it is easy to either strip the threads or crack the lens.

X (1999) models onward

4 Remove the seat (see Chapter 8).

5 Turn the bulbholder anti-clockwise and withdraw it from the tail light **(see illustration).**

6 Carefully pull the bulb out of the socket **(see illustration).** Check the socket terminals for corrosion and clean them if necessary. Install the new bulb by pushing it into the socket – it can be installed either way round.

7 Fit the bulbholder into the tail light and turn it clockwise to secure it.

8 Install the seat.

License plate light bulb

9 Unscrew the bolts securing the license plate bracket and light and detach them from the rear mudguard.

11.2a Turn signal relay (arrowed) – V and W (1997 and 1998) models

10 Undo the screws on the back of the light and detach the lens cover and lens.

11 Push the bulb into the holder and twist it anti-clockwise to remove it. Check the socket terminals for corrosion and clean them if necessary. Line up the pins of the new bulb with the slots in the socket, then push the bulb in and turn it clockwise until it locks into place. *It is a good idea to use a paper towel or dry cloth when handling the new bulb to prevent injury if the bulb should break and to increase bulb life.*

12 Fit the lens and its cover back onto the light. Secure the light to the bracket, then fit the assembly back on the mudguard.

10 Tail light assembly – removal and installation

Tail light

1 Remove the seat (see Chapter 8).

2 On V and W (1997 and 1998) models disconnect the tail light wiring connector, and remove the bulbs if required (see Section 9). Unscrew the bolts securing the tail light assembly and carefully withdraw it from the back of the bike.

3 On X (1999) models onward, turn the bulbholders anti-clockwise and withdraw them from the tail light **(see illustration 9.5).** Unscrew the nuts securing the tail light assembly and carefully withdraw it from the back of the bike **(see illustration).**

11.2b Turn signal relay (arrowed) – X (1999) models onward

4 Installation is the reverse of removal. Check the operation of the tail and brake lights.

License plate light

5 Remove the seat (see Chapter 8).

6 Trace the wiring and disconnect it at the connector. Feed the wiring through to the light.

7 Unscrew the bolts securing the license plate bracket and light and detach them from the rear mudguard. If required, undo the screws and separate the light from the bracket.

8 Installation is the reverse of removal. Check the operation of the light.

11 Turn signal circuit – check

Note: *On US models the front turn signals also function as running lights and have dual filament bulbs. When checking for faults, refer to the wiring diagram at the end of this Chapter.*

1 Most turn signal problems are the result of a burned out bulb or corroded socket. This is especially true when the turn signals function properly in one direction, but fail to flash in the other direction. If this is the case, first check the bulbs, the sockets and the wiring connectors. If all the turn signals fail to work, first check the fuse (see Section 5), and then the relay (see below). If they are good, the problem lies in the wiring or connectors, or the switch. Refer to Section 20 for the switch testing procedures, and also to the wiring diagrams at the end of this Chapter.

2 To check the relay, remove the seat (see Chapter 8). The relay is mounted behind the battery **(see illustrations).** The easiest way to tell if the relay is faulty is to substitute it with another one, if available. If the turn signals then work, replace the faulty relay with a new one.

3 If a substitute is not available, or if it does not solve the problem, displace the relay and disconnect the wiring connector. Check for battery voltage at the white/green wire terminal on the loom side of the connector with the ignition ON. Turn the ignition OFF

when the check is complete. If no voltage was present, check the wiring from the relay to the ignition (main) switch (via the fusebox) for continuity. If voltage was present, check the green wire from the connector for continuity to earth (ground). Repair or renew the wiring or connectors as necessary.

4 Using a jumper wire, connect between the white/green and grey wire terminals on the connector. Turn the ignition ON and operate the turn signal switch. If the turn signals now work, replace the relay with a new one.

5 If the turn signals still don't work, use the appropriate wiring diagram at the end of this Chapter and check the wiring and connectors between the relay, turn signal switch and turn signal lights for continuity. Repair or renew the wiring, connectors or switch as necessary.

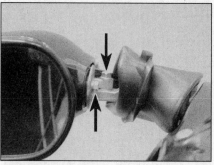

12.1a Pull back the boot, then unscrew the bolts (arrowed) . . .

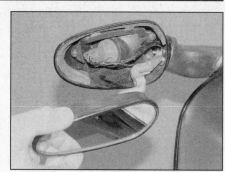

12.1b . . . and remove the mirror

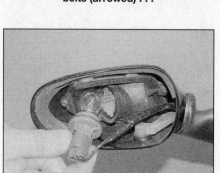

12.2a Release the bulbholder . . .

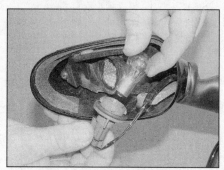

12.2b . . . and remove the bulb

12 Turn signal bulbs – replacement

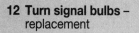

Note: *It is a good idea to use a paper towel or dry cloth when handling the new bulb to prevent injury if the bulb should break and to increase bulb life.*

Front

1 To replace the front turn signal bulbs, pull the rubber boot back off the mirror, then unscrew the bolts securing the mirror in its housing and remove it **(see illustrations)**.

2 Turn the bulbholder anti-clockwise and withdraw it from the lens **(see illustration)**. Push the bulb into the holder and twist it anti-clockwise to remove it **(see illustration)**. Check the socket terminals for corrosion and clean them if necessary. Line up the pins of the new bulb with the slots in the socket, then push the bulb in and turn it clockwise until it locks into place. Note that on US models the front turn signals double as running lights and the bulbs have offset pins.

3 Fit the bulbholder back into the lens, making sure it is securely held, then install the mirror and secure it with its bolts. Fit the boot back around the mirror.

Rear

4 To replace the rear turn signal bulbs, remove the screw securing the lens and detach the lens from the housing, noting how it fits **(see illustration)**. Remove the rubber gasket if it is free, and discard it if it is damaged, deformed or deteriorated.

5 Push the bulb into the holder and twist it anti-clockwise to remove it **(see illustration)**. Check the socket terminals for corrosion and clean them if necessary. Line up the pins of the new bulb with the slots in the socket, then push the bulb in and turn it clockwise until it locks into place.

6 Fit a new rubber gasket onto the housing if required, and make sure it is properly seated and does not get pinched by the lens. Fit the lens engaging the tab with the cutout and

install the screw. Do not overtighten the screw as it is easy to strip the threads or crack the lens.

13 Turn signal assemblies – removal and installation

Front turn signals

1 Pull the rubber boot back off the mirror, then unscrew the bolts securing the mirror in its housing and remove it **(see illustrations 12.1a and b)**.

2 Turn the bulbholder anti-clockwise and withdraw it from the lens **(see illustration 12.2a)**.

3 Undo the two screws securing the lens unit

12.4a Remove the screw . . .

12.4b . . . and detach the lens . . .

12.5 . . . then remove the bulb from the holder – V, W, X and Y type shown

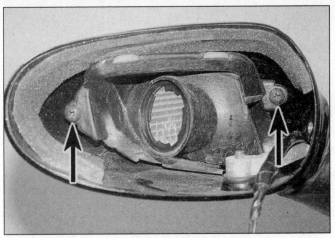

13.3 Undo the screws (arrowed) and remove the lens unit

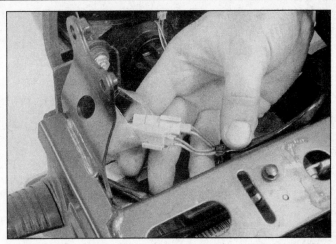

13.5 Rear turn signal wiring connectors – later type connector shown, early models have bullet connectors

in the mirror housing and remove it **(see illustration)**.

4 Installation is the reverse of removal. Check the operation of the turn signals.

Rear turn signals

5 Remove the seat (see Chapter 8). Disconnect the turn signal wiring connector **(see illustration)**. Carefully draw the wiring through to the stem under the mudguard, taking care not to it.

6 Unscrew the nut securing the stem to the inside of the rear mudguard and remove the mounting plate. Remove the turn signal, again taking care as you draw the wiring through.

7 Installation is the reverse of removal. Check the operation of the turn signals.

14 Brake light switches – check and replacement

Circuit check

1 Before checking the switches, and if not already done, check the brake light circuit (see Section 6, Steps 8 and 9). Ensure that the rear brake light switch is correctly adjusted – see Chapter 1, Section 14.

2 The front brake light switch is mounted on the underside of the brake master cylinder. Disconnect the wiring connectors from the switch **(see illustration)**. Using a continuity tester, connect the probes to the terminals of the switch. With the brake lever at rest, there should be no continuity. With the brake lever applied, there should be continuity. If the switch does not behave as described, replace it with a new one.

3 The rear brake light switch is mounted on the inside of the rider's right-hand footrest bracket, above the brake pedal **(see illustration)**. Remove the seat to access the wiring connector (see Chapter 8). Trace the wiring from the switch and disconnect it at the connector **(see illustration)**. Using a continuity tester, connect the probes to the terminals on the switch side of the wiring connector. With the brake pedal at rest, there should be no continuity. With the brake pedal applied, there should be continuity. If the switch does not behave as described, replace it with a new one.

4 If the switches are good, check for voltage at the black/green (front) or white/green (rear switch) wire terminal on the connector with the ignition switch ON – there should be battery voltage. If there's no voltage present, check the wiring between the switch and the

ignition switch via the fusebox (see the *wiring diagrams* at the end of this Chapter). If voltage is present, check the black/yellow (front) or green/yellow (rear) wire for continuity to the brake light bulb wiring connector, referring to the relevant Wiring Diagram. Repair or renew the wiring as necessary.

Switch replacement

Front brake

5 The switch is mounted on the underside of the brake master cylinder. Disconnect the wiring connectors from the switch **(see illustration 14.2)**.

6 Remove the single screw securing the switch to the master cylinder and remove the switch.

7 Installation is the reverse of removal. The switch isn't adjustable.

Rear brake

8 The rear brake light switch is mounted on the inside of the right-hand riders footrest bracket, above the brake pedal **(see illustration 14.3a)**. Remove the seat to access the wiring connector (see Chapter 8). Trace the wiring from the switch and disconnect it at the connector **(see illustration 14.3b)**.

9 Detach the lower end of the switch spring

14.2 Front brake switch wiring connectors (arrowed)

14.3a Rear brake light switch (arrowed)

14.3b Rear brake light switch wiring connector

15.3 Instrument cluster mounting nuts (arrowed)

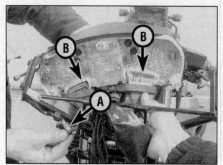

15.4 Immobiliser indicator wiring connector (A), instrument cluster wiring connectors (B) – X (1999) models onward shown

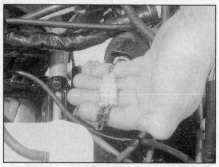

16.2 Disconnect the speed sensor wiring connector

from the brake pedal, then either release the switch with its adjustment nut from the mounting by squeezing the tabs on the underside of the nut, or thread the switch itself out of the nut, leaving the nut in the mounting.

10 Installation is the reverse of removal. Make sure the brake light is activated just before the rear brake pedal takes effect. If adjustment is necessary, hold the switch body and turn the adjustment nut as required (either raising or lowering the switch) until the brake light is activated correctly.

15 Instrument cluster – removal and installation

Removal

1 Remove the fairing (see Chapter 8).
2 On European X (1999) models onward, disconnect the immobiliser system wiring connector **(see illustration 15.4)**.
3 Unscrew the three nuts and remove the washers securing the instrument cluster, then displace it from the bracket **(see illustration)**. Note the rubber grommets fitted in the mounts.
4 Pull back the rubber boots and disconnect the large wiring connector(s) **(see illustration)**.

Installation

5 Installation is the reverse of removal. Check the rubber grommets for damage,

deformation and deterioration and replace them with new ones if necessary. Make sure that the wiring connector(s) are correctly routed and secured.

16 Instruments and speed sensor – check and replacement

Speedometer and speed sensor

Check

1 First check the fuse (see Section 5).
2 Raise or remove the fuel tank (see Chapter 4). Trace the wiring from the speed sensor, which is mounted on the crankcase behind the cylinders, and disconnect it at the 3-pin white connector inside the rubber boot **(see illustration)**. With the ignition switch ON, check for battery voltage between the black/brown and green/black wire terminals on the wiring loom side of the connector. If there is no voltage, refer to the wiring diagrams and check the circuit.
3 If there is voltage, remove the fairing (see Chapter 8). Disconnect the instrument cluster wiring connectors and check for loose or broken connections, then reconnect them **(see illustration 15.4)**. With the ignition switch ON, check for battery voltage between the black/brown and green/black speedometer wire terminals on the back of the instrument cluster. If there is no voltage,

refer to the wiring diagrams and check the wiring.
4 If there is voltage, with the ignition switch OFF check for continuity between the pink/green wire terminal on the loom side of the speed sensor wiring connector and the pink/green wire terminal on the rear of the instrument cluster. If there is no continuity, check the circuit for loose or broken connections.
5 If there is continuity, connect a voltmeter between the pink/green and green/black wire terminals on the rear of the instrument cluster. With the machine on its centrestand and the ignition switch ON, turn the rear wheel by hand and check that a fluctuating voltage reading between 0 – 5 volts is obtained. If a reading is obtained, the speedometer is probably faulty. Special instruments are required to properly check the operation of the speedometer. Take the machine to a Honda dealer service department or other qualified repair shop for diagnosis. If no reading is obtained, and the wiring is good, then the speed sensor is faulty.

Replacement

Speedometer

6 Remove the instrument cluster (see Section 15).
7 Remove the front cover screws from the back of the housing and lift off the cover **(see illustrations)**.
8 On V, W, X and Y (1997 to 2000) models, remove the screws securing the speedometer, then carefully remove it from the housing **(see illustration)**.

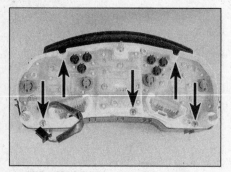

16.7a Undo the screws (arrowed) . . .

16.7b . . . and remove the front cover

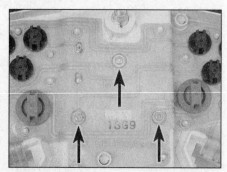

16.8 Speedometer screws (arrowed)

16.13a Unscrew the bolts (arrowed) . . .

16.13b . . . and withdraw the sensor

9 On 1 (2001) models onward, remove the complete instrument panel from the housing. Individual components are not available, so the entire assembly must be renewed if it is faulty.

10 Installation is the reverse of removal.

Speed Sensor

11 Remove the fuel tank (see Chapter 4).

12 Trace the wiring from the speed sensor, which is mounted on the crankcase behind the cylinders, and disconnect it at the 3-pin white connector inside the rubber boot **(see illustration 16.2)**. Release the wiring from its clip.

13 Unscrew the sensor mounting bolts and remove the sensor **(see illustrations)**. Remove and discard its O-ring as a new one must be used. Plug the sensor orifice with clean rag to prevent anything falling into the engine.

14 Installation is the reverse of removal, using a new O-ring.

Tachometer

Check

15 Remove the seat and the fairing (see Chapter 8).

16 Check for battery voltage between the black/brown and green/black tachometer wire terminals on the back of the instrument cluster with the ignition ON. If no voltage is

present, refer to the wiring diagrams and check the wiring and connectors.

17 Disconnect the ignition control unit or ECM wiring connector, according to your model (see Chapter 5 or 4). Check for continuity in the yellow/green wire between the ignition control unit or ECM wiring connector and its terminal on the back of the instrument cluster. If there is no continuity there is a break in the wire or faulty connector. Refer to the wiring diagrams and trace and rectify the fault.

18 If continuity exists, either the tachometer or the ignition control unit could be faulty. Reconnect the wiring connectors. Special instruments are required to properly check this voltage (see Step 19), and the use of other instruments could lead to false readings. If the instruments are not available, check for an input voltage using a normal meter. With the engine running, there should be an input voltage from the module to the tachometer at the yellow/green wire terminal. If no voltage is measured and the wire is good, then it is likely the ignition control unit or ECM is faulty. If a voltage is measured, then it is likely the tachometer is faulty. Take the machine to a Honda dealer service department or other qualified repair shop for further diagnosis.

19 Honda specify their own Imrie diagnostic tester (model 625), or the peak voltage adapter (Pt. No. 07HGJ-0020100) with an

aftermarket digital multimeter having an impedance of 10 M-ohm/DCV minimum, for this test. Connect the positive (+) lead of the voltmeter and peak voltage adapter arrangement to the instrument cluster yellow/green terminal and the negative (–) lead to earth (ground). Start the engine and measure the tachometer input peak voltage; this should be at least 10.5 volts. If the peak voltage exceeds this amount then the tachometer or instrument cluster printed circuit board is faulty. If there is no reading then the ignition control unit or ECM is at fault (see Chapter 5 or 4 according to model).

Replacement

20 Remove the instrument cluster (see Section 15).

21 Remove the front cover screws from the back of the housing and lift off the cover **(see illustrations 16.7a and b)**.

22 On V, W, X and Y (1997 to 2000) models, remove the screws securing the tachometer, then carefully remove it from the housing **(see illustration)**.

23 On 1 (2001) models onward, remove the complete instrument panel from the housing. Individual components are not available, so the entire assembly must be renewed if it is faulty.

24 Installation is the reverse of removal.

Coolant temperature gauge

Check

25 See Chapter 3.

Replacement

26 Remove the instrument cluster (see Section 15).

27 Remove the front cover screws from the back of the housing and lift off the cover **(see illustrations 16.7a and b)**.

28 On V, W, X and Y (1997 to 2000) models, remove the screws securing the coolant temperature/fuel gauge assembly (an integral component), then carefully remove it from the housing **(see illustration)**.

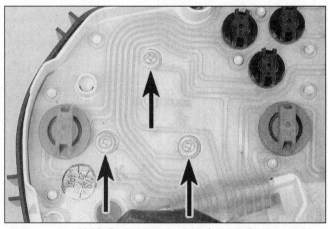

16.22 Tachometer screws (arrowed)

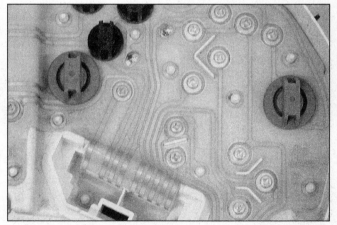

16.28 Coolant temperature gauge, fuel gauge, clock and FI indicator screws

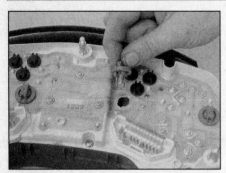

17.2a Release the bulbholder . . .

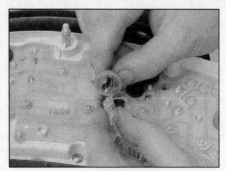

17.2b . . . and remove the bulb

29 On 1 (2001) models onward, remove the complete instrument panel from the housing. Individual components are not available, so the entire assembly must be renewed if it is faulty.
30 Installation is the reverse of removal.

Fuel gauge

Check
31 See Chapter 4.

Replacement
32 Remove the instrument cluster (see Section 15).
33 Remove the front cover screws from the back of the housing and lift off the cover (see illustrations 16.7a and b).
34 On V, W, X and Y (1997 to 2000) models, remove the screws securing the fuel/coolant temperature gauge assembly (an integral component), then carefully remove it from the housing (see illustration 16.28).
35 On 1 (2001) models onward, remove the complete instrument panel from the housing. Individual components are not available, so the entire assembly must be renewed if it is faulty.
36 Installation is the reverse of removal.

Clock

Check
37 Remove the fairing (see Chapter 8). With the ignition switch OFF, check for battery voltage between the red/green and green/black clock wire terminals on the back of the instrument cluster. There should be voltage at all times. If no voltage is present, check the wires for continuity and solid connections. If voltage is present, the clock is faulty.

Replacement
38 Remove the instrument cluster (see Section 15).
39 Remove the front cover screws from the back of the housing and lift off the cover (see illustrations 16.7a and b).
40 On V, W, X and Y (1997 to 2000) models, remove the screws securing the clock, then carefully remove it from the housing (see illustration 16.28).
41 On 1 (2001) models onward, remove the

complete instrument panel from the housing. Individual components are not available, so the entire assembly must be renewed if it is faulty.
42 Installation is the reverse of removal.

17 Instrument and warning light bulbs – replacement

V, W, X and Y (1997 to 2000) models

1 Remove the windshield (see Chapter 8). Many of the bulbs are accessible with the instrument cluster in place. If access is restricted, remove the fairing (see Chapter 8) and displace the cluster from the bracket (see Section 15).
2 Twist the bulbholder to release it and pull it out of the instrument housing, then pull the bulb out of the bulbholder (see illustrations). If the socket contacts are dirty or corroded, scrape them clean and spray with electrical contact cleaner before a new bulb is installed. Carefully push the new bulb into the holder, then fit the holder into the housing.
3 Install the instrument cluster, fairing or windshield as required (see Chapter 8).

1 (2001) models onward

4 Remove the windshield (see Chapter 8). The tachometer bulbs are the only ones that can be renewed individually. All other instrument and warning lights are LED's, which are not available individually. If one of the LED's fails the entire instrument panel must be renewed.
5 For easiest access, remove the fairing (see Chapter 8) and displace the cluster from the bracket (see Section 15). Twist the bulbholder to release it and pull it out of the instrument housing, then pull the bulb out of the bulbholder (see illustrations). If the socket contacts are dirty or corroded, scrape them clean and spray with electrical contact cleaner before a new bulb is installed. Carefully push the new bulb into the holder, then fit the holder into the housing.
6 Install the instrument cluster (see Chapter 8).

18 Oil pressure switch – check, removal and installation

Check
1 The oil pressure warning light should come on when the ignition (main) switch is turned ON and extinguish a few seconds after the engine is started. If the oil pressure warning light comes on whilst the engine is running, stop the engine immediately and carry out an oil level check, and if the level is correct, an oil pressure check (see Chapter 1).
2 If the oil pressure warning light does not come on when the ignition is turned on, check the bulb (see Section 17) and fuse (see Section 5).
3 The oil pressure switch is screwed into the crankcase on the right-hand side. Remove the right-hand fairing side panel for access (see Chapter 8). Pull the rubber cover off the switch and remove the screw securing the wiring connector (see illustration). With the ignition switched ON, earth (ground) the wire on the crankcase and check that the warning light comes on. If the light comes on, the switch is defective and must be replaced with a new one.
4 If the light still does not come on, check for voltage at the wire terminal. If there is no voltage present, check the wire between the switch, the instrument cluster and fusebox for continuity (see the wiring diagrams at the end of this Chapter).
5 If the warning light comes on whilst the engine is running, yet the oil pressure is satisfactory, remove the wire from the oil pressure switch. With the wire detached and the ignition switched ON the light should be out. If it is illuminated, the wire between the switch and instrument cluster must be earthed (grounded) at some point. If the wiring is good, the switch must be assumed faulty and replaced.

Removal
6 Remove the right-hand fairing side panel (see Chapter 8).
7 Pull the rubber cover off the switch, then

18.3 Pull back the rubber then remove the terminal screw and detach the wiring

18.8 Unscrew and remove the switch

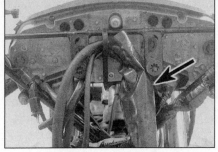

19.1 The wiring connector is inside the rubber boot (arrowed)

19.9 The ignition switch is secured by two shear-head bolts (arrowed)

remove the screw securing the wiring connector **(see illustration 18.3)**.

8 Unscrew the oil pressure switch and withdraw it from the crankcase **(see illustration)**.

Installation

9 Apply a suitable sealant to the upper portion of the switch threads near the switch body, leaving the bottom 3 to 4 mm of thread clean. Install the switch in the crankcase and tighten it to the torque setting specified at the beginning of the Chapter **(see illustration 18.8)**. Attach the wiring connector and secure it with the screw, then fit the rubber cover **(see illustration 18.3)**.

10 Run the engine and check that the switch operates correctly without leakage.

11 Install the fairing side panel (see Chapter 8).

 19 Ignition (main) switch – check, removal and installation

⚠ **Warning: To prevent the risk of short circuits, disconnect the battery negative (–) lead before making any ignition (main) switch checks.**

Note: *Two shear-head bolts mount the ignition switch to the underside of the top yoke – these bolts can only be used once. Obtain new bolts before starting.*

Check

1 Remove the fairing (see Chapter 8). Trace the wiring from the ignition switch and disconnect it at the 3-pin white connector inside the black rubber boot on the front of the instrument cluster **(see illustration)**.

2 Using an ohmmeter or a continuity tester, check the continuity of the connector terminal pairs (see the *Wiring Diagrams* at the end of this Chapter). Continuity should exist between the terminals connected by a solid line on the diagram when the switch is in the indicated position.

3 If the switch fails any of the tests, replace it with a new one.

Removal

4 Remove the fuel tank (see Chapter 4) and the fairing (see Chapter 8). This will prevent the possibility of damage should a tool slip.

5 Trace the wiring from the ignition switch and disconnect it at the 3-pin white connector inside the black rubber boot on the front of the instrument cluster **(see illustration 19.1)**. Work back along the harness, freeing it from any clips and ties, noting its correct routing.

6 Displace the handlebars from the top yoke (see Chapter 6). Support them so the master cylinders are upright to prevent the possibility of fluid leakage. There is no need to remove assemblies from the handlebars.

7 Displace the top yoke from the forks and steering stem as described in Chapter 1, Section 18, following the relevant Steps.

8 On models fitted with the HISS immobiliser system, undo the screws securing the receiver around the ignition switch and remove it, noting how it fits.

9 Two shear-head bolts mount the ignition switch to the underside of the top yoke **(see illustration)**. The heads of the bolts must be drifted round using a suitable punch or drift, or drilled or ground off, before the switch can be removed. Mount the yoke in a vice equipped with soft jaws and padded out with rags to do this. Remove the bolts and withdraw the switch from the top yoke.

Installation

10 Installation is the reverse of removal. Tighten the new bolts until the heads shear off. Make sure wiring connectors are securely connected and correctly routed.

11 Fit the top yoke onto the steering stem and forks as described in Chapter 1, Section 18, following the relevant Steps.

12 Install the handlebars (see Chapter 6), the fuel tank (see Chapter 4), and the fairing (see Chapter 8).

20 Handlebar switches – check

1 Generally speaking, the switches are reliable and trouble-free. Most troubles, when

they do occur, are caused by dirty or corroded contacts, but wear and breakage of internal parts is a possibility that should not be overlooked. If breakage does occur, the entire switch and related wiring harness will have to be replaced with a new one, as individual parts are not available.

2 The switches can be checked for continuity using an ohmmeter or a continuity test light. Always disconnect the battery negative (–) cable, which will prevent the possibility of a short circuit, before making the checks.

3 Remove the fairing (see Chapter 8). Trace the wiring harness of the switch in question and disconnect it at its connector inside the black rubber boot in front of the instrument cluster – the connector for the right-hand switchgear is red, and for the left-hand is black **(see illustration 19.1)**.

4 Check for continuity between the terminals of the switch connector with the switch in the various positions (i.e. switch off – no continuity, switch on – continuity) – see the *wiring diagrams* at the end of this Chapter. Continuity should exist between the terminals connected by a solid line on the diagram when the switch is in the indicated position.

5 If the continuity check indicates a problem exists, refer to Section 21, displace the switch housing and spray the switch contacts with electrical contact cleaner (there is no need to remove the switch completely). If they are accessible, the contacts can be scraped clean with a knife or polished with crocus cloth. If switch components are damaged or broken, it will be obvious when the switch is disassembled.

21 Handlebar switches – removal and installation

Removal

1 If the switch is to be removed from the bike, rather than just displaced from the handlebar, remove the fairing (see Chapter 8). Trace the wiring harness of the switch in question and disconnect it at its connector inside the black rubber boot in front of the instrument cluster – the connector for the right-hand switchgear is

21.4 Left-hand switch housing screws (arrowed)

22.2a Neutral switch (arrowed)

22.2b Disconnect the wiring connector from the switch

red, and for the left-hand is black **(see illustration 19.1)**. Work back along the harness, freeing it from any clips and ties, noting its correct routing.

2 Disconnect the two wires from the brake light switch (if removing the right-hand switch) or the clutch switch (if removing the left-hand switch) **(see illustration 14.2 or 24.2)**.

3 When working on the right-hand switch, refer to Chapter 4 for removal of the throttle cables, which involves separating the switch from the handlebars. Free the throttle cables from the twistgrip and remove them from the housing.

4 When working on the left-hand switch, unscrew the two handlebar switch screws and free the switch from the handlebar by separating the halves **(see illustration)**. On V and W (1997 and 1998) models, free the choke cable and lever from the housing. On X (1999) models onward, note the blanking cap that fits in the housing.

Installation

5 Installation is the reverse of removal. Make sure the locating pin in the switch housing locates in the hole in the handlebar. Refer to Chapter 4 for installation of the throttle and choke cables.

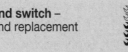

22 Neutral switch – check, removal and installation

Check

1 Before checking the electrical circuit, check the bulb (see Section 17) and fuse (see Section 5).

2 The switch is located in the left-hand side of the transmission casing below the front sprocket cover **(see illustration)**. Remove the left-hand fairing side panel (see Chapter 8). Detach the wiring connector from the switch **(see illustration)**. Make sure the transmission is in neutral.

3 With the connector disconnected and the ignition switch ON, the neutral light should be out. If not, the wire between the connector and instrument cluster must be earthed (grounded) at some point.

4 Check for continuity between the switch terminal and the crankcase. With the transmission in neutral, there should be continuity. With the transmission in gear, there should be no continuity. If the tests prove otherwise, then the switch is faulty.

5 If the continuity tests prove the switch is good, check for voltage at the wire terminal using a test light. If there's no voltage present, check the wire between the switch, the instrument cluster and fusebox (see the *wiring diagrams* at the end of this Chapter).

Removal

6 The switch is located in the left-hand side of the transmission casing below the front sprocket cover **(see illustration 22.2a)**. Remove the left-hand fairing side panel (see Chapter 8).

7 Detach the wiring connector from the switch **(see illustration 22.2b)**.

8 Unscrew the switch and withdraw it from the transmission casing. Discard the sealing washer as a new one should be used.

Installation

9 Install the switch using as new washer and tighten it to the torque setting specified at the beginning of the Chapter.

10 Connect the wiring connector and check the operation of the neutral light **(see illustration 22.2b)**.

11 Install the fairing side panel (see Chapter 6).

---

23 Sidestand switch – check and replacement

Check

1 The sidestand switch is mounted on the front of the sidestand. The switch is part of the safety circuit which prevents or stops the engine running if the transmission is in gear whilst the sidestand is down, and prevents the engine from starting if the transmission is in gear unless the sidestand is up, and unless the clutch is pulled in. Before checking the electrical circuit, check the fuse (see Section 5), and on V and W (1997 and 1998)

models the warning bulb (see Section 17)

2 Raise or remove the fuel tank (see Chapter 4). Trace the wiring back from the switch and disconnect at the 3-pin (V and W (1997 and 1998) models) or 2-pin (X (1999) models onward) green wiring connector inside the rubber boot **(see illustration)**.

3 Check the operation of the switch using an ohmmeter or continuity test light. Connect the meter between the green/white and green wires on the switch side of the connector. With the sidestand up there should be continuity (zero resistance) between the terminals, and with the stand down there should be no continuity (infinite resistance). On V and W (1997 and 1998) models, now connect the meter to the yellow/black and green wires on the switch side of the connector. With the sidestand down there should be continuity (zero resistance) between the terminals, and with the stand up there should be no continuity (infinite resistance).

4 If the switch does not perform as expected, it is faulty and must be replaced with a new one.

5 If the switch is good, check the wiring and connectors between the various components in the starter safety circuit using a continuity tester (see the *wiring diagrams* at the end of this book). Also check for voltage at the green/white, and on V and W (1997 and 1998) models the yellow/black wire terminal with the ignition ON. Repair or renew the wiring as required

Replacement

6 The sidestand switch is mounted on the

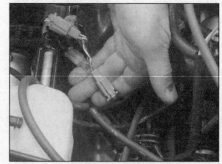

23.2 Sidestand switch wiring connector

23.6 Sidestand switch mounting bolt (arrowed)

24.2 Clutch switch wiring connectors (arrowed)

front of the sidestand **(see illustration)**. Raise or remove the fuel tank (see Chapter 4). Trace the wiring back from the switch and disconnect at the 3-pin (V and W (1997 and 1998) models) or 2-pin (X (1999) models onward) green wiring connector inside the rubber boot **(see illustration 23.2)**. Work back along the switch wiring, freeing it from any clips and ties, noting its correct routing.

7 Unscrew the switch bolt and remove the switch from the stand, noting how it fits.

8 Fit the new switch onto the sidestand, making sure the pin locates in the hole in the sidestand, and the lug for the spring on the stand bracket locates into the cutout in the switch body. Secure the switch with its bolt and tighten it to the torque setting specified at the beginning of the Chapter **(see illustration 23.6)**.

9 Make sure the wiring is correctly routed up to the connector and retained by any clips and ties.

10 Reconnect the wiring connector and check the operation of the sidestand switch **(see illustration 23.2)**.

11 Install the fuel tank (see Chapter 4).

24 Clutch switch –
check and replacement

Check

1 The clutch switch is mounted on the front of the clutch master cylinder. The switch is part of the safety circuit which prevents or stops the engine running if the transmission is in gear whilst the sidestand is down, and prevents the engine from starting if the transmission is in gear unless the sidestand is up and the clutch lever is pulled in. The switch isn't adjustable.

2 To check the switch, disconnect the wiring connectors from it **(see illustration)**. Connect the probes of an ohmmeter or a continuity test light to the two switch terminals. With the clutch lever pulled in, continuity should be indicated. With the clutch lever out, no continuity (infinite resistance) should be indicated.

3 If the switch is good, check the other components in the starter circuit as described in the relevant sections of this Chapter. If all components are good, check the wiring

between the various components (see the *wiring diagrams* at the end of this book).

Replacement

4 The clutch switch is mounted on the front of the clutch master cylinder.

5 Disconnect the wiring connectors from the switch **(see illustration 24.2)**. Undo the screw and remove the switch, noting how it fits.

6 Installation is the reverse of removal.

25 Diode –
check and replacement

Check

1 The diode is a small block that plugs into a connector in the fusebox, which is located under the seat. The diode is part of the safety circuit which prevents or stops the engine running if the transmission is in gear whilst the sidestand is down, and prevents the engine from starting if the transmission is in gear unless the sidestand is up and the clutch lever is pulled in.

2 Remove the seat (see Chapter 8), open the fusebox lid and pull the diode out of its socket **(see illustrations 5.2a and b)**.

3 Using an ohmmeter or continuity tester, connect the positive (+) probe to one of the outer terminals of the diode and the negative (–) probe to the middle terminal of the diode. The diode should show continuity. Now reverse the probes. The diode should show no continuity. Repeat the tests between the other outer terminal and the middle terminal. The same results should be achieved. If it doesn't behave as stated, replace the diode with a new one.

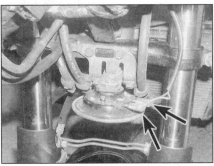

26.2 Horn wiring connectors (arrowed)

4 If the diode is good, check the other components in the starter circuit as described in the relevant sections of this Chapter. If all components are good, check the wiring between the various components (see the *wiring diagrams* at the end of this book).

Replacement

5 The diode is a small block that plugs into a connector in the fusebox, which is located under the seat.

6 Remove the seat (see Chapter 8), open the fusebox lid and pull the diode out of its socket **(see illustrations 5.2a and b)**.

26 Horn –
check and replacement

Check

1 The horn is mounted on the bottom yoke – remove the fairing for access (see Chapter 8).

2 Unplug the wiring connectors from the horn **(see illustration)**. Using two jumper wires, apply battery voltage directly to the terminals on the horn. If the horn sounds, check the switch (see Section 21). Also check for voltage at the light green wire connector with the ignition ON and the horn button pressed. If voltage is present, check the green wire for continuity to earth. If no voltage was present, check the light green wire for continuity between the horn and the switch, and in the white/green wire from the switch to the fusebox, and then to the ignition switch (see the *wiring diagrams* at the end of this Chapter). With the ignition switch ON, there should be voltage at the white/green wire to the horn button in the left-hand switch gear.

3 If the horn doesn't sound, replace it with a new one.

Replacement

4 The horn is mounted on the bottom yoke – remove the fairing for access (see Chapter 8).

5 Unplug the wiring connectors from the horn **(see illustration 26.2)**. Unscrew the bolt securing the horn and remove it from the bike **(see illustration)**.

6 Install the horn and securely tighten the bolt. Connect the wiring to the horn. Check that it works, then install the fairing (see Chapter 8).

26.5 Horn mounting bolt (arrowed)

27.2 Starter relay (arrowed)

27.9a Disconnect the wiring connector . . .

27.9b . . . then pull back the cover and unscrew the terminal bolts

27 Starter relay – check and replacement

Check

1 If the starter circuit is faulty, first check the fuse (see Section 5).
2 The starter relay is located behind the seat cowling on the left-hand side of the bike **(see illustration)** – remove the seat cowling for access (see Chapter 8).
3 Lift the rubber terminal cover and unscrew the bolt securing the starter motor lead **(see illustration 27.9b)**; position the lead away from the relay terminal. With the ignition switch ON, the engine kill switch in the RUN position, and the transmission in neutral, press the starter switch. The relay should be heard to click.
4 If the relay doesn't click, switch off the ignition and remove the relay as described below; test it as follows.
5 Set a multimeter to the ohms x 1 scale and connect it across the relay's starter motor and battery lead terminals **(see illustration 27.3)**. There should be no continuity. Using a fully-charged 12 volt battery and two insulated jumper wires, connect the positive (+) terminal of the battery to the yellow/red wire terminal of the relay, and the negative (–) terminal to the green/red wire terminal of the relay. At this point the relay should be heard to click and the multimeter read 0 ohms (continuity). If this

is the case the relay is proved good. If the relay does not click when battery voltage is applied and indicates no continuity (infinite resistance) across its terminals, it is faulty and must be replaced with a new one.
6 If the relay is good, check for battery voltage at the yellow/red wire when the starter button is pressed. If there is no voltage, check the wiring between the relay wiring connector and the starter button. If voltage is present, check that there is continuity to earth in the green/red wire with the transmission in neutral, the clutch lever pulled in and the sidestand up (note that there will be a very slight resistance due to the diode). If there is no continuity, check the other components in the starter circuit as described in the relevant sections of this Chapter. If all components are good, check the wiring between the various components (see the *wiring diagrams* at the end of this book).

Replacement

7 The starter relay is located behind the seat cowling on the left-hand side of the bike **(see illustration 27.2)** – remove the seat cowling for access (see Chapter 8).
8 Disconnect the battery terminals, remembering to disconnect the negative (–) terminal first.
9 Disconnect the relay wiring connector, then lift the insulating cover and unscrew the bolts securing the starter motor and battery leads to the relay and detach the leads **(see illustrations)**. Remove the relay with its rubber sleeve from its mounting lug on the

frame. If the relay is being replaced with a new one, remove the main fuse from the relay, and remove the relay from its sleeve.
10 Installation is the reverse of removal. Make sure the terminal bolts are securely tightened. Do not forget to fit the main fuse into the relay, if removed. Connect the negative (–) lead last when reconnecting the battery.

28 Starter motor – removal and installation

Removal

1 Remove the seat (see Chapter 8). Disconnect the battery negative (–) lead. The starter motor is mounted on the crankcase behind the cylinders on the left-hand side.
2 Drain the cooling system (see Chapter 1). Remove the fuel tank (see Chapter 4).
3 Unscrew the two bolts securing the coolant inlet union to the engine and detach the union **(see illustration)**. There is no need to disconnect the hose, but on V and W (1997 and 1998) models, you may need to detach the small hose from the thermostat housing to access the left-hand union bolt. Discard the union O-ring as a new one must be used.
4 Peel back the rubber terminal cover on the starter motor **(see illustration)**. Unscrew the nut securing the starter lead to the motor and detach the lead **(see illustration)**.

28.3 Unscrew the bolts (arrowed) and detach the union

28.4a Pull back the terminal cover . . .

28.4b . . . then unscrew the nut and detach the lead

28.5 Unscrew the two bolts (arrowed), noting the earth lead (A), and remove the starter motor

28.7 Fit a new O-ring and lubricate it . . .

28.8a . . . then install the starter motor . . .

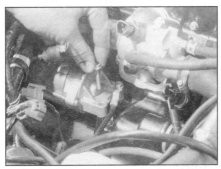

28.8b . . . and secure it with the bolts

28.10 Fit the union using a new O-ring

5 Unscrew the two bolts securing the starter motor to the crankcase, noting the earth lead secured by on eof the bolts **(see illustration)**. Slide the starter motor out and remove it.

6 Remove the O-ring on the end of the starter motor and discard it as a new one must be used.

Installation

7 Fit a new O-ring onto the end of the starter motor, making sure it is seated in its groove **(see illustration)**. Apply a smear of engine oil to the O-ring to aid installation.

8 Manoeuvre the motor into position and slide it into the crankcase **(see illustration)**. Ensure that the starter motor teeth mesh correctly with those of the starter idle/reduction gear. Install the mounting bolts, not forgetting to secure the earth lead, and tighten them securely **(see illustration)**.

9 Connect the starter lead to the motor and secure it with the nut **(see illustration 28.4b)**. Fit the rubber cover over the terminal **(see illustration 28.4a)**.

10 Fit the coolant union onto the engine using a new O-ring and tighten its bolts securely **(see illustration)**. On V and W (1997 and 1998) models, connect the hose to the thermostat housing if detached.

11 Fill the cooling system (see Chapter 1).

12 Install the fuel tank (see Chapter 4). Connect the battery negative (–) lead and install the fairing side panels and the seat (see Chapter 8).

---

29 Starter motor – disassembly, inspection and reassembly

Disassembly

1 Remove the starter motor (see Section 28) **(see illustration)**.

2 Note the alignment marks between the main housing and the front and rear covers, or

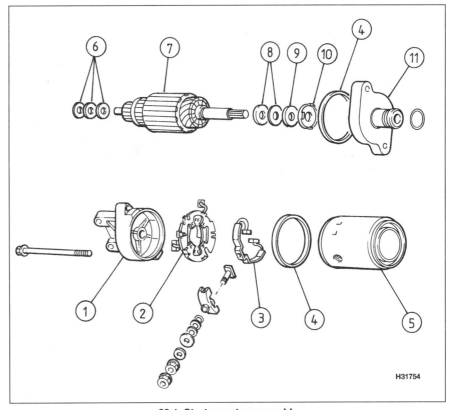

29.1 Starter motor assembly

1 Rear cover	5 Main housing	9 Insulated washer
2 Brush plate	6 Shims	10 Tabbed washer
3 Brush holder	7 Armature	11 Front cover
4 Sealing ring	8 Shims	

H31754

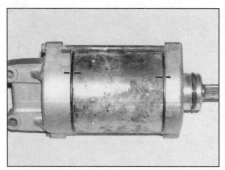

29.2 Note the alignment marks between the housing and the covers

29.3a Unscrew and remove the two bolts (arrowed) . . .

29.3b . . . then remove the front cover and sealing ring (arrowed)

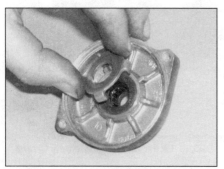

29.3c Remove the tabbed washer . . .

29.3d . . . and the shims

make your own if they aren't clear (see illustration).

3 Unscrew the two long bolts then remove the front cover from the motor along with its sealing ring (see illustration). Discard the sealing ring as a new one must be used. Remove the tabbed washer from the cover and slide the insulating washer and shim(s) from the front end of the armature, noting the number of shims and their correct fitted order (see illustrations).

4 Remove the rear cover from the motor along with its sealing ring (see illustration). Discard the sealing ring as a new one must be used. Remove the shim(s) from the rear end of the armature noting how many and their correct fitted positions (see illustration).

5 Withdraw the armature from the main housing (see illustration).

6 Lift each brush spring end onto the top of each brush housing and slide the brushes out (see illustrations).

7 At this stage check for continuity between the terminal bolt and the two brushes with yellow insulation. There should be continuity (zero resistance). Check for continuity between the terminal bolt and the housing. There should be no continuity (infinite resistance). Also check for continuity between the brushes with uninsulated wires and the brushplate. There should be continuity (zero resistance). If there is no continuity when

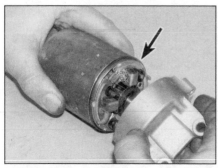

29.4a Remove the rear cover and its sealing ring (arrowed) . . .

29.4b . . . and remove the shims

29.5 Withdraw the armature from the housing

29.6a Place the brush spring ends onto the top of the brush housings . . .

29.6b . . . and slide the brushes out

29.8a Unscrew the nut and remove the washers and O-ring

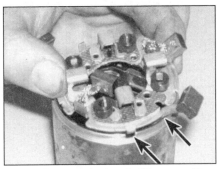

29.8b Remove the brushplate assembly, noting how it locates (arrows) . . .

29.8c . . . and remove the insulator

there should be or vice versa, identify the faulty component and replace it with a new one.

8 Noting the correct fitted location of each component, unscrew the nut from the terminal bolt and remove the plain washer, the one large and two small insulating washers and the rubber O-ring **(see illustration)**. Remove the brushplate assembly and terminal bolt from the main housing, noting how it locates, and recover the insulator **(see illustrations)**.

Inspection

9 The parts of the starter motor that are most likely to require attention are the brushes. Measure the length of each brush and compare the results to the Specifications at the beginning of the Chapter. If any of the brushes are worn beyond the service limit, replace the brush holder and/or brushplate assembly with a new one. If the brushes are not worn excessively, nor cracked, chipped, or otherwise damaged, they may be re-used.

10 Inspect the commutator bars on the armature for scoring, scratches and discoloration. The commutator can be cleaned and polished with crocus cloth, but do not use sandpaper or emery paper. After cleaning, wipe away any residue with a cloth soaked in electrical system cleaner or denatured alcohol.

11 Using an ohmmeter or a continuity test light, check for continuity between the

commutator bars **(see illustration)**. Continuity should exist between each bar and all of the others. Also, check for continuity between the commutator bars and the armature shaft **(see illustration)**. There should be no continuity (infinite resistance) between the commutator and the shaft. If the checks indicate otherwise, the armature is defective.

12 Check the starter pinion gear for worn, cracked, chipped and broken teeth. If the gear is damaged or worn, replace the starter motor.

13 Inspect the end covers for signs of cracks or wear. Check the needle bearing in the front cover and the bush in the rear cover for wear and damage **(see illustration)**. Inspect the magnets in the main housing and the housing itself for cracks.

14 Inspect the insulating washers, O-ring and front cover oil seal for signs of damage and renew if necessary.

Reassembly

15 Fit the insulator into the main housing **(see illustration 29.8c)**, then install the brush holder and insert the terminal bolt through it and the housing **(see illustrations)**. Slide the rubber O-ring and small insulating washers onto the terminal bolt, followed by the large insulating washer and the plain washer **(see illustration 29.8a)**. Fit the nut onto the terminal bolt and tighten it securely.

16 Install the brushplate assembly, making

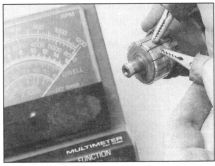

29.11a Continuity should exist between the commutator bars

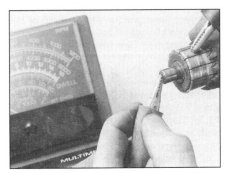

29.11b There should be no continuity between the commutator bars and the armature shaft

29.13 There is a needle bearing in the front cover (arrow)

29.15a Fit the brush holder . . .

29.15b . . . and the terminal bolt

29.18 Locate the spring ends onto the brushes

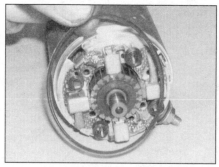

29.20 Fit a new sealing ring onto the rear of the housing

29.22 Fit a new sealing ring onto the front of the housing

sure its tab is correctly located in the housing slot, and that each of the insulated brush wires sits in its cutout in the brushplate **(see illustration 29.8b)**.
17 Slide all the brushes back into position in their housings **(see illustration 29.6b)**. Make sure that each brush spring is retained against the top of its housing so that it will not exert any pressure on the brush **(see illustration 29.6a)**.

 Lifting the end of the brush spring so that it is against the top of the brush holder and not pressing the brush inwards makes it much easier to install the armature on reassembly.

18 Insert the armature into the front of the housing and locate the brushes on the commutator bars **(see illustration 29.5)**. Slip each brush spring end off the top of the brush housing and onto the brush end **(see illustration)**. Check that each brush is securely pressed against the commutator by its spring and is free to move easily in its housing.
19 Fit the shims onto the rear of the armature shaft **(see illustration 29.4b)**. Apply a smear of grease to the end of the shaft.
20 Fit a new sealing ring onto the rear of the housing **(see illustration)**. Align the rear cover groove with the brushplate outer tab and install the cover – aligning the marks between the cover and housing (Step 2) will help **(see illustration 29.4a)**.

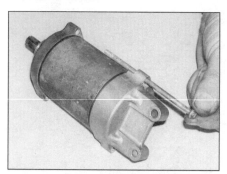

29.23 Fit the long bolts and tighten them securely

21 Apply a smear of grease to the front cover oil seal lip. Fit the toothed washer into the cover so that its teeth are correctly located with the cover ribs **(see illustration 29.3c)**.
22 Fit a new sealing ring onto the front of the housing **(see illustration)**. Slide the shim(s) onto the front end of the armature shaft then fit the insulating washer **(see illustration 29.3d)**. Slide the front cover into position, aligning the marks made on removal **(see illustration 29.3b)**.
23 Check the marks made on removal are correctly aligned then fit the long bolts and tighten them securely **(see illustration)**.
24 Install the starter motor (see Section 28).

30 Charging system testing – general information and precautions

1 If the performance of the charging system is suspect, the system as a whole should be checked first, followed by testing of the individual components. **Note:** *Before beginning the checks, make sure the battery is fully charged and that all system connections are clean and tight.*
2 Checking the output of the charging system and the performance of the various

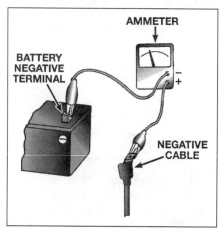

31.3 Checking the charging system leakage rate – connect the meter as shown

components within the charging system requires the use of a multimeter (with voltage, current and resistance checking facilities).
3 When making the checks, follow the procedures carefully to prevent incorrect connections or short circuits, as irreparable damage to electrical system components may result if short circuits occur.
4 If a multimeter is not available, the job of checking the charging system should be left to a Honda dealer.

31 Charging system – leakage and output test

1 If the charging system of the machine is thought to be faulty, remove the seat (see Chapter 8) and perform the following checks.

Leakage test

Caution: Always connect an ammeter in series, never in parallel with the battery, otherwise it will be damaged. Do not turn the ignition ON or operate the starter motor when the ammeter is connected – a sudden surge in current will blow the meter's fuse.

2 Turn the ignition switch OFF and disconnect the lead from the battery negative (–) terminal.
3 Set the multimeter to the Amps function and connect its negative (–) probe to the battery negative (–) terminal, and positive (+) probe to the disconnected negative (–) lead **(see illustration)**. Always set the meter to a high amps range initially and then bring it down to the mA (milli Amps) range; if there is a high current flow in the circuit it may blow the meter's fuse.
4 If the current leakage indicated exceeds the amount specified at the beginning of the Chapter, there is probably a short circuit in the wiring. Use the wiring diagrams at the end of this book and systematically disconnect individual electrical components until the source is identified.
5 Disconnect the meter and connect the negative (–) lead to the battery, tightening it securely,

Output test

6 Start the engine and warm it up to normal operating temperature.

7 To check the voltage output, allow the engine to idle and connect a multimeter set to the 0 – 20 volts DC scale (voltmeter) across the terminals of the battery (positive (+) lead to battery positive (+) terminal, negative (–) lead to battery negative (–) terminal). Slowly increase the engine speed to 5000 rpm and note the reading obtained. The regulated voltage should be as specified at the beginning of the Chapter. If the voltage is outside these limits, check the alternator and the regulator (see Sections 32 and 33).

 HAYNES HINT *Clues to a faulty regulator are constantly blowing bulbs, with brightness varying considerably with engine speed, and battery overheating.*

32 Alternator – check, removal and installation

Check

1 Remove the seat cowling (see Chapter 8).
2 On V and W (1997 and 1998) models, disconnect the wiring connector from the regulator/rectifier, which is on the left-hand side of the rear sub-frame. On X (1999) models onward, disconnect the white wiring connector containing the three yellow wires in the rubber boot below the regulator/rectifier **(see illustration 33.1b)**. Check the connector terminals for corrosion and security.
3 Using a multimeter set to the ohms x 1 (ohmmeter) scale measure the resistance between each of the yellow wires on the alternator side of the connector, taking a total of three readings, then check for continuity between each terminal and ground (earth). If the stator coil windings are in good condition the three readings should be within the range shown in the Specifications at the start of this

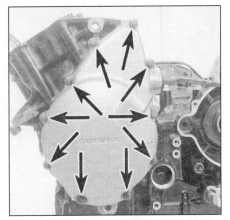

32.6 Alternator cover bolts (arrowed)

Chapter and there should be no continuity (infinite resistance) between any of the terminals and ground (earth). If not, the alternator stator coil assembly is at fault and should be replaced with a new one. **Note:** *Before condemning the stator coils, check the fault is not due to damaged wiring between the connector and the coils. On V and W (1997 and 1998) models, raise or remove the fuel tank (see Chapter 4) and check the other 3-pin white alternator wiring connector inside the rubber boot.*

Removal

4 On V and W (1997 and 1998) models, raise or remove the fuel tank (see Chapter 4). On X (1999) models onward, remove the seat cowling (see Chapter 8). On all models, remove the left-hand fairing side panel (see Chapter 8). Either drain the engine oil (see Chapter 1), or place a container under the engine to catch the oil that will come out when the alternator cover is removed.
5 Trace the wiring back from the alternator cover on the left-hand side of the engine and disconnect it at the 3-pin white connector containing the three yellow wires – on V and W (1997 and 1998) models the connector is inside the rubber boot above the crankcase, and on X (1999) models onward the connector is inside the rubber boot next to the regulator/rectifier **(see illustration 32.2)**. Free

32.7 Withdraw the shaft and remove the gear

the wiring from any clips or guides and feed it through to the alternator cover.
6 Working in a criss-cross pattern, evenly slacken the alternator cover bolts **(see illustration)**. Lift the cover away from the engine, noting that it will be restrained by the force of the rotor magnets, and be prepared to catch any residual oil. Remove the gasket and discard it. Remove the dowel from either the cover or the crankcase if it is loose.
7 Withdraw the idle/reduction gear shaft from the crankcase and remove the gear, noting which way round it fits **(see illustration)**.
8 To remove the rotor bolt it is necessary to stop the rotor from turning. The best way is to use a commercially available rotor strap **(see illustration)**. If one is not available, try placing the transmission in gear and having an assistant apply the rear brake hard. Unscrew the bolt. Note the washer fitted with the bolt.
9 To remove the rotor from the shaft it is necessary to use a rotor puller (Honda pt. no. 07733-0020001 or 07933-3950000, or a commercially available equivalent). Thread the rotor puller into the centre of the rotor and turn it until the rotor is displaced from the shaft, holding the rotor to prevent the engine turning **(see illustration)**. Remove the Woodruff key from its slot in the crankcase if it is loose **(see illustration)**. Separate the starter clutch from the rotor if required (see Chapter 2).
10 To remove the stator from the cover, unscrew the bolts securing the stator, and the bolt securing the wiring clamp, then remove

32.8 Using a rotor strap to hold the rotor while unscrewing the bolt

32.9a Using a puller to remove the rotor

32.9b Remove the Woodruff key if it is loose

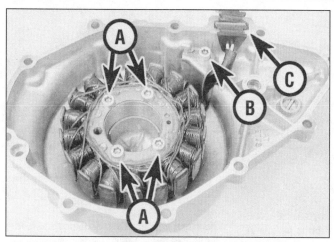

32.10 Unscrew the stator bolts (A) and the wiring clamp bolt (B) and free the grommet (C)

32.13 Slide the rotor onto the shaft, aligning the cutout (arrowed) with the Woodruff key

the assembly, noting how the rubber wiring grommet fits **(see illustration)**.

Installation

11 Fit the stator into the cover, aligning the rubber wiring grommet with the groove **(see illustration 32.10)**. Apply a suitable non-permanent thread locking compound to the stator bolt threads, then install the bolts and tighten them to the torque setting specified at the beginning of the Chapter. Apply a suitable sealant to the wiring grommet, then press it into the cut-out in the cover. Secure the wiring with its clamp and tighten the bolt securely.

32.14a Install the bolt with its washer . . .

12 If separated, fit the starter clutch onto the back of the rotor (see Chapter 2). Apply some oil to the needle bearing in the starter clutch.
13 Clean the tapered end of the crankshaft and the corresponding mating surface on the inside of the rotor with a suitable solvent. Fit the Woodruff key into its slot in the crankshaft if removed **(see illustration 32.9b)**. Make sure that no metal objects have attached themselves to the magnet on the inside of the rotor. Slide the rotor onto the shaft, making sure the groove on the inside of the rotor is aligned with and fits over the Woodruff key **(see illustration)**. Make sure the Woodruff key does not become dislodged when installing the rotor.
14 Apply some clean oil to the rotor bolt threads and the underside of the head. Install the rotor bolt with its washer and tighten it to the torque setting specified at the beginning of the Chapter, using the method employed on removal to prevent the rotor from turning **(see illustrations)**.
15 Lubricate the idle/reduction gear shaft with clean engine oil. Position the gear in the crankcase, making sure the larger pinion faces outwards, and the teeth of the smaller pinion mesh correctly with the teeth of the starter driven gear, and the teeth of the larger

pinion mesh correctly with the teeth of the starter motor shaft, then slide the shaft into the gear **(see illustration 32.7)**.
16 Apply a smear of suitable sealant to the area around the crankcase joints. Fit the dowel into the crankcase if removed. Install the alternator cover using a new gasket, making sure they locate onto the dowel **(see illustrations)**. Tighten the cover bolts evenly in a criss-cross sequence to the specified torque setting.
17 Reconnect the wiring at the connector and secure it with any clips or ties **(see illustration 32.2)**.
18 Fill the engine with oil, or top it up to the correct level, according to you removal method (see Chapter 1). Install the fairing side panel and seat cowling or fuel tank, according to model (see Chapters 8 and 4).

33 Regulator/rectifier – check and replacement

Check

1 Remove the seat cowling (see Chapter 8). The regulator/rectifier is mounted on the left-

32.14b . . . and tighten it to the specified torque

32.16a Locate the new gasket onto the dowel . . .

32.16b . . . then install the cover

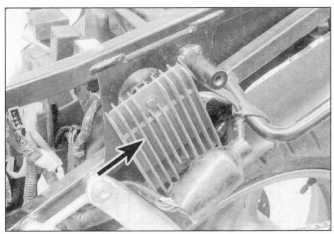

33.1a Regulator/rectifier (arrowed) – X (1999) models onward

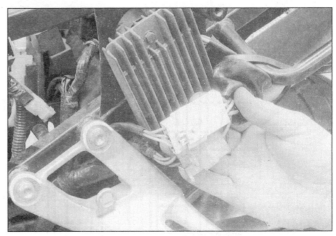

33.1b Regulator/rectifier wiring connectors –
X (1999) models onward

hand side of the rear sub-frame **(see illustration)**. Disconnect the wiring connector(s) and check for loose, damaged or corroded terminals **(see illustration)**.

2 Set the multimeter to the 0-20 dc volts setting. Connect the meter positive (+) probe to the red/white (V and W (1997 and 1998) models) or red (X (1999) models onward) wire terminal on the connector and the negative (–) probe to a suitable ground (earth) point and check for voltage. Full battery voltage should be present at all times.

3 Switch the multimeter to the resistance (ohms) scale. Check for continuity in the green wire between the terminal in the wiring connector and ground (earth). There should be continuity.

4 Set the multimeter to the ohms x 1

(ohmmeter) scale and measure the resistance between each of the yellow wires on the alternator side of the connector, taking a total of three readings, then check for continuity between each terminal and ground (earth). The three readings should be within the range shown in the Specifications for the alternator stator coil at the start of this Chapter, and there should be no continuity (infinite resistance) between any of the terminals and ground (earth).

5 If the above checks do not provide the expected results check the wiring and connectors between the battery, regulator/rectifier and alternator for shorts, breaks, and loose or corroded terminals (see the *wiring diagrams* at the end of this book).

6 If the wiring checks out, the

regulator/rectifier unit is probably faulty. Honda provide no test data for the unit itself. Take it to a Honda dealer for confirmation of its condition before replacing it with a new one.

Replacement

7 Remove the seat cowling (see Chapter 8). The regulator/rectifier is mounted on the left-hand side of the rear sub-frame **(see illustration 33.1a)**.

8 Disconnect the wiring connector(s) **(see illustration 33.1b)**.

9 Unscrew the two bolts securing the regulator/rectifier and remove it.

10 Install the new unit and tighten its bolts securely. Connect the wiring connector(s).

11 Install the seat cowling (see Chapter 8).

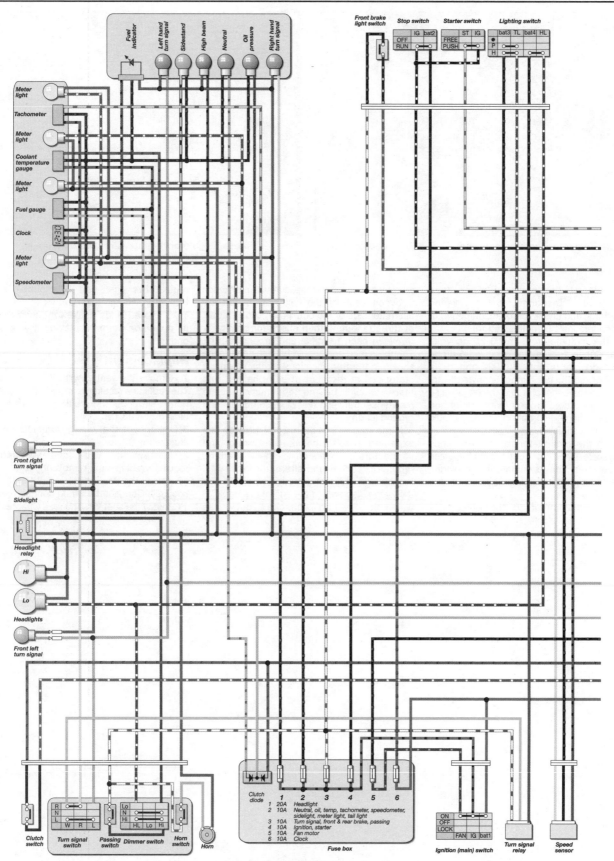

1997 and 1998 (V and W) Europe models

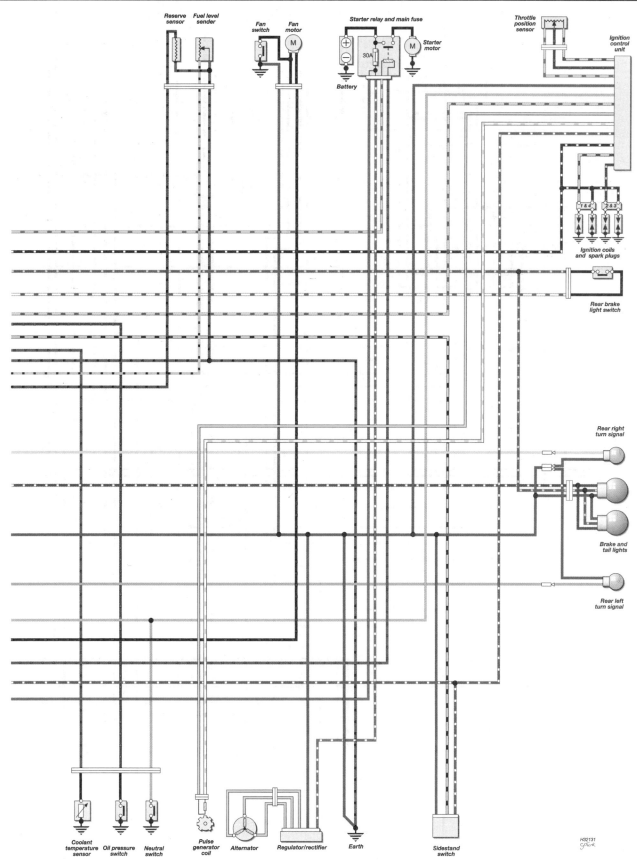

1997 and 1998 (V and W) Europe models

H32131

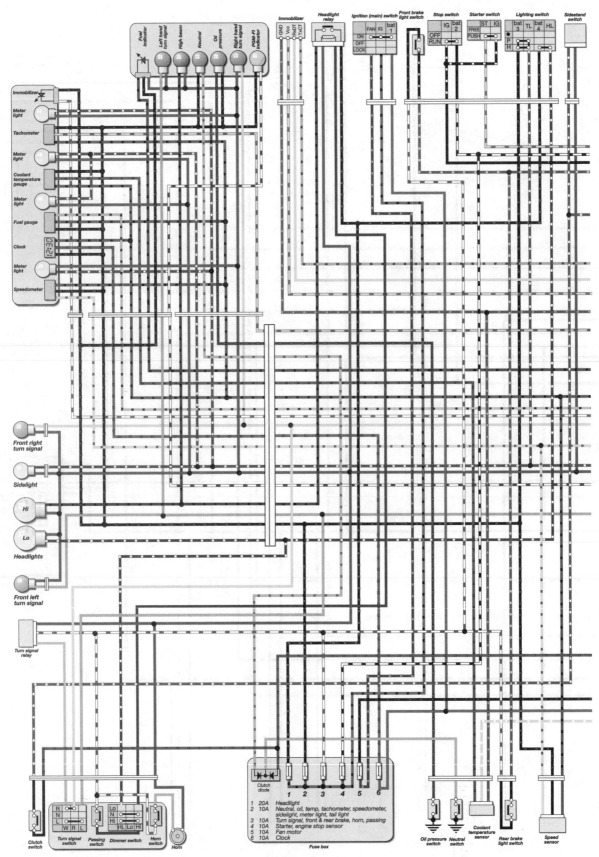

1999 and 2000 (X and Y) Europe models

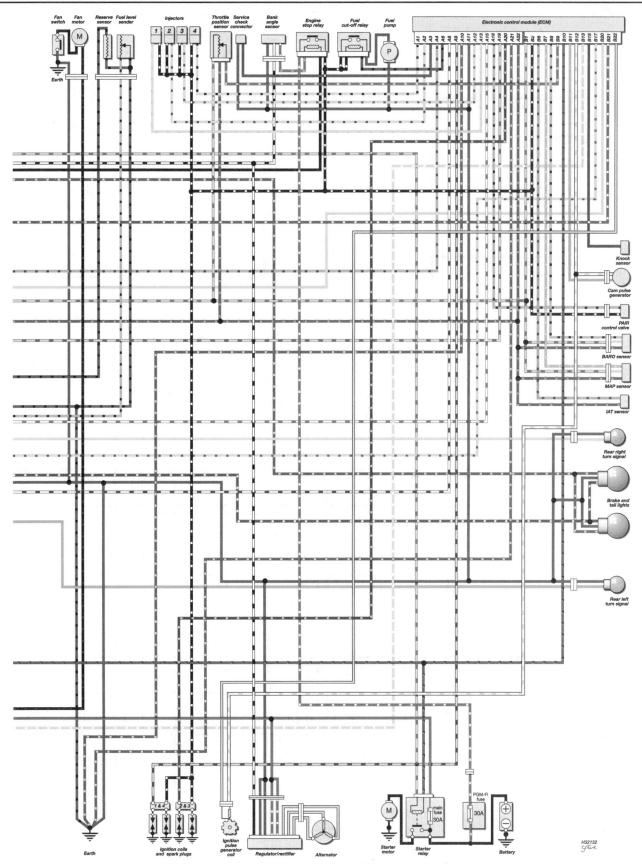

1999 and 2000 (X and Y) Europe models

H32132

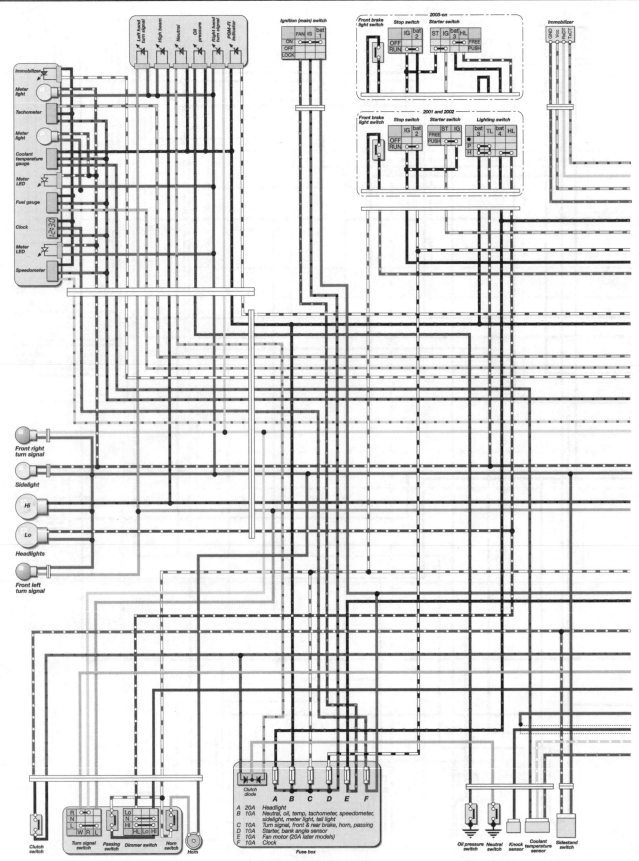

2001 models onward - Europe

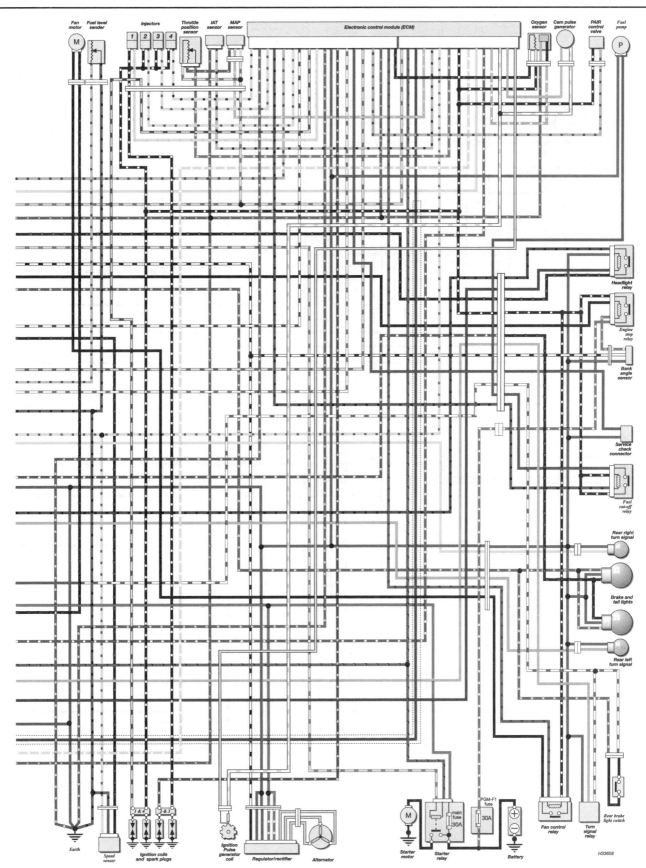

Fan motor | Fuel level sender | Injectors | Throttle position sensor | IAT sensor | MAP sensor | Electronic control module (ECM) | Oxygen sensor | Cam pulse generator | PAIR control valve | Fuel pump

Headlight relay
Engine stop relay
Bank angle sensor
Service check connector
Fuel cut-off relay
Rear right turn signal
Brake and tail lights
Rear left turn signal
Rear brake light switch

Earth | Speed sensor | Ignition coils and spark plugs | Ignition Pulse generator coil | Regulator/rectifier | Alternator | Starter motor | Starter relay | PGM-F1 fuse | Battery | Fan control relay | Turn signal relay

main fuse 30A | 30A

H33658

2001 models onward - Europe

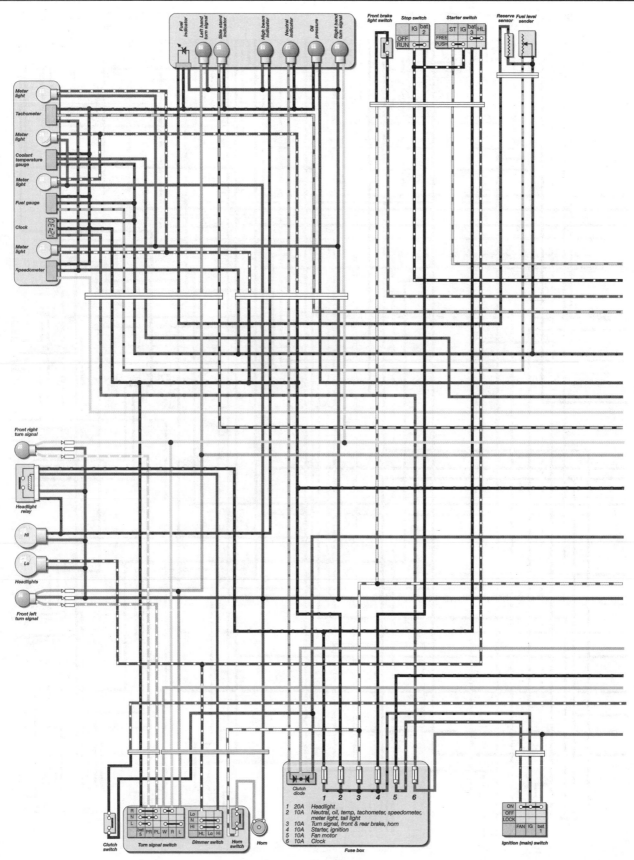

1997 and 1998 (V and W) US models

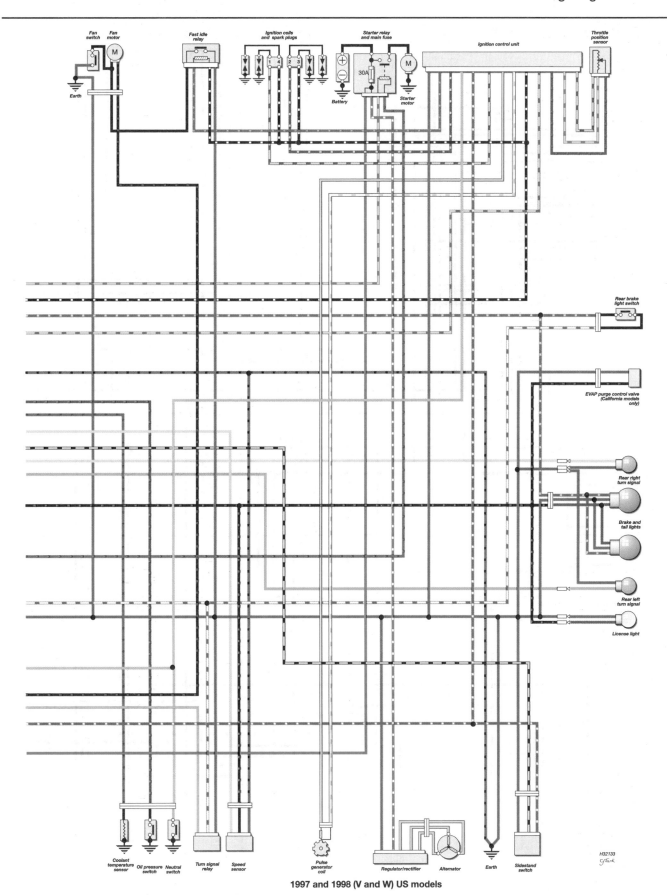

1997 and 1998 (V and W) US models

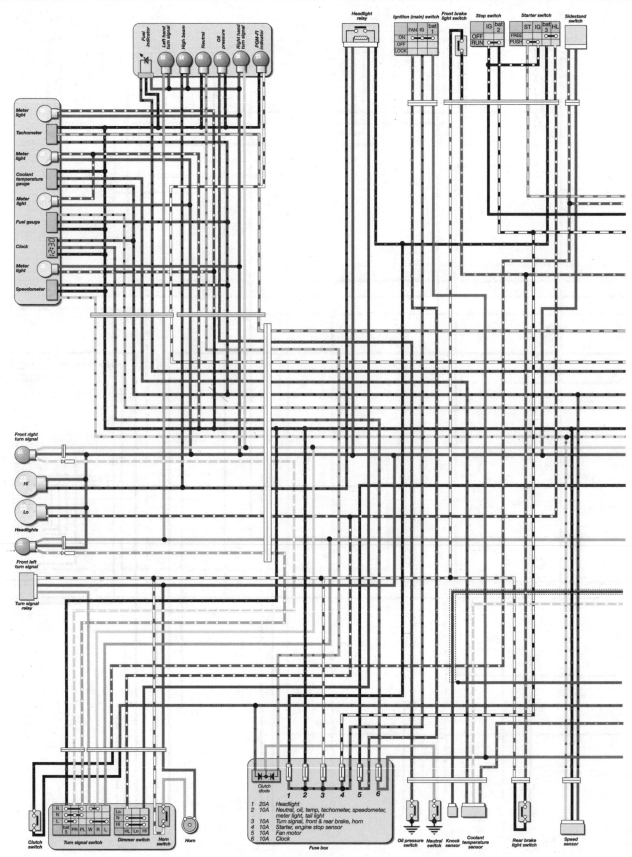

1999 and 2000 (X and Y) US models

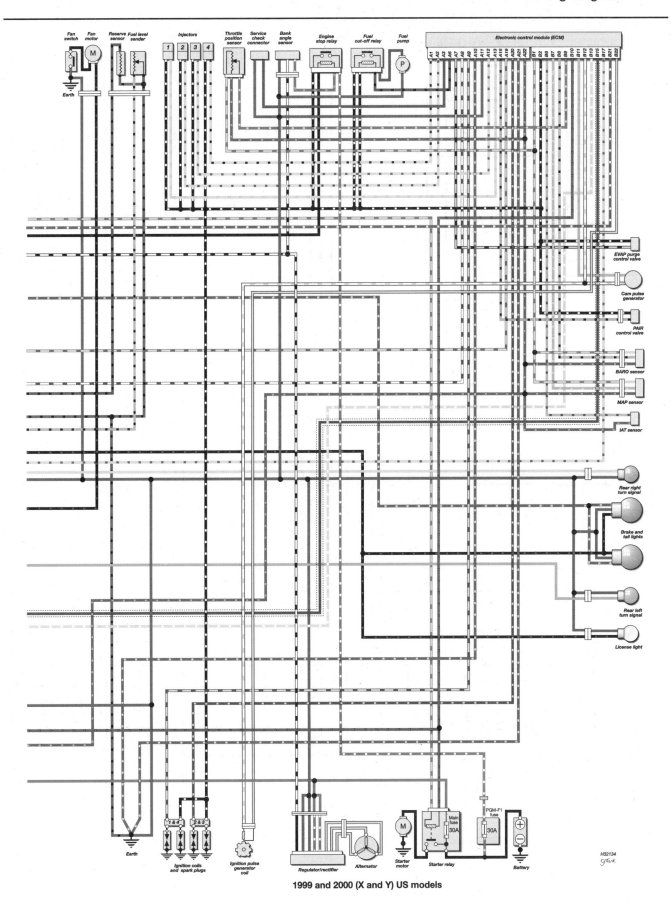

1999 and 2000 (X and Y) US models

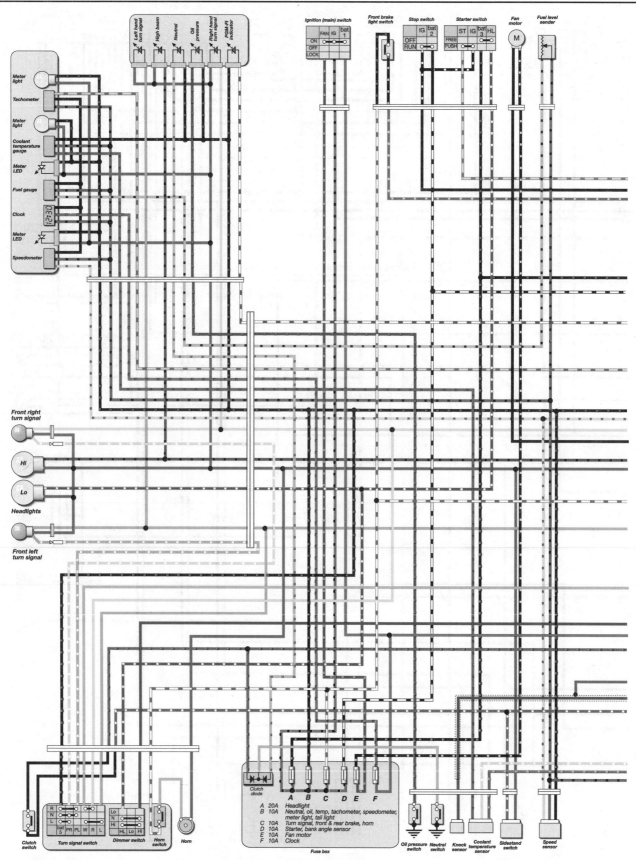

2001 models onwards – US models

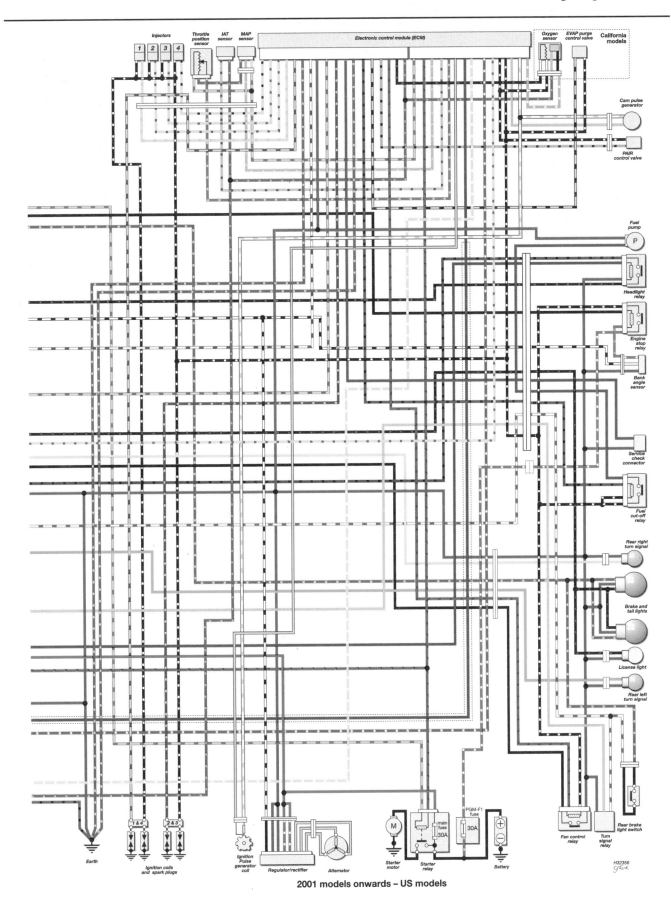

2001 models onwards – US models

Notes

Reference

Tools and Workshop Tips

● Building up a tool kit and equipping your workshop ● Using tools ● Understanding bearing, seal, fastener and chain sizes and markings ● Repair techniques

Security

● Locks and chains ● U-locks ● Disc locks ● Alarms and immobilisers ● Security marking systems ● Tips on how to prevent bike theft

Lubricants and fluids

● Engine oils ● Transmission (gear) oils ● Coolant/anti-freeze ● Fork oils and suspension fluids ● Brake/clutch fluids ● Spray lubes, degreasers and solvents

Conversion Factors

34 Nm x 0.738
= 25 lbf ft

● Formulae for conversion of the metric (SI) units used throughout the manual into Imperial measures

MOT Test Checks

● A guide to the UK MOT test ● Which items are tested ● How to prepare your motorcycle for the test and perform a pre-test check

Storage

● How to prepare your motorcycle for going into storage and protect essential systems ● How to get the motorcycle back on the road

Fault Finding

● Common faults and their likely causes ● How to check engine cylinder compression ● How to make electrical tests and use test meters

Technical Terms Explained

● Component names, technical terms and common abbreviations explained

Index

Buying tools

A toolkit is a fundamental requirement for servicing and repairing a motorcycle. Although there will be an initial expense in building up enough tools for servicing, this will soon be offset by the savings made by doing the job yourself. As experience and confidence grow, additional tools can be added to enable the repair and overhaul of the motorcycle. Many of the specialist tools are expensive and not often used so it may be preferable to hire them, or for a group of friends or motorcycle club to join in the purchase.

As a rule, it is better to buy more expensive, good quality tools. Cheaper tools are likely to wear out faster and need to be renewed more often, nullifying the original saving.

> **Warning: To avoid the risk of a poor quality tool breaking in use, causing injury or damage to the component being worked on, always aim to purchase tools which meet the relevant national safety standards.**

The following lists of tools do not represent the manufacturer's service tools, but serve as a guide to help the owner decide which tools are needed for this level of work. In addition, items such as an electric drill, hacksaw, files, soldering iron and a workbench equipped with a vice, may be needed. Although not classed as tools, a selection of bolts, screws, nuts, washers and pieces of tubing always come in useful.

For more information about tools, refer to the Haynes *Motorcycle Workshop Practice TechBook* (Bk. No. 3470).

Manufacturer's service tools

Inevitably certain tasks require the use of a service tool. Where possible an alternative tool or method of approach is recommended, but sometimes there is no option if personal injury or damage to the component is to be avoided. Where required, service tools are referred to in the relevant procedure.

Service tools can usually only be purchased from a motorcycle dealer and are identified by a part number. Some of the commonly-used tools, such as rotor pullers, are available in aftermarket form from mail-order motorcycle tool and accessory suppliers.

Maintenance and minor repair tools

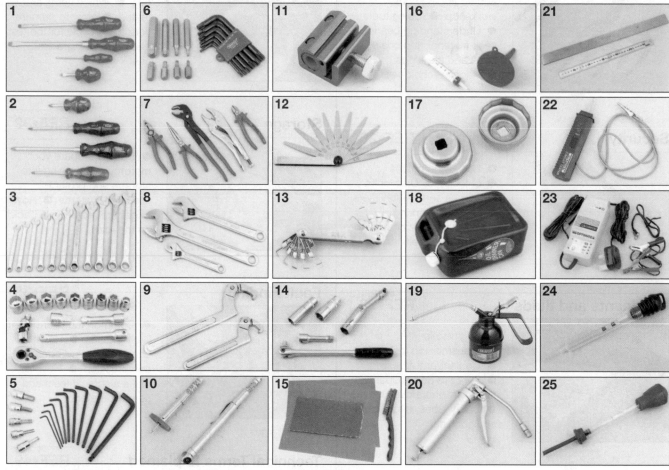

1 Set of flat-bladed screwdrivers
2 Set of Phillips head screwdrivers
3 Combination open-end and ring spanners
4 Socket set (3/8 inch or 1/2 inch drive)
5 Set of Allen keys or bits
6 Set of Torx keys or bits
7 Pliers, cutters and self-locking grips (Mole grips)
8 Adjustable spanners
9 C-spanners
10 Tread depth gauge and tyre pressure gauge
11 Cable oiler clamp
12 Feeler gauges
13 Spark plug gap measuring tool
14 Spark plug spanner or deep plug sockets
15 Wire brush and emery paper
16 Calibrated syringe, measuring vessel and funnel
17 Oil filter adapters
18 Oil drainer can or tray
19 Pump type oil can
20 Grease gun
21 Straight-edge and steel rule
22 Continuity tester
23 Battery charger
24 Hydrometer (for battery specific gravity check)
25 Anti-freeze tester (for liquid-cooled engines)

Repair and overhaul tools

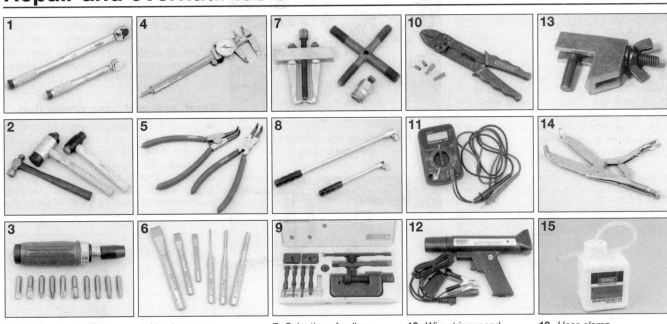

1 Torque wrench
   (small and mid-ranges)
2 Conventional, plastic or
   soft-faced hammers
3 Impact driver set

4 Vernier gauge
5 Circlip pliers (internal and
   external, or combination)
6 Set of cold chisels
   and punches

7 Selection of pullers
8 Breaker bars
9 Chain breaking/
   riveting tool set

10 Wire stripper and
   crimper tool
11 Multimeter (measures
   amps, volts and ohms)
12 Stroboscope (for
   dynamic timing checks)

13 Hose clamp
   (wingnut type shown)
14 Clutch holding tool
15 One-man brake/clutch
   bleeder kit

Specialist tools

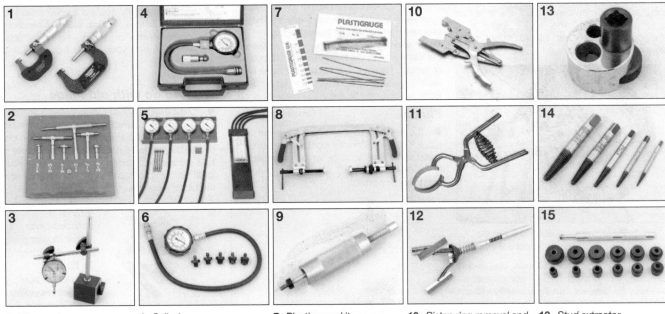

1 Micrometers
   (external type)
2 Telescoping gauges
3 Dial gauge

4 Cylinder
   compression gauge
5 Vacuum gauges (left) or
   manometer (right)
6 Oil pressure gauge

7 Plastigauge kit
8 Valve spring compressor
   (4-stroke engines)
9 Piston pin drawbolt tool

10 Piston ring removal and
   installation tool
11 Piston ring clamp
12 Cylinder bore hone
   (stone type shown)

13 Stud extractor
14 Screw extractor set
15 Bearing driver set

1 Workshop equipment and facilities

The workbench

● Work is made much easier by raising the bike up on a ramp - components are much more accessible if raised to waist level. The hydraulic or pneumatic types seen in the dealer's workshop are a sound investment if you undertake a lot of repairs or overhauls **(see illustration 1.1)**.

1.1 Hydraulic motorcycle ramp

● If raised off ground level, the bike must be supported on the ramp to avoid it falling. Most ramps incorporate a front wheel locating clamp which can be adjusted to suit different diameter wheels. When tightening the clamp, take care not to mark the wheel rim or damage the tyre - use wood blocks on each side to prevent this.
● Secure the bike to the ramp using tie-downs **(see illustration 1.2)**. If the bike has only a sidestand, and hence leans at a dangerous angle when raised, support the bike on an auxiliary stand.

1.2 Tie-downs are used around the passenger footrests to secure the bike

● Auxiliary (paddock) stands are widely available from mail order companies or motorcycle dealers and attach either to the wheel axle or swingarm pivot **(see illustration 1.3)**. If the motorcycle has a centrestand, you can support it under the crankcase to prevent it toppling whilst either wheel is removed **(see illustration 1.4)**.

1.3 This auxiliary stand attaches to the swingarm pivot

1.4 Always use a block of wood between the engine and jack head when supporting the engine in this way

Fumes and fire

● Refer to the Safety first! page at the beginning of the manual for full details. Make sure your workshop is equipped with a fire extinguisher suitable for fuel-related fires (Class B fire - flammable liquids) - it is not sufficient to have a water-filled extinguisher.
● Always ensure adequate ventilation is available. Unless an exhaust gas extraction system is available for use, ensure that the engine is run outside of the workshop.
● If working on the fuel system, make sure the workshop is ventilated to avoid a build-up of fumes. This applies equally to fume build-up when charging a battery. Do not smoke or allow anyone else to smoke in the workshop.

Fluids

● If you need to drain fuel from the tank, store it in an approved container marked as suitable for the storage of petrol (gasoline) **(see illustration 1.5)**. Do not store fuel in glass jars or bottles.

1.5 Use an approved can only for storing petrol (gasoline)

● Use proprietary engine degreasers or solvents which have a high flash-point, such as paraffin (kerosene), for cleaning off oil, grease and dirt - never use petrol (gasoline) for cleaning. Wear rubber gloves when handling solvent and engine degreaser. The fumes from certain solvents can be dangerous - always work in a well-ventilated area.

Dust, eye and hand protection

● Protect your lungs from inhalation of dust particles by wearing a filtering mask over the nose and mouth. Many frictional materials still contain asbestos which is dangerous to your health. Protect your eyes from spouts of liquid and sprung components by wearing a pair of protective goggles **(see illustration 1.6)**.

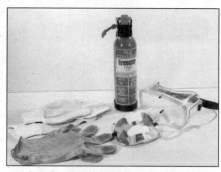

1.6 A fire extinguisher, goggles, mask and protective gloves should be at hand in the workshop

● Protect your hands from contact with solvents, fuel and oils by wearing rubber gloves. Alternatively apply a barrier cream to your hands before starting work. If handling hot components or fluids, wear suitable gloves to protect your hands from scalding and burns.

What to do with old fluids

● Old cleaning solvent, fuel, coolant and oils should not be poured down domestic drains or onto the ground. Package the fluid up in old oil containers, label it accordingly, and take it to a garage or disposal facility. Contact your local authority for location of such sites or ring the oil care hotline.

OIL CARE
FOLLOW THE CODE

OIL BANK LINE
0800 66 33 66
www.oilbankline.org.uk

Note: It is antisocial and illegal to dump oil down the drain. To find the location of your local oil recycling bank, call this number free.

In the USA, note that any oil supplier must accept used oil for recycling.

2 Fasteners -
screws, bolts and nuts

Fastener types and applications

Bolts and screws

● Fastener head types are either of hexagonal, Torx or splined design, with internal and external versions of each type **(see illustrations 2.1 and 2.2)**; splined head fasteners are not in common use on motorcycles. The conventional slotted or Phillips head design is used for certain screws. Bolt or screw length is always measured from the underside of the head to the end of the item **(see illustration 2.11)**.

2.1 Internal hexagon/Allen (A), Torx (B) and splined (C) fasteners, with corresponding bits

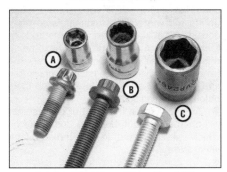

2.2 External Torx (A), splined (B) and hexagon (C) fasteners, with corresponding sockets

● Certain fasteners on the motorcycle have a tensile marking on their heads, the higher the marking the stronger the fastener. High tensile fasteners generally carry a 10 or higher marking. Never replace a high tensile fastener with one of a lower tensile strength.

Washers **(see illustration 2.3)**

● Plain washers are used between a fastener head and a component to prevent damage to the component or to spread the load when torque is applied. Plain washers can also be used as spacers or shims in certain assemblies. Copper or aluminium plain washers are often used as sealing washers on drain plugs.

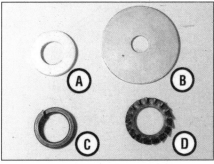

2.3 Plain washer (A), penny washer (B), spring washer (C) and serrated washer (D)

● The split-ring spring washer works by applying axial tension between the fastener head and component. If flattened, it is fatigued and must be renewed. If a plain (flat) washer is used on the fastener, position the spring washer between the fastener and the plain washer.

● Serrated star type washers dig into the fastener and component faces, preventing loosening. They are often used on electrical earth (ground) connections to the frame.

● Cone type washers (sometimes called Belleville) are conical and when tightened apply axial tension between the fastener head and component. They must be installed with the dished side against the component and often carry an OUTSIDE marking on their outer face. If flattened, they are fatigued and must be renewed.

● Tab washers are used to lock plain nuts or bolts on a shaft. A portion of the tab washer is bent up hard against one flat of the nut or bolt to prevent it loosening. Due to the tab washer being deformed in use, a new tab washer should be used every time it is disturbed.

● Wave washers are used to take up endfloat on a shaft. They provide light springing and prevent excessive side-to-side play of a component. Can be found on rocker arm shafts.

Nuts and split pins

● Conventional plain nuts are usually six-sided **(see illustration 2.4)**. They are sized by thread diameter and pitch. High tensile nuts carry a number on one end to denote their tensile strength.

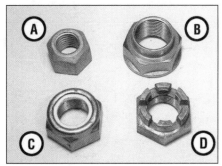

2.4 Plain nut (A), shouldered locknut (B), nylon insert nut (C) and castellated nut (D)

● Self-locking nuts either have a nylon insert, or two spring metal tabs, or a shoulder which is staked into a groove in the shaft - their advantage over conventional plain nuts is a resistance to loosening due to vibration. The nylon insert type can be used a number of times, but must be renewed when the friction of the nylon insert is reduced, ie when the nut spins freely on the shaft. The spring tab type can be reused unless the tabs are damaged. The shouldered type must be renewed every time it is disturbed.

● Split pins (cotter pins) are used to lock a castellated nut to a shaft or to prevent slackening of a plain nut. Common applications are wheel axles and brake torque arms. Because the split pin arms are deformed to lock around the nut a new split pin must always be used on installation - always fit the correct size split pin which will fit snugly in the shaft hole. Make sure the split pin arms are correctly located around the nut **(see illustrations 2.5 and 2.6)**.

2.5 Bend split pin (cotter pin) arms as shown (arrows) to secure a castellated nut

2.6 Bend split pin (cotter pin) arms as shown to secure a plain nut

Caution: If the castellated nut slots do not align with the shaft hole after tightening to the torque setting, tighten the nut until the next slot aligns with the hole - never slacken the nut to align its slot.

● R-pins (shaped like the letter R), or slip pins as they are sometimes called, are sprung and can be reused if they are otherwise in good condition. Always install R-pins with their closed end facing forwards **(see illustration 2.7)**.

**2.7 Correct fitting of R-pin.
Arrow indicates forward direction**

Circlips (see illustration 2.8)

● Circlips (sometimes called snap-rings) are used to retain components on a shaft or in a housing and have corresponding external or internal ears to permit removal. Parallel-sided (machined) circlips can be installed either way round in their groove, whereas stamped circlips (which have a chamfered edge on one face) must be installed with the chamfer facing away from the direction of thrust load **(see illustration 2.9)**.

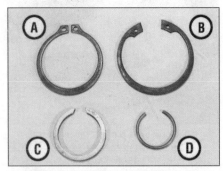

2.8 External stamped circlip (A), internal stamped circlip (B), machined circlip (C) and wire circlip (D)

● Always use circlip pliers to remove and install circlips; expand or compress them just enough to remove them. After installation, rotate the circlip in its groove to ensure it is securely seated. If installing a circlip on a splined shaft, always align its opening with a shaft channel to ensure the circlip ends are well supported and unlikely to catch **(see illustration 2.10)**.

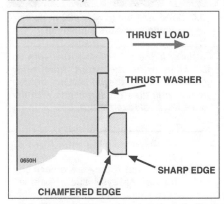

2.9 Correct fitting of a stamped circlip

THRUST LOAD

THRUST WASHER

SHARP EDGE

CHAMFERED EDGE

0650H

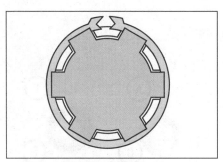

**2.10 Align circlip opening
with shaft channel**

● Circlips can wear due to the thrust of components and become loose in their grooves, with the subsequent danger of becoming dislodged in operation. For this reason, renewal is advised every time a circlip is disturbed.

● Wire circlips are commonly used as piston pin retaining clips. If a removal tang is provided, long-nosed pliers can be used to dislodge them, otherwise careful use of a small flat-bladed screwdriver is necessary. Wire circlips should be renewed every time they are disturbed.

Thread diameter and pitch

● Diameter of a male thread (screw, bolt or stud) is the outside diameter of the threaded portion **(see illustration 2.11)**. Most motorcycle manufacturers use the ISO (International Standards Organisation) metric system expressed in millimetres, eg M6 refers to a 6 mm diameter thread. Sizing is the same for nuts, except that the thread diameter is measured across the valleys of the nut.

● Pitch is the distance between the peaks of the thread **(see illustration 2.11)**. It is expressed in millimetres, thus a common bolt size may be expressed as 6.0 x 1.0 mm (6 mm thread diameter and 1 mm pitch). Generally pitch increases in proportion to thread diameter, although there are always exceptions.

● Thread diameter and pitch are related for conventional fastener applications and the accompanying table can be used as a guide. Additionally, the AF (Across Flats), spanner or socket size dimension of the bolt or nut **(see illustration 2.11)** is linked to thread and pitch specification. Thread pitch can be measured with a thread gauge **(see illustration 2.12)**.

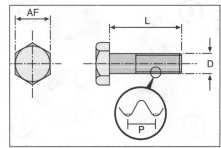

**2.11 Fastener length (L), thread diameter
(D), thread pitch (P) and head size (AF)**

AF

L

D

P

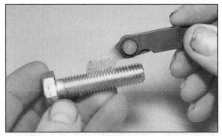

**2.12 Using a thread gauge
to measure pitch**

AF size	Thread diameter x pitch (mm)
8 mm	M5 x 0.8
8 mm	M6 x 1.0
10 mm	M6 x 1.0
12 mm	M8 x 1.25
14 mm	M10 x 1.25
17 mm	M12 x 1.25

● The threads of most fasteners are of the right-hand type, ie they are turned clockwise to tighten and anti-clockwise to loosen. The reverse situation applies to left-hand thread fasteners, which are turned anti-clockwise to tighten and clockwise to loosen. Left-hand threads are used where rotation of a component might loosen a conventional right-hand thread fastener.

Seized fasteners

● Corrosion of external fasteners due to water or reaction between two dissimilar metals can occur over a period of time. It will build up sooner in wet conditions or in countries where salt is used on the roads during the winter. If a fastener is severely corroded it is likely that normal methods of removal will fail and result in its head being ruined. When you attempt removal, the fastener thread should be heard to crack free and unscrew easily - if it doesn't, stop there before damaging something.

● A smart tap on the head of the fastener will often succeed in breaking free corrosion which has occurred in the threads **(see illustration 2.13)**.

● An aerosol penetrating fluid (such as WD-40) applied the night beforehand may work its way down into the thread and ease removal. Depending on the location, you may be able to make up a Plasticine well around the fastener head and fill it with penetrating fluid.

**2.13 A sharp tap on the head of a fastener
will often break free a corroded thread**

● If you are working on an engine internal component, corrosion will most likely not be a problem due to the well lubricated environment. However, components can be very tight and an impact driver is a useful tool in freeing them **(see illustration 2.14)**.

2.14 Using an impact driver to free a fastener

● Where corrosion has occurred between dissimilar metals (eg steel and aluminium alloy), the application of heat to the fastener head will create a disproportionate expansion rate between the two metals and break the seizure caused by the corrosion. Whether heat can be applied depends on the location of the fastener - any surrounding components likely to be damaged must first be removed **(see illustration 2.15)**. Heat can be applied using a paint stripper heat gun or clothes iron, or by immersing the component in boiling water - wear protective gloves to prevent scalding or burns to the hands.

2.15 Using heat to free a seized fastener

● As a last resort, it is possible to use a hammer and cold chisel to work the fastener head unscrewed **(see illustration 2.16)**. This will damage the fastener, but more importantly extreme care must be taken not to damage the surrounding component.

Caution: Remember that the component being secured is generally of more value than the bolt, nut or screw - when the fastener is freed, do not unscrew it with force, instead work the fastener back and forth when resistance is felt to prevent thread damage.

2.16 Using a hammer and chisel to free a seized fastener

Broken fasteners and damaged heads

● If the shank of a broken bolt or screw is accessible you can grip it with self-locking grips. The knurled wheel type stud extractor tool or self-gripping stud puller tool is particularly useful for removing the long studs which screw into the cylinder mouth surface of the crankcase or bolts and screws from which the head has broken off **(see illustration 2.17)**. Studs can also be removed by locking two nuts together on the threaded end of the stud and using a spanner on the lower nut **(see illustration 2.18)**.

2.17 Using a stud extractor tool to remove a broken crankcase stud

2.18 Two nuts can be locked together to unscrew a stud from a component

● A bolt or screw which has broken off below or level with the casing must be extracted using a screw extractor set. Centre punch the fastener to centralise the drill bit, then drill a hole in the fastener **(see illustration 2.19)**. Select a drill bit which is approximately half to three-quarters the

2.19 When using a screw extractor, first drill a hole in the fastener . . .

diameter of the fastener and drill to a depth which will accommodate the extractor. Use the largest size extractor possible, but avoid leaving too small a wall thickness otherwise the extractor will merely force the fastener walls outwards wedging it in the casing thread.

● If a spiral type extractor is used, thread it anti-clockwise into the fastener. As it is screwed in, it will grip the fastener and unscrew it from the casing **(see illustration 2.20)**.

2.20 . . . then thread the extractor anti-clockwise into the fastener

● If a taper type extractor is used, tap it into the fastener so that it is firmly wedged in place. Unscrew the extractor (anti-clockwise) to draw the fastener out.

> ⚠ *Warning: Stud extractors are very hard and may break off in the fastener if care is not taken - ask an engineer about spark erosion if this happens.*

● Alternatively, the broken bolt/screw can be drilled out and the hole retapped for an oversize bolt/screw or a diamond-section thread insert. It is essential that the drilling is carried out squarely and to the correct depth, otherwise the casing may be ruined - if in doubt, entrust the work to an engineer.

● Bolts and nuts with rounded corners cause the correct size spanner or socket to slip when force is applied. Of the types of spanner/socket available always use a six-point type rather than an eight or twelve-point type - better grip

2.21 Comparison of surface drive ring spanner (left) with 12-point type (right)

is obtained. Surface drive spanners grip the middle of the hex flats, rather than the corners, and are thus good in cases of damaged heads **(see illustration 2.21)**.

● Slotted-head or Phillips-head screws are often damaged by the use of the wrong size screwdriver. Allen-head and Torx-head screws are much less likely to sustain damage. If enough of the screw head is exposed you can use a hacksaw to cut a slot in its head and then use a conventional flat-bladed screwdriver to remove it. Alternatively use a hammer and cold chisel to tap the head of the fastener around to slacken it. Always replace damaged fasteners with new ones, preferably Torx or Allen-head type.

HAYNES
HiNT

A dab of valve grinding compound between the screw head and screw-driver tip will often give a good grip.

Thread repair

● Threads (particularly those in aluminium alloy components) can be damaged by overtightening, being assembled with dirt in the threads, or from a component working loose and vibrating. Eventually the thread will fail completely, and it will be impossible to tighten the fastener.
● If a thread is damaged or clogged with old locking compound it can be renovated with a thread repair tool (thread chaser) **(see illustrations 2.22 and 2.23)**; special thread

2.22 A thread repair tool being used to correct an internal thread

2.23 A thread repair tool being used to correct an external thread

chasers are available for spark plug hole threads. The tool will not cut a new thread, but clean and true the original thread. Make sure that you use the correct diameter and pitch tool. Similarly, external threads can be cleaned up with a die or a thread restorer file **(see illustration 2.24)**.

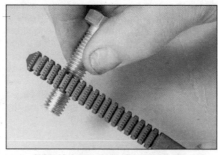

2.24 Using a thread restorer file

● It is possible to drill out the old thread and retap the component to the next thread size. This will work where there is enough surrounding material and a new bolt or screw can be obtained. Sometimes, however, this is not possible - such as where the bolt/screw passes through another component which must also be suitably modified, also in cases where a spark plug or oil drain plug cannot be obtained in a larger diameter thread size.
● The diamond-section thread insert (often known by its popular trade name of Heli-Coil) is a simple and effective method of renewing the thread and retaining the original size. A kit can be purchased which contains the tap, insert and installing tool **(see illustration 2.25)**. Drill out the damaged thread with the size drill specified **(see illustration 2.26)**. Carefully retap the thread **(see illustration 2.27)**. Install the

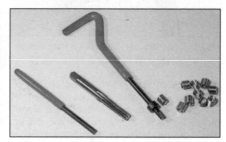

2.25 Obtain a thread insert kit to suit the thread diameter and pitch required

2.26 To install a thread insert, first drill out the original thread . . .

2.27 . . . tap a new thread . . .

2.28 . . . fit insert on the installing tool . . .

2.29 . . . and thread into the component . . .

2.30 . . . break off the tang when complete

insert on the installing tool and thread it slowly into place using a light downward pressure **(see illustrations 2.28 and 2.29)**. When positioned between a 1/4 and 1/2 turn below the surface withdraw the installing tool and use the break-off tool to press down on the tang, breaking it off **(see illustration 2.30)**.
● There are epoxy thread repair kits on the market which can rebuild stripped internal threads, although this repair should not be used on high load-bearing components.

Thread locking and sealing compounds

● Locking compounds are used in locations where the fastener is prone to loosening due to vibration or on important safety-related items which might cause loss of control of the motorcycle if they fail. It is also used where important fasteners cannot be secured by other means such as lockwashers or split pins.

● Before applying locking compound, make sure that the threads (internal and external) are clean and dry with all old compound removed. Select a compound to suit the component being secured - a non-permanent general locking and sealing type is suitable for most applications, but a high strength type is needed for permanent fixing of studs in castings. Apply a drop or two of the compound to the first few threads of the fastener, then thread it into place and tighten to the specified torque. Do not apply excessive thread locking compound otherwise the thread may be damaged on subsequent removal.

● Certain fasteners are impregnated with a dry film type coating of locking compound on their threads. Always renew this type of fastener if disturbed.

● Anti-seize compounds, such as copper-based greases, can be applied to protect threads from seizure due to extreme heat and corrosion. A common instance is spark plug threads and exhaust system fasteners.

3 Measuring tools and gauges

Feeler gauges

● Feeler gauges (or blades) are used for measuring small gaps and clearances (see illustration 3.1). They can also be used to measure endfloat (sideplay) of a component on a shaft where access is not possible with a dial gauge.

● Feeler gauge sets should be treated with care and not bent or damaged. They are etched with their size on one face. Keep them clean and very lightly oiled to prevent corrosion build-up.

3.1 Feeler gauges are used for measuring small gaps and clearances - thickness is marked on one face of gauge

● When measuring a clearance, select a gauge which is a light sliding fit between the two components. You may need to use two gauges together to measure the clearance accurately.

Micrometers

● A micrometer is a precision tool capable of measuring to 0.01 or 0.001 of a millimetre. It should always be stored in its case and not in the general toolbox. It must be kept clean and never dropped, otherwise its frame or measuring anvils could be distorted resulting in inaccurate readings.

● External micrometers are used for measuring outside diameters of components and have many more applications than internal micrometers. Micrometers are available in different size ranges, eg 0 to 25 mm, 25 to 50 mm, and upwards in 25 mm steps; some large micrometers have interchangeable anvils to allow a range of measurements to be taken. Generally the largest precision measurement you are likely to take on a motorcycle is the piston diameter.

● Internal micrometers (or bore micrometers) are used for measuring inside diameters, such as valve guides and cylinder bores. Telescoping gauges and small hole gauges are used in conjunction with an external micro-meter, whereas the more expensive internal micrometers have their own measuring device.

External micrometer

Note: *The conventional analogue type instrument is described. Although much easier to read, digital micrometers are considerably more expensive.*

● Always check the calibration of the micrometer before use. With the anvils closed (0 to 25 mm type) or set over a test gauge (for

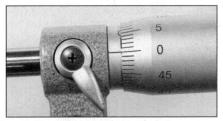

3.2 Check micrometer calibration before use

the larger types) the scale should read zero (see illustration 3.2); make sure that the anvils (and test piece) are clean first. Any discrepancy can be adjusted by referring to the instructions supplied with the tool. Remember that the micrometer is a precision measuring tool - don't force the anvils closed, use the ratchet (4) on the end of the micrometer to close it. In this way, a measured force is always applied.

● To use, first make sure that the item being measured is clean. Place the anvil of the micrometer (1) against the item and use the thimble (2) to bring the spindle (3) lightly into contact with the other side of the item (see illustration 3.3). Don't tighten the thimble down because this will damage the micrometer - instead use the ratchet (4) on the end of the micrometer. The ratchet mechanism applies a measured force preventing damage to the instrument.

● The micrometer is read by referring to the linear scale on the sleeve and the annular scale on the thimble. Read off the sleeve first to obtain the base measurement, then add the fine measurement from the thimble to obtain the overall reading. The linear scale on the sleeve represents the measuring range of the micrometer (eg 0 to 25 mm). The annular scale

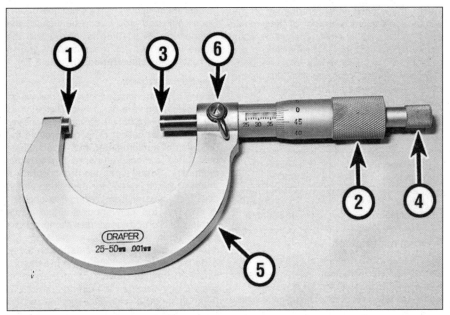

3.3 Micrometer component parts

1	Anvil	3	Spindle	5	Frame
2	Thimble	4	Ratchet	6	Locking lever

on the thimble will be in graduations of 0.01 mm (or as marked on the frame) - one full revolution of the thimble will move 0.5 mm on the linear scale. Take the reading where the datum line on the sleeve intersects the thimble's scale. Always position the eye directly above the scale otherwise an inaccurate reading will result.

In the example shown the item measures 2.95 mm (see illustration 3.4):

Linear scale	2.00 mm
Linear scale	0.50 mm
Annular scale	0.45 mm
Total figure	**2.95 mm**

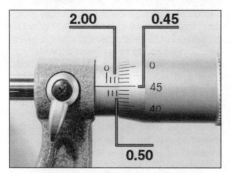

3.4 Micrometer reading of 2.95 mm

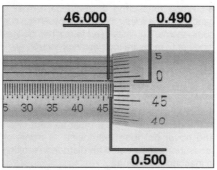

3.5 Micrometer reading of 46.99 mm on linear and annular scales . . .

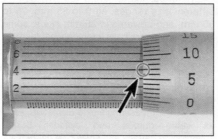

3.6 . . . and 0.004 mm on vernier scale

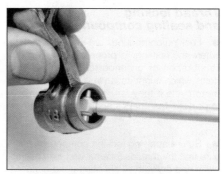

3.7 Expand the telescoping gauge in the bore, lock its position . . .

3.8 . . . then measure the gauge with a micrometer

3.9 Expand the small hole gauge in the bore, lock its position . . .

3.10 . . . then measure the gauge with a micrometer

Most micrometers have a locking lever (6) on the frame to hold the setting in place, allowing the item to be removed from the micrometer.
● Some micrometers have a vernier scale on their sleeve, providing an even finer measurement to be taken, in 0.001 increments of a millimetre. Take the sleeve and thimble measurement as described above, then check which graduation on the vernier scale aligns with that of the annular scale on the thimble Note: *The eye must be perpendicular to the scale when taking the vernier reading - if necessary rotate the body of the micrometer to ensure this.* Multiply the vernier scale figure by 0.001 and add it to the base and fine measurement figures.

In the example shown the item measures 46.994 mm (see illustrations 3.5 and 3.6):

Linear scale (base)	46.000 mm
Linear scale (base)	00.500 mm
Annular scale (fine)	00.490 mm
Vernier scale	00.004 mm
Total figure	**46.994 mm**

Internal micrometer

● Internal micrometers are available for measuring bore diameters, but are expensive and unlikely to be available for home use. It is suggested that a set of telescoping gauges and small hole gauges, both of which must be used with an external micrometer, will suffice for taking internal measurements on a motorcycle.
● Telescoping gauges can be used to measure internal diameters of components. Select a gauge with the correct size range, make sure its ends are clean and insert it into the bore. Expand the gauge, then lock its position and withdraw it from the bore (see illustration 3.7). Measure across the gauge ends with a micrometer (see illustration 3.8).
● Very small diameter bores (such as valve guides) are measured with a small hole gauge. Once adjusted to a slip-fit inside the component, its position is locked and the gauge withdrawn for measurement with a micrometer (see illustrations 3.9 and 3.10).

Vernier caliper

Note: *The conventional linear and dial gauge type instruments are described. Digital types are easier to read, but are far more expensive.*
● The vernier caliper does not provide the precision of a micrometer, but is versatile in being able to measure internal and external diameters. Some types also incorporate a depth gauge. It is ideal for measuring clutch plate friction material and spring free lengths.
● To use the conventional linear scale vernier, slacken off the vernier clamp screws (1) and set its jaws over (2), or inside (3), the item to be measured (see illustration 3.11). Slide the jaw into contact, using the thumbwheel (4) for fine movement of the sliding scale (5) then tighten the clamp screws (1). Read off the main scale (6) where the zero on the sliding scale (5) intersects it, taking the whole number to the left of the zero; this provides the base measurement. View along the sliding scale and select the division which lines up exactly with any of the divisions on the main scale, noting that the divisions usually represents 0.02 of a millimetre. Add this fine measurement to the base measurement to obtain the total reading.

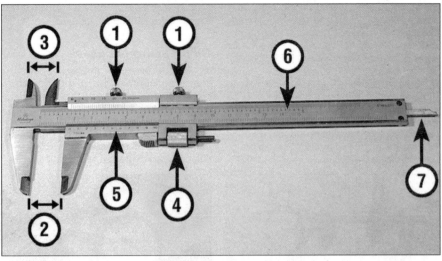

3.11 Vernier component parts (linear gauge)

| 1 | Clamp screws | 3 | Internal jaws | 5 | Sliding scale | 7 | Depth gauge |
| 2 | External jaws | 4 | Thumbwheel | 6 | Main scale | | |

In the example shown the item measures 55.92 mm **(see illustration 3.12)**:

3.12 Vernier gauge reading of 55.92 mm

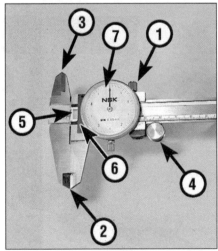

3.13 Vernier component parts (dial gauge)

1	Clamp screw	5	Main scale
2	External jaws	6	Sliding scale
3	Internal jaws	7	Dial gauge
4	Thumbwheel		

Base measurement	55.00 mm
Fine measurement	00.92 mm
Total figure	**55.92 mm**

● Some vernier calipers are equipped with a dial gauge for fine measurement. Before use, check that the jaws are clean, then close them fully and check that the dial gauge reads zero. If necessary adjust the gauge ring accordingly. Slacken the vernier clamp screw (1) and set its jaws over (2), or inside (3), the item to be measured **(see illustration 3.13)**. Slide the jaws into contact, using the thumbwheel (4) for fine movement. Read off the main scale (5) where the edge of the sliding scale (6) intersects it, taking the whole number to the left of the zero; this provides the base measurement. Read off the needle position on the dial gauge (7) scale to provide the fine measurement; each division represents 0.05 of a millimetre. Add this fine measurement to the base measurement to obtain the total reading.

In the example shown the item measures 55.95 mm **(see illustration 3.14)**:

Base measurement	55.00 mm
Fine measurement	00.95 mm
Total figure	**55.95 mm**

3.14 Vernier gauge reading of 55.95 mm

Plastigauge

● Plastigauge is a plastic material which can be compressed between two surfaces to measure the oil clearance between them. The width of the compressed Plastigauge is measured against a calibrated scale to determine the clearance.

● Common uses of Plastigauge are for measuring the clearance between crankshaft journal and main bearing inserts, between crankshaft journal and big-end bearing inserts, and between camshaft and bearing surfaces. The following example describes big-end oil clearance measurement.

● Handle the Plastigauge material carefully to prevent distortion. Using a sharp knife, cut a length which corresponds with the width of the bearing being measured and place it carefully across the journal so that it is parallel with the shaft **(see illustration 3.15)**. Carefully install both bearing shells and the connecting rod. Without rotating the rod on the journal tighten its bolts or nuts (as applicable) to the specified torque. The connecting rod and bearings are then disassembled and the crushed Plastigauge examined.

3.15 Plastigauge placed across shaft journal

● Using the scale provided in the Plastigauge kit, measure the width of the material to determine the oil clearance **(see illustration 3.16)**. Always remove all traces of Plastigauge after use using your fingernails.

Caution: Arriving at the correct clearance demands that the assembly is torqued correctly, according to the settings and sequence (where applicable) provided by the motorcycle manufacturer.

3.16 Measuring the width of the crushed Plastigauge

Dial gauge or DTI (Dial Test Indicator)

● A dial gauge can be used to accurately measure small amounts of movement. Typical uses are measuring shaft runout or shaft endfloat (sideplay) and setting piston position for ignition timing on two-strokes. A dial gauge set usually comes with a range of different probes and adapters and mounting equipment.

● The gauge needle must point to zero when at rest. Rotate the ring around its periphery to zero the gauge.

● Check that the gauge is capable of reading the extent of movement in the work. Most gauges have a small dial set in the face which records whole millimetres of movement as well as the fine scale around the face periphery which is calibrated in 0.01 mm divisions. Read off the small dial first to obtain the base measurement, then add the measurement from the fine scale to obtain the total reading.

In the example shown the gauge reads 1.48 mm **(see illustration 3.17)**:

Base measurement	1.00 mm
Fine measurement	0.48 mm
Total figure	**1.48 mm**

3.17 Dial gauge reading of 1.48 mm

● If measuring shaft runout, the shaft must be supported in vee-blocks and the gauge mounted on a stand perpendicular to the shaft. Rest the tip of the gauge against the centre of the shaft and rotate the shaft slowly whilst watching the gauge reading **(see illustration 3.18)**. Take several measurements along the length of the shaft and record the

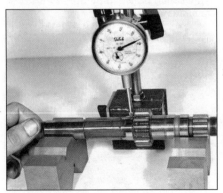

3.18 Using a dial gauge to measure shaft runout

maximum gauge reading as the amount of runout in the shaft. **Note:** *The reading obtained will be total runout at that point - some manufacturers specify that the runout figure is halved to compare with their specified runout limit.*

● Endfloat (sideplay) measurement requires that the gauge is mounted securely to the surrounding component with its probe touching the end of the shaft. Using hand pressure, push and pull on the shaft noting the maximum endfloat recorded on the gauge **(see illustration 3.19)**.

3.19 Using a dial gauge to measure shaft endfloat

● A dial gauge with suitable adapters can be used to determine piston position BTDC on two-stroke engines for the purposes of ignition timing. The gauge, adapter and suitable length probe are installed in the place of the spark plug and the gauge zeroed at TDC. If the piston position is specified as 1.14 mm BTDC, rotate the engine back to 2.00 mm BTDC, then slowly forwards to 1.14 mm BTDC.

Cylinder compression gauges

● A compression gauge is used for measuring cylinder compression. Either the rubber-cone type or the threaded adapter type can be used. The latter is preferred to ensure a perfect seal against the cylinder head. A 0 to 300 psi (0 to 20 Bar) type gauge (for petrol/gasoline engines) will be suitable for motorcycles.

● The spark plug is removed and the gauge either held hard against the cylinder head (cone type) or the gauge adapter screwed into the cylinder head (threaded type) **(see illustration 3.20)**. Cylinder compression is measured with the engine turning over, but not running - carry out the compression test as described in

3.20 Using a rubber-cone type cylinder compression gauge

Fault Finding Equipment. The gauge will hold the reading until manually released.

Oil pressure gauge

● An oil pressure gauge is used for measuring engine oil pressure. Most gauges come with a set of adapters to fit the thread of the take-off point **(see illustration 3.21)**. If the take-off point specified by the motorcycle manufacturer is an external oil pipe union, make sure that the specified replacement union is used to prevent oil starvation.

3.21 Oil pressure gauge and take-off point adapter (arrow)

● Oil pressure is measured with the engine running (at a specific rpm) and often the manufacturer will specify pressure limits for a cold and hot engine.

Straight-edge and surface plate

● If checking the gasket face of a component for warpage, place a steel rule or precision straight-edge across the gasket face and measure any gap between the straight-edge and component with feeler gauges **(see illustration 3.22)**. Check diagonally across the component and between mounting holes **(see illustration 3.23)**.

3.22 Use a straight-edge and feeler gauges to check for warpage

3.23 Check for warpage in these directions

4 Torque and leverage

What is torque?

● Torque describes the twisting force about a shaft. The amount of torque applied is determined by the distance from the centre of the shaft to the end of the lever and the amount of force being applied to the end of the lever; distance multiplied by force equals torque.

● The manufacturer applies a measured torque to a bolt or nut to ensure that it will not slacken in use and to hold two components securely together without movement in the joint. The actual torque setting depends on the thread size, bolt or nut material and the composition of the components being held.

● Too little torque may cause the fastener to loosen due to vibration, whereas too much torque will distort the joint faces of the component or cause the fastener to shear off. Always stick to the specified torque setting.

Using a torque wrench

● Check the calibration of the torque wrench and make sure it has a suitable range for the job. Torque wrenches are available in Nm (Newton-metres), kgf m (kilograms-force metre), lbf ft (pounds-feet), lbf in (inch-pounds). Do not confuse lbf ft with lbf in.

● Adjust the tool to the desired torque on the scale (see illustration 4.1). If your torque wrench is not calibrated in the units specified, carefully convert the figure (see Conversion Factors). A manufacturer sometimes gives a torque setting as a range (8 to 10 Nm) rather than a single figure - in this case set the tool midway between the two settings. The same torque may be expressed as 9 Nm ± 1 Nm. Some torque wrenches have a method of locking the setting so that it isn't inadvertently altered during use.

4.1 Set the torque wrench index mark to the setting required, in this case 12 Nm

● Install the bolts/nuts in their correct location and secure them lightly. Their threads must be clean and free of any old locking compound. Unless specified the threads and flange should be dry - oiled threads are necessary in certain circumstances and the manufacturer will take this into account in the specified torque figure. Similarly, the manufacturer may also specify the application of thread-locking compound.

● Tighten the fasteners in the specified sequence until the torque wrench clicks, indicating that the torque setting has been reached. Apply the torque again to double-check the setting. Where different thread diameter fasteners secure the component, as a rule tighten the larger diameter ones first.

● When the torque wrench has been finished with, release the lock (where applicable) and fully back off its setting to zero - do not leave the torque wrench tensioned. Also, do not use a torque wrench for slackening a fastener.

Angle-tightening

● Manufacturers often specify a figure in degrees for final tightening of a fastener. This usually follows tightening to a specific torque setting.

● A degree disc can be set and attached to the socket (see illustration 4.2) or a protractor can be used to mark the angle of movement on the bolt/nut head and the surrounding casting (see illustration 4.3).

4.2 Angle tightening can be accomplished with a torque-angle gauge . . .

4.3 . . . or by marking the angle on the surrounding component

Loosening sequences

● Where more than one bolt/nut secures a component, loosen each fastener evenly a little at a time. In this way, not all the stress of the joint is held by one fastener and the components are not likely to distort.

● If a tightening sequence is provided, work in the REVERSE of this, but if not, work from the outside in, in a criss-cross sequence (see illustration 4.4).

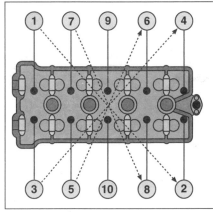

4.4 When slackening, work from the outside inwards

Tightening sequences

● If a component is held by more than one fastener it is important that the retaining bolts/nuts are tightened evenly to prevent uneven stress build-up and distortion of sealing faces. This is especially important on high-compression joints such as the cylinder head.

● A sequence is usually provided by the manufacturer, either in a diagram or actually marked in the casting. If not, always start in the centre and work outwards in a criss-cross pattern (see illustration 4.5). Start off by securing all bolts/nuts finger-tight, then set the torque wrench and tighten each fastener by a small amount in sequence until the final torque is reached. By following this practice,

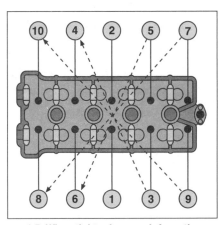

4.5 When tightening, work from the inside outwards

● Checking individual components for warpage, such as clutch plain (metal) plates, requires a perfectly flat plate or piece or plate glass and feeler gauges.

the joint will be held evenly and will not be distorted. Important joints, such as the cylinder head and big-end fasteners often have two- or three-stage torque settings.

Applying leverage

● Use tools at the correct angle. Position a socket wrench or spanner on the bolt/nut so that you pull it towards you when loosening. If this can't be done, push the spanner without curling your fingers around it **(see illustration 4.6)** - the spanner may slip or the fastener loosen suddenly, resulting in your fingers being crushed against a component.

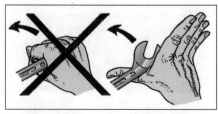

4.6 If you can't pull on the spanner to loosen a fastener, push with your hand open

● Additional leverage is gained by extending the length of the lever. The best way to do this is to use a breaker bar instead of the regular length tool, or to slip a length of tubing over the end of the spanner or socket wrench.
● If additional leverage will not work, the fastener head is either damaged or firmly corroded in place (see *Fasteners*).

5 Bearings

Bearing removal and installation

Drivers and sockets

● Before removing a bearing, always inspect the casing to see which way it must be driven out - some casings will have retaining plates or a cast step. Also check for any identifying markings on the bearing and if installed to a certain depth, measure this at this stage. Some roller bearings are sealed on one side - take note of the original fitted position.
● Bearings can be driven out of a casing using a bearing driver tool (with the correct size head) or a socket of the correct diameter. Select the driver head or socket so that it contacts the outer race of the bearing, not the balls/rollers or inner race. Always support the casing around the bearing housing with wood blocks, otherwise there is a risk of fracture. The bearing is driven out with a few blows on the driver or socket from a heavy mallet. Unless access is severely restricted (as with wheel bearings), a pin-punch is not recommended unless it is moved around the bearing to keep it square in its housing.

● The same equipment can be used to install bearings. Make sure the bearing housing is supported on wood blocks and line up the bearing in its housing. Fit the bearing as noted on removal - generally they are installed with their marked side facing outwards. Tap the bearing squarely into its housing using a driver or socket which bears only on the bearing's outer race - contact with the bearing balls/rollers or inner race will destroy it **(see illustrations 5.1 and 5.2)**.
● Check that the bearing inner race and balls/rollers rotate freely.

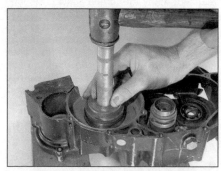

5.1 Using a bearing driver against the bearing's outer race

5.2 Using a large socket against the bearing's outer race

Pullers and slide-hammers

● Where a bearing is pressed on a shaft a puller will be required to extract it **(see illustration 5.3)**. Make sure that the puller clamp or legs fit securely behind the bearing and are unlikely to slip out. If pulling a bearing

5.3 This bearing puller clamps behind the bearing and pressure is applied to the shaft end to draw the bearing off

off a gear shaft for example, you may have to locate the puller behind a gear pinion if there is no access to the race and draw the gear pinion off the shaft as well **(see illustration 5.4)**.

> *Caution: Ensure that the puller's centre bolt locates securely against the end of the shaft and will not slip when pressure is applied. Also ensure that puller does not damage the shaft end.*

5.4 Where no access is available to the rear of the bearing, it is sometimes possible to draw off the adjacent component

● Operate the puller so that its centre bolt exerts pressure on the shaft end and draws the bearing off the shaft.
● When installing the bearing on the shaft, tap only on the bearing's inner race - contact with the balls/rollers or outer race with destroy the bearing. Use a socket or length of tubing as a drift which fits over the shaft end **(see illustration 5.5)**.

5.5 When installing a bearing on a shaft use a piece of tubing which bears only on the bearing's inner race

● Where a bearing locates in a blind hole in a casing, it cannot be driven or pulled out as described above. A slide-hammer with a knife-edged bearing puller attachment will be required. The puller attachment passes through the bearing and when tightened expands to fit firmly behind the bearing **(see illustration 5.6)**. By operating the slide-hammer part of the tool the bearing is jarred out of its housing **(see illustration 5.7)**.
● It is possible, if the bearing is of reasonable weight, for it to drop out of its housing if the casing is heated as described opposite. If this

5.6 Expand the bearing puller so that it locks behind the bearing . . .

5.7 . . . attach the slide hammer to the bearing puller

method is attempted, first prepare a work surface which will enable the casing to be tapped face down to help dislodge the bearing - a wood surface is ideal since it will not damage the casing's gasket surface. Wearing protective gloves, tap the heated casing several times against the work surface to dislodge the bearing under its own weight **(see illustration 5.8)**.

5.8 Tapping a casing face down on wood blocks can often dislodge a bearing

● Bearings can be installed in blind holes using the driver or socket method described above.

Drawbolts

● Where a bearing or bush is set in the eye of a component, such as a suspension linkage arm or connecting rod small-end, removal by drift may damage the component. Furthermore, a rubber bushing in a shock absorber eye cannot successfully be driven out of position. If access is available to a engineering press, the task is straightforward. If not, a drawbolt can be fabricated to extract the bearing or bush.

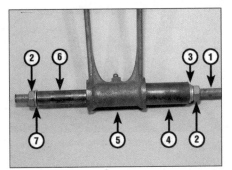

5.9 Drawbolt component parts assembled on a suspension arm

1. Bolt or length of threaded bar
2. Nuts
3. Washer (external diameter greater than tubing internal diameter)
4. Tubing (internal diameter sufficient to accommodate bearing)
5. Suspension arm with bearing
6. Tubing (external diameter slightly smaller than bearing)
7. Washer (external diameter slightly smaller than bearing)

5.10 Drawing the bearing out of the suspension arm

● To extract the bearing/bush you will need a long bolt with nut (or piece of threaded bar with two nuts), a piece of tubing which has an internal diameter larger than the bearing/bush, another piece of tubing which has an external diameter slightly smaller than the bearing/ bush, and a selection of washers **(see illustrations 5.9 and 5.10)**. Note that the pieces of tubing must be of the same length, or longer, than the bearing/bush.

● The same kit (without the pieces of tubing) can be used to draw the new bearing/bush back into place **(see illustration 5.11)**.

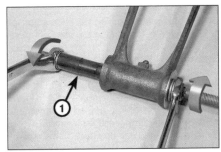

5.11 Installing a new bearing (1) in the suspension arm

Temperature change

● If the bearing's outer race is a tight fit in the casing, the aluminium casing can be heated to release its grip on the bearing. Aluminium will expand at a greater rate than the steel bearing outer race. There are several ways to do this, but avoid any localised extreme heat (such as a blow torch) - aluminium alloy has a low melting point.

● Approved methods of heating a casing are using a domestic oven (heated to 100°C) or immersing the casing in boiling water **(see illustration 5.12)**. Low temperature range localised heat sources such as a paint stripper heat gun or clothes iron can also be used **(see illustration 5.13)**. Alternatively, soak a rag in boiling water, wring it out and wrap it around the bearing housing.

> ⚠ **Warning: All of these methods require care in use to prevent scalding and burns to the hands. Wear protective gloves when handling hot components.**

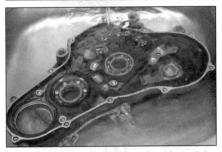

5.12 A casing can be immersed in a sink of boiling water to aid bearing removal

5.13 Using a localised heat source to aid bearing removal

● If heating the whole casing note that plastic components, such as the neutral switch, may suffer - remove them beforehand.

● After heating, remove the bearing as described above. You may find that the expansion is sufficient for the bearing to fall out of the casing under its own weight or with a light tap on the driver or socket.

● If necessary, the casing can be heated to aid bearing installation, and this is sometimes the recommended procedure if the motorcycle manufacturer has designed the housing and bearing fit with this intention.

● Installation of bearings can be eased by placing them in a freezer the night before installation. The steel bearing will contract slightly, allowing easy insertion in its housing. This is often useful when installing steering head outer races in the frame.

Bearing types and markings

● Plain shell bearings, ball bearings, needle roller bearings and tapered roller bearings will all be found on motorcycles (see illustrations 5.14 and 5.15). The ball and roller types are usually caged between an inner and outer race, but uncaged variations may be found.

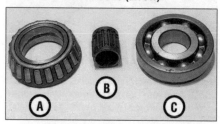

5.14 Shell bearings are either plain or grooved. They are usually identified by colour code (arrow)

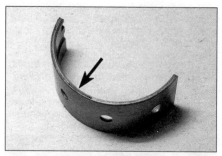

5.15 Tapered roller bearing (A), needle roller bearing (B) and ball journal bearing (C)

● Shell bearings (often called inserts) are usually found at the crankshaft main and connecting rod big-end where they are good at coping with high loads. They are made of a phosphor-bronze material and are impregnated with self-lubricating properties.

● Ball bearings and needle roller bearings consist of a steel inner and outer race with the balls or rollers between the races. They require constant lubrication by oil or grease and are good at coping with axial loads. Taper roller bearings consist of rollers set in a tapered cage set on the inner race; the outer race is separate. They are good at coping with axial loads and prevent movement along the shaft - a typical application is in the steering head.

● Bearing manufacturers produce bearings to ISO size standards and stamp one face of the bearing to indicate its internal and external diameter, load capacity and type (see illustration 5.16).

● Metal bushes are usually of phosphor-bronze material. Rubber bushes are used in suspension mounting eyes. Fibre bushes have also been used in suspension pivots.

5.16 Typical bearing marking

Bearing fault finding

● If a bearing outer race has spun in its housing, the housing material will be damaged. You can use a bearing locking compound to bond the outer race in place if damage is not too severe.

● Shell bearings will fail due to damage of their working surface, as a result of lack of lubrication, corrosion or abrasive particles in the oil (see illustration 5.17). Small particles of dirt in the oil may embed in the bearing material whereas larger particles will score the bearing and shaft journal. If a number of short journeys are made, insufficient heat will be generated to drive off condensation which has built up on the bearings.

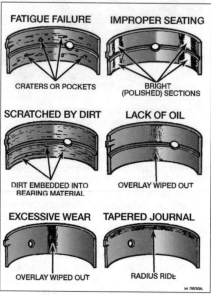

5.17 Typical bearing failures

● Ball and roller bearings will fail due to lack of lubrication or damage to the balls or rollers. Tapered-roller bearings can be damaged by overloading them. Unless the bearing is sealed on both sides, wash it in paraffin (kerosene) to remove all old grease then allow it to dry. Make a visual inspection looking to dented balls or rollers, damaged cages and worn or pitted races (see illustration 5.18).

● A ball bearing can be checked for wear by listening to it when spun. Apply a film of light oil to the bearing and hold it close to the ear - hold the outer race with one hand and spin the inner

5.18 Example of ball journal bearing with damaged balls and cages

5.19 Hold outer race and listen to inner race when spun

race with the other hand (see illustration 5.19). The bearing should be almost silent when spun; if it grates or rattles it is worn.

6 Oil seals

Oil seal removal and installation

● Oil seals should be renewed every time a component is dismantled. This is because the seal lips will become set to the sealing surface and will not necessarily reseal.

● Oil seals can be prised out of position using a large flat-bladed screwdriver (see illustration 6.1). In the case of crankcase seals, check first that the seal is not lipped on the inside, preventing its removal with the crankcases joined.

6.1 Prise out oil seals with a large flat-bladed screwdriver

● New seals are usually installed with their marked face (containing the seal reference code) outwards and the spring side towards the fluid being retained. In certain cases, such as a two-stroke engine crankshaft seal, a double lipped seal may be used due to there being fluid or gas on each side of the joint.

● Use a bearing driver or socket which bears only on the outer hard edge of the seal to install it in the casing - tapping on the inner edge will damage the sealing lip.

Oil seal types and markings

● Oil seals are usually of the single-lipped type. Double-lipped seals are found where a liquid or gas is on both sides of the joint.
● Oil seals can harden and lose their sealing ability if the motorcycle has been in storage for a long period - renewal is the only solution.
● Oil seal manufacturers also conform to the ISO markings for seal size - these are moulded into the outer face of the seal **(see illustration 6.2)**.

6.2 These oil seal markings indicate inside diameter, outside diameter and seal thickness

7 Gaskets and sealants

Types of gasket and sealant

● Gaskets are used to seal the mating surfaces between components and keep lubricants, fluids, vacuum or pressure contained within the assembly. Aluminium gaskets are sometimes found at the cylinder joints, but most gaskets are paper-based. If the mating surfaces of the components being joined are undamaged the gasket can be installed dry, although a dab of sealant or grease will be useful to hold it in place during assembly.
● RTV (Room Temperature Vulcanising) silicone rubber sealants cure when exposed to moisture in the atmosphere. These sealants are good at filling pits or irregular gasket faces, but will tend to be forced out of the joint under very high torque. They can be used to replace a paper gasket, but first make sure that the width of the paper gasket is not essential to the shimming of internal components. RTV sealants should not be used on components containing petrol (gasoline).
● Non-hardening, semi-hardening and hard setting liquid gasket compounds can be used with a gasket or between a metal-to-metal joint. Select the sealant to suit the application: universal non-hardening sealant can be used on virtually all joints; semi-hardening on joint faces which are rough or damaged; hard setting sealant on joints which require a permanent bond and are subjected to high temperature and pressure. **Note:** *Check first if the paper gasket has a bead of sealant*

impregnated in its surface before applying additional sealant.
● When choosing a sealant, make sure it is suitable for the application, particularly if being applied in a high-temperature area or in the vicinity of fuel. Certain manufacturers produce sealants in either clear, silver or black colours to match the finish of the engine. This has a particular application on motorcycles where much of the engine is exposed.
● Do not over-apply sealant. That which is squeezed out on the outside of the joint can be wiped off, whereas an excess of sealant on the inside can break off and clog oilways.

Breaking a sealed joint

● Age, heat, pressure and the use of hard setting sealant can cause two components to stick together so tightly that they are difficult to separate using finger pressure alone. Do not resort to using levers unless there is a pry point provided for this purpose **(see illustration 7.1)** or else the gasket surfaces will be damaged.
● Use a soft-faced hammer **(see illustration 7.2)** or a wood block and conventional hammer to strike the component near the mating surface. Avoid hammering against cast extremities since they may break off. If this method fails, try using a wood wedge between the two components.

Caution: If the joint will not separate, double-check that you have removed all the fasteners.

7.1 If a pry point is provided, apply gently pressure with a flat-bladed screwdriver

7.2 Tap around the joint with a soft-faced mallet if necessary - don't strike cooling fins

Removal of old gasket and sealant

● Paper gaskets will most likely come away complete, leaving only a few traces stuck on

Most components have one or two hollow locating dowels between the two gasket faces. If a dowel cannot be removed, do not resort to gripping it with pliers - it will almost certainly be distorted. Install a close-fitting socket or Phillips screwdriver into the dowel and then grip the outer edge of the dowel to free it.

the sealing faces of the components. It is imperative that all traces are removed to ensure correct sealing of the new gasket.
● Very carefully scrape all traces of gasket away making sure that the sealing surfaces are not gouged or scored by the scraper **(see illustrations 7.3, 7.4 and 7.5)**. Stubborn deposits can be removed by spraying with an aerosol gasket remover. Final preparation of

7.3 Paper gaskets can be scraped off with a gasket scraper tool . . .

7.4 . . . a knife blade . . .

7.5 . . . or a household scraper

7.6 Fine abrasive paper is wrapped around a flat file to clean up the gasket face

7.7 A kitchen scourer can be used on stubborn deposits

the gasket surface can be made with very fine abrasive paper or a plastic kitchen scourer **(see illustrations 7.6 and 7.7)**.

● Old sealant can be scraped or peeled off components, depending on the type originally used. Note that gasket removal compounds are available to avoid scraping the components clean; make sure the gasket remover suits the type of sealant used.

8 Chains

Breaking and joining final drive chains

● Drive chains for all but small bikes are continuous and do not have a clip-type connecting link. The chain must be broken using a chain breaker tool and the new chain securely riveted together using a new soft rivet-type link. Never use a clip-type connecting link instead of a rivet-type link, except in an emergency. Various chain breaking and riveting tools are available, either as separate tools or combined as illustrated in the accompanying photographs - read the instructions supplied with the tool carefully.

> ⚠ **Warning: The need to rivet the new link pins correctly cannot be overstressed - loss of control of the motorcycle is very likely to result if the chain breaks in use.**

● Rotate the chain and look for the soft link. The soft link pins look like they have been

8.1 Tighten the chain breaker to push the pin out of the link . . .

8.2 . . . withdraw the pin, remove the tool . . .

8.3 . . . and separate the chain link

deeply centre-punched instead of peened over like all the other pins **(see illustration 8.9)** and its sideplate may be a different colour. Position the soft link midway between the sprockets and assemble the chain breaker tool over one of the soft link pins **(see illustration 8.1)**. Operate the tool to push the pin out through the chain **(see illustration 8.2)**. On an O-ring chain, remove the O-rings **(see illustration 8.3)**. Carry out the same procedure on the other soft link pin.

> *Caution: Certain soft link pins (particularly on the larger chains) may require their ends to be filed or ground off before they can be pressed out using the tool.*

● Check that you have the correct size and strength (standard or heavy duty) new soft link - do not reuse the old link. Look for the size marking on the chain sideplates **(see illustration 8.10)**.

● Position the chain ends so that they are engaged over the rear sprocket. On an O-ring

8.4 Insert the new soft link, with O-rings, through the chain ends . . .

8.5 . . . install the O-rings over the pin ends . . .

8.6 . . . followed by the sideplate

chain, install a new O-ring over each pin of the link and insert the link through the two chain ends **(see illustration 8.4)**. Install a new O-ring over the end of each pin, followed by the sideplate (with the chain manufacturer's marking facing outwards) **(see illustrations 8.5 and 8.6)**. On an unsealed chain, insert the link through the two chain ends, then install the sideplate with the chain manufacturer's marking facing outwards.

● Note that it may not be possible to install the sideplate using finger pressure alone. If using a joining tool, assemble it so that the plates of the tool clamp the link and press the sideplate over the pins **(see illustration 8.7)**. Otherwise, use two small sockets placed over

8.7 Push the sideplate into position using a clamp

8.8 Assemble the chain riveting tool over one pin at a time and tighten it fully

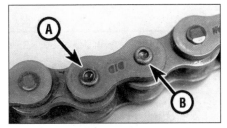

8.9 Pin end correctly riveted (A), pin end unriveted (B)

the rivet ends and two pieces of the wood between a G-clamp. Operate the clamp to press the sideplate over the pins.

● Assemble the joining tool over one pin (following the maker's instructions) and tighten the tool down to spread the pin end securely **(see illustrations 8.8 and 8.9)**. Do the same on the other pin.

 Warning: Check that the pin ends are secure and that there is no danger of the sideplate coming loose. If the pin ends are cracked the soft link must be renewed.

Final drive chain sizing

● Chains are sized using a three digit number, followed by a suffix to denote the chain type **(see illustration 8.10)**. Chain type is either standard or heavy duty (thicker sideplates), and also unsealed or O-ring/X-ring type.

● The first digit of the number relates to the pitch of the chain, ie the distance from the centre of one pin to the centre of the next pin **(see illustration 8.11)**. Pitch is expressed in eighths of an inch, as follows:

8.10 Typical chain size and type marking

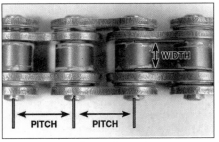

8.11 Chain dimensions

Sizes commencing with a 4 (eg 428) have a pitch of 1/2 inch (12.7 mm)
Sizes commencing with a 5 (eg 520) have a pitch of 5/8 inch (15.9 mm)
Sizes commencing with a 6 (eg 630) have a pitch of 3/4 inch (19.1 mm)

● The second and third digits of the chain size relate to the width of the rollers, again in imperial units, eg the 525 shown has 5/16 inch (7.94 mm) rollers **(see illustration 8.11)**.

9 Hoses

Clamping to prevent flow

● Small-bore flexible hoses can be clamped to prevent fluid flow whilst a component is worked on. Whichever method is used, ensure that the hose material is not permanently distorted or damaged by the clamp.

a) A brake hose clamp available from auto accessory shops *(see illustration 9.1)*.
b) A wingnut type hose clamp *(see illustration 9.2)*.

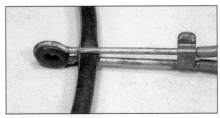

9.1 Hoses can be clamped with an automotive brake hose clamp . . .

9.2 . . . a wingnut type hose clamp . . .

c) Two sockets placed each side of the hose and held with straight-jawed self-locking grips *(see illustration 9.3)*.
d) Thick card each side of the hose held between straight-jawed self-locking grips *(see illustration 9.4)*.

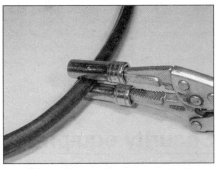

9.3 . . . two sockets and a pair of self-locking grips . . .

9.4 . . . or thick card and self-locking grips

Freeing and fitting hoses

● Always make sure the hose clamp is moved well clear of the hose end. Grip the hose with your hand and rotate it whilst pulling it off the union. If the hose has hardened due to age and will not move, slit it with a sharp knife and peel its ends off the union **(see illustration 9.5)**.

● Resist the temptation to use grease or soap on the unions to aid installation; although it helps the hose slip over the union it will equally aid the escape of fluid from the joint. It is preferable to soften the hose ends in hot water and wet the inside surface of the hose with water or a fluid which will evaporate.

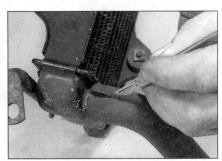

9.5 Cutting a coolant hose free with a sharp knife

Introduction

In less time than it takes to read this introduction, a thief could steal your motorcycle. Returning only to find your bike has gone is one of the worst feelings in the world. Even if the motorcycle is insured against theft, once you've got over the initial shock, you will have the inconvenience of dealing with the police and your insurance company.

The motorcycle is an easy target for the professional thief and the joyrider alike and

the official figures on motorcycle theft make for depressing reading; on average a motorcycle is stolen every 16 minutes in the UK!

Motorcycle thefts fall into two categories, those stolen 'to order' and those taken by opportunists. The thief stealing to order will be on the look out for a specific make and model and will go to extraordinary lengths to obtain that motorcycle. The opportunist thief on the other hand will look for easy targets which can be stolen with the minimum of effort and risk.

Whilst it is never going to be possible to make your machine 100% secure, it is estimated that around half of all stolen motorcycles are taken by opportunist thieves. Remember that the opportunist thief is always on the look out for the easy option: if there are two similar motorcycles parked side-by-side, they will target the one with the lowest level of security. By taking a few precautions, you can reduce the chances of your motorcycle being stolen.

Security equipment

There are many specialised motorcycle security devices available and the following text summarises their applications and their good and bad points.

Once you have decided on the type of security equipment which best suits your needs, we recommended that you read one of the many equipment tests regularly carried

Ensure the lock and chain you buy is of good quality and long enough to shackle your bike to a solid object

out by the motorcycle press. These tests compare the products from all the major manufacturers and give impartial ratings on their effectiveness, value-for-money and ease of use.

No one item of security equipment can provide complete protection. It is highly recommended that two or more of the items described below are combined to increase the security of your motorcycle (a lock and chain plus an alarm system is just about ideal). The more security measures fitted to the bike, the less likely it is to be stolen.

Lock and chain

Pros: *Very flexible to use; can be used to secure the motorcycle to almost any immovable object. On some locks and chains, the lock can be used on its own as a disc lock (see below).*

Cons: *Can be very heavy and awkward to carry on the motorcycle, although some types*

will be supplied with a carry bag which can be strapped to the pillion seat.

● Heavy-duty chains and locks are an excellent security measure **(see illustration 1)**. Whenever the motorcycle is parked, use the lock and chain to secure the machine to a solid, immovable object such as a post or railings. This will prevent the machine from being ridden away or being lifted into the back of a van.

● When fitting the chain, always ensure the chain is routed around the motorcycle frame or swingarm **(see illustrations 2 and 3)**. Never merely pass the chain around one of the wheel rims; a thief may unbolt the wheel and lift the rest of the machine into a van, leaving you with just the wheel! Try to avoid having excess chain free, thus making it difficult to use cutting tools, and keep the chain and lock off the ground to prevent thieves attacking it with a cold chisel. Position the lock so that its lock barrel is facing downwards; this will make it harder for the thief to attack the lock mechanism.

Pass the chain through the bike's frame, rather than just through a wheel . . .

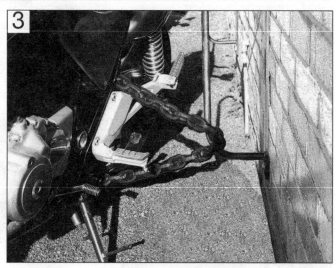

. . . and loop it around a solid object

U-locks

Pros: *Highly effective deterrent which can be used to secure the bike to a post or railings. Most U-locks come with a carrier which allows the lock to be easily carried on the bike.*

Cons: *Not as flexible to use as a lock and chain.*

● These are solid locks which are similar in use to a lock and chain. U-locks are lighter than a lock and chain but not so flexible to use. The length and shape of the lock shackle limit the objects to which the bike can be secured **(see illustration 4)**.

Disc locks

Pros: *Small, light and very easy to carry; most can be stored underneath the seat.*

Cons: *Does not prevent the motorcycle being lifted into a van. Can be very embarrassing if you*

U-locks can be used to secure the bike to a solid object – ensure you purchase one which is long enough

forget to remove the lock before attempting to ride off!

● Disc locks are designed to be attached to the front brake disc. The lock passes through one of the holes in the disc and prevents the wheel rotating by jamming against the fork/brake caliper **(see illustration 5)**. Some are equipped with an alarm siren which sounds if the disc lock is moved; this not only acts as a theft deterrent but also as a handy reminder if you try to move the bike with the lock still fitted.

● Combining the disc lock with a length of cable which can be looped around a post or railings provides an additional measure of security **(see illustration 6)**.

Alarms and immobilisers

Pros: *Once installed it is completely hassle-free to use. If the system is 'Thatcham' or 'Sold Secure-approved', insurance companies may give you a discount.*

Cons: *Can be expensive to buy and complex to install. No system will prevent the motorcycle from being lifted into a van and taken away.*

● Electronic alarms and immobilisers are available to suit a variety of budgets. There are three different types of system available: pure alarms, pure immobilisers, and the more expensive systems which are combined alarm/immobilisers **(see illustration 7)**.
● An alarm system is designed to emit an audible warning if the motorcycle is being tampered with.
● An immobiliser prevents the motorcycle being started and ridden away by disabling its electrical systems.
● When purchasing an alarm/immobiliser system, check the cost of installing the system unless you are able to do it yourself. If the motorcycle is not used regularly, another consideration is the current drain of the system. All alarm/immobiliser systems are powered by the motorcycle's battery; purchasing a system with a very low current drain could prevent the battery losing its charge whilst the motorcycle is not being used.

A typical disc lock attached through one of the holes in the disc

A disc lock combined with a security cable provides additional protection

A typical alarm/immobiliser system

Indelible markings can be applied to most areas of the bike – always apply the manufacturer's sticker to warn off thieves

Chemically-etched code numbers can be applied to main body panels . . .

. . . again, always ensure that the kit manufacturer's sticker is applied in a prominent position

Security marking kits

Pros: *Very cheap and effective deterrent. Many insurance companies will give you a discount on your insurance premium if a recognised security marking kit is used on your motorcycle.*

Cons: *Does not prevent the motorcycle being stolen by joyriders.*

● There are many different types of security marking kits available. The idea is to mark as many parts of the motorcycle as possible with a unique security number (**see illustrations 8, 9 and 10**). A form will be included with the kit to register your personal details and those of the motorcycle with the kit manufacturer. This register is made available to the police to help them trace the rightful owner of any motorcycle or components which they recover should all other forms of identification have been removed. Always apply the warning stickers provided with the kit to deter thieves.

Ground anchors, wheel clamps and security posts

Pros: *An excellent form of security which will deter all but the most determined of thieves.*

Cons: *Awkward to install and can be expensive.*

● Whilst the motorcycle is at home, it is a good idea to attach it securely to the floor or a solid wall, even if it is kept in a securely locked garage. Various types of ground anchors, security posts and wheel clamps are available for this purpose (**see illustration 11**). These security devices are either bolted to a solid concrete or brick structure or can be cemented into the ground.

Permanent ground anchors provide an excellent level of security when the bike is at home

Security at home

A high percentage of motorcycle thefts are from the owner's home. Here are some things to consider whenever your motorcycle is at home:
✔ Where possible, always keep the motorcycle in a securely locked garage. Never rely solely on the standard lock on the garage door, these are usual hopelessly inadequate. Fit an additional locking mechanism to the door and consider having the garage alarmed. A security light, activated by a movement sensor, is also a good investment.

✔ Always secure the motorcycle to the ground or a wall, even if it is inside a securely locked garage.
✔ Do not regularly leave the motorcycle outside your home, try to keep it out of sight wherever possible. If a garage is not available, fit a motorcycle cover over the bike to disguise its true identity.
✔ It is not uncommon for thieves to follow a motorcyclist home to find out where the bike is kept. They will then return at a later date. Be aware of this whenever you are returning

home on your motorcycle. If you suspect you are being followed, do not return home, instead ride to a garage or shop and stop as a precaution.
✔ When selling a motorcycle, do not provide your home address or the location where the bike is normally kept. Arrange to meet the buyer at a location away from your home. Thieves have been known to pose as potential buyers to find out where motorcycles are kept and then return later to steal them.

Security away from the home

As well as fitting security equipment to your motorcycle here are a few general rules to follow whenever you park your motorcycle.
✔ Park in a busy, public place.
✔ Use car parks which incorporate security features, such as CCTV.

✔ At night, park in a well-lit area, preferably directly underneath a street light.
✔ Engage the steering lock.
✔ Secure the motorcycle to a solid, immovable object such as a post or railings with an additional lock. If this is not possible,

secure the bike to a friend's motorcycle. Some public parking places provide security loops for motorcycles.
✔ Never leave your helmet or luggage attached to the motorcycle. Take them with you at all times.

Lubricants and fluids

A wide range of lubricants, fluids and cleaning agents is available for motor-cycles. This is a guide as to what is available, its applications and properties.

Four-stroke engine oil

● Engine oil is without doubt the most important component of any four-stroke engine. Modern motorcycle engines place a lot of demands on their oil and choosing the right type is essential. Using an unsuitable oil will lead to an increased rate of engine wear and could result in serious engine damage. Before purchasing oil, always check the recommended oil specification given by the manufacturer. The manufacturer will state a recommended 'type or classification' and also a specific 'viscosity' range for engine oil.

● The oil 'type or classification' is identified by its API (American Petroleum Institute) rating. The API rating will be in the form of two letters, e.g. SG. The S identifies the oil as being suitable for use in a petrol (gasoline) engine (S stands for spark ignition) and the second letter, ranging from A to J, identifies the oil's performance rating. The later this letter, the higher the specification of the oil; for example API SG oil exceeds the requirements of API SF oil. **Note:** *On some oils there may also be a second rating consisting of another two letters, the first letter being C, e.g. API SF/CD. This rating indicates the oil is also suitable for use in a diesel engines (the C stands for compression ignition) and is thus of no relevance for motorcycle use.*

● The 'viscosity' of the oil is identified by its SAE (Society of Automotive Engineers) rating. All modern engines require multigrade oils and the SAE rating will consist of two numbers, the first followed by a W, e.g.

10W/40. The first number indicates the viscosity rating of the oil at low temperatures (W stands for winter – tested at –20°C) and the second number represents the viscosity of the oil at high temperatures (tested at 100°C). The lower the number, the thinner the oil. For example an oil with an SAE 10W/40 rating will give better cold starting and running than an SAE 15W/40 oil.

● As well as ensuring the 'type' and 'viscosity' of the oil match the recommendations, another consideration to make when buying engine oil is whether to purchase a standard mineral-based oil, a semi-synthetic oil (also known as a synthetic blend or synthetic-based oil) or a fully-synthetic oil. Although all oils will have a similar rating and viscosity, their cost will vary considerably; mineral-based oils are the cheapest, the fully-synthetic oils the most expensive with the semi-synthetic oils falling somewhere in-between. This decision is very much up to the owner, but it should be noted that modern synthetic oils have far better lubricating and cleaning qualities than traditional mineral-based oils and tend to retain these properties for far longer. Bearing in mind the operating conditions inside a modern, high-revving motorcycle engine it is highly recommended that a fully synthetic oil is used. The extra expense at each service could save you money in the long term by preventing premature engine wear.

● As a final note always ensure that the oil is specifically designed for use in motorcycle engines. Engine oils designed primarily for use in car engines sometimes contain additives or friction modifiers which could cause clutch slip on a motorcycle fitted with a wet-clutch.

Two-stroke engine oil

● Modern two-stroke engines, with their high power outputs, place high demands on their oil. If engine seizure is to be avoided it is essential that a high-quality oil is used. Two-stroke oils differ hugely from four-stroke oils. The oil lubricates only the crankshaft and piston(s) (the transmission has its own lubricating oil) and is used on a total-loss basis where it is burnt completely during the combustion process.

● The Japanese have recently introduced a classification system for two-stroke oils, the JASO rating. This rating is in the form of two letters, either FA, FB or FC – FA is the lowest classification and FC the highest. Ensure the oil being used meets or exceeds the recommended rating specified by the manufacturer.

● As well as ensuring the oil rating matches the recommendation, another consideration to make when buying engine oil is whether to purchase a standard mineral-based oil, a semi-synthetic oil (also known as a synthetic blend or synthetic-based oil) or a fully-synthetic oil. The cost of each type of oil varies considerably; mineral-based oils are the cheapest, the fully-synthetic oils the most expensive with the semi-synthetic oils falling somewhere in-between. This decision is very much up to the owner, but it should be noted that modern synthetic oils have far better lubricating properties and burn cleaner than traditional mineral-based oils. It is therefore recommended that a fully synthetic oil is used. The extra expense could save you money in the long term by preventing premature engine wear, engine performance will be improved, carbon deposits and exhaust smoke will be reduced.

● Always ensure that the oil is specifically designed for use in an injector system. Many high quality two-stroke oils are designed for competition use and need to be pre-mixed with fuel. These oils are of a much higher viscosity and are not designed to flow through the injector pumps used on road-going two-stroke motorcycles.

Transmission (gear) oil

● On a two-stroke engine, the transmission and clutch are lubricated by their own separate oil bath which must be changed in accordance with the Maintenance Schedule.
● Although the engine and transmission units of most four-strokes use a common lubrication supply, there are some exceptions where the engine and gearbox have separate oil reservoirs and a dry clutch is used.
● Motorcycle manufacturers will either recommend a monograde transmission oil or a four-stroke multigrade engine oil to lubricate the transmission.
● Transmission oils, or gear oils as they are often called, are designed specifically for use in transmission systems. The viscosity of these oils is represented by an SAE number, but the scale of measurement applied is different to that used to grade engine oils. As a rough guide a SAE90 gear oil will be of the same viscosity as an SAE50 engine oil.

Shaft drive oil
● On models equipped with shaft final drive, the shaft drive gears are will have their own oil supply. The manufacturer will state a recommended 'type or classification' and also a specific 'viscosity' range in the same manner as for four-stroke engine oil.
● Gear oil classification is given by the number which follows the API GL (GL standing for gear lubricant) rating, the higher the number, the higher the specification of the oil, e.g. API GL5 oil is a higher specification than API GL4 oil. Ensure the oil meets or

exceeds the classification specified and is of the correct viscosity. The viscosity of gear oils is also represented by an SAE number but the scale of measurement used is different to that used to grade engine oils. As a rough guide an SAE90 gear oil will be of the same viscosity as an SAE50 engine oil.
● If the use of an EP (Extreme Pressure) gear oil is specified, ensure the oil purchased is suitable.

Fork oil and suspension fluid

● Conventional telescopic front forks are hydraulic and require fork oil to work. To ensure the forks function correctly, the fork oil must be changed in accordance with the Maintenance Schedule.
● Fork oil is available in a variety of viscosities, identified by their SAE rating; fork oil ratings vary from light (SAE 5) to heavy (SAE 30). When purchasing fork oil, ensure the viscosity rating matches that specified by the manufacturer.
● Some lubricant manufacturers also produce a range of high-quality suspension fluids which are very similar to fork oil but are designed mainly for competition use. These fluids may have a different viscosity rating system which is not to be confused with the SAE rating of normal fork oil. Refer to the manufacturer's instructions if in any doubt.

Brake and clutch fluid
● All disc brake systems and some clutch systems are hydraulically operated. To ensure correct operation, the hydraulic fluid must be changed in accordance with the Maintenance Schedule.
● Brake and clutch fluid is classified by its DOT rating with most motorcycle manufacturers specifying DOT 3 or 4 fluid. Both fluid types are glycol-based and can be mixed together without adverse effect; DOT 4 fluid exceeds the requirements of DOT 3

fluid. Although it is safe to use DOT 4 fluid in a system designed for use with DOT 3 fluid, never use DOT 3 fluid in a system which specifies the use of DOT 4 as this will adversely affect the system's performance. The type required for the system will be marked on the fluid reservoir cap.
● Some manufacturers also produce a DOT 5 hydraulic fluid. DOT 5 hydraulic fluid is silicone-based and is not compatible with the glycol-based DOT 3 and 4 fluids. Never mix DOT 5 fluid with DOT 3 or 4 fluid as this will seriously affect the performance of the hydraulic system.

Coolant/antifreeze
● When purchasing coolant/antifreeze, always ensure it is suitable for use in an aluminium engine and contains corrosion inhibitors to prevent possible blockages of the internal coolant passages of the system. As a general rule, most coolants are designed to be used neat and should not be diluted whereas antifreeze can be mixed with distilled water to provide a coolant solution of the required strength. Refer to the manufacturer's instructions on the bottle.

● Ensure the coolant is changed in accordance with the Maintenance Schedule.

Chain lube
● Chain lube is an aerosol-type spray lubricant specifically designed for use on motorcycle final drive chains. Chain lube has two functions, to minimise friction between the final drive chain and sprockets and to prevent corrosion of the chain. Regular use of a good-quality chain lube will extend the life of the drive chain and sprockets and thus maximise the power being transmitted from the transmission to the rear wheel.

● When using chain lube, always allow some time for the solvents in the lube to evaporate before riding the motorcycle. This will minimise the amount of lube which will 'fling' off from the chain when the motorcycle is used. If the motorcycle is equipped with an 'O-ring' chain, ensure the chain lube is labelled as being suitable for use on 'O-ring' chains.

Degreasers and solvents

● There are many different types of solvents and degreasers available to remove the grime and grease which accumulate around the motorcycle during normal use. Degreasers and solvents are usually available as an aerosol-type spray or as a liquid which you apply with a brush. Always closely follow the manufacturer's instructions and wear eye protection during use. Be aware that many solvents are flammable and may give off noxious fumes; take adequate precautions when using them (see Safety First!).

● For general cleaning, use one of the many solvents or degreasers available from most motorcycle accessory shops. These solvents are usually applied then left for a certain time before being washed off with water.

Brake cleaner is a solvent specifically designed to remove all traces of oil, grease and dust from braking system components. Brake cleaner is designed to evaporate quickly and leaves behind no residue.

Carburettor cleaner is an aerosol-type solvent specifically designed to clear carburettor blockages and break down the hard deposits and gum often found inside carburettors during overhaul.

Contact cleaner is an aerosol-type solvent designed for cleaning electrical components. The cleaner will remove all traces of oil and dirt from components such as switch contacts or fouled spark plugs and then dry, leaving behind no residue.

Gasket remover is an aerosol-type solvent designed for removing stubborn gaskets from engine components during overhaul. Gasket remover will minimise the amount of scraping required to remove the gasket and therefore reduce the risk of damage to the mating surface.

Spray lubricants

● Aerosol-based spray lubricants are widely available and are excellent for lubricating lever pivots and exposed cables and switches. Try to use a lubricant which is of the dry-film type as the fluid evaporates, leaving behind a dry-film of lubricant. Lubricants which leave behind an oily residue will attract dust and dirt which will increase the rate of wear of the cable/lever.

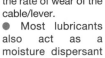

● Most lubricants also act as a moisture dispersant and a penetrating fluid. This means they can also be used to 'dry out' electrical components such as wiring connectors or switches as well as helping to free seized fasteners.

Greases

● Grease is used to lubricate many of the pivot-points. A good-quality multi-purpose grease is suitable for most applications but some manufacturers will specify the use of specialist greases for use on components such as swingarm and suspension linkage bushes. These specialist greases can be purchased from most motorcycle (or car) accessory shops; commonly specified types include molybdenum disulphide grease, lithium-based grease, graphite-based grease, silicone-based grease and high-temperature copper-based grease.

Gasket sealing compounds

● Gasket sealing compounds can be used in conjunction with gaskets, to improve their sealing capabilities, or on their own to seal metal-to-metal joints. Depending on their type, sealing compounds either set hard or stay relatively soft and pliable.

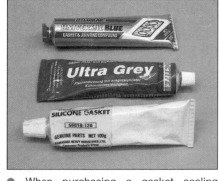

● When purchasing a gasket sealing compound, ensure that it is designed specifically for use on an internal combustion engine. General multi-purpose sealants available from DIY stores may appear visibly similar but they are not designed to withstand the extreme heat or contact with fuel and oil encountered when used on an engine (see 'Tools and Workshop Tips' for further information).

Thread locking compound

● Thread locking compounds are used to secure certain threaded fasteners in position to prevent them from loosening due to vibration. Thread locking compounds can be purchased from most motorcycle (and car) accessory shops. Ensure the threads of the both components are completely clean and dry before sparingly applying the locking compound (see 'Tools and Workshop Tips' for further information).

Fuel additives

● Fuel additives which protect and clean the fuel system components are widely available. These additives are designed to remove all traces of deposits that build up on the carburettors/injectors and prevent wear, helping the fuel system to operate more efficiently. If a fuel additive is being used, check that it is suitable for use with your motorcycle, especially if your motorcycle is equipped with a catalytic converter.

● Octane boosters are also available. These additives are designed to improve the performance of highly-tuned engines being run on normal pump-fuel and are of no real use on standard motorcycles.

Length (distance)

Inches (in)	x 25.4	= Millimetres (mm)	x 0.0394	=	Inches (in)
Feet (ft)	x 0.305	= Metres (m)	x 3.281	=	Feet (ft)
Miles	x 1.609	= Kilometres (km)	x 0.621	=	Miles

Volume (capacity)

Cubic inches (cu in; in³)	x 16.387	= Cubic centimetres (cc; cm³)	x 0.061	=	Cubic inches (cu in; in³)
Imperial pints (Imp pt)	x 0.568	= Litres (l)	x 1.76	=	Imperial pints (Imp pt)
Imperial quarts (Imp qt)	x 1.137	= Litres (l)	x 0.88	=	Imperial quarts (Imp qt)
Imperial quarts (Imp qt)	x 1.201	= US quarts (US qt)	x 0.833	=	Imperial quarts (Imp qt)
US quarts (US qt)	x 0.946	= Litres (l)	x 1.057	=	US quarts (US qt)
Imperial gallons (Imp gal)	x 4.546	= Litres (l)	x 0.22	=	Imperial gallons (Imp gal)
Imperial gallons (Imp gal)	x 1.201	= US gallons (US gal)	x 0.833	=	Imperial gallons (Imp gal)
US gallons (US gal)	x 3.785	= Litres (l)	x 0.264	=	US gallons (US gal)

Mass (weight)

Ounces (oz)	x 28.35	= Grams (g)	x 0.035	=	Ounces (oz)
Pounds (lb)	x 0.454	= Kilograms (kg)	x 2.205	=	Pounds (lb)

Force

Ounces-force (ozf; oz)	x 0.278	= Newtons (N)	x 3.6	=	Ounces-force (ozf; oz)
Pounds-force (lbf; lb)	x 4.448	= Newtons (N)	x 0.225	=	Pounds-force (lbf; lb)
Newtons (N)	x 0.1	= Kilograms-force (kgf; kg)	x 9.81	=	Newtons (N)

Pressure

Pounds-force per square inch (psi; lbf/in²; lb/in²)	x 0.070	= Kilograms-force per square centimetre (kgf/cm²; kg/cm²)	x 14.223	=	Pounds-force per square inch (psi; lbf/in²; lb/in²)
Pounds-force per square inch (psi; lbf/in²; lb/in²)	x 0.068	= Atmospheres (atm)	x 14.696	=	Pounds-force per square inch (psi; lbf/in²; lb/in²)
Pounds-force per square inch (psi; lbf/in²; lb/in²)	x 0.069	= Bars	x 14.5	=	Pounds-force per square inch (psi; lbf/in²; lb/in²)
Pounds-force per square inch (psi; lbf/in²; lb/in²)	x 6.895	= Kilopascals (kPa)	x 0.145	=	Pounds-force per square inch (psi; lbf/in²; lb/in²)
Kilopascals (kPa)	x 0.01	= Kilograms-force per square centimetre (kgf/cm²; kg/cm²)	x 98.1	=	Kilopascals (kPa)
Millibar (mbar)	x 100	= Pascals (Pa)	x 0.01	=	Millibar (mbar)
Millibar (mbar)	x 0.0145	= Pounds-force per square inch (psi; lbf/in²; lb/in²)	x 68.947	=	Millibar (mbar)
Millibar (mbar)	x 0.75	= Millimetres of mercury (mmHg)	x 1.333	=	Millibar (mbar)
Millibar (mbar)	x 0.401	= Inches of water (inH₂O)	x 2.491	=	Millibar (mbar)
Millimetres of mercury (mmHg)	x 0.535	= Inches of water (inH₂O)	x 1.868	=	Millimetres of mercury (mmHg)
Inches of water (inH₂O)	x 0.036	= Pounds-force per square inch (psi; lbf/in²; lb/in²)	x 27.68	=	Inches of water (inH₂O)

Torque (moment of force)

Pounds-force inches (lbf in; lb in)	x 1.152	= Kilograms-force centimetre (kgf cm; kg cm)	x 0.868	=	Pounds-force inches (lbf in; lb in)
Pounds-force inches (lbf in; lb in)	x 0.113	= Newton metres (Nm)	x 8.85	=	Pounds-force inches (lbf in; lb in)
Pounds-force inches (lbf in; lb in)	x 0.083	= Pounds-force feet (lbf ft; lb ft)	x 12	=	Pounds-force inches (lbf in; lb in)
Pounds-force feet (lbf ft; lb ft)	x 0.138	= Kilograms-force metres (kgf m; kg m)	x 7.233	=	Pounds-force feet (lbf ft; lb ft)
Pounds-force feet (lbf ft; lb ft)	x 1.356	= Newton metres (Nm)	x 0.738	=	Pounds-force feet (lbf ft; lb ft)
Newton metres (Nm)	x 0.102	= Kilograms-force metres (kgf m; kg m)	x 9.804	=	Newton metres (Nm)

Power

Horsepower (hp)	x 745.7	= Watts (W)	x 0.0013	=	Horsepower (hp)

Velocity (speed)

Miles per hour (miles/hr; mph)	x 1.609	= Kilometres per hour (km/hr; kph)	x 0.621	=	Miles per hour (miles/hr; mph)

Fuel consumption*

Miles per gallon (mpg)	x 0.354	= Kilometres per litre (km/l)	x 2.825	=	Miles per gallon (mpg)

Temperature

Degrees Fahrenheit = (°C x 1.8) + 32   Degrees Celsius (Degrees Centigrade; °C) = (°F - 32) x 0.56

It is common practice to convert from miles per gallon (mpg) to litres/100 kilometres (l/100km), where mpg x l/100 km = 282

About the MOT Test

In the UK, all vehicles more than three years old are subject to an annual test to ensure that they meet minimum safety requirements. A current test certificate must be issued before a machine can be used on public roads, and is required before a road fund licence can be issued. Riding without a current test certificate will also invalidate your insurance.

For most owners, the MOT test is an annual cause for anxiety, and this is largely due to owners not being sure what needs to be checked prior to submitting the motorcycle for testing. The simple answer is that a fully roadworthy motorcycle will have no difficulty in passing the test.

This is a guide to getting your motorcycle through the MOT test. Obviously it will not be possible to examine the motorcycle to the same standard as the professional MOT

tester, particularly in view of the equipment required for some of the checks. However, working through the following procedures will enable you to identify any problem areas before submitting the motorcycle for the test.

It has only been possible to summarise the test requirements here, based on the regulations in force at the time of printing. Test standards are becoming increasingly stringent, although there are some exemptions for older vehicles. More information about the MOT test can be obtained from the TSO publications, *How Safe is your Motorcycle* and *The MOT Inspection Manual for Motorcycle Testing*.

Many of the checks require that one of the wheels is raised off the ground. If the motorcycle doesn't have a centre stand, note that an auxiliary stand will be required. Additionally, the help of an assistant may prove useful.

Certain exceptions apply to machines under 50 cc, machines without a lighting system, and Classic bikes - if in doubt about any of the requirements listed below seek confirmation from an MOT tester prior to submitting the motorcycle for the test.

Check that the frame number is clearly visible.

> **HAYNES HiNT** *If a component is in borderline condition, the tester has discretion in deciding whether to pass or fail it. If the motorcycle presented is clean and evidently well cared for, the tester may be more inclined to pass a borderline component than if the motorcycle is scruffy and apparently neglected.*

Electrical System

Lights, turn signals, horn and reflector

✔ With the ignition on, check the operation of the following electrical components. **Note:** *The electrical components on certain small-capacity machines are powered by the generator, requiring that the engine is run for this check.*

a) Headlight and tail light. Check that both illuminate in the low and high beam switch positions.

b) Position lights. Check that the front position (or sidelight) and tail light illuminate in this switch position.

c) Turn signals. Check that all flash at the correct rate, and that the warning light(s) function correctly. Check that the turn signal switch works correctly.

d) Hazard warning system (where fitted). Check that all four turn signals flash in this switch position.

e) Brake stop light. Check that the light comes on when the front and rear brakes are independently applied. Models first used on or after 1st April 1986 must have a brake light switch on each brake.

f) Horn. Check that the sound is continuous and of reasonable volume.

✔ Check that there is a red reflector on the rear of the machine, either mounted separately or as part of the tail light lens.

✔ Check the condition of the headlight, tail light and turn signal lenses.

Headlight beam height

✔ The MOT tester will perform a headlight beam height check using specialised beam setting equipment **(see illustration 1)**. This equipment will not be available to the home mechanic, but if you suspect that the headlight is incorrectly set or may have been maladjusted in the past, you can perform a rough test as follows.

✔ Position the bike in a straight line facing a brick wall. The bike must be off its stand, upright and with a rider seated. Measure the height from the ground to the centre of the headlight and mark a horizontal line on the wall at this height. Position the motorcycle 3.8 metres from the wall and draw a vertical

Headlight beam height checking equipment

line up the wall central to the centreline of the motorcycle. Switch to dipped beam and check that the beam pattern falls slightly lower than the horizontal line and to the left of the vertical line **(see illustration 2)**.

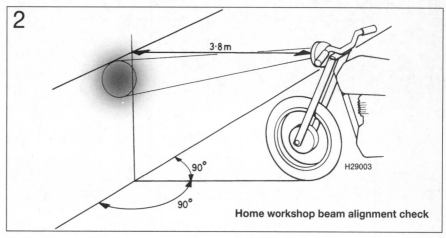

Home workshop beam alignment check

Exhaust System and Final Drive

Exhaust

✔ Check that the exhaust mountings are secure and that the system does not foul any of the rear suspension components.
✔ Start the motorcycle. When the revs are increased, check that the exhaust is neither holed nor leaking from any of its joints. On a linked system, check that the collector box is not leaking due to corrosion.

✔ Note that the exhaust decibel level ("loudness" of the exhaust) is assessed at the discretion of the tester. If the motorcycle was first used on or after 1st January 1985 the silencer must carry the BSAU 193 stamp, or a marking relating to its make and model, or be of OE (original equipment) manufacture. If the silencer is marked NOT FOR ROAD USE, RACING USE ONLY or similar, it will fail the MOT.

Final drive

✔ On chain or belt drive machines, check that the chain/belt is in good condition and does not have excessive slack. Also check that the sprocket is securely mounted on the rear wheel hub. Check that the chain/belt guard is in place.
✔ On shaft drive bikes, check for oil leaking from the drive unit and fouling the rear tyre.

Steering and Suspension

Steering

✔ With the front wheel raised off the ground, rotate the steering from lock to lock. The handlebar or switches must not contact the fuel tank or be close enough to trap the rider's hand. Problems can be caused by damaged lock stops on the lower yoke and frame, or by the fitting of non-standard handlebars.
✔ When performing the lock to lock check, also ensure that the steering moves freely without drag or notchiness. Steering movement can be impaired by poorly routed cables, or by overtight head bearings or worn bearings. The tester will perform a check of the steering head bearing lower race by mounting the front wheel on a surface plate, then performing a lock to

lock check with the weight of the machine on the lower bearing (see illustration 3).
✔ Grasp the fork sliders (lower legs) and attempt to push and pull on the forks (see

Front wheel mounted on a surface plate for steering head bearing lower race check

illustration 4). Any play in the steering head bearings will be felt. Note that in extreme cases, wear of the front fork bushes can be misinterpreted for head bearing play.
✔ Check that the handlebars are securely mounted.
✔ Check that the handlebar grip rubbers are secure. They should by bonded to the bar left end and to the throttle cable pulley on the right end.

Front suspension

✔ With the motorcycle off the stand, hold the front brake on and pump the front forks up and down (see illustration 5). Check that they are adequately damped.

Checking the steering head bearings for freeplay

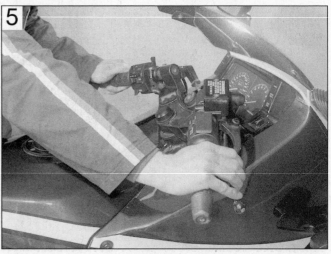

Hold the front brake on and pump the front forks up and down to check operation

Inspect the area around the fork dust seal for oil leakage (arrow)

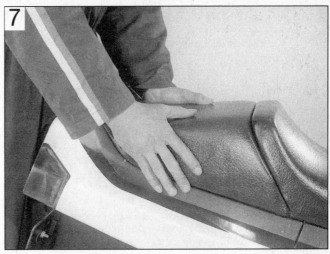

Bounce the rear of the motorcycle to check rear suspension operation

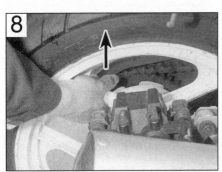

Checking for rear suspension linkage play

✔ Inspect the area above and around the front fork oil seals **(see illustration 6)**. There should be no sign of oil on the fork tube (stanchion) nor leaking down the slider (lower leg). On models so equipped, check that there is no oil leaking from the anti-dive units.

✔ On models with swingarm front suspension, check that there is no freeplay in the linkage when moved from side to side.

Rear suspension

✔ With the motorcycle off the stand and an assistant supporting the motorcycle by its handlebars, bounce the rear suspension **(see illustration 7)**. Check that the suspension components do not foul on any of the cycle parts and check that the shock absorber(s) provide adequate damping.

✔ Visually inspect the shock absorber(s) and check that there is no sign of oil leakage from its damper. This is somewhat restricted on certain single shock models due to the location of the shock absorber.

✔ With the rear wheel raised off the ground, grasp the wheel at the highest point and attempt to pull it up **(see illustration 8)**. Any play in the swingarm pivot or suspension linkage bearings will be felt as movement. **Note:** *Do not confuse play with actual suspension movement.* Failure to lubricate suspension linkage bearings can lead to bearing failure **(see illustration 9)**.

✔ With the rear wheel raised off the ground, grasp the swingarm ends and attempt to move the swingarm from side to side and forwards and backwards - any play indicates wear of the swingarm pivot bearings **(see illustration 10)**.

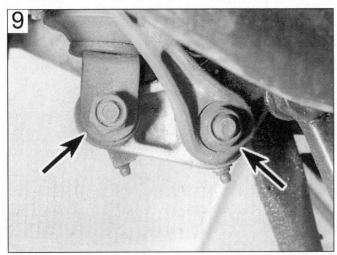

Worn suspension linkage pivots (arrows) are usually the cause of play in the rear suspension

Grasp the swingarm at the ends to check for play in its pivot bearings

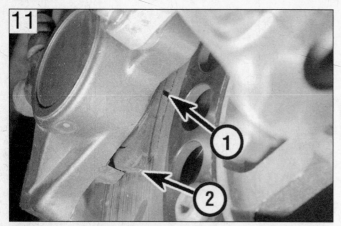

Brake pad wear can usually be viewed without removing the caliper. Most pads have wear indicator grooves (1) and some also have indicator tangs (2)

On drum brakes, check the angle of the operating lever with the brake fully applied. Most drum brakes have a wear indicator pointer and scale.

Brakes, Wheels and Tyres

Brakes

✔ With the wheel raised off the ground, apply the brake then free it off, and check that the wheel is about to revolve freely without brake drag.

✔ On disc brakes, examine the disc itself. Check that it is securely mounted and not cracked.

✔ On disc brakes, view the pad material through the caliper mouth and check that the pads are not worn down beyond the limit (see illustration 11).

✔ On drum brakes, check that when the brake is applied the angle between the operating lever and cable or rod is not too great (see illustration 12). Check also that the operating lever doesn't foul any other components.

✔ On disc brakes, examine the flexible hoses from top to bottom. Have an assistant hold the brake on so that the fluid in the hose is under pressure, and check that there is no sign of fluid leakage, bulges or cracking. If there are any metal brake pipes or unions, check that these are free from corrosion and damage. Where a brake-linked anti-dive system is fitted, check the hoses to the anti-dive in a similar manner.

✔ Check that the rear brake torque arm is secure and that its fasteners are secured by self-locking nuts or castellated nuts with split-pins or R-pins (see illustration 13).

✔ On models with ABS, check that the self-check warning light in the instrument panel works.

✔ The MOT tester will perform a test of the motorcycle's braking efficiency based on a calculation of rider and motorcycle weight. Although this cannot be carried out at home, you can at least ensure that the braking systems are properly maintained. For hydraulic disc brakes, check the fluid level, lever/pedal feel (bleed of air if its spongy) and pad material. For drum brakes, check adjustment, cable or rod operation and shoe lining thickness.

Wheels and tyres

✔ Check the wheel condition. Cast wheels should be free from cracks and if of the built-up design, all fasteners should be secure. Spoked wheels should be checked for broken, corroded, loose or bent spokes.

✔ With the wheel raised off the ground, spin the wheel and visually check that the tyre and wheel run true. Check that the tyre does not foul the suspension or mudguards.

✔ With the wheel raised off the ground, grasp the wheel and attempt to move it about the axle (spindle) (see illustration 14). Any play felt here indicates wheel bearing failure.

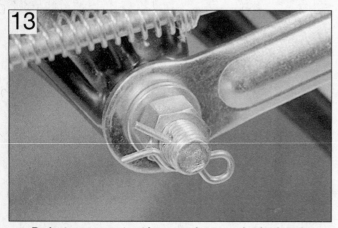

Brake torque arm must be properly secured at both ends

Check for wheel bearing play by trying to move the wheel about the axle (spindle)

Checking the tyre tread depth

Tyre direction of rotation arrow can be found on tyre sidewall

Castellated type wheel axle (spindle) nut must be secured by a split pin or R-pin

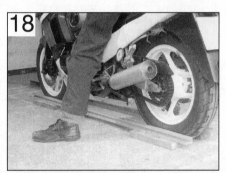

Two straightedges are used to check wheel alignment

✔ Check the tyre tread depth, tread condition and sidewall condition **(see illustration 15)**.
✔ Check the tyre type. Front and rear tyre types must be compatible and be suitable for road use. Tyres marked NOT FOR ROAD USE, COMPETITION USE ONLY or similar, will fail the MOT.

✔ If the tyre sidewall carries a direction of rotation arrow, this must be pointing in the direction of normal wheel rotation **(see illustration 16)**.
✔ Check that the wheel axle (spindle) nuts (where applicable) are properly secured. A self-locking nut or castellated nut with a split-pin or R-pin can be used **(see illustration 17)**.
✔ Wheel alignment is checked with the motorcycle off the stand and a rider seated. With the front wheel pointing straight ahead, two perfectly straight lengths of metal or wood and placed against the sidewalls of both tyres **(see illustration 18)**. The gap each side of the front tyre must be equidistant on both sides. Incorrect wheel alignment may be due to a cocked rear wheel (often as the result of poor chain adjustment) or in extreme cases, a bent frame.

General checks and condition

✔ Check the security of all major fasteners, bodypanels, seat, fairings (where fitted) and mudguards.

✔ Check that the rider and pillion footrests, handlebar levers and brake pedal are securely mounted.

✔ Check for corrosion on the frame or any load-bearing components. If severe, this may affect the structure, particularly under stress.

Sidecars

A motorcycle fitted with a sidecar requires additional checks relating to the stability of the machine and security of attachment and swivel joints, plus specific wheel alignment (toe-in) requirements. Additionally, tyre and lighting requirements differ from conventional motorcycle use. Owners are advised to check MOT test requirements with an official test centre.

Preparing for storage

Before you start

If repairs or an overhaul is needed, see that this is carried out now rather than left until you want to ride the bike again.

Give the bike a good wash and scrub all dirt from its underside. Make sure the bike dries completely before preparing for storage.

Engine

● Remove the spark plug(s) and lubricate the cylinder bores with approximately a teaspoon of motor oil using a spout-type oil can (**see illustration 1**). Reinstall the spark plug(s). Crank the engine over a couple of times to coat the piston rings and bores with oil. If the bike has a kickstart, use this to turn the engine over. If not, flick the kill switch to the OFF position and crank the engine over on the starter (**see illustration 2**). If the nature on the ignition system prevents the starter operating with the kill switch in the OFF position,

remove the spark plugs and fit them back in their caps; ensure that the plugs are earthed (grounded) against the cylinder head when the starter is operated (**see illustration 3**).

 Warning: It is important that the plugs are earthed (grounded) away from the spark plug holes otherwise there is a risk of atomised fuel from the cylinders igniting.

HAYNES HiNT *On a single cylinder four-stroke engine, you can seal the combustion chamber completely by positioning the piston at TDC on the compression stroke.*

● Drain the carburettor(s) otherwise there is a risk of jets becoming blocked by gum deposits from the fuel (**see illustration 4**).

● If the bike is going into long-term storage, consider adding a fuel stabiliser to the fuel in the tank. If the tank is drained completely, corrosion of its internal surfaces may occur if left unprotected for a long period. The tank can be treated with a rust preventative especially for this purpose. Alternatively, remove the tank and pour half a litre of motor oil into it, install the filler cap and shake the tank to coat its internals with oil before draining off the excess. The same effect can also be achieved by spraying WD40 or a similar water-dispersant around the inside of the tank via its flexible nozzle.

● Make sure the cooling system contains the correct mix of antifreeze. Antifreeze also contains important corrosion inhibitors.

● The air intakes and exhaust can be sealed off by covering or plugging the openings. Ensure that you do not seal in any condensation; run the engine until it is hot,

Squirt a drop of motor oil into each cylinder

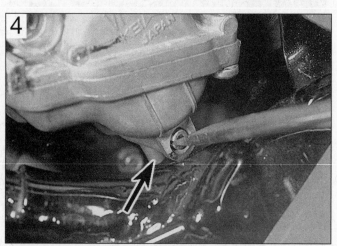

Flick the kill switch to OFF . . .

. . . and ensure that the metal bodies of the plugs (arrows) are earthed against the cylinder head

Connect a hose to the carburettor float chamber drain stub (arrow) and unscrew the drain screw

5

Exhausts can be sealed off with a plastic bag

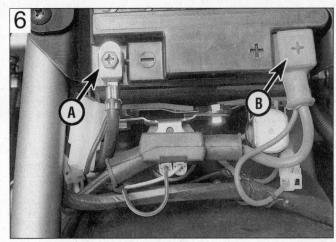

6

Disconnect the negative lead (A) first, followed by the positive lead (B)

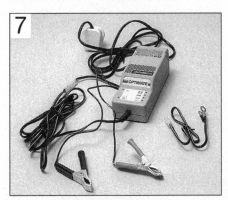

7

Use a suitable battery charger - this kit also assess battery condition

then switch off and allow to cool. Tape a piece of thick plastic over the silencer end(s) **(see illustration 5)**. Note that some advocate pouring a tablespoon of motor oil into the silencer(s) before sealing them off.

Battery

● Remove it from the bike - in extreme cases of cold the battery may freeze and crack its case **(see illustration 6)**.

● Check the electrolyte level and top up if necessary (conventional refillable batteries). Clean the terminals.
● Store the battery off the motorcycle and away from any sources of fire. Position a wooden block under the battery if it is to sit on the ground.
● Give the battery a trickle charge for a few hours every month **(see illustration 7)**.

Tyres

● Place the bike on its centrestand or an auxiliary stand which will support the motorcycle in an upright position. Position wood blocks under the tyres to keep them off the ground and to provide insulation from damp. If the bike is being put into long-term storage, ideally both tyres should be off the ground; not only will this protect the tyres, but will also ensure that no load is placed on the steering head or wheel bearings.
● Deflate each tyre by 5 to 10 psi, no more or the beads may unseat from the rim, making subsequent inflation difficult on tubeless tyres.

Pivots and controls

● Lubricate all lever, pedal, stand and

footrest pivot points. If grease nipples are fitted to the rear suspension components, apply lubricant to the pivots.
● Lubricate all control cables.

Cycle components

● Apply a wax protectant to all painted and plastic components. Wipe off any excess, but don't polish to a shine. Where fitted, clean the screen with soap and water.
● Coat metal parts with Vaseline (petroleum jelly). When applying this to the fork tubes, do not compress the forks otherwise the seals will rot from contact with the Vaseline.
● Apply a vinyl cleaner to the seat.

Storage conditions

● Aim to store the bike in a shed or garage which does not leak and is free from damp.
● Drape an old blanket or bedspread over the bike to protect it from dust and direct contact with sunlight (which will fade paint). This also hides the bike from prying eyes. Beware of tight-fitting plastic covers which may allow condensation to form and settle on the bike.

Getting back on the road

Engine and transmission

● Change the oil and replace the oil filter. If this was done prior to storage, check that the oil hasn't emulsified - a thick whitish substance which occurs through condensation.
● Remove the spark plugs. Using a spout-type oil can, squirt a few drops of oil into the cylinder(s). This will provide initial lubrication as the piston rings and bores comes back into contact. Service the spark plugs, or fit new ones, and install them in the engine.

● Check that the clutch isn't stuck on. The plates can stick together if left standing for some time, preventing clutch operation. Engage a gear and try rocking the bike back and forth with the clutch lever held against the handlebar. If this doesn't work on cable-operated clutches, hold the clutch lever back against the handlebar with a strong elastic band or cable tie for a couple of hours **(see illustration 8)**.
● If the air intakes or silencer end(s) were blocked off, remove the bung or cover used.
● If the fuel tank was coated with a rust

8

Hold clutch lever back against the handlebar with elastic bands or a cable tie

preventative, oil or a stabiliser added to the fuel, drain and flush the tank and dispose of the fuel sensibly. If no action was taken with the fuel tank prior to storage, it is advised that the old fuel is disposed of since it will go off over a period of time. Refill the fuel tank with fresh fuel.

Frame and running gear

● Oil all pivot points and cables.
● Check the tyre pressures. They will definitely need inflating if pressures were reduced for storage.
● Lubricate the final drive chain (where applicable).
● Remove any protective coating applied to the fork tubes (stanchions) since this may well destroy the fork seals. If the fork tubes weren't protected and have picked up rust spots, remove them with very fine abrasive paper and refinish with metal polish.
● Check that both brakes operate correctly. Apply each brake hard and check that it's not possible to move the motorcycle forwards, then check that the brake frees off again once released. Brake caliper pistons can stick due to corrosion around the piston head, or on the sliding caliper types, due to corrosion of the slider pins. If the brake doesn't free after repeated operation, take the caliper off for examination. Similarly drum brakes can stick due to a seized operating cam, cable or rod linkage.
● If the motorcycle has been in long-term storage, renew the brake fluid and clutch fluid (where applicable).
● Depending on where the bike has been stored, the wiring, cables and hoses may have been nibbled by rodents. Make a visual check and investigate disturbed wiring loom tape.

Battery

● If the battery has been previously removal and given top up charges it can simply be reconnected. Remember to connect the positive cable first and the negative cable last.
● On conventional refillable batteries, if the battery has not received any attention, remove it from the motorcycle and check its electrolyte level. Top up if necessary then charge the battery. If the battery fails to hold a charge and a visual checks show heavy white sulphation of the plates, the battery is probably defective and must be renewed. This is particularly likely if the battery is old. Confirm battery condition with a specific gravity check.
● On sealed (MF) batteries, if the battery has not received any attention, remove it from the motorcycle and charge it according to the information on the battery case - if the battery fails to hold a charge it must be renewed.

Starting procedure

● If a kickstart is fitted, turn the engine over a couple of times with the ignition OFF to distribute oil around the engine. If no kickstart is fitted, flick the engine kill switch OFF and the ignition ON and crank the engine over a couple of times to work oil around the upper cylinder components. If the nature of the ignition system is such that the starter won't work with the kill switch OFF, remove the spark plugs, fit them back into their caps and earth (ground) their bodies on the cylinder head. Reinstall the spark plugs afterwards.
● Switch the kill switch to RUN, operate the choke and start the engine. If the engine won't start don't continue cranking the engine - not only will this flatten the battery, but the starter motor will overheat. Switch the ignition off and try again later. If the engine refuses to start, go through the fault finding procedures in this manual. **Note:** *If the bike has been in storage for a long time, old fuel or a carburettor blockage may be the problem. Gum deposits in carburettors can block jets - if a carburettor cleaner doesn't prove successful the carburettors must be dismantled for cleaning.*
● Once the engine has started, check that the lights, turn signals and horn work properly.
● Treat the bike gently for the first ride and check all fluid levels on completion. Settle the bike back into the maintenance schedule.

This Section provides an easy reference-guide to the more common faults that are likely to afflict your machine. Obviously, the opportunities are almost limitless for faults to occur as a result of obscure failures, and to try and cover all eventualities would require a book. Indeed, a number have been written on the subject.

Successful troubleshooting is not a mysterious 'black art' but the application of a bit of knowledge combined with a systematic and logical approach to the problem. Approach any troubleshooting by first accurately identifying the symptom and then checking through the list of possible causes, starting with the simplest or most obvious and progressing in stages to the most complex.

Take nothing for granted, but above all apply liberal quantities of common sense.

The main symptom of a fault is given in the text as a major heading below which are listed the various systems or areas which may contain the fault. Details of each possible cause for a fault and the remedial action to be taken are given, in brief, in the paragraphs below each heading. Further information should be sought in the relevant Chapter.

1 Engine doesn't start or is difficult to start
- [ ] Starter motor doesn't rotate
- [ ] Starter motor rotates but engine does not turn over
- [ ] Starter works but engine won't turn over (seized)
- [ ] No fuel flow
- [ ] Engine flooded
- [ ] No spark or weak spark
- [ ] Compression low
- [ ] Stalls after starting
- [ ] Rough idle

2 Poor running at low speed
- [ ] Spark weak
- [ ] Fuel/air mixture incorrect
- [ ] Compression low
- [ ] Poor acceleration

3 Poor running or no power at high speed
- [ ] Firing incorrect
- [ ] Fuel/air mixture incorrect
- [ ] Compression low
- [ ] Knocking or pinking
- [ ] Miscellaneous causes

4 Overheating
- [ ] Engine overheats
- [ ] Firing incorrect
- [ ] Fuel/air mixture incorrect
- [ ] Compression too high
- [ ] Engine load excessive
- [ ] Lubrication inadequate
- [ ] Miscellaneous causes

5 Clutch problems
- [ ] Clutch slipping
- [ ] Clutch not disengaging completely

6 Gear changing problems
- [ ] Doesn't go into gear, or lever doesn't return
- [ ] Jumps out of gear
- [ ] Overshifts

7 Abnormal engine noise
- [ ] Knocking or pinking
- [ ] Piston slap or rattling
- [ ] Valve noise
- [ ] Other noise

8 Abnormal driveline noise
- [ ] Clutch noise
- [ ] Transmission noise
- [ ] Final drive noise

9 Abnormal frame and suspension noise
- [ ] Front end noise
- [ ] Shock absorber noise
- [ ] Brake noise

10 Oil pressure warning light comes on
- [ ] Engine lubrication system
- [ ] Electrical system

11 Excessive exhaust smoke
- [ ] White smoke
- [ ] Black smoke
- [ ] Brown smoke

12 Poor handling or stability
- [ ] Handlebar hard to turn
- [ ] Handlebar shakes or vibrates excessively
- [ ] Handlebar pulls to one side
- [ ] Poor shock absorbing qualities

13 Braking problems
- [ ] Brakes are spongy, don't hold
- [ ] Brake lever or pedal pulsates
- [ ] Brakes drag

14 Electrical problems
- [ ] Battery dead or weak
- [ ] Battery overcharged

1 Engine doesn't start or is difficult to start

Starter motor doesn't rotate

- ☐ Engine kill switch OFF.
- ☐ Fuse blown. Check main fuse and starter circuit fuse (Chapter 9).
- ☐ Battery voltage low. Check and recharge battery (Chapter 9).
- ☐ Starter motor defective. Make sure the wiring to the starter is secure. Make sure the starter relay clicks when the start button is pushed. If the relay clicks, then the fault is in the wiring or motor.
- ☐ Starter relay faulty. Check it according to the procedure in Chapter 9.
- ☐ Starter switch not contacting. The contacts could be wet, corroded or dirty. Disassemble and clean the switch (Chapter 9).
- ☐ Wiring open or shorted. Check all wiring connections and harnesses to make sure that they are dry, tight and not corroded. Also check for broken or frayed wires that can cause a short to ground (earth) (see wiring diagram, Chapter 9).
- ☐ Ignition (main) switch defective. Check the switch according to the procedure in Chapter 9. Replace the switch with a new one if it is defective.
- ☐ Engine kill switch defective. Check for wet, dirty or corroded contacts. Clean or replace the switch as necessary (Chapter 9).
- ☐ Faulty neutral, side stand or clutch switch. Check the wiring to each switch and the switch itself according to the procedures in Chapter 9.

Starter motor rotates but engine does not turn over

- ☐ Starter clutch defective. Inspect and repair or replace (Chapter 2).
- ☐ Damaged idle/reduction or starter gears. Inspect and replace the damaged parts (Chapter 2).

Starter works but engine won't turn over (seized)

- ☐ Seized engine caused by one or more internally damaged components. Failure due to wear, abuse or lack of lubrication. Damage can include seized valves, followers, camshafts, pistons, crankshaft, connecting rod bearings, or transmission gears or bearings. Refer to Chapter 2 for engine disassembly.

No fuel flow

- ☐ No fuel in tank.
- ☐ Fuel tank breather hose obstructed.
- ☐ Fuel tap filter (carburettor models) or fuel pump assembly filter (fuel injected models) clogged. Remove the tap or pump and clean or renew the filter (Chapter 1 and 4).
- ☐ Fuel tap vacuum hose split or detached (carburettor models). Check the hose.
- ☐ Fuel tap diaphragm split (carburettor models). Remove the tap and check the diaphragm (Chapter 4).
- ☐ Fuel line clogged. Pull the fuel line loose and carefully blow through it.
- ☐ Float needle valve clogged (carburettor models). For all of the valves to be clogged, either a very bad batch of fuel with an unusual additive has been used, or some other foreign material has entered the tank. Many times after a machine has been stored for many months without running, the fuel turns to a varnish-like liquid and forms deposits on the inlet needle valves and jets. The carburettors should be removed and overhauled if draining the float chambers doesn't solve the problem.
- ☐ Fuel pump or relay faulty (fuel injected models). Check the fuel pump and relay (Chapter 4).

Engine flooded (carburettor models)

- ☐ Float height too high. Check as described in Chapter 4.
- ☐ Float needle valve worn or stuck open. A piece of dirt, rust or other debris can cause the valve to seat improperly, causing excess fuel to be admitted to the float chamber. In this case, the float chamber should be cleaned and the needle valve and seat inspected. If the needle and seat are worn, then the leaking will persist and the parts should be replaced with new ones (Chapter 4).

☐ Starting technique incorrect. Under normal circumstances (i.e., if all the carburettor functions are sound) the machine should start with little or no throttle. When the engine is cold, the choke should be operated and the engine started without opening the throttle. When the engine is at operating temperature, only a very slight amount of throttle should be necessary. If the engine is flooded, raise the fuel tank and turn the fuel tap OFF and hold the throttle open while cranking the engine. This will allow additional air to reach the cylinders. Remember to turn the fuel tap back ON after the engine starts.

Engine flooded (fuel injected models)

- ☐ Faulty pressure regulator – if it is stuck closed there could be excessive pressure in the fuel rail. Check as described in Chapter 4.
- ☐ Injector(s) stuck open, allowing a constant flow of fuel into the engine. Check as described in Chapter 4.
- ☐ Starting technique incorrect. Under normal circumstances (i.e., if all the carburettor functions are sound) the machine should start with little or no throttle. When the engine is cold, the choke should be operated and the engine started without opening the throttle. When the engine is at operating temperature, only a very slight amount of throttle should be necessary. If the engine is flooded, raise the fuel tank and turn the fuel tap OFF and hold the throttle open while cranking the engine. This will allow additional air to reach the cylinders. Remember to turn the fuel tap back ON after the engine starts.

No spark or weak spark

- ☐ Ignition switch OFF.
- ☐ Engine kill switch turned to the OFF position.
- ☐ Battery voltage low. Check and recharge the battery as necessary (Chapter 9).
- ☐ Spark plugs dirty, defective or worn out. Locate reason for fouled plugs using spark plug condition chart and follow the plug maintenance procedures (Chapter 1).
- ☐ Spark plug caps or secondary (HT) wiring faulty. Check condition. Replace either or both components if cracks or deterioration are evident (Chapter 5).
- ☐ Spark plug caps not making good contact. Make sure that the plug caps fit snugly over the plug ends.
- ☐ Ignition control unit (carburettor models) or ECM (fuel injected models) defective. Check the unit, referring to Chapter 5 or 4 for details.
- ☐ Pulse generator defective. Check the unit, referring to Chapter 5 (carburettor models) or 4 (fuel injected models) for details.
- ☐ Ignition HT coils defective. Check the coils, referring to Chapter 5.
- ☐ Ignition or kill switch shorted. This is usually caused by water, corrosion, damage or excessive wear. The switches can be disassembled and cleaned with electrical contact cleaner. If cleaning does not help, replace the switches (Chapter 9).
- ☐ Wiring shorted or broken between:
  - a)   Ignition (main) switch and engine kill switch (or blown fuse)
  - b)   Ignition control unit or ECM and engine kill switch
  - c)   Ignition control unit or ECM and ignition HT coils
  - d)   Ignition HT coils and spark plugs
  - e)   Ignition control unit or ECM and pulse generator
- ☐ Make sure that all wiring connections are clean, dry and tight. Look for chafed and broken wires (Chapters 5 and 9).

Compression low

- ☐ Spark plugs loose. Remove the plugs and inspect their threads. Reinstall and tighten to the specified torque (Chapter 1).
- ☐ Cylinder heads not sufficiently tightened down. If a cylinder head is suspected of being loose, then there's a chance that the gasket or head is damaged if the problem has persisted for any length of time. The head bolts should be tightened to the proper torque in the correct sequence (Chapter 2).

1 Engine doesn't start or is difficult to start (continued)

☐ Incorrect valve clearance. This means that the valve is not closing completely and compression pressure is leaking past the valve. Check and adjust the valve clearances (Chapter 1).
☐ Cylinder and/or piston worn. Excessive wear will cause compression pressure to leak past the rings. This is usually accompanied by worn rings as well. A top-end overhaul is necessary (Chapter 2).
☐ Piston rings worn, weak, broken, or sticking. Broken or sticking piston rings usually indicate a lubrication or carburation problem that causes excess carbon deposits or seizures to form on the pistons and rings. Top-end overhaul is necessary (Chapter 2).
☐ Piston ring-to-groove clearance excessive. This is caused by excessive wear of the piston ring lands. Piston replacement is necessary (Chapter 2).
☐ Cylinder head gasket damaged. If a head is allowed to become loose, or if excessive carbon build-up on the piston crown and combustion chamber causes extremely high compression, the head gasket may leak. Retorquing the head is not always sufficient to restore the seal, so gasket replacement is necessary (Chapter 2).
☐ Cylinder head warped. This is caused by overheating or improperly tightened head bolts. Machine shop resurfacing or head replacement is necessary (Chapter 2).
☐ Valve spring broken or weak. Caused by component failure or wear; the springs must be replaced (Chapter 2).
☐ Valve not seating properly. This is caused by a bent valve (from over-revving or improper valve adjustment), burned valve or seat (improper carburation) or an accumulation of carbon deposits on the seat (from carburation or lubrication problems). The valves must be cleaned and/or replaced and the seats serviced if possible (Chapter 2).

Stalls after starting

☐ Improper choke action (carburettor models). Make sure the choke

linkage shaft is getting a full stroke and staying in the out position (Chapter 4).
☐ Ignition malfunction. See Chapter 5.
☐ Carburettor or fuel injection system malfunction. See Chapter 4.
☐ Fuel contaminated. The fuel can be contaminated with either dirt or water, or can change chemically if the machine is allowed to sit for several months or more. Drain the tank and float chambers (Chapter 4). Also check that the fuel flows freely and is not being restricted.
☐ Intake air leak. Check for loose carburettor or throttle body-to-intake manifold connections, loose or missing vacuum gauge adapter screws or hoses, or loose carburettor tops (Chapter 4).
☐ Engine idle speed incorrect. Turn idle adjusting screw until the engine idles at the specified rpm (Chapter 1). On fuel injected models, also check the first idle system wax unit and starter valves (See Chapter 4).

Rough idle

☐ Ignition malfunction. See Chapter 5.
☐ Idle speed incorrect. See Chapter 1.
☐ Carburettors or throttle bodies (starter valves) not synchronised. Adjust with vacuum gauge or manometer set as described in Chapter 1.
☐ Carburettor or throttle body (starter valve) or fuel injection system malfunction. See Chapter 4.
☐ Fuel contaminated. The fuel can be contaminated with either dirt or water, or can change chemically if the machine is allowed to sit for several months or more. Drain the tank and float chambers (Chapter 4).
☐ Intake air leak. Check for loose carburettor or throttle body-to-intake manifold connections, loose or missing vacuum gauge adapter screws or hoses, or loose carburettor tops (Chapter 4).
☐ Air filter clogged. Clean or replace the air filter element (Chapter 1).

2 Poor running at low speeds

Spark weak

☐ Battery voltage low. Check and recharge battery (Chapter 9).
☐ Spark plugs fouled, defective or worn out. Refer to Chapter 1 for spark plug maintenance.
☐ Spark plug cap or HT wiring defective. Refer to Chapters 1 and 5 for details on the ignition system.
☐ Spark plug caps not making contact.
☐ Incorrect spark plugs. Wrong type, heat range or cap configuration. Check and install correct plugs listed in Chapter 1.
☐ Ignition control unit (carburettor models) or ECM (fuel injected models) defective. Check the unit, referring to Chapter 5 or 4 for details.
☐ Pulse generator defective. See Chapter 5.
☐ Ignition HT coils defective. See Chapter 5.

Fuel/air mixture incorrect

Carburettor models

☐ Pilot screws out of adjustment (Chapter 4).
☐ Pilot jet or air passage clogged. Remove and overhaul the carburettors (Chapter 4).
☐ Air bleed holes clogged. Remove carburettor and blow out all passages (Chapter 4).
☐ Fuel level too high or too low. Check the float height (Chapter 4).

☐ Carburettor intake manifolds loose. Check for cracks, breaks, tears or loose clamps. Replace the rubber intake manifold joints if split or perished.

Fuel injected models

☐ Fuel injection system malfunction (see Chapter 4).
☐ Fuel injector clogged (see Chapter 4).
☐ Fuel pump or pressure regulator faulty (see Chapter 4).
☐ Throttle body intake manifolds loose. Check for cracks, breaks, tears or loose clamps. Replace the rubber intake manifold joints if split or perished.

All models

☐ Air filter clogged, poorly sealed or missing (Chapter 1).
☐ Air filter housing poorly sealed. Look for cracks, holes or loose clamps and replace or repair defective parts.
☐ Fuel tank breather hose obstructed.

Compression low

☐ Spark plugs loose. Remove the plugs and inspect their threads. Reinstall and tighten to the specified torque (Chapter 1).
☐ Cylinder heads not sufficiently tightened down. If a cylinder head is suspected of being loose, then there's a chance that the gasket and head are damaged if the problem has persisted for any length of time. The head bolts should be tightened to the proper torque in the correct sequence (Chapter 2).

2 Poor running at low speeds (continued)

☐ Incorrect valve clearance. This means that the valve is not closing completely and compression pressure is leaking past the valve. Check and adjust the valve clearances (Chapter 1).

☐ Cylinder and/or piston worn. Excessive wear will cause compression pressure to leak past the rings. This is usually accompanied by worn rings as well. A top end overhaul is necessary (Chapter 2).

☐ Piston rings worn, weak, broken, or sticking. Broken or sticking piston rings usually indicate a lubrication or carburation problem that causes excess carbon deposits or seizures to form on the pistons and rings. Top-end overhaul is necessary (Chapter 2).

☐ Piston ring-to-groove clearance excessive. This is caused by excessive wear of the piston ring lands. Piston replacement is necessary (Chapter 2).

☐ Cylinder head gasket damaged. If a head is allowed to become loose, or if excessive carbon build-up on the piston crown and combustion chamber causes extremely high compression, the head gasket may leak. Retorquing the head is not always sufficient to restore the seal, so gasket replacement is necessary (Chapter 2).

☐ Cylinder head warped. This is caused by overheating or improperly tightened head bolts. Machine shop resurfacing or head replacement is necessary (Chapter 2).

☐ Valve spring broken or weak. Caused by component failure or wear; the springs must be replaced (Chapter 2).

☐ Valve not seating properly. This is caused by a bent valve (from over-revving or improper valve adjustment), burned valve or seat (improper carburation) or an accumulation of carbon deposits on the seat (from carburation, lubrication problems). The valves must be cleaned and/or replaced and the seats serviced if possible (Chapter 2).

Poor acceleration

☐ Carburettors or throttle bodies leaking or dirty. Overhaul them (Chapter 4).

☐ Fuel injection system malfunction, faulty fuel pump or pressure regulator (Chapter 4).

☐ Timing not advancing. The pulse generator or the ignition control module or ECM may be defective. If so, they must be replaced with new ones, as they can't be repaired. Check them (see Chapter 4 or 5).

☐ Carburettors or throttle bodies (starter valves) not synchronised. Adjust them with a vacuum gauge set or manometer (Chapter 1).

☐ Engine oil viscosity too high. Using a heavier oil than that recommended in Chapter 1 can damage the oil pump or lubrication system and cause drag on the engine.

☐ Brakes dragging. Usually caused by debris which has entered the brake piston seals, or from a warped disc or bent axle. Repair as necessary (Chapter 7).

3 Poor running or no power at high speed

Firing incorrect

☐ Air filter restricted. Clean or replace filter (Chapter 1).

☐ Spark plugs fouled, defective or worn out. See Chapter 1 for spark plug maintenance.

☐ Spark plug caps or HT wiring defective. See Chapters 1 and 5 for details of the ignition system.

☐ Spark plug caps not in good contact. See Chapter 5.

☐ Incorrect spark plugs. Wrong type, heat range or cap configuration. Check and install correct plugs listed in Chapter 1.

☐ Ignition control unit defective. See Chapter 5.

☐ Ignition coils defective. See Chapter 5.

Fuel/air mixture incorrect

Carburettor models

☐ Main jet clogged. Dirt, water or other contaminants can clog the main jets. Clean the fuel tap filter, the in-line filter, the float chamber area, and the jets and carburettor orifices (Chapter 4).

☐ Main jet wrong size. The standard jetting is for sea level atmospheric pressure and oxygen content.

☐ Throttle shaft-to-carburettor body clearance excessive. Refer to Chapter 4 for inspection and part replacement procedures.

☐ Air bleed holes clogged. Remove carburettor and blow out all passages (Chapter 4).

☐ Fuel level too high or too low. Check the float height (Chapter 4).

☐ Carburettor intake manifolds loose. Check for cracks, breaks, tears or loose clamps. Replace the rubber intake manifold joints if split or perished.

Fuel injected models

☐ Fuel injection system malfunction (see Chapter 4).

☐ Fuel injector clogged (see Chapter 4).

☐ Fuel pump or pressure regulator faulty (see Chapter 4).

☐ Throttle body intake manifolds loose. Check for cracks, breaks, tears or loose clamps. Replace the rubber intake manifold joints if split or perished.

All models

☐ Air filter clogged, poorly sealed or missing (Chapter 1).

☐ Air filter housing poorly sealed. Look for cracks, holes or loose clamps and replace or repair defective parts.

☐ Fuel tank breather hose obstructed.

Compression low

☐ Spark plugs loose. Remove the plugs and inspect their threads. Reinstall and tighten to the specified torque (Chapter 1).

☐ Cylinder heads not sufficiently tightened down. If a cylinder head is suspected of being loose, then there's a chance that the gasket and head are damaged if the problem has persisted for any length of time. The head bolts should be tightened to the proper torque in the correct sequence (Chapter 2).

☐ Incorrect valve clearance. This means that the valve is not closing completely and compression pressure is leaking past the valve. Check and adjust the valve clearances (Chapter 1).

☐ Cylinder and/or piston worn. Excessive wear will cause compression pressure to leak past the rings. This is usually accompanied by worn rings as well. A top-end overhaul is necessary (Chapter 2).

☐ Piston rings worn, weak, broken, or sticking. Broken or sticking piston rings usually indicate a lubrication or carburation problem that causes excess carbon deposits or seizures to form on the pistons and rings. Top-end overhaul is necessary (Chapter 2).

☐ Piston ring-to-groove clearance excessive. This is caused by excessive wear of the piston ring lands. Piston replacement is necessary (Chapter 2).

☐ Cylinder head gasket damaged. If a head is allowed to become loose, or if excessive carbon build-up on the piston crown and combustion chamber causes extremely high compression, the head gasket may leak. Retorquing the head is not always sufficient to restore the seal, so gasket replacement is necessary (Chapter 2).

☐ Cylinder head warped. This is caused by overheating or improperly tightened head bolts. Machine shop resurfacing or head replacement is necessary (Chapter 2).

☐ Valve spring broken or weak. Caused by component failure or wear; the springs must be replaced (Chapter 2).

☐ Valve not seating properly. This is caused by a bent valve (from over-revving or improper valve adjustment), burned valve or seat (improper carburation) or an accumulation of carbon deposits on the seat (from carburation or lubrication problems). The valves must be cleaned and/or replaced and the seats serviced if possible (Chapter 2).

3 Poor running or no power at high speed (continued)

Knocking or pinking

- ☐ Carbon build-up in combustion chamber. Use of a fuel additive that will dissolve the adhesive bonding the carbon particles to the crown and chamber is the easiest way to remove the build-up. Otherwise, the cylinder heads will have to be removed and decarbonized (Chapter 2).
- ☐ Incorrect or poor quality fuel. Old or improper grades of fuel can cause detonation. This causes the piston to rattle, thus the knocking or pinging sound. Drain old fuel and always use the recommended fuel grade.
- ☐ Spark plug heat range incorrect. Uncontrolled detonation indicates the plug heat range is too hot. The plug in effect becomes a glow plug, raising cylinder temperatures. Install the proper heat range plug (Chapter 1).
- ☐ Improper air/fuel mixture. This will cause the cylinders to run hot, which leads to detonation. Clogged jets or an air leak can cause this imbalance. See Chapter 4.
- ☐ Faulty knock sensor (fuel injected models – see Chapter 4).

Miscellaneous causes

- ☐ Throttle valve doesn't open fully. Adjust the throttle grip freeplay (Chapter 1).
- ☐ Clutch slipping. May be caused by loose or worn clutch components. Refer to Chapter 2 for clutch overhaul procedures.
- ☐ Timing not advancing – faulty ignition control unit or ECM.
- ☐ Engine oil viscosity too high. Using a heavier oil than the one recommended in Chapter 1 can damage the oil pump or lubrication system and cause drag on the engine.
- ☐ Brakes dragging. Usually caused by debris which has entered the brake piston seals, or from a warped disc or bent axle. Repair as necessary.

4 Overheating

Engine overheats

- ☐ Coolant level low. Check and add coolant (Chapter 1).
- ☐ Leak in cooling system. Check cooling system hoses and radiator for leaks and other damage. Repair or replace parts as necessary (Chapter 3).
- ☐ Thermostat sticking open or closed. Check and replace as described in Chapter 3.
- ☐ Faulty radiator cap. Remove the cap and have it pressure tested.
- ☐ Coolant passages clogged. Have the entire system drained and flushed, then refill with fresh coolant.
- ☐ Water pump defective. Remove the pump and check the components (Chapter 3).
- ☐ Clogged radiator fins. Clean them by blowing compressed air through the fins from the backside.
- ☐ Cooling fan or fan switch fault (Chapter 3).

Firing incorrect

- ☐ Spark plugs fouled, defective or worn out. See Chapter 1 for spark plug maintenance.
- ☐ Incorrect spark plugs.
- ☐ Ignition control unit or ECM defective (Chapter 4 or 5).
- ☐ Pulse generator faulty (Chapter 4 or 5).
- ☐ Faulty ignition HT coils (Chapter 5).

Fuel/air mixture incorrect

Carburettor models

- ☐ Main jet clogged. Dirt, water or other contaminants can clog the main jets. Clean the fuel tap filter, the in-line filter, the float chamber area, and the jets and carburettor orifices (Chapter 4).
- ☐ Main jet wrong size. The standard jetting is for sea level atmospheric pressure and oxygen content.
- ☐ Throttle shaft-to-carburettor body clearance excessive. Refer to Chapter 4 for inspection and part replacement procedures.
- ☐ Air bleed holes clogged. Remove carburettor and blow out all passages (Chapter 4).
- ☐ Fuel level too high or too low. Check the float height (Chapter 4).
- ☐ Carburettor intake manifolds loose. Check for cracks, breaks, tears or loose clamps. Replace the rubber intake manifold joints if split or perished.

Fuel injected models

- ☐ Fuel injection system malfunction (see Chapter 4).
- ☐ Fuel injector clogged (see Chapter 4).
- ☐ Fuel pump or pressure regulator faulty (see Chapter 4).
- ☐ Throttle body intake manifolds loose. Check for cracks, breaks, tears or loose clamps. Replace the rubber intake manifold joints if split or perished.

All models

- ☐ Air filter clogged, poorly sealed or missing (Chapter 1).
- ☐ Air filter housing poorly sealed. Look for cracks, holes or loose clamps and replace or repair defective parts.
- ☐ Fuel tank breather hose obstructed.

Compression too high

- ☐ Carbon build-up in combustion chamber. Use of a fuel additive that will dissolve the adhesive bonding the carbon particles to the piston crown and chamber is the easiest way to remove the build-up. Otherwise, the cylinder heads will have to be removed and decarbonized (Chapter 2).
- ☐ Improperly machined head surface or installation of incorrect gasket during engine assembly.

Engine load excessive

- ☐ Clutch slipping. Can be caused by damaged, loose or worn clutch components. Refer to Chapter 2 for overhaul procedures.
- ☐ Engine oil level too high. The addition of too much oil will cause pressurisation of the crankcase and inefficient engine operation. Check Specifications and drain to proper level (Chapter 1).
- ☐ Engine oil viscosity too high. Using a heavier oil than the one recommended in Chapter 1 can damage the oil pump or lubrication system as well as cause drag on the engine.
- ☐ Brakes dragging. Usually caused by debris which has entered the brake piston seals, or from a warped disc or bent axle. Repair as necessary.

Lubrication inadequate

- ☐ Engine oil level too low. Friction caused by intermittent lack of lubrication or from oil that is overworked can cause overheating. The oil provides a definite cooling function in the engine. Check the oil level (Chapter 1).
- ☐ Poor quality engine oil or incorrect viscosity or type. Oil is rated not only according to viscosity but also according to type. Some oils are not rated high enough for use in this engine. Check the Specifications section and change to the correct oil (Chapter 1).

Miscellaneous causes

- ☐ Modification to exhaust system. Most aftermarket exhaust systems cause the engine to run leaner, which make them run hotter. On V and W (1997 and 1998) models, when installing an accessory exhaust system, always rejet the carburettors.

5 Clutch problems

Clutch slipping

- ☐ Clutch fluid level too high. Check and adjust (see Daily (pre-ride) checks).
- ☐ Friction plates worn or warped. Overhaul the clutch assembly (Chapter 2).
- ☐ Plain plates warped (Chapter 2).
- ☐ Clutch springs broken or weak. Old or heat-damaged (from slipping clutch) springs should be replaced with new ones (Chapter 2).
- ☐ Clutch release mechanism defective. Replace any defective parts (Chapter 2).
- ☐ Clutch centre or housing unevenly worn. This causes improper engagement of the plates. Replace the damaged or worn parts (Chapter 2).

Clutch not disengaging completely

- ☐ Clutch fluid level too high. Check and adjust (see Daily (pre-ride) checks).
- ☐ Air in hydraulic release system. Bleed the system (see Chapter 2).
- ☐ Clutch plates warped or damaged. This will cause clutch drag, which in turn will cause the machine to creep. Overhaul the clutch assembly (Chapter 2).
- ☐ Clutch spring tension uneven. Usually caused by a sagged or broken spring. Check and replace the springs as a set (Chapter 2).
- ☐ Engine oil deteriorated. Old, thin, worn out oil will not provide proper lubrication for the plates, causing the clutch to drag. Replace the oil and filter (Chapter 1).
- ☐ Engine oil viscosity too high. Using a heavier oil than recommended in Chapter 1 can cause the plates to stick together, putting a drag on the engine. Change to the correct weight oil (Chapter 1).
- ☐ Clutch housing guide seized on mainshaft. Lack of lubrication, severe wear or damage can cause the guide to seize on the shaft. Overhaul of the clutch, and perhaps transmission, may be necessary to repair the damage (Chapter 2).
- ☐ Clutch release mechanism defective. Overhaul the master and release (slave) cylinders (Chapter 2). Check the hoses for bulges and leaks.
- ☐ Loose clutch centre nut. Causes housing and centre misalignment putting a drag on the engine. Engagement adjustment continually varies. Overhaul the clutch assembly (Chapter 2).

6 Gear changing problems

Doesn't go into gear or lever doesn't return

- ☐ Clutch not disengaging. See above.
- ☐ Selector fork(s) bent or seized. Often caused by dropping the machine or from lack of lubrication. Overhaul the transmission (Chapter 2).
- ☐ Gear(s) stuck on shaft. Most often caused by a lack of lubrication or excessive wear in transmission bearings and bushings. Overhaul the transmission (Chapter 2).
- ☐ Selector drum binding. Caused by lubrication failure or excessive wear. Replace the drum and bearing (Chapter 2).
- ☐ Gearchange lever return spring weak or broken (Chapter 2).
- ☐ Gearchange lever broken. Splines stripped out of lever or shaft, caused by allowing the lever to get loose or from dropping the machine. Replace necessary parts (Chapter 2).
- ☐ Gearchange mechanism stopper arm broken or worn. Full engagement and rotary movement of shift drum results. Replace the arm (Chapter 2).
- ☐ Stopper arm spring broken. Allows arm to float, causing sporadic shift operation. Replace spring (Chapter 2).

Jumps out of gear

- ☐ Selector fork(s) worn. Overhaul the transmission (Chapter 2).
- ☐ Gear groove(s) worn. Overhaul the transmission (Chapter 2).
- ☐ Gear dogs or dog slots worn or damaged. The gears should be inspected and replaced. No attempt should be made to service the worn parts.

Overshifts

- ☐ Stopper arm spring weak or broken (Chapter 2).
- ☐ Gearchange shaft return spring post broken or distorted (Chapter 2).

7 Abnormal engine noise

Knocking or pinking

- ☐ Carbon build-up in combustion chamber. Use of a fuel additive that will dissolve the adhesive bonding the carbon particles to the piston crown and chamber is the easiest way to remove the build-up. Otherwise, the cylinder head will have to be removed and decarbonized (Chapter 2).
- ☐ Incorrect or poor quality fuel. Old or improper fuel can cause detonation. This causes the pistons to rattle, thus the knocking or pinging sound. Drain the old fuel and always use the recommended grade fuel (Chapter 4).
- ☐ Spark plug heat range incorrect. Uncontrolled detonation indicates that the plug heat range is too hot. The plug in effect becomes a glow plug, raising cylinder temperatures. Install the proper heat range plug (Chapter 1).
- ☐ Improper fuel/air mixture. This will cause the cylinders to run hot and lead to detonation. Clogged jets or an air leak can cause this imbalance. See Chapter 4.
- ☐ Faulty knock sensor (fuel injected models – see Chapter 4).

Piston slap or rattling

- ☐ Cylinder-to-piston clearance excessive. Caused by improper assembly. Inspect and overhaul top-end parts (Chapter 2).
- ☐ Connecting rod bent. Caused by over-revving, trying to start a badly flooded engine or from ingesting a foreign object into the combustion chamber. Replace the damaged parts (Chapter 2).
- ☐ Piston pin or piston pin bore worn or seized from wear or lack of lubrication. Replace damaged parts (Chapter 2).
- ☐ Piston ring(s) worn, broken or sticking. Overhaul the top-end (Chapter 2).
- ☐ Piston seizure damage. Usually from lack of lubrication or overheating. Replace the pistons and bore the cylinders, as necessary (Chapter 2).
- ☐ Connecting rod upper or lower end clearance excessive. Caused by excessive wear or lack of lubrication. Replace worn parts.

Valve noise

- ☐ Incorrect valve clearances. Adjust the clearances by referring to Chapter 1.
- ☐ Valve spring broken or weak. Check and replace weak valve springs (Chapter 2).
- ☐ Camshaft or cylinder head worn or damaged. Lack of lubrication at high rpm is usually the cause of damage. Insufficient oil or failure to change the oil at the recommended intervals are the chief causes. Since there are no replaceable bearings in the head, the head itself will have to be replaced if there is excessive wear or damage (Chapter 2).

Other noise

- ☐ Cylinder head gasket leaking.
- ☐ Exhaust pipe leaking at cylinder head connection. Caused by improper fit of pipe(s) or loose exhaust flange. All exhaust fasteners should be tightened evenly and carefully. Failure to do this will lead to a leak.
- ☐ Crankshaft runout excessive. Caused by a bent crankshaft (from over-revving) or damage from an upper cylinder component failure. Can also be attributed to dropping the machine on either of the crankshaft ends.
- ☐ Engine mounting bolts loose. Tighten all engine mount bolts (Chapter 2).
- ☐ Crankshaft bearings worn (Chapter 2).
- ☐ Camshaft drive gear assembly defective. Replace according to the procedure in Chapter 2.

8 Abnormal driveline noise

Clutch noise

- ☐ Clutch outer drum/friction plate clearance excessive (Chapter 2).
- ☐ Loose or damaged clutch pressure plate and/or bolts (Chapter 2).

Transmission noise

- ☐ Bearings worn. Also includes the possibility that the shafts are worn. Overhaul the transmission (Chapter 2).
- ☐ Gears worn or chipped (Chapter 2).
- ☐ Metal chips jammed in gear teeth. Probably pieces from a broken clutch, gear or shift mechanism that were picked up by the gears. This will cause early bearing failure (Chapter 2).
- ☐ Engine oil level too low. Causes a howl from transmission. Also affects engine power and clutch operation (Chapter 1).

Final drive noise

- ☐ Chain not adjusted properly (Chapter 1).
- ☐ Front or rear sprocket loose. Tighten fasteners (Chapter 6).
- ☐ Sprockets worn. Renew sprockets (Chapter 6).
- ☐ Rear sprocket warped. Renew sprockets (Chapter 6).
- ☐ Rubber dampers in rear wheel hub worn. Check and renew (Chapter 7).

9 Abnormal frame and suspension noise

Front end noise

☐ Low fluid level or improper viscosity oil in forks. This can sound like spurting and is usually accompanied by irregular fork action (Chapter 6).

☐ Spring weak or broken. Makes a clicking or scraping sound. Fork oil, when drained, will have a lot of metal particles in it (Chapter 6).

☐ Steering head bearings loose or damaged. Clicks when braking. Check and adjust or replace as necessary (Chapters 1 and 6).

☐ Fork yokes loose. Make sure all clamp pinch bolts are tightened to the specified torque (Chapter 6).

☐ Fork tube bent. Good possibility if machine has been dropped. Replace tube with a new one (Chapter 6).

☐ Front axle bolt or axle clamp bolts loose. Tighten them to the specified torque (Chapter 7).

☐ Loose or worn wheel bearings. Check and replace as needed (Chapter 7).

Shock absorber noise

☐ Fluid level incorrect. Indicates a leak caused by defective seal. Shock will be covered with oil. Replace shock or seek advice on repair from a Honda dealer (Chapter 6).

☐ Defective shock absorber with internal damage. This is in the body of the shock and can't be remedied. The shock must be replaced with a new one (Chapter 6).

☐ Bent or damaged shock body. Replace the shock with a new one (Chapter 6).

☐ Loose or worn suspension linkage or swingarm components. Check and replace as necessary (Chapter 6).

Brake noise

☐ Squeal caused by pad shim not installed or positioned correctly (where fitted) (Chapter 7).

☐ Squeal caused by dust on brake pads. Usually found in combination with glazed pads. Clean using brake cleaning solvent (Chapter 7).

☐ Contamination of brake pads. Oil, brake fluid or dirt causing brake to chatter or squeal. Clean or replace pads (Chapter 7).

☐ Pads glazed. Caused by excessive heat from prolonged use or from contamination. Do not use sandpaper, emery cloth, carborundum cloth or any other abrasive to roughen the pad surfaces as abrasives will stay in the pad material and damage the disc. A very fine flat file can be used, but pad replacement is suggested as a cure (Chapter 7).

☐ Disc warped. Can cause a chattering, clicking or intermittent squeal. Usually accompanied by a pulsating lever and uneven braking. Replace the disc (Chapter 7).

☐ Loose or worn wheel bearings. Check and replace as needed (Chapter 7).

10 Oil pressure warning light comes on

Engine lubrication system

☐ Engine oil pump defective, blocked oil strainer gauze or failed relief valve. Carry out oil pressure check (Chapter 2).

☐ Engine oil level low. Inspect for leak or other problem causing low oil level and add recommended oil (Chapter 1).

☐ Engine oil viscosity too low. Very old, thin oil or an improper weight of oil used in the engine. Change to correct oil (Chapter 1).

☐ Camshaft or journals worn. Excessive wear causing drop in oil pressure. Replace cam and/or cylinder head. Abnormal wear could be caused by oil starvation at high rpm from low oil level or improper weight or type of oil (Chapter 1).

☐ Crankshaft and/or bearings worn. Same problems as above. Check and replace crankshaft and/or bearings (Chapter 2).

Electrical system

☐ Oil pressure switch defective. Check the switch according to the procedure in Chapter 9. Replace it if it is defective.

☐ Oil pressure indicator light circuit defective. Check for pinched, shorted, disconnected or damaged wiring (Chapter 9).

11 Excessive exhaust smoke

White smoke

- [ ] Piston oil ring worn. The ring may be broken or damaged, causing oil from the crankcase to be pulled past the piston into the combustion chamber. Replace the rings with new ones (Chapter 2).
- [ ] Cylinders worn, cracked, or scored. Caused by overheating or oil starvation. The cylinders will have to be rebored and new pistons installed.
- [ ] Valve oil seal damaged or worn. Replace oil seals with new ones (Chapter 2).
- [ ] Valve guide worn. Perform a complete valve job (Chapter 2).
- [ ] Engine oil level too high, which causes the oil to be forced past the rings. Drain oil to the proper level (Chapter 1).
- [ ] Head gasket broken between oil return and cylinder. Causes oil to be pulled into the combustion chamber. Replace the head gasket and check the head for warpage (Chapter 2).
- [ ] Abnormal crankcase pressurisation, which forces oil past the rings. Clogged breather is usually the cause.

Black smoke

Carburettor models

- [ ] Main jet too large or loose. Compare the jet size to the Specifications (Chapter 4).
- [ ] Choke cable or linkage shaft stuck, causing fuel to be pulled through choke circuit (Chapter 4).

- [ ] Fuel level too high. Check and adjust the float height(s) as necessary (Chapter 4).
- [ ] Float needle valve held off needle seat. Clean the float chambers and fuel line and replace the needles and seats if necessary (Chapter 4).
- [ ] Air filter clogged (Chapter 1).

Fuel injected models

- [ ] Fuel injection system malfunction (see Chapter 4).
- [ ] Air filter clogged (Chapter 1).

Brown smoke

Carburettor models

- [ ] Main jet too small or clogged. Lean condition caused by wrong size main jet or by a restricted orifice. Clean float chambers and jets and compare jet size to Specifications (Chapter 4).
- [ ] Fuel flow insufficient. Float needle valve stuck closed due to chemical reaction with old fuel. Float height incorrect. Restricted fuel line. Clean line and float chamber and adjust floats if necessary.
- [ ] Carburettor intake manifold clamps loose (Chapter 4).
- [ ] Air filter poorly sealed or not installed (Chapter 1).

Fuel injected models

- [ ] Fuel injection system malfunction (see Chapter 4).
- [ ] Faulty fuel pump or pressure regulator (see Chapter 4).
- [ ] Air filter poorly sealed or not installed (Chapter 1).

12 Poor handling or stability

Handlebar hard to turn

- [ ] Steering head bearing adjuster nut too tight. Check adjustment as described in Chapter 1.
- [ ] Bearings damaged. Roughness can be felt as the bars are turned from side-to-side. Replace bearings and races (Chapter 6).
- [ ] Races dented or worn. Denting results from wear in only one position (e.g., straight ahead), from a collision or hitting a pothole or from dropping the machine. Replace races and bearings (Chapter 6
- [ ] Steering stem lubrication inadequate. Causes are grease getting hard from age or being washed out by high pressure car washes. Disassemble steering head and repack bearings (Chapter 6).
- [ ] Steering stem bent. Caused by a collision, hitting a pothole or by dropping the machine. Replace damaged part. Don't try to straighten the steering stem (Chapter 6).
- [ ] Front tyre air pressure too low (Chapter 1).

Handlebar shakes or vibrates excessively

- [ ] Tyres worn or out of balance (Chapter 7).
- [ ] Swingarm bearings worn. Replace worn bearings (Chapter 6).
- [ ] Wheel rim(s) warped or damaged. Inspect wheels for runout (Chapter 7).
- [ ] Wheel bearings worn. Worn front or rear wheel bearings can cause poor tracking. Worn front bearings will cause wobble (Chapter 7).
- [ ] Handlebar clamp bolts loose (Chapter 6).
- [ ] Fork yoke bolts loose. Tighten them to the specified torque (Chapter 6).
- [ ] Engine mounting bolts loose. Will cause excessive vibration with increased engine rpm (Chapter 2).

Handlebar pulls to one side

- [ ] Frame bent. Definitely suspect this if the machine has been dropped. May or may not be accompanied by cracking near the bend. Replace the frame (Chapter 6).
- [ ] Wheels out of alignment. Caused by improper location of axle spacers or from bent steering stem or frame (Chapter 6).
- [ ] Swingarm bent or twisted. Caused by age (metal fatigue) or impact damage. Replace the arm (Chapter 6).
- [ ] Steering stem bent. Caused by impact damage or by dropping the motorcycle. Replace the steering stem (Chapter 6).
- [ ] Fork tube bent. Disassemble the forks and replace the damaged parts (Chapter 6).
- [ ] Fork oil level uneven. Check and add or drain as necessary (Chapter 6).

Poor shock absorbing qualities

- [ ] Too hard:
  - a) Fork oil level excessive (Chapter 6).
  - b) Fork oil viscosity too high. Use a lighter oil (see the Specifications in Chapter 6).
  - c) Fork tube bent. Causes a harsh, sticking feeling (Chapter 6).
  - d) Shock shaft or body bent or damaged (Chapter 6).
  - e) Fork internal damage (Chapter 6).
  - f) Shock internal damage.
  - g) Tyre pressure too high (Chapter 1).
- [ ] Too soft:
  - a) Fork or shock oil insufficient and/or leaking (Chapter 6).
  - b) Fork oil level too low (Chapter 6).
  - c) Fork oil viscosity too light (Chapter 6).
  - d) Fork springs weak or broken (Chapter 6).
  - e) Shock internal damage or leakage (Chapter 6).

13 Braking problems

Brakes are spongy, or lack power

☐ Air in brake line. Caused by inattention to master cylinder fluid level or by leakage. Locate problem and bleed brakes (Chapter 7).
☐ Pad or disc worn (Chapters 1 and 7).
☐ Brake fluid leak. See paragraph 1.
☐ Contaminated pads. Caused by contamination with oil, grease, brake fluid, etc. Clean or replace pads. Clean disc thoroughly with brake cleaner (Chapter 7).
☐ Brake fluid deteriorated. Fluid is old or contaminated. Drain system, replenish with new fluid and bleed the system (Chapter 7).
☐ Master cylinder internal parts worn or damaged causing fluid to bypass (Chapter 7).
☐ Master cylinder bore scratched by foreign material or broken spring. Repair or replace master cylinder (Chapter 7).
☐ Disc warped. Replace disc (Chapter 7).
☐ Fault in Dual-CBS system – could be the delay valve or the proportional control valve (see Chapter 7).

Brake lever or pedal pulsates

☐ Disc warped. Replace disc (Chapter 7).
☐ Axle bent. Replace axle (Chapter 7).

☐ Brake caliper bolts loose (Chapter 7).
☐ Brake caliper sliders damaged or sticking, causing caliper to bind. Lubricate the sliders or replace them if they are corroded or bent (Chapter 7).
☐ Wheel warped or otherwise damaged (Chapter 7).
☐ Wheel bearings damaged or worn (Chapter 7).

Brakes drag

☐ Master cylinder piston seized. Caused by wear or damage to piston or cylinder bore (Chapter 7).
☐ Lever balky or stuck. Check pivot and lubricate (Chapter 7).
☐ Brake caliper binds on bracket. Caused by inadequate lubrication or damage to caliper sliders (Chapter 7).
☐ Brake caliper piston seized in bore. Caused by wear or ingestion of dirt past deteriorated seal (Chapter 7).
☐ Brake pad damaged. Pad material separated from backing plate. Usually caused by faulty manufacturing process or from contact with chemicals. Replace pads (Chapter 7).
☐ Pads improperly installed (Chapter 7).
☐ Fault in Dual-CBS system – could be the delay valve or the proportional control valve (see Chapter 7).

14 Electrical problems

Battery dead or weak

☐ Battery faulty. Caused by sulphated plates which are shorted through sedimentation. Also, broken battery terminal making only occasional contact (Chapter 9).
☐ Battery cables making poor contact (Chapter 9).
☐ Load excessive. Caused by addition of high wattage lights or other electrical accessories.
☐ Ignition (main) switch defective. Switch either grounds (earths) internally or fails to shut off system. Replace the switch (Chapter 9).
☐ Regulator/rectifier defective (Chapter 9).

☐ Alternator stator coil open or shorted (Chapter 9).
☐ Wiring faulty. Wiring grounded (earthed) or connections loose in ignition, charging or lighting circuits (Chapter 9).

Battery overcharged

☐ Regulator/rectifier defective. Overcharging is noticed when battery gets excessively warm (Chapter 9).
☐ Battery defective. Replace battery with a new one (Chapter 9).
☐ Battery amperage too low, wrong type or size. Install manufacturer's specified amp-hour battery to handle charging load (Chapter 9).

Checking engine compression

● Low compression will result in exhaust smoke, heavy oil consumption, poor starting and poor performance. A compression test will provide useful information about an engine's condition and if performed regularly, can give warning of trouble before any other symptoms become apparent.

● A compression gauge will be required, along with an adapter to suit the spark plug hole thread size. Note that the screw-in type gauge/adapter set up is preferable to the rubber cone type.

● Before carrying out the test, first check the valve clearances as described in Chapter 1.

1 Run the engine until it reaches normal operating temperature, then stop it and remove the spark plug(s), taking care not to scald your hands on the hot components.

2 Install the gauge adapter and compression gauge in No. 1 cylinder spark plug hole **(see illustration 1)**.

Screw the compression gauge adapter into the spark plug hole, then screw the gauge into the adapter

3 On kickstart-equipped motorcycles, make sure the ignition switch is OFF, then open the throttle fully and kick the engine over a couple of times until the gauge reading stabilises.

4 On motorcycles with electric start only, the procedure will differ depending on the nature of the ignition system. Flick the engine kill switch (engine stop switch) to OFF and turn the ignition switch ON; open the throttle fully and crank the engine over on the starter motor for a couple of revolutions until the gauge reading stabilises. If the starter will not operate with the kill switch OFF, turn the ignition switch OFF and refer to the next paragraph.

5 Install the plugs back in their caps and arrange the plug electrodes so that their metal bodies are earthed (grounded) against the cylinder head; this is essential to prevent damage to the engine management system **(see illustration 2)**. Position the plugs well away from the plug holes otherwise there is a

All spark plugs must be earthed (grounded) against the cylinder head

risk of atomised fuel escaping from the plug holes and igniting. As a safety precaution, cover the cylinder head with rag. Also on fuel injected models disconnect the fuel tank wiring connector (see illustration 2.15a in Chapter 4). Turn the ignition switch and kill switch ON, open the throttle fully and crank the engine over on the starter motor for a couple of revolutions until the gauge reading stabilises.

6 After one or two revolutions the pressure should build up to a maximum figure and then stabilise. Take a note of this reading and on multi-cylinder engines repeat the test on the remaining cylinders.

7 The correct pressures are given in Chapter 1. If the results fall within the specified range and on multi-cylinder engines all are relatively equal, the engine is in good condition. If there is a marked difference between the readings, or if the readings are lower than specified, inspection of the top-end components will be required.

8 Low compression pressure may be due to worn cylinder bores, pistons or rings, failure of the cylinder head gasket, worn valve seals, or poor valve seating.

9 To distinguish between cylinder/piston wear and valve leakage, pour a small quantity of oil into the bore to temporarily seal the piston rings, then repeat the compression tests **(see illustration 3)**. If the readings show

Bores can be temporarily sealed with a squirt of motor oil

a noticeable increase in pressure this confirms that the cylinder bore, piston, or rings are worn. If, however, no change is indicated, the cylinder head gasket or valves should be examined.

10 High compression pressure indicates excessive carbon build-up in the combustion chamber and on the piston crown. If this is the case the cylinder head should be removed and the deposits removed. Note that excessive carbon build-up is less likely with the used on modern fuels.

Checking battery open-circuit voltage

 Warning: The gases produced by the battery are explosive - never smoke or create any sparks in the vicinity of the battery. Never allow the electrolyte to contact your skin or clothing - if it does, wash it off and seek immediate medical attention.

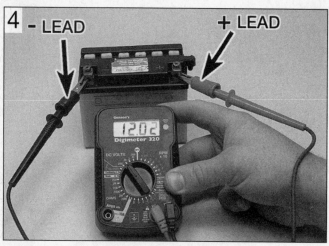

4 - LEAD   + LEAD

Measuring open-circuit battery voltage

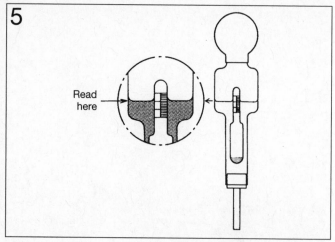

5

Read here

Float-type hydrometer for measuring battery specific gravity

● Before any electrical fault is investigated the battery should be checked.

● You'll need a dc voltmeter or multimeter to check battery voltage. Check that the leads are inserted in the correct terminals on the meter, red lead to positive (+ve), black lead to negative (-ve). Incorrect connections can damage the meter.

● A sound fully-charged 12 volt battery should produce between 12.3 and 12.6 volts across its terminals (12.8 volts for a maintenance-free battery). On machines with a 6 volt battery, voltage should be between 6.1 and 6.3 volts.

1 Set a multimeter to the 0 to 20 volts dc range and connect its probes across the battery terminals. Connect the meter's positive (+ve) probe, usually red, to the battery positive (+ve) terminal, followed by the meter's negative (-ve) probe, usually black, to the battery negative terminal (-ve) **(see illustration 4)**.

2 If battery voltage is low (below 10 volts on a 12 volt battery or below 4 volts on a six volt battery), charge the battery and test the voltage again. If the battery repeatedly goes flat, investigate the motorcycle's charging system.

Checking battery specific gravity (SG)

⚠️ *Warning: The gases produced by the battery are explosive - never smoke or create any sparks in the vicinity of the battery. Never allow the electrolyte to contact your skin or clothing - if it does, wash it off and seek immediate medical attention.*

● The specific gravity check gives an indication of a battery's state of charge.

● A hydrometer is used for measuring specific gravity. Make sure you purchase one

which has a small enough hose to insert in the aperture of a motorcycle battery.

● Specific gravity is simply a measure of the electrolyte's density compared with that of water. Water has an SG of 1.000 and fully-charged battery electrolyte is about 26% heavier, at 1.260.

● Specific gravity checks are not possible on maintenance-free batteries. Testing the open-circuit voltage is the only means of determining their state of charge.

1 To measure SG, remove the battery from the motorcycle and remove the first cell cap. Draw

some electrolyte into the hydrometer and note the reading **(see illustration 5)**. Return the electrolyte to the cell and install the cap.

2 The reading should be in the region of 1.260 to 1.280. If SG is below 1.200 the battery needs charging. Note that SG will vary with temperature; it should be measured at 20°C (68°F). Add 0.007 to the reading for every 10°C above 20°C, and subtract 0.007 from the reading for every 10°C below 20°C. Add 0.004 to the reading for every 10°F above 68°F, and subtract 0.004 from the reading for every 10°F below 68°F.

3 When the check is complete, rinse the hydrometer thoroughly with clean water.

Checking for continuity

● The term continuity describes the uninterrupted flow of electricity through an electrical circuit. A continuity check will determine whether an **open-circuit** situation exists.

● Continuity can be checked with an ohmmeter, multimeter, continuity tester or battery and bulb test circuit **(see illustrations 6, 7 and 8)**.

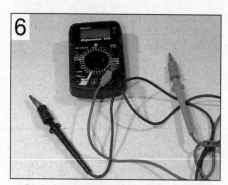

6

Digital multimeter can be used for all electrical tests

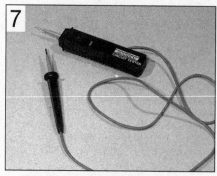

7

Battery-powered continuity tester

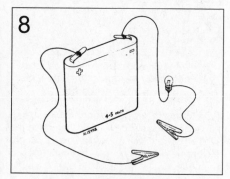

8

Battery and bulb test circuit

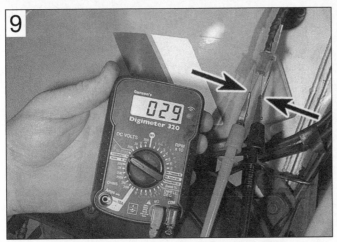

Continuity check of front brake light switch using a meter - note split pins used to access connector terminals

Continuity check of rear brake light switch using a continuity tester

● All of these instruments are self-powered by a battery, therefore the checks are made with the ignition OFF.

● As a safety precaution, always disconnect the battery negative (-ve) lead before making checks, particularly if ignition switch checks are being made.

● If using a meter, select the appropriate ohms scale and check that the meter reads infinity (∞). Touch the meter probes together and check that meter reads zero; where necessary adjust the meter so that it reads zero.

● After using a meter, always switch it OFF to conserve its battery.

Switch checks

1 If a switch is at fault, trace its wiring up to the wiring connectors. Separate the wire connectors and inspect them for security and condition. A build-up of dirt or corrosion here will most likely be the cause of the problem - clean up and apply a water dispersant such as WD40.

2 If using a test meter, set the meter to the ohms x 10 scale and connect its probes across the wires from the switch (see illustration 9). Simple ON/OFF type switches, such as brake light switches, only have two wires whereas combination switches, like the

ignition switch, have many internal links. Study the wiring diagram to ensure that you are connecting across the correct pair of wires. Continuity (low or no measurable resistance - 0 ohms) should be indicated with the switch ON and no continuity (high resistance) with it OFF.

3 Note that the polarity of the test probes doesn't matter for continuity checks, although care should be taken to follow specific test procedures if a diode or solid-state component is being checked.

4 A continuity tester or battery and bulb circuit can be used in the same way. Connect its probes as described above (see illustration 10). The light should come on to indicate continuity in the ON switch position, but should extinguish in the OFF position.

Wiring checks

● Many electrical faults are caused by damaged wiring, often due to incorrect routing or chaffing on frame components.

● Loose, wet or corroded wire connectors can also be the cause of electrical problems, especially in exposed locations.

1 A continuity check can be made on a single length of wire by disconnecting it at each end and connecting a meter or continuity tester

across both ends of the wire (see illustration 11).

2 Continuity (low or no resistance - 0 ohms) should be indicated if the wire is good. If no continuity (high resistance) is shown, suspect a broken wire.

Checking for voltage

● A voltage check can determine whether current is reaching a component.

● Voltage can be checked with a dc voltmeter, multimeter set on the dc volts scale, test light or buzzer (see illustrations 12 and 13). A meter has the advantage of being able to measure actual voltage.

● When using a meter, check that its leads are inserted in the correct terminals on the meter, red to positive (+ve), black to negative (-ve). Incorrect connections can damage the meter.

● A voltmeter (or multimeter set to the dc volts scale) should always be connected in parallel (across the load). Connecting it in series will not harm the meter, but the reading will not be meaningful.

● Voltage checks are made with the ignition ON.

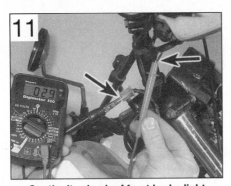

Continuity check of front brake light switch sub-harness

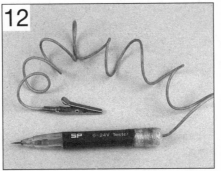

A simple test light can be used for voltage checks

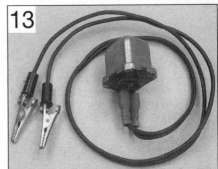

A buzzer is useful for voltage checks

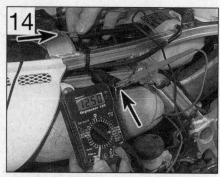

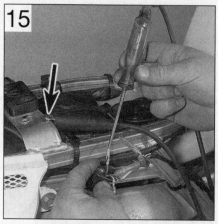

Checking for voltage at the rear brake light power supply wire using a meter . . .

1 First identify the relevant wiring circuit by referring to the wiring diagram at the end of this manual. If other electrical components share the same power supply (ie are fed from the same fuse), take note whether they are working correctly - this is useful information in deciding where to start checking the circuit.
2 If using a meter, check first that the meter leads are plugged into the correct terminals on the meter (see above). Set the meter to the dc volts function, at a range suitable for the battery voltage. Connect the meter red probe (+ve) to the power supply wire and the black probe to a good metal earth (ground) on the motorcycle's frame or directly to the battery negative (-ve) terminal **(see illustration 14)**. Battery voltage should be shown on the meter

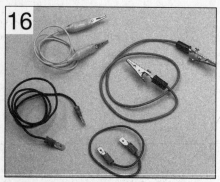

A selection of jumper wires for making earth (ground) checks

. . . or a test light - note the earth connection to the frame (arrow)

with the ignition switched ON.
3 If using a test light or buzzer, connect its positive (+ve) probe to the power supply terminal and its negative (-ve) probe to a good earth (ground) on the motorcycle's frame or directly to the battery negative (-ve) terminal **(see illustration 15)**. With the ignition ON, the test light should illuminate or the buzzer sound.
4 If no voltage is indicated, work back towards the fuse continuing to check for voltage. When you reach a point where there is voltage, you know the problem lies between that point and your last check point.

Checking the earth (ground)

● Earth connections are made either directly to the engine or frame (such as sensors, neutral switch etc. which only have a positive feed) or by a separate wire into the earth circuit of the wiring harness. Alternatively a short earth wire is sometimes run directly from the component to the motorcycle's frame.
● Corrosion is often the cause of a poor earth connection.
● If total failure is experienced, check the security of the main earth lead from the

negative (-ve) terminal of the battery and also the main earth (ground) point on the wiring harness. If corroded, dismantle the connection and clean all surfaces back to bare metal.
1 To check the earth on a component, use an insulated jumper wire to temporarily bypass its earth connection **(see illustration 16)**. Connect one end of the jumper wire between the earth terminal or metal body of the component and the other end to the motorcycle's frame.
2 If the circuit works with the jumper wire installed, the original earth circuit is faulty. Check the wiring for open-circuits or poor connections. Clean up direct earth connections, removing all traces of corrosion and remake the joint. Apply petroleum jelly to the joint to prevent future corrosion.

Tracing a short-circuit

● A short-circuit occurs where current shorts to earth (ground) bypassing the circuit components. This usually results in a blown fuse.

● A short-circuit is most likely to occur where the insulation has worn through due to wiring chafing on a component, allowing a direct path to earth (ground) on the frame.

1 Remove any bodypanels necessary to access the circuit wiring.
2 Check that all electrical switches in the circuit are OFF, then remove the circuit fuse and connect a test light, buzzer or voltmeter (set to the dc scale) across the fuse terminals. No voltage should be shown.
3 Move the wiring from side to side whilst observing the test light or meter. When the test light comes on, buzzer sounds or meter shows voltage, you have found the cause of the short. It will usually shown up as damaged or burned insulation.
4 Note that the same test can be performed on each component in the circuit, even the switch.

A

ABS (Anti-lock braking system) A system, usually electronically controlled, that senses incipient wheel lockup during braking and relieves hydraulic pressure at wheel which is about to skid.
Aftermarket Components suitable for the motorcycle, but not produced by the motorcycle manufacturer.
Allen key A hexagonal wrench which fits into a recessed hexagonal hole.
Alternating current (ac) Current produced by an alternator. Requires converting to direct current by a rectifier for charging purposes.
Alternator Converts mechanical energy from the engine into electrical energy to charge the battery and power the electrical system.
Ampere (amp) A unit of measurement for the flow of electrical current. Current = Volts ÷ Ohms.
Ampere-hour (Ah) Measure of battery capacity.
Angle-tightening A torque expressed in degrees. Often follows a conventional tightening torque for cylinder head or main bearing fasteners **(see illustration)**.

Angle-tightening cylinder head bolts

Antifreeze A substance (usually ethylene glycol) mixed with water, and added to the cooling system, to prevent freezing of the coolant in winter. Antifreeze also contains chemicals to inhibit corrosion and the formation of rust and other deposits that would tend to clog the radiator and coolant passages and reduce cooling efficiency.
Anti-dive System attached to the fork lower leg (slider) to prevent fork dive when braking hard.
Anti-seize compound A coating that reduces the risk of seizing on fasteners that are subjected to high temperatures, such as exhaust clamp bolts and nuts.
API American Petroleum Institute. A quality standard for 4-stroke motor oils.
Asbestos A natural fibrous mineral with great heat resistance, commonly used in the composition of brake friction materials. Asbestos is a health hazard and the dust created by brake systems should never be inhaled or ingested.
ATF Automatic Transmission Fluid. Often used in front forks.
ATU Automatic Timing Unit. Mechanical device for advancing the ignition timing on early engines.
ATV All Terrain Vehicle. Often called a Quad.
Axial play Side-to-side movement.
Axle A shaft on which a wheel revolves. Also known as a spindle.

B

Backlash The amount of movement between meshed components when one component is held still. Usually applies to gear teeth.
Ball bearing A bearing consisting of a hardened inner and outer race with hardened steel balls between the two races.
Bearings Used between two working surfaces to prevent wear of the components and a build-up of heat. Four types of bearing are commonly used on motorcycles: plain shell bearings, ball bearings, tapered roller bearings and needle roller bearings.
Bevel gears Used to turn the drive through 90°. Typical applications are shaft final drive and camshaft drive **(see illustration)**.

Bevel gears are used to turn the drive through 90°

BHP Brake Horsepower. The British measurement for engine power output. Power output is now usually expressed in kilowatts (kW).
Bias-belted tyre Similar construction to radial tyre, but with outer belt running at an angle to the wheel rim.
Big-end bearing The bearing in the end of the connecting rod that's attached to the crankshaft.
Bleeding The process of removing air from an hydraulic system via a bleed nipple or bleed screw.
Bottom-end A description of an engine's crankcase components and all components contained there-in.
BTDC Before Top Dead Centre in terms of piston position. Ignition timing is often expressed in terms of degrees or millimetres BTDC.
Bush A cylindrical metal or rubber component used between two moving parts.
Burr Rough edge left on a component after machining or as a result of excessive wear.

C

Cam chain The chain which takes drive from the crankshaft to the camshaft(s).
Canister The main component in an evaporative emission control system (California market only); contains activated charcoal granules to trap vapours from the fuel system rather than allowing them to vent to the atmosphere.
Castellated Resembling the parapets along the top of a castle wall. For example, a castellated wheel axle or spindle nut.
Catalytic converter A device in the exhaust system of some machines which converts certain pollutants in the exhaust gases into less harmful substances.
Charging system Description of the components which charge the battery, ie the alternator, rectifier and regulator.
Circlip A ring-shaped clip used to prevent endwise movement of cylindrical parts and shafts. An internal circlip is installed in a groove in a housing; an external circlip fits into a groove on the outside of a cylindrical piece such as a shaft. Also known as a snap-ring.
Clearance The amount of space between two parts. For example, between a piston and a cylinder, between a bearing and a journal, etc.
Coil spring A spiral of elastic steel found in various sizes throughout a vehicle, for example as a springing medium in the suspension and in the valve train.
Compression Reduction in volume, and increase in pressure and temperature, of a gas, caused by squeezing it into a smaller space.
Compression damping Controls the speed the suspension compresses when hitting a bump.
Compression ratio The relationship between cylinder volume when the piston is at top dead centre and cylinder volume when the piston is at bottom dead centre.
Continuity The uninterrupted path in the flow of electricity. Little or no measurable resistance.
Continuity tester Self-powered bleeper or test light which indicates continuity.
Cp Candlepower. Bulb rating commonly found on US motorcycles.
Crossply tyre Tyre plies arranged in a criss-cross pattern. Usually four or six plies used, hence 4PR or 6PR in tyre size codes.
Cush drive Rubber damper segments fitted between the rear wheel and final drive sprocket to absorb transmission shocks **(see illustration)**.

Cush drive rubbers dampen out transmission shocks

D

Degree disc Calibrated disc for measuring piston position. Expressed in degrees.
Dial gauge Clock-type gauge with adapters for measuring runout and piston position. Expressed in mm or inches.
Diaphragm The rubber membrane in a master cylinder or carburettor which seals the upper chamber.
Diaphragm spring A single sprung plate often used in clutches.
Direct current (dc) Current produced by a dc generator.

Decarbonisation The process of removing carbon deposits - typically from the combustion chamber, valves and exhaust port/system.

Detonation Destructive and damaging explosion of fuel/air mixture in combustion chamber instead of controlled burning.

Diode An electrical valve which only allows current to flow in one direction. Commonly used in rectifiers and starter interlock systems.

Disc valve (or rotary valve) A induction system used on some two-stroke engines.

Double-overhead camshaft (DOHC) An engine that uses two overhead camshafts, one for the intake valves and one for the exhaust valves.

Drivebelt A toothed belt used to transmit drive to the rear wheel on some motorcycles. A drivebelt has also been used to drive the camshafts. Drivebelts are usually made of Kevlar.

Driveshaft Any shaft used to transmit motion. Commonly used when referring to the final driveshaft on shaft drive motorcycles.

E

Earth return The return path of an electrical circuit, utilising the motorcycle's frame.

ECU (Electronic Control Unit) A computer which controls (for instance) an ignition system, or an anti-lock braking system.

EGO Exhaust Gas Oxygen sensor. Sometimes called a Lambda sensor.

Electrolyte The fluid in a lead-acid battery.

EMS (Engine Management System) A computer controlled system which manages the fuel injection and the ignition systems in an integrated fashion.

Endfloat The amount of lengthways movement between two parts. As applied to a crankshaft, the distance that the crankshaft can move side-to-side in the crankcase.

Endless chain A chain having no joining link. Common use for cam chains and final drive chains.

EP (Extreme Pressure) Oil type used in locations where high loads are applied, such as between gear teeth.

Evaporative emission control system Describes a charcoal filled canister which stores fuel vapours from the tank rather than allowing them to vent to the atmosphere. Usually only fitted to California models and referred to as an EVAP system.

Expansion chamber Section of two-stroke engine exhaust system so designed to improve engine efficiency and boost power.

F

Feeler blade or gauge A thin strip or blade of hardened steel, ground to an exact thickness, used to check or measure clearances between parts.

Final drive Description of the drive from the transmission to the rear wheel. Usually by chain or shaft, but sometimes by belt.

Firing order The order in which the engine cylinders fire, or deliver their power strokes, beginning with the number one cylinder.

Flooding Term used to describe a high fuel level in the carburettor float chambers, leading to fuel overflow. Also refers to excess fuel in the combustion chamber due to incorrect starting technique.

Free length The no-load state of a component when measured. Clutch, valve and fork spring lengths are measured at rest, without any preload.

Freeplay The amount of travel before any action takes place. The looseness in a linkage, or an assembly of parts, between the initial application of force and actual movement. For example, the distance the rear brake pedal moves before the rear brake is actuated.

Fuel injection The fuel/air mixture is metered electronically and directed into the engine intake ports (indirect injection) or into the cylinders (direct injection). Sensors supply information on engine speed and conditions.

Fuel/air mixture The charge of fuel and air going into the engine. See **Stoichiometric ratio**.

Fuse An electrical device which protects a circuit against accidental overload. The typical fuse contains a soft piece of metal which is calibrated to melt at a predetermined current flow (expressed as amps) and break the circuit.

G

Gap The distance the spark must travel in jumping from the centre electrode to the side electrode in a spark plug. Also refers to the distance between the ignition rotor and the pickup coil in an electronic ignition system.

Gasket Any thin, soft material - usually cork, cardboard, asbestos or soft metal - installed between two metal surfaces to ensure a good seal. For instance, the cylinder head gasket seals the joint between the block and the cylinder head.

Gauge An instrument panel display used to monitor engine conditions. A gauge with a movable pointer on a dial or a fixed scale is an analogue gauge. A gauge with a numerical readout is called a digital gauge.

Gear ratios The drive ratio of a pair of gears in a gearbox, calculated on their number of teeth.

Glaze-busting see **Honing**

Grinding Process for renovating the valve face and valve seat contact area in the cylinder head.

Gudgeon pin The shaft which connects the connecting rod small-end with the piston. Often called a piston pin or wrist pin.

H

Helical gears Gear teeth are slightly curved and produce less gear noise that straight-cut gears. Often used for primary drives.

Installing a Helicoil thread insert in a cylinder head

Helicoil A thread insert repair system. Commonly used as a repair for stripped spark plug threads **(see illustration)**.

Honing A process used to break down the glaze on a cylinder bore (also called glaze-busting). Can also be carried out to roughen a rebored cylinder to aid ring bedding-in.

HT (High Tension) Description of the electrical circuit from the secondary winding of the ignition coil to the spark plug.

Hydraulic A liquid filled system used to transmit pressure from one component to another. Common uses on motorcycles are brakes and clutches.

Hydrometer An instrument for measuring the specific gravity of a lead-acid battery.

Hygroscopic Water absorbing. In motorcycle applications, braking efficiency will be reduced if DOT 3 or 4 hydraulic fluid absorbs water from the air - care must be taken to keep new brake fluid in tightly sealed containers.

I

lbf ft Pounds-force feet. An imperial unit of torque. Sometimes written as ft-lbs.

lbf in Pound-force inch. An imperial unit of torque, applied to components where a very low torque is required. Sometimes written as in-lbs.

IC Abbreviation for Integrated Circuit.

Ignition advance Means of increasing the timing of the spark at higher engine speeds. Done by mechanical means (ATU) on early engines or electronically by the ignition control unit on later engines.

Ignition timing The moment at which the spark plug fires, expressed in the number of crankshaft degrees before the piston reaches the top of its stroke, or in the number of millimetres before the piston reaches the top of its stroke.

Infinity (∞) Description of an open-circuit electrical state, where no continuity exists.

Inverted forks (upside down forks) The sliders or lower legs are held in the yokes and the fork tubes or stanchions are connected to the wheel axle (spindle). Less unsprung weight and stiffer construction than conventional forks.

J

JASO Quality standard for 2-stroke oils.

Joule The unit of electrical energy.

Journal The bearing surface of a shaft.

K

Kickstart Mechanical means of turning the engine over for starting purposes. Only usually fitted to mopeds, small capacity motorcycles and off-road motorcycles.

Kill switch Handebar-mounted switch for emergency ignition cut-out. Cuts the ignition circuit on all models, and additionally prevent starter motor operation on others.

km Symbol for kilometre.

kmh Abbreviation for kilometres per hour.

L

Lambda (λ) sensor A sensor fitted in the exhaust system to measure the exhaust gas oxygen content (excess air factor).

Lapping see **Grinding**.
LCD Abbreviation for Liquid Crystal Display.
LED Abbreviation for Light Emitting Diode.
Liner A steel cylinder liner inserted in a aluminium alloy cylinder block.
Locknut A nut used to lock an adjustment nut, or other threaded component, in place.
Lockstops The lugs on the lower triple clamp (yoke) which abut those on the frame, preventing handlebar-to-fuel tank contact.
Lockwasher A form of washer designed to prevent an attaching nut from working loose.
LT Low Tension Description of the electrical circuit from the power supply to the primary winding of the ignition coil.

M

Main bearings The bearings between the crankshaft and crankcase.
Maintenance-free (MF) battery A sealed battery which cannot be topped up.
Manometer Mercury-filled calibrated tubes used to measure intake tract vacuum. Used to synchronise carburettors on multi-cylinder engines.
Micrometer A precision measuring instrument that measures component outside diameters **(see illustration)**.

Tappet shims are measured with a micrometer

MON (Motor Octane Number) A measure of a fuel's resistance to knock.
Monograde oil An oil with a single viscosity, eg SAE80W.
Monoshock A single suspension unit linking the swingarm or suspension linkage to the frame.
mph Abbreviation for miles per hour.
Multigrade oil Having a wide viscosity range (eg 10W40). The W stands for Winter, thus the viscosity ranges from SAE10 when cold to SAE40 when hot.
Multimeter An electrical test instrument with the capability to measure voltage, current and resistance. Some meters also incorporate a continuity tester and buzzer.

N

Needle roller bearing Inner race of caged needle rollers and hardened outer race. Examples of uncaged needle rollers can be found on some engines. Commonly used in rear suspension applications and in two-stroke engines.
Nm Newton metres.
NOx Oxides of Nitrogen. A common toxic pollutant emitted by petrol engines at higher temperatures.

O

Octane The measure of a fuel's resistance to knock.
OE (Original Equipment) Relates to components fitted to a motorcycle as standard or replacement parts supplied by the motorcycle manufacturer.
Ohm The unit of electrical resistance. Ohms = Volts ÷ Current.
Ohmmeter An instrument for measuring electrical resistance.
Oil cooler System for diverting engine oil outside of the engine to a radiator for cooling purposes.
Oil injection A system of two-stroke engine lubrication where oil is pump-fed to the engine in accordance with throttle position.
Open-circuit An electrical condition where there is a break in the flow of electricity - no continuity (high resistance).
O-ring A type of sealing ring made of a special rubber-like material; in use, the O-ring is compressed into a groove to provide the sealing action.
Oversize (OS) Term used for piston and ring size options fitted to a rebored cylinder.
Overhead cam (sohc) engine An engine with single camshaft located on top of the cylinder head.
Overhead valve (ohv) engine An engine with the valves located in the cylinder head, but with the camshaft located in the engine block or crankcase.
Oxygen sensor A device installed in the exhaust system which senses the oxygen content in the exhaust and converts this information into an electric current. Also called a Lambda sensor.

P

Plastigauge A thin strip of plastic thread, available in different sizes, used for measuring clearances. For example, a strip of Plastigauge is laid across a bearing journal. The parts are assembled and dismantled; the width of the crushed strip indicates the clearance between journal and bearing.
Polarity Either negative or positive earth (ground), determined by which battery lead is connected to the frame (earth return). Modern motorcycles are usually negative earth.
Pre-ignition A situation where the fuel/air mixture ignites before the spark plug fires. Often due to a hot spot in the combustion chamber caused by carbon build-up. Engine has a tendency to 'run-on'.
Pre-load (suspension) The amount a spring is compressed when in the unloaded state. Preload can be applied by gas, spacer or mechanical adjuster.
Premix The method of engine lubrication on older two-stroke engines. Engine oil is mixed with the petrol in the fuel tank in a specific ratio. The fuel/oil mix is sometimes referred to as "petroil".
Primary drive Description of the drive from the crankshaft to the clutch. Usually by gear or chain.
PS Pfedestärke - a German interpretation of BHP.
PSI Pounds-force per square inch. Imperial measurement of tyre pressure and cylinder pressure measurement.
PTFE Polytetrafluoroethylene. A low friction substance.

Pulse secondary air injection system A process of promoting the burning of excess fuel present in the exhaust gases by routing fresh air into the exhaust ports.

Q

Quartz halogen bulb Tungsten filament surrounded by a halogen gas. Typically used for the headlight **(see illustration)**.

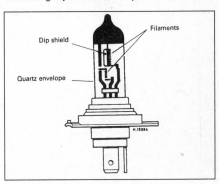

Quartz halogen headlight bulb construction

R

Rack-and-pinion A pinion gear on the end of a shaft that mates with a rack (think of a geared wheel opened up and laid flat). Sometimes used in clutch operating systems.
Radial play Up and down movement about a shaft.
Radial ply tyres Tyre plies run across the tyre (from bead to bead) and around the circumference of the tyre. Less resistant to tread distortion than other tyre types.
Radiator A liquid-to-air heat transfer device designed to reduce the temperature of the coolant in a liquid cooled engine.
Rake A feature of steering geometry - the angle of the steering head in relation to the vertical **(see illustration)**.

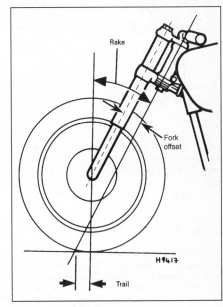

Steering geometry

Rebore Providing a new working surface to the cylinder bore by boring out the old surface. Necessitates the use of oversize piston and rings.

Rebound damping A means of controlling the oscillation of a suspension unit spring after it has been compressed. Resists the spring's natural tendency to bounce back after being compressed.

Rectifier Device for converting the ac output of an alternator into dc for battery charging.

Reed valve An induction system commonly used on two-stroke engines.

Regulator Device for maintaining the charging voltage from the generator or alternator within a specified range.

Relay A electrical device used to switch heavy current on and off by using a low current auxiliary circuit.

Resistance Measured in ohms. An electrical component's ability to pass electrical current.

RON (Research Octane Number) A measure of a fuel's resistance to knock.

rpm revolutions per minute.

Runout The amount of wobble (in-and-out movement) of a wheel or shaft as it's rotated. The amount a shaft rotates 'out-of-true'. The out-of-round condition of a rotating part.

S

SAE (Society of Automotive Engineers) A standard for the viscosity of a fluid.

Sealant A liquid or paste used to prevent leakage at a joint. Sometimes used in conjunction with a gasket.

Service limit Term for the point where a component is no longer useable and must be renewed.

Shaft drive A method of transmitting drive from the transmission to the rear wheel.

Shell bearings Plain bearings consisting of two shell halves. Most often used as big-end and main bearings in a four-stroke engine. Often called bearing inserts.

Shim Thin spacer, commonly used to adjust the clearance or relative positions between two parts. For example, shims inserted into or under tappets or followers to control valve clearances. Clearance is adjusted by changing the thickness of the shim.

Short-circuit An electrical condition where current shorts to earth (ground) bypassing the circuit components.

Skimming Process to correct warpage or repair a damaged surface, eg on brake discs or drums.

Slide-hammer A special puller that screws into or hooks onto a component such as a shaft or bearing; a heavy sliding handle on the shaft bottoms against the end of the shaft to knock the component free.

Small-end bearing The bearing in the upper end of the connecting rod at its joint with the gudgeon pin.

Spalling Damage to camshaft lobes or bearing journals shown as pitting of the working surface.

Specific gravity (SG) The state of charge of the electrolyte in a lead-acid battery. A measure of the electrolyte's density compared with water.

Straight-cut gears Common type gear used on gearbox shafts and for oil pump and water pump drives.

Stanchion The inner sliding part of the front forks, held by the yokes. Often called a fork tube.

Stoichiometric ratio The optimum chemical air/fuel ratio for a petrol engine, said to be 14.7 parts of air to 1 part of fuel.

Sulphuric acid The liquid (electrolyte) used in a lead-acid battery. Poisonous and extremely corrosive.

Surface grinding (lapping) Process to correct a warped gasket face, commonly used on cylinder heads.

T

Tapered-roller bearing Tapered inner race of caged needle rollers and separate tapered outer race. Examples of taper roller bearings can be found on steering heads.

Tappet A cylindrical component which transmits motion from the cam to the valve stem, either directly or via a pushrod and rocker arm. Also called a cam follower.

TCS Traction Control System. An electronically-controlled system which senses wheel spin and reduces engine speed accordingly.

TDC Top Dead Centre denotes that the piston is at its highest point in the cylinder.

Thread-locking compound Solution applied to fastener threads to prevent slackening. Select type to suit application.

Thrust washer A washer positioned between two moving components on a shaft. For example, between gear pinions on gearshaft.

Timing chain See **Cam Chain**.

Timing light Stroboscopic lamp for carrying out ignition timing checks with the engine running.

Top-end A description of an engine's cylinder block, head and valve gear components.

Torque Turning or twisting force about a shaft.

Torque setting A prescribed tightness specified by the motorcycle manufacturer to ensure that the bolt or nut is secured correctly. Undertightening can result in the bolt or nut coming loose or a surface not being sealed. Overtightening can result in stripped threads, distortion or damage to the component being retained.

Torx key A six-point wrench.

Tracer A stripe of a second colour applied to a wire insulator to distinguish that wire from another one with the same colour insulator. For example, Br/W is often used to denote a brown insulator with a white tracer.

Trail A feature of steering geometry. Distance from the steering head axis to the tyre's central contact point.

Triple clamps The cast components which extend from the steering head and support the fork stanchions or tubes. Often called fork yokes.

Turbocharger A centrifugal device, driven by exhaust gases, that pressurises the intake air. Normally used to increase the power output from a given engine displacement.

TWI Abbreviation for Tyre Wear Indicator. Indicates the location of the tread depth indicator bars on tyres.

U

Universal joint or U-joint (UJ) A double-pivoted connection for transmitting power from a driving to a driven shaft through an angle. Typically found in shaft drive assemblies.

Unsprung weight Anything not supported by the bike's suspension (ie the wheel, tyres, brakes, final drive and bottom (moving) part of the suspension).

V

Vacuum gauges Clock-type gauges for measuring intake tract vacuum. Used for carburettor synchronisation on multi-cylinder engines.

Valve A device through which the flow of liquid, gas or vacuum may be stopped, started or regulated by a moveable part that opens, shuts or partially obstructs one or more ports or passageways. The intake and exhaust valves in the cylinder head are of the poppet type.

Valve clearance The clearance between the valve tip (the end of the valve stem) and the rocker arm or tappet/follower. The valve clearance is measured when the valve is closed. The correct clearance is important - if too small the valve won't close fully and will burn out, whereas if too large noisy operation will result.

Valve lift The amount a valve is lifted off its seat by the camshaft lobe.

Valve timing The exact setting for the opening and closing of the valves in relation to piston position.

Vernier caliper A precision measuring instrument that measures inside and outside dimensions. Not quite as accurate as a micrometer, but more convenient.

VIN Vehicle Identification Number. Term for the bike's engine and frame numbers.

Viscosity The thickness of a liquid or its resistance to flow.

Volt A unit for expressing electrical "pressure" in a circuit. Volts = current x ohms.

W

Water pump A mechanically-driven device for moving coolant around the engine.

Watt A unit for expressing electrical power. Watts = volts x current.

Wear limit see **Service limit**

Wet liner A liquid-cooled engine design where the pistons run in liners which are directly surrounded by coolant **(see illustration)**.

Wet liner arrangement

Wheelbase Distance from the centre of the front wheel to the centre of the rear wheel.

Wiring harness or loom Describes the electrical wires running the length of the motorcycle and enclosed in tape or plastic sheathing. Wiring coming off the main harness is usually referred to as a sub harness.

Woodruff key A key of semi-circular or square section used to locate a gear to a shaft. Often used to locate the alternator rotor on the crankshaft.

Wrist pin Another name for gudgeon or piston pin.

Note: *References throughout this index are in the form - "Chapter number" • "Page number"*

Haynes Motorcycle Manuals – The Complete List

Title	Book No
APRILIA RS50 (99 - 06) & RS125 (93 - 06)	4298
Aprilia RSV1000 Mille (98 - 03) ♦	4255
BMW 2-valve Twins (70 - 96) ♦	0249
BMW K100 & 75 2-valve Models (83 - 96) ♦	1373
BMW R850, 1100 & 1150 4-valve Twins (93 - 04) ♦	3466
BMW R1200 (04 - 06) ♦	4598
BSA Bantam (48 - 71)	0117
BSA Unit Singles (58 - 72)	0127
BSA Pre-unit Singles (54 - 61)	0326
BSA A7 & A10 Twins (47 - 62)	0121
BSA A50 & A65 Twins (62 - 73)	0155
DUCATI 600, 620, 750 and 900 2-valve V-Twins (91 - 05) ♦	3290
Ducati MK III & Desmo Singles (69 - 76) ◊	0445
Ducati 748, 916 & 996 4-valve V-Twins (94 - 01) ♦	3756
GILERA Runner, DNA, Ice & SKP/Stalker (97 - 07)	4163
HARLEY-DAVIDSON Sportsters (70 - 03) ♦	2534
Harley-Davidson Shovelhead and Evolution Big Twins (70 - 99) ♦	2536
Harley-Davidson Twin Cam 88 (99 - 03) ♦	2478
HONDA NB, ND, NP & NS50 Melody (81 - 85) ◊	0622
Honda NE/NB50 Vision & SA50 Vision Met-in (85 - 95) ◊	1278
Honda MB, MBX, MT & MTX50 (80 - 93)	0731
Honda C50, C70 & C90 (67 - 03)	0324
Honda XR80/100R & CRF80/100F (85 - 04)	2218
Honda XL/XR 80, 100, 125, 185 & 200 2-valve Models (78 - 87)	0566
Honda H100 & H100S Singles (80 - 92) ◊	0734
Honda CB/CD125T & CM125C Twins (77 - 88) ◊	0571
Honda CG125 (76 - 07) ◊	0433
Honda NS125 (86 - 93)	3056
Honda CBR125R (04 - 07)	4620
Honda MBX/MTX125 & MTX200 (83 - 93)	1132
Honda CD/CM185 200T & CM250C 2-valve Twins (77 - 85)	0572
Honda XL/XR 250 & 500 (78 - 84)	0567
Honda XR250L, XR250R & XR400R (86 - 03)	2219
Honda CB250 & CB400N Super Dreams (78 - 84) ◊	0540
Honda CR Motocross Bikes (86 - 01)	2222
Honda CRF250 & CRF450 (02 - 06)	2630
Honda CBR400RR Fours (88 - 99) ◊ ♦	3552
Honda VFR400 (NC30) & RVF400 (NC35) V-Fours (89 - 98) ◊ ♦	3496
Honda CB500 (93 - 01) ◊	3753
Honda CB400 & CB550 Fours (73 - 77)	0262
Honda CX/GL500 & 650 V-Twins (78 - 86)	0442
Honda CBX550 Four (82 - 86) ◊	0940
Honda XL600R & XR600R (83 - 00)	2183
Honda XL600/650V Transalp & XRV750 Africa Twin (87 to 07) ♦	3919
Honda CBR600F1 & 1000F Fours (87 - 96) ♦	1730
Honda CBR600F2 & F3 Fours (91 - 98) ♦	2070
Honda CBR600F4 (99 - 06) ♦	3911
Honda CB600F Hornet & CBF600 (98 - 06) ◊ ♦	3915
Honda CBR600RR (03 - 06) ♦	4590
Honda CB650 sohc Fours (78 - 84)	0665
Honda NTV600 Revere, NTV650 and NT650V Deauville (88 - 05) ◊ ♦	3243
Honda Shadow VT600 & 750 (USA) (88 - 03)	2312
Honda CB750 sohc Four (69 - 79)	0131
Honda V45/65 Sabre & Magna (82 - 88)	0820
Honda VFR750 & 700 V-Fours (86 - 97) ♦	2101
Honda VFR800 V-Fours (97 - 01) ♦	3703
Honda VFR800 V-Tec V-Fours (02 - 05) ♦	4196
Honda CB750 & CB900 dohc Fours (78 - 84)	0535
Honda VTR1000 (FireStorm, Super Hawk) & XL1000V (Varadero) (97 - 00) ♦	3744
Honda CBR900RR FireBlade (92 - 99) ♦	2161
Honda CBR900RR FireBlade (00 - 03) ♦	4060
Honda CBR1000RR Fireblade (04 - 07) ♦	4604
Honda CBR1100XX Super Blackbird (97 - 07) ♦	3901
Honda ST1100 Pan European V-Fours (90 - 02) ♦	3384
Honda Shadow VT1100 (USA) (85 - 98)	2313
Honda GL1000 Gold Wing (75 - 79)	0309
Honda GL1100 Gold Wing (79 - 81)	0669

Title	Book No
Honda Gold Wing 1200 (USA) (84 - 87)	2199
Honda Gold Wing 1500 (USA) (88 - 00)	2225
KAWASAKI AE/AR 50 & 80 (81 - 95)	1007
Kawasaki KC, KE & KH100 (75 - 99)	1371
Kawasaki KMX125 & 200 (86 - 02) ◊	3046
Kawasaki 250, 350 & 400 Triples (72 - 79)	0134
Kawasaki 400 & 440 Twins (74 - 81)	0281
Kawasaki 400, 500 & 550 Fours (79 - 91)	0910
Kawasaki EN450 & 500 Twins (Ltd/Vulcan) (85 - 04)	2053
Kawasaki EX500 (GPZ500S) & ER500 (ER-5) (87 - 05) ♦	2052
Kawasaki ZX600 (ZZ-R600 & Ninja ZX-6) (90 - 06) ♦	2146
Kawasaki ZX-6R Ninja Fours (95 - 02) ♦	3541
Kawasaki ZX-6R (03 - 06) ♦	4742
Kawasaki ZX600 (GPZ600R, GPX600R, Ninja 600R & RX) & ZX750 (GPX750R, Ninja 750R) ♦	1780
Kawasaki 650 Four (76 - 78)	0373
Kawasaki Vulcan 700/750 & 800 (85 - 04) ♦	2457
Kawasaki 750 Air-cooled Fours (80 - 91)	0574
Kawasaki ZR550 & 750 Zephyr Fours (90 - 97) ♦	3382
Kawasaki Z750 & Z1000 (03 - 08) ♦	4762
Kawasaki ZX750 (Ninja ZX-7 & ZXR750) Fours (89 - 96) ♦	2054
Kawasaki Ninja ZX-7R & ZX-9R (94 - 04) ♦	3721
Kawasaki 900 & 1000 Fours (73 - 77)	0222
Kawasaki ZX900, 1000 & 1100 Liquid-cooled Fours (83 - 97) ♦	1681
KTM EXC Enduro & SX Motocross (00 - 07) ♦	4629
MOTO GUZZI 750, 850 & 1000 V-Twins (74 - 78)	0339
MZ ETZ Models (81 - 95) ◊	1680
NORTON 500, 600, 650 & 750 Twins (57 - 70)	0187
Norton Commando (68 - 77)	0125
PEUGEOT Speedfight, Trekker & Vivacity Scooters (96 - 05) ◊	3920
PIAGGIO (Vespa) Scooters (91 - 06)	3492
SUZUKI GT, ZR & TS50 (77 - 90)	0799
Suzuki TS50X (84 - 00)	1599
Suzuki 100, 125, 185 & 250 Air-cooled Trail bikes (79 - 89)	0797
Suzuki GP100 & 125 Singles (78 - 93)	0576
Suzuki GS, GN, GZ & DR125 Singles (82 - 05) ◊	0888
Suzuki 250 & 350 Twins (68 - 78)	0120
Suzuki GT250X7, GT200X5 & SB200 Twins (78 - 83) ◊	0469
Suzuki GS/GSX250, 400 & 450 Twins (79 - 85)	0736
Suzuki GS500 Twin (89 - 06) ♦	3238
Suzuki GS550 (77 - 82) & GS750 Fours (76 - 79)	0363
Suzuki GS/GSX550 4-valve Fours (83 - 88)	1133
Suzuki SV650 & SV650S (99 - 05) ♦	3912
Suzuki GSX-R600 & 750 (96 - 00) ♦	3553
Suzuki GSX-R600 (01 - 03), GSX-R750 (00 - 03) & GSX-R1000 (01 - 02) ♦	3986
Suzuki GSX-R600/750 (04 - 05) & GSX-R1000 (03 - 06) ♦	4382
Suzuki GSF600, 650 & 1200 Bandit Fours (95 - 06) ♦	3367
Suzuki Intruder, Marauder, Volusia & Boulevard (85 - 06) ♦	2618
Suzuki GS850 Fours (78 - 88)	0536
Suzuki GS1000 Four (77 - 79)	0484
Suzuki GSX-R750, GSX-R1100 (85 - 92), GSX600F, GSX750F, GSX1100F (Katana) Fours ♦	2055
Suzuki GSX600/750F & GSX750 (98 - 02) ♦	3987
Suzuki GS/GSX1000, 1100 & 1150 4-valve Fours (79 - 88)	0737
Suzuki TL1000S/R & DL1000 V-Strom (97 - 04) ♦	4083
Suzuki GSX1300R Hayabusa (99 - 04) ♦	4184
Suzuki GSX1400 (02 - 07) ♦	4758
TRIUMPH Tiger Cub & Terrier (52 - 68)	0414
Triumph 350 & 500 Unit Twins (58 - 73)	0137
Triumph Pre-Unit Twins (47 - 62)	0251
Triumph 650 & 750 2-valve Unit Twins (63 - 83)	0122
Triumph Trident & BSA Rocket 3 (69 - 75)	0136
Triumph Bonneville (01 - 07) ♦	4364
Triumph Daytona, Speed Triple, Sprint & Tiger (97 - 05) ♦	3755
Triumph Triples and Fours (carburettor engines) (91 - 04) ♦	2162
VESPA P/PX125, 150 & 200 Scooters (78 - 06)	0707
Vespa Scooters (59 - 78)	0126
YAMAHA DT50 & 80 Trail Bikes (78 - 95) ◊	0800
Yamaha T50 & 80 Townmate (83 - 95) ◊	1247
Yamaha YB100 Singles (73 - 91) ◊	0474

Title	Book No
Yamaha RS/RXS100 & 125 Singles (74 - 95)	0331
Yamaha RD & DT125LC (82 - 87) ◊	0887
Yamaha TZR125 (87 - 93) & DT125R (88 - 02) ◊	1655
Yamaha TY50, 80, 125 & 175 (74 - 84) ◊	0464
Yamaha XT & SR125 (82 - 03) ◊	1021
Yamaha Trail Bikes (81 - 00)	2350
Yamaha 2-stroke Motocross Bikes 1986 - 2006	2662
Yamaha YZ & WR 4-stroke Motocross Bikes (98 - 07)	2689
Yamaha 250 & 350 Twins (70 - 79)	0040
Yamaha XS250, 360 & 400 sohc Twins (75 - 84)	0378
Yamaha RD250 & 350LC Twins (80 - 82)	0803
Yamaha RD350 YPVS Twins (83 - 95)	1158
Yamaha RD400 Twin (75 - 79)	0333
Yamaha XT, TT & SR500 Singles (75 - 83)	0342
Yamaha XZ550 Vision V-Twins (82 - 85)	0821
Yamaha FJ, FZ, XJ & YX600 Radian (84 - 92)	2100
Yamaha XJ600S (Diversion, Seca II) & XJ600N Fours (92 - 03) ♦	2145
Yamaha YZF600R Thundercat & FZS600 Fazer (96 - 03) ♦	3702
Yamaha FZ-6 Fazer (04 - 07) ♦	4751
Yamaha YZF-R6 (99 - 02) ♦	3900
Yamaha YZF-R6 (03 - 05) ♦	4601
Yamaha 650 Twins (70 - 83)	0341
Yamaha XJ650 & 750 Fours (80 - 84) ♦	0738
Yamaha XS750 & 850 Triples (76 - 85)	0340
Yamaha TDM850, TRX850 & XTZ750 (89 - 99) ◊ ♦	3540
Yamaha YZF750R & YZF1000R Thunderace (93 - 00) ♦	3720
Yamaha FZR600, 750 & 1000 Fours (87 - 96) ♦	2056
Yamaha XV (Virago) V-Twins (81 - 03) ♦	0802
Yamaha XVS650 & 1100 Drag Star/V-Star (97 - 05) ♦	4195
Yamaha XJ900F Fours (83 - 94) ♦	3239
Yamaha XJ900S Diversion (94 - 01) ♦	3739
Yamaha YZF-R1 (98 - 03) ♦	3754
Yamaha YZF-R1 (04 - 06) ♦	4605
Yamaha FZS1000 Fazer (01 - 05) ♦	4287
Yamaha FJ1100 & 1200 Fours (84 - 96) ♦	2057
Yamaha XJR1200 & 1300 (95 - 06) ♦	3981
Yamaha V-Max (85 - 03) ♦	4072

ATVs

Title	Book No
Honda ATC70, 90, 110, 185 & 200 (71 - 85)	0565
Honda Rancher, Recon & TRX250EX ATVs	2553
Honda TRX300 Shaft Drive ATVs (88 - 00)	2125
Honda TRX300EX, TRX400EX & TRX450ER/ER ATVs (93 - 06)	2318
Kawasaki Bayou 220/250/300 & Prairie 300 ATVs (86 - 03)	2351
Polaris ATVs (85 - 97)	2302
Polaris ATVs (98 - 06)	2508
Yamaha YFS200 Blaster ATV (88 - 02)	2317
Yamaha YFB250 Timberwolf ATVs (92 - 00)	2217
Yamaha YFM350 & YFM400 (ER and Big Bear) ATVs (87 - 03)	2126
Yamaha Banshee and Warrior ATVs (87 - 03)	2314
Yamaha Kodiak and Grizzly ATVs (93 - 05)	2567
ATV Basics	10450

TECHBOOK SERIES

Title	Book No
Twist and Go (automatic transmission) Scooters Service and Repair Manual	4082
Motorcycle Basics TechBook (2nd Edition)	3515
Motorcycle Electrical TechBook (3rd Edition)	3471
Motorcycle Fuel Systems TechBook	3514
Motorcycle Maintenance TechBook	4071
Motorcycle Modifying	4272
Motorcycle Workshop Practice TechBook (2nd Edition)	3470

◊ = not available in the USA   ♦ = Superbike

The manuals on this page are available through good motorcycle dealers and accessory shops.
In case of difficulty, contact: **Haynes Publishing**
(UK) +44 1963 442030   (USA) +1 805 498 6703
(SV) +46 18 124016
(Australia/New Zealand) +61 3 9763 8100

MCL23.12/07

Preserving Our Motoring Heritage

< *The Model J Duesenberg Derham Tourster. Only eight of these magnificent cars were ever built – this is the only example to be found outside the United States of America*

Almost every car you've ever loved, loathed or desired is gathered under one roof at the Haynes Motor Museum. Over 300 immaculately presented cars and motorbikes represent every aspect of our motoring heritage, from elegant reminders of bygone days, such as the superb Model J Duesenberg to curiosities like the bug-eyed BMW Isetta. There are also many old friends and flames. Perhaps you remember the 1959 Ford Popular that you did your courting in? The magnificent 'Red Collection' is a spectacle of classic sports cars including AC, Alfa Romeo, Austin Healey, Ferrari, Lamborghini, Maserati, MG, Riley, Porsche and Triumph.

A Perfect Day Out

Each and every vehicle at the Haynes Motor Museum has played its part in the history and culture of Motoring. Today, they make a wonderful spectacle and a great day out for all the family. Bring the kids, bring Mum and Dad, but above all bring your camera to capture those golden memories for ever. You will also find an impressive array of motoring memorabilia, a comfortable 70 seat video cinema and one of the most extensive transport book shops in Britain. The Pit Stop Cafe serves everything from a cup of tea to wholesome, home-made meals or, if you prefer, you can enjoy the large picnic area nestled in the beautiful rural surroundings of Somerset.

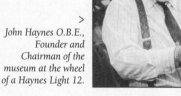

> *John Haynes O.B.E., Founder and Chairman of the museum at the wheel of a Haynes Light 12.*

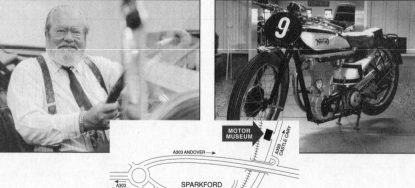

< *The 1936 490cc sohc-engined International Norton – well known for its racing success*

The Museum is situated on the A359 Yeovil to Frome road at Sparkford, just off the A303 in Somerset. It is about 40 miles south of Bristol, and 25 minutes drive from the M5 intersection at Taunton.

Open 9.30am - 5.30pm (10.00am - 4.00pm Winter) 7 days a week, *except Christmas Day, Boxing Day and New Years Day*

Special rates available for schools, coach parties and outings Charitable Trust No. 292048